WALTER HORATIO PATER was born   time in Enfield before the Pater househo   Walter attended the King's School, proc   Oxford, as an undergraduate. In 1864,   was made a fellow of Brasenose College, where he taught Classics and Philosophy. He retained his fellowship for the rest of his life. From around the time of this appointment, Pater began publishing critical essays on literature and art, gradually gaining a reputation for fine, idiosyncratic prose, sceptical philosophy, and a distinctive aestheticist outlook. Some of these essays were included in his first book, *Studies in the History of the Renaissance* (1873), which made his name not only as a stylist and perceptive critic, but also as a controversial thinker whose sympathy with the 'pagan' sensibility and the 'epicurean' mode of life attracted considerable hostility. Other critical essays were collected in the 1889 volume *Appreciations*, while Pater's historical novel *Marius the Epicurean* had appeared in 1885, and some of his works of short fiction had been gathered together in a volume entitled *Imaginary Portraits* in 1887. Living with his two unmarried sisters and dividing his time between West London and his Oxford college, Pater had become one of the most important figures in the British Aesthetic Movement. His essays on critical theory helped to shape the values of many younger writers and artists, while his subtle representations of various aesthetic and philosophical temperaments, both in his critical studies and in his fictional narratives, exercised a large influence on notions of conduct, taste and moral feeling in certain artistic and intellectual spheres. In 1893 was published his final book, *Plato and Platonism*, based on a series of lectures he had delivered to Oxford students. After an attack of rheumatic fever or pleurisy, Pater died suddenly of heart failure in Oxford in 1894. His grave may be seen there in the Holywell Cemetery. In the following years Pater's friends oversaw the publication of several further volumes of previously uncollected essays, including *Greek Studies* (1895), *Miscellaneous Studies* (1895), and *Essays from the Guardian* (1896), as well as an unfinished novel, *Gaston de Latour* (1896).

ALEX WONG is a literary scholar living in Cambridge, where he is currently a Research Fellow of St John's College. His critical book, *The Poetry of Kissing in Early Modern Europe*, is published by D.S. Brewer (2017), and his studies of English literature have appeared in various periodicals. *Poems Without Irony*, a first collection of his own verse, was published by Carcanet in 2016, and for Carcanet Classics (formally the Fyfield series) he has also edited the *Selected Verse* of Algernon Charles Swinburne (2015).

SELECTED ESSAYS

OF

WALTER PATER

EDITED BY

ALEX WONG

Carcanet Classics

First published in Great Britain in 2018 by

Carcanet Press Ltd
Floor 4 Alliance House, 30 Cross Street
Manchester M2 7AQ

Selection, introduction and notes © Alex Wong, 2018.

The right of Alex Wong to be identified as the editor of this volume, and the author of its introduction and notes, has been asserted in accordance with the Copyright, Designs and Patents Act of 1988. All rights reserved.

Printed in England by SRP Ltd.
A CIP catalogue record for this book is available from the British Library.
ISBN 9781784106263.

The publisher acknowledges financial assistance
from Arts Council England.

Contents

Acknowledgements	7
Introduction	9
Note on the Text	39

from THE RENAISSANCE

Preface	41
Pico Della Mirandola	45
Sandro Botticelli	55
Leonardo Da Vinci	61
The School of Giorgione	76
Joachim Du Bellay	88
from Winckelmann	99
Conclusion	114

from APPRECIATIONS

Style	117
Wordsworth	135
from Coleridge	148
Charles Lamb	162
Sir Thomas Browne	171
from Shakespeare's English Kings	189
Dante Gabriel Rossetti	196
Postscript	203

from PLATO AND PLATONISM

EXTRACTS FROM CHAPTERS 1 TO 5:

i. Three Kinds of Criticism	213
ii. "Perpetual Flux"	215
iii. The Eleatic School	219

iv. The Mania for Nonentity	222
v. Pythagoras	223
vi. The Centrifugal and the Centripetal	226
The Genius of Plato	228
from The Doctrine of Plato, Part I:	
The Theory of Ideas	241
The Doctrine of Plato, Part II:	
Dialectic	245
from Lacedæmon	256
Plato's Æsthetics	268

ESSAYS POSTHUMOUSLY COLLECTED

"GREEK STUDIES"

A Study of Dionysus	277
The Beginnings of Greek Sculpture, Part I:	
The Heroic Age of Greek Art	298
from FURTHER CHAPTERS ON GREEK SCULPTURE:	
i. The First True School of Greek Sculpture	316
ii. (a) The "Discobolus" of Myron	320
ii. (b) The "Diadumenus" of Polycleitus	324
ii. (c) The "Discobolus at Rest"	325

"MISCELLANEOUS STUDIES"

Prosper Mérimée	326
Raphael	339
from Pascal	350
Notre-Dame D'Amiens	353
The Child in the House	361

Explanatory Notes	373

Acknowledgements

My first thanks are to Michael Schmidt for suggesting this addition to what has hitherto been known as Carcanet's 'Fyfield' series, henceforth re-baptized 'Carcanet Classics'. My thanks extend, of course, to everyone else at Carcanet, and above all to my editor Luke Allan; also to Andrew Latimer, who helped the book through its last few days of preparation. I am also grateful to Alison Hennegan, for advice and cheering conversation regarding Pater and this selection; to Tess Somervell, for her helpful answers to a number of queries related to the literature of the Romantic period; to Arabella Milbank and James Robinson, for guidance on theological matters; to Alexander Schmidt of the University of Jena, for locating an elusive passage in Schiller; and to Seamus Perry for reinforcement in the search for some still more elusive references concerning Coleridge. Several friends and colleagues at St John's, Cambridge, kindly helped me with problems in preparing the explanatory notes: especially Stacey McDowell and, for all things Platonic, Malcolm Schofield; also Elena Giusti, Renaud Lejosne and Andrew Chen. Then, in the very final stages of preparing the book, I received help and welcome encouragement from a number of scholars of Pater, especially Lene Østermark-Johansen, Kenneth Daley and Lesley Higgins. Particular thanks are due to Martin Golding of my former college, Peterhouse, for detailed observations and ruminations on a number of puzzles; and most of all, not only for thoughts and 'second thoughts' about Paterian matters, but for support of many kinds, to Sarah Green.

None of my academic colleagues, however, has had the opportunity to correct my errors, all of which therefore remain solely my own responsibility. I like to fancy Pater would have understood.

A.W.

Introduction

WALTER PATER (1839-94) was the central figure, 'virtually the founder', of the Aesthetic Movement that dominated the artistic culture of Britain in the final third of the nineteenth century.[1] He was also one of the most individual stylists of the Victorian age, a model 'prosaist' for the aesthetically-minded aspirants of a time that was eager to cultivate prose as a fine art, emphatic in its fineness. Pater's literary manner, with its urbane and diffident charm characteristically controlled by evident care and effort, and with touches of lyricism rising provocatively out of a background of discursive calm, was the indispensable medium in which he was able to propose and exemplify a subtly worked-out aesthetic sensibility, as well as a critical method. His thinking, virtually impossible to disengage from the special qualities of its expression, was founded upon principles of scepticism and subjectivism, and directed towards a desired state of discriminating attentiveness. Intensity and authenticity of experience, precisely understood by oneself through a continual process of honest self-scrutiny, was the first aim, 'appreciation' being the resultant mode in critical work, and 'sympathy' the pre-eminent moral virtue. Pater's philosophy, his approach to the intellectual tasks he selected for himself, and the rarefied idiosyncrasies of the style itself, allured and animated many of his readers while earning the scorn of others.

In the twentieth century Pater was not so much forgotten as resisted, and frequently misrepresented, by most of the authoritative voices of the Anglophone literary world. Even if lately he has been the object of renewed scholarly interest, he is still oddly neglected beyond the academic pale, and it seems his full significance really has been largely forgotten. Nonetheless, that Pater has been 'a shade or trace in virtually every writer of any significance from Hopkins and Wilde to Ashbery', is a claim that has seemed reasonable to one recent critic, and it is not such a gross exaggeration that others might not think it possible to defend the notion.[2] Between late Romanticism and nascent Modernism the writings of Walter Pater occupy an important place.

PATER'S *OEUVRE*

Studies in the History of the Renaissance (1873), Pater's first book, attracted more attention than its author had probably been expecting, and has remained the most famous of his works. It is a series of independent essays, mostly concerned with individual artists and writers: Botticelli, Leonardo, Joachim Du Bellay, and so on. These are anticipated by a methodological 'Preface' concerned with critical theory, and terminate in a 'Conclusion' which broadens the critical method into an apparently more general philosophy of life. The whole volume offers a celebration of the sensuous and intellectual achievements of classical humanism, or of what Pater calls the 'Greek' or 'pagan' spirit, discerned in its various phases as it re-infuses European culture from the end of the 'Middle Ages' down to the passionate Hellenism of Winckelmann, lover and historian of ancient art, in the eighteenth century.

The stir caused by the publication of this book seems to have been the great event in a generally quiet life, spent as a fellow of Brasenose College, Oxford, and latterly as a shy but much-courted man of letters resident in London during the University vacations. Pater's *Renaissance*, the first and most forthright expression, on a large scale, of his critical and ethical principles, met with a mixed response from its early reviewers: some qualified praise, coming largely from liberal and secularist quarters; some sarcastic disparagement of its intellectual rigour or scholarly plausibility; and a good deal of indignant condemnation on moral and spiritual grounds, for its undisguised religious scepticism and ostensible commendation of a life of sensation and self-involvement. To others, and chiefly to the younger readers about whose moral wellbeing some of the more exasperated critics professed themselves anxious, its extraordinary prose and exhilarating late-Romantic ideals came as a rousing surprise, if not a revelation: a new style in English literature, and an approach to art which, despite the recent activities of a handful of critics, such as the poet Swinburne, had hitherto seemed much more at home on the opposite side of the English Channel. *The Renaissance* became the essential literary work of the Aesthetic Movement, and remained a canonical title during the so-called 'Decadence', distilled from that earlier aestheticism, that flourished in the 1890s. Oscar Wilde, according to the memoirs of W.B. Yeats, called it his 'golden book' and declared: 'I never travel anywhere without it; but it is the very flower of decadence: the last trumpet should have sounded the moment it was written'.[3]

Pater continued to write critical essays for various magazines, but his next book, containing what Yeats thought 'the only great prose in modern English', was not published until nearly twelve years later. *Marius the Epicurean: His Sensations and Ideas* (1885) is a two-volume novel, set in and around Rome during the reign of Marcus Aurelius. Its fictional protagonist, who has been made 'intentionally not very individual', as one critic puts it,[4] but who patently bears some temperamental resemblance to his creator, is a young man of an aesthetic and contemplative cast of mind, whose mental development—rather than anything one could call a 'plot'—gives the book what it has of narrative. The chapters represent successively the operation of particular philosophical systems and environmental circumstances upon this delicate temperament, as Marius refines and modifies his 'epicurean' scheme of life, and negotiates the influence upon his moral sensibility of the Christian community to whom he finds himself mysteriously drawn. *Marius* was acknowledged as a major work, and for at least a couple of decades it was as much a point of common reference for aesthetically-minded readers as *The Renaissance* had been, if not more so. In the long interval between *The Renaissance* and *Marius*, Pater's fame had grown, but hostile critical notices had not ceased to accumulate. And in 1874 had occurred, it appears, another incident in a life of few dramatic incidents, although one about the precise nature, scale and significance of which we are left in the dark. A talented student at Oxford named William Hardinge, apparently notorious as a flirt and nicknamed 'the Balliol Bugger', was temporarily sent down from the University for inappropriate behaviour, and the few letters between his friends which form almost all our extant evidence about the situation imply that Pater had been implicated, and that some flirtation, at the least, is likely.[5] There were rumours, in any case, which did not entirely vanish; and also, it may be gathered, some letters which *have* vanished—though one early source suggests that the threat of their being publicised may have been a considerable burden on Pater for some time.[6] Suspicions about the erotic orientation of the always unmarried Oxford don, who in many places throughout his work discusses such topics as romantic friendships between men, or the beauty of the youthful male physique, were thus elided with the notion of the supposed 'danger' his sceptical, aestheticist philosophy might pose to the morals of young men. Still it is hardly clear that unease of this nature constituted the sole, or even the primary reason for the disapproval he continued to face from reviewers, churchmen and colleagues. To many or most of these, the other problems with Pater's outlook—his seeming atheism and hedonism—would have been, and perhaps were, quite enough to damn him on their own.

In *Marius the Epicurean*, Pater attempted without the loss of integrity to answer some of the misgivings with which *The Renaissance* had been received. But he was also reformulating his principles and expanding them, as was only natural after more than a decade of pondering, much of which must have been carried on in a defensive mood. The depiction of Marius, safely transposed to Antonine Rome, constitutes a much more detailed account of the 'epicurean' elements of Pater's ethic than had been possible in the brief and more narrowly limited 'Conclusion' to his first book, where his moral philosophy had received its clearest expression so far; but it also shows the growth of the protagonist's mind, movements in his habits of thought, as some of those elements come at length to seem insufficient. Pater's great novel, in which there are scarcely any external events to speak of, was a due consideration of the moral ramifications which the 'Conclusion' had left unexplored.

Pater had been a fellow of Brasenose, Oxford, since 1864. He held his fellowship until his death. But in 1885, the year of *Marius*, he and his two unmarried sisters, with whom he shared a home, moved to a house in London. There they lived, outside of term-time, until their final return to Oxford in 1893, the year before Pater's unexpected death. In the London years he continued to write substantial critical essays, but much of his attention was now given to a series of 'Imaginary Portraits', in which he combined the forms and conventions of the essay and the short story. Each was an imaginative experiment with temperament and cultural context, which allowed the critic interested by the subtleties and mysteries of subjective experience free rein to deal with characters who, though they had never existed in reality, could be used to work out and symbolically represent the various aspects of Pater's own thinking, the relationships between his leading ideas. In some, we are made witness to the mental life of a personality born outside of its proper element, or searching for the unattainable, or surprised by unanticipated impulses. In others the spirit of one phase of culture is thrown artificially into the embrace of another, in order to test—again symbolically, or in microcosm—how something like the 'Renaissance' might have happened, or been thwarted, under different and less appropriate circumstances. Thus, in two of them, the Greek gods Apollo and Dionysus, surviving *incognito* into the Christian age, bring both delight and disorder to Medieval communities.

The first of Pater's 'Imaginary Portraits' had in fact been published as early as 1878. This is one of Pater's most beloved works, 'The Child in the House', the least storylike of them all. It contains some of his subtlest thinking about the psychology of the aesthetic temperament: a Paterian or 'Pateresque' temperament, even if in outward fact the portrait is not strictly autobiographical. In other pieces, however, such as the four that were included in the book called *Imaginary Portraits*, Pater's third volume, in 1887, certain traits of personality are conspicuously exaggerated: the cold and inhumane idealism, for instance, of 'Sebastian van Storck', a Dutch youth of the seventeenth century rather too wholly given to the philosophy of Spinoza. After the 1887 volume a few other pieces of short fiction, not all explicitly identified as 'Imaginary Portraits', but in a markedly similar vein, were published in various magazines, and these were collected after Pater's death.[7]

The fictional works were central to Pater's *oeuvre*, and the truth is that the boundary between his fictional and non-fictional writing is possible to locate only when thinking of the *whole* of each work, since this or that specific passage in the fiction is very likely to be of indeterminate genre when judged in isolation, and may in fact resemble criticism much more than storytelling; while on the other hand, the creative and speculative nature of Pater's critical writing might sometimes be thought, with good reason, to approach the condition of fiction. In preparing the present selection, however, with space limited and the disjointing of fictional narratives (such as they are) undesirable, I have chosen to hold to a distinction between 'essays' and 'fiction' that is starker than it otherwise ought to be. To detach the essayistic passages from *Marius*, for example, has proven in practice too messy to be worthwhile for the reader or just to the writer. The one exception to my rule is 'The Child in the House', the last piece in the anthology, included for reasons that my comments above may begin to explain.

Appreciations, with an Essay on Style (1889), Pater's fourth book, is a collection of literary-critical essays. Most of these had been previously published in periodicals over a span of more than two decades, stretching back as far as 1866. The 'Essay on Style', which opens the volume, is one of Pater's most important and revealing statements of his own literary values, with Flaubert as paradigmatic saint and martyr of fine writing. It shows the price Pater set on scrupulousness, sincerity, and 'impersonality', these last two qualities offering no contradiction in his usage. Taken as a whole, *Appreciations* is Pater's best claim to a distinguished place as a critic of literature specifically. In it can be found not only some of his best prose (though none of the most famous passages), but also much of the writing—parts, for instance, of the essays on 'Dante Gabriel Rossetti' and 'Wordsworth'—that retains the highest likelihood of striking today's reader as still valid criticism, judged purely as such. The book's title reminds us that critical appreciation was Pater's natural mode, and that he knew it: adverse criticism, denigration, denunciation, did not form part of his repertoire as a writer, full though his essays are of gentle qualifications and doubts.

The fifth and final book Pater published before his death is perhaps the most surprising title, at least for those who have inherited the conventional view of him as the decadent dilettante, and it has probably been the most neglected of his major works during the past century. This was his study of *Plato and Platonism*, which appeared in 1893 and collected in print a series of lectures Pater had given a couple of years earlier to undergraduate audiences at Oxford. In a scrutiny of Plato's thought he grappled with a central tension in his own: between philosophical idealism, with its eye on the abstract and its heart set on the mysterious absolute, and the aestheticism that in his own work had generally sustained the upper hand—worldly, particularizing, focussed on what lay visibly around one. 'The book', as Edward Thomas put it in his strangely ambivalent study of Pater, 'is in fact a hymn to visible beauty—intellectual beauty often, but always visible'.[8] For in Pater's conception of Platonism, even ideas and moral values can make an aesthetic appeal to the sensitive, and they find material forms, however imperfect, in earthly things and persons.

After his death in 1894 at the early age of fifty-four, Pater's friends and literary executors issued four further volumes with Macmillan. *Greek Studies*, a collection of previously published articles on Greek sculpture, myth and religion, came first, appearing in 1895. It includes some of Pater's most accomplished work. It was followed in the same year by *Miscellaneous Studies*, which presented a range of essays on art, architecture and literature, together with three more 'Imaginary Portraits'. Essays from both of these books have been included in the present anthology. A third volume, *Essays from the Guardian*, appeared in a small edition in 1896, issued by the Chiswick Press (it was added later to Pater's *Collected Works* in Macmillan's 'Library Edition'). This contained a set of book reviews that Pater had contributed anonymously, between 1886 and 1890, to an Anglican weekly called *The Church Guardian*. The review-essays give important insights into Pater's literary and ethical values, and are carefully and beautifully, if perhaps more rapidly, written; but placed beside his more important and highly finished essays they might seem relatively slight or 'occasional', and so for want of space, and very reluctantly, I have left them out of this selection.[9]

The final major addition to Pater's *oeuvre* was an unfinished second novel, *Gaston de Latour*, set in sixteenth-century France.[10] The general construction of the book is similar to that of *Marius*, bringing its protagonist into contact with such figures as the essayist Montaigne, the poet Ronsard, and the esoteric philosopher Giordano Bruno, as well as putting him through the horror of the Saint Bartholomew's Day Massacre. *Gaston* too appeared in 1896, with a preface by Pater's close friend C.L. Shadwell which explained that no more posthumous works were forthcoming. The full set of Pater's *Works*, then, in the Macmillan edition, extends to nine titles in ten volumes, *Marius* filling two. Yet in spite of Shadwell's decisive statement, several more reviews and other writings did eventually appear, in two American editions whose contents are largely but not entirely shared: an *Uncollected Essays* (1903), and a volume called *Sketches and Reviews* (1919). These books are much less common than the Macmillan ones, and their contents—which certainly do not include *all* of Pater's previously uncollected journalism—have been generally less well known.

THEORY AND DOUBT

In matters of philosophy and religion, Pater was inclined from his youth to scepticism. Despite the scrupulous conventionality of his personal manners, he seems to have had an 'antinomian' streak in his personality not wholly dissimilar from that which he bestows upon the young Marius: 'A vein of subjective philosophy, with the individual as the standard of all things, there would be always in his intellectual scheme of the world and of conduct, with a certain incapacity wholly to accept other men's valuations.'[11]

An early and sympathetic critic called Pater a 'deep though unwilling sceptic'.[12] He himself, recognising the sceptical tendency of the ancient philosophies by which he was most exercised, considered such doubt to be a central element just as well of 'modernity'. Hard to escape, then: at least for all those, like himself, for whom a strong religious faith did not seem to be possible. Modernity, as we see in Pater's essay on 'Coleridge', meant for him the triumph of the spirit of relativity, the rejection of the absolute; and with this modern spirit comes an elevation in the moral and intellectual value of individualism. For if absolute standards have become impossible to take seriously, the individual must then be 'the standard of all things', and a mental stress upon the dignity of the individual, each set amid the diversity of so many other individuals, might come to seem an ethical good in itself, as well as making for an interesting field of study for the critical mind excited, as Pater was, by the heterogeneity of human nature. Imbued with this 'modern' spirit, and being temperamentally an aesthete and a critic (rather than a philosopher in the mould, say, of Hume), Pater is attracted to what may broadly be called the epicurean mode of thought. But his published work, especially *Marius*, suggests that he worried about the way in which his qualified espousal of such an ethic might be, and had been, interpreted, and that he felt compelled to emphasise the moral and emotional discipline which in his view inhered in it.

One of the crucial chapters in *Marius* is headed by the title 'Second Thoughts', while in *Gaston de Latour* there is one entitled 'Suspended Judgement'. Both phrases recur in Pater's writings, and they help to define his approach. He is forever reconsidering, making space for reconsideration. And he values those writers and artists who go about things likewise, distrusting the decisiveness of first impressions without dishonouring or forgetting them. Subtlety of understanding is what he looks for, which comes of a reaching past the face of things, past what is superficial: he takes a special pleasure in objects that reward such complexified, meditative thought. Sir Thomas Browne, one of Pater's favoured authors, speaks of *deuteroscopy*, the 'second view' of things, and this is apparently Pater's aim. And, since there may always be a third view, or a fourth, one's final judgement must always be held in suspension.

Pater is a writer from whom it is possible to extract, in fact nearly impossible *not* to extract, something approaching to a 'system' of thought and values, but whose manner of writing nevertheless provides considerable and intentional resistance to the over-systematic interpreter. He carefully avoids the reductiveness inevitably risked by those who commit to stark or schematic expression. For Pater it is important never to reduce the world to stereotypes, since 'it is only the roughness of the eye that makes any two persons, things, situations, seem alike'.[13] The aesthetic critic, like the true 'essayist'—Pater is pre-eminently both—should never substitute preconception, classification, rigid structures of thought, for an attentive experience of the specific object itself. Such a writer will proceed flexibly and responsively, 'never judging system-wise of things, but fastening on particulars', as Pater repeats approvingly from Charles Lamb.[14] And so to his early biographer, A.C. Benson, we can fairly presume that it did not seem any self-contradiction to say, on one page, that Pater was an author exceptionally 'preoccupied with a theory', and then, only a few pages later, that he could 'hardly be said to have had any philosophical system'.[15]

A temperamental difference in this regard seems to separate Pater from an older English writer on aesthetics and morality to whom he owed a great deal, John Ruskin (1819–1900). In reading Ruskin one feels the force, and at times the frustration, of a systematizing, if not always systematic, mind; yet one that is so acutely and passionately observant of real particularities that it must struggle continually to adjust the stated principles, to accommodate what has been newly realized, to come to terms with exceptions to the rule. This partly explains why Ruskin's 'second thoughts' sometimes come as moments of intellectual crisis, or at least in troubling conflict with earlier pronouncements. Pater, on the other hand, develops a style which, without eliminating pronouncement altogether, nevertheless attempts to see its matter from various points of view at the same time, or in immediate succession, so that judgements may be effectively kept suspended, or at least confessed to be questionable. We see how we *might* concur with this or that notion, imagine what it *might* be like to hold by the given fix on truth. From the middle of the 1870s especially, Pater attempted to incorporate 'second thoughts', or the possibility of them, into the very fabric of each essay or argument. Those who condemn Ruskin tend to think him too dogmatic; but Pater's detractors complain of indecision, lack of commitment, vacillation.

If Pater was 'preoccupied with a theory', therefore, it was a theory always undergoing a process of refinement. Or else one might prefer to remove from Benson's phrase the indefinite article. But the theoretic preoccupations perceptible in all of Pater's writings did have implications for *practice*, both in the sphere of critical method and in the larger sphere of morals. These, in fact, are best imagined as concentric spheres, since for Pater the aesthetic and the intellectual were separable only artificially, and in the abstract, from ethics. Ethics, that is, in the broadest sense: the conduct of life, inwardly and outwardly.

To begin with the smaller sphere, the 'Preface' to *The Renaissance* offers up the clearest and most succinct iteration of Pater's critical principles:

"To see the object as in itself it really is," has been justly said to be the aim of all true criticism whatever, and in æsthetic criticism the first step towards seeing one's object as it really is, is to know one's own impression as it really is, to discriminate it, to realise it distinctly.[16]

It was Matthew Arnold (1822–88) who had defined the critical thought of modern Europe as 'the endeavour, in all branches of knowledge, theology, philosophy, history, art, science, to see the object as in itself it really is'. The comment had first been printed in 1861 in Arnold's study *On Translating Homer*, and was afterwards made more famous by its repetition at the beginning of his classic meditation on 'The Function of Criticism at the Present Time'.[17] Pater does not dismiss the aim as Arnold sees it. He doubts its practical attainability. 'Things-in-themselves' may exist in a noumenal realm, to use the Kantian terminology; but we have access to them only at second hand, being confined to the realm of appearances or 'phenomena'. Pater, as he will make clear later in the same volume, is far from sure that even our *sense* of these appearances can be truly shared, still less that they might be or even should be agreed upon. If criticism is what Arnold says it is, then the goal is dauntingly far off: one can only begin by analysing one's own impressions of things, with scrupulous care, with clarity of articulation, and as far as possible maintain an honesty of both thought and expression. Of any interesting object we must start by asking: 'How is my nature modified by its presence, and under its influence?' As Pater reminds us, 'one must realise such primary data for one's self, or not at all'.[18]

The expansion of this mode of thinking beyond the methods of strictly critical enquiry is suggested—or suggestively assayed—in the much-decried and much-celebrated 'Conclusion' that lies at the other end of *The Renaissance*. Modern philosophy, Pater says, puts us in great doubt about our ability ever to know the world outside our own insular subjectivities. We have only 'impressions', and lack the wherewithal to test their true relation to external realities. 'Experience, already reduced to a group of impressions, is ringed round for each one of us by that thick wall of personality through which no real voice has ever pierced on its way to us, or from us to that which we can only conjecture to be without.' Or so we are encouraged to think, at least, by cogent philosophical traditions both ancient and modern. Meanwhile our impressions, which are all we really know (and that only if we really take the trouble to get to know them), are in perpetual flux: ungraspable, unfixable and transient, like the ever-changing physical world by which they are occasioned. 'A counted number of pulses only is given to us of a variegated, dramatic life', says Pater. And so by intense, discriminating attentiveness, which needs always to be renewed, we must make the best of what is offered.

Then comes the sentence that has ever afterwards been held up, too frequently in a misleading isolation, as an epitome of Pater's thought: 'To burn always with this hard, gemlike flame, to maintain this ecstasy, is success in life.'[19]

Reviewers, noting the unmistakable religious scepticism beneath these speculations, as well as the larger epistemological doubt, detected in all of this a 'pagan' morality. 'Mr Pater lays himself open', said one, 'to the charge of being a heathen, or of trying to become one'.[20] They were not unjustified: the whole book, virtually, is a celebration of the revival of antiquity, or, as Pater prefers to say, of the Greek spirit or sensibility. In the essay on 'Winckelmann' he explains that 'Greek sensuousness' had been in the ancient world, and for some souls in the modern world still might be, 'shameless and childlike'; for the Greek had been contented with material reality, 'at unity with himself, with his physical nature, with the outward world'. This 'pagan sentiment', as Pater apprehends it, survives in the Christian world, the source and explanation of that 'sadness with which the human mind is filled, whenever its thoughts wander far from what is here, and now'.[21] Yet the modern sensibility, imbued by cultural heredity with both pagan and Christian sentiments, might in fact find itself driven by this sadness, this 'sense of the splendour of our experience and of its awful brevity', into the world of experience with only the greater urgency—'gathering all we are into one desperate effort to see and touch'.[22]

Even in a passage based, as the whole 'Conclusion' is, on avowedly hypothetical premises, the writer who would later come to place a high value on 'reserve' in literature had gone too far for comfort, been too unguarded, in the positing of moral 'conclusions'. Of course, Pater's suggestion that 'our one chance' consists in 'getting as many pulsations as possible into the given time' was bound to be seen as a call for solipsistic epicureanism, mere pleasure-seeking and self-cultivation, all the worse for its seeming lack of regard for otherworldly benefits.[23] To some of his more censorious readers, and those who knew of Pater only by swelling repute, he had become a sort of marauding hedonistic radical, a dandy evangelist among the impressionable youth of Oxford University, who were thought all too ready, in their precarious innocence, to catch this dubious fire. He had the distinction of being denounced by the Bishop of Oxford, and as broad-minded a person as George Eliot called *The Renaissance* a 'poisonous' book. A colleague at Brasenose, John Wordsworth, whom Pater had once briefly taught, wrote to him that although he admired 'the beauty of style and felicity of thought', he was 'grieved' by the moral conclusions of the book, as he understood them; namely, 'that no fixed principles either of religion or morality can be regarded as certain, that the only thing worth living for is momentary enjoyment and that probably or certainly the soul dissolves at death into elements which are destined never to reunite.' The letter is far from intemperate; it helps us to form a fair idea both of the real disquiet the book must have caused to some of Pater's friends and students, and also of the distress Pater himself must have felt at the strength of their reactions:—

> Could you indeed have known the dangers into which you were likely to lead minds weaker than your own, you would, I believe, have paused. Could you have known the grief your words would be to many of your Oxford contemporaries you might even have found no ignoble pleasure in refraining from uttering them.[24]

Pater withdrew the 'Conclusion' from the second edition of *The Renaissance* (1877), also rewriting some other sensitive sections. He replaced it, in an altered form, only in the third edition (1888), by which time he had already published a number of other works in which he had clarified his position, and been more explicit about the ethical implications of his aesthetic thought.

STYLE AND THE ESSAY

In the 'Conclusion', experience is reduced to a sequence of passing impressions, every moment or incident 'gone while we try to apprehend it'. The aesthetic writer, therefore, must try first to apprehend, and then to comprehend, the elements of experience through and within the medium of language. The criticism Pater performs is a sensitive literary operation, entirely dependent upon his style. It relies on the ability of his prose to catch up for examination the fleeting subjective response, or to evoke a penetrating imaginative reconstruction, and through these means get closer to the ultimately unknowable thing, or personality—maybe the thoughts or feelings of another, to which we have no certain access; maybe their manifestation through artistic forms. His arguments and his mode of enquiry proceed by delicate expression and re-expression in a recognizably fastidious choice of words, as the essential condition of thought—of Pater's kind of thought—on any subject. His syntax registers the shifting and self-correcting movements of a doubting but minutely attentive mind in the act of rumination.

Pater was renowned, and by many intensely admired, for his style. It was 'unlike all other styles', according to the novelist George Moore (1852–1933), who also calls Pater's writing 'the only prose that I never weary of'.[25] Among the younger generation, Moore was just one of many strivers after finely crafted English 'art prose' who had been inspired by the example of Pater's *Renaissance* and *Marius*. 'I went about the fields', he recalls of his first reading of the latter book, 'saying to myself: the English language is still alive, Pater has raised it from the dead.'[26] In the 'Essay on Style', Pater commends the painstaking dedication of Flaubert to an unflagging pursuit of the perfect, inevitable word, at all costs; and his own writing seems to have been comparably careful and laborious. Edmund Gosse (1849–1928), another younger friend and follower, remarked: 'I have known writers of every degree, but never one to whom the act of composition was such a travail and an agony as it was to Pater'.[27] If Pater was a prose virtuoso, he was of the kind that does *not* make brilliance appear effortless.

It is Pater's meticulousness that warrants his hesitancy in statement and argumentation. 'Conscientious inconsistency', to borrow an appealing phrase from Marianne Moore; certainly a conscientious indecision, though in a mind which nevertheless thinks habitually and deeply about what decisiveness in various directions would be like. Such *may* be the case, or *might* be supposed: what we are examining is *a kind of* ——, or *a sort of* ——. Is he hedging his bets, a modern critic or scholar might ask, having been taught to distrust or condemn a style full of ostensible evasions—*perhaps*, *so to speak*, *as it were*? 'In a sense it might even be said', for example, is a curiously doubtful expression in what has widely been taken as a credo or manifesto, the notorious 'Conclusion'.[28]

Yet what to some readers looks like imprecision is, from another point of view, only a way of intimating the desire for yet more precision, or the appeal to a precise *sense* of something which nevertheless eludes adequate articulation. This is why Pater sometimes sounds as though he were talking to himself, or seems to speak to the reader as if it were taken for granted that one understood what he meant, however insufficient the words. The notion of a shared connoisseurship becomes an implicit standard to be gestured towards. It is a genial manner as well as a critical strategy. Few writers, probably, use the word 'so' as often as Pater does, and when he tells us that a thing is *so* strange, *so* characteristic, *so* comely, the bid for precision is referred to our own sense of the matter—even if this is thoroughly conditioned by Pater's own suggestions. 'Just', as an adverb, is another frequent word in his idiolect: *just here*, or *just there*; just *this* thought, just *that* quality. And the effect is comparable. Other favourites are 'precisely', as one expects from an aesthete; 'really', an intensifier usually asking us to heighten our sensitivity to some special quality or state; and 'literally', which in Pater does not mean what people nowadays require it to mean ('unfigurative'), but rather conveys a demand that we stop to think about the etymology of a word, or the particular sense in which it is being used. All these words are inviting us to pay more attention. The writing continually reminds its reader how serious it is in the search for accuracy, the *mot juste*, without obliging itself to summarise or define; having intuited the meaning cumulatively from the complex and often hesitant discussion, we are persuaded to do without the firm formula. Not definition, in a strict or inflexible way, but circumscription is the aim of such prose: getting all the way around something and then gradually moving inward.

Even when writing *about* Pater, one finds oneself often reproducing the characteristics of his syntax: not only because of the seductiveness of the manner, but because in order to reduce the risk of misrepresenting his 'many-sided' thoughts and opinions one needs frequently to refine upon simple statements, usually by the employment of subordinate and parallel clauses that slightly modify the foregoing. Pater's meandering, self-refining sentences may have been formed in the hope of 'getting his prose to flow to a murmurous melody', as George Moore supposes.[29] But it has a philosophical function also. It expresses a turn of mind, the 'Pateresque' attitude to the business of verbal articulation as the basis of critical thought. 'He had a parenthetical mind', another early critic perceptively said; 'The very Genius of Qualification followed him through all his thinking'.[30] And if this is the main charge brought against Pater as a stylist, in particular by those who associate verbal precision above all with economical expression and decisiveness, to admirers it is one of his laudable virtues, producing a different kind of critical scrupulosity. Qualification, after all, does not mean only the weakening of statements by caveats and conditions, but the accounting for and making of *qualities*, the attempt to put a finger on what things are actually like.

It is worth adding that the idiosyncratic mood or tone of Pater's writing is in part a result of the tension between a very obvious artifice in the style, and on the other hand a colloquial, almost spontaneous address to the reader. 'Well!', he says affably, at the start of many sentences and paragraphs; and he flatters or teases his audience, even when speaking of esoteric matters, with phrases like 'as you know', or 'as you recall'. For all the meditated artistry of his prose, he is still operating within the tradition of the English 'familiar essay' as practised by Hazlitt, De Quincey or Lamb. Rhapsodic passages, such as the wonderful and immoderately famous 'purple panel' on *La Gioconda* (the 'Mona Lisa') in the essay on 'Leonardo Da Vinci', are relatively uncommon and therefore hardly representative.[31] Yet even at its purplest, Pater's prose always balances the deliberate discipline of its calmly evolving, hypotactic periods with the more casual fluency of sophisticated, gently wayward table talk.

Pater's style, as I have portrayed it, is a formal expression of certain values and principles he appears to have espoused in some form or degree from the beginning of his writing life, though he developed them more and more explicitly after the reaction to *The Renaissance*. To examine these it is useful to make a leap into the later years of his career.

In the early 1890s, nearly two decades after that first period of notoriety, Pater was writing the series of articles and Oxford lectures that would become his last completed book, *Plato and Platonism*. He set out to describe the attitude of Socrates and Plato to the pursuit of knowledge. This method of thought he calls the 'dialectic method'. The dialogues of Plato, in which Socrates conducts his philosophical enquiries through conversation with a range of interlocutors, while himself professing—with some measure of irony—not to know where the conversation will lead, are 'dialectic' in the most literal sense. Plato does not write treatises, which show patiently, by gradual argumentation from distinct premises, that a premeditated hypothesis is viable; instead he approaches his problems by taking into account and putting into contest diverse points of view (represented by the characters of the dialogue), and allowing Socrates to discount some of these as he proceeds, by showing their shortcomings. Total consensus is the closest thing, in such a composition, to the indication of the 'truth' of an argument. Pater shows that the 'essayist', represented primarily by Montaigne, adopts a similar method, proceeding not by dialogue with others, however, but by a continual internal dialogue: the testing and qualifying of one's own ideas. The aim is a 'many-sided but hesitant consciousness of the truth'.[32] By explicitly connecting this spirit of 'dialectic' with the form of the essay, his own chosen medium, Pater has allowed his readers to see clearly that in speaking thus of Plato, or Montaigne, he is at the same time reflecting on his own practice and showing the traditions to which he belongs. The essay, he says—and we should remember that even in fiction he is typically essayistic in style—is 'that characteristic literary type of our own time, a time so rich and various in special apprehensions of truth, so tentative and dubious in its sense of their *ensemble*, and issues'.[33]

Only 'issues', we may note. Not quite 'conclusions'. Indeed, in the course of Pater's remarks on dialectic, he ends a paragraph (pointedly, it is hard not to feel) by admiring, among the intellectual characteristics of Socrates, his way of 'always faithfully registering just so much light as is given, and, so to speak, never concluding'.[34] Is it possible that this was meant as a wry and subtle joke, coming from an author who, though his works must have struck most readers as decidedly *in*conclusive, had attracted censure and derision particularly, all those years ago, with a 'Conclusion'? In the meantime the offending chapter had been withdrawn, re-written and replaced, as we have seen, and other works had been largely engaged in a clarification and reformation of its supposed tenets, so that although Pater did not turn his back on the 'Conclusion' it is hardly unreasonable to see much of his subsequent work as a sustained attempt to recast, redirect and justify it. He seems to have adopted more consciously, and perhaps more cautiously, the habit or rule of 'never concluding', especially in ethical matters. His fictions, the ones that are finished, end ambiguously; his essays show tendencies, preferences, values, but are wary of fixed principles;

tensions in his moral thought become increasingly emphatic, and are held in suspension. When he reprinted his essay on 'Romanticism' as the final chapter of *Appreciations*, he called it not a 'Conclusion' but only a 'Postscript'. Valéry's saying, well known to English readers because quoted by Auden, to the effect that poems 'are never finished, but only abandoned', has perhaps some valid application to Pater's dialectic method, which does not, and *should* not, tie up all its loose ends in a strict and neat conclusion. To 'shut up totally' the question in hand, as the word *conclude* literally implies, would be alien to its mode of courting wisdom.

This dialectic or essayistic approach is also associated with two other important Paterian values: 'reserve' and 'irony'. Charles Lamb was for Pater an illuminating example of both. 'Glimpses, suggestions, delightful half-apprehensions', are what Lamb gives us; 'profound thoughts of old philosophers, hints of the innermost reason in things, the full knowledge of which is held in reserve'. Such is the stuff, according to Pater, 'of which genuine essays are made'.[35] And yet, as usual under his analysis, this *method* is also revealed as a personal trait, inviting sympathetic psychological imagination. And the personal element only heightens the effect. Lamb's habit of 'reserve', we are given to understand, may not be unconnected with the 'genuinely tragic element' in his private life: misfortunes kept private, but a knowledge of which contributes shades of feeling to the ostensibly 'slight' and 'humorous' things which are presented on the surface.[36] His grief, his anxiety and vulnerability, are among the things thus 'held in reserve', and may be taken as partly explanatory of his need to wear literary masks, hiding behind an *alter ego*, and employing so often 'that dangerous figure', as Lamb himself calls it: irony.[37]

Pater's own avoidance of dogma, together with his tendency to dwell upon the finer points of aesthetic discrimination and appreciation, may mean that his writing too seems 'slight', or even 'quaint', to some; and although his humour or irony has not been as fully grasped by modern critics as by early readers, the characteristic of reserve must strike any reader looking in vain for bald expressions of personal opinion, or overt autobiography. As a writer highly conscious of the controversial nature of his thinking, especially after the publication of *The Renaissance*; as an aesthete and belletrist of wide interests, who had become an Oxford don and was surrounded by scholars of more rigorously 'academic' methods and, though not always deeper, more narrowly focussed expertise than his own; as a man whose erotic feelings seem to have been directed primarily, perhaps exclusively, towards young men, in a situation in which many such youths were in his charge, and at a time when homosexual acts were judged immoral by many and ruled illegal; and, after all, merely as a sensitive and bookish individual, Walter Pater may very well have had his own personal or psychological reasons, like Lamb's, for the cultivation of reserve in utterance.

A.C. Benson records that Pater was known at Brasenose to be a paradoxical conversationalist, 'apt to talk, gently and persistently, of trivial topics, using his conversation rather as a shield against undue intimacy'.[38] Of this ironical reticence Benson gives a convincing explanation, the more convincing (rightly or wrongly) because it sounds so much like the kind of thing Pater himself might have said about one of his subjects:

> Probably this habit arose from the fact that he was of a shy and sensitive temperament, and that to give a real and serious opinion was a trial to him. He disliked the possibility of dissent or disapproval, and took refuge in this habit of irony, so as to baffle his hearers and erect a sort of fence between them and his own personality.[39]

His putative fear of giving 'a real and serious opinion' may try the patience of some readers. But it was also a habit, even a merit, assigned by Pater to the venerable Socrates, whose irony may have been useful and 'welcome', he says, 'as affording a means of escape from the full responsibilities of his teaching'. This in itself might sound like a fault, a failure of intellectual responsibilities, but the next sentence establishes its value: 'It belonged, in truth, to the tentative character of dialectic'.[40] And so the custom of never concluding may have been a *bona fide* philosophical method, a symptom of personal temperament, and a mere excuse, all at once. We know that Pater read with interest the correspondence of Flaubert with Louise Colet, since he quotes from it extensively in the 'Essay on Style'. One wonders if he noted down with special pleasure a passage from the letter of 27 September 1846, in which Flaubert confesses, not without irony: 'I observe much, and never make conclusions: an infallible way of not being mistaken'.

PATER'S DEVELOPING THOUGHT

If Pater's thinking after 1873 was, as I have said, largely preoccupied with the same questions as had been addressed already in *The Renaissance* and its 'Conclusion', let us consider some of the ways in which he refined his earlier thoughts in returning to them. 'Not the fruit of experience, but experience itself, is the end', Pater had said in 1873. In an essay on Wordsworth published the following year and later heavily revised for *Appreciations* (from which I quote this only lightly retouched passage), such thoughts are laid out again, but with a more explicit moral emphasis:

That the end of life is not action but contemplation—*being* as distinct from *doing*—a certain disposition of the mind: is, in some shape or other, the principle of all the higher morality. In poetry, in art, if you enter into their true spirit at all, you touch this principle, in a measure: these, by their very sterility, are a type of beholding for the mere joy of beholding. To treat life in the spirit of art, is to make life a thing in which means and ends are identified: to encourage such treatment, the true moral significance of art and poetry. Wordsworth, and other poets who have been like him in ancient or more recent times, are the masters, the experts, in this art of impassioned contemplation.[41]

For Pater, a conception of life which confines its attention to the practical pursuit of material aims and the strategies for their attainment is, if not actually and irredeemably distasteful, at least a view requiring impassioned contemplation as a moral antidote. 'Against this predominance of machinery in our existence', he continues, 'Wordsworth's poetry, like all great art and poetry, is a continual protest.' Contemplation, then—not, as before, mere 'experience', but *contemplative* experience—is here deemed an 'end-in-itself'.

Pater's experiments in fiction gave him the presumably welcome freedom to explore such ethical considerations with even less danger of binding himself to firm statements of principle, and *Marius the Epicurean* shows its protagonist developing a similar sense of morality as a matter of '*being* as distinct from *doing*'—even if, as will be seen in a moment, he is also convinced by the force of his own conscience that mere acquiescence in what is morally unsatisfactory in the world is an unacceptable position.

Marius develops his 'epicurean' outlook early in life, and the chapters which delineate its contours and development in his mind, recalling, while they explain and justify, the scepticism and aestheticism of the 'Conclusion', take pains to show that Marius is no sensualist, and neither immoral nor amoral, but sensitive and humane. Nevertheless there does come a change in his ideas. In the chapter called 'Second Thoughts', the essayistic narrator explains the mental evolution of the young protagonist as a natural alteration in the point of view of a person growing older. Epicureanism is 'ever the characteristic philosophy of youth'—

> ardent, but narrow in its survey—sincere, but apt to become one-sided, or even fanatical. It is one of those subjective and partial ideals, based on vivid, because limited, apprehension of the truth of one aspect of experience (in this case, of the beauty of the world and the brevity of man's life there) which it may be said to be the special vocation of the young to express.[42]

What this presumably communicates to most readers familiar with Pater's other work is the author's sense of having outgrown some of his old ideas, his need to place them now in a wider context; yet without repudiating or abandoning them, and with the sincerity of the earlier thinking, both his own and that of Marius, re-affirmed. Or perhaps, if the distinction is truly valid, it may have been the *expression* of the principles, rather than the principles themselves, that needed reworking. The subjectivism Pater has always insisted upon is now enlisted to defend, so long as they are sincere, and within certain limits, the respectability of 'partial ideals'—varying between individuals, of course, but also evolving throughout the mental history of the same individual under the unconstant pressure of second thoughts. There is no implication that Marius has been foolish, no suggestion that he ought to have reached his later perspective at an earlier date, and no offensive narratorial knowingness: only the delicate dramatic irony we see here, as the narrator steps back from the free indirect. Marius remains 'the Epicurean' by temperament, and by the lasting effect on his psyche of his youthful ideas, but in the rest of the novel he is looking for something more. In contact with Stoicism, idealism of various kinds, a humanistic view of cultural heritage, and finally the spiritual, aesthetic and familial values of Christianity, he gradually achieves an enlargement of his sensibility: a 'many-sidedness'.

In *Marius*, then, and also in *Gaston de Latour*, changes of mind are necessary, natural events in the life of the thinking and feeling individual, but they need not involve a complete rejection of former ideas. Instead they are effects of the mind's ongoing conversation with itself while accosted by the multiplicity of exterior reality, including the ideas of other people. First thoughts, refined and modified, are incorporated with second thoughts so that the one-sided outlook becomes many-sided; limitations are identified and routes around them are found, but the evolution of sensibility is a cumulative process driven by the dialectic spirit. Paterian subjectivism leads not to mere hedonistic solipsism, the contented imprisonment of each consciousness in its own dense epistemological atmosphere, but rather to a broad intellectual sympathy in which strictly contradictory visions of the world are taken to be simultaneously valid, based on criteria of sincerity, attentiveness, and so on, rather than any criterion of absolute truth. This is a notion that steals upon Marius after a night-time chat with Apuleius, the author of *The Golden Ass*:

> Yes! the reception of theory, of hypothesis, of beliefs, did depend a great deal on temperament. They were, so to speak, mere equivalents of temperament. [...] For himself, it was clear, he must still hold by what his eyes really saw. Only, he had to concede also, that the very boldness of such theory [*as that*

expounded by Apuleius] bore witness, at least, to a variety of human disposition and a consequent variety of mental view, which might—who can tell?—be correspondent to, be defined by and define, varieties of facts, of truths, just "behind the veil," regarding the world all alike had actually before them as their original premiss or starting-point; a world, wider, perhaps, in its possibilities than all possible fancies concerning it.[43]

Scepticism about the capacity of human minds in concert to ascertain a common truth with regard to any object or question, let alone in the search for a general philosophy, ultimately gives way to an exciting sense of the relativity of truth, enjoyed for its variousness almost as one enjoys variety and diversity in aesthetic matters. And indeed this subjectivism, not despairing but sympathetic and imaginative, does become an aesthetic value for Pater. Truth, as he says in the 'Essay on Style', is essential to literary art: 'there can be no merit, no craft at all, without that'. But truth in this context is a question of 'the finer accommodation of speech to that vision within'. It consists in the lucid and effective representation of the writer's special 'sense of fact', which will naturally differ from yours or mine. 'Soul-facts', rather than 'facts' supposedly standing independent of a specific perceiving mind, are Pater's prime subjects, both in his critical studies and in his explorations of fictional personalities.[44] As a writer on art and literature what he wants to articulate is, in a favourite phrase of his, the *vraie verité* of the artist or the work. *Vraie verité*, the 'true truth', is a phrase which both insists on the truthfulness of the truth discovered, and at the same time gently implies that other 'truths'—still true, therefore, but less so—might also have been advanced. It makes the truth truer while also subjectivizing it.

In Pater's late work, especially in *Gaston de Latour*, the rather bleak sense of mental isolation detectable in the earlier 'Conclusion', in which each of us had been 'a solitary prisoner' possessed only of our own 'dream of a world', changes into a more enlivening and morally constructive sense of the surprisingness and mysteriousness of things and persons outside us. 'On all sides we are beset by the incalculable.'[45] Objects out there in the world are crowding around us, waiting to be understood for what they are, and not simply configured with a 'stereotyped' scheme of the world. This even becomes a principle of ethics. According to Pater, a sense of the unpredictable variousness in humanity ('The diversity, the undulancy, of human nature!')[46] was so profound in Montaigne that even he himself 'seemed to be ever changing colour sympathetically therewith'.[47]

A.C. Benson thought that Pater's whole ethical outlook involved the substitution of 'sympathy for conscience', which may not be accurate but is worthwhile food for thought.[48] Was Pater reflecting on his own character, for example, when he said of Botticelli that 'his morality was all sympathy'?[49] As for the changing of colour, it may be thought that Pater was a chameleon with a limited palette: 'narrowness of range' was one of the traits attributed to him in an admiring article by Havelock Ellis in 1885.[50] But, in the end, there are limits to our sympathy, and it makes good sense for critics to confine themselves to subjects they feel especially able to understand or 'appreciate'. Furthermore it is probably significant that the word Pater usually chooses is 'sympathy' (feeling *with*), and not 'empathy' (feeling *into*). Breadth of sympathy is an important ethical quality or function for Pater, and must involve some empathetic reaching; but in his selection of critical and fictional material, the fellow-feeling is much more a matter of 'elective affinities'.

On the other hand, Pater's commitment to sustained inner debate has the effect of pushing his sympathies simultaneously in opposite directions, so that the things which he appears to value are sometimes tensely antithetical to one another, on the surface. The unconventional, 'antinomian' side of Pater inspired outrage and suspicion, excitement and intellectual *frisson*. He can write with enthusiasm about 'rebellion', whether in personal feeling or cultural history. He praises the 'pagan' view of life with an apparent conviction that some might have thought it prudent to disguise. Even in later works, in which he is supposed by some to have been disablingly over-cautious, ostensibly homoerotic material is presented with notable frankness. Yet he has also what one might call his conventional or conservative side—though relatively apolitical in the practical sense. He can enter at least provisionally into the spirit of Plato's *Republic*, repressive to the arts; and his seeming admiration, possibly with a touch of repugnance, for the rigidly anti-individualist culture of classical Sparta, in the essay on 'Lacedæmon', may even be somewhat disturbing to modern readers. His early essay 'Diaphaneité', which ends with thoughts of 'the regeneration of the world', tries to imagine an ideal type of character, from which 'the pedant, or the conservative' is sharply distinguished; but then again, so is 'anything rash and irreverent'.[51] In short, we are obliged to take into account many contradictions in Pater's work, and to join him in negotiating a balance. The dialectic process should therefore be understood as an unending search for the most acceptable combination of, or compromise between, opposing values. Despite his admiration for revolutionary thinkers and questioners, and despite the splash he himself had made in the early years of his fame, he is also attracted to character types, like 'Emerald Uthwart' in one of his 'Imaginary Portraits', who exemplify an instinct for submissiveness, orderliness, deference to tradition.

 . . . Despite the splash—or because of it? In any case, not even Uthwart can resist the one fatal outbreak of a quite different impulse, the one romantic and heroic eruption from order, 'an act of thoughtless bravery, almost the sole irregular or undisciplined act of Uthwart's life'—which results, to his surprise, but also with a sense of inevitability, in a lasting and haunting dishonour: fair or not, depending on one's point of view.[52] There was glamour as well as nobility in the reckless act.

It might be argued that Pater was more in the habit of changing the colour of his subjects to match himself, than the other way around. Complaining of critics who re-make Shakespeare's Hamlet after their own image, T. S. Eliot suavely quipped: 'We should be thankful that Walter Pater did not fix his attention on this play'.[53] The witty laconicism of the remark suggests that Eliot expected his readers to *know* that Pater was guilty of the sin imputed, though it also invites those familiar with Pater's work to consider his famous style in relation to the indecisiveness commonly said to be Hamlet's defining trait. It might have been too fatal a temptation, we are encouraged to infer — too easy an identification.

But Pater, it appears, knew what he was doing. Perhaps this can be seen in what he says of Lamb, in whom 'the desire of self-portraiture is, below all more superficial tendencies, the real motive in writing at all'. Moreover, he goes on, such a desire is to be seen as 'closely connected with that intimacy, that modern subjectivity, which may be called the *Montaignesque* element in literature'.[54] And in *Gaston de Latour* he says the following about Montaigne:

> And what was the purport, what the justification, of this undissembled egotism? It was the recognition, over against, or in continuation of, that world of floating doubt, of the individual mind, as for each one severally, at once the unique organ, and the only matter, of knowledge, — the wonderful energy, the reality and authority of that, in its absolute loneliness, conforming all things to its law, without witnesses as without judge, without appeal, save to itself.[55]

Although the world must be *conformed* to the mind if it is to be registered at all, now at least the individual mind may think of itself as existing *in continuation of* the dubious world. It is no longer the 'solitary prisoner' we recall from the still-resounding 'Conclusion', cut off from, and impervious to, any 'real' communication or knowledge. Subjectivism has gained, or confers upon the particular consciousness, 'energy', 'reality', 'authority'; is not regarded merely as the last shred of philosophical security left for us to believe in, but gives to the impressions of the contemplative person an authority 'wonderful' and vital in itself. Pater's criticism is candidly and at last triumphantly subjective. We must expect, as an inevitable fact, the conformation of object with subject in some degree. We may thus also expect the critical mind to seek out, for its study, the objects most profitably conformable with itself.

'To burn always with this hard, gemlike flame'. This was certainly an arresting figure. It is easy to see why many readers, both then and now, might balk at the ethical consequences of what at first sight seems a retreat into experiential isolationism. But the loneliness of the individual immured behind impenetrable walls of subjectivity is a prospect which we are invited to find troubling as well as bracing, and from which Pater derives a melancholy pathos. And it is not often enough noticed that when the famous sentence continues, clarifying its metaphor, '*to maintain this ecstasy*', the precise implication—especially in the work of a writer who takes such care over classical etymologies—is that one's experience is to involve not merely a one-way traffic of impressions inward from the mysterious outer world, but the displacement of the subject from its own confines: '*ecstasy*', a lifting *out* of oneself, out of one's settled place.

But outward to where? If sometimes to the external world of palpable things, then also, at times, to an even less knowable world of the ideal, the metaphysical. Devotion to physical reality is strong in Pater, but so is an attraction to abstract speculation. He readily sympathises with philosophical idealism so long as it does not result in a contempt for the concrete or the humane. Pater's celebration of sensuous experience was therefore never a strident materialism, if the 'materialist' is taken to be one who cares little for the spiritual or the ideal. If we are really capable of determining only our *impressions* of external reality, then things come to criticism always in the form of their impress on the particular human mind—namely that of the artist, whose impression or apprehension is relayed to the critic in place of the original stimulus—or else on a group of minds, as interpreted by the critic's historical sense. Inanimate things presumed to have their own existence are received by criticism wrapped in general or accumulated ideas. For Pater the objective world is always made inward, or approached through the particular inwardness of some other character, real or fictional. And if the world is full of variety in itself, this viewing of its objects under such various human lights has the effect of almost infinitely multiplying that variousness. The things, the facts, are presented to the critical mind as 'soul-facts'. Idealist philosophy, indeed all abstract or metaphysical thinking, is from one point of view a realm made up entirely of soul-facts.

Plato and Platonism displays constantly the aesthete grappling with the idealist. It is not simply Pater *vs.* Plato, however, but a more complex accommodation between two authors each presumed to have instincts tending in either direction. There are two sides of Pater, two faces of Plato. The 'Dorian' element in Plato, 'centripetal', 'reserved', and somewhat austere, is aligned with some of Pater's own habits of thought. And yet the Victorian critic was also faced with the task of proving satisfactorily that this aspect of Plato (his unworldliness and suspicion of the arts) did not actually cancel out another aspect: the earthly, humanistic Plato, affectionately attentive to the concrete details of the physical world. This was Plato the 'lover', as Pater says; lover of young men, but also of all visible or material beauty. His 'intimate concern with, his power over, the sensible world' must therefore be given particular emphasis, in order to make him more than purely an antagonist to modern aestheticism.[56] Pater's friend and disciple, the poet and critic Lionel Johnson, wrote in a review of the book: 'Mr. Pater has shown us how fruitful of good things is this visible world, with its garniture and furniture for every sense'.[57] Not necessarily what one would expect from a book about Platonism, but natural in a book by Walter Pater. He sees the beauty of 'renunciation', its 'eternal moral charm'.[58] But it must be something truly desired and highly valued that is renounced.

Théophile Gautier once said of himself, and Pater, repeating him, says again of Plato, that he was 'a man for whom the visible world really existed'.[59] Throughout his work, Pater shows himself to be another such character. Even with his early-settled and never-resolved scepticism, even with his relativism, to him the visible, external world of things and people was never without *existence*—a reality that had an exigent claim upon his attention. Gautier's words are no contradiction to Pater's epistemological uncertainties; they do not break down the distinction between things 'in themselves' and their mere appearances, nor solve the problem of the questionable coincidence of my impression and yours. There are people, he implies, to whom the visible world does *not* really exist; those who, through lack of care, or absorption in abstract considerations, do not recognise its claims, charms or subtleties. Once more it is a matter of temperament. There *is* a visible world: but to each individual it must be visible differently, and in different degrees, and with different points of emphasis.

ETHICS, AESTHETICS AND CRITICISM

'It may be said, I think, that he never returned to Christianity in the orthodox or intellectual sense', Pater's friend, the novelist Mary Humphry Ward, wrote of him. 'But his heart returned to it.'[60] That is, he does not appear ever to have arrived at a condition of Christian faith, but his published works show a sustained and probably deepening susceptibility to the moral beauty of such a state. In ending one of his essays on classical Greek sculpture, he is moved to the following, somewhat unexpected reflection about the pagan spirit of the ancient Greek:

He had been faithful, we cannot help saying, as we pass from that youthful company, in what comparatively is perhaps little—in the culture, the administration, of the visible world; and he merited, so we might go on to say—he merited Revelation, something which should solace his heart in the inevitable fading of that.[61]

For an author as much interested in 'the visible world' as Pater was, and such an eager advocate on behalf of its careful 'culture', this may seem an unusual comment. It is all a matter of 'perhaps'. It is what one 'might go on to say'. And yet the coy tone, the delaying dash, the momentary self-repetition ('he merited'), make the comment seem only the more personal in effect, more loaded with significance for the speaker, as we watch him acknowledging irresolution, and then dramatizing the moment at which it is overcome. Without expressing any faith of his own, Pater appears to suppose that merely living in the age of 'Revelation' is to feel at least the *possibility* of a solace such as the Greek could never have known.

The mere possibility can make a considerable difference. It does so, certainly, for Marius, as he moves from a pagan world into the embrace of a Christian community. And in a review of Mary Ward's own novel, *Robert Elsmere*, Pater writes this:

> It is philosophical, doubtless, and a duty to the intellect to recognize our doubts, to locate them, perhaps to give them practical effect. It may be also a moral duty to do this. But then there is also a large class of minds which cannot be sure it is false [*i.e. the basis of Christian religion*]—minds of very various degrees of conscientiousness and intellectual power, up to the highest. They will think those who are quite sure it is false unphilosophical through lack of doubt. For their part, they make allowance in their scheme of life for a great possibility, and with some of them that bare concession of possibility (the subject of it being what it is) becomes the most important fact in the world.[62]

Deliberately elusive again, he stands behind another scrupulously impersonal but feelingful statement. It is characteristic of Pater that *possibilities* themselves become mental *facts*, in this case the fact of an uncertainty, while supposedly definite *facts* are softened into *possibilities*, differing with perspective: 'soul-facts'.

As for *Robert Elsmere* itself, the terms in which Pater praises it are those in which his later moral thinking is often formulated: 'it abounds in sympathy with people as we find them, in aspiration towards something better—towards a certain ideal'. Also, returning to this favourite phrase, he finds in it 'a refreshing sense of second thoughts everywhere'.⁶³ One must sympathise with people as they really are, in all their variousness, just as one must remain attentive to the sensuous world as we really find it; but ethically it is also good to be aspiring to a higher ideal.

This instinctive aim for the improvement of the moral world is a preoccupation much more frequently encountered in Pater's work after *The Renaissance*. Marius, for instance, finds fault at last with the Emperor's equable attitude of detachment from social realities: the Stoic Aurelius, it seems to him, has 'too much of a complacent acquiescence in the world as it is'. His philosophic idealism is too remote from his earthly dominion. The failing is for once quite bluntly put: 'It amounted to a tolerance of evil'.⁶⁴ Though Pater remained ostensibly committed to an ideal of morality more concerned with *being* than with *doing*, the existence of evil is presented by him as a fact which appeals loudly for redress, and requires at least a decisive rejection by the individual; evil that is 'real as an aching in the head or heart, which one instinctively desires to have cured'. It is imagined with sinister liveliness, 'an enemy with whom no terms could be made, visible, hatefully visible, in a thousand forms—the apparent waste of men's gifts in an early, or even in a late grave; the death, as such, of men, and even of animals; the disease and pain of the body'.⁶⁵

Walter Pater has sometimes been mistaken for an amoral writer. It may at least be said fairly that he is far from being a 'moralist' in the sense that can be easily applied to Ruskin, Carlyle, Morris, Newman or Mill: all writers naturally related to him in one way or another. Nevertherless he was a moral thinker from the very beginning. Aesthetic sensibility was a part of moral character, a matter of *mores* and values; and some of the artistic values that Pater admires, such as fastidiousness, reserve, or *ascesis*, are clearly moral qualities as well.

Precision, sincerity, sympathy, suspended judgement, a refusal to acquiesce in the unjust or the sordid—but still a readiness for the critic to give aesthetic credit wherever due, even in the midst of sordor or cruelty, as in the case of Mérimée—these are some of the ethical principles one might collect from the full range of Pater's works. In his essay on *Measure for Measure* he depicted the kind of moral delicacy he valued:

> The idea of justice involves the idea of rights. But at bottom rights are equivalent to that which really is, to facts; and the recognition of his rights therefore, the justice he requires of our hands, or our thoughts, is the recognition of that which the person, in his inmost nature, really is; and as sympathy alone can discover that which really is in matters of feeling and thought, true justice is in its essence a finer knowledge through love. [...] It is for this finer justice, a justice based on a more delicate appreciation

of the true conditions of men and things, a true respect of persons in our estimate of actions, that the people in *Measure for Measure* cry out as they pass before us [...]. It is not always that poetry can be the exponent of morality; but it is this aspect of morals which it represents most naturally, for this true justice is dependent on just those finer appreciations which poetry cultivates in us the power of making, those peculiar valuations of action and its effect which poetry actually requires.[66]

To some modern readers, Pater's moral or political attitude must seem little better than a passive wistfulness; but one regularly encounters defences of the moral status of the 'aesthetic', or of the arts, that are much less persuasive than this. 'Finer knowledge through love'—a refinement of understanding, and so of justice, by the operation of an active and curious sympathy—is the moral ambition of Pater's humane 'observer' (the word is his). And it correlates both with the artistic ambition of the writer for refinement of language and thought, and with the answering ambition of the critic for finer appreciation and comprehension. So the *mot juste*, or the writer's search for it as portrayed in the 'Essay on Style', is naturally akin to 'justice' in the ethical sphere.

Fineness as justice; rightness in, and by means of, *finesse*. Finish emerges as an ethical as well as an aesthetic commitment, entailing effort. Criticism, meaning 'judgement', not only becomes, in its pronouncement, a moral action, but is always—even privately and in suspension—a question of moral relationships, and of the attitude with which its objects are regarded: the temper, the carefully sustained state of mind, in which one agrees to meet them. Self-criticism, too, must be a habit of discipline, inevitably moral in character and implication; and this is the foundation for artistic expression. Pater was at all times both artist *and* critic. 'Scholarship', in his special sense of the word, meaning a careful sensitivity and disciplined curiosity, was the necessary aspiration behind the exercise of either function, insofar as they might truly be divisible. Whether we are thinking of art or, in the very largest sense, criticism, the moral value of care with language may today be one of the most important things Pater can cause us to re-examine. He is a writer devoted to fairness, which implies both beauty and justice. Pater is interested in both, and in their relationship.

The moral dimension in Pater's aesthetics is not a question of didacticism in art, but of sympathetic scrupulousness spreading from aesthetic experience into larger moral habits: an extension outward of the 'fineness' of response, and the 'respect' for things, which a devotion to art instils. At the end of the previous century, Friedrich Schiller, an author Pater seems often to have had in his thoughts, wrote that art should give its beholders 'the *direction* towards the good', and that it should do so not by preaching, but through aesthetic means. 'Drive away lawlessness, frivolity and coarseness from their pleasure, and you will imperceptibly banish them from their actions, and finally from their dispositions.'[67] Pater likewise hoped that the proper 'aesthetic education' of the individual, which must go hand in hand with a process of moral self-cultivation, might ultimately make a contribution to the good of society in general. And yet for the individual, and perhaps for society, he clearly accepts no single ideal of perfection. How could a thinker won over by the 'undulancy' of human nature reduce the perfect moral life to a single type?

'There are some', Pater observes, 'to whom nothing has any real interest, or real meaning, except as operative in a given person'. Those for whom this is true are they who tend or prefer to take all things as personally as possible; readers, for instance, who 'seem to know a *person*, in a book'.[68] He is not explicitly speaking of himself, but the evidence of Pater's work suggests that he might have been. The essays show again and again that this was either his own instinctive experience, or else, at any rate, a large part of his purpose in writing; and it is worth noting that he was an admirer, in some ways a follower, of the French critic Sainte-Beuve and his biographical method of criticism. But even abstract ideas could become personal, in the sense of their being regarded like a person—demanding the respect and soliciting the affection due to real people. We hear this more than once in the course of the lectures on Plato, while in *Marius* it is significant that the protagonist's epiphanic experience, alone on the hills around Rome, takes hold of him through a 'sense of companionship, of a person beside him'. Marius in this instant has 'apprehended the *Great Ideal*', and for once not merely as a cold abstraction, but in the feeling of 'a friendly hand laid upon him amid the shadows of the world'.[69]

'In whom did the stir, the genius, the sentiment of the period find itself', Pater asks in the 'Preface' to *The Renaissance*. One of the distinctive qualities of modernity, as he sees it, is its cultivation of 'the historic sense, which, by an imaginative act, throws itself back into a world unlike one's own, and estimates every intellectual creation in its connexion with the age from which it proceeded'.[70] He believes in the Hegelian Time-Spirit or *Zeit-Geist* of history. The character and fashions of a time and place, the ephemeral details of life as well as the modes of feeling and terms of thought, intrigue him and appeal to his imagination, partly because they are so elusive. Yet his primary emphasis almost everywhere is on the exceptional individual, the sensibility that comes a little early, or late, or out of place, or that interprets in a special way the prevailing conditions; and on the particular artistic and intellectual creations—idiosyncratic or typical, and very often both—of persons who are both *of* their age, in whatever way, and above it. The European Renaissance, in one aspect at least, meant to Pater the emergence and the triumph of the modern individual. The revival of antiquity had involved, he felt, a restoration of dignity to the human body, allied to a deepened dignity of the soul.

Humanity, the *human* or *humane*, are concepts to which Pater frequently appeals, and in his writing the 'humanities' may refer to just about any field of activity in which sensitive people have refined upon the thoughts, arts and manners proper to individuals living freely in a civilized society; 'liberal arts', in a much widened sense. The Time-Spirit moves onward, but these humanities accrue, and the modern critical mind is still able, perhaps obliged, to put an intelligent sympathy to work on the human experience of the past, especially as it is recorded in the works of its writers and artists. Sir Thomas Browne, in the seventeenth century, may have been prone to as many fallacies as he tried to disprove; Coleridge, at the start of the nineteenth, may have been a struggler in vain against the 'relative spirit' of modernity itself; and Pico della Mirandola in the Florentine Renaissance is judged to have been wholly lacking in the true 'historic sense' itself. But the relativistic, historically-minded Pater is also a humanist ready to find value in unexpected places, and does not need to *agree* in order to appreciate and value highly. So what he finally says of Pico, after having shown his limitations, may perhaps also serve today as a thought-provoking comment—valuably suggestive, however overstated—on Pater himself, once we have made any necessary allowances for whatever in his critical practice we ourselves now find antiquated:

> The essence of humanism is that belief of which he seems never to have doubted, that nothing which has ever interested living men and women can wholly lose its vitality—no language they have spoken, nor oracle beside which they have hushed their voices, no dream which has once been entertained by actual human minds, nothing about which they have ever been passionate, or expended time and zeal.[71]

Notes

For texts included in the present selection, paragraph references are given; other quotations from Pater refer to the Library Edition (1910). Abbreviations are explained in the preface to the Explanatory Notes at the end of this volume.

1. Quotation from Richard Le Gallienne, *The Romantic '90s* (London and New York: Putnam, 1926), p. 74.
2. Denis Donoghue, *Walter Pater: Lover of Strange Souls* (New York: Knopf, 1995), p. 6.
3. Yeats, *Collected Works*, vol. 3: *Autobiographies*, ed. William H. O'Donnell and Douglas N. Archibald (New York: Scribner, 1999), p. 124.
4. Osbert Burdett, 'Introduction' to his Everyman's Library edn of *Marius the Epicurean* (London: Dent, 1934), p. viii.
5. The relevant documents are printed and discussed in Billie Andrew Inman, 'Estrangement and Connection: Walter Pater, Benjamin Jowett, and William M. Hardinge', in *Pater in the 1990s*, ed. Laurel Brake and Ian Small (Greensboro: ELT Press, 1991), pp. 1–20.
6. The source is the diary of A.C. Benson, who heard it from Edmund Gosse in 1905, some years after Pater's death (and after Benson had already finished his own critical biography of Pater). But neither Gosse nor Benson committed these details to print.
7. Lene Østermark-Johansen has produced a critical edition of Pater's *Imaginary Portraits* (London: MHRA, 2014), collecting all of his short fiction and not only those printed in 1887. She is also the editor of the new volume dedicated to the 'portraits' in the ten-volume edition of Pater's *Collected Works* that is currently in preparation for Oxford University Press.
8. Edward Thomas, *Walter Pater: A Critical Study* (London: Secker, 1913), p. 224.
9. A number of other review-essays, written for a range of periodicals, have so far remained uncollected, though they will certainly be included in the forthcoming OUP *Collected Works*.
10. Drafts for some additional chapters were left in manuscript and have been incorporated into a modern critical edition, *Gaston de Latour: The Revised Text*, ed. Gerald Monsman (Greensboro: ELT Press, 1995). They will also be included in the OUP *Collected Works*.
11. *Marius*, Lib. Edn, vol. 1, p. 25 (ch. 2).
12. Arthur Christopher Benson, *Walter Pater* (London: Macmillan, 1906), p. 174.
13. *Ren.*, 'Conclusion', ¶4.
14. *App.*, 'Charles Lamb', ¶13 (and see notes for source).
15. Benson, *op. cit.*, pp. 156, 164.
16. *Ren.*, 'Preface', ¶2.
17. The latter essay is the first in Arnold's *Essays in Criticism, First Series* (London: Macmillan, 1865).
18. *Ren.*, 'Preface', ¶2.
19. All these quotations are from *Ren.*, 'Conclusion'.
20. Sarah B. Wister, 'Pater, Rio, and Burckhardt,' *North American Review*, vol. 121, no. 248 (July 1875), pp. 155–90.
21. *Ren.*, 'Winckelmann', ¶40, ¶41, ¶22.
22. *Ren.* 'Conclusion', ¶4.
23. *Ibid.*, ¶5.
24. See R.M. Seiler (ed.), *Walter Pater: The Critical Heritage*, pp. 61–63 (item 4).
25. George Moore, *Avowals* (London: Heinemann, 1924; first published 1919), pp. 191, 85.
26. *Ibid.*, p. 170.

27. Edmund Gosse, 'Walter Pater', in *Critical Kit-Kats* (London: Heinemann, 1896, repr. 1913), pp. 239–72; p. 262.
28. *Ren.*, 'Conclusion', ¶4.
29. Moore, *op. cit.*, p. 187.
30. Ferris Greenslet, *Walter Pater* (London: Heinemann, 1905), p. 96.
31. 'Purple panel' is what George Saintsbury names it, reluctant to call it a 'patch'; *A History of English Prose Rhythm* (London: Macmillan, 1912), p. 421. The much-anthologized passage in question comprises ¶29–30, but esp. ¶30, as given here.
32. *PP*, 'The Doctrine of Plato, Pt II: Dialectic', ¶4.
33. *Ibid.*, ¶2.
34. *Ibid.*, ¶4.
35. *App.*, 'Charles Lamb', ¶13.
36. *Ibid.*, ¶18.
37. Lamb, 'A Character of the Late Elia' (1823), later added to the *Last Essays of Elia*.
38. Benson, *op. cit.*, pp. 191, 180.
39. *Ibid.*, p. 192.
40. *PP*, 'Dialectic', ¶16.
41. *App.*, 'Wordsworth', ¶25. Subsequent quotations from ¶24, ¶22.
42. *Marius*, Lib. Edn, vol. 2, p. 15 (ch. 16).
43. *Ibid.*, pp. 90–91 (ch. 20).
44. *App.*, 'Style', ¶4–6.
45. *Gaston*, Lib. Edn, p. 100 (ch. 5).
46. *Ibid.*, p. 91 (ch. 5).
47. *Ibid.*
48. Benson, *op. cit.*, p. 48.
49. *Ren.*, 'Sandro Botticelli', ¶6.
50. From the essay 'The Present Position of English Criticism', *Time* (Dec. 1885), pp. 669–78. Find in Seiler, *Critical Heritage*, pp. 109–12; p. 110.
51. 'Diaphaneité', in *MS*, Lib. Edn, p. 254.
52. 'Emerald Uthwart', in *MS*, Lib. Edn, p. 230.
53. T.S. Eliot, 'Hamlet' (1919), in *Selected Essays*, 3rd edn (London: Faber, 1951, repr. 1999), pp. 141–46; p. 141.
54. *App.*, 'Charles Lamb', ¶14.
55. *Gaston*, Lib. Edn, p. 105 (ch. 5).
56. *PP*, 'The Genius of Plato', ¶11.
57. Lionel Johnson, 'Mr. Pater Upon Plato' (1893), in *Post Liminium: Essays and Critical Papers* (London: Elkin Mathews, 1912), pp. 1–10; p. 3.
58. 'Robert Elsmere', in *EG*, Lib. Edn, pp. 55–70; p. 62.
59. *PP*, 'The Genius of Plato', ¶3 (and see notes for source).
60. Mrs Humphry Ward, *A Writer's Recollections* (London: Harper & Brothers, 1918), vol. 1, p. 162.
61. *GS*, 'The Age of Athletic Prizemen' (extracts on Greek Sculpture, extr. [ii.c]), ¶26.
62. 'Robert Elsmere', in *EG*, Lib. Edn, pp. 67–68.
63. *Ibid.*, p. 55.
64. *Marius*, Lib. Edn, vol. 2, p. 51 (ch. 18).
65. *Ibid.*, p. 53.
66. 'Measure for Measure', in *App.*, Lib. Edn, pp. 170–84; pp. 183–84.
67. Friedrich Schiller, *On the Aesthetic Education of Man* (1794), trans. Reginald Snell (New Haven: Yale University Press, 1954), pp. 50–55 (letter 9).
68. *App.*, 'Style', ¶16.
69. See *PP*, 'The Genius of Plato', ¶5; *Marius*, vol. 2, p. 71 (ch. 19).
70. *Ren.*, 'Pico Della Mirandola', ¶4.
71. *Ibid.*, ¶16.

Note on the Text

The essays and extracts in this selection are reproduced from the text of the 'Library Edition' of Pater's *Works*, first published by Macmillan in 1910 and several times reprinted, which included the five books Pater published during his lifetime, in each case following the text of the final edition overseen by the author himself, as well as the four further volumes published posthumously by Pater's friends, the contents of which, with the one exception of 'The Child in the House', had never been reprinted by Pater, and so had never been revised. The Library Edition superseded the 'Edition De Luxe' of 1900-01, which had been somewhat inconsistent in its choice of texts, not always honouring Pater's last revisions. The rationale behind the choice of the 1910 text for the present anthology has been governed by a wish to respect the 'second thoughts' of a careful writer.

The arrangement of the essays according the volumes in which they eventually appeared, rather than in chronological order of composition or first publication (in periodicals), is partly motivated by the consideration that most of Pater's readers, from his own day down to ours, have encountered his writings in books rather than journals, and that there is a value in retaining for the modern reader the sense of companionship between essays, and the identity of the whole volumes, as they have been generally conceived and remembered. But of course there is another, more practical motivation, which proceeds from the choice of copy-texts: for by giving priority to the latest authorial text, and incorporating all revisions, in many cases one is necessarily providing a version quite different from the earliest publication. A chronological disposition of the material based on the *date* of the first publication, but the *text* of the last, would be nonsensical and misleading.

The Library Edition is not without its problems. Misprints which are clearly no more than typesetting errors have been silently corrected in the present selection, with reference to earlier editions. But mistakes of this sort are extremely few. Other suggested corrections, dubious readings, or unexplained deviations from the final authorial texts have been remarked and discussed in the notes at the end of the volume. Finally, it may be worth stating clearly that the numbering of paragraphs should be regarded as part of the editorial apparatus, having been judged preferable to the numbering of lines on every page. Paragraph numbers are not printed in any of the early editions.

from THE RENAISSANCE

PREFACE

Many attempts have been made by writers on art and poetry to define beauty in the abstract, to express it in the most general terms, to find some universal formula for it. The value of these attempts has most often been in the suggestive and penetrating things said by the way. Such discussions help us very little to enjoy what has been well done in art or poetry, to discriminate between what is more and what is less excellent in them, or to use words like beauty, excellence, art, poetry, with a more precise meaning than they would otherwise have. Beauty, like all other qualities presented to human experience, is relative; and the definition of it becomes unmeaning and useless in proportion to its abstractness. To define beauty, not in the most abstract but in the most concrete terms possible, to find not its universal formula, but the formula which expresses most adequately this or that special manifestation of it, is the aim of the true student of æsthetics.

2. "To see the object as in itself it really is," has been justly said to be the aim of all true criticism whatever; and in æsthetic criticism the first step towards seeing one's object as it really is, is to know one's own impression as it really is, to discriminate it, to realise it distinctly. The objects with which æsthetic criticism deals—music, poetry, artistic and accomplished forms of human life—are indeed receptacles of so many powers or forces: they possess, like the products of nature, so many virtues or qualities. What is this song or picture, this engaging personality presented in life or in a book, to *me*? What effect does it really produce on me? Does it give me pleasure? and if so, what sort or degree of pleasure? How is my nature modified by its presence, and under its influence? The answers to these questions are the original facts with which the æsthetic critic has to do; and, as in the study of light, of morals, of number, one must realise such primary data for one's self, or not at all. And he who experiences these impressions strongly, and drives directly at the discrimination and analysis of them, has no need to trouble himself with the abstract question what beauty is in itself, or what its exact relation to truth or experience—metaphysical questions, as unprofitable as metaphysical questions elsewhere. He may pass them all by as being, answerable or not, of no interest to him.

3. The æsthetic critic, then, regards all the objects with which he has to do, all works of art, and the fairer forms of nature and human life, as powers or forces producing pleasurable sensations, each of a more or less peculiar or unique kind. This influence he feels, and wishes to explain, by analysing and

reducing it to its elements. To him, the picture, the landscape, the engaging personality in life or in a book, *La Gioconda*, the hills of Carrara, Pico of Mirandola, are valuable for their virtues, as we say, in speaking of a herb, a wine, a gem; for the property each has of affecting one with a special, a unique, impression of pleasure. Our education becomes complete in proportion as our susceptibility to these impressions increases in depth and variety. And the function of the æsthetic critic is to distinguish, to analyse, and separate from its adjuncts, the virtue by which a picture, a landscape, a fair personality in life or in a book, produces this special impression of beauty or pleasure, to indicate what the source of that impression is, and under what conditions it is experienced. His end is reached when he has disengaged that virtue, and noted it, as a chemist notes some natural element, for himself and others; and the rule for those who would reach this end is stated with great exactness in the words of a recent critic of Sainte-Beuve:—*De se borner à connaître de près les belles choses, et à s'en nourrir en exquis amateurs, en humanistes accomplis.*

4. What is important, then, is not that the critic should possess a correct abstract definition of beauty for the intellect, but a certain kind of temperament, the power of being deeply moved by the presence of beautiful objects. He will remember always that beauty exists in many forms. To him all periods, types, schools of taste, are in themselves equal. In all ages there have been some excellent workmen, and some excellent work done. The question he asks is always:—In whom did the stir, the genius, the sentiment of the period find itself? where was the receptacle of its refinement, its elevation, its taste? "The ages are all equal," says William Blake, "but genius is always above its age."

5. Often it will require great nicety to disengage this virtue from the commoner elements with which it may be found in combination. Few artists, not Goethe or Byron even, work quite cleanly, casting off all *débris*, and leaving us only what the heat of their imagination has wholly fused and transformed. Take, for instance, the writings of Wordsworth. The heat of his genius, entering into the substance of his work, has crystallised a part, but only a part, of it; and in that great mass of verse there is much which might well be forgotten. But scattered up and down it, sometimes fusing and transforming entire compositions, like the Stanzas on *Resolution and Independence*, or the *Ode on the Recollections of Childhood*, sometimes, as if at random, depositing a fine crystal here or there, in a matter it does not wholly search through and transmute, we trace the action of his unique, incommunicable faculty, that strange, mystical sense of a life in natural things, and of man's life as a part of nature, drawing strength and colour and character from local influences, from the hills and streams, and from natural sights and sounds. Well! that is the *virtue*, the active principle in Wordsworth's poetry; and then the function

of the critic of Wordsworth is to follow up that active principle, to disengage it, to mark the degree in which it penetrates his verse.

6. The subjects of the following studies are taken from the history of the *Renaissance*, and touch what I think the chief points in that complex, many-sided movement. I have explained in the first of them what I understand by the word, giving it a much wider scope than was intended by those who originally used it to denote that revival of classical antiquity in the fifteenth century which was only one of many results of a general excitement and enlightening of the human mind, but of which the great aim and achievements of what, as Christian art, is often falsely opposed to the Renaissance, were another result. This outbreak of the human spirit may be traced far into the middle age itself, with its motives already clearly pronounced, the care for physical beauty, the worship of the body, the breaking down of those limits which the religious system of the middle age imposed on the heart and the imagination. I have taken as an example of this movement, this earlier Renaissance within the middle age itself, and as an expression of its qualities, two little compositions in early French; not because they constitute the best possible expression of them, but because they help the unity of my series, inasmuch as the Renaissance ends also in France, in French poetry, in a phase of which the writings of Joachim du Bellay are in many ways the most perfect illustration. The Renaissance, in truth, put forth in France an aftermath, a wonderful later growth, the products of which have to the full that subtle and delicate sweetness which belongs to a refined and comely decadence, just as its earliest phases have the freshness which belongs to all periods of growth in art, the charm of *ascêsis*, of the austere and serious girding of the loins in youth.

7. But it is in Italy, in the fifteenth century, that the interest of the Renaissance mainly lies,—in that solemn fifteenth century which can hardly be studied too much, not merely for its positive results in the things of the intellect and the imagination, its concrete works of art, its special and prominent personalities, with their profound æsthetic charm, but for its general spirit and character, for the ethical qualities of which it is a consummate type.

8. The various forms of intellectual activity which together make up the culture of an age, move for the most part from different starting-points, and by unconnected roads. As products of the same generation they partake indeed of a common character, and unconsciously illustrate each other; but of the producers themselves, each group is solitary, gaining what advantage or disadvantage there may be in intellectual isolation. Art and poetry, philosophy and the religious life, and that other life of refined pleasure and action in the conspicuous places of the world, are each of them confined to its own circle of ideas, and those who prosecute either of them are generally little curious

of the thoughts of others. There come, however, from time to time, eras of more favourable conditions, in which the thoughts of men draw nearer together than is their wont, and the many interests of the intellectual world combine in one complete type of general culture. The fifteenth century in Italy is one of these happier eras, and what is sometimes said of the age of Pericles is true of that of Lorenzo:—it is an age productive in personalities, many-sided, centralised, complete. Here, artists and philosophers and those whom the action of the world has elevated and made keen, do not live in isolation, but breathe a common air, and catch light and heat from each other's thoughts. There is a spirit of general elevation and enlightenment in which all alike communicate. The unity of this spirit gives unity to all the various products of the Renaissance; and it is to this intimate alliance with mind, this participation in the best thoughts which that age produced, that the art of Italy in the fifteenth century owes much of its grave dignity and influence.

9. I have added an essay on Winckelmann, as not incongruous with the studies which precede it, because Winckelmann, coming in the eighteenth century, really belongs in spirit to an earlier age. By his enthusiasm for the things of the intellect and the imagination for their own sake, by his Hellenism, his life-long struggle to attain to the Greek spirit, he is in sympathy with the humanists of a previous century. He is the last fruit of the Renaissance, and explains in a striking way its motive and tendencies.

1873.

PICO DELLA MIRANDOLA

No account of the Renaissance can be complete without some notice of the attempt made by certain Italian scholars of the fifteenth century to reconcile Christianity with the religion of ancient Greece. To reconcile forms of sentiment which at first sight seem incompatible, to adjust the various products of the human mind to one another in one many-sided type of intellectual culture, to give humanity, for heart and imagination to feed upon, as much as it could possibly receive, belonged to the generous instincts of that age. An earlier and simpler generation had seen in the gods of Greece so many malignant spirits, the defeated but still living centres of the religion of darkness, struggling, not always in vain, against the kingdom of light. Little by little, as the natural charm of pagan story reasserted itself over minds emerging out of barbarism, the religious significance which had once belonged to it was lost sight of, and it came to be regarded as the subject of a purely artistic or poetical treatment. But it was inevitable that from time to time minds should arise, deeply enough impressed by its beauty and power to ask themselves whether the religion of Greece was indeed a rival of the religion of Christ; for the older gods had rehabilitated themselves, and men's allegiance was divided. And the fifteenth century was an impassioned age, so ardent and serious in its pursuit of art that it consecrated everything with which art had to do as a religious object. The restored Greek literature had made it familiar, at least in Plato, with a style of expression concerning the earlier gods, which had about it something of the warmth and unction of a Christian hymn. It was too familiar with such language to regard mythology as a mere story; and it was too serious to play with a religion.

2. "Let me briefly remind the reader"—says Heine, in the *Gods in Exile*, an essay full of that strange blending of sentiment which is characteristic of the traditions of the middle age concerning the pagan religions—"how the gods of the older world, at the time of the definite triumph of Christianity, that is, in the third century, fell into painful embarrassments, which greatly resembled certain tragical situations of their earlier life. They now found themselves beset by the same troublesome necessities to which they had once before been exposed during the primitive ages, in that revolutionary epoch when the Titans broke out of the custody of Orcus, and, piling Pelion on Ossa, scaled Olympus. Unfortunate gods! They had then to take flight ignominiously, and hide themselves among us here on earth, under all sorts of disguises. The larger number betook themselves to Egypt, where for greater security they assumed the forms of animals, as is

generally known. Just in the same way, they had to take flight again, and seek entertainment in remote hiding-places, when those iconoclastic zealots, the black brood of monks, broke down all the temples, and pursued the gods with fire and curses. Many of these unfortunate emigrants, now entirely deprived of shelter and ambrosia, must needs take to vulgar handicrafts, as a means of earning their bread. Under these circumstances, many whose sacred groves had been confiscated, let themselves out for hire as wood-cutters in Germany, and were forced to drink beer instead of nectar. Apollo seems to have been content to take service under graziers, and as he had once kept the cows of Admetus, so he lived now as a shepherd in Lower Austria. Here, however, having become suspected on account of his beautiful singing, he was recognised by a learned monk as one of the old pagan gods, and handed over to the spiritual tribunal. On the rack he confessed that he was the god Apollo; and before his execution he begged that he might be suffered to play once more upon the lyre, and to sing a song. And he played so touchingly, and sang with such magic, and was withal so beautiful in form and feature, that all the women wept, and many of them were so deeply impressed that they shortly afterwards fell sick. Some time afterwards the people wished to drag him from the grave again, that a stake might be driven through his body, in the belief that he had been a vampire, and that the sick women would by this means recover. But they found the grave empty."

3. The Renaissance of the fifteenth century was, in many things, great rather by what it designed than by what it achieved. Much which it aspired to do, and did but imperfectly or mistakenly, was accomplished in what is called the *éclaircissement* of the eighteenth century, or in our own generation; and what really belongs to the revival of the fifteenth century is but the leading instinct, the curiosity, the initiatory idea. It is so with this very question of the reconciliation of the religion of antiquity with the religion of Christ. A modern scholar occupied by this problem might observe that all religions may be regarded as natural products, that, at least in their origin, their growth, and decay, they have common laws, and are not to be isolated from the other movements of the human mind in the periods in which they respectively prevailed; that they arise spontaneously out of the human mind, as expressions of the varying phases of its sentiment concerning the unseen world; that every intellectual product must be judged from the point of view of the age and the people in which it was produced. He might go on to observe that each has contributed something to the development of the religious sense, and ranging them as so many stages in the gradual education of the human mind, justify the existence of each. The basis of the reconciliation of the religions of the world would thus be the inexhaustible activity and creativeness of the human mind itself, in which all religions alike have their root, and in which all alike

are reconciled; just as the fancies of childhood and the thoughts of old age meet and are laid to rest, in the experience of the individual.

4. Far different was the method followed by the scholars of the fifteenth century. They lacked the very rudiments of the historic sense, which, by an imaginative act, throws itself back into a world unlike one's own, and estimates every intellectual creation in its connexion with the age from which it proceeded. They had no idea of development, of the differences of ages, of the process by which our race has been "educated." In their attempts to reconcile the religions of the world, they were thus thrown back upon the quicksand of allegorical interpretation. The religions of the world were to be reconciled, not as successive stages in a regular development of the religious sense, but as subsisting side by side, and substantially in agreement with one another. And here the first necessity was to misrepresent the language, the conceptions, the sentiments, it was proposed to compare and reconcile. Plato and Homer must be made to speak agreeably to Moses. Set side by side, the mere surfaces could never unite in any harmony of design. Therefore one must go below the surface, and bring up the supposed secondary, or still more remote meaning,—that diviner signification held in reserve, *in recessu divinius aliquid*, latent in some stray touch of Homer, or figure of speech in the books of Moses.

5. And yet as a curiosity of the human mind, a "madhouse-cell," if you will, into which we may peep for a moment, and see it at work weaving strange fancies, the allegorical interpretation of the fifteenth century has its interest. With its strange web of imagery, its quaint conceits, its unexpected combinations and subtle moralising, it is an element in the local colour of a great age. It illustrates also the faith of that age in all oracles, its desire to hear all voices, its generous belief that nothing which had ever interested the human mind could wholly lose its vitality. It is the counterpart, though certainly the feebler counterpart, of that practical truce and reconciliation of the gods of Greece with the Christian religion, which is seen in the art of the time. And it is for his share in this work, and because his own story is a sort of analogue or visible equivalent to the expression of this purpose in his writings, that something of a general interest still belongs to the name of Pico della Mirandola, whose life, written by his nephew Francis, seemed worthy, for some touch of sweetness in it, to be translated out of the original Latin by Sir Thomas More, that great lover of Italian culture, among whose works the life of Pico, *Earl of Mirandola, and a great lord of Italy*, as he calls him, may still be read, in its quaint, antiquated English.

6. Marsilio Ficino has told us how Pico came to Florence. It was the very day—some day probably in the year 1482—on which Ficino had finished his famous translation of Plato into Latin, the work to which he had been dedicated from childhood by Cosmo de' Medici, in furtherance of his desire to

resuscitate the knowledge of Plato among his fellow-citizens. Florence indeed, as M. Renan has pointed out, had always had an affinity for the mystic and dreamy philosophy of Plato, while the colder and more practical philosophy of Aristotle had flourished in Padua, and other cities of the north; and the Florentines, though they knew perhaps very little about him, had had the name of the great idealist often on their lips. To increase this knowledge, Cosmo had founded the Platonic academy, with periodical discussions at the Villa Careggi. The fall of Constantinople in 1453, and the council in 1438 for the reconciliation of the Greek and Latin Churches, had brought to Florence many a needy Greek scholar. And now the work was completed, the door of the mystical temple lay open to all who could construe Latin, and the scholar rested from his labour; when there was introduced into his study, where a lamp burned continually before the bust of Plato, as other men burned lamps before their favourite saints, a young man fresh from a journey, "of feature and shape seemly and beauteous, of stature goodly and high, of flesh tender and soft, his visage lovely and fair, his colour white, intermingled with comely reds, his eyes grey, and quick of look, his teeth white and even, his hair yellow and abundant," and trimmed with more than the usual artifice of the time.

7. It is thus that Sir Thomas More translates the words of the biographer of Pico, who, even in outward form and appearance, seems an image of that inward harmony and completeness, of which he is so perfect an example. The word *mystic* has been usually derived from a Greek word which signifies *to shut*, as if one *shut one's lips* brooding on what cannot be uttered; but the Platonists themselves derive it rather from the act of *shutting the eyes*, that one may see the more, inwardly. Perhaps the eyes of the mystic Ficino, now long past the midway of life, had come to be thus half-closed; but when a young man, not unlike the archangel Raphael, as the Florentines of that age depicted him in his wonderful walk with Tobit, or Mercury, as he might have appeared in a painting by Sandro Botticelli or Piero di Cosimo, entered his chamber, he seems to have thought there was something not wholly earthly about him; at least, he ever afterwards believed that it was not without the co-operation of the stars that the stranger had arrived on that day. For it happened that they fell into a conversation, deeper and more intimate than men usually fall into at first sight. During this conversation Ficino formed the design of devoting his remaining years to the translation of Plotinus, that new Plato, in whom the mystical element in the Platonic philosophy had been worked out to the utmost limit of vision and ecstasy; and it is in dedicating this translation to Lorenzo de' Medici that Ficino has recorded these incidents.

8. It was after many wanderings, wanderings of the intellect as well as physical journeys, that Pico came to rest at Florence. Born in 1463, he was

then about twenty years old. He was called Giovanni at baptism, Pico, like all his ancestors, from Picus, nephew of the Emperor Constantine, from whom they claimed to be descended, and Mirandola from the place of his birth, a little town afterwards part of the duchy of Modena, of which small territory his family had long been the feudal lords. Pico was the youngest of the family, and his mother, delighting in his wonderful memory, sent him at the age of fourteen to the famous school of law at Bologna. From the first, indeed, she seems to have had some presentiment of his future fame, for, with a faith in omens characteristic of her time, she believed that a strange circumstance had happened at the time of Pico's birth—the appearance of a circular flame which suddenly vanished away, on the wall of the chamber where she lay. He remained two years at Bologna; and then, with an inexhaustible, unrivalled thirst for knowledge, the strange, confused, uncritical learning of that age, passed through the principal schools of Italy and France, penetrating, as he thought, into the secrets of all ancient philosophies, and many Eastern languages. And with this flood of erudition came the generous hope, so often disabused, of reconciling the philosophers with one another, and all alike with the Church. At last he came to Rome. There, like some knight-errant of philosophy, he offered to defend nine hundred bold paradoxes, drawn from the most opposite sources, against all comers. But the pontifical court was led to suspect the orthodoxy of some of these propositions, and even the reading of the book which contained them was forbidden by the Pope. It was not until 1493 that Pico was finally absolved, by a brief of Alexander the Sixth. Ten years before that date he had arrived at Florence; an early instance of those who, after following the vain hope of an impossible reconciliation from system to system, have at last fallen back unsatisfied on the simplicities of their childhood's belief.

9. The oration which Pico composed for the opening of this philosophical tournament still remains; its subject is the dignity of human nature, the greatness of man. In common with nearly all medieval speculation, much of Pico's writing has this for its drift; and in common also with it, Pico's theory of that dignity is founded on a misconception of the place in nature both of the earth and of man. For Pico the earth is the centre of the universe: and around it, as a fixed and motionless point, the sun and moon and stars revolve, like diligent servants or ministers. And in the midst of all is placed man, *nodus et vinculum mundi*, the bond or copula of the world, and the "interpreter of nature": that famous expression of Bacon's really belongs to Pico. *Tritum est in scholis*, he says, *esse hominem minorem mundum, in quo mixtum ex elementis corpus et spiritus coelestis et plantarum anima vegetalis et brutorum sensus et ratio et angelica mens et Dei similitudo conspicitur.*—"It is a commonplace of the

schools that man is a little world, in which we may discern a body mingled of earthy elements, and ethereal breath, and the vegetable life of plants, and the senses of the lower animals, and reason, and the intelligence of angels, and a likeness to God."

10. A commonplace of the schools! But perhaps it had some new significance and authority, when men heard one like Pico reiterate it; and, false as its basis was, the theory had its use. For this high dignity of man, thus bringing the dust under his feet into sensible communion with the thoughts and affections of the angels, was supposed to belong to him, not as renewed by a religious system, but by his own natural right. The proclamation of it was a counterpoise to the increasing tendency of medieval religion to depreciate man's nature, to sacrifice this or that element in it, to make it ashamed of itself, to keep the degrading or painful accidents of it always in view. It helped man onward to that reassertion of himself, that rehabilitation of human nature, the body, the senses, the heart, the intelligence, which the Renaissance fulfils. And yet to read a page of one of Pico's forgotten books is like a glance into one of those ancient sepulchres, upon which the wanderer in classical lands has sometimes stumbled, with the old disused ornaments and furniture of a world wholly unlike ours still fresh in them. That whole conception of nature is so different from our own. For Pico the world is a limited place, bounded by actual crystal walls, and a material firmament; it is like a painted toy, like that map or system of the world, held, as a great target or shield, in the hands of the creative *Logos*, by whom the Father made all things, in one of the earlier frescoes of the *Campo Santo* at Pisa. How different from this childish dream is our own conception of nature, with its unlimited space, its innumerable suns, and the earth but a mote in the beam; how different the strange new awe, or superstition, with which it fills our minds! "The silence of those infinite spaces," says Pascal, contemplating a starlight night, "the silence of those infinite spaces terrifies me":—*Le silence éternel de ces espaces infinis m'effraie.*

11. He was already almost wearied out when he came to Florence. He had loved much and been beloved by women, "wandering over the crooked hills of delicious pleasure"; but their reign over him was over, and long before Savonarola's famous "bonfire of vanities," he had destroyed those love-songs in the vulgar tongue, which would have been so great a relief to us, after the scholastic prolixity of his Latin writings. It was in another spirit that he composed a Platonic commentary, the only work of his in Italian which has come down to us, on the "Song of Divine Love"—*secondo la mente ed opinione dei Platonici*—"according to the mind and opinion of the Platonists," by his friend Hieronymo Beniveni, in which, with an ambitious array of every sort of learning, and a profusion of imagery borrowed indifferently from

the astrologers, the Cabala, and Homer, and Scripture, and Dionysius the Areopagite, he attempts to define the stages by which the soul passes from the earthly to the unseen beauty. A change indeed had passed over him, as if the chilling touch of the abstract and disembodied beauty Platonists profess to long for were already upon him. Some sense of this, perhaps, coupled with that over-brightness which in the popular imagination always betokens an early death, made Camilla Rucellai, one of those prophetic women whom the preaching of Savonarola had raised up in Florence, declare, seeing him for the first time, that he would depart in the time of lilies—prematurely, that is, like the field-flowers which are withered by the scorching sun almost as soon as they are sprung up. He now wrote down those thoughts on the religious life which Sir Thomas More turned into English, and which another English translator thought worthy to be added to the books of the *Imitation*. "It is not hard to know God, provided one will not force oneself to define Him":—has been thought a great saying of Joubert's. "Love God," Pico writes to Angelo Politian, "we rather may, than either know Him, or by speech utter Him. And yet had men liefer by knowledge never find that which they seek, than by love possess that thing, which also without love were in vain found."

12. Yet he who had this fine touch for spiritual things did not—and in this is the enduring interest of his story—even after his conversion, forget the old gods. He is one of the last who seriously and sincerely entertained the claim on men's faith of the pagan religions; he is anxious to ascertain the true significance of the obscurest legend, the lightest tradition concerning them. With many thoughts and many influences which led him in that direction, he did not become a monk; only he became gentle and patient in disputation; retaining "somewhat of the old plenty, in dainty viand and silver vessel," he gave over the greater part of his property to his friend, the mystical poet Beniveni, to be spent by him in works of charity, chiefly in the sweet charity of providing marriage-dowries for the peasant girls of Florence. His end came in 1494, when, amid the prayers and sacraments of Savonarola, he died of fever, on the very day on which Charles the Eighth entered Florence, the seventeenth of November, yet in the time of lilies—the lilies of the shield of France, as the people now said, remembering Camilla's prophecy. He was buried in the conventual church of Saint Mark, in the hood and white frock of the Dominican order.

13. It is because the life of Pico, thus lying down to rest in the Dominican habit, yet amid thoughts of the older gods, himself like one of those comely divinities, reconciled indeed to the new religion, but still with a tenderness for the earlier life, and desirous literally to "bind the ages each to each by natural piety"—it is because this life is so perfect a parallel to the attempt made in

his writings to reconcile Christianity with the ideas of paganism, that Pico, in spite of the scholastic character of those writings, is really interesting. Thus, in the *Heptaplus, or Discourse on the Seven Days of the Creation*, he endeavours to reconcile the accounts which pagan philosophy had given of the origin of the world with the account given in the books of Moses—the *Timæus* of Plato with the book of *Genesis*. The *Heptaplus* is dedicated to Lorenzo the Magnificent, whose interest, the preface tells us, in the secret wisdom of Moses is well known. If Moses seems in his writings simple and even popular, rather than either a philosopher or a theologian, that is because it was an institution with the ancient philosophers, either not to speak of divine things at all, or to speak of them dissemblingly: hence their doctrines were called mysteries. Taught by them, Pythagoras became so great a "master of silence," and wrote almost nothing, thus hiding the words of God in his heart, and speaking wisdom only among the perfect. In explaining the harmony between Plato and Moses, Pico lays hold on every sort of figure and analogy, on the double meanings of words, the symbols of the Jewish ritual, the secondary meanings of obscure stories in the later Greek mythologists. Everywhere there is an unbroken system of correspondences. Every object in the terrestrial world is an analogue, a symbol or counterpart, of some higher reality in the starry heavens, and this again of some law of the angelic life in the world beyond the stars. There is the element of fire in the material world; the sun is the fire of heaven; and in the super-celestial world there is the fire of the seraphic intelligence. "But behold how they differ! The elementary fire burns, the heavenly fire vivifies, the super-celestial fire loves." In this way, every natural object, every combination of natural forces, every accident in the lives of men, is filled with higher meanings. Omens, prophecies, supernatural coincidences, accompany Pico himself all through life. There are oracles in every tree and mountain-top, and a significance in every accidental combination of the events of life.

14. This constant tendency to symbolism and imagery gives Pico's work a figured style, by which it has some real resemblance to Plato's, and he differs from other mystical writers of his time by a genuine desire to know his authorities at first hand. He reads Plato in Greek, Moses in Hebrew, and by this his work really belongs to the higher culture. Above all, we have a constant sense in reading him, that his thoughts, however little their positive value may be, are connected with springs beneath them of deep and passionate emotion; and when he explains the grades or steps by which the soul passes from the love of a physical object to the love of unseen beauty, and unfolds the analogies between this process and other movements upward of human thought, there is a glow and vehemence in his words which remind one of the manner in which his own brief existence flamed itself away.

15. I said that the Renaissance of the fifteenth century was, in many things, great rather by what it designed or aspired to do, than by what it actually achieved. It remained for a later age to conceive the true method of effecting a scientific reconciliation of Christian sentiment with the imagery, the legends, the theories about the world, of pagan poetry and philosophy. For that age the only possible reconciliation was an imaginative one, and resulted from the efforts of artists, trained in Christian schools, to handle pagan subjects; and of this artistic reconciliation work like Pico's was but the feebler counterpart. Whatever philosophers had to say on one side or the other, whether they were successful or not in their attempts to reconcile the old to the new, and to justify the expenditure of so much care and thought on the dreams of a dead faith, the imagery of the Greek religion, the direct charm of its story, were by artists valued and cultivated for their own sake. Hence a new sort of mythology, with a tone and qualities of its own. When the ship-load of sacred earth from the soil of Jerusalem was mingled with the common clay in the *Campo Santo* at Pisa, a new flower grew up from it, unlike any flower men had seen before, the anemone with its concentric rings of strangely blended colour, still to be found by those who search long enough for it, in the long grass of the Maremma. Just such a strange flower was that mythology of the Italian Renaissance, which grew up from the mixture of two traditions, two sentiments, the sacred and the profane. Classical story was regarded as so much imaginative material to be received and assimilated. It did not come into men's minds to ask curiously of science, concerning the origin of such story, its primary form and import, its meaning for those who projected it. The thing sank into their minds, to issue forth again with all the tangle about it of medieval sentiment and ideas. In the *Doni* Madonna in the *Tribune* of the *Uffizii*, Michelangelo actually brings the pagan religion, and with it the unveiled human form, the sleepy-looking fauns of a Dionysiac revel, into the presence of the Madonna, as simpler painters had introduced there other products of the earth, birds or flowers, while he has given to that Madonna herself much of the uncouth energy of the older and more primitive "Mighty Mother."

16. This picturesque union of contrasts, belonging properly to the art of the close of the fifteenth century, pervades, in Pico della Mirandola, an actual person, and that is why the figure of Pico is so attractive. He will not let one go; he wins one on, in spite of one's self, to turn again to the pages of his forgotten books, although we know already that the actual solution proposed in them will satisfy us as little as perhaps it satisfied him. It is said that in his eagerness for mysterious learning he once paid a great sum for a collection of cabalistic manuscripts, which turned out to be forgeries; and the story might well stand as a parable of all he ever seemed to gain in the way of actual knowledge. He

had sought knowledge, and passed from system to system, and hazarded much; but less for the sake of positive knowledge than because he believed there was a spirit of order and beauty in knowledge, which would come down and unite what men's ignorance had divided, and renew what time had made dim. And so, while his actual work has passed away, yet his own qualities are still active, and himself remains, as one alive in the grave, *cæsiis et vigilibus oculis*, as his biographer describes him, and with that sanguine, clear skin, *decenti rubore interspersa*, as with the light of morning upon it; and he has a true place in that group of great Italians who fill the end of the fifteenth century with their names, he is a true *humanist*. For the essence of humanism is that belief of which he seems never to have doubted, that nothing which has ever interested living men and women can wholly lose its vitality—no language they have spoken, nor oracle beside which they have hushed their voices, no dream which has once been entertained by actual human minds, nothing about which they have ever been passionate, or expended time and zeal.

1871.

SANDRO BOTTICELLI

In Leonardo's treatise on painting only one contemporary is mentioned by name—Sandro Botticelli. This pre-eminence may be due to chance only, but to some will rather appear a result of deliberate judgment; for people have begun to find out the charm of Botticelli's work, and his name, little known in the last century, is quietly becoming important. In the middle of the fifteenth century he had already anticipated much of that meditative subtlety, which is sometimes supposed peculiar to the great imaginative workmen of its close. Leaving the simple religion which had occupied the followers of Giotto for a century, and the simple naturalism which had grown out of it, a thing of birds and flowers only, he sought inspiration in what to him were works of the modern world, the writings of Dante and Boccaccio, and in new readings of his own of classical stories: or, if he painted religious incidents, painted them with an under-current of original sentiment, which touches you as the real matter of the picture through the veil of its ostensible subject. What is the peculiar sensation, what is the peculiar quality of pleasure, which his work has the property of exciting in us, and which we cannot get elsewhere? For this, especially when he has to speak of a comparatively unknown artist, is always the chief question which a critic has to answer.

2. In an age when the lives of artists were full of adventure, his life is almost colourless. Criticism indeed has cleared away much of the gossip which Vasari accumulated, has touched the legend of Lippo and Lucrezia, and rehabilitated the character of Andrea del Castagno. But in Botticelli's case there is no legend to dissipate. He did not even go by his true name: Sandro is a nickname, and his true name is Filipepi, Botticelli being only the name of the goldsmith who first taught him art. Only two things happened to him, two things which he shared with other artists:—he was invited to Rome to paint in the Sistine Chapel, and he fell in later life under the influence of Savonarola, passing apparently almost out of men's sight in a sort of religious melancholy, which lasted till his death in 1515, according to the received date. Vasari says that he plunged into the study of Dante, and even wrote a comment on the *Divine Comedy*. But it seems strange that he should have lived on inactive so long; and one almost wishes that some document might come to light, which, fixing the date of his death earlier, might relieve one, in thinking of him, of his dejected old age.

3. He is before all things a poetical painter, blending the charm of story and sentiment, the medium of the art of poetry, with the charm of line and colour,

the medium of abstract painting. So he becomes the illustrator of Dante. In a few rare examples of the edition of 1481, the blank spaces, left at the beginning of every canto for the hand of the illuminator, have been filled, as far as the nineteenth canto of the *Inferno*, with impressions of engraved plates, seemingly by way of experiment, for in the copy in the Bodleian Library, one of the three impressions it contains has been printed upside down, and much awry, in the midst of the luxurious printed page. Giotto, and the followers of Giotto, with their almost childish religious aim, had not learned to put that weight of meaning into outward things, light, colour, everyday gesture, which the poetry of the *Divine Comedy* involves, and before the fifteenth century Dante could hardly have found an illustrator. Botticelli's illustrations are crowded with incident, blending, with a naïve carelessness of pictorial propriety, three phases of the same scene into one plate. The grotesques, so often a stumbling-block to painters, who forget that the words of a poet, which only feebly present an image to the mind, must be lowered in key when translated into visible form, make one regret that he has not rather chosen for illustration the more subdued imagery of the *Purgatorio*. Yet in the scene of those who "go down quick into hell," there is an inventive force about the fire taking hold on the upturned soles of the feet, which proves that the design is no mere translation of Dante's words, but a true painter's vision; while the scene of the Centaurs wins one at once, for, forgetful of the actual circumstances of their appearance, Botticelli has gone off with delight on the thought of the Centaurs themselves, bright, small creatures of the woodland, with arch baby faces and mignon forms, drawing tiny bows.

4. Botticelli lived in a generation of naturalists, and he might have been a mere naturalist among them. There are traces enough in his work of that alert sense of outward things, which, in the pictures of that period, fills the lawns with delicate living creatures, and the hillsides with pools of water, and the pools of water with flowering reeds. But this was not enough for him; he is a visionary painter, and in his visionariness he resembles Dante. Giotto, the tried companion of Dante, Masaccio, Ghirlandajo even, do but transcribe, with more or less refining, the outward image; they are dramatic, not visionary painters; they are almost impassive spectators of the action before them. But the genius of which Botticelli is the type usurps the data before it as the exponent of ideas, moods, visions of its own; in this interest it plays fast and loose with those data, rejecting some and isolating others, and always combining them anew. To him, as to Dante, the scene, the colour, the outward image or gesture, comes with all its incisive and importunate reality; but awakes in him, moreover, by some subtle law of his own structure, a mood which it awakes in no one else, of which it is the double or repetition, and which it clothes, that all may share

it, with visible circumstance.

5. But he is far enough from accepting the conventional orthodoxy of Dante which, referring all human action to the simple formula of purgatory, heaven and hell, leaves an insoluble element of prose in the depths of Dante's poetry. One picture of his, with the portrait of the donor, Matteo Palmieri, below, had the credit or discredit of attracting some shadow of ecclesiastical censure. This Matteo Palmieri, (two dim figures move under that name in contemporary history,) was the reputed author of a poem, still unedited, *La Città Divina*, which represented the human race as an incarnation of those angels who, in the revolt of Lucifer, were neither for Jehovah nor for His enemies, a fantasy of that earlier Alexandrian philosophy about which the Florentine intellect in that century was so curious. Botticelli's picture may have been only one of those familiar compositions in which religious reverie has recorded its impressions of the various forms of beatified existence—*Glorias*, as they were called, like that in which Giotto painted the portrait of Dante; but somehow it was suspected of embodying in a picture the wayward dream of Palmieri, and the chapel where it hung was closed. Artists so entire as Botticelli are usually careless about philosophical theories, even when the philosopher is a Florentine of the fifteenth century, and his work a poem in *terza rima*. But Botticelli, who wrote a commentary on Dante, and became the disciple of Savonarola, may well have let such theories come and go across him. True or false, the story interprets much of the peculiar sentiment with which he infuses his profane and sacred persons, comely, and in a certain sense like angels, but with a sense of displacement or loss about them—the wistfulness of exiles, conscious of a passion and energy greater than any known issue of them explains, which runs through all his varied work with a sentiment of ineffable melancholy.

6. So just what Dante scorns as unworthy alike of heaven and hell, Botticelli accepts, that middle world in which men take no side in great conflicts, and decide no great causes, and make great refusals. He thus sets for himself the limits within which art, undisturbed by any moral ambition, does its most sincere and surest work. His interest is neither in the untempered goodness of Angelico's saints, nor the untempered evil of Orcagna's *Inferno*; but with men and women, in their mixed and uncertain condition, always attractive, clothed sometimes by passion with a character of loveliness and energy, but saddened perpetually by the shadow upon them of the great things from which they shrink. His morality is all sympathy; and it is this sympathy, conveying into his work somewhat more than is usual of the true complexion of humanity, which makes him, visionary as he is, so forcible a realist.

7. It is this which gives to his Madonnas their unique expression and charm.

He has worked out in them a distinct and peculiar type, definite enough in his own mind, for he has painted it over and over again, sometimes one might think almost mechanically, as a pastime during that dark period when his thoughts were so heavy upon him. Hardly any collection of note is without one of these circular pictures, into which the attendant angels depress their heads so naïvely. Perhaps you have sometimes wondered why those peevish-looking Madonnas, conformed to no acknowledged or obvious type of beauty, attract you more and more, and often come back to you when the Sistine Madonna and the Virgins of Fra Angelico are forgotten. At first, contrasting them with those, you may have thought that there was something in them mean or abject even, for the abstract lines of the face have little nobleness, and the colour is wan. For with Botticelli she too, though she holds in her hands the "Desire of all nations," is one of those who are neither for Jehovah nor for His enemies; and her choice is on her face. The white light on it is cast up hard and cheerless from below, as when snow lies upon the ground, and the children look up with surprise at the strange whiteness of the ceiling. Her trouble is in the very caress of the mysterious child, whose gaze is always far from her, and who has already that sweet look of devotion which men have never been able altogether to love, and which still makes the born saint an object almost of suspicion to his earthly brethren. Once, indeed, he guides her hand to transcribe in a book the words of her exaltation, the *Ave*, and the *Magnificat*, and the *Gaude Maria*, and the young angels, glad to rouse her for a moment from her dejection, are eager to hold the inkhorn and to support the book. But the pen almost drops from her hand, and the high cold words have no meaning for her, and her true children are those others, among whom, in her rude home, the intolerable honour came to her, with that look of wistful inquiry on their irregular faces which you see in startled animals—gipsy children, such as those who, in Apennine villages, still hold out their long brown arms to beg of you, but on Sundays become *enfants du chœur*, with their thick black hair nicely combed, and fair white linen on their sunburnt throats.

8. What is strangest is that he carries this sentiment into classical subjects, its most complete expression being a picture in the *Uffizii*, of Venus rising from the sea, in which the grotesque emblems of the middle age, and a landscape full of its peculiar feeling, and even its strange draperies, powdered all over in the Gothic manner with a quaint conceit of daisies, frame a figure that reminds you of the faultless nude studies of Ingres. At first, perhaps, you are attracted only by a quaintness of design, which seems to recall all at once whatever you have read of Florence in the fifteenth century; afterwards you may think that this quaintness must be incongruous with the subject, and that the colour is cadaverous or at least cold. And yet, the more you come to understand what

imaginative colouring really is, that all colour is no mere delightful quality of natural things, but a spirit upon them by which they become expressive to the spirit, the better you will like this peculiar quality of colour; and you will find that quaint design of Botticelli's a more direct inlet into the Greek temper than the works of the Greeks themselves even of the finest period. Of the Greeks as they really were, of their difference from ourselves, of the aspects of their outward life, we know far more than Botticelli, or his most learned contemporaries; but for us long familiarity has taken off the edge of the lesson, and we are hardly conscious of what we owe to the Hellenic spirit. But in pictures like this of Botticelli's you have a record of the first impression made by it on minds turned back towards it, in almost painful aspiration, from a world in which it had been ignored so long; and in the passion, the energy, the industry of realisation, with which Botticelli carries out his intention, is the exact measure of the legitimate influence over the human mind of the imaginative system of which this is perhaps the central myth. The light is indeed cold—mere sunless dawn; but a later painter would have cloyed you with sunshine; and you can see the better for that quietness in the morning air each long promontory, as it slopes down to the water's edge. Men go forth to their labours until the evening; but she is awake before them, and you might think that the sorrow in her face was at the thought of the whole long day of love yet to come. An emblematical figure of the wind blows hard across the grey water, moving forward the dainty-lipped shell on which she sails, the sea "showing his teeth," as it moves, in thin lines of foam, and sucking in, one by one, the falling roses, each severe in outline, plucked off short at the stalk, but embrowned a little, as Botticelli's flowers always are. Botticelli meant all this imagery to be altogether pleasurable; and it was partly an incompleteness of resources, inseparable from the art of that time, that subdued and chilled it. But this predilection for minor tones counts also; and what is unmistakable is the sadness with which he has conceived the goddess of pleasure, as the depositary of a great power over the lives of men.

9. I have said that the peculiar character of Botticelli is the result of a blending in him of a sympathy for humanity in its uncertain condition, its attractiveness, its investiture at rarer moments in a character of loveliness and energy, with his consciousness of the shadow upon it of the great things from which it shrinks, and that this conveys into his work somewhat more than painting usually attains of the true complexion of humanity. He paints the story of the goddess of pleasure in other episodes besides that of her birth from the sea, but never without some shadow of death in the grey flesh and wan flowers. He paints Madonnas, but they shrink from the pressure of the divine child, and plead in unmistakable undertones for a warmer, lower

humanity. The same figure—tradition connects it with Simonetta, the Mistress of Giuliano de' Medici—appears again as Judith, returning home across the hill country, when the great deed is over, and the moment of revulsion come, when the olive branch in her hand is becoming a burthen; as *Justice*, sitting on a throne, but with a fixed look of self-hatred which makes the sword in her hand seem that of a suicide; and again as *Veritas*, in the allegorical picture of *Calumnia*, where one may note in passing the suggestiveness of an accident which identifies the image of Truth with the person of Venus. We might trace the same sentiment through his engravings; but his share in them is doubtful, and the object of this brief study has been attained, if I have defined aright the temper in which he worked.

10. But, after all, it may be asked, is a painter like Botticelli—a secondary painter, a proper subject for general criticism? There are a few great painters, like Michelangelo or Leonardo, whose work has become a force in general culture, partly for this very reason that they have absorbed into themselves all such workmen as Sandro Botticelli; and, over and above mere technical or antiquarian criticism, general criticism may be very well employed in that sort of interpretation which adjusts the position of these men to general culture, whereas smaller men can be the proper subjects only of technical or antiquarian treatment. But, besides those great men, there is a certain number of artists who have a distinct faculty of their own by which they convey to us a peculiar quality of pleasure which we cannot get elsewhere; and these too have their place in general culture, and must be interpreted to it by those who have felt their charm strongly, and are often the object of a special diligence and a consideration wholly affectionate, just because there is not about them the stress of a great name and authority. Of this select number Botticelli is one. He has the freshness, the uncertain and diffident promise, which belong to the earlier Renaissance itself, and make it perhaps the most interesting period in the history of the mind. In studying his work one begins to understand to how great a place in human culture the art of Italy had been called.

1870.

LEONARDO DA VINCI

Homo Minister et Interpres Naturæ

In Vasari's life of Leonardo da Vinci as we now read it there are some variations from the first edition. There, the painter who has fixed the outward type of Christ for succeeding centuries was a bold speculator, holding lightly by other men's beliefs, setting philosophy above Christianity. Words of his, trenchant enough to justify this impression, are not recorded, and would have been out of keeping with a genius of which one characteristic is the tendency to lose itself in a refined and graceful mystery. The suspicion was but the time-honoured mode in which the world stamps its appreciation of one who has thoughts for himself alone, his high indifference, his intolerance of the common forms of things; and in the second edition the image was changed into something fainter and more conventional. But it is still by a certain mystery in his work, and something enigmatical beyond the usual measure of great men, that he fascinates, or perhaps half repels. His life is one of sudden revolts, with intervals in which he works not at all, or apart from the main scope of his work. By a strange fortune the pictures on which his more popular fame rested disappeared early from the world, like the *Battle of the Standard*; or are mixed obscurely with the product of meaner hands, like the *Last Supper*. His type of beauty is so exotic that it fascinates a larger number than it delights, and seems more than that of any other artist to reflect ideas and views and some scheme of the world within; so that he seemed to his contemporaries to be the possessor of some unsanctified and secret wisdom; as to Michelet and others to have anticipated modern ideas. He trifles with his genius, and crowds all his chief work into a few tormented years of later life; yet he is so possessed by his genius that he passes unmoved through the most tragic events, overwhelming his country and friends, like one who comes across them by chance on some secret errand.

2. His *legend*, as the French say, with the anecdotes which every one remembers, is one of the most brilliant chapters of Vasari. Later writers merely copied it, until, in 1804, Carlo Amoretti applied to it a criticism which left hardly a date fixed, and not one of those anecdotes untouched. The various questions thus raised have since that time become, one after another, subjects of special study, and mere antiquarianism has in this direction little more to do. For others remain the editing of the thirteen books of his manuscripts, and the separation by technical criticism of what in his reputed works is really his, from what is only half his, or the work of his pupils. But a lover of strange

souls may still analyse for himself the impression made on him by those works, and try to reach through it a definition of the chief elements of Leonardo's genius. The *legend*, as corrected and enlarged by its critics, may now and then intervene to support the results of this analysis.

3. His life has three divisions—thirty years at Florence, nearly twenty years at Milan, then nineteen years of wandering, till he sinks to rest under the protection of Francis the First at the *Château de Clou*. The dishonour of illegitimacy hangs over his birth. Piero Antonio, his father, was of a noble Florentine house, of Vinci in the *Val d'Arno*, and Leonardo, brought up delicately among the true children of that house, was the love-child of his youth, with the keen, puissant nature such children often have. We see him in his boyhood fascinating all men by his beauty, improvising music and songs, buying the caged birds and setting them free, as he walked the streets of Florence, fond of odd bright dresses and spirited horses.

4. From his earliest years he designed many objects, and constructed models in relief, of which Vasari mentions some of women smiling. His father, pondering over this promise in the child, took him to the workshop of Andrea del Verrocchio, then the most famous artist in Florence. Beautiful objects lay about there—reliquaries, pyxes, silver images for the pope's chapel at Rome, strange fancy-work of the middle age, keeping odd company with fragments of antiquity, then but lately discovered. Another student Leonardo may have seen there—a lad into whose soul the level light and aërial illusions of Italian sunsets had passed, in after days famous as Perugino. Verrocchio was an artist of the earlier Florentine type, carver, painter, and worker in metals, in one; designer, not of pictures only, but of all things for sacred or household use, drinking-vessels, ambries, instruments of music, making them all fair to look upon, filling the common ways of life with the reflexion of some far-off brightness; and years of patience had refined his hand till his work was now sought after from distant places.

5. It happened that Verrocchio was employed by the brethren of Vallombrosa to paint the Baptism of Christ, and Leonardo was allowed to finish an angel in the left-hand corner. It was one of those moments in which the progress of a great thing—here, that of the art of Italy—presses hard on the happiness of an individual, through whose discouragement and decrease, humanity, in more fortunate persons, comes a step nearer to its final success.

6. For beneath the cheerful exterior of the mere well-paid craftsman, chasing brooches for the copes of *Santa Maria Novella*, or twisting metal screens for the tombs of the Medici, lay the ambitious desire to expand the destiny of Italian art by a larger knowledge and insight into things, a purpose in art not unlike Leonardo's still unconscious purpose; and often, in the modelling of

drapery, or of a lifted arm, or of hair cast back from the face, there came to him something of the freer manner and richer humanity of a later age. But in this *Baptism* the pupil had surpassed the master; and Verrocchio turned away as one stunned, and as if his sweet earlier work must thereafter be distasteful to him, from the bright animated angel of Leonardo's hand.

7. The angel may still be seen in Florence, a space of sunlight in the cold, laboured old picture; but the legend is true only in sentiment, for painting had always been the art by which Verrocchio set least store. And as in a sense he anticipates Leonardo, so to the last Leonardo recalls the studio of Verrocchio, in the love of beautiful toys, such as the vessel of water for a mirror, and lovely needle-work about the implicated hands in the *Modesty and Vanity*, and of reliefs, like those cameos which in the *Virgin of the Balances* hang all round the girdle of Saint Michael, and of bright variegated stones, such as the agates in the *Saint Anne*, and in a hieratic preciseness and grace, as of a sanctuary swept and garnished. Amid all the cunning and intricacy of his Lombard manner this never left him. Much of it there must have been in that lost picture of *Paradise*, which he prepared as a cartoon for tapestry, to be woven in the looms of Flanders. It was the perfection of the older Florentine style of miniature-painting, with patient putting of each leaf upon the trees and each flower in the grass, where the first man and woman were standing.

8. And because it was the perfection of that style, it awoke in Leonardo some seed of discontent which lay in the secret places of his nature. For the way to perfection is through a series of disgusts; and this picture—all that he had done so far in his life at Florence—was after all in the old slight manner. His art, if it was to be something in the world, must be weighted with more of the meaning of nature and purpose of humanity. Nature was "the true mistress of higher intelligences." He plunged, then, into the study of nature. And in doing this he followed the manner of the older students; he brooded over the hidden virtues of plants and crystals, the lines traced by the stars as they moved in the sky, over the correspondences which exist between the different orders of living things, through which, to eyes opened, they interpret each other; and for years he seemed to those about him as one listening to a voice, silent for other men.

9. He learned here the art of going deep, of tracking the sources of expression to their subtlest retreats, the power of an intimate presence in the things he handled. He did not at once or entirely desert his art; only he was no longer the cheerful, objective painter, through whose soul, as through clear glass, the bright figures of Florentine life, only made a little mellower and more pensive by the transit, passed on to the white wall. He wasted many days in curious tricks of design, seeming to lose himself in the spinning of intricate devices of

line and colour. He was smitten with a love of the impossible—the perforation of mountains, changing the course of rivers, raising great buildings, such as the church of *San Giovanni*, in the air; all those feats for the performance of which natural magic professed to have the key. Later writers, indeed, see in these efforts an anticipation of modern mechanics; in him they were rather dreams, thrown off by the overwrought and labouring brain. Two ideas were especially confirmed in him, as reflexes of things that had touched his brain in childhood beyond the depth of other impressions—the smiling of women and the motion of great waters.

10. And in such studies some interfusion of the extremes of beauty and terror shaped itself, as an image that might be seen and touched, in the mind of this gracious youth, so fixed that for the rest of his life it never left him. As if catching glimpses of it in the strange eyes or hair of chance people, he would follow such about the streets of Florence till the sun went down, of whom many sketches of his remain. Some of these are full of a curious beauty, that remote beauty which may be apprehended only by those who have sought it carefully; who, starting with acknowledged types of beauty, have refined as far upon these, as these refine upon the world of common forms. But mingled inextricably with this there is an element of mockery also; so that, whether in sorrow or scorn, he caricatures Dante even. Legions of grotesques sweep under his hand; for has not nature too her grotesques—the rent rock, the distorting lights of evening on lonely roads, the unveiled structure of man in the embryo, or the skeleton?

11. All these swarming fancies unite in the *Medusa* of the *Uffizii*. Vasari's story of an earlier Medusa, painted on a wooden shield, is perhaps an invention; and yet, properly told, has more of the air of truth about it than anything else in the whole legend. For its real subject is not the serious work of a man, but the experiment of a child. The lizards and glow-worms and other strange small creatures which haunt an Italian vineyard bring before one the whole picture of a child's life in a Tuscan dwelling—half castle, half farm—and are as true to nature as the pretended astonishment of the father for whom the boy has prepared a surprise. It was not in play that he painted that other Medusa, the one great picture which he left behind him in Florence. The subject has been treated in various ways; Leonardo alone cuts to its centre; he alone realises it as the head of a corpse, exercising its powers through all the circumstances of death. What may be called the fascination of corruption penetrates in every touch its exquisitely finished beauty. About the dainty lines of the cheek the bat flits unheeded. The delicate snakes seem literally strangling each other in terrified struggle to escape from the Medusa brain. The hue which violent death always brings with it is in the features; features singularly massive

and grand, as we catch them inverted, in a dexterous foreshortening, crown foremost, like a great calm stone against which the wave of serpents breaks.

12. The science of that age was all divination, clairvoyance, unsubjected to our exact modern formulas, seeking in an instant of vision to concentrate a thousand experiences. Later writers, thinking only of the well-ordered treatise on painting which a Frenchman, Raffaelle du Fresne, a hundred years afterwards, compiled from Leonardo's bewildered manuscripts, written strangely, as his manner was, from right to left, have imagined a rigid order in his inquiries. But this rigid order would have been little in accordance with the restlessness of his character; and if we think of him as the mere reasoner who subjects design to anatomy, and composition to mathematical rules, we shall hardly have that impression which those around Leonardo received from him. Poring over his crucibles, making experiments with colour, trying, by a strange variation of the alchemist's dream, to discover the secret, not of an elixir to make man's natural life immortal, but of giving immortality to the subtlest and most delicate effects of painting, he seemed to them rather the sorcerer or the magician, possessed of curious secrets and a hidden knowledge, living in a world of which he alone possessed the key. What his philosophy seems to have been most like is that of Paracelsus or Cardan; and much of the spirit of the older alchemy still hangs about it, with its confidence in short cuts and odd byways to knowledge. To him philosophy was to be something giving strange swiftness and double sight, divining the sources of springs beneath the earth or of expression beneath the human countenance, clairvoyant of occult gifts in common or uncommon things, in the reed at the brook-side, or the star which draws near to us but once in a century. How, in this way, the clear purpose was overclouded, the fine chaser's hand perplexed, we but dimly see; the mystery which at no point quite lifts from Leonardo's life is deepest here. But it is certain that at one period of his life he had almost ceased to be an artist.

13. The year 1483—the year of the birth of Raphael and the thirty-first of Leonardo's life—is fixed as the date of his visit to Milan by the letter in which he recommends himself to Ludovico Sforza, and offers to tell him, for a price, strange secrets in the art of war. It was that Sforza who murdered his young nephew by slow poison, yet was so susceptible of religious impressions that he blended mere earthly passion with a sort of religious sentimentalism, and who took for his device the mulberry-tree—symbol, in its long delay and sudden yielding of flowers and fruit together, of a wisdom which economises all forces for an opportunity of sudden and sure effect. The fame of Leonardo had gone before him, and he was to model a colossal statue of Francesco, the first Duke of Milan. As for Leonardo himself, he came not as an artist at all, or careful of the fame of one; but as a player on the harp, a strange harp of

silver of his own construction, shaped in some curious likeness to a horse's skull. The capricious spirit of Ludovico was susceptible also to the power of music, and Leonardo's nature had a kind of spell in it. Fascination is always the word descriptive of him. No portrait of his youth remains; but all tends to make us believe that up to this time some charm of voice and aspect, strong enough to balance the disadvantage of his birth, had played about him. His physical strength was great; it was said that he could bend a horse-shoe like a coil of lead.

14. The *Duomo*, work of artists from beyond the Alps, so fantastic to the eye of a Florentine used to the mellow, unbroken surfaces of Giotto and Arnolfo, was then in all its freshness; and below, in the streets of Milan, moved a people as fantastic, changeful, and dreamlike. To Leonardo least of all men could there be anything poisonous in the exotic flowers of sentiment which grew there. It was a life of brilliant sins and exquisite amusements: Leonardo became a celebrated designer of pageants; and it suited the quality of his genius, composed, in almost equal parts, of curiosity and the desire of beauty, to take things as they came.

15. Curiosity and the desire of beauty—these are the two elementary forces in Leonardo's genius; curiosity often in conflict with the desire of beauty, but generating, in union with it, a type of subtle and curious grace.

16. The movement of the fifteenth century was twofold; partly the Renaissance, partly also the coming of what is called the "modern spirit," with its realism, its appeal to experience. It comprehended a return to antiquity, and a return to nature. Raphael represents the return to antiquity, and Leonardo the return to nature. In this return to nature, he was seeking to satisfy a boundless curiosity by her perpetual surprises, a microscopic sense of finish by her *finesse*, or delicacy of operation, that *subtilitas naturæ* which Bacon notices. So we find him often in intimate relations with men of science,—with Fra Luca Paccioli the mathematician, and the anatomist Marc Antonio della Torre. His observations and experiments fill thirteen volumes of manuscript; and those who can judge describe him as anticipating long before, by rapid intuition, the later ideas of science. He explained the obscure light of the unilluminated part of the moon, knew that the sea had once covered the mountains which contain shells, and of the gathering of the equatorial waters above the polar.

17. He who thus penetrated into the most secret parts of nature preferred always the more to the less remote, what, seeming exceptional, was an instance of law more refined, the construction about things of a peculiar atmosphere and mixed lights. He paints flowers with such curious felicity that different writers have attributed to him a fondness for particular flowers, as Clement the cyclamen, and Rio the jasmin; while, at Venice, there is a stray leaf from his

portfolio dotted all over with studies of violets and the wild rose. In him first appears the taste for what is *bizarre* or *recherché* in landscape; hollow places full of the green shadow of bituminous rocks, ridged reefs of trap-rock which cut the water into quaint sheets of light,—their exact antitype is in our own western seas; all the solemn effects of moving water. You may follow it springing from its distant source among the rocks on the heath of the *Madonna of the Balances*, passing, as a little fall, into the treacherous calm of the *Madonna of the Lake*, as a goodly river next, below the cliffs of the *Madonna of the Rocks*, washing the white walls of its distant villages, stealing out in a network of divided streams in *La Gioconda* to the seashore of the *Saint Anne*—that delicate place, where the wind passes like the hand of some fine etcher over the surface, and the untorn shells are lying thick upon the sand, and the tops of the rocks, to which the waves never rise, are green with grass, grown fine as hair. It is the landscape, not of dreams or of fancy, but of places far withdrawn, and hours selected from a thousand with a miracle of *finesse*. Through Leonardo's strange veil of sight things reach him so; in no ordinary night or day, but as in faint light of eclipse, or in some brief interval of falling rain at daybreak, or through deep water.

18. And not into nature only; but he plunged also into human personality, and became above all a painter of portraits; faces of a modelling more skilful than has been seen before or since, embodied with a reality which almost amounts to illusion, on the dark air. To take a character as it was, and delicately sound its stops, suited one so curious in observation, curious in invention. He painted thus the portraits of Ludovico's mistresses, Lucretia Crivelli and Cecilia Galerani the poetess, of Ludovico himself, and the Duchess Beatrice. The portrait of Cecilia Galerani is lost, but that of Lucretia Crivelli has been identified with *La Belle Feronière* of the Louvre, and Ludovico's pale, anxious face still remains in the Ambrosian library. Opposite is the portrait of Beatrice d'Este, in whom Leonardo seems to have caught some presentiment of early death, painting her precise and grave, full of the refinement of the dead, in sad earth-coloured raiment, set with pale stones.

19. Sometimes this curiosity came in conflict with the desire of beauty; it tended to make him go too far below that outside of things in which art really begins and ends. This struggle between the reason and its ideas, and the senses, the desire of beauty, is the key to Leonardo's life at Milan—his restlessness, his endless re-touchings, his odd experiments with colour. How much must he leave unfinished, how much recommence! His problem was the transmutation of ideas into images. What he had attained so far had been the mastery of that earlier Florentine style, with its naïve and limited sensuousness. Now he was to entertain in this narrow medium those divinations of a humanity too wide for it, that larger vision of the opening world, which is only not too much for

the great, irregular art of Shakespeare; and everywhere the effort is visible in the work of his hands. This agitation, this perpetual delay, give him an air of weariness and *ennui*. To others he seems to be aiming at an impossible effect, to do something that art, that painting, can never do. Often the expression of physical beauty at this or that point seems strained and marred in the effort, as in those heavy German foreheads—too heavy and German for perfect beauty.

20. For there was a touch of Germany in that genius which, as Goethe said, had "thought itself weary"—*müde sich gedacht*. What an anticipation of modern Germany, for instance, in that debate on the question whether sculpture or painting is the nobler art![1] But there is this difference between him and the German, that, with all that curious science, the German would have thought nothing more was needed. The name of Goethe himself reminds one how great for the artist may be the danger of overmuch science; how Goethe, who, in the *Elective Affinities* and the first part of *Faust*, does transmute ideas into images, who wrought many such transmutations, did not invariably find the spell-word, and in the second part of *Faust* presents us with a mass of science which has almost no artistic character at all. But Leonardo will never work till the happy moment comes—that moment of *bien-être*, which to imaginative men is a moment of invention. On this he waits with a perfect patience; other moments are but a preparation, or after-taste of it. Few men distinguish between them as jealously as he. Hence so many flaws even in the choicest work. But for Leonardo the distinction is absolute, and, in the moment of *bien-être*, the alchemy complete: the idea is stricken into colour and imagery: a cloudy mysticism is refined to a subdued and graceful mystery, and painting pleases the eye while it satisfies the soul.

21. This curious beauty is seen above all in his drawings, and in these chiefly in the abstract grace of the bounding lines. Let us take some of these drawings, and pause over them awhile; and, first, one of those at Florence—the heads of a woman and a little child, set side by side, but each in its own separate frame. First of all, there is much pathos in the reappearance, in the fuller curves of the face of the child, of the sharper, more chastened lines of the worn and older face, which leaves no doubt that the heads are those of a little child and its mother. A feeling for maternity is indeed always characteristic of Leonardo; and this feeling is further indicated here by the half-humorous pathos of the diminutive, rounded shoulders of the child. You may note a like pathetic power in drawings of a young man, seated in a stooping posture, his face in his hands, as in sorrow; of a slave sitting in an uneasy inclined attitude, in

---

1. How princely, how characteristic of Leonardo, the answer, *Quanto più, un' arte porta seco fatica di corpo, tanto più è vile!*

some brief interval of rest; of a small Madonna and Child, peeping sideways in half-reassured terror, as a mighty griffin with batlike wings, one of Leonardo's finest *inventions*, descends suddenly from the air to snatch up a great wild beast wandering near them. But note in these, as that which especially belongs to art, the contour of the young man's hair, the poise of the slave's arm above his head, and the curves of the head of the child, following the little skull within, thin and fine as some sea-shell worn by the wind.

22. Take again another head, still more full of sentiment, but of a different kind, a little drawing in red chalk which every one will remember who has examined at all carefully the drawings by old masters at the Louvre. It is a face of doubtful sex, set in the shadow of its own hair, the cheek-line in high light against it, with something voluptuous and full in the eye-lids and the lips. Another drawing might pass for the same face in childhood, with parched and feverish lips, but much sweetness in the loose, short-waisted childish dress, with necklace and *bulla*, and in the daintily bound hair. We might take the thread of suggestion which these two drawings offer, when thus set side by side, and, following it through the drawings at Florence, Venice, and Milan, construct a sort of series, illustrating better than anything else Leonardo's type of womanly beauty. Daughters of Herodias, with their fantastic head-dresses knotted and folded so strangely to leave the dainty oval of the face disengaged, they are not of the Christian family, or of Raphael's. They are the clairvoyants, through whom, as through delicate instruments, one becomes aware of the subtler forces of nature, and the modes of their action, all that is magnetic in it, all those finer conditions wherein material things rise to that subtlety of operation which constitutes them spiritual, where only the finer nerve and the keener touch can follow. It is as if in certain significant examples we actually saw those forces at their work on human flesh. Nervous, electric, faint always with some inexplicable faintness, these people seem to be subject to exceptional conditions, to feel powers at work in the common air unfelt by others, to become, as it were, the receptacle of them, and pass them on to us in a chain of secret influences.

23. But among the more youthful heads there is one at Florence which Love chooses for its own—the head of a young man, which may well be the likeness of Andrea Salaino, beloved of Leonardo for his curled and waving hair—*belli capelli ricci e inanellati*—and afterwards his favourite pupil and servant. Of all the interests in living men and women which may have filled his life at Milan, this attachment alone is recorded. And in return Salaino identified himself so entirely with Leonardo, that the picture of *Saint Anne*, in the Louvre, has been attributed to him. It illustrates Leonardo's usual choice of pupils, men of some natural charm of person or intercourse like Salaino, or men of birth and

princely habits of life like Francesco Melzi—men with just enough genius to be capable of initiation into his secret, for the sake of which they were ready to efface their own individuality. Among them, retiring often to the villa of the Melzi at *Canonica al Vaprio*, he worked at his fugitive manuscripts and sketches, working for the present hour, and for a few only, perhaps chiefly for himself. Other artists have been as careless of present or future applause, in self-forgetfulness, or because they set moral or political ends above the ends of art; but in him this solitary culture of beauty seems to have hung upon a kind of self-love, and a carelessness in the work of art of all but art itself. Out of the secret places of a unique temperament he brought strange blossoms and fruits hitherto unknown; and for him, the novel impression conveyed, the exquisite effect woven, counted as an end in itself—a perfect end.

24. And these pupils of his acquired his manner so thoroughly, that though the number of Leonardo's authentic works is very small indeed, there is a multitude of other men's pictures through which we undoubtedly see him, and come very near to his genius. Sometimes, as in the little picture of the *Madonna of the Balances*, in which, from the bosom of His mother, Christ weighs the pebbles of the brook against the sins of men, we have a hand, rough enough by contrast, working upon some fine hint or sketch of his. Sometimes, as in the subjects of the *Daughter of Herodias* and the *Head of John the Baptist*, the lost originals have been re-echoed and varied upon again and again by Luini and others. At other times the original remains, but has been a mere theme or motive, a type of which the accessories might be modified or changed; and these variations have but brought out the more the purpose, or expression of the original. It is so with the so-called *Saint John the Baptist* of the Louvre—one of the few naked figures Leonardo painted—whose delicate brown flesh and woman's hair no one would go out into the wilderness to seek, and whose treacherous smile would have us understand something far beyond the outward gesture or circumstance. But the long, reedlike cross in the hand, which suggests Saint John the Baptist, becomes faint in a copy at the Ambrosian Library, and disappears altogether in another version, in the *Palazzo Rosso* at Genoa. Returning from the latter to the original, we are no longer surprised by Saint John's strange likeness to the *Bacchus* which hangs near it, and which set Théophile Gautier thinking of Heine's notion of decayed gods, who, to maintain themselves, after the fall of paganism, took employment in the new religion. We recognise one of those symbolical inventions in which the ostensible subject is used, not as matter for definite pictorial realisation, but as the starting-point of a train of sentiment, subtle and vague as a piece of music. No one ever ruled over the mere *subject* in hand more entirely than Leonardo, or bent it more dexterously to purely artistic ends. And so it comes to pass that though he handles sacred subjects

continually, he is the most profane of painters; the given person or subject, Saint John in the Desert, or the Virgin on the knees of Saint Anne, is often merely the pretext for a kind of work which carries one altogether beyond the range of its conventional associations.

25. About the *Last Supper*, its decay and restorations, a whole literature has risen up, Goethe's pensive sketch of its sad fortunes being perhaps the best. The death in childbirth of the Duchess Beatrice was followed in Ludovico by one of those paroxysms of religious feeling which in him were constitutional. The low, gloomy Dominican church of *Saint Mary of the Graces* had been the favourite oratory of Beatrice. She had spent her last days there, full of sinister presentiments; at last it had been almost necessary to remove her from it by force; and now it was here that mass was said a hundred times a day for her repose. On the damp wall of the refectory, oozing with mineral salts, Leonardo painted the *Last Supper*. Effective anecdotes were told about it, his retouchings and delays. They show him refusing to work except at the moment of invention, scornful of any one who supposed that art could be a work of mere industry and rule, often coming the whole length of Milan to give a single touch. He painted it, not in fresco, where all must be *impromptu*, but in oils, the new method which he had been one of the first to welcome, because it allowed of so many after-thoughts, so refined a working out of perfection. It turned out that on a plastered wall no process could have been less durable. Within fifty years it had fallen into decay. And now we have to turn back to Leonardo's own studies, above all to one drawing of the central head at the *Brera*, which, in a union of tenderness and severity in the face-lines, reminds one of the monumental work of Mino da Fiesole, to trace it as it was.

26. Here was another effort to lift a given subject out of the range of its traditional associations. Strange, after all the mystic developments of the middle age, was the effort to see the Eucharist, not as the pale Host of the altar, but as one taking leave of his friends. Five years afterwards the young Raphael, at Florence, painted it with sweet and solemn effect in the refectory of Saint Onofrio; but still with all the mystical unreality of the school of Perugino. Vasari pretends that the central head was never finished. But finished or unfinished, or owing part of its effect to a mellowing decay, the head of Jesus does but consummate the sentiment of the whole company—ghosts through which you see the wall, faint as the shadows of the leaves upon the wall on autumn afternoons. This figure is but the faintest, the most spectral of them all.

27. The *Last Supper* was finished in 1497; in 1498 the French entered Milan, and whether or not the Gascon bowmen used it as a mark for their arrows, the model of Francesco Sforza certainly did not survive. What, in that age, such work was capable of being—of what nobility, amid what racy truthfulness

to fact—we may judge from the bronze statue of Bartolomeo Colleoni on horseback, modelled by Leonardo's master, Verrocchio (he died of grief, it was said, because, the mould accidentally failing, he was unable to complete it), still standing in the *piazza* of Saint John and Saint Paul at Venice. Some traces of the thing may remain in certain of Leonardo's drawings, and perhaps also, by a singular circumstance, in a far-off town of France. For Ludovico became a prisoner, and ended his days at Loches in Touraine. After many years of captivity in the dungeons below, where all seems sick with barbarous feudal memories, he was allowed at last, it is said, to breathe fresher air for awhile in one of the rooms of the great tower still shown, its walls covered with strange painted arabesques, ascribed by tradition to his hand, amused a little, in this way, through the tedious years. In those vast helmets and human faces and pieces of armour, among which, in great letters, the motto *Infelix Sum* is woven in and out, it is perhaps not too fanciful to see the fruit of a wistful after-dreaming over Leonardo's sundry experiments on the armed figure of the great duke, which had occupied the two so much during the days of their good fortune at Milan.

28. The remaining years of Leonardo's life are more or less years of wandering. From his brilliant life at court he had saved nothing, and he returned to Florence a poor man. Perhaps necessity kept his spirit excited: the next four years are one prolonged rapture or ecstasy of invention. He painted now the pictures of the Louvre, his most authentic works, which came there straight from the cabinet of Francis the First, at Fontainebleau. One picture of his, the *Saint Anne*—not the *Saint Anne* of the Louvre, but a simple cartoon, now in London—revived for a moment a sort of appreciation more common in an earlier time, when good pictures had still seemed miraculous. For two days a crowd of people of all qualities passed in naïve excitement through the chamber where it hung, and gave Leonardo a taste of the "triumph" of Cimabue. But his work was less with the saints than with the living women of Florence. For he lived still in the polished society that he loved, and in the houses of Florence, left perhaps a little subject to light thoughts by the death of Savonarola—the latest gossip (1869) is of an undraped Monna Lisa, found in some out-of-the-way corner of the late *Orleans* collection—he saw Ginevra di Benci, and Lisa, the young third wife of Francesco del Giocondo. As we have seen him using incidents of sacred story, not for their own sake, or as mere subjects for pictorial realisation, but as a cryptic language for fancies all his own, so now he found a vent for his thought in taking one of these languid women, and raising her, as Leda or Pomona, as Modesty or Vanity, to the seventh heaven of symbolical expression.

29. *La Gioconda* is, in the truest sense, Leonardo's masterpiece, the

revealing instance of his mode of thought and work. In suggestiveness, only the *Melancholia* of Dürer is comparable to it; and no crude symbolism disturbs the effect of its subdued and graceful mystery. We all know the face and hands of the figure, set in its marble chair, in that circle of fantastic rocks, as in some faint light under sea. Perhaps of all ancient pictures time has chilled it least.[1] As often happens with works in which invention seems to reach its limit, there is an element in it given to, not invented by, the master. In that inestimable folio of drawings, once in the possession of Vasari, were certain designs by Verrocchio, faces of such impressive beauty that Leonardo in his boyhood copied them many times. It is hard not to connect with these designs of the elder, by-past master, as with its germinal principle, the unfathomable smile, always with a touch of something sinister in it, which plays over all Leonardo's work. Besides, the picture is a portrait. From childhood we see this image defining itself on the fabric of his dreams; and but for express historical testimony, we might fancy that this was but his ideal lady, embodied and beheld at last. What was the relationship of a living Florentine to this creature of his thought? By what strange affinities had the dream and the person grown up thus apart, and yet so closely together? Present from the first incorporeally in Leonardo's brain, dimly traced in the designs of Verrocchio, she is found present at last in *Il Giocondo's* house. That there is much of mere portraiture in the picture is attested by the legend that by artificial means, the presence of mimes and flute-players, that subtle expression was protracted on the face. Again, was it in four years and by renewed labour never really completed, or in four months and as by stroke of magic, that the image was projected?

30. The presence that rose thus so strangely beside the waters, is expressive of what in the ways of a thousand years men had come to desire. Hers is the head upon which all "the ends of the world are come," and the eyelids are a little weary. It is a beauty wrought out from within upon the flesh, the deposit, little cell by cell, of strange thoughts and fantastic reveries and exquisite passions. Set it for a moment beside one of those white Greek goddesses or beautiful women of antiquity, and how would they be troubled by this beauty, into which the soul with all its maladies has passed! All the thoughts and experience of the world have etched and moulded there, in that which they have of power to refine and make expressive the outward form, the animalism of Greece, the lust of Rome, the mysticism of the middle age with its spiritual ambition and imaginative loves, the return of the Pagan world, the sins of the Borgias. She is older than the rocks among which she sits; like the vampire, she has been dead many times, and learned the secrets of the grave; and has

---

1. Yet for Vasari there was some further magic of crimson in the lips and cheeks, lost for us.

been a diver in deep seas, and keeps their fallen day about her; and trafficked for strange webs with Eastern merchants: and, as Leda, was the mother of Helen of Troy, and, as Saint Anne, the mother of Mary; and all this has been to her but as the sound of lyres and flutes, and lives only in the delicacy with which it has moulded the changing lineaments, and tinged the eyelids and the hands. The fancy of a perpetual life, sweeping together ten thousand experiences, is an old one; and modern philosophy has conceived the idea of humanity as wrought upon by, and summing up in itself, all modes of thought and life. Certainly Lady Lisa might stand as the embodiment of the old fancy, the symbol of the modern idea.

31. During these years at Florence Leonardo's history is the history of his art; for himself, he is lost in the bright cloud of it. The outward history begins again in 1502, with a wild journey through central Italy, which he makes as the chief engineer of Cæsar Borgia. The biographer, putting together the stray jottings of his manuscripts, may follow him through every day of it, up the strange tower of Siena, elastic like a bent bow, down to the seashore at Piombino, each place appearing as fitfully as in a fever dream.

32. One other great work was left for him to do, a work all trace of which soon vanished, *The Battle of the Standard*, in which he had Michelangelo for his rival. The citizens of Florence, desiring to decorate the walls of the great council-chamber, had offered the work for competition, and any subject might be chosen from the Florentine wars of the fifteenth century. Michelangelo chose for his cartoon an incident of the war with Pisa, in which the Florentine soldiers, bathing in the Arno, are surprised by the sound of trumpets, and run to arms. His design has reached us only in an old engraving, which helps us less perhaps than our remembrance of the background of his *Holy Family* in the *Uffizii* to imagine in what superhuman form, such as might have beguiled the heart of an earlier world, those figures ascended out of the water. Leonardo chose an incident from the battle of Anghiari, in which two parties of soldiers fight for a standard. Like Michelangelo's, his cartoon is lost, and has come to us only in sketches, and in a fragment of Rubens. Through the accounts given we may discern some lust of terrible things in it, so that even the horses tore each other with their teeth. And yet one fragment of it, in a drawing of his at Florence, is far different — a waving field of lovely armour, the chased edgings running like lines of sunlight from side to side. Michelangelo was twenty-seven years old; Leonardo more than fifty; and Raphael, then nineteen years of age, visiting Florence for the first time, came and watched them as they worked.

33. We catch a glimpse of Leonardo again, at Rome in 1514, surrounded by his mirrors and vials and furnaces, making strange toys that seemed alive of wax and quicksilver. The hesitation which had haunted him all through life,

and made him like one under a spell, was upon him now with double force. No one had ever carried political indifferentism farther; it had always been his philosophy to "fly before the storm"; he is for the Sforzas, or against them, as the tide of their fortune turns. Yet now, in the political society of Rome, he came to be suspected of secret French sympathies. It paralysed him to find himself among enemies; and he turned wholly to France, which had long courted him.

34. France was about to become an Italy more Italian than Italy itself. Francis the First, like Lewis the Twelfth before him, was attracted by the *finesse* of Leonardo's work; *La Gioconda* was already in his cabinet, and he offered Leonardo the little *Château de Clou*, with its vineyards and meadows, in the pleasant valley of the Masse, just outside the walls of the town of Amboise, where, especially in the hunting season, the court then frequently resided. *A Monsieur Lyonard, peinteur du Roy pour Amboyse*—so the letter of Francis the First is headed. It opens a prospect, one of the most interesting in the history of art, where, in a peculiarly blent atmosphere, Italian art dies away as a French exotic.

35. Two questions remain, after much busy antiquarianism, concerning Leonardo's death—the question of the exact form of his religion, and the question whether Francis the First was present at the time. They are of about equally little importance in the estimate of Leonardo's genius. The directions in his will concerning the thirty masses and the great candles for the church of Saint Florentin are things of course, their real purpose being immediate and practical; and on no theory of religion could these hurried offices be of much consequence. We forget them in speculating how one who had been always so desirous of beauty, but desired it always in such precise and definite forms, as hands or flowers or hair, looked forward now into the vague land, and experienced the last curiosity.

1869.

THE SCHOOL OF GIORGIONE

It is the mistake of much popular criticism to regard poetry, music, and painting—all the various products of art—as but translations into different languages of one and the same fixed quantity of imaginative thought, supplemented by certain technical qualities of colour, in painting; of sound, in music; of rhythmical words, in poetry. In this way, the sensuous element in art, and with it almost everything in art that is essentially artistic, is made a matter of indifference; and a clear apprehension of the opposite principle—that the sensuous material of each art brings with it a special phase or quality of beauty, untranslatable into the forms of any other, an order of impressions distinct in kind—is the beginning of all true æsthetic criticism. For, as art addresses not pure sense, still less the pure intellect, but the "imaginative reason" through the senses, there are differences of kind in æsthetic beauty, corresponding to the differences in kind of the gifts of sense themselves. Each art, therefore, having its own peculiar and untranslatable sensuous charm, has its own special mode of reaching the imagination, its own special responsibilities to its material. One of the functions of æsthetic criticism is to define these limitations; to estimate the degree in which a given work of art fulfils its responsibilities to its special material; to note in a picture that true pictorial charm, which is neither a mere poetical thought or sentiment, on the one hand, nor a mere result of communicable technical skill in colour or design, on the other; to define in a poem that true poetical quality, which is neither descriptive nor meditative merely, but comes of an inventive handling of rhythmical language, the element of song in the singing; to note in music the musical charm, that essential music, which presents no words, no matter of sentiment or thought, separable from the special form in which it is conveyed to us.

2. To such a philosophy of the variations of the beautiful, Lessing's analysis of the spheres of sculpture and poetry, in the *Laocoon*, was an important contribution. But a true appreciation of these things is possible only in the light of a whole system of such art-casuistries. Now painting is the art in the criticism of which this truth most needs enforcing, for it is in popular judgments on pictures that the false generalisation of all art into forms of poetry is most prevalent. To suppose that all is mere technical acquirement in delineation or touch, working through and addressing itself to the intelligence, on the one side, or a merely poetical, or what may be called literary interest, addressed also to the pure intelligence, on the other:—this is the way of most spectators, and of many critics, who have never caught sight all the time of

that true pictorial quality which lies between, unique pledge, as it is, of the possession of the pictorial gift, that inventive or creative handling of pure line and colour, which, as almost always in Dutch painting, as often also in the works of Titian or Veronese, is quite independent of anything definitely poetical in the subject it accompanies. It is the *drawing*—the design projected from that peculiar pictorial temperament or constitution, in which, while it may possibly be ignorant of true anatomical proportions, all things whatever, all poetry, all ideas however abstract or obscure, float up as visible scene or image: it is the *colouring*—that weaving of light, as of just perceptible gold threads, through the dress, the flesh, the atmosphere, in Titian's *Lace-girl*, that staining of the whole fabric of the thing with a new, delightful physical quality. This *drawing*, then—the arabesque traced in the air by Tintoret's flying figures, by Titian's forest branches; this colouring—the magic conditions of light and hue in the atmosphere of Titian's *Lace-girl*, or Rubens's *Descent from the Cross*:—these essential pictorial qualities must first of all delight the sense, delight it as directly and sensuously as a fragment of Venetian glass; and through this delight alone become the vehicle of whatever poetry or science may lie beyond them in the intention of the composer. In its primary aspect, a great picture has no more definite message for us than an accidental play of sunlight and shadow for a few moments on the wall or floor: is itself, in truth, a space of such fallen light, caught as the colours are in an Eastern carpet, but refined upon, and dealt with more subtly and exquisitely than by nature itself. And this primary and essential condition fulfilled, we may trace the coming of poetry into painting, by fine gradations upwards; from Japanese fan-painting, for instance, where we get, first, only abstract colour; then, just a little interfused sense of the poetry of flowers; then, sometimes, perfect flower-painting; and so, onwards, until in Titian we have, as his poetry in the *Ariadne*, so actually a touch of true childlike humour in the diminutive, quaint figure with its silk gown, which ascends the temple stairs, in his picture of the *Presentation of the Virgin*, at Venice.

3. But although each art has thus its own specific order of impressions, and an untranslatable charm, while a just apprehension of the ultimate differences of the arts is the beginning of æsthetic criticism; yet it is noticeable that, in its special mode of handling its given material, each art may be observed to pass into the condition of some other art, by what German critics term an *Anders-streben*—a partial alienation from its own limitations, through which the arts are able, not indeed to supply the place of each other, but reciprocally to lend each other new forces.

4. Thus some of the most delightful music seems to be always approaching to figure, to pictorial definition. Architecture, again, though it has its own laws—laws esoteric enough, as the true architect knows only too well—yet

sometimes aims at fulfilling the conditions of a picture, as in the *Arena* chapel; or of sculpture, as in the flawless unity of Giotto's tower at Florence; and often finds a true poetry, as in those strangely twisted staircases of the *châteaux* of the country of the Loire, as if it were intended that among their odd turnings the actors in a theatrical mode of life might pass each other unseen; there being a poetry also of memory and of the mere effect of time, by which architecture often profits greatly. Thus, again, sculpture aspires out of the hard limitation of pure form towards colour, or its equivalent; poetry also, in many ways, finding guidance from the other arts, the analogy between a Greek tragedy and a work of Greek sculpture, between a sonnet and a relief, of French poetry generally with the art of engraving, being more than mere figures of speech; and all the arts in common aspiring towards the principle of music; music being the typical, or ideally consummate art, the object of the great *Anders-streben* of all art, of all that is artistic, or partakes of artistic qualities.

5. *All art constantly aspires towards the condition of music.* For while in all other kinds of art it is possible to distinguish the matter from the form, and the understanding can always make this distinction, yet it is the constant effort of art to obliterate it. That the mere matter of a poem, for instance, its subject, namely, its given incidents or situation—that the mere matter of a picture, the actual circumstances of an event, the actual topography of a landscape—should be nothing without the form, the spirit, of the handling, that this form, this mode of handling, should become an end in itself, should penetrate every part of the matter: this is what all art constantly strives after, and achieves in different degrees.

6. This abstract language becomes clear enough, if we think of actual examples. In an actual landscape we see a long white road, lost suddenly on the hill-verge. That is the matter of one of the etchings of M. Alphonse Legros: only, in this etching, it is informed by an indwelling solemnity of expression, seen upon it or half-seen, within the limits of an exceptional moment, or caught from his own mood perhaps, but which he maintains as the very essence of the thing, throughout his work. Sometimes a momentary tint of stormy light may invest a homely or too familiar scene with a character which might well have been drawn from the deep places of the imagination. Then we might say that this particular effect of light, this sudden inweaving of gold thread through the texture of the haystack, and the poplars, and the grass, gives the scene artistic qualities, that it is like a picture. And such tricks of circumstance are commonest in landscape which has little salient character of its own; because, in such scenery, all the material details are so easily absorbed by that informing expression of passing light, and elevated, throughout their whole extent, to a new and delightful effect by it. And hence the superiority, for most conditions

of the picturesque, of a river-side in France to a Swiss valley, because, on the French river-side, mere topography, the simple material, counts for so little, and, all being very pure, untouched, and tranquil in itself, mere light and shade have such easy work in modulating it to one dominant tone. The Venetian landscape, on the other hand, has in its material conditions much which is hard, or harshly definite; but the masters of the Venetian school have shown themselves little burdened by them. Of its Alpine background they retain certain abstracted elements only, of cool colour and tranquillising line; and they use its actual details, the brown windy turrets, the straw-coloured fields, the forest arabesques, but as the notes of a music which duly accompanies the presence of their men and women, presenting us with the spirit or essence only of a certain sort of landscape—a country of the pure reason or half-imaginative memory.

7. Poetry, again, works with words addressed in the first instance to the pure intelligence; and it deals, most often, with a definite subject or situation. Sometimes it may find a noble and quite legitimate function in the conveyance of moral or political aspiration, as often in the poetry of Victor Hugo. In such instances it is easy enough for the understanding to distinguish between the matter and the form, however much the matter, the subject, the element which is addressed to the mere intelligence, has been penetrated by the informing, artistic spirit. But the ideal types of poetry are those in which this distinction is reduced to its *minimum*; so that lyrical poetry, precisely because in it we are least able to detach the matter from the form, without a deduction of something from that matter itself, is, at least artistically, the highest and most complete form of poetry. And the very perfection of such poetry often appears to depend, in part, on a certain suppression or vagueness of mere subject, so that the meaning reaches us through ways not distinctly traceable by the understanding, as in some of the most imaginative compositions of William Blake, and often in Shakespeare's songs, as pre-eminently in that song of Mariana's page in *Measure for Measure*, in which the kindling force and poetry of the whole play seems to pass for a moment into an actual strain of music.

8. And this principle holds good of all things that partake in any degree of artistic qualities, of the furniture of our houses, and of dress, for instance, of life itself, of gesture and speech, and the details of daily intercourse; these also, for the wise, being susceptible of a suavity and charm, caught from the way in which they are done, which gives them a worth in themselves. Herein, again, lies what is valuable and justly attractive, in what is called the fashion of a time, which elevates the trivialities of speech, and manner, and dress, into "ends in themselves," and gives them a mysterious grace and attractiveness in the doing of them.

9. Art, then, is thus always striving to be independent of the mere intelligence,

to become a matter of pure perception, to get rid of its responsibilities to its subject or material; the ideal examples of poetry and painting being those in which the constituent elements of the composition are so welded together, that the material or subject no longer strikes the intellect only; nor the form, the eye or the ear only; but form and matter, in their union or identity, present one single effect to the "imaginative reason," that complex faculty for which every thought and feeling is twin-born with its sensible analogue or symbol.

10. It is the art of music which most completely realises this artistic ideal, this perfect identification of matter and form. In its consummate moments, the end is not distinct from the means, the form from the matter, the subject from the expression; they inhere in and completely saturate each other; and to it, therefore, to the condition of its perfect moments, all the arts may be supposed constantly to tend and aspire. In music, then, rather than in poetry, is to be found the true type or measure of perfected art. Therefore, although each art has its incommunicable element, its untranslatable order of impressions, its unique mode of reaching the "imaginative reason," yet the arts may be represented as continually struggling after the law or principle of music, to a condition which music alone completely realises; and one of the chief functions of æsthetic criticism, dealing with the products of art, new or old, is to estimate the degree in which each of those products approaches, in this sense, to musical law.

11. By no school of painters have the necessary limitations of the art of painting been so unerringly though instinctively apprehended, and the essence of what is pictorial in a picture so justly conceived, as by the school of Venice; and the train of thought suggested in what has been now said is, perhaps, a not unfitting introduction to a few pages about Giorgione, who, though much has been taken by recent criticism from what was reputed to be his work, yet, more entirely than any other painter, sums up, in what we know of himself and his art, the spirit of the Venetian school.

12. The beginnings of Venetian painting link themselves to the last, stiff, half-barbaric splendours of Byzantine decoration, and are but the introduction into the crust of marble and gold on the walls of the *Duomo* of Murano, or of Saint Mark's, of a little more of human expression. And throughout the course of its later development, always subordinate to architectural effect, the work of the Venetian school never escaped from the influence of its beginnings. Unassisted, and therefore unperplexed, by naturalism, religious mysticism, philosophical theories, it had no Giotto, no Angelico, no Botticelli. Exempt from the stress of thought and sentiment, which taxed so severely the resources of the generations of Florentine artists, those earlier Venetian painters, down

to Carpaccio and the Bellini, seem never for a moment to have been so much as tempted to lose sight of the scope of their art in its strictness, or to forget that painting must be before all things decorative, a thing for the eye, a space of colour on the wall, only more dexterously blent than the marking of its precious stone or the chance interchange of sun and shade upon it:—this, to begin and end with; whatever higher matter of thought, or poetry, or religious reverie might play its part therein, between. At last, with final mastery of all the technical secrets of his art, and with somewhat more than "a spark of the divine fire" to his share, comes Giorgione. He is the inventor of *genre*, of those easily movable pictures which serve neither for uses of devotion, nor of allegorical or historic teaching—little groups of real men and women, amid congruous furniture or landscape—morsels of actual life, conversation or music or play, but refined upon or idealised, till they come to seem like glimpses of life from afar. Those spaces of more cunningly blent colour, obediently filling their places, hitherto, in a mere architectural scheme, Giorgione detaches from the wall. He frames them by the hands of some skilful carver, so that people may move them readily and take with them where they go, as one might a poem in manuscript, or a musical instrument, to be used, at will, as a means of self-education, stimulus or solace, coming like an animated presence, into one's cabinet, to enrich the air as with some choice aroma, and, like persons, live with us, for a day or a lifetime. Of all art such as this, art which has played so large a part in men's culture since that time, Giorgione is the initiator. Yet in him too that old Venetian clearness or justice, in the apprehension of the essential limitations of the pictorial art, is still undisturbed. While he interfuses his painted work with a high-strung sort of poetry, caught directly from a singularly rich and high-strung sort of life, yet in his selection of subject, or phase of subject, in the subordination of mere subject to pictorial design, to the main purpose of a picture, he is typical of that aspiration of all the arts towards music, which I have endeavoured to explain,—towards the perfect identification of matter and form.

13. Born so near to Titian, though a little before him, that these two companion pupils of the aged Giovanni Bellini may almost be called contemporaries, Giorgione stands to Titian in something like the relationship of Sordello to Dante, in Browning's poem. Titian, when he leaves Bellini, becomes, in turn, the pupil of Giorgione. He lives in constant labour more than sixty years after Giorgione is in his grave; and with such fruit, that hardly one of the greater towns of Europe is without some fragment of his work. But the slightly older man, with his so limited actual product (what remains to us of it seeming, when narrowly explained, to reduce itself to almost one picture, like Sordello's one fragment of lovely verse), yet expresses, in elementary motive and principle,

that spirit—itself the final acquisition of all the long endeavours of Venetian art—which Titian spreads over his whole life's activity.

14. And, as we might expect, something fabulous and illusive has always mingled itself in the brilliancy of Giorgione's fame. The exact relationship to him of many works—drawings, portraits, painted idylls—often fascinating enough, which in various collections went by his name, was from the first uncertain. Still, six or eight famous pictures at Dresden, Florence and the Louvre, were with no doubt attributed to him, and in these, if anywhere, something of the splendour of the old Venetian humanity seemed to have been preserved. But of those six or eight famous pictures it is now known that only one is certainly from Giorgione's hand. The accomplished science of the subject has come at last, and, as in other instances, has not made the past more real for us, but assured us only that we possess less of it than we seemed to possess. Much of the work on which Giorgione's immediate fame depended, work done for instantaneous effect, in all probability passed away almost within his own age, like the frescoes on the façade of the *fondaco dei Tedeschi* at Venice, some crimson traces of which, however, still give a strange additional touch of splendour to the scene of the *Rialto*. And then there is a barrier or borderland, a period about the middle of the sixteenth century, in passing through which the tradition miscarries, and the true outlines of Giorgione's work and person are obscured. It became fashionable for wealthy lovers of art, with no critical standard of authenticity, to collect so-called works of Giorgione, and a multitude of imitations came into circulation. And now, in the "new Vasari,"[1] the great traditional reputation, woven with so profuse demand on men's admiration, has been scrutinised thread by thread; and what remains of the most vivid and stimulating of Venetian masters, a live flame, as it seemed, in those old shadowy times, has been reduced almost to a name by his most recent critics.

15. Yet enough remains to explain why the legend grew up above the name, why the name attached itself, in many instances, to the bravest work of other men. The *Concert* in the *Pitti* Palace, in which a monk, with cowl and tonsure, touches the keys of a harpsichord, while a clerk, placed behind him, grasps the handle of the viol, and a third, with cap and plume, seems to wait upon the true interval for beginning to sing, is undoubtedly Giorgione's. The outline of the lifted finger, the trace of the plume, the very threads of the fine linen, which fasten themselves on the memory, in the moment before they are lost altogether in that calm unearthly glow, the skill which has caught the waves of wandering sound, and fixed them for ever on the lips and hands—these are indeed the master's own; and the criticism which, while dismissing so

---

1. Crowe and Cavalcaselle: *History of Painting in North Italy*.

much hitherto believed to be Giorgione's, has established the claims of this one picture, has left it among the most precious things in the world of art.

16. It is noticeable that the "distinction" of this *Concert*, its sustained evenness of perfection, alike in design, in execution, and in choice of personal type, becomes for the "new Vasari" the standard of Giorgione's genuine work. Finding here sufficient to explain his influence, and the true seal of mastery, its authors assign to Pellegrino da San Daniele the *Holy Family* in the Louvre, in consideration of certain points where it comes short of this standard. Such shortcoming, however, will hardly diminish the spectator's enjoyment of a singular charm of liquid air, with which the whole picture seems instinct, filling the eyes and lips, the very garments, of its sacred personages, with some wind-searched brightness and energy; of which fine air the blue peak, clearly defined in the distance, is, as it were, the visible pledge. Similarly, another favourite picture in the Louvre, the subject of a delightful sonnet by a poet[2] whose own painted work often comes to mind as one ponders over these precious things—the *Fête Champêtre*, is assigned to an imitator of Sebastian del Piombo; and the *Tempest*, in the Academy at Venice, to Paris Bordone, or perhaps to "some advanced craftsman of the sixteenth century." From the gallery at Dresden, the *Knight embracing a Lady*, where the knight's broken gauntlets seem to mark some well-known pause in a story we would willingly hear the rest of, is conceded to "a Brescian hand," and *Jacob meeting Rachel* to a pupil of Palma. And then, whatever their charm, we are called on to give up the *Ordeal*, and the *Finding of Moses* with its jewel-like pools of water, perhaps to Bellini.

17. Nor has the criticism, which thus so freely diminishes the number of his authentic works, added anything important to the well-known outline of the life and personality of the man: only, it has fixed one or two dates, one or two circumstances, a little more exactly. Giorgione was born before the year 1477, and spent his childhood at Castelfranco, where the last crags of the Venetian Alps break down romantically, with something of parklike grace, to the plain. A natural child of the family of the Barbarelli by a peasant-girl of Vedelago, he finds his way early into the circle of notable persons—people of courtesy. He is initiated into those differences of personal type, manner, and even of dress, which are best understood there—that "distinction" of the *Concert* of the *Pitti* Palace. Not far from his home lives Catherine of Cornara, formerly Queen of Cyprus; and, up in the towers which still remain, Tuzio Costanzo, the famous *condottiere*—a picturesque remnant of medieval manners, amid a civilisation rapidly changing. Giorgione paints their portraits; and when

---

2. Dante Gabriel Rossetti.

Tuzio's son, Matteo, dies in early youth, adorns in his memory a chapel in the church of Castelfranco, painting on this occasion, perhaps, the altar-piece, foremost among his authentic works, still to be seen there, with the figure of the warrior-saint, Liberale, of which the original little study in oil, with the delicately gleaming, silver-grey armour, is one of the greater treasures of the National Gallery. In that figure, as in some other knightly personages attributed to him, people have supposed the likeness of the painter's own presumably gracious presence. Thither, at last, he is himself brought home from Venice, early dead, but celebrated. It happened, about his thirty-fourth year, that in one of those parties at which he entertained his friends with music, he met a certain lady of whom he became greatly enamoured, and "they rejoiced greatly," says Vasari, "the one and the other, in their loves." And two quite different legends concerning it agree in this, that it was through this lady he came by his death; Ridolfi relating that, being robbed of her by one of his pupils, he died of grief at the double treason; Vasari, that she being secretly stricken of the plague, and he making his visits to her as usual, Giorgione took the sickness from her mortally, along with her kisses, and so briefly departed.

18. But, although the number of Giorgione's extant works has been thus limited by recent criticism, all is not done when the real and the traditional elements in what concerns him have been discriminated; for, in what is connected with a great name, much that is not real is often very stimulating. For the æsthetic philosopher, therefore, over and above the real Giorgione and his authentic extant works, there remains the *Giorgionesque* also—an influence, a spirit or type in art, active in men so different as those to whom many of his supposed works are really assignable. A veritable school, in fact, grew together out of all those fascinating works rightly or wrongly attributed to him; out of many copies from, or variations on him, by unknown or uncertain workmen, whose drawings and designs were, for various reasons, prized as his; out of the immediate impression he made upon his contemporaries, and with which he continued in men's minds; out of many traditions of subject and treatment, which really descend from him to our own time, and by retracing which we fill out the original image. Giorgione thus becomes a sort of impersonation of Venice itself, its projected reflex or ideal, all that was intense or desirable in it crystallising about the memory of this wonderful young man.

19. And now, finally, let me illustrate some of the characteristics of this *School of Giorgione*, as we may call it, which, for most of us, notwithstanding all that negative criticism of the "new Vasari," will still identify itself with those famous pictures at Florence, at Dresden and Paris. A certain artistic ideal is there defined for us—the conception of a peculiar aim and procedure

in art, which we may understand as the *Giorgionesque*, wherever we find it, whether in Venetian work generally, or in work of our own time. Of this the *Concert*, that undoubted work of Giorgione in the *Pitti* Palace, is the typical instance, and a pledge authenticating the connexion of the school, and the spirit of the school, with the master.

20. I have spoken of a certain interpenetration of the matter or subject of a work of art with the form of it, a condition realised absolutely only in music, as the condition to which every form of art is perpetually aspiring. In the art of painting, the attainment of this ideal condition, this perfect interpenetration of the subject with the elements of colour and design, depends, of course, in great measure, on dexterous choice of that subject, or phase of subject; and such choice is one of the secrets of Giorgione's school. It is the school of *genre*, and employs itself mainly with "painted idylls," but, in the production of this pictorial poetry, exercises a wonderful tact in the selecting of such matter as lends itself most readily and entirely to pictorial form, to complete expression by drawing and colour. For although its productions are painted poems, they belong to a sort of poetry which tells itself without an articulated story. The master is pre-eminent for the resolution, the ease and quickness, with which he reproduces instantaneous motion—the lacing-on of armour, with the head bent back so stately—the fainting lady—the embrace, rapid as the kiss, caught with death itself from dying lips—some momentary conjunction of mirrors and polished armour and still water, by which all the sides of a solid image are exhibited at once, solving that casuistical question whether painting can present an object as completely as sculpture. The sudden act, the rapid transition of thought, the passing expression—this he arrests with that vivacity which Vasari has attributed to him, *il fuoco Giorgionesco*, as he terms it. Now it is part of the ideality of the highest sort of dramatic poetry, that it presents us with a kind of profoundly significant and animated instants, a mere gesture, a look, a smile, perhaps—some brief and wholly concrete moment—into which, however, all the motives, all the interests and effects of a long history, have condensed themselves, and which seem to absorb past and future in an intense consciousness of the present. Such ideal instants the school of Giorgione selects, with its admirable tact, from that feverish, tumultuously coloured world of the old citizens of Venice—exquisite pauses in time, in which, arrested thus, we seem to be spectators of all the fulness of existence, and which are like some consummate extract or quintessence of life.

21. It is to the law or condition of music, as I said, that all art like this is really aspiring; and, in the school of Giorgione, the perfect moments of music itself, the making or hearing of music, song or its accompaniment, are themselves prominent as subjects. On that background of the silence of Venice,

so impressive to the modern visitor, the world of Italian music was then forming. In choice of subject, as in all besides, the *Concert* of the *Pitti* Palace is typical of everything that Giorgione, himself an admirable musician, touched with his influence. In sketch or finished picture, in various collections, we may follow it through many intricate variations—men fainting at music; music at the pool-side while people fish, or mingled with the sound of the pitcher in the well, or heard across running water, or among the flocks; the tuning of instruments; people with intent faces, as if listening, like those described by Plato in an ingenious passage of the *Republic*, to detect the smallest interval of musical sound, the smallest undulation in the air, or feeling for music in thought on a stringless instrument, ear and finger refining themselves infinitely, in the appetite for sweet sound; a momentary touch of an instrument in the twilight, as one passes through some unfamiliar room, in a chance company.

22. In these then, the favourite incidents of Giorgione's school, music or the musical intervals in our existence, life itself is conceived as a sort of listening—listening to music, to the reading of Bandello's novels, to the sound of water, to time as it flies. Often such moments are really our moments of play, and we are surprised at the unexpected blessedness of what may seem our least important part of time; not merely because play is in many instances that to which people really apply their own best powers, but also because at such times, the stress of our servile, everyday attentiveness being relaxed, the happier powers in things without are permitted free passage, and have their way with us. And so, from music, the school of Giorgione passes often to the play which is like music; to those masques in which men avowedly do but play at real life, like children "dressing up," disguised in the strange old Italian dresses, parti-coloured, or fantastic with embroidery and furs, of which the master was so curious a designer, and which, above all the spotless white linen at wrist and throat, he painted so dexterously.

23. But when people are happy in this thirsty land water will not be far off; and in the school of Giorgione, the presence of water—the well, or marble-rimmed pool, the drawing or pouring of water, as the woman pours it from a pitcher with her jewelled hand in the *Fête Champêtre*, listening, perhaps, to the cool sound as it falls, blent with the music of the pipes—is as characteristic, and almost as suggestive, as that of music itself. And the landscape feels, and is glad of it also—a landscape full of clearness, of the effects of water, of fresh rain newly passed through the air, and collected into the grassy channels. The air, moreover, in the school of Giorgione, seems as vivid as the people who breathe it, and literally empyrean, all impurities being burnt out of it, and no taint, no floating particle of anything but its own proper elements allowed to subsist within it.

24. Its scenery is such as in England we call "park scenery," with some elusive refinement felt about the rustic buildings, the choice grass, the grouped trees, the undulations deftly economised for graceful effect. Only, in Italy all natural things are as it were woven through and through with gold thread, even the cypress revealing it among the folds of its blackness. And it is with gold dust, or gold thread, that these Venetian painters seem to work, spinning its fine filaments, through the solemn human flesh, away into the white plastered walls of the thatched huts. The harsher details of the mountains recede to a harmonious distance, the one peak of rich blue above the horizon remaining but as the sensible warrant of that due coolness which is all we need ask here of the Alps, with their dark rains and streams. Yet what real, airy space, as the eye passes from level to level, through the long-drawn valley in which Jacob embraces Rachel among the flocks! Nowhere is there a truer instance of that balance, that modulated unison of landscape and persons—of the human image and its accessories—already noticed as characteristic of the Venetian school, so that, in it, neither personage nor scenery is ever a mere pretext for the other.

25. Something like this seems to me to be the *vraie vérité* about Giorgione, if I may adopt a serviceable expression, by which the French recognise those more liberal and durable impressions which, in respect of any really considerable person or subject, anything that has at all intricately occupied men's attention, lie beyond, and must supplement, the narrower range of the strictly ascertained facts about it. In this, Giorgione is but an illustration of a valuable general caution we may abide by in all criticism. As regards Giorgione himself, we have indeed to take note of all those negations and exceptions, by which, at first sight, a "new Vasari" seems merely to have confused our apprehension of a delightful object, to have explained away in our inheritance from past time what seemed of high value there. Yet it is not with a full understanding even of those exceptions that one can leave off just at this point. Properly qualified, such exceptions are but a salt of genuineness in our knowledge; and beyond all those strictly ascertained facts, we must take note of that indirect influence by which one like Giorgione, for instance, enlarges his permanent efficacy and really makes himself felt in our culture. In a just impression of that, is the essential truth, the *vraie vérité*, concerning him.

1877.

JOACHIM DU BELLAY

In the middle of the sixteenth century, when the spirit of the Renaissance was everywhere, and people had begun to look back with distaste on the works of the middle age, the old Gothic manner had still one chance more, in borrowing something from the rival which was about to supplant it. In this way there was produced, chiefly in France, a new and peculiar phase of taste with qualities and a charm of its own, blending the somewhat attenuated grace of Italian ornament with the general outlines of Northern design. It created the *Château de Gaillon*, as you may still see it in the delicate engravings of Israël Silvestre—a Gothic donjon veiled faintly by a surface of dainty Italian traceries—Chenonceaux, Blois, Chambord, and the church of Brou. In painting, there came from Italy workmen like *Maître Roux* and the masters of the school of Fontainebleau, to have their later Italian voluptuousness attempered by the naïve and silvery qualities of the native style; and it was characteristic of these painters that they were most successful in painting on glass, an art so essentially medieval. Taking it up where the middle age had left it, they found their whole work among the last subtleties of colour and line; and keeping within the true limits of their material, they got quite a new order of effects from it, and felt their way to refinements on colour never dreamed of by those older workmen, the glass-painters of Chartres or Le Mans. What is called the *Renaissance in France* is thus not so much the introduction of a wholly new taste ready-made from Italy, but rather the finest and subtlest phase of the middle age itself, its last fleeting splendour and temperate Saint Martin's summer. In poetry, the Gothic spirit in France had produced a thousand songs; so in the Renaissance, French poetry too did but borrow something to blend with a native growth, and the poems of Ronsard, with their ingenuity, their delicately figured surfaces, their slightness, their fanciful combinations of rhyme, are the correlative of the traceries of the house of Jacques Cœur at Bourges, or the *Maison de Justice* at Rouen.

2. There was indeed something in the native French taste naturally akin to that Italian *finesse*. The characteristic of French work had always been a certain nicety, a remarkable daintiness of hand, *une netteté remarquable d'exécution*. In the paintings of François Clouet, for example, or rather of the Clouets—for there was a whole family of them—painters remarkable for their resistance to Italian influences, there is a silveriness of colour and a clearness of expression which distinguish them very definitely from their Flemish neighbours, Hemling or the Van Eycks. And this nicety is not less characteristic of old French poetry. A light, aërial delicacy, a simple elegance—*une netteté remarquable*

d'exécution: these are essential characteristics alike of Villon's poetry, and of the *Hours of Anne of Brittany*. They are characteristic too of a hundred French Gothic carvings and traceries. Alike in the old Gothic cathedrals, and in their counterpart, the old Gothic *chansons de geste*, the rough and ponderous mass becomes, as if by passing for a moment into happier conditions, or through a more gracious stratum of air, graceful and refined, like the carved ferneries on the granite church at Folgoat, or the lines which describe the fair priestly hands of Archbishop Turpin, in the song of Roland; although below both alike there is a fund of mere Gothic strength, or heaviness.[1]

3. Now Villon's songs and Clouet's painting are like these. It is the higher touch making itself felt here and there, betraying itself, like nobler blood in a lower stock, by a fine line or gesture or expression, the turn of a wrist, the tapering of a finger. In Ronsard's time that rougher element seemed likely to predominate. No one can turn over the pages of Rabelais without feeling how much need there was of softening, of castigation. To effect this softening is the object of the revolution in poetry which is connected with Ronsard's name. Casting about for the means of thus refining upon and saving the character of French literature, he accepted that influx of Renaissance taste, which, leaving the buildings, the language, the art, the poetry of France, at bottom, what they were, old French Gothic still, gilds their surfaces with a strange, delightful, foreign aspect passing over all that Northern land, in itself neither deeper nor more permanent than a chance effect of light. He reinforces, he doubles the French daintiness by Italian *finesse*. Thereupon, nearly all the force and all the seriousness of French work disappear; only the elegance, the aërial touch, the perfect manner remain. But this elegance, this manner, this daintiness of execution are consummate, and have an unmistakable æsthetic value.

4. So the old French *chanson*, which, like the old northern Gothic ornament, though it sometimes refined itself into a sort of weird elegance, was often, in its essence, something rude and formless, became in the hands of Ronsard a Pindaric ode. He gave it structure, a sustained system, *strophe* and *antistrophe*, and taught it a changefulness and variety of metre which keep the curiosity always excited, so that the very aspect of it, as it lies written on the page, carries the eye lightly onwards, and of which this is a good instance:—

> *Avril, la grace, et le ris*
> *De Cypris,*
> *Le flair et la douce haleine;*

---

1. The purely artistic aspects of this subject have been interpreted, in a work of great taste and learning, by Mrs. Mark Pattison:—*The Renaissance of Art in France.*

> *Avril, le parfum des dieux,*
>   *Qui, des cieux,*
> *Sentent l'odeur de la plaine;*
>
> *C'est toy, courtois et gentil,*
>   *Qui, d exil*
> *Retire ces passageres,*
> *Ces arondelles qui vont,*
>   *Et qui sont*
> *Du printemps les messageres.*

That is not by Ronsard, but by Remy Belleau, for Ronsard soon came to have a school. Six other poets threw in their lot with him in his literary revolution,— this Remy Belleau, Antoine de Baif, Pontus de Tyard, Étienne Jodelle, Jean Daurat, and lastly Joachim du Bellay; and with that strange love of emblems which is characteristic of the time, which covered all the works of Francis the First with the salamander, and all the works of Henry the Second with the double crescent, and all the works of Anne of Brittany with the knotted cord, they called themselves the *Pleiad*; seven in all, although, as happens with the celestial Pleiad, if you scrutinise this constellation of poets more carefully you may find there a great number of minor stars.

5. The first note of this literary revolution was struck by Joachim du Bellay in a little tract written at the early age of twenty-four, which coming to us through three centuries seems of yesterday, so full is it of those delicate critical distinctions which are sometimes supposed peculiar to modern writers. The piece has for its title *La Deffense et Illustration de la langue Françoyse*; and its problem is how to illustrate or ennoble the French language, to give it lustre. We are accustomed to speak of the varied critical and creative movement of the fifteenth and sixteenth centuries as the *Renaissance*, and because we have a single name for it we may sometimes fancy that there was more unity in the thing itself than there really was. Even the Reformation, that other great movement of the fifteenth and sixteenth centuries, had far less unity, far less of combined action, than is at first sight supposed; and the Renaissance was infinitely less united, less conscious of combined action, than the Reformation. But if anywhere the Renaissance became conscious, as a German philosopher might say, if ever it was understood as a systematic movement by those who took part in it, it is in this little book of Joachim du Bellay's, which it is impossible to read without feeling the excitement, the animation, of change, of discovery. "It is a remarkable fact," says M. Sainte-Beuve, "and an inversion of what is true of other languages, that, in French, prose has always had the

precedence over poetry." Du Bellay's prose is perfectly transparent, flexible, and chaste. In many ways it is a more characteristic example of the culture of the *Pleiad* than any of its verse; and those who love the whole movement of which the *Pleiad* is a part, for a weird foreign grace in it, and may be looking about for a true specimen of it, cannot have a better than Joachim du Bellay and this little treatise of his.

6. Du Bellay's object is to adjust the existing French culture to the rediscovered classical culture; and in discussing this problem, and developing the theories of the *Pleiad*, he has lighted upon many principles of permanent truth and applicability. There were some who despaired of the French language altogether, who thought it naturally incapable of the fulness and elegance of Greek and Latin—*cette élégance et copie qui est en la langue Greque et Romaine*—that science could be adequately discussed, and poetry nobly written, only in the dead languages. "Those who speak thus," says Du Bellay, "make me think of the relics which one may only see through a little pane of glass, and must not touch with one's hands. That is what these people do with all branches of culture, which they keep shut up in Greek and Latin books, not permitting one to see them otherwise, or transport them out of dead words into those which are alive, and wing their way daily through the mouths of men." "Languages," he says again, "are not born like plants and trees, some naturally feeble and sickly, others healthy and strong and apter to bear the weight of men's conceptions, but all their virtue is generated in the world of choice and men's freewill concerning them. Therefore, I cannot blame too strongly the rashness of some of our countrymen, who being anything rather than Greeks or Latins, depreciate and reject with more than stoical disdain everything written in French; nor can I express my surprise at the odd opinion of some learned men who think that our vulgar tongue is wholly incapable of erudition and good literature."

7. It was an age of translations. Du Bellay himself translated two books of the *Æneid*, and other poetry, old and new, and there were some who thought that the translation of the classical literature was the true means of *ennobling* the French language:—strangers are ever favourites with us—*nous favorisons toujours les étrangers*. Du Bellay moderates their expectations. "I do not believe that one can learn the right use of them"—he is speaking of figures and ornament in language—"from translations, because it is impossible to reproduce them with the same grace with which the original author used them. For each language has I know not what peculiarity of its own; and if you force yourself to express the naturalness (*le naïf*) of this in another language, observing the law of translation,—not to expatiate beyond the limits of the author himself, your words will be constrained, cold and ungraceful." Then he fixes the test

of all good translation:—"To prove this, read me Demosthenes and Homer in Latin, Cicero and Virgil in French, and see whether they produce in you the same affections which you experience in reading those authors in the original."

8. In this effort to ennoble the French language, to give it grace, number, perfection, and as painters do to their pictures, that last, so desirable, touch—*cette dernière main que nous désirons*—what Du Bellay is really pleading for is his mother-tongue, the language, that is, in which one will have the utmost degree of what is moving and passionate. He recognised of what force the music and dignity of languages are, how they enter into the inmost part of things; and in pleading for the cultivation of the French language, he is pleading for no merely scholastic interest, but for freedom, impulse, reality, not in literature only, but in daily communion of speech. After all, it was impossible to have this impulse in Greek and Latin, dead languages shut up in books as in reliquaries—*péris et mises en reliquaires de livres*. By aid of this starveling stock—*pauvre plante et vergette*—of the French language, he must speak delicately, movingly, if he is ever to speak so at all: that, or none, must be for him the medium of what he calls, in one of his great phrases, *le discours fatal des choses mondaines*—that discourse about affairs which decides men's fates. And it is his patriotism not to despair of it; he sees it already perfect in all elegance and beauty of words—*parfait en toute élégance et vénusté de paroles*.

9. Du Bellay was born in the disastrous year 1525, the year of the battle of Pavia, and the captivity of Francis the First. His parents died early, and to him, as the younger son, his mother's little estate, *ce petit Liré*, the beloved place of his birth, descended. He was brought up by a brother only a little older than himself; and left to themselves, the two boys passed their lives in day-dreams of military glory. Their education was neglected; "The time of my youth," says Du Bellay, "was lost, like the flower which no shower waters, and no hand cultivates." He was just twenty years old when the elder brother died, leaving Joachim to be the guardian of his child. It was with regret, with a shrinking sense of incapacity, that he took upon him the burden of this responsibility. Hitherto he had looked forward to the profession of a soldier, hereditary in his family. But at this time a sickness attacked him which brought him cruel sufferings, and seemed likely to be mortal. It was then for the first time that he read the Greek and Latin poets. These studies came too late to make him what he so much desired to be, a trifler in Greek and Latin verse, like so many others of his time now forgotten; instead, they made him a lover of his own homely native tongue, that poor starveling stock of the French language. It was through this fortunate shortcoming in his education that he became national and modern; and he learned afterwards to look back on that wild garden of his youth with only a half regret. A certain Cardinal du Bellay

was the successful member of the family, a man often employed in high official business. To him the thoughts of Joachim turned when it became necessary to choose a profession, and in 1552 he accompanied the Cardinal to Rome. He remained there nearly five years, burdened with the weight of affairs, and languishing with home-sickness. Yet it was under these circumstances that his genius yielded its best fruits. From Rome, so full of pleasurable sensation for men of an imaginative temperament such as his, with all the curiosities of the Renaissance still fresh in it, his thoughts went back painfully, longingly, to the country of the Loire, with its wide expanse of waving corn, its homely pointed roofs of grey slate, and its far-off scent of the sea. He reached home at last, but only to die there, quite suddenly, one wintry day, at the early age of thirty-five.

10. Much of Du Bellay's poetry illustrates rather the age and school to which he belonged than his own temper and genius. As with the writings of Ronsard and the other poets of the *Pleiad*, its interest depends not so much on the impress of individual genius upon it, as on the circumstance that it was once poetry *à la mode*, that it is part of the manner of a time—a time which made much of manner, and carried it to a high degree of perfection. It is one of the decorations of an age which threw a large part of its energy into the work of decoration. We feel a pensive pleasure in gazing on these faded adornments, and observing how a group of actual men and women pleased themselves long ago. Ronsard's poems are a kind of epitome of his age. Of one side of that age, it is true, of the strenuous, the progressive, the serious movement, which was then going on, there is little; but of the catholic side, the losing side, the forlorn hope, hardly a figure is absent. The Queen of Scots, at whose desire Ronsard published his odes, reading him in her northern prison, felt that he was bringing back to her the true flavour of her early days in the court of Catherine at the Louvre, with its exotic Italian gaieties. Those who disliked that poetry, disliked it because they found that age itself distasteful. The poetry of Malherbe came, with its sustained style and weighty sentiment, but with nothing that set people singing; and the lovers of such poetry saw in the poetry of the *Pleiad* only the latest trumpery of the middle age. But the time arrived when the school of Malherbe also had had its day; and the *Romanticists*, who in their eagerness for excitement, for strange music and imagery, went back to the works of the middle age, accepted the *Pleiad* too with the rest; and in that new middle age which their genius has evoked, the poetry of the *Pleiad* has found its place. At first, with Malherbe, you may think it, like the architecture, the whole mode of life, the very dresses of that time, fantastic, faded, *rococo*. But if you look long enough to understand it, to conceive its sentiment, you will find that those wanton lines have a spirit guiding their caprices. For there is *style* there; one temper has shaped the whole; and everything that has style,

that has been done as no other man or age could have done it, as it could never, for all our trying, be done again, has its true value and interest. Let us dwell upon it for a moment, and try to gather from it that special flower, *ce fleur particulier*, which Ronsard himself tells us every garden has.

11. It is poetry not for the people, but for a confined circle, for courtiers, great lords and erudite persons, people who desire to be humoured, to gratify a certain refined voluptuousness they have in them. Ronsard loves, or dreams that he loves, a rare and peculiar type of beauty, *la petite pucelle Angevine*, with golden hair and dark eyes. But he has the ambition not only of being a courtier and a lover, but a great scholar also; he is anxious about orthography, about the letter *è Grecque*, the true spelling of Latin names in French writing, and the restoration of the letter *i* to its primitive liberty—*del' i voyelle en sa première liberté*. His poetry is full of quaint, remote learning. He is just a little pedantic, true always to his own express judgment, that to be natural is not enough for one who in poetry desires to produce work worthy of immortality. And therewithal a certain number of Greek words, which charmed Ronsard and his circle by their gaiety and daintiness, and a certain air of foreign elegance about them, crept into the French language; as there were other strange words which the poets of the *Pleiad* forged for themselves, and which had only an ephemeral existence.

12. With this was united the desire to taste a more exquisite and various music than that of the older French verse, or of the classical poets. The music of the measured, scanned verse of Latin and Greek poetry is one thing; the music of the rhymed, unscanned verse of Villon and the old French poets, *la poésie chantée*, is another. To combine these two kinds of music in a new school of French poetry, to make verse which should scan and rhyme as well, to search out and harmonise the measure of every syllable, and unite it to the swift, flitting, swallow-like motion of rhyme, to penetrate their poetry with a double music—this was the ambition of the *Pleiad*. They are insatiable of music, they cannot have enough of it; they desire a music of greater compass perhaps than words can possibly yield, to drain out the last drops of sweetness which a certain note or accent contains.

13. It was Goudimel, the serious and protestant Goudimel, who set Ronsard's songs to music; but except in this eagerness for music the poets of the *Pleiad* seem never quite in earnest. The old Greek and Roman mythology, which the great Italians had found a motive so weighty and severe, becomes with them a mere toy. That "Lord of terrible aspect," *Amor*, has become Love the boy, or the babe. They are full of fine railleries; they delight in diminutives, *ondelette, fontelette, doucelette, Cassandrette*. Their loves are only half real, a vain effort to prolong the imaginative loves of the middle age beyond their natural lifetime.

They write love-poems for hire. Like that party of people who tell the tales in Boccaccio's *Decameron*, they form a circle which in an age of great troubles, losses, anxieties, can amuse itself with art, poetry, intrigue. But they amuse themselves with wonderful elegance. And sometimes their gaiety becomes satiric, for, as they play, real passions insinuate themselves, and at least the reality of death. Their dejection at the thought of leaving this fair abode of our common daylight—*le beau sejour du commun jour*—is expressed by them with almost wearisome reiteration. But with this sentiment too they are able to trifle. The imagery of death serves for delicate ornament, and they weave into the airy nothingness of their verses their trite reflections on the vanity of life. Just so the grotesque details of the charnel-house nest themselves, together with birds and flowers and the fancies of the pagan mythology, in the traceries of the architecture of that time, which wantons in its graceful arabesques with the images of old age and death.

14. Ronsard became deaf at sixteen; and it was this circumstance which finally determined him to be a man of letters instead of a diplomatist, significantly, one might fancy, of a certain premature agedness, and of the tranquil, temperate sweetness appropriate to that, in the school of poetry which he founded. Its charm is that of a thing not vigorous or original, but full of the grace which comes of long study and reiterated refinements, and many steps repeated, and many angles worn down, with an exquisite faintness, *une fadeur exquise*, a certain tenuity and caducity, as for those who can bear nothing vehement or strong; for princes weary of love, like Francis the First, or of pleasure, like Henry the Third, or of action, like Henry the Fourth. Its merits are those of the old,—grace and finish, perfect in minute detail. For these people are a little jaded, and have a constant desire for a subdued and delicate excitement, to warm their creeping fancy a little. They love a constant change of rhyme in poetry, and in their houses that strange, fantastic interweaving of thin, reed-like lines, which are a kind of rhetoric in architecture.

15. But the poetry of the *Pleiad* is true not only to the physiognomy of its age, but also to its country—*ce pays du Vendomois*—the names and scenery of which so often recur in it:—the great Loire, with its long spaces of white sand; the little river Loir; the heathy, upland country, with its scattered pools of water and waste road-sides, and retired manors, with their crazy old feudal defences half fallen into decay; *La Beauce*, where the vast rolling fields seem to anticipate the great western sea itself. It is full of the traits of that country. We see Du Bellay and Ronsard gardening, or hunting with their dogs, or watch the pastimes of a rainy day; and with all this is connected a domesticity, a homeliness and simple goodness, by which the Northern country gains upon the South. They have the love of the aged for warmth, and understand the

poetry of winter; for they are not far from the Atlantic, and the west wind which comes up from it, turning the poplars white, spares not this new Italy in France. So the fireside often appears, with the pleasures of the frosty season, about the vast emblazoned chimneys of the time, and with a *bonhomie* as of little children, or old people.

16. It is in Du Bellay's *Olive*, a collection of sonnets in praise of a half-imaginary lady, *Sonnetz a la louange d'Olive*, that these characteristics are most abundant. Here is a perfectly crystallised example:—

>   *D'amour, de grace, et de haulte valeur*
>   *Les feux divins estoient ceinctz et les cieulx*
>   *S'estoient vestuz d'un manteau precieux*
>   *A raiz ardens de diverse couleur:*
>   *Tout estoit plein de beauté, de bonheur,*
>   *La mer tranquille, et le vent gracieulx,*
>   *Quand celle la nasquit en ces bas lieux*
>   *Qui a pillé du monde tout l'honneur.*
>   *Ell' prist son teint des beux lyz blanchissans,*
>   *Son chef de l'or, ses deux levres des rozes,*
>   *Et du soleil ses yeux resplandissans:*
>   *Le ciel usant de libéralité,*
>   *Mist en l'esprit ses semences encloses,*
>   *Son nom des Dieux prist l'immortalité.*

17. That he is thus a characteristic specimen of the poetical taste of that age, is indeed Du Bellay's chief interest. But if his work is to have the highest sort of interest, if it is to do something more than satisfy curiosity, if it is to have an æsthetic as distinct from an historical value, it is not enough for a poet to have been the true child of his age, to have conformed to its æsthetic conditions, and by so conforming to have charmed and stimulated that age; it is necessary that there should be perceptible in his work something individual, inventive, unique, the impress there of the writer's own temper and personality. This impress M. Sainte-Beuve thought he found in the *Antiquités de Rome*, and the *Regrets*, which he ranks as what has been called *poésie intime*, that intensely modern sort of poetry in which the writer has for his aim the portraiture of his own most intimate moods, and to take the reader into his confidence. That age had other instances of this intimacy of sentiment: Montaigne's *Essays* are full of it, the carvings of the church of Brou are full of it. M. Sainte-Beuve has perhaps exaggerated the influence of this quality in Du Bellay's *Regrets*; but the very name of the book has a touch of Rousseau about it, and reminds one of a whole

generation of self-pitying poets in modern times. It was in the atmosphere of Rome, to him so strange and mournful, that these pale flowers grew up. For that journey to Italy, which he deplored as the greatest misfortune of his life, put him in full possession of his talent, and brought out all its originality. And in effect you do find intimacy, *intimité*, here. The trouble of his life is analysed, and the sentiment of it conveyed directly to our minds; not a great sorrow or passion, but only the sense of loss in passing days, the *ennui* of a dreamer who must plunge into the world's affairs, the opposition between actual life and the ideal, a longing for rest, nostalgia, home-sickness—that pre-eminently childish, but so suggestive sorrow, as significant of the final regret of all human creatures for the familiar earth and limited sky.

18. The feeling for landscape is often described as a modern one; still more so is that for antiquity, the sentiment of ruins. Du Bellay has this sentiment. The duration of the hard, sharp outlines of things is a grief to him, and passing his wearisome days among the ruins of ancient Rome, he is consoled by the thought that all must one day end, by the sentiment of the grandeur of nothingness—*la grandeur du rien*. With a strange touch of far-off mysticism, he thinks that the great whole—*le grand tout*—into which all other things pass and lose themselves, ought itself sometimes to perish and pass away. Nothing less can relieve his weariness. From the stately aspects of Rome his thoughts went back continually to France, to the smoking chimneys of his little village, the longer twilight of the North, the soft climate of Anjou—*La douceur Angevine*; yet not so much to the real France, we may be sure, with its dark streets and roofs of rough-hewn slate, as to that other country, with slenderer towers, and more winding rivers, and trees like flowers, and with softer sunshine on more gracefully-proportioned fields and ways, which the fancy of the exile, and the pilgrim, and of the schoolboy far from home, and of those kept at home unwillingly, everywhere builds up before or behind them.

19. He came home at last, through the *Grisons*, by slow journeys; and there, in the cooler air of his own country, under its skies of milkier blue, the sweetest flower of his genius sprang up. There have been poets whose whole fame has rested on one poem, as Gray's on the *Elegy in a Country Churchyard*, or Ronsard's, as many critics have thought, on the eighteen lines of one famous ode. Du Bellay has almost been the poet of one poem; and this one poem of his is an Italian product transplanted into that green country of Anjou; out of the Latin verses of Andrea Navagero, into French. But it is a composition in which the matter is almost nothing, and the form almost everything; and the form of the poem as it stands, written in old French, is all Du Bellay's own. It is a song which the winnowers are supposed to sing as they winnow the corn, and they invoke the winds to lie lightly on the grain.

D'UN VANNEUR DE BLE AUX VENTS.[1]

A vous trouppe legère
  Qui d'aile passagère
  Par le monde volez,
  Et d'un sifflant murmure
  L'ombrageuse verdure
  Doulcement esbranlez.

J'offre ces violettes,
  Ces lis & ces fleurettes,
  Et ces roses icy,
  Ces vermeillettes roses
  Sont freschement écloses,
  Et ces œlliets aussi.

De vostre doulce haleine
  Eventez ceste plaine
  Eventez ce sejour;
  Ce pendant que j'ahanne
  A mon blè que je vanne
  A la chaleur du jour.

20. That has, in the highest degree, the qualities, the value, of the whole Pleiad school of poetry, of the whole phase of taste from which that school derives—a certain silvery grace of fancy, nearly all the pleasure of which is in the surprise at the happy and dexterous way in which a thing slight in itself is handled. The sweetness of it is by no means to be got at by crushing, as you crush wild herbs to get at their perfume. One seems to hear the measured motion of the fans, with a child's pleasure on coming across the incident for the first time, in one of those great barns of Du Bellay's own country, *La Beauce*, the granary of France. A sudden light transfigures some trivial thing, a weather-vane, a wind-mill, a winnowing fan, the dust in the barn door. A moment—and the thing has vanished, because it was pure effect; but it leaves a relish behind it, a longing that the accident may happen again.

1872.

---

1. A graceful translation of this and some other poems of the *Pleiad* may be found in *Ballads and Lyrics of Old France*, by Mr. Andrew Lang.

from WINCKELMANN
Et Ego in Arcadia Fui

[...] In one of the frescoes of the Vatican, Raphael has commemorated the tradition of the Catholic religion. Against a space of tranquil sky, broken in upon by the beatific vision, are ranged the great personages of Christian history, with the Sacrament in the midst. Another fresco of Raphael in the same apartment presents a very different company, Dante alone appearing in both. Surrounded by the muses of Greek mythology, under a thicket of laurel, sits Apollo, with the sources of Castalia at his feet. On either side are grouped those on whom the spirit of Apollo descended, the classical and Renaissance poets, to whom the waters of Castalia come down, a river making glad this other "city of God." In this fresco it is the classical tradition, the orthodoxy of taste, that Raphael commemorates. Winckelmann's intellectual history authenticates the claims of this tradition in human culture. In the countries where that tradition arose, where it still lurked about its own artistic relics, and changes of language had not broken its continuity, national pride might sometimes light up anew an enthusiasm for it. Aliens might imitate that enthusiasm, and classicism become from time to time an intellectual fashion. But Winckelmann was not further removed by language, than by local aspects and associations, from those vestiges of the classical spirit; and he lived at a time when, in Germany, classical studies were out of favour. Yet, remote in time and place, he feels after the Hellenic world, divines those channels of ancient art, in which its life still circulates, and, like Scyles, the half-barbarous yet Hellenising king, in the beautiful story of Herodotus, is irresistibly attracted by it. This testimony to the authority of the Hellenic tradition, its fitness to satisfy some vital requirement of the intellect, which Winckelmann contributes as a solitary man of genius, is offered also by the general history of the mind. The spiritual forces of the past, which have prompted and informed the culture of a succeeding age, live, indeed, within that culture, but with an absorbed, underground life. The Hellenic element alone has not been so absorbed, or content with this underground life; from time to time it has started to the surface; culture has been drawn back to its sources to be clarified and corrected. Hellenism is not merely an absorbed element in our intellectual life; it is a conscious tradition in it.

20. Again, individual genius works ever under conditions of time and place: its products are coloured by the varying aspects of nature, and type of human form, and outward manners of life. There is thus an element of change in art; criticism must never for a moment forget that "the artist is the child of his time."

But besides these conditions of time and place, and independent of them, there is also an element of permanence, a standard of taste, which genius confesses. This standard is maintained in a purely intellectual tradition. It acts upon the artist, not as one of the influences of his own age, but through those artistic products of the previous generation which first excited, while they directed into a particular channel, his sense of beauty. The supreme artistic products of succeeding generations thus form a series of elevated points, taking each from each the reflection of a strange light, the source of which is not in the atmosphere around and above them, but in a stage of society remote from ours. The standard of taste, then, was fixed in Greece, at a definite historical period. A tradition for all succeeding generations, it originates in a spontaneous growth out of the influences of Greek society. What were the conditions under which this ideal, this standard of artistic orthodoxy, was generated? How was Greece enabled to force its thought upon Europe?

21. Greek art, when we first catch sight of it, is entangled with Greek religion. We are accustomed to think of Greek religion as the religion of art and beauty, the religion of which the Olympian Zeus and the Athena Polias are the idols, the poems of Homer the sacred books. Thus Cardinal Newman speaks of "the classical polytheism which was gay and graceful, as was natural in a civilised age." Yet such a view is only a partial one. In it the eye is fixed on the sharp, bright edge of high Hellenic culture, but loses sight of the sombre world across which it strikes. Greek religion, where we can observe it most distinctly, is at once a magnificent ritualistic system, and a cycle of poetical conceptions. Religions, as they grow by natural laws out of man's life, are modified by whatever modifies his life. They brighten under a bright sky, they become liberal as the social range widens, they grow intense and shrill in the clefts of human life, where the spirit is narrow and confined, and the stars are visible at noonday; and a fine analysis of these differences is one of the gravest functions of religious criticism. Still, the broad foundation, in mere human nature, of all religions as they exist for the greatest number, is a universal pagan sentiment, a paganism which existed before the Greek religion, and has lingered far onward into the Christian world, ineradicable, like some persistent vegetable growth, because its seed is an element of the very soil out of which it springs.

22. This pagan sentiment measures the sadness with which the human mind is filled, whenever its thoughts wander far from what is here, and now. It is beset by notions of irresistible natural powers, for the most part ranged against man, but the secret also of his fortune, making the earth golden and the grape fiery for him. He makes gods in his own image, gods smiling and flower-crowned, or bleeding by some sad fatality, to console him by their wounds, never closed from generation to generation. It is with a rush of home-sickness that the thought

of death presents itself. He would remain at home for ever on the earth if he could. As it loses its colour and the senses fail, he clings ever closer to it; but since the mouldering of bones and flesh must go on to the end, he is careful for charms and talismans, which may chance to have some friendly power in them, when the inevitable shipwreck comes. Such sentiment is a part of the eternal basis of all religions, modified indeed by changes of time and place, but indestructible, because its root is so deep in the earth of man's nature. The breath of religious initiators passes over them; a few "rise up with wings as eagles," but the broad level of religious life is not permanently changed. Religious progress, like all purely spiritual progress, is confined to a few. This sentiment attaches itself in the earliest times to certain usages of patriarchal life, the kindling of fire, the washing of the body, the slaughter of the flock, the gathering of harvest, holidays and dances. Here are the beginnings of a ritual, at first as occasional and unfixed as the sentiment which it expresses, but destined to become the permanent element of religious life. The usages of patriarchal life change; but this germ of ritual remains, promoted now with a consciously religious motive, losing its domestic character, and therefore becoming more and more inexplicable with each generation. Such pagan worship, in spite of local variations, essentially one, is an element in all religions. It is the anodyne which the religious principle, like one administering opiates to the incurable, has added to the law which makes life sombre for the vast majority of mankind.

23. More definite religious conceptions come from other sources, and fix themselves upon this ritual in various ways, changing it, and giving it new meanings. In Greece they were derived from mythology, itself not due to a religious source at all, but developing in the course of time into a body of religious conceptions, entirely human in form and character. To the unprogressive ritual element it brought these conceptions, itself—ἡ πτεροῦ δύναμις, the power of the wing—an element of refinement, of ascension, with the promise of an endless destiny. While the ritual remains unchanged, the æsthetic element, only accidentally connected with it, expands with the freedom and mobility of the things of the intellect. Always, the fixed element is the religious observance; the fluid, unfixed element is the myth, the religious conception. This religion is itself pagan, and has in any broad view of it the pagan sadness. It does not at once, and for the majority, become the higher Hellenic religion. The country people, of course, cherish the unlovely idols of an earlier time, such as those which Pausanias found still devoutly preserved in Arcadia. Athenæus tells the story of one who, coming to a temple of Latona, had expected to find some worthy presentment of the mother of Apollo, and laughed on seeing only a shapeless wooden figure. The wilder people have wilder gods, which, however, in Athens, or Corinth, or

Lacedæmon, changing ever with the worshippers in whom they live and move and have their being, borrow something of the lordliness and distinction of human nature there. Greek religion too has its mendicants, its purifications, its antinomian mysticism, its garments offered to the gods, its statues worn with kissing, its exaggerated superstitions for the vulgar only, its worship of sorrow, its *addolorata*, its mournful mysteries. Scarcely a wild or melancholy note of the medieval church but was anticipated by Greek polytheism! What should we have thought of the vertiginous prophetess at the very centre of Greek religion? The supreme Hellenic culture is a sharp edge of light across this gloom. The fiery, stupefying wine becomes in a happier climate clear and exhilarating. The Dorian worship of Apollo, rational, chastened, debonair, with his unbroken daylight, always opposed to the sad Chthonian divinities, is the aspiring element, by force and spring of which Greek religion sublimes itself. Out of Greek religion, under happy conditions, arises Greek art, to minister to human culture. It was the privilege of Greek religion to be able to transform itself into an artistic ideal.

24. For the thoughts of the Greeks about themselves, and their relation to the world generally, were ever in the happiest readiness to be transformed into objects for the senses. In this lies the main distinction between Greek art and the mystical art of the Christian middle age, which is always struggling to express thoughts beyond itself. Take, for instance, a characteristic work of the middle age, Angelico's *Coronation of the Virgin*, in the cloister of *Saint Mark's* at Florence. In some strange halo of a moon Jesus and the Virgin Mother are seated, clad in mystical white raiment, half shroud, half priestly linen. Jesus, with rosy nimbus and the long pale hair—*tanquam lana alba et tanquam nix*—of the figure in the Apocalypse, with slender finger-tips is setting a crown of pearl on the head of Mary, who, corpse-like in her refinement, is bending forward to receive it, the light lying like snow upon her forehead. Certainly, it cannot be said of Angelico's fresco that it throws into a sensible form our highest thoughts about man and his relation to the world; but it did not do this adequately even for Angelico. For him, all that is outward or sensible in his work—the hair like wool, the rosy nimbus, the crown of pearl—is only the symbol or type of a really inexpressible world, to which he wishes to direct the thoughts; he would have shrunk from the notion that what the eye apprehended was all. Such forms of art, then, are inadequate to the matter they clothe; they remain ever below its level. Something of this kind is true also of oriental art. As in the middle age from an exaggerated inwardness, so in the East from a vagueness, a want of definition, in thought, the matter presented to art is unmanageable, and the forms of sense struggle vainly with it. The many-headed gods of the East, the orientalised, many-breasted Diana

of Ephesus, like Angelico's fresco, are at best overcharged symbols, a means of hinting at an idea which art cannot fitly or completely express, which still remains in the world of shadows.

25. But take a work of Greek art,—the Venus of Melos. That is in no sense a symbol, a suggestion, of anything beyond its own victorious fairness. The mind begins and ends with the finite image, yet loses no part of the spiritual motive. That motive is not lightly and loosely attached to the sensuous form, as its meaning to an allegory, but saturates and is identical with it. The Greek mind had advanced to a particular stage of self-reflexion, but was careful not to pass beyond it. In oriental thought there is a vague conception of life everywhere, but no true appreciation of itself by the mind, no knowledge of the distinction of man's nature: in its consciousness of itself, humanity is still confused with the fantastic, indeterminate life of the animal and vegetable world. In Greek thought, on the other hand, the "lordship of the soul" is recognised; that lordship gives authority and divinity to human eyes and hands and feet; inanimate nature is thrown into the background. But just there Greek thought finds its happy limit; it has not yet become too inward; the mind has not yet learned to boast its independence of the flesh; the spirit has not yet absorbed everything with its emotions, nor reflected its own colour everywhere. It has indeed committed itself to a train of reflexion which must end in defiance of form, of all that is outward, in an exaggerated idealism. But that end is still distant: it has not yet plunged into the depths of religious mysticism.

26. This ideal art, in which the thought does not outstrip or lie beyond the proper range of its sensible embodiment, could not have arisen out of a phase of life that was uncomely or poor. That delicate pause in Greek reflexion was joined, by some supreme good luck, to the perfect animal nature of the Greeks. Here are the two conditions of an artistic ideal. The influences which perfected the animal nature of the Greeks are part of the process by which "the ideal" was evolved. Those "Mothers" who, in the second part of *Faust*, mould and remould the typical forms that appear in human history, preside, at the beginning of Greek culture, over such a concourse of happy physical conditions as ever generates by natural laws some rare type of intellectual or spiritual life. That delicate air, "nimbly and sweetly recommending itself" to the senses, the finer aspects of nature, the finer lime and clay of the human form, and modelling of the dainty framework of the human countenance:—these are the good luck of the Greek when he enters upon life. Beauty becomes a distinction, like genius, or noble place.

27. "By no people," says Winckelmann, "has beauty been so highly esteemed as by the Greeks. The priests of a youthful Jupiter at Ægæ, of the Ismenian Apollo, and the priest who at Tanagra led the procession of Mercury, bearing a

lamb upon his shoulders, were always youths to whom the prize of beauty had been awarded. The citizens of Egesta erected a monument to a certain Philip, who was not their fellow-citizen, but of Croton, for his distinguished beauty; and the people made offerings at it. In an ancient song, ascribed to Simonides or Epicharmus, of four wishes, the first was health, the second beauty. And as beauty was so longed for and prized by the Greeks, every beautiful person sought to become known to the whole people by this distinction, and above all to approve himself to the artists, because they awarded the prize; and this was for the artists an occasion for having supreme beauty ever before their eyes. Beauty even gave a right to fame; and we find in Greek histories the most beautiful people distinguished. Some were famous for the beauty of one single part of their form; as Demetrius Phalereus, for his beautiful eyebrows, was called *Charito-blepharos*. It seems even to have been thought that the procreation of beautiful children might be promoted by prizes. This is shown by the existence of contests for beauty, which in ancient times were established by Cypselus, King of Arcadia, by the river Alpheus; and, at the feast of Apollo of Philæ, a prize was offered to the youths for the deftest kiss. This was decided by an umpire; as also at Megara, by the grave of Diocles. At Sparta, and at Lesbos, in the temple of Juno, and among the Parrhasii, there were contests for beauty among women. The general esteem for beauty went so far, that the Spartan women set up in their bedchambers a Nireus, a Narcissus, or a Hyacinth, that they might bear beautiful children."

28. So, from a few stray antiquarianisms, a few faces cast up sharply from the waves, Winckelmann, as his manner was, divines the temperament of the antique world, and that in which it had delight. It has passed away with that distant age, and we may venture to dwell upon it. What sharpness and reality it has is the sharpness and reality of suddenly arrested life. The Greek system of gymnastics originated as part of a religious ritual. The worshipper was to recommend himself to the gods by becoming fleet and fair, white and red, like them. The beauty of the *palæstra*, and the beauty of the artist's workshop, reacted on one another. The youth tried to rival his gods; and his increased beauty passed back into them.—"I take the gods to witness, I had rather have a fair body than a king's crown"—Ὄμνυμι πάντας θεοὺς μὴ ἑλέσθαι ἄν τὴν βασιλέως ἀρχὴν ἀντὶ τοῦ καλὸς εἶναι.—that is the form in which one age of the world chose the higher life.—A perfect world, if the gods could have seemed for ever only fleet and fair, white and red! Let us not regret that this unperplexed youth of humanity, satisfied with the vision of itself, passed, at the due moment, into a mournful maturity; for already the deep joy was in store for the spirit, of finding the ideal of that youth still red with life in the grave.

29. It followed that the Greek ideal expressed itself pre-eminently in sculpture.

All art has a sensuous element, colour, form, sound—in poetry a dexterous recalling of these, together with the profound, joyful sensuousness of motion, and each of them may be a medium for the ideal: it is partly accident which in any individual case makes the born artist, poet, or painter rather than sculptor. But as the mind itself has had an historical development, one form of art, by the very limitations of its material, may be more adequate than another for the expression of any one phase of that development. Different attitudes of the imagination have a native affinity with different types of sensuous form, so that they combine together, with completeness and ease. The arts may thus be ranged in a series, which corresponds to a series of developments in the human mind itself. Architecture, which begins in a practical need, can only express by vague hint or symbol the spirit or mind of the artist. He closes his sadness over him, or wanders in the perplexed intricacies of things, or projects his purpose from him clean-cut and sincere, or bares himself to the sunlight. But these spiritualities, felt rather than seen, can but lurk about architectural form as volatile effects, to be gathered from it by reflexion. Their expression is, indeed, not really sensuous at all. As human form is not the subject with which it deals, architecture is the mode in which the artistic effort centres, when the thoughts of man concerning himself are still indistinct, when he is still little preoccupied with those harmonies, storms, victories, of the unseen and intellectual world, which, wrought out into the bodily form, give it an interest and significance communicable to it alone. The art of Egypt, with its supreme architectural effects, is, according to Hegel's beautiful comparison, a Memnon waiting for the day, the day of the Greek spirit, the humanistic spirit, with its power of speech.

30. Again, painting, music, and poetry, with their endless power of complexity, are the special arts of the romantic and modern ages. Into these, with the utmost attenuation of detail, may be translated every delicacy of thought and feeling, incidental to a consciousness brooding with delight over itself. Through their gradations of shade, their exquisite intervals, they project in an external form that which is most inward in passion or sentiment. Between architecture and those romantic arts of painting, music, and poetry, comes sculpture, which, unlike architecture, deals immediately with man, while it contrasts with the romantic arts, because it is not self-analytical. It has to do more exclusively than any other art with the human form, itself one entire medium of spiritual expression, trembling, blushing, melting into dew, with inward excitement. That spirituality which only lurks about architecture as a volatile effect, in sculpture takes up the whole given material, and penetrates it with an imaginative motive; and at first sight sculpture, with its solidity of form, seems a thing more real and full than the faint, abstract world of

poetry or painting. Still the fact is the reverse. Discourse and action show man as he is, more directly than the play of the muscles and the moulding of the flesh; and over these poetry has command. Painting, by the flushing of colour in the face and dilatation of light in the eye—music, by its subtle range of tones—can refine most delicately upon a single moment of passion, unravelling its subtlest threads.

31. But why should sculpture thus limit itself to pure form? Because, by this limitation, it becomes a perfect medium of expression for one peculiar motive of the imaginative intellect. It therefore renounces all those attributes of its material which do not forward that motive. It has had, indeed, from the beginning an unfixed claim to colour; but this element of colour in it has always been more or less conventional, with no melting or modulation of tones, never permitting more than a very limited realism. It was maintained chiefly as a religious tradition. In proportion as the art of sculpture ceased to be merely decorative, and subordinate to architecture, it threw itself upon pure form. It renounces the power of expression by lower or heightened tones. In it, no member of the human form is more significant than the rest; the eye is wide, and without pupil; the lips and brow are hardly less significant than hands, and breasts, and feet. But the limitation of its resources is part of its pride: it has no backgrounds, no sky or atmosphere, to suggest and interpret a train of feeling; a little of suggested motion, and much of pure light on its gleaming surfaces, with pure form—only these. And it gains more than it loses by this limitation to its own distinguishing motives; it unveils man in the repose of his unchanging characteristics. That white light, purged from the angry, blood-like stains of action and passion, reveals, not what is accidental in man, but the tranquil godship in him, as opposed to the restless accidents of life. The art of sculpture records the first naïve, unperplexed recognition of man by himself; and it is a proof of the high artistic capacity of the Greeks, that they apprehended and remained true to these exquisite limitations, yet, in spite of them, gave to their creations a mobile, a vital, individuality.

32. *Heiterkeit*—blitheness or repose, and *Allgemeinheit*—generality or breadth, are, then, the supreme characteristics of the Hellenic ideal. But that generality or breadth has nothing in common with the lax observation, the unlearned thought, the flaccid execution, which have sometimes claimed superiority in art, on the plea of being "broad" or "general." Hellenic breadth and generality come of a culture minute, severe, constantly renewed, rectifying and concentrating its impressions into certain pregnant types.

33. The basis of all artistic genius lies in the power of conceiving humanity in a new and striking way, of putting a happy world of its own creation in place of the meaner world of our common days, generating around itself an atmosphere

with a novel power of refraction, selecting, transforming, recombining the images it transmits, according to the choice of the imaginative intellect. In exercising this power, painting and poetry have a variety of subject almost unlimited. The range of characters or persons open to them is as various as life itself; no character, however trivial, misshapen, or unlovely, can resist their magic. That is because those arts can accomplish their function in the choice and development of some special situation, which lifts or glorifies a character, in itself not poetical. To realise this situation, to define, in a chill and empty atmosphere, the focus where rays, in themselves pale and impotent, unite and begin to burn, the artist may have, indeed, to employ the most cunning detail, to complicate and refine upon thought and passion a thousand-fold. Let us take a brilliant example from the poems of Robert Browning. His poetry is pre-eminently the poetry of situations. The characters themselves are always of secondary importance; often they are characters in themselves of little interest; they seem to come to him by strange accidents from the ends of the world. His gift is shown by the way in which he accepts such a character, throws it into some situation, or apprehends it in some delicate pause of life, in which for a moment it becomes ideal. In the poem entitled *Le Byron de nos Jours*, in his *Dramatis Personæ*, we have a single moment of passion thrown into relief after this exquisite fashion. Those two jaded Parisians are not intrinsically interesting: they begin to interest us only when thrown into a choice situation. But to discriminate that moment, to make it appreciable by us, that we may "find" it, what a cobweb of allusions, what double and treble reflexions of the mind upon itself, what an artificial light is constructed and broken over the chosen situation; on how fine a needle's point that little world of passion is balanced! Yet, in spite of this intricacy, the poem has the clear ring of a central motive. We receive from it the impression of one imaginative tone, of a single creative act.

34. To produce such effects at all requires all the resources of painting, with its power of indirect expression, of subordinate but significant detail, its atmosphere, its foregrounds and backgrounds. To produce them in a pre-eminent degree requires all the resources of poetry, language in its most purged form, its remote associations and suggestions, its double and treble lights. These appliances sculpture cannot command. In it, therefore, not the special situation, but the type, the general character of the subject to be delineated, is all-important. In poetry and painting, the situation predominates over the character; in sculpture, the character over the situation. Excluded by the proper limitation of its material from the development of exquisite situations, it has to choose from a select number of types intrinsically interesting—interesting, that is, independently of any special situation into which they may be thrown.

Sculpture finds the secret of its power in presenting these types, in their broad, central, incisive lines. This it effects not by accumulation of detail, but by abstracting from it. All that is accidental, all that distracts the simple effect upon us of the supreme types of humanity, all traces in them of the commonness of the world, it gradually purges away.

35. Works of art produced under this law, and only these, are really characterised by Hellenic generality or breadth. In every direction it is a law of restraint. It keeps passion always below that degree of intensity at which it must necessarily be transitory, never winding up the features to one note of anger, or desire, or surprise. In some of the feebler allegorical designs of the middle age, we find isolated qualities portrayed as by so many masks; its religious art has familiarised us with faces fixed immovably into blank types of placid reverie. Men and women, again, in the hurry of life, often wear the sharp impress of one absorbing motive, from which it is said death sets their features free. All such instances may be ranged under the *grotesque*; and the Hellenic ideal has nothing in common with the grotesque. It allows passion to play lightly over the surface of the individual form, losing thereby nothing of its central impassivity, its depth and repose. To all but the highest culture, the reserved faces of the gods will ever have something of insipidity.

36. Again, in the best Greek sculpture, the archaic immobility has been stirred, its forms are in motion; but it is a motion ever kept in reserve, and very seldom committed to any definite action. Endless as are the attitudes of Greek sculpture, exquisite as is the invention of the Greeks in this direction, the actions or situations it permits are simple and few. There is no Greek Madonna; the goddesses are always childless. The actions selected are those which would be without significance, except in a divine person—binding on a sandal or preparing for the bath. When a more complex and significant action is permitted, it is most often represented as just finished, so that eager expectancy is excluded, as in the image of Apollo just after the slaughter of the Python, or of Venus with the apple of Paris already in her hand. The *Laocoon*, with all that patient science through which it has triumphed over an almost unmanageable subject, marks a period in which sculpture has begun to aim at effects legitimate, because delightful, only in painting.

37. The hair, so rich a source of expression in painting, because, relatively to the eye or the lip, it is mere drapery, is withdrawn from attention; its texture, as well as its colour, is lost, its arrangement but faintly and severely indicated, with no broken or enmeshed light. The eyes are wide and directionless, not fixing anything with their gaze, nor riveting the brain to any special external object, the brows without hair. Again, Greek sculpture deals almost exclusively with youth, where the moulding of the bodily organs is still as if suspended

between growth and completion, indicated but not emphasised; where the transition from curve to curve is so delicate and elusive, that Winckelmann compares it to a quiet sea, which, although we understand it to be in motion, we nevertheless regard as an image of repose; where, therefore, the exact degree of development is so hard to apprehend. If a single product only of Hellenic art were to be saved in the wreck of all beside, one might choose perhaps from the "beautiful multitude" of the Panathenaic frieze, that line of youths on horseback, with their level glances, their proud, patient lips, their chastened reins, their whole bodies in exquisite service. This colourless, unclassified purity of life, with its blending and interpenetration of intellectual, spiritual, and physical elements, still folded together, pregnant with the possibilities of a whole world closed within it, is the highest expression of the indifference which lies beyond all that is relative or partial. Everywhere there is the effect of an awaking, of a child's sleep just disturbed. All these effects are united in a single instance—the *adorante* of the museum of Berlin, a youth who has gained the wrestler's prize, with hands lifted and open, in praise for the victory. Fresh, unperplexed, it is the image of a man as he springs first from the sleep of nature, his white light taking no colour from any one-sided experience. He is characterless, so far as *character* involves subjection to the accidental influences of life.

38. "This sense," says Hegel, "for the consummate modelling of divine and human forms was pre-eminently at home in Greece. In its poets and orators, its historians and philosophers, Greece cannot be conceived from a central point, unless one brings, as a key to the understanding of it, an insight into the ideal forms of sculpture, and regards the images of statesmen and philosophers, as well as epic and dramatic heroes, from the artistic point of view. For those who act, as well as those who create and think, have, in those beautiful days of Greece, this plastic character. They are great and free, and have grown up on the soil of their own individuality, creating themselves out of themselves, and moulding themselves to what they were, and willed to be. The age of Pericles was rich in such characters; Pericles himself, Pheidias, Plato, above all Sophocles, Thucydides also, Xenophon and Socrates, each in his own order, the perfection of one remaining undiminished by that of the others. They are ideal artists of themselves, cast each in one flawless mould, works of art, which stand before us as an immortal presentment of the gods. Of this modelling also are those bodily works of art, the victors in the Olympic games; yes! and even Phryne, who, as the most beautiful of women, ascended naked out of the water, in the presence of assembled Greece."

39. This key to the understanding of the Greek spirit, Winckelmann possessed in his own nature, itself like a relic of classical antiquity, laid open by

accident to our alien, modern atmosphere. To the criticism of that consummate Greek modelling he brought not only his culture but his temperament. We have seen how definite was the leading motive of that culture; how, like some central root-fibre, it maintained the well-rounded unity of his life through a thousand distractions. Interests not his, nor meant for him, never disturbed him. In morals, as in criticism, he followed the clue of instinct, of an unerring instinct. Penetrating into the antique world by his passion, his temperament, he enunciated no formal principles, always hard and one-sided. Minute and anxious as his culture was, he never became one-sidedly self-analytical. Occupied ever with himself, perfecting himself and developing his genius, he was not content, as so often happens with such natures, that the atmosphere between him and other minds should be thick and clouded; he was ever jealously refining his meaning into a form, express, clear, objective. This temperament he nurtured and invigorated by friendships which kept him always in direct contact with the spirit of youth. The beauty of the Greek statues was a sexless beauty: the statues of the gods had the least traces of sex. Here there is a moral sexlessness, a kind of ineffectual wholeness of nature, yet with a true beauty and significance of its own.

40. One result of this temperament is a serenity—*Heiterkeit*—which characterises Winckelmann's handling of the sensuous side of Greek art. This serenity is, perhaps, in great measure, a negative quality: it is the absence of any sense of want, or corruption, or shame. With the sensuous element in Greek art he deals in the pagan manner; and what is implied in that? It has been sometimes said that art is a means of escape from "the tyranny of the senses." It may be so for the spectator: he may find that the spectacle of supreme works of art takes from the life of the senses something of its turbid fever. But this is possible for the spectator only because the artist, in producing those works, has gradually sunk his intellectual and spiritual ideas in sensuous form. He may live, as Keats lived, a pure life; but his soul, like that of Plato's false astronomer, becomes more and more immersed in sense, until nothing which lacks the appeal to sense has interest for him. How could such an one ever again endure the greyness of the ideal or spiritual world? The spiritualist is satisfied as he watches the escape of the sensuous elements from his conceptions; his interest grows, as the dyed garment bleaches in the keener air. But the artist steeps his thought again and again into the fire of colour. To the Greek this immersion in the sensuous was, religiously, at least, indifferent. Greek sensuousness, therefore, does not fever the conscience: it is shameless and childlike. Christian asceticism, on the other hand, discrediting the slightest touch of sense, has from time to time provoked into strong emphasis the contrast or antagonism to itself, of the artistic life, with its inevitable sensuousness.—*I did but taste*

a little honey with the end of the rod that was in mine hand, and lo! I must die. —It has sometimes seemed hard to pursue that life without something of conscious disavowal of a spiritual world; and this imparts to genuine artistic interests a kind of intoxication. From this intoxication Winckelmann is free: he fingers those pagan marbles with unsinged hands, with no sense of shame or loss. That is to deal with the sensuous side of art in the pagan manner.

41. The longer we contemplate that Hellenic ideal, in which man is at unity with himself, with his physical nature, with the outward world, the more we may be inclined to regret that he should ever have passed beyond it, to contend for a perfection that makes the blood turbid, and frets the flesh, and discredits the actual world about us. But if he was to be saved from the *ennui* which ever attaches itself to realisation, even the realisation of the perfect life, it was necessary that a conflict should come, that some sharper note should grieve the existing harmony, and the spirit chafed by it beat out at last only a larger and profounder music. In Greek tragedy this conflict has begun: man finds himself face to face with rival claims. Greek tragedy shows how such a conflict may be treated with serenity, how the evolution of it may be a spectacle of the dignity, not of the impotence, of the human spirit. But it is not only in tragedy that the Greek spirit showed itself capable of thus bringing joy out of matter in itself full of discouragements. Theocritus too strikes often a note of romantic sadness. But what a blithe and steady poise, above these discouragements, in a clear and sunny stratum of the air!

42. Into this stage of Greek achievement Winckelmann did not enter. Supreme as he is where his true interest lay, his insight into the typical unity and repose of the highest sort of sculpture seems to have involved limitation in another direction. His conception of art excludes that bolder type of it which deals confidently and serenely with life, conflict, evil. Living in a world of exquisite but abstract and colourless form, he could hardly have conceived of the subtle and penetrative, yet somewhat grotesque art of the modern world. What would he have thought of Gilliatt, in Victor Hugo's *Travailleurs de la Mer*, or of the bleeding mouth of Fantine in the first part of *Les Misérables*, penetrated as those books are with a sense of beauty, as lively and transparent as that of a Greek? Nay, a sort of preparation for the romantic temper is noticeable even within the limits of the Greek ideal itself, which for his part Winckelmann failed to see. For Greek religion has not merely its mournful mysteries of Adonis, of Hyacinthus, of Demeter, but it is conscious also of the fall of earlier divine dynasties. Hyperion gives way to Apollo, Oceanus to Poseidon. Around the feet of that tranquil Olympian family still crowd the weary shadows of an earlier, more formless, divine world. The placid minds even of Olympian gods are troubled with thoughts of a limit to duration, of inevitable

decay, of dispossession. Again, the supreme and colourless abstraction of those divine forms, which is the secret of their repose, is also a premonition of the fleshless, consumptive refinements of the pale, medieval artists. That high indifference to the outward, that impassivity, has already a touch of the corpse in it: we see already Angelico and the *Master of the Passion* in the artistic future. The suppression of the sensuous, the shutting of the door upon it, the ascetic interest, may be even now foreseen. Those abstracted gods, "ready to melt out their essence fine into the winds," who can fold up their flesh as a garment, and still remain themselves, seem already to feel that bleak air, in which, like Helen of Troy, they wander as the spectres of the middle age.

43. Gradually, as the world came into the church, an artistic interest, native in the human soul, reasserted its claims. But Christian art was still dependent on pagan examples, building the shafts of pagan temples into its churches, perpetuating the form of the *basilica*, in later times working the disused amphitheatres as stone quarries. The sensuous expression of ideas which unreservedly discredit the world of sense, was the delicate problem which Christian art had before it. If we think of medieval painting, as it ranges from the early German schools, still with something of the air of the charnel-house about them, to the clear loveliness of Perugino, we shall see how that problem was solved. In the very "worship of sorrow" the native blitheness of art asserted itself. The religious spirit, as Hegel says, "smiled through its tears." So perfectly did the young Raphael infuse that *Heiterkeit*, that pagan blitheness, into religious works, that his picture of Saint Agatha at Bologna became to Goethe a step in the evolution of *Iphigenie*.[1] But in proportion as the gift of smiling was found once more, there came also an aspiration towards that lost antique art, some relics of which Christian art had buried in itself, ready to work wonders when their day came.

44. The history of art has suffered as much as any history by trenchant and absolute divisions. Pagan and Christian art are sometimes harshly opposed, and the Renaissance is represented as a fashion which set in at a definite period. That is the superficial view: the deeper view is that which preserves the identity of European culture. The two are really continuous; and there is a sense in which it may be said that the Renaissance was an uninterrupted effort of the middle age, that it was ever taking place. When the actual relics of the antique were restored to the world, in the view of the Christian ascetic it was as if an ancient plague-pit had been opened. All the world took the contagion of the life of nature and of the senses. And now it was seen that the medieval spirit

---

1. *Italiänische Reise. Bologna*, 19 Oct. 1776.

too had done something for the new fortunes of the antique. By hastening the decline of art, by withdrawing interest from it and yet keeping unbroken the thread of its traditions, it had suffered the human mind to repose itself, that when day came it might awake, with eyes refreshed, to those ancient, ideal forms. [...]

1867.

CONCLUSION [1]

Λέγει που Ἡράκλειτος ὅτι πάντα χωρεῖ καὶ οὐδὲν μένει

To regard all things and principles of things as inconstant modes or fashions has more and more become the tendency of modern thought. Let us begin with that which is without—our physical life. Fix upon it in one of its more exquisite intervals, the moment, for instance, of delicious recoil from the flood of water in summer heat. What is the whole physical life in that moment but a combination of natural elements to which science gives their names? But those elements, phosphorus and lime and delicate fibres, are present not in the human body alone: we detect them in places most remote from it. Our physical life is a perpetual motion of them—the passage of the blood, the waste and repairing of the lenses of the eye, the modification of the tissues of the brain under every ray of light and sound—processes which science reduces to simpler and more elementary forces. Like the elements of which we are composed, the action of these forces extends beyond us: it rusts iron and ripens corn. Far out on every side of us those elements are broadcast, driven in many currents; and birth and gesture and death and the springing of violets from the grave are but a few out of ten thousand resultant combinations. That clear, perpetual outline of face and limb is but an image of ours, under which we group them—a design in a web, the actual threads of which pass out beyond it. This at least of flamelike our life has, that it is but the concurrence, renewed from moment to moment, of forces parting sooner or later on their ways.

2. Or if we begin with the inward world of thought and feeling, the whirlpool is still more rapid, the flame more eager and devouring. There it is no longer the gradual darkening of the eye, the gradual fading of colour from the wall—movements of the shore-side, where the water flows down indeed, though in apparent rest—but the race of the mid-stream, a drift of momentary acts of sight and passion and thought. At first sight experience seems to bury us under a flood of external objects, pressing upon us with a sharp and importunate reality, calling us out of ourselves in a thousand forms of action. But when reflexion begins to play upon these objects they are dissipated under its influence; the cohesive force seems suspended like some trick of magic; each object

---

1. This brief "Conclusion" was omitted in the second edition of this book, as I conceived it might possibly mislead some of those young men into whose hands it might fall. On the whole, I have thought it best to reprint it here, with some slight changes which bring it closer to my original meaning. I have dealt more fully in *Marius the Epicurean* with the thoughts suggested by it.

is loosed into a group of impressions—colour, odour, texture—in the mind of the observer. And if we continue to dwell in thought on this world, not of objects in the solidity with which language invests them, but of impressions, unstable, flickering, inconsistent, which burn and are extinguished with our consciousness of them, it contracts still further: the whole scope of observation is dwarfed into the narrow chamber of the individual mind. Experience, already reduced to a group of impressions, is ringed round for each one of us by that thick wall of personality through which no real voice has ever pierced on its way to us, or from us to that which we can only conjecture to be without. Every one of those impressions is the impression of the individual in his isolation, each mind keeping as a solitary prisoner its own dream of a world. Analysis goes a step farther still, and assures us that those impressions of the individual mind to which, for each one of us, experience dwindles down, are in perpetual flight; that each of them is limited by time, and that as time is infinitely divisible, each of them is infinitely divisible also; all that is actual in it being a single moment, gone while we try to apprehend it, of which it may ever be more truly said that it has ceased to be than that it is. To such a tremulous wisp constantly re-forming itself on the stream, to a single sharp impression, with a sense in it, a relic more or less fleeting, of such moments gone by, what is real in our life fines itself down. It is with this movement, with the passage and dissolution of impressions, images, sensations, that analysis leaves off—that continual vanishing away, that strange, perpetual weaving and unweaving of ourselves.

3. *Philosophiren*, says Novalis, *ist dephlegmatisiren, vivificiren*. The service of philosophy, of speculative culture, towards the human spirit, is to rouse, to startle it to a life of constant and eager observation. Every moment some form grows perfect in hand or face; some tone on the hills or the sea is choicer than the rest; some mood of passion or insight or intellectual excitement is irresistibly real and attractive to us,—for that moment only. Not the fruit of experience, but experience itself, is the end. A counted number of pulses only is given to us of a variegated, dramatic life. How may we see in them all that is to be seen in them by the finest senses? How shall we pass most swiftly from point to point, and be present always at the focus where the greatest number of vital forces unite in their purest energy?

4. To burn always with this hard, gemlike flame, to maintain this ecstasy, is success in life. In a sense it might even be said that our failure is to form habits: for, after all, habit is relative to a stereotyped world, and meantime it is only the roughness of the eye that makes any two persons, things, situations, seem alike. While all melts under our feet, we may well grasp at any exquisite passion, or any contribution to knowledge that seems by a lifted horizon to

set the spirit free for a moment, or any stirring of the senses, strange dyes, strange colours, and curious odours, or work of the artist's hands, or the face of one's friend. Not to discriminate every moment some passionate attitude in those about us, and in the very brilliancy of their gifts some tragic dividing of forces on their ways, is, on this short day of frost and sun, to sleep before evening. With this sense of the splendour of our experience and of its awful brevity, gathering all we are into one desperate effort to see and touch, we shall hardly have time to make theories about the things we see and touch. What we have to do is to be for ever curiously testing new opinions and courting new impressions, never acquiescing in a facile orthodoxy of Comte, or of Hegel, or of our own. Philosophical theories or ideas, as points of view, instruments of criticism, may help us to gather up what might otherwise pass unregarded by us. "Philosophy is the microscope of thought." The theory or idea or system which requires of us the sacrifice of any part of this experience, in consideration of some interest into which we cannot enter, or some abstract theory we have not identified with ourselves, or of what is only conventional, has no real claim upon us.

5. One of the most beautiful passages of Rousseau is that in the sixth book of the *Confessions*, where he describes the awakening in him of the literary sense. An undefinable taint of death had clung always about him, and now in early manhood he believed himself smitten by mortal disease. He asked himself how he might make as much as possible of the interval that remained; and he was not biassed by anything in his previous life when he decided that it must be by intellectual excitement, which he found just then in the clear, fresh writings of Voltaire. Well! we are all *condamnés*, as Victor Hugo says: we are all under sentence of death but with a sort of indefinite reprieve—*les hommes sont tous condamnés à mort avec des sursis indéfinis*: we have an interval, and then our place knows us no more. Some spend this interval in listlessness, some in high passions, the wisest, at least among "the children of this world," in art and song. For our one chance lies in expanding that interval, in getting as many pulsations as possible into the given time. Great passions may give us this quickened sense of life, ecstasy and sorrow of love, the various forms of enthusiastic activity, disinterested or otherwise, which come naturally to many of us. Only be sure it is passion—that it does yield you this fruit of a quickened, multiplied consciousness. Of such wisdom, the poetic passion, the desire of beauty, the love of art for its own sake, has most. For art comes to you proposing frankly to give nothing but the highest quality to your moments as they pass, and simply for those moments' sake.

1868.

from *APPRECIATIONS*

STYLE

Since all progress of mind consists for the most part in differentiation, in the resolution of an obscure and complex object into its component aspects, it is surely the stupidest of losses to confuse things which right reason has put asunder, to lose the sense of achieved distinctions, the distinction between poetry and prose, for instance, or, to speak more exactly, between the laws and characteristic excellences of verse and prose composition. On the other hand, those who have dwelt most emphatically on the distinction between prose and verse, prose and poetry, may sometimes have been tempted to limit the proper functions of prose too narrowly; and this again is at least false economy, as being, in effect, the renunciation of a certain means or faculty, in a world where after all we must needs make the most of things. Critical efforts to limit art *a priori*, by anticipations regarding the natural incapacity of the material with which this or that artist works, as the sculptor with solid form, or the prose-writer with the ordinary language of men, are always liable to be discredited by the facts of artistic production; and while prose is actually found to be a coloured thing with Bacon, picturesque with Livy and Carlyle, musical with Cicero and Newman, mystical and intimate with Plato and Michelet and Sir Thomas Browne, exalted or florid, it may be, with Milton and Taylor, it will be useless to protest that it can be nothing at all, except something very tamely and narrowly confined to mainly practical ends—a kind of "good round-hand;" as useless as the protest that poetry might not touch prosaic subjects as with Wordsworth, or an abstruse matter as with Browning, or treat contemporary life nobly as with Tennyson. In subordination to one essential beauty in all good literary style, in all literature as a fine art, as there are many beauties of poetry so the beauties of prose are many, and it is the business of criticism to estimate them as such; as it is good in the criticism of verse to look for those hard, logical, and quasi-prosaic excellences which that too has, or needs. To find in the poem, amid the flowers, the allusions, the mixed perspectives, of *Lycidas* for instance, the thought, the logical structure:—how wholesome! how delightful! as to identify in prose what we call the poetry, the imaginative power, not treating it as out of place and a kind of vagrant intruder, but by way of an estimate of its rights, that is, of its achieved powers, there.

2. Dryden, with the characteristic instinct of his age, loved to emphasise the distinction between poetry and prose, the protest against their confusion with

each other, coming with somewhat diminished effect from one whose poetry was so prosaic. In truth, his sense of prosaic excellence affected his verse rather than his prose, which is not only fervid, richly figured, poetic, as we say, but vitiated, all unconsciously, by many a scanning line. Setting up correctness, that humble merit of prose, as the central literary excellence, he is really a less correct writer than he may seem, still with an imperfect mastery of the relative pronoun. It might have been foreseen that, in the rotations of mind, the province of poetry in prose would find its assertor; and, a century after Dryden, amid very different intellectual needs, and with the need therefore of great modifications in literary form, the range of the poetic force in literature was effectively enlarged by Wordsworth. The true distinction between prose and poetry he regarded as the almost technical or accidental one of the absence or presence of metrical beauty, or, say! metrical restraint; and for him the opposition came to be between verse and prose of course; but, as the essential dichotomy in this matter, between imaginative and unimaginative writing, parallel to De Quincey's distinction between "the literature of power and the literature of knowledge," in the former of which the composer gives us not fact, but his peculiar sense of fact, whether past or present.

3. Dismissing then, under sanction of Wordsworth, that harsher opposition of poetry to prose, as savouring in fact of the arbitrary psychology of the last century, and with it the prejudice that there can be but one only beauty of prose style, I propose here to point out certain qualities of all literature as a fine art, which, if they apply to the literature of fact, apply still more to the literature of the imaginative sense of fact, while they apply indifferently to verse and prose, so far as either is really imaginative—certain conditions of true art in both alike, which conditions may also contain in them the secret of the proper discrimination and guardianship of the peculiar excellences of either.

4. The line between fact and something quite different from external fact is, indeed, hard to draw. In Pascal, for instance, in the persuasive writers generally, how difficult to define the point where, from time to time, argument which, if it is to be worth anything at all, must consist of facts or groups of facts, becomes a pleading—a theorem no longer, but essentially an appeal to the reader to catch the writer's spirit, to think with him, if one can or will—an expression no longer of fact but of his sense of it, his peculiar intuition of a world, prospective, or discerned below the faulty conditions of the present, in either case changed somewhat from the actual world. In science, on the other hand, in history so far as it conforms to scientific rule, we have a literary domain where the imagination may be thought to be always an intruder. And as, in all science, the functions of literature reduce themselves eventually to the transcribing of fact, so all the excellences of literary form in regard

to science are reducible to various kinds of painstaking; this good quality being involved in all "skilled work" whatever, in the drafting of an act of parliament, as in sewing. Yet here again, the writer's sense of fact, in history especially, and in all those complex subjects which do but lie on the borders of science, will still take the place of fact, in various degrees. Your historian, for instance, with absolutely truthful intention, amid the multitude of facts presented to him must needs select, and in selecting assert something of his own humour, something that comes not of the world without but of a vision within. So Gibbon moulds his unwieldy material to a preconceived view. Livy, Tacitus, Michelet, moving full of poignant sensibility amid the records of the past, each, after his own sense, modifies—who can tell where and to what degree?—and becomes something else than a transcriber; each, as he thus modifies, passing into the domain of art proper. For just in proportion as the writer's aim, consciously or unconsciously, comes to be the transcribing, not of the world, not of mere fact, but of his sense of it, he becomes an artist, his work *fine* art; and good art (as I hope ultimately to show) in proportion to the truth of his presentment of that sense; as in those humbler or plainer functions of literature also, truth—truth to bare fact, there—is the essence of such artistic quality as they may have. Truth! there can be no merit, no craft at all, without that. And further, all beauty is in the long run only *fineness* of truth, or what we call expression, the finer accommodation of speech to that vision within.

5. —The transcript of his sense of fact rather than the fact, as being preferable, pleasanter, more beautiful to the writer himself. In literature, as in every other product of human skill, in the moulding of a bell or a platter for instance, wherever this sense asserts itself, wherever the producer so modifies his work as, over and above its primary use or intention, to make it pleasing (to himself, of course, in the first instance) there, "fine" as opposed to merely serviceable art, exists. Literary art, that is, like all art which is in any way imitative or reproductive of fact—form, or colour, or incident—is the representation of such fact as connected with soul, of a specific personality, in its preferences, its volition and power.

6. Such is the matter of imaginative or artistic literature—this transcript, not of mere fact, but of fact in its infinite variety, as modified by human preference in all its infinitely varied forms. It will be good literary art not because it is brilliant or sober, or rich, or impulsive, or severe, but just in proportion as its representation of that sense, that soul-fact, is true, verse being only one department of such literature, and imaginative prose, it may be thought, being the special art of the modern world. That imaginative prose should be the special and opportune art of the modern world results from two important facts about the latter: first, the chaotic variety and complexity of its interests,

making the intellectual issue, the really master currents of the present time incalculable—a condition of mind little susceptible of the restraint proper to verse form, so that the most characteristic verse of the nineteenth century has been lawless verse; and secondly, an all-pervading naturalism, a curiosity about everything whatever as it really is, involving a certain humility of attitude, cognate to what must, after all, be the less ambitious form of literature. And prose thus asserting itself as the special and privileged artistic faculty of the present day, will be, however critics may try to narrow its scope, as varied in its excellence as humanity itself reflecting on the facts of its latest experience—an instrument of many stops, meditative, observant, descriptive, eloquent, analytic, plaintive, fervid. Its beauties will be not exclusively "pedestrian": it will exert, in due measure, all the varied charms of poetry, down to the rhythm which, as in Cicero, or Michelet, or Newman, at their best, gives its musical value to every syllable.[1]

7. The literary artist is of necessity a scholar, and in what he proposes to do will have in mind, first of all, the scholar and the scholarly conscience—the male conscience in this matter, as we must think it, under a system of education which still to so large an extent limits real scholarship to men. In his self-criticism, he supposes always that sort of reader who will go (full of eyes) warily, considerately, though without consideration for him, over the ground which the female conscience traverses so lightly, so amiably. For the material in which he works is no more a creation of his own than the sculptor's marble. Product of a myriad various minds and contending tongues, compact of obscure and minute association, a language has its own abundant and often recondite laws, in the habitual and summary recognition of which scholarship consists. A writer, full of a matter he is before all things anxious to express, may think of those laws, the limitations of vocabulary, structure, and the like, as a restriction, but if a real artist will find in them an opportunity. His punctilious observance of the proprieties of his medium will diffuse through all he writes a general air of sensibility, of refined usage. *Exclusiones debitæ naturæ*—the exclusions, or rejections, which nature demands—we know how large a part these play, according to Bacon, in the science of nature. In a somewhat changed sense, we might say that the art of the scholar is summed

---

1. Mr. Saintsbury, in his *Specimens of English Prose, from Malory to Macaulay*, has succeeded in tracing, through successive English prose-writers, the tradition of that severer beauty in them, of which this admirable scholar of our literature is known to be a lover. *English Prose, from Mandeville to Thackeray*, more recently "chosen and edited" by a younger scholar, Mr. Arthur Galton, of New College, Oxford, a lover of our literature at once enthusiastic and discreet, aims at a more various illustration of the eloquent powers of English prose, and is a delightful companion.

up in the observance of those rejections demanded by the nature of his medium, the material he must use. Alive to the value of an atmosphere in which every term finds its utmost degree of expression, and with all the jealousy of a lover of words, he will resist a constant tendency on the part of the majority of those who use them to efface the distinctions of language, the facility of writers often reinforcing in this respect the work of the vulgar. He will feel the obligation not of the laws only, but of those affinities, avoidances, those mere preferences, of his language, which through the associations of literary history have become a part of its nature, prescribing the rejection of many a neology, many a license, many a gipsy phrase which might present itself as actually expressive. His appeal, again, is to the scholar, who has great experience in literature, and will show no favour to short-cuts, or hackneyed illustration, or an affectation of learning designed for the unlearned. Hence a contention, a sense of self-restraint and renunciation, having for the susceptible reader the effect of a challenge for minute consideration; the attention of the writer, in every minutest detail, being a pledge that it is worth the reader's while to be attentive too, that the writer is dealing scrupulously with his instrument, and therefore, indirectly, with the reader himself also, that he has the science of the instrument he plays on, perhaps, after all, with a freedom which in such case will be the freedom of a master.

8. For meanwhile, braced only by those restraints, he is really vindicating his liberty in the making of a vocabulary, an entire system of composition, for himself, his own true manner; and when we speak of the manner of a true master we mean what is essential in his art. Pedantry being only the scholarship of *le cuistre* (we have no English equivalent) he is no pedant, and does but show his intelligence of the rules of language in his freedoms with it, addition or expansion, which like the spontaneities of manner in a well-bred person will still further illustrate good taste.—The right vocabulary! Translators have not invariably seen how all-important that is in the work of translation, driving for the most part at idiom or construction; whereas, if the original be first-rate, one's first care should be with its elementary particles, Plato, for instance, being often reproducible by an exact following, with no variation in structure, of word after word, as the pencil follows a drawing under tracing-paper, so only each word or syllable be not of false colour, to change my illustration a little.

9. Well! that is because any writer worth translating at all has winnowed and searched through his vocabulary, is conscious of the words he would select in systematic reading of a dictionary, and still more of the words he would reject were the dictionary other than Johnson's; and doing this with his peculiar sense of the world ever in view, in search of an instrument for the adequate expression of that, he begets a vocabulary faithful to the colouring of his own

spirit, and in the strictest sense original. That living authority which language needs lies, in truth, in its scholars, who recognising always that every language possesses a genius, a very fastidious genius, of its own, expand at once and purify its very elements, which must needs change along with the changing thoughts of living people. Ninety years ago, for instance, great mental force, certainly, was needed by Wordsworth, to break through the consecrated poetic associations of a century, and speak the language that was his, that was to become in a measure the language of the next generation. But he did it with the tact of a scholar also. English, for a quarter of a century past, has been assimilating the phraseology of pictorial art; for half a century, the phraseology of the great German metaphysical movement of eighty years ago; in part also the language of mystical theology: and none but pedants will regret a great consequent increase of its resources. For many years to come its enterprise may well lie in the naturalisation of the vocabulary of science, so only it be under the eye of a sensitive scholarship—in a liberal naturalisation of the ideas of science too, for after all the chief stimulus of good style is to possess a full, rich, complex matter to grapple with. The literary artist, therefore, will be well aware of physical science; science also attaining, in its turn, its true literary ideal. And then, as the scholar is nothing without the historic sense, he will be apt to restore not really obsolete or really worn-out words, but the finer edge of words still in use: *ascertain, communicate, discover*—words like these it has been part of our "business" to misuse. And still, as language was made for man, he will be no authority for correctnesses which, limiting freedom of utterance, were yet but accidents in their origin; as if one vowed not to say "*its*," which ought to have been in Shakespeare; "*his*" and "*hers*," for inanimate objects, being but a barbarous and really inexpressive survival. Yet we have known many things like this. Racy Saxon monosyllables, close to us as touch and sight, he will intermix readily with those long, savoursome, Latin words, rich in "second intention." In this late day certainly, no critical process can be conducted reasonably without eclecticism. Of such eclecticism we have a justifying example in one of the first poets of our time. How illustrative of monosyllabic effect, of sonorous Latin, of the phraseology of science, of metaphysic, of colloquialism even, are the writings of Tennyson; yet with what a fine, fastidious scholarship throughout!

10. A scholar writing for the scholarly, he will of course leave something to the willing intelligence of his reader. "To go preach to the first passer-by," says Montaigne, "to become tutor to the ignorance of the first I meet, is a thing I abhor;" a thing, in fact, naturally distressing to the scholar, who will therefore ever be shy of offering uncomplimentary assistance to the reader's wit. To really strenuous minds there is a pleasurable stimulus in the challenge for a

continuous effort on their part, to be rewarded by securer and more intimate grasp of the author's sense. Self-restraint, a skilful economy of means, *ascêsis*, that too has a beauty of its own; and for the reader supposed there will be an æsthetic satisfaction in that frugal closeness of style which makes the most of a word, in the exaction from every sentence of a precise relief, in the just spacing out of word to thought, in the logically filled space connected always with the delightful sense of difficulty overcome.

11. Different classes of persons, at different times, make, of course, very various demands upon literature. Still, scholars, I suppose, and not only scholars, but all disinterested lovers of books, will always look to it, as to all other fine art, for a refuge, a sort of cloistral refuge, from a certain vulgarity in the actual world. A perfect poem like *Lycidas*, a perfect fiction like *Esmond*, the perfect handling of a theory like Newman's *Idea of a University*, has for them something of the uses of a religious "retreat." Here, then, with a view to the central need of a select few, those "men of a finer thread" who have formed and maintain the literary ideal, everything, every component element, will have undergone exact trial, and, above all, there will be no uncharacteristic or tarnished or vulgar decoration, permissible ornament being for the most part structural, or necessary. As the painter in his picture, so the artist in his book, aims at the production by honourable artifice of a peculiar atmosphere. "The artist," says Schiller, "may be known rather by what he *omits*"; and in literature, too, the true artist may be best recognised by his tact of omission. For to the grave reader words too are grave; and the ornamental word, the figure, the accessory form or colour or reference, is rarely content to die to thought precisely at the right moment, but will inevitably linger awhile, stirring a long "brain-wave" behind it of perhaps quite alien associations.

12. Just there, it may be, is the detrimental tendency of the sort of scholarly attentiveness of mind I am recommending. But the true artist allows for it. He will remember that, as the very word ornament indicates what is in itself non-essential, so the "one beauty" of all literary style is of its very essence, and independent, in prose and verse alike, of all removable decoration; that it may exist in its fullest lustre, as in Flaubert's *Madame Bovary*, for instance, or in Stendhal's *Le Rouge et Le Noir*, in a composition utterly unadorned, with hardly a single suggestion of visibly beautiful things. Parallel, allusion, the allusive way generally, the flowers in the garden:—he knows the narcotic force of these upon the negligent intelligence to which any *diversion*, literally, is welcome, any vagrant intruder, because one can go wandering away with it from the immediate subject. Jealous, if he have a really quickening motive within, of all that does not hold directly to that, of the facile, the otiose, he will never depart from the strictly pedestrian process, unless he gains a ponderable

something thereby. Even assured of its congruity, he will still question its serviceableness. Is it worth while, can we afford, to attend to just that, to just that figure or literary reference, just then?—Surplusage! he will dread that, as the runner on his muscles. For in truth all art does but consist in the removal of surplusage, from the last finish of the gem-engraver blowing away the last particle of invisible dust, back to the earliest divination of the finished work to be, lying somewhere, according to Michelangelo's fancy, in the rough-hewn block of stone.

13. And what applies to figure or flower must be understood of all other accidental or removable ornaments of writing whatever; and not of specific ornament only, but of all that latent colour and imagery which language as such carries in it. A lover of words for their own sake, to whom nothing about them is unimportant, a minute and constant observer of their physiognomy, he will be on the alert not only for obviously mixed metaphors of course, but for the metaphor that is mixed in all our speech, though a rapid use may involve no cognition of it. Currently recognising the incident, the colour, the physical elements or particles in words like *absorb*, *consider*, *extract*, to take the first that occur, he will avail himself of them, as further adding to the resources of expression. The elementary particles of language will be realised as colour and light and shade through his scholarly living in the full sense of them. Still opposing the constant degradation of language by those who use it carelessly, he will not treat coloured glass as if it were clear; and while half the world is using figure unconsciously, will be fully aware not only of all that latent figurative texture in speech, but of the vague, lazy, half-formed personification—a rhetoric, depressing, and worse than nothing, because it has no really rhetorical motive—which plays so large a part there, and, as in the case of more ostentatious ornament, scrupulously exact of it, from syllable to syllable, its precise value.

14. So far I have been speaking of certain conditions of the literary art arising out of the medium or material in or upon which it works, the essential qualities of language and its aptitudes for contingent ornamentation, matters which define scholarship as science and good taste respectively. They are both subservient to a more intimate quality of good style: more intimate, as coming nearer to the artist himself. The otiose, the facile, surplusage: why are these abhorrent to the true literary artist, except because, in literary as in all other art, structure is all-important, felt, or painfully missed, everywhere?—that architectural conception of work, which foresees the end in the beginning and never loses sight of it, and in every part is conscious of all the rest, till the last sentence does but, with undiminished vigour, unfold and justify the first—a condition of literary art, which, in contradistinction to another quality of the

artist himself, to be spoken of later, I shall call the necessity of *mind* in style.

15. An acute philosophical writer, the late Dean Mansel (a writer whose works illustrate the literary beauty there may be in closeness, and with obvious repression or economy of a fine rhetorical gift) wrote a book, of fascinating precision in a very obscure subject, to show that all the technical laws of logic are but means of securing, in each and all of its apprehensions, the unity, the strict identity with itself, of the apprehending mind. All the laws of good writing aim at a similar unity or identity of the mind in all the processes by which the word is associated to its import. The term is right, and has its essential beauty, when it becomes, in a manner, what it signifies, as with the names of simple sensations. To give the phrase, the sentence, the structural member, the entire composition, song, or essay, a similar unity with its subject and with itself:—style is in the right way when it tends towards that. All depends upon the original unity, the vital wholeness and identity, of the initiatory apprehension or view. So much is true of all art, which therefore requires always its logic, its comprehensive reason—insight, foresight, retrospect, in simultaneous action—true, most of all, of the literary art, as being of all the arts most closely cognate to the abstract intelligence. Such logical coherency may be evidenced not merely in the lines of composition as a whole, but in the choice of a single word, while it by no means interferes with, but may even prescribe, much variety, in the building of the sentence for instance, or in the manner, argumentative, descriptive, discursive, of this or that part or member of the entire design. The blithe, crisp sentence, decisive as a child's expression of its needs, may alternate with the long-contending, victoriously intricate sentence; the sentence, born with the integrity of a single word, relieving the sort of sentence in which, if you look closely, you can see much contrivance, much adjustment, to bring a highly qualified matter into compass at one view. For the literary architecture, if it is to be rich and expressive, involves not only foresight of the end in the beginning, but also development or growth of design, in the process of execution, with many irregularities, surprises, and afterthoughts; the contingent as well as the necessary being subsumed under the unity of the whole. As truly, to the lack of such architectural design, of a single, almost visual, image, vigorously informing an entire, perhaps very intricate, composition, which shall be austere, ornate, argumentative, fanciful, yet true from first to last to that vision within, may be attributed those weaknesses of conscious or unconscious repetition of word, phrase, motive, or member of the whole matter, indicating, as Flaubert was aware, an original structure in thought not organically complete. With such foresight, the actual conclusion will most often get itself written out of hand, before, in the more obvious sense, the work is finished. With some strong and leading sense of the world, the tight

hold of which secures true *composition* and not mere loose accretion, the literary artist, I suppose, goes on considerably, setting joint to joint, sustained by yet restraining the productive ardour, retracing the negligences of his first sketch, repeating his steps only that he may give the reader a sense of secure and restful progress, readjusting mere assonances even, that they may soothe the reader, or at least not interrupt him on his way; and then, somewhere before the end comes, is burdened, inspired, with his conclusion, and betimes delivered of it, leaving off, not in weariness and because he finds *himself* at an end, but in all the freshness of volition. His work now structurally complete, with all the accumulating effect of secondary shades of meaning, he finishes the whole up to the just proportion of that ante-penultimate conclusion, and all becomes expressive. The house he has built is rather a body he has informed. And so it happens, to its greater credit, that the better interest even of a narrative to be recounted, a story to be told, will often be in its second reading. And though there are instances of great writers who have been no artists, an unconscious tact sometimes directing work in which we may detect, very pleasurably, many of the effects of conscious art, yet one of the greatest pleasures of really good prose literature is in the critical tracing out of that conscious artistic structure, and the pervading sense of it as we read. Yet of poetic literature too; for, in truth, the kind of constructive intelligence here supposed is one of the forms of the imagination.

16. That is the special function of mind, in style. Mind and soul:—hard to ascertain philosophically, the distinction is real enough practically, for they often interfere, are sometimes in conflict, with each other. Blake, in the last century, is an instance of preponderating soul, embarrassed, at a loss, in an era of preponderating mind. As a quality of style, at all events, soul is a fact, in certain writers—the way they have of absorbing language, of attracting it into the peculiar spirit they are of, with a subtlety which makes the actual result seem like some inexplicable inspiration. By mind, the literary artist reaches us, through static and objective indications of design in his work, legible to all. By soul, he reaches us, somewhat capriciously perhaps, one and not another, through vagrant sympathy and a kind of immediate contact. Mind we cannot choose but approve where we recognise it; soul may repel us, not because we misunderstand it. The way in which theological interests sometimes avail themselves of language is perhaps the best illustration of the force I mean to indicate generally in literature, by the word *soul*. Ardent religious persuasion may exist, may make its way, without finding any equivalent heat in language: or, again, it may enkindle words to various degrees, and when it really takes hold of them doubles its force. Religious history presents many remarkable instances in which, through no mere phrase-worship, an unconscious literary

tact has, for the sensitive, laid open a privileged pathway from one to another. "The altar-fire," people say, "has touched those lips!" The Vulgate, the English Bible, the English Prayer-Book, the writings of Swedenborg, the Tracts for the Times:—there, we have instances of widely different and largely diffused phases of religious feeling in operation as soul in style. But something of the same kind acts with similar power in certain writers of quite other than theological literature, on behalf of some wholly personal and peculiar sense of theirs. Most easily illustrated by theological literature, this quality lends to profane writers a kind of religious influence. At their best, these writers become, as we say sometimes, "prophets"; such character depending on the effect not merely of their matter, but of their matter as allied to, in "electric affinity" with, peculiar form, and working in all cases by an immediate sympathetic contact, on which account it is that it may be called soul, as opposed to mind, in style. And this too is a faculty of choosing and rejecting what is congruous or otherwise, with a drift towards unity—unity of atmosphere here, as there of design—soul securing colour (or perfume, might we say?) as mind secures form, the latter being essentially finite, the former vague or infinite, as the influence of a living person is practically infinite. There are some to whom nothing has any real interest, or real meaning, except as operative in a given person; and it is they who best appreciate the quality of soul in literary art. They seem to know a *person*, in a book, and make way by intuition: yet, although they thus enjoy the completeness of a personal information, it is still a characteristic of soul, in this sense of the word, that it does but suggest what can never be uttered, not as being different from, or more obscure than, what actually gets said, but as containing that plenary substance of which there is only one phase or facet in what is there expressed.

17. If all high things have their martyrs, Gustave Flaubert might perhaps rank as the martyr of literary style. In his printed correspondence, a curious series of letters, written in his twenty-fifth year, records what seems to have been his one other passion—a series of letters which, with its fine casuistries, its firmly repressed anguish, its tone of harmonious grey, and the sense of disillusion in which the whole matter ends, might have been, a few slight changes supposed, one of his own fictions. Writing to Madame X. certainly he does display, by "taking thought" mainly, by constant and delicate pondering, as in his love for literature, a heart really moved, but still more, and as the pledge of that emotion, a loyalty to his work. Madame X., too, is a literary artist, and the best gifts he can send her are precepts of perfection in art, counsels for the effectual pursuit of that better love. In his love-letters it is the pains and pleasures of art he insists on, its solaces: he communicates secrets, reproves, encourages, with a view to that. Whether the lady was dissatisfied with such divided or

indirect service, the reader is not enabled to see; but sees that, on Flaubert's part at least, a living person could be no rival of what was, from first to last, his leading passion, a somewhat solitary and exclusive one.

I must scold you (he writes) for one thing, which shocks, scandalises me, the small concern, namely, you show for art just now. As regards glory be it so: there, I approve. But for art!—the one thing in life that is good and real—can you compare with it an earthly love?—prefer the adoration of a relative beauty to the *cultus* of the true beauty? Well! I tell you the truth. That is the one thing good in me: the one thing I have, to me estimable. For yourself, you blend with the beautiful a heap of alien things, the useful, the agreeable, what not?—

The only way not to be unhappy is to shut yourself up in art, and count everything else as nothing. Pride takes the place of all beside when it is established on a large basis. Work! God wills it. That, it seems to me, is clear.—

I am reading over again the *Æneid*, certain verses of which I repeat to myself to satiety. There are phrases there which stay in one's head, by which I find myself beset, as with those musical airs which are for ever returning, and cause you pain, you love them so much. I observe that I no longer laugh much, and am no longer depressed. I am ripe. You talk of my serenity, and envy me. It may well surprise you. Sick, irritated, the prey a thousand times a day of cruel pain, I continue my labour like a true working-man, who, with sleeves turned up, in the sweat of his brow, beats away at his anvil, never troubling himself whether it rains or blows, for hail or thunder. I was not like that formerly. The change has taken place naturally, though my will has counted for something in the matter.—

Those who write in good style are sometimes accused of a neglect of ideas, and of the moral end, as if the end of the physician were something else than healing, of the painter than painting—as if the end of art were not, before all else, the beautiful.

18. What, then, did Flaubert understand by beauty, in the art he pursued with so much fervour, with so much self-command? Let us hear a sympathetic commentator:—

Possessed of an absolute belief that there exists but one way of expressing one thing, one word to call it by, one adjective to qualify, one verb to animate it, he gave himself to superhuman labour for the discovery, in every phrase, of that word, that verb, that epithet. In this way, he believed in some mysterious harmony of expression, and when a true word seemed to him to lack euphony still went on seeking another, with invincible patience, certain that he had not yet got hold of the *unique* word.... A thousand preoccupations would beset him at the same moment, always with this desperate certitude fixed in his spirit: Among all the expressions in the world, all forms and turns of expression, there is but *one*—one form, one mode—to express what I want to say.

19. The one word for the one thing, the one thought, amid the multitude of words, terms, that might just do: the problem of style was there!—the unique word, phrase, sentence, paragraph, essay, or song, absolutely proper to the single mental presentation or vision within. In that perfect justice, over and above the many contingent and removable beauties with which beautiful style may charm us, but which it can exist without, independent of them yet dexterously availing itself of them, omnipresent in good work, in function at every point, from single epithets to the rhythm of a whole book, lay the specific, indispensable, very intellectual, beauty of literature, the possibility of which constitutes it a fine art.

20. One seems to detect the influence of a philosophic idea there, the idea of a natural economy, of some pre-existent adaptation, between a relative, somewhere in the world of thought, and its correlative, somewhere in the world of language—both alike, rather, somewhere in the mind of the artist, desiderative, expectant, inventive—meeting each other with the readiness of "soul and body reunited," in Blake's rapturous design; and, in fact, Flaubert was fond of giving his theory philosophical expression.—

There are no beautiful thoughts (he would say) without beautiful forms, and conversely. As it is impossible to extract from a physical body the qualities which really constitute it—colour, extension, and the like—without reducing it to a hollow abstraction, in a word, without destroying it; just so it is impossible to detach the form from the idea, for the idea only exists by virtue of the form.

21. All the recognised flowers, the removable ornaments of literature (including harmony and ease in reading aloud, very carefully considered by him) counted, certainly; for these too are part of the actual value of what one says. But still, after all, with Flaubert, the search, the unwearied research, was not for the smooth, or winsome, or forcible word, as such, as with false Ciceronians, but quite simply and honestly, for the word's adjustment to its meaning. The first condition of this must be, of course, to know yourself, to

have ascertained your own sense exactly. Then, if we suppose an artist, he says to the reader,—I want you to see precisely what I see. Into the mind sensitive to "form," a flood of random sounds, colours, incidents, is ever penetrating from the world without, to become, by sympathetic selection, a part of its very structure, and, in turn, the visible vesture and expression of that other world it sees so steadily within, nay, already with a partial conformity thereto, to be refined, enlarged, corrected, at a hundred points; and it is just there, just at those doubtful points that the function of style, as tact or taste, intervenes. The unique term will come more quickly to one than another, at one time than another, according also to the kind of matter in question. Quickness and slowness, ease and closeness alike, have nothing to do with the artistic character of the true word found at last. As there is a charm of ease, so there is also a special charm in the signs of discovery, of effort and contention towards a due end, as so often with Flaubert himself—in the style which has been pliant, as only obstinate, durable metal can be, to the inherent perplexities and recusancy of a certain difficult thought.

22. If Flaubert had not told us, perhaps we should never have guessed how tardy and painful his own procedure really was, and after reading his confession may think that his almost endless hesitation had much to do with diseased nerves. Often, perhaps, the felicity supposed will be the product of a happier, a more exuberant nature than Flaubert's. Aggravated, certainly, by a morbid physical condition, that anxiety in "seeking the phrase," which gathered all the other small *ennuis* of a really quiet existence into a kind of battle, was connected with his lifelong contention against facile poetry, facile art—art, facile and flimsy; and what constitutes the true artist is not the slowness or quickness of the process, but the absolute success of the result. As with those labourers in the parable, the prize is independent of the mere length of the actual day's work. "You talk," he writes, odd, trying lover, to Madame X.—

"You talk of the exclusiveness of my literary tastes. That might have enabled you to divine what kind of a person I am in the matter of love. I grow so hard to please as a literary artist, that I am driven to despair. I shall end by not writing another line."

23. "Happy," he cries, in a moment of discouragement at that patient labour, which for him, certainly, was the condition of a great success—

Happy those who have no doubts of themselves! who lengthen out, as the pen runs on, all that flows forth from their brains. As for me, I hesitate, I disappoint myself, turn round upon myself in despite: my taste is augmented in proportion as my natural vigour decreases, and I afflict my soul over some dubious word out of all proportion to the pleasure I get from a whole page of good writing. One would have to live two centuries to attain a true idea of any matter whatever. What Buffon said is a big blasphemy: genius is not long-continued patience. Still, there is some truth in the statement, and more than people think, especially as regards our own day. Art! art! art! bitter deception! phantom that glows with light, only to lead one on to destruction.

24. Again—

I am growing so peevish about my writing. I am like a man whose ear is true but who plays falsely on the violin: his fingers refuse to reproduce precisely those sounds of which he has the inward sense. Then the tears come rolling down from the poor scraper's eyes and the bow falls from his hand.

25. Coming slowly or quickly, when it comes, as it came with so much labour of mind, but also with so much lustre, to Gustave Flaubert, this discovery of the word will be, like all artistic success and felicity, incapable of strict analysis: effect of an intuitive condition of mind, it must be recognised by like intuition on the part of the reader, and a sort of immediate sense. In every one of those masterly sentences of Flaubert there was, below all mere contrivance, shaping and afterthought, by some happy instantaneous concourse of the various faculties of the mind with each other, the exact apprehension of what was *needed* to carry the meaning. And that it fits with absolute justice will be a judgment of immediate sense in the appreciative reader. We all feel this in what may be called inspired translation. Well! all language involves translation from inward to outward. In literature, as in all forms of art, there are the absolute and the merely relative or accessory beauties; and precisely in that exact proportion of the term to its purpose is the absolute beauty of style, prose or verse. All the good qualities, the beauties, of verse also, are such, only as precise expression.

26. In the highest as in the lowliest literature, then, the one indispensable beauty is, after all, truth:—truth to bare fact in the latter, as to some personal sense of fact, diverted somewhat from men's ordinary sense of it, in the former; truth there as accuracy, truth here as expression, that finest and most intimate form of truth, the *vraie vérité*. And what an eclectic principle this really is! employing for its one sole purpose—that absolute accordance of expression to idea—all other literary beauties and excellences whatever: how many kinds of style it covers, explains, justifies, and at the same time safeguards! Scott's facility, Flaubert's deeply pondered evocation of "the phrase," are equally

good art. Say what you have to say, what you have a will to say, in the simplest, the most direct and exact manner possible, with no surplusage:—there, is the justification of the sentence so fortunately born, "entire, smooth, and round," that it needs no punctuation, and also (that is the point!) of the most elaborate period, if it be right in its elaboration. Here is the office of ornament: here also the purpose of restraint in ornament. As the exponent of truth, that austerity (the beauty, the function, of which in literature Flaubert understood so well) becomes not the correctness or purism of the mere scholar, but a security against the otiose, a jealous exclusion of what does not really tell towards the pursuit of relief, of life and vigour in the portraiture of one's sense. License again, the making free with rule, if it be indeed, as people fancy, a habit of genius, flinging aside or transforming all that opposes the liberty of beautiful production, will be but faith to one's own meaning. The seeming baldness of *Le Rouge et Le Noir* is nothing in itself; the wild ornament of *Les Misérables* is nothing in itself; and the restraint of Flaubert, amid a real natural opulence, only redoubled beauty—the phrase so large and so precise at the same time, hard as bronze, in service to the more perfect adaptation of words to their matter. Afterthoughts, retouchings, finish, will be of profit only so far as they too really serve to bring out the original, initiative, generative, sense in them.

27. In this way, according to the well-known saying, "The style is the man," complex or simple, in his individuality, his plenary sense of what he really has to say, his sense of the world; all cautions regarding style arising out of so many natural scruples as to the medium through which alone he can expose that inward sense of things, the purity of this medium, its laws or tricks of refraction: nothing is to be left there which might give conveyance to any matter save that. Style in all its varieties, reserved or opulent, terse, abundant, musical, stimulant, academic, so long as each is really characteristic or expressive, finds thus its justification, the sumptuous good taste of Cicero being as truly the man himself, and not another, justified, yet insured inalienably to him, thereby, as would have been his portrait by Raffaelle, in full consular splendour, on his ivory chair.

28. A relegation, you may say perhaps—a relegation of style to the subjectivity, the mere caprice, of the individual, which must soon transform it into mannerism. Not so! since there is, under the conditions supposed, for those elements of the man, for every lineament of the vision within, the one word, the one acceptable word, recognisable by the sensitive, by others "who have intelligence" in the matter, as absolutely as ever anything can be in the evanescent and delicate region of human language. The style, the manner, would be the man, not in his unreasoned and really uncharacteristic caprices, involuntary or affected, but in absolutely sincere apprehension of what is most

real to him. But let us hear our French guide again.—

Styles (says Flaubert's commentator), *Styles*, as so many peculiar moulds, each of which bears the mark of a particular writer, who is to pour into it the whole content of his ideas, were no part of his theory. What he believed in was *Style*: that is to say, a certain absolute and unique manner of expressing a thing, in all its intensity and colour. For him the *form* was the work itself. As in living creatures, the blood, nourishing the body, determines its very contour and external aspect, just so, to his mind, the *matter*, the basis, in a work of art, imposed, necessarily, the unique, the just expression, the measure, the rhythm—the *form* in all its characteristics.

29. If the style be the man, in all the colour and intensity of a veritable apprehension, it will be in a real sense "impersonal."

30. I said, thinking of books like Victor Hugo's *Les Misérables*, that prose literature was the characteristic art of the nineteenth century, as others, thinking of its triumphs since the youth of Bach, have assigned that place to music. Music and prose literature are, in one sense, the opposite terms of art; the art of literature presenting to the imagination, through the intelligence, a range of interests, as free and various as those which music presents to it through sense. And certainly the tendency of what has been here said is to bring literature too under those conditions, by conformity to which music takes rank as the typically perfect art. If music be the ideal of all art whatever, precisely because in music it is impossible to distinguish the form from the substance or matter, the subject from the expression, then, literature, by finding its specific excellence in the absolute correspondence of the term to its import, will be but fulfilling the condition of all artistic quality in things everywhere, of all good art.

31. Good art, but not necessarily great art; the distinction between great art and good art depending immediately, as regards literature at all events, not on its form, but on the matter. Thackeray's *Esmond*, surely, is greater art than *Vanity Fair*, by the greater dignity of its interests. It is on the quality of the matter it informs or controls, its compass, its variety, its alliance to great ends, or the depth of the note of revolt, or the largeness of hope in it, that the greatness of literary art depends, as *The Divine Comedy*, *Paradise Lost*, *Les Misérables*, *The English Bible*, are great art. Given the conditions I have tried to explain as constituting good art;—then, if it be devoted further to the increase of men's happiness, to the redemption of the oppressed, or the enlargement of our sympathies with each other, or to such presentment of new or old truth about ourselves and our relation to the world as may ennoble and fortify us in

our sojourn here, or immediately, as with Dante, to the glory of God, it will be also great art; if, over and above those qualities I summed up as mind and soul—that colour and mystic perfume, and that reasonable structure, it has something of the soul of humanity in it, and finds its logical, its architectural place, in the great structure of human life.

1888.

WORDSWORTH

Some English critics at the beginning of the present century had a great deal to say concerning a distinction, of much importance, as they thought, in the true estimate of poetry, between the *Fancy*, and another more powerful faculty—the *Imagination*. This metaphysical distinction, borrowed originally from the writings of German philosophers, and perhaps not always clearly apprehended by those who talked of it, involved a far deeper and more vital distinction, with which indeed all true criticism more or less directly has to do, the distinction, namely, between higher and lower degrees of intensity in the poet's perception of his subject, and in his concentration of himself upon his work. Of those who dwelt upon the metaphysical distinction between the Fancy and the Imagination, it was Wordsworth who made the most of it, assuming it as the basis for the final classification of his poetical writings; and it is in these writings that the deeper and more vital distinction, which, as I have said, underlies the metaphysical distinction, is most needed, and may best be illustrated.

2. For nowhere is there so perplexed a mixture as in Wordsworth's own poetry, of work touched with intense and individual power, with work of almost no character at all. He has much conventional sentiment, and some of that insincere poetic diction, against which his most serious critical efforts were directed: the reaction in his political ideas, consequent on the excesses of 1795, makes him, at times, a mere declaimer on moral and social topics; and he seems, sometimes, to force an unwilling pen, and write by rule. By making the most of these blemishes it is possible to obscure the true æsthetic value of his work, just as his life also, a life of much quiet delicacy and independence, might easily be placed in a false focus, and made to appear a somewhat tame theme in illustration of the more obvious parochial virtues. And those who wish to understand his influence, and experience his peculiar savour, must bear with patience the presence of an alien element in Wordsworth's work, which never coalesced with what is really delightful in it, nor underwent his special power. Who that values his writings most has not felt the intrusion there, from time to time, of something tedious and prosaic? Of all poets equally great, he would gain most by a skilfully made anthology. Such a selection would show, in truth, not so much what he was, or to himself or others seemed to be, as what, by the more energetic and fertile quality in his writings, he was ever tending to become. And the mixture in his work, as it actually stands, is so perplexed, that one fears to miss the least promising composition even, lest

some precious morsel should be lying hidden within—the few perfect lines, the phrase, the single word perhaps, to which he often works up mechanically through a poem, almost the whole of which may be tame enough. He who thought that in all creative work the larger part was *given* passively, to the recipient mind, who waited so dutifully upon the gift, to whom so large a measure was sometimes given, had his times also of desertion and relapse; and he has permitted the impress of these too to remain in his work. And this duality there—the fitfulness with which the higher qualities manifest themselves in it, gives the effect in his poetry of a power not altogether his own, or under his control, which comes and goes when it will, lifting or lowering a matter, poor in itself; so that that old fancy which made the poet's art an enthusiasm, a form of divine possession, seems almost literally true of him.

3. This constant suggestion of an absolute duality between higher and lower moods, and the work done in them, stimulating one always to look below the surface, makes the reading of Wordsworth an excellent sort of training towards the things of art and poetry. It begets in those, who, coming across him in youth, can bear him at all, a habit of reading between the lines, a faith in the effect of concentration and collectedness of mind in the right appreciation of poetry, an expectation of things, in this order, coming to one by means of a right discipline of the temper as well as of the intellect. He meets us with the promise that he has much, and something very peculiar, to give us, if we will follow a certain difficult way, and seems to have the secret of a special and privileged state of mind. And those who have undergone his influence, and followed this difficult way, are like people who have passed through some initiation, a *disciplina arcani*, by submitting to which they become able constantly to distinguish in art, speech, feeling, manners, that which is organic, animated, expressive, from that which is only conventional, derivative, inexpressive.

4. But although the necessity of selecting these precious morsels for oneself is an opportunity for the exercise of Wordsworth's peculiar influence, and induces a kind of just criticism and true estimate of it, yet the purely literary product would have been more excellent, had the writer himself purged away that alien element. How perfect would have been the little treasury, shut between the covers of how thin a book! Let us suppose the desired separation made, the electric thread untwined, the golden pieces, great and small, lying apart together.[1] What are the peculiarities of this residue? What special sense does Wordsworth exercise, and what instincts does he satisfy? What are the subjects and the motives which in him excite the imaginative faculty? What

---

1. Since this essay was written, such selections have been made, with excellent taste, by Matthew Arnold and Professor Knight.

are the qualities in things and persons which he values, the impression and sense of which he can convey to others, in an extraordinary way?

5. An intimate consciousness of the expression of natural things, which weighs, listens, penetrates, where the earlier mind passed roughly by, is a large element in the complexion of modern poetry. It has been remarked as a fact in mental history again and again. It reveals itself in many forms; but is strongest and most attractive in what is strongest and most attractive in modern literature. It is exemplified, almost equally, by writers as unlike each other as Senancour and Théophile Gautier: as a singular chapter in the history of the human mind, its growth might be traced from Rousseau to Chateaubriand, from Chateaubriand to Victor Hugo: it has doubtless some latent connexion with those pantheistic theories which locate an intelligent soul in material things, and have largely exercised men's minds in some modern systems of philosophy: it is traceable even in the graver writings of historians: it makes as much difference between ancient and modern landscape art, as there is between the rough masks of an early mosaic and a portrait by Reynolds or Gainsborough. Of this new sense, the writings of Wordsworth are the central and elementary expression: he is more simply and entirely occupied with it than any other poet, though there are fine expressions of precisely the same thing in so different a poet as Shelley. There was in his own character a certain contentment, a sort of inborn religious placidity, seldom found united with a sensibility so mobile as his, which was favourable to the quiet, habitual observation of inanimate, or imperfectly animate, existence. His life of eighty years is divided by no very profoundly felt incidents: its changes are almost wholly inward, and it falls into broad, untroubled, perhaps somewhat monotonous spaces. What it most resembles is the life of one of those early Italian or Flemish painters, who, just because their minds were full of heavenly visions, passed, some of them, the better part of sixty years in quiet, systematic industry. This placid life matured a quite unusual sensibility, really innate in him, to the sights and sounds of the natural world—the flower and its shadow on the stone, the cuckoo and its echo. The poem of *Resolution and Independence* is a storehouse of such records: for its fulness of imagery it may be compared to Keats's *Saint Agnes' Eve*. To read one of his longer pastoral poems for the first time, is like a day spent in a new country: the memory is crowded for a while with its precise and vivid incidents—

> The pliant harebell swinging in the breeze
> On some grey rock;—

> The single sheep and the one blasted tree
> And the bleak music from that old stone wall;—
>
> In the meadows and the lower ground
> Was all the sweetness of a common dawn;—
>
> And that green corn all day is rustling in thine ears.

6. Clear and delicate at once, as he is in the outlining of visible imagery, he is more clear and delicate still, and finely scrupulous, in the noting of sounds; so that he conceives of noble sound as even moulding the human countenance to nobler types, and as something actually "profaned" by colour, by visible form, or image. He has a power likewise of realising, and conveying to the consciousness of the reader, abstract and elementary impressions—silence, darkness, absolute motionlessness: or, again, the whole complex sentiment of a particular place, the abstract expression of desolation in the long white road, of peacefulness in a particular folding of the hills. In the airy building of the brain, a special day or hour even, comes to have for him a sort of personal identity, a spirit or angel given to it, by which, for its exceptional insight, or the happy light upon it, it has a presence in one's history, and acts there, as a separate power or accomplishment; and he has celebrated in many of his poems the "efficacious spirit," which, as he says, resides in these "particular spots" of time.

7. It is to such a world, and to a world of congruous meditation thereon, that we see him retiring in his but lately published poem of *The Recluse*—taking leave, without much count of costs, of the world of business, of action and ambition, as also of all that for the majority of mankind counts as sensuous enjoyment.[1]

---

1. In Wordsworth's prefatory advertisement to the first edition of *The Prelude*, published in 1850, it is stated that that work was intended to be introductory to *The Recluse*; and that *The Recluse*, if completed, would have consisted of three parts. The second part is *The Excursion*. The third part was only planned; but the first book of the first part was left in manuscript by Wordsworth—though in manuscript, it is said, in no great condition of forwardness for the printers. This book, now for the first time printed *in extenso* (a very noble passage from it found place in that prose advertisement to *The Excursion*), is included in the latest edition of Wordsworth by Mr. John Morley. It was well worth adding to the poet's great bequest to English literature. A true student of his work, who has formulated for himself what he supposes to be the leading characteristics of Wordsworth's genius, will feel, we think, lively interest in testing them by the various fine passages in what is here presented for the first time. Let the following serve for a sample:—

> Thickets full of songsters, and the voice
> Of lordly birds, an unexpected sound

8. And so it came about that this sense of a life in natural objects, which in most poetry is but a rhetorical artifice, is with Wordsworth the assertion of what for him is almost literal fact. To him every natural object seemed to possess more or less of a moral or spiritual life, to be capable of a companionship with man, full of expression, of inexplicable affinities and delicacies of intercourse. An emanation, a particular spirit, belonged, not to the moving leaves or water only, but to the distant peak of the hills arising suddenly, by some change of perspective, above the nearer horizon, to the passing space of light across the plain, to the lichened Druidic stone even, for a certain weird fellowship in it with the moods of men. It was like a "survival," in the peculiar intellectual temperament of a man of letters at the end of the eighteenth century, of that primitive condition, which some philosophers have traced in the general history of human culture, wherein all outward objects alike, including even the works of men's hands, were believed to be endowed with animation, and the world was "full of souls"—that mood in which the old Greek gods were first begotten, and which had many strange aftergrowths.

9. In the early ages, this belief, delightful as its effects on poetry often are, was but the result of a crude intelligence. But, in Wordsworth, such power of seeing life, such perception of a soul, in inanimate things, came of an exceptional susceptibility to the impressions of eye and ear, and was, in its essence, a kind

---

> Heard now and then from morn to latest eve,
> Admonishing the man who walks below
> Of solitude and silence in the sky:—
> These have we, and a thousand nooks of earth
> Have also these, but nowhere else is found,
> Nowhere (or is it fancy?) can be found
> The one sensation that is here; 'tis here,
> Here as it found its way into my heart
> In childhood, here as it abides by day,
> By night, here only; or in chosen minds
> That take it with them hence, where'er they go.
> —'Tis, but I cannot name it, 'tis the sense
> Of majesty, and beauty, and repose,
> A blended holiness of earth and sky,
> Something that makes this individual spot,
> This small abiding-place of many men,
> A termination, and a last retreat,
> A centre, come from wheresoe'er you will,
> A whole without dependence or defect,
> Made for itself, and happy in itself,
> Perfect contentment, Unity entire.

of sensuousness. At least, it is only in a temperament exceptionally susceptible on the sensuous side, that this sense of the expressiveness of outward things comes to be so large a part of life. That he awakened "a sort of thought in sense," is Shelley's just estimate of this element in Wordsworth's poetry.

10. And it was through nature, thus ennobled by a semblance of passion and thought, that he approached the spectacle of human life. Human life, indeed, is for him, at first, only an additional, accidental grace on an expressive landscape. When he thought of man, it was of man as in the presence and under the influence of these effective natural objects, and linked to them by many associations. The close connexion of man with natural objects, the habitual association of his thoughts and feelings with a particular spot of earth, has sometimes seemed to degrade those who are subject to its influence, as if it did but reinforce that physical connexion of our nature with the actual lime and clay of the soil, which is always drawing us nearer to our end. But for Wordsworth, these influences tended to the dignity of human nature, because they tended to tranquillise it. By raising nature to the level of human thought he gives it power and expression: he subdues man to the level of nature, and gives him thereby a certain breadth and coolness and solemnity. The leech-gatherer on the moor, the woman "stepping westward," are for him natural objects, almost in the same sense as the aged thorn, or the lichened rock on the heath. In this sense the leader of the "Lake School," in spite of an earnest preoccupation with man, his thoughts, his destiny, is the poet of nature. And of nature, after all, in its modesty. The English lake country has, of course, its grandeurs. But the peculiar function of Wordsworth's genius, as carrying in it a power to open out the soul of apparently little or familiar things, would have found its true test had he become the poet of Surrey, say! and the prophet of its life. The glories of Italy and Switzerland, though he did write a little about them, had too potent a material life of their own to serve greatly his poetic purpose.

11. Religious sentiment, consecrating the affections and natural regrets of the human heart, above all, that pitiful awe and care for the perishing human clay, of which relic-worship is but the corruption, has always had much to do with localities, with the thoughts which attach themselves to actual scenes and places. Now what is true of it everywhere, is truest of it in those secluded valleys where one generation after another maintains the same abiding-place; and it was on this side, that Wordsworth apprehended religion most strongly. Consisting, as it did so much, in the recognition of local sanctities, in the habit of connecting the stones and trees of a particular spot of earth with the great events of life, till the low walls, the green mounds, the half-obliterated epitaphs seemed full of voices, and a sort of natural oracles, the very religion of these people of the dales appeared but as another link between them and the

earth, and was literally a religion of nature. It tranquillised them by bringing them under the placid rule of traditional and narrowly localised observances. "Grave livers," they seemed to him, under this aspect, with stately speech, and something of that natural dignity of manners, which underlies the highest courtesy.

12. And, seeing man thus as a part of nature, elevated and solemnised in proportion as his daily life and occupations brought him into companionship with permanent natural objects, his very religion forming new links for him with the narrow limits of the valley, the low vaults of his church, the rough stones of his home, made intense for him now with profound sentiment, Wordsworth was able to appreciate passion in the lowly. He chooses to depict people from humble life, because, being nearer to nature than others, they are on the whole more impassioned, certainly more direct in their expression of passion, than other men: it is for this direct expression of passion, that he values their humble words. In much that he said in exaltation of rural life, he was but pleading indirectly for that sincerity, that perfect fidelity to one's own inward presentations, to the precise features of the picture within, without which any profound poetry is impossible. It was not for their tameness, but for this passionate sincerity, that he chose incidents and situations from common life, "related in a selection of language really used by men." He constantly endeavours to bring his language near to the real language of men: to the real language of men, however, not on the dead level of their ordinary intercourse, but in select moments of vivid sensation, when this language is winnowed and ennobled by excitement. There are poets who have chosen rural life as their subject, for the sake of its passionless repose, and times when Wordsworth himself extols the mere calm and dispassionate survey of things as the highest aim of poetical culture. But it was not for such passionless calm that he preferred the scenes of pastoral life; and the meditative poet, sheltering himself, as it might seem, from the agitations of the outward world, is in reality only clearing the scene for the great exhibitions of emotion, and what he values most is the almost elementary expression of elementary feelings.

13. And so he has much for those who value highly the concentrated presentment of passion, who appraise men and women by their susceptibility to it, and art and poetry as they afford the spectacle of it. Breaking from time to time into the pensive spectacle of their daily toil, their occupations near to nature, come those great elementary feelings, lifting and solemnising their language and giving it a natural music. The great, distinguishing passion came to Michael by the sheepfold, to Ruth by the wayside, adding these humble children of the furrow to the true aristocracy of passionate souls. In this respect, Wordsworth's work resembles most that of George Sand, in those of her novels

which depict country life. With a penetrative pathos, which puts him in the same rank with the masters of the sentiment of pity in literature, with Meinhold and Victor Hugo, he collects all the traces of vivid excitement which were to be found in that pastoral world—the girl who rung her father's knell; the unborn infant feeling about its mother's heart; the instinctive touches of children; the sorrows of the wild creatures, even—their home-sickness, their strange yearnings; the tales of passionate regret that hang by a ruined farm-building, a heap of stones, a deserted sheepfold; that gay, false, adventurous, outer world, which breaks in from time to time to bewilder and deflower these quiet homes; not "passionate sorrow" only, for the overthrow of the soul's beauty, but the loss of, or carelessness for personal beauty even, in those whom men have wronged—their pathetic wanness; the sailor "who, in his heart, was half a shepherd on the stormy seas"; the wild woman teaching her child to pray for her betrayer; incidents like the making of the shepherd's staff, or that of the young boy laying the first stone of the sheepfold;—all the pathetic episodes of their humble existence, their longing, their wonder at fortune, their poor pathetic pleasures, like the pleasures of children, won so hardly in the struggle for bare existence; their yearning towards each other, in their darkened houses, or at their early toil. A sort of biblical depth and solemnity hangs over this strange, new, passionate, pastoral world, of which he first raised the image, and the reflection of which some of our best modern fiction has caught from him.

14. He pondered much over the philosophy of his poetry, and reading deeply in the history of his own mind, seems at times to have passed the borders of a world of strange speculations, inconsistent enough, had he cared to note such inconsistencies, with those traditional beliefs, which were otherwise the object of his devout acceptance. Thinking of the high value he set upon customariness, upon all that is habitual, local, rooted in the ground, in matters of religious sentiment, you might sometimes regard him as one tethered down to a world, refined and peaceful indeed, but with no broad outlook, a world protected, but somewhat narrowed, by the influence of received ideas. But he is at times also something very different from this, and something much bolder. A chance expression is overheard and placed in a new connexion, the sudden memory of a thing long past occurs to him, a distant object is relieved for a while by a random gleam of light—accidents turning up for a moment what lies below the surface of our immediate experience—and he passes from the humble graves and lowly arches of "the little rock-like pile" of a Westmoreland church, on bold trains of speculative thought, and comes, from point to point, into strange contact with thoughts which have visited, from time to time, far more venturesome, perhaps errant, spirits.

15. He had pondered deeply, for instance, on those strange reminiscences and forebodings, which seem to make our lives stretch before and behind us, beyond where we can see or touch anything, or trace the lines of connexion. Following the soul, backwards and forwards, on these endless ways, his sense of man's dim, potential powers became a pledge to him, indeed, of a future life, but carried him back also to that mysterious notion of an earlier state of existence—the fancy of the Platonists—the old heresy of Origen. It was in this mood that he conceived those oft-reiterated regrets for a half-ideal childhood, when the relics of Paradise still clung about the soul—a childhood, as it seemed, full of the fruits of old age, lost for all, in a degree, in the passing away of the youth of the world, lost for each one, over again, in the passing away of actual youth. It is this ideal childhood which he celebrates in his famous *Ode on the Recollections of Childhood*, and some other poems which may be grouped around it, such as the lines on *Tintern Abbey*, and something like what he describes was actually truer of himself than he seems to have understood; for his own most delightful poems were really the instinctive productions of earlier life, and most surely for him, "the first diviner influence of this world" passed away, more and more completely, in his contact with experience.

16. Sometimes as he dwelt upon those moments of profound, imaginative power, in which the outward object appears to take colour and expression, a new nature almost, from the prompting of the observant mind, the actual world would, as it were, dissolve and detach itself, flake by flake, and he himself seemed to be the creator, and when he would the destroyer, of the world in which he lived—that old isolating thought of many a brain-sick mystic of ancient and modern times.

17. At other times, again, in those periods of intense susceptibility, in which he appeared to himself as but the passive recipient of external influences, he was attracted by the thought of a spirit of life in outward things, a single, all-pervading mind in them, of which man, and even the poet's imaginative energy, are but moments—that old dream of the *anima mundi*, the mother of all things and their grave, in which some had desired to lose themselves, and others had become indifferent to the distinctions of good and evil. It would come, sometimes, like the sign of the *macrocosm* to Faust in his cell: the network of man and nature was seen to be pervaded by a common, universal life: a new, bold thought lifted him above the furrow, above the green turf of the Westmoreland churchyard, to a world altogether different in its vagueness and vastness, and the narrow glen was full of the brooding power of one universal spirit.

18. And so he has something, also, for those who feel the fascination of bold speculative ideas, who are really capable of rising upon them to conditions of

poetical thought. He uses them, indeed, always with a very fine apprehension of the limits within which alone philosophical imaginings have any place in true poetry; and using them only for poetical purposes, is not too careful even to make them consistent with each other. To him, theories which for other men bring a world of technical diction, brought perfect form and expression, as in those two lofty books of *The Prelude*, which describe the decay and the restoration of Imagination and Taste. Skirting the borders of this world of bewildering heights and depths, he got but the first exciting influence of it, that joyful enthusiasm which great imaginative theories prompt, when the mind first comes to have an understanding of them; and it is not under the influence of these thoughts that his poetry becomes tedious or loses its blitheness. He keeps them, too, always within certain ethical bounds, so that no word of his could offend the simplest of those simple souls which are always the largest portion of mankind. But it is, nevertheless, the contact of these thoughts, the speculative boldness in them, which constitutes, at least for some minds, the secret attraction of much of his best poetry—the sudden passage from lowly thoughts and places to the majestic forms of philosophical imagination, the play of these forms over a world so different, enlarging so strangely the bounds of its humble churchyards, and breaking such a wild light on the graves of christened children.

19. And these moods always brought with them faultless expression. In regard to expression, as with feeling and thought, the duality of the higher and lower moods was absolute. It belonged to the higher, the imaginative mood, and was the pledge of its reality, to bring the appropriate language with it. In him, when the really poetical motive worked at all, it united, with absolute justice, the word and the idea; each, in the imaginative flame, becoming inseparably one with the other, by that fusion of matter and form, which is the characteristic of the highest poetical expression. His words are themselves thought and feeling; not eloquent, or musical words merely, but that sort of creative language which carries the reality of what it depicts, directly, to the consciousness.

20. The music of mere metre performs but a limited, yet a very peculiar and subtly ascertained function, in Wordsworth's poetry. With him, metre is but an additional grace, accessory to that deeper music of words and sounds, that moving power, which they exercise in the nobler prose no less than in formal poetry. It is a sedative to that excitement, an excitement sometimes almost painful, under which the language, alike of poetry and prose, attains a rhythmical power, independent of metrical combination, and dependent rather on some subtle adjustment of the elementary sounds of words themselves to the image or feeling they convey. Yet some of his pieces, pieces prompted by a sort of half-playful mysticism, like the *Daffodils* and *The Two April*

Mornings, are distinguished by a certain quaint gaiety of metre, and rival by their perfect execution, in this respect, similar pieces among our own Elizabethan, or contemporary French poetry. And those who take up these poems after an interval of months, or years perhaps, may be surprised at finding how well old favourites wear, how their strange, inventive turns of diction or thought still send through them the old feeling of surprise. Those who lived about Wordsworth were all great lovers of the older English literature, and oftentimes there came out in him a noticeable likeness to our earlier poets. He quotes unconsciously, but with new power of meaning, a clause from one of Shakespeare's sonnets; and, as with some other men's most famous work, the *Ode on the Recollections of Childhood* had its anticipator.[1] He drew something too from the unconscious mysticism of the old English language itself, drawing out the inward significance of its racy idiom, and the not wholly unconscious poetry of the language used by the simplest people under strong excitement—language, therefore, at its origin.

21. The office of the poet is not that of the moralist, and the first aim of Wordsworth's poetry is to give the reader a peculiar kind of pleasure. But through his poetry, and through this pleasure in it, he does actually convey to the reader an extraordinary wisdom in the things of practice. One lesson, if men must have lessons, he conveys more clearly than all, the supreme importance of contemplation in the conduct of life.

22. Contemplation—impassioned contemplation—that, is with Wordsworth the end-in-itself, the perfect end. We see the majority of mankind going most often to definite ends, lower or higher ends, as their own instincts may determine; but the end may never be attained, and the means not be quite the right means, great ends and little ones alike being, for the most part, distant, and the ways to them, in this dim world, somewhat vague. Meantime, to higher or lower ends, they move too often with something of a sad countenance, with hurried and ignoble gait, becoming, unconsciously, something like thorns, in their anxiety to bear grapes; it being possible for people, in the pursuit of even great ends, to become themselves thin and impoverished in spirit and temper, thus diminishing the sum of perfection in the world, at its very sources. We understand this when it is a question of mean, or of intensely selfish ends—of Grandet, or Javert. We think it bad morality to say that the end justifies the means, and we know how false to all higher conceptions of the religious life is the type of one who is ready to do evil that good may come. We contrast with such dark, mistaken eagerness, a type like that of Saint Catherine of Siena,

---

1. Henry Vaughan, in *The Retreat*.

who made the means to her ends so attractive, that she has won for herself an undying place in the *House Beautiful*, not by her rectitude of soul only, but by its "fairness"—by those quite different qualities which commend themselves to the poet and the artist.

23. Yet, for most of us, the conception of means and ends covers the whole of life, and is the exclusive type or figure under which we represent our lives to ourselves. Such a figure, reducing all things to machinery, though it has on its side the authority of that old Greek moralist who has fixed for succeeding generations the outline of the theory of right living, is too like a mere picture or description of men's lives as we actually find them, to be the basis of the higher ethics. It covers the meanness of men's daily lives, and much of the dexterity and the vigour with which they pursue what may seem to them the good of themselves or of others; but not the intangible perfection of those whose ideal is rather in *being* than in *doing*—not those *manners* which are, in the deepest as in the simplest sense, *morals*, and without which one cannot so much as offer a cup of water to a poor man without offence—not the part of "antique Rachel," sitting in the company of Beatrice; and even the moralist might well endeavour rather to withdraw men from the too exclusive consideration of means and ends, in life.

24. Against this predominance of machinery in our existence, Wordsworth's poetry, like all great art and poetry, is a continual protest. Justify rather the end by the means, it seems to say: whatever may become of the fruit, make sure of the flowers and the leaves. It was justly said, therefore, by one who had meditated very profoundly on the true relation of means to ends in life, and on the distinction between what is desirable in itself and what is desirable only as machinery, that when the battle which he and his friends were waging had been won, the world would need more than ever those qualities which Wordsworth was keeping alive and nourishing.[1]

25. That the end of life is not action but contemplation—*being* as distinct from *doing*—a certain disposition of the mind: is, in some shape or other, the principle of all the higher morality. In poetry, in art, if you enter into their true spirit at all, you touch this principle, in a measure: these, by their very sterility, are a type of beholding for the mere joy of beholding. To treat life in the spirit of art, is to make life a thing in which means and ends are identified: to encourage such treatment, the true moral significance of art and poetry. Wordsworth, and other poets who have been like him in ancient or more recent times, are the masters, the experts, in this art of impassioned contemplation.

---

1. See an interesting paper, by Mr. John Morley, on "The Death of Mr. Mill," *Fortnightly Review*, June 1873.

Their work is, not to teach lessons, or enforce rules, or even to stimulate us to noble ends; but to withdraw the thoughts for a little while from the mere machinery of life, to fix them, with appropriate emotions, on the spectacle of those great facts in man's existence which no machinery affects, "on the great and universal passions of men, the most general and interesting of their occupations, and the entire world of nature,"—on "the operations of the elements and the appearances of the visible universe, on storm and sunshine, on the revolutions of the seasons, on cold and heat, on loss of friends and kindred, on injuries and resentments, on gratitude and hope, on fear and sorrow." To witness this spectacle with appropriate emotions is the aim of all culture; and of these emotions poetry like Wordsworth's is a great nourisher and stimulant. He sees nature full of sentiment and excitement; he sees men and women as parts of nature, passionate, excited, in strange grouping and connexion with the grandeur and beauty of the natural world:—images, in his own words, "of man suffering, amid awful forms and powers."

26. Such is the figure of the more powerful and original poet, hidden away, in part, under those weaker elements in Wordsworth's poetry, which for some minds determine their entire character; a poet somewhat bolder and more passionate than might at first sight be supposed, but not too bold for true poetical taste; an unimpassioned writer, you might sometimes fancy, yet thinking the chief aim, in life and art alike, to be a certain deep emotion; seeking most often the great elementary passions in lowly places; having at least this condition of all impassioned work, that he aims always at an absolute sincerity of feeling and diction, so that he is the true forerunner of the deepest and most passionate poetry of our own day; yet going back also, with something of a protest against the conventional fervour of much of the poetry popular in his own time, to those older English poets, whose unconscious likeness often comes out in him.

1874.

from COLERIDGE[1]

Forms of intellectual and spiritual culture sometimes exercise their subtlest and most artful charm when life is already passing from them. Searching and irresistible as are the changes of the human spirit on its way to perfection, there is yet so much elasticity of temper that what must pass away sooner or later is not disengaged all at once, even from the highest order of minds. Nature, which by one law of development evolves ideas, hypotheses, modes of inward life, and represses them in turn, has in this way provided that the earlier growth should propel its fibres into the later, and so transmit the whole of its forces in an unbroken continuity of life. Then comes the spectacle of the reserve of the elder generation exquisitely refined by the antagonism of the new. That current of new life chastens them while they contend against it. Weaker minds fail to perceive the change: the clearest minds abandon themselves to it. To feel the change everywhere, yet not abandon oneself to it, is a situation of difficulty and contention. Communicating, in this way, to the passing stage of culture, the charm of what is chastened, high-strung, athletic, they yet detach the highest minds from the past, by pressing home its difficulties and finally proving it impossible. Such has been the charm of many leaders of lost causes in philosophy and in religion. It is the special charm of Coleridge, in connexion with those older methods of philosophic inquiry, over which the empirical philosophy of our day has triumphed.

2. Modern thought is distinguished from ancient by its cultivation of the "relative" spirit in place of the "absolute." Ancient philosophy sought to arrest every object in an eternal outline, to fix thought in a necessary formula, and the varieties of life in a classification by "kinds," or *genera*. To the modern spirit nothing is, or can be rightly known, except relatively and under conditions. The philosophical conception of the relative has been developed in modern times through the influence of the sciences of observation. Those sciences reveal types of life evanescing into each other by inexpressible refinements of change. Things pass into their opposites by accumulation of undefinable quantities. The growth of those sciences consists in a continual analysis of facts of rough and general observation into groups of facts more precise and minute. The faculty for truth is recognised as a power of distinguishing and fixing delicate and fugitive detail. The moral world is ever in contact with the

---

1. The latter part of this paper, like that on Dante Gabriel Rossetti, was contributed to Mr. T. H. Ward's *English Poets*.

physical, and the relative spirit has invaded moral philosophy from the ground of the inductive sciences. There it has started a new analysis of the relations of body and mind, good and evil, freedom and necessity. Hard and abstract moralities are yielding to a more exact estimate of the subtlety and complexity of our life. Always, as an organism increases in perfection, the conditions of its life become more complex. Man is the most complex of the products of nature. Character merges into temperament: the nervous system refines itself into intellect. Man's physical organism is played upon not only by the physical conditions about it, but by remote laws of inheritance, the vibration of long-past acts reaching him in the midst of the new order of things in which he lives. When we have estimated these conditions he is still not yet simple and isolated; for the mind of the race, the character of the age, sway him this way or that through the medium of language and current ideas. It seems as if the most opposite statements about him were alike true: he is so receptive, all the influences of nature and of society ceaselessly playing upon him, so that every hour in his life is unique, changed altogether by a stray word, or glance, or touch. It is the truth of these relations that experience gives us, not the truth of eternal outlines ascertained once for all, but a world of fine gradations and subtly linked conditions, shifting intricately as we ourselves change—and bids us, by a constant clearing of the organs of observation and perfecting of analysis, to make what we can of these. To the intellect, the critical spirit, just these subtleties of effect are more precious than anything else. What is lost in precision of form is gained in intricacy of expression. It is no vague scholastic abstraction that will satisfy the speculative instinct in our modern minds. Who would change the colour or curve of a rose-leaf for that οὐσία ἀχρώματος, ἀσχημάτιστος, ἀναφὴς—that colourless, formless, intangible, being—Plato put so high? For the true illustration of the speculative temper is not the Hindoo mystic, lost to sense, understanding, individuality, but one such as Goethe, to whom every moment of life brought its contribution of experimental, individual knowledge; by whom no touch of the world of form, colour, and passion was disregarded.

3. Now the literary life of Coleridge was a disinterested struggle against the relative spirit. With a strong native bent towards the tracking of all questions, critical or practical, to first principles, he is ever restlessly scheming to "apprehend the absolute," to affirm it effectively, to get it acknowledged. It was an effort, surely, an effort of sickly thought, that saddened his mind, and limited the operation of his unique poetic gift.

4. So what the reader of our own generation will least find in Coleridge's prose writings is the excitement of the literary sense. And yet, in those grey volumes, we have the larger part of the production of one who made way

ever by a charm, the charm of voice, of aspect, of language, above all by the intellectual charm of new, moving, luminous ideas. Perhaps the chief offence in Coleridge is an excess of seriousness, a seriousness arising not from any moral principle, but from a misconception of the perfect manner. There is a certain shade of unconcern, the perfect manner of the eighteenth century, which may be thought to mark complete culture in the handling of abstract questions. The humanist, the possessor of that complete culture, does not "weep" over the failure of "a theory of the quantification of the predicate," nor "shriek" over the fall of a philosophical formula. A kind of humour is, in truth, one of the conditions of the just mental attitude, in the criticism of by-past stages of thought. Humanity cannot afford to be too serious about them, any more than a man of good sense can afford to be too serious in looking back upon his own childhood. Plato, whom Coleridge claims as the first of his spiritual ancestors, Plato, as we remember him, a true humanist, holds his theories lightly, glances with a somewhat blithe and naive inconsequence from one view to another, not anticipating the burden of importance "views" will one day have for men. In reading him one feels how lately it was that Crœsus thought it a paradox to say that external prosperity was not necessarily happiness. But on Coleridge lies the whole weight of the sad reflection that has since come into the world, with which for us the air is full, which the "children in the market-place" repeat to each other. His very language is forced and broken lest some saving formula should be lost—*distinctities, enucleation, pentad of operative Christianity*; he has a whole armoury of these terms, and expects to turn the tide of human thought by fixing the sense of such expressions as "reason," "understanding," "idea." Again, he lacks the jealousy of a true artist in excluding all associations that have no colour, or charm, or gladness in them; and everywhere allows the impress of a somewhat inferior theological literature.

5. "I was driven from life in motion to life in thought and sensation:" so Coleridge sums up his childhood, with its delicacy, its sensitiveness, and passion. But at twenty-five he was exercising a wonderful charm, and had already defined for himself his peculiar line of intellectual activity. He had an odd, attractive gift of conversation, or rather of monologue, as Madame de Staël observed of him, full of *bizarreries*, with the rapid alternations of a dream, and here or there an unexpected summons into a world strange to the hearer, abounding in images drawn from a sort of divided imperfect life, the consciousness of the opium-eater, as of one to whom the external world penetrated only in part, and, blent with all this, passages of deep obscurity, precious, if at all, only for their musical cadence, echoes in Coleridge of the eloquence of those older English writers of whom he was so ardent a lover. And all through this brilliant early manhood we may discern the power of the "Asiatic" temperament, of

that voluptuousness, which is connected perhaps with his appreciation of the intimacy, the almost mystical communion of touch, between nature and man. "I am much better," he writes, "and my new and tender health is all over me like a voluptuous feeling." And whatever fame, or charm, or life-inspiring gift he has had as a speculative thinker, is the vibration of the interest he excited then, the propulsion into years which clouded his early promise of that first buoyant, irresistible, self-assertion. So great is even the indirect power of a sincere effort towards the ideal life, of even a temporary escape of the spirit from routine.

6. In 1798 he visited Germany, then, the only half-known, "promised land," of the metaphysical, the "absolute," philosophy. A beautiful fragment of this period remains, describing a spring excursion to the Brocken. His excitement still vibrates in it. Love, all joyful states of mind, are self-expressive: they loosen the tongue, they fill the thoughts with sensuous images, they harmonise one with the world of sight. We hear of the "rich graciousness and courtesy" of Coleridge's manner, of the white and delicate skin, the abundant black hair, the full, almost animal lips—that whole physiognomy of the dreamer, already touched with narcotism. One says, of the beginning of one of his Unitarian sermons: "His voice rose like a stream of rich, distilled perfumes;" another, "He talks like an angel, and does—nothing!"

7. The *Aids to Reflection*, *The Friend*, *The Biographia Literaria*: those books came from one whose vocation was in the world of the imagination, the theory and practice of poetry. And yet, perhaps, of all books that have been influential in modern times, they are furthest from artistic form—bundles of notes; the original matter inseparably mixed up with that borrowed from others; the whole, just that mere preparation for an artistic effect which the finished literary artist would be careful one day to destroy. Here, again, we have a trait profoundly characteristic of Coleridge. He sometimes attempts to reduce a phase of thought, subtle and exquisite, to conditions too rough for it. He uses a purely speculative gift for direct moral edification. Scientific truth is a thing fugitive, relative, full of fine gradations: he tries to fix it in absolute formulas. The *Aids to Reflection*, *The Friend*, are efforts to propagate the volatile spirit of conversation into the less ethereal fabric of a written book; and it is only here or there that the poorer matter becomes vibrant, is really lifted by the spirit.

8. De Quincey said of him that "he wanted better bread than can be made with wheat:" Lamb, that from childhood he had "hungered for eternity." Yet the faintness, the continuous dissolution, whatever its cause, which soon supplanted the buoyancy of his first wonderful years, had its own consumptive refinements, and even brought, as to the "Beautiful Soul" in *Wilhelm Meister*, a faint religious ecstasy—that "singing in the sails" which is not of the breeze. Here again is one of his occasional notes:—

9. "In looking at objects of nature while I am thinking, as at yonder moon, dim-glimmering through the window-pane, I seem rather to be seeking, as it were asking, a symbolical language for something within me, that already and for ever exists, than observing anything new. Even when the latter is the case, yet still I have always an obscure feeling, as if that new phenomenon were the dim awaking of a forgotten or hidden truth of my inner nature. While I was preparing the pen to make this remark, I lost the train of thought which had led me to it."

10. What a distemper of the eye of the mind! What an almost bodily distemper there is in that!

11. Coleridge's intellectual sorrows were many; but he had one singular intellectual happiness. With an inborn taste for transcendental philosophy, he lived just at the time when that philosophy took an immense spring in Germany, and connected itself with an impressive literary movement. He had the good luck to light upon it in its freshness, and introduce it to his countrymen. What an opportunity for one reared on the colourless analytic English philosophies of the last century, but who feels an irresistible attraction towards bold metaphysical synthesis! How rare are such occasions of intellectual contentment! This transcendental philosophy, chiefly as systematised by the mystic Schelling, Coleridge applied with an eager, unwearied subtlety, to the questions of theology, and poetic or artistic criticism. It is in his theory of poetry, of art, that he comes nearest to principles of permanent truth and importance: that is the least fugitive part of his prose work. What, then, is the essence of his philosophy of art—of imaginative production?

12. Generally, it may be described as an attempt to reclaim the world of art as a world of fixed laws, to show that the creative activity of genius and the simplest act of thought are but higher and lower products of the laws of a universal logic. Criticism, feeling its own inadequacy in dealing with the greater works of art, is sometimes tempted to make too much of those dark and capricious suggestions of *genius*, which even the intellect possessed by them is unable to explain or recall. It has seemed due to the half-sacred character of those works to ignore all analogy between the productive process by which they had their birth, and the simpler processes of mind. Coleridge, on the other hand, assumes that the highest phases of thought must be more, not less, than the lower, subject to law.

13. With this interest, in the *Biographia Literaria*, he refines Schelling's "Philosophy of Nature" into a theory of art. "There can be no plagiarism in philosophy," says Heine:—*Es giebt kein Plagiat in der Philosophie*, in reference to the charge brought against Schelling of unacknowledged borrowing from Bruno; and certainly that which is common to Coleridge and Schelling and Bruno

alike is of far earlier origin than any of them. Schellingism, the "Philosophy of Nature," is indeed a constant tradition in the history of thought: it embodies a permanent type of the speculative temper. That mode of conceiving nature as a mirror or reflex of the intelligence of man may be traced up to the first beginnings of Greek speculation. There are two ways of envisaging those aspects of nature which seem to bear the impress of reason or intelligence. There is the deist's way, which regards them merely as marks of design, which separates the informing mind from its result in nature, as the mechanist from the machine; and there is the pantheistic way, which identifies the two, which regards nature itself as the living energy of an intelligence of the same kind as though vaster in scope than the human. Partly through the influence of mythology, the Greek mind became early possessed with the conception of nature as living, thinking, almost speaking to the mind of man. This unfixed poetical prepossession, reduced to an abstract form, petrified into an idea, is the force which gives unity of aim to Greek philosophy. Little by little, it works out the substance of the Hegelian formula: "Whatever is, is according to reason: whatever is according to reason, that is." Experience, which has gradually saddened the earth's colours for us, stiffened its motions, withdrawn from it some blithe and debonair presence, has quite changed the character of the science of nature, as we understand it. The "positive" method, in truth, makes very little account of marks of intelligence in nature: in its wider view of phenomena, it sees that those instances are a minority, and may rank as happy coincidences: it absorbs them in the larger conception of universal mechanical law. But the suspicion of a mind latent in nature, struggling for release, and intercourse with the intellect of man through true ideas, has never ceased to haunt a certain class of minds. Started again and again in successive periods by enthusiasts on the antique pattern, in each case the thought may have seemed paler and more fantastic amid the growing consistency and sharpness of outline of other and more positive forms of knowledge. Still, wherever the speculative instinct has been united with a certain poetic inwardness of temperament, as in Bruno, in Schelling, there that old Greek conception, like some seed floating in the air, has taken root and sprung up anew. Coleridge, thrust inward upon himself, driven from "life in thought and sensation" to life in thought only, feels already, in his dark London school, a thread of the Greek mind on this matter vibrating strongly in him. At fifteen he is discoursing on Plotinus, as in later years he reflects from Schelling that flitting intellectual tradition. He supposes a subtle, sympathetic co-ordination between the ideas of the human reason and the laws of the natural world. Science, the real knowledge of that natural world, is to be attained, not by observation, experiment, analysis, patient generalisation, but by the evolution or recovery of those ideas directly from within, by a sort of Platonic "recollection"; every group of observed facts remaining an enigma until the appropriate idea is struck upon them from the mind of a Newton, or a Cuvier, the genius in whom sympathy with the universal reason becomes entire. In the next place, he conceives that this reason or intelligence in nature becomes reflective, or self-conscious. He fancies he can trace, through all the simpler forms of life, fragments of an eloquent prophecy about the human mind. The whole of nature he regards as a development of higher forms out of the lower, through shade after shade of systematic change. The dim stir of chemical atoms towards the axis of crystal form, the trance-like life of plants, the animal troubled by strange irritabilities, are stages which anticipate consciousness. All through the ever-increasing movement of life that was shaping itself; every successive phase of life, in its unsatisfied susceptibilities, seeming to be drawn out of its own limits by the more pronounced current of life on its confines, the "shadow of approaching humanity" gradually deepening, the latent intelligence winning a way to the surface. And at this point the law of development does not lose itself in caprice: rather it becomes more constraining and incisive. From the lowest to the very highest acts of the conscious intelligence, there is another series of refining shades. Gradually the mind concentrates itself, frees itself from the limitations of the particular, the individual, attains a strange power of modifying and centralising what it receives from without, according to the pattern of an inward ideal. At last, in imaginative genius, ideas become effective: the intelligence of nature, all its discursive elements now connected and justified, is clearly reflected; the interpretation of its latent purposes being embodied in the great central products of creative art. The secret of creative genius would be an exquisitely purged sympathy with nature, with the reasonable soul antecedent there. Those associative conceptions of the imagination, those eternally fixed types of action and passion, would come, not so much from the conscious invention of the artist, as from his self-surrender to the suggestions of an abstract reason or ideality in things: they would be evolved by the stir of nature itself, realising the highest reach of its dormant reason: they would have a kind of prevenient necessity to rise at some time to the surface of the human mind.

14. It is natural that Shakespeare should be the favourite illustration of such criticism, whether in England or Germany. The first suggestion in Shakespeare is that of capricious detail, of a waywardness that plays with the parts careless of the impression of the whole; what supervenes is the constraining unity of effect, the ineffaceable impression, of Hamlet or Macbeth. His hand moving freely is curved round as if by some law of gravitation from within: an energetic unity or identity makes itself visible amid an abounding variety. This unity

or identity Coleridge exaggerates into something like the identity of a natural organism, and the associative act which effected it into something closely akin to the primitive power of nature itself. "In the Shakespearian drama," he says, "there is a vitality which grows and evolves itself from within."

15. Again—

He, too, worked in the spirit of nature, by evolving the germ from within, by the imaginative power, according to the idea. For as the power of seeing is to light, so is an idea in mind to a law in nature. They are correlatives which suppose each other.

16. Again—

The organic form is innate: it shapes, as it develops, itself from within, and the fulness of its development is one and the same with the perfection of its outward form. Such as the life is, such is the form. Nature, the prime, genial artist, inexhaustible in diverse powers, is equally inexhaustible in forms: each exterior is the physiognomy of the being within, and even such is the appropriate excellence of Shakespeare, himself a nature humanised, a genial understanding, directing self-consciously a power and an implicit wisdom deeper even than our consciousness.

17. In this late age we are become so familiarised with the greater works of art as to be little sensitive of the act of creation in them: they do not impress us as a new presence in the world. Only sometimes, in productions which realise immediately a profound influence and enforce a change in taste, we are actual witnesses of the moulding of an unforeseen type by some new principle of association; and to that phenomenon Coleridge wisely recalls our attention. What makes his view a one-sided one is, that in it the artist has become almost a mechanical agent: instead of the most luminous and self-possessed phase of consciousness, the associative act in art or poetry is made to look like some blindly organic process of assimilation. The work of art is likened to a living organism. That expresses truly the sense of a self-delighting, independent life which the finished work of art gives us: it hardly figures the process by which such work was produced. Here there is no blind ferment of lifeless elements towards the realisation of a type. By exquisite analysis the artist attains clearness of idea; then, through many stages of refining, clearness of expression. He moves slowly over his work, calculating the tenderest tone, and restraining the subtlest curve, never letting hand or fancy move at large, gradually enforcing flaccid spaces to the higher degree of expressiveness. The

philosophic critic, at least, will value, even in works of imagination, seemingly the most intuitive, the power of the understanding in them, their logical process of construction, the spectacle of a supreme intellectual dexterity which they afford. [...]

28. *Christabel*, though not printed till 1816, was written mainly in the year 1797: *The Rhyme of the Ancient Mariner* was printed as a contribution to the *Lyrical Ballads* in 1798; and these two poems belong to the great year of Coleridge's poetic production, his twenty-fifth year. In poetic quality, above all in that most poetic of all qualities, a keen sense of, and delight in beauty, the infection of which lays hold upon the reader, they are quite out of proportion to all his other compositions. The form in both is that of the ballad, with some of its terminology, and some also of its quaint conceits. They connect themselves with that revival of ballad literature, of which Percy's *Relics*, and, in another way, Macpherson's *Ossian* are monuments, and which afterwards so powerfully affected Scott—

> Young-eyed poesy
> All deftly masked as hoar antiquity.

29. *The Ancient Mariner*, as also, in its measure, *Christabel*, is a "romantic" poem, impressing us by bold invention, and appealing to that taste for the supernatural, that longing for *le frisson*, a shudder, to which the "romantic" school in Germany, and its derivations in England and France, directly ministered. In Coleridge, personally, this taste had been encouraged by his odd and out-of-the-way reading in the old-fashioned literature of the marvellous—books like Purchas's *Pilgrims*, early voyages like Hakluyt's, old naturalists and visionary moralists, like Thomas Burnet, from whom he quotes the motto of *The Ancient Mariner*, "*Facile credo, plures esse naturas invisibiles quam visibiles in rerum universitate, etc.*" Fancies of the strange things which may very well happen, even in broad daylight, to men shut up alone in ships far off on the sea, seem to have occurred to the human mind in all ages with a peculiar readiness, and often have about them, from the story of the stealing of Dionysus downwards, the fascination of a certain dreamy grace, which distinguishes them from other kinds of marvellous inventions. This sort of fascination *The Ancient Mariner* brings to its highest degree: it is the delicacy, the dreamy grace, in his presentation of the marvellous, which makes Coleridge's work so remarkable. The too palpable intruders from a spiritual world in almost all ghost literature, in Scott and Shakespeare even, have a kind of crudity or coarseness. Coleridge's power is in the very fineness

with which, as by some really ghostly finger, he brings home to our inmost sense his inventions, daring as they are—the skeleton ship, the polar spirit, the inspiriting of the dead corpses of the ship's crew. *The Rhyme of the Ancient Mariner* has the plausibility, the perfect adaptation to reason and the general aspect of life, which belongs to the marvellous, when actually presented as part of a credible experience in our dreams. Doubtless, the mere experience of the opium-eater, the habit he must almost necessarily fall into of noting the more elusive phenomena of dreams, had something to do with that: in its essence, however, it is connected with a more purely intellectual circumstance in the development of Coleridge's poetic gift. Some one once asked William Blake, to whom Coleridge has many resemblances, when either is at his best (that whole episode of the re-inspiriting of the ship's crew in *The Ancient Mariner* being comparable to Blake's well-known design of the "Morning Stars singing together") whether he had ever seen a ghost, and was surprised when the famous seer, who ought, one might think, to have seen so many, answered frankly, "Only once!" His "spirits," at once more delicate, and so much more real, than any ghost—the burden, as they were the privilege, of his *temperament*—like it, were an integral element in his everyday life. And the difference of mood expressed in that question and its answer, is indicative of a change of temper in regard to the supernatural which has passed over the whole modern mind, and of which the true measure is the influence of the writings of Swedenborg. What that change is we may see if we compare the vision by which Swedenborg was "called," as he thought, to his work, with the ghost which called Hamlet, or the spells of Marlowe's *Faust* with those of Goethe's. The modern mind, so minutely self-scrutinising, if it is to be affected at all by a sense of the supernatural, needs to be more finely touched than was possible in the older, romantic presentment of it. The spectral object, so crude, so impossible, has become plausible, as

> The blot upon the brain,
> That *will* show itself without;

and is understood to be but a condition of one's own mind, for which, according to the scepticism, latent at least, in so much of our modern philosophy, the so-called real things themselves are but *spectra* after all.

30. It is this finer, more delicately marvellous supernaturalism, fruit of his more delicate psychology, that Coleridge infuses into romantic adventure, itself also then a new or revived thing in English literature; and with a fineness of weird effect in *The Ancient Mariner*, unknown in those older, more simple, romantic legends and ballads. It is a flower of medieval or later German romance,

growing up in the peculiarly compounded atmosphere of modern psychological speculation, and putting forth in it wholly new qualities. The quaint prose commentary, which runs side by side with the verse of *The Ancient Mariner*, illustrates this—a composition of quite a different shade of beauty and merit from that of the verse which it accompanies, connecting this, the chief poem of Coleridge, with his philosophy, and emphasising therein that psychological interest of which I have spoken, its curious soul-lore.

31. Completeness, the perfectly rounded wholeness and unity of the impression it leaves on the mind of a reader who fairly gives himself to it—that, too, is one of the characteristics of a really excellent work, in the poetic as in every other kind of art; and by this completeness, *The Ancient Mariner* certainly gains upon *Christabel*—a completeness, entire as that of Wordsworth's *Leech-gatherer*, or Keats's *Saint Agnes' Eve*, each typical in its way of such wholeness or entirety of effect on a careful reader. It is Coleridge's one great complete work, the one really finished thing, in a life of many beginnings. *Christabel* remained a fragment. In *The Ancient Mariner* this unity is secured in part by the skill with which the incidents of the marriage-feast are made to break in dreamily from time to time upon the main story. And then, how pleasantly, how reassuringly, the whole nightmare story itself is made to end, among the clear fresh sounds and lights of the bay, where it began, with

> The moon-light steeped in silentness,
> The steady weather-cock.

32. So different from *The Rhyme of the Ancient Mariner* in regard to this completeness of effect, *Christabel* illustrates the same complexion of motives, a like intellectual situation. Here, too, the work is of a kind peculiar to one who touches the characteristic motives of the old romantic ballad, with a spirit made subtle and fine by modern reflection; as we feel, I think, in such passages as—

> But though my slumber had gone by,
> This dream it would not pass away—
> It seems to live upon mine eye;—

and—

> For she, belike, hath drunken deep
> Of all the blessedness of sleep;

and again—

> With such perplexity of mind
> As dreams too lively leave behind.

33. And that gift of handling the finer passages of human feeling, at once with power and delicacy, which was another result of his finer psychology, of his exquisitely refined habit of self-reflection, is illustrated by a passage on Friendship in the *Second Part*—

> Alas! they had been friends in youth;
> But whispering tongues can poison truth;
> And constancy lives in realms above;
> And life is thorny; and youth is vain;
> And to be wroth with one we love,
> Doth work like madness in the brain.
> And thus it chanced, as I divine,
> With Roland and Sir Leoline.
> Each spake words of high disdain
> And insult to his heart's best brother:
> They parted—ne'er to meet again!
> But never either found another
> To free the hollow heart from paining—
> They stood aloof, the scars remaining,
> Like cliffs which had been rent asunder;
> A dreary sea now flows between;
> But neither heat, nor frost, nor thunder,
> Shall wholly do away, I ween,
> The marks of that which once hath been.

34. I suppose these lines leave almost every reader with a quickened sense of the beauty and compass of human feeling; and it is the sense of such richness and beauty which, in spite of his "dejection," in spite of that burden of his morbid lassitude, accompanies Coleridge himself through life. A warm poetic joy in everything beautiful, whether it be a moral sentiment, like the friendship of Roland and Leoline, or only the flakes of falling light from the water-snakes—this joy, visiting him, now and again, after sickly dreams, in sleep or waking, as a relief not to be forgotten, and with such a power of felicitous expression that the infection of it passes irresistibly to the reader—such is the predominant element in the matter of his poetry, as cadence is the predominant quality of its form. "We bless thee for our creation!" he might have said, in his later period of definite religious assent, "because the world is so beautiful:

the world of ideas—living spirits, detached from the divine nature itself, to inform and lift the heavy mass of material things; the world of man, above all in his melodious and intelligible speech; the world of living creatures and natural scenery; the world of dreams." What he really did say, by way of *A Tombless Epitaph*, is true enough of himself—

> Sickness, 'tis true,
> Whole years of weary days, besieged him close,
> Even to the gates and inlets of his life!
> But it is true, no less, that strenuous, firm,
> And with a natural gladness, he maintained
> The citadel unconquered, and in joy
> Was strong to follow the delightful Muse.
> For not a hidden path, that to the shades
> Of the beloved Parnassian forest leads,
> Lurked undiscovered by him; not a rill
> There issues from the fount of Hippocrene,
> But he had traced it upward to its source,
> Through open glade, dark glen, and secret dell,
> Knew the gay wild flowers on its banks, and culled
> Its med'cinable herbs. Yea, oft alone,
> Piercing the long-neglected holy cave,
> The haunt obscure of old Philosophy,
> He bade with lifted torch its starry walls
> Sparkle, as erst they sparkled to the flame
> Of odorous lamps tended by saint and sage.
> O framed for calmer times and nobler hearts!
> O studious Poet, eloquent for truth!
> Philosopher! contemning wealth and death,
> Yet docile, childlike, full of Life and Love.

35. The student of empirical science asks, Are absolute principles attainable? What are the limits of knowledge? The answer he receives from science itself is not ambiguous. What the moralist asks is, Shall we gain or lose by surrendering human life to the relative spirit? Experience answers that the dominant tendency of life is to turn ascertained truth into a dead letter, to make us all the phlegmatic servants of routine. The relative spirit, by its constant dwelling on the more fugitive conditions or circumstances of things, breaking through a thousand rough and brutal classifications, and giving elasticity to inflexible principles, begets an intellectual *finesse* of which the ethical result

is a delicate and tender justice in the criticism of human life. Who would gain more than Coleridge by criticism in such a spirit? We know how his life has appeared when judged by absolute standards. We see him trying to "apprehend the absolute," to stereotype forms of faith and philosophy, to attain, as he says, "fixed principles" in politics, morals, and religion, to fix one mode of life as the essence of life, refusing to see the parts as parts only; and all the time his own pathetic history pleads for a more elastic moral philosophy than his, and cries out against every formula less living and flexible than life itself.

36. "From his childhood he hungered for eternity." There, after all, is the incontestable claim of Coleridge. The perfect flower of any elementary type of life must always be precious to humanity, and Coleridge is a true flower of the *ennuyé*, of the type of René. More than Childe Harold, more than Werther, more than René himself, Coleridge, by what he did, what he was, and what he failed to do, represents that inexhaustible discontent, languor, and homesickness, that endless regret, the chords of which ring all through our modern literature. It is to the romantic element in literature that those qualities belong. One day, perhaps, we may come to forget the distant horizon, with full knowledge of the situation, to be content with "what is here and now"; and herein is the essence of classical feeling. But by us of the present moment, certainly—by us for whom the Greek spirit, with its engaging naturalness, simple, chastened, debonair, τρυφῆς, ἁβρότητος, χλιδῆς, χαρίτων, ἱμέρου, πόθου πατήρ, is itself the Sangrail of an endless pilgrimage, Coleridge, with his passion for the absolute, for something fixed where all is moving, his faintness, his broken memory, his intellectual disquiet, may still be ranked among the interpreters of one of the constituent elements of our life.

1865, 1880.

CHARLES LAMB

Those English critics who at the beginning of the present century introduced from Germany, together with some other subtleties of thought transplanted hither not without advantage, the distinction between the *Fancy* and the *Imagination*, made much also of the cognate distinction between *Wit* and *Humour*, between that unreal and transitory mirth, which is as the crackling of thorns under the pot, and the laughter which blends with tears and even with the sublimities of the imagination, and which, in its most exquisite motives, is one with pity—the laughter of the comedies of Shakespeare, hardly less expressive than his moods of seriousness or solemnity, of that deeply stirred soul of sympathy in him, as flowing from which both tears and laughter are alike genuine and contagious.

2. This distinction between wit and humour, Coleridge and other kindred critics applied, with much effect, in their studies of some of our older English writers. And as the distinction between imagination and fancy, made popular by Wordsworth, found its best justification in certain essential differences of stuff in Wordsworth's own writings, so this other critical distinction, between wit and humour, finds a sort of visible interpretation and instance in the character and writings of Charles Lamb;—one who lived more consistently than most writers among subtle literary theories, and whose remains are still full of curious interest for the student of literature as a fine art.

3. The author of the *English Humourists of the Eighteenth Century*, coming to the humourists of the nineteenth, would have found, as is true pre-eminently of Thackeray himself, the springs of pity in them deepened by the deeper subjectivity, the intenser and closer living with itself, which is characteristic of the temper of the later generation; and therewith, the mirth also, from the amalgam of which with pity humour proceeds, has become, in Charles Dickens, for example, freer and more boisterous.

4. To this more high-pitched feeling, since predominant in our literature, the writings of Charles Lamb, whose life occupies the last quarter of the eighteenth century and the first quarter of the nineteenth, are a transition; and such union of grave, of terrible even, with gay, we may note in the circumstances of his life, as reflected thence into his work. We catch the aroma of a singular, homely sweetness about his first years, spent on Thames' side, amid the red bricks and terraced gardens, with their rich historical memories of old-fashioned legal London. Just above the poorer class, deprived, as he says, of the "sweet food of academic institution," he is fortunate enough to be reared in the

classical languages at an ancient school, where he becomes the companion of Coleridge, as at a later period he was his enthusiastic disciple. So far, the years go by with less than the usual share of boyish difficulties; protected, one fancies, seeing what he was afterwards, by some attraction of temper in the quaint child, small and delicate, with a certain Jewish expression in his clear, brown complexion, eyes not precisely of the same colour, and a slow walk adding to the staidness of his figure; and whose infirmity of speech, increased by agitation, is partly engaging.

5. And the cheerfulness of all this, of the mere aspect of Lamb's quiet subsequent life also, might make the more superficial reader think of him as in himself something slight, and of his mirth as cheaply bought. Yet we know that beneath this blithe surface there was something of the fateful domestic horror, of the beautiful heroism and devotedness too, of old Greek tragedy. His sister Mary, ten years his senior, in a sudden paroxysm of madness, caused the death of her mother, and was brought to trial for what an overstrained justice might have construed as the greatest of crimes. She was released on the brother's pledging himself to watch over her; and to this sister, from the age of twenty-one, Charles Lamb sacrificed himself, "seeking thenceforth," says his earliest biographer, "no connexion which could interfere with her supremacy in his affections, or impair his ability to sustain and comfort her." The "feverish, romantic tie of love," he cast away in exchange for the "charities of home." Only, from time to time, the madness returned, affecting him too, once; and we see the brother and sister voluntarily yielding to restraint. In estimating the humour of *Elia*, we must no more forget the strong undercurrent of this great misfortune and pity, than one could forget it in his actual story. So he becomes the best critic, almost the discoverer, of Webster, a dramatist of genius so sombre, so heavily coloured, so *macabre*. *Rosamund Grey*, written in his twenty-third year, a story with something bitter and exaggerated, an almost insane fixedness of gloom perceptible in it, strikes clearly this note in his work.

6. For himself, and from his own point of view, the exercise of his gift, of his literary art, came to gild or sweeten a life of monotonous labour, and seemed, as far as regarded others, no very important thing; availing to give them a little pleasure, and inform them a little, chiefly in a retrospective manner, but in no way concerned with the turning of the tides of the great world. And yet this very modesty, this unambitious way of conceiving his work, has impressed upon it a certain exceptional enduringness. For of the remarkable English writers contemporary with Lamb, many were greatly preoccupied with ideas of practice—religious, moral, political—ideas which have since, in some sense or other, entered permanently into the general consciousness; and, these having no longer any stimulus for a generation provided with a different

stock of ideas, the writings of those who spent so much of themselves in their propagation have lost, with posterity, something of what they gained by them in immediate influence. Coleridge, Wordsworth, Shelley even—sharing so largely in the unrest of their own age, and made personally more interesting thereby, yet, of their actual work, surrender more to the mere course of time than some of those who may have seemed to exercise themselves hardly at all in great matters, to have been little serious, or a little indifferent, regarding them.

7. Of this number of the disinterested servants of literature, smaller in England than in France, Charles Lamb is one. In the making of prose he realises the principle of art for its own sake, as completely as Keats in the making of verse. And, working ever close to the concrete, to the details, great or small, of actual things, books, persons, and with no part of them blurred to his vision by the intervention of mere abstract theories, he has reached an enduring moral effect also, in a sort of boundless sympathy. Unoccupied, as he might seem, with great matters, he is in immediate contact with what is real, especially in its caressing littleness, that littleness in which there is much of the whole woeful heart of things, and meets it more than half-way with a perfect understanding of it. What sudden, unexpected touches of pathos in him!—bearing witness how the sorrow of humanity, the *Weltschmerz*, the constant aching of its wounds, is ever present with him: but what a gift also for the enjoyment of life in its subtleties, of enjoyment actually refined by the need of some thoughtful economies and making the most of things! Little arts of happiness he is ready to teach to others. The quaint remarks of children which another would scarcely have heard, he preserves—little flies in the priceless amber of his Attic wit—and has his "Praise of chimney-sweepers" (as William Blake has written, with so much natural pathos, the Chimney-sweeper's Song) valuing carefully their white teeth, and fine enjoyment of white sheets in stolen sleep at Arundel Castle, as he tells the story, anticipating something of the mood of our deep humourists of the last generation. His simple mother-pity for those who suffer by accident, or unkindness of nature, blindness for instance, or fateful disease of mind like his sister's, has something primitive in its largeness; and on behalf of ill-used animals he is early in composing a *Pity's Gift*.

8. And if, in deeper or more superficial sense, the dead *do* care at all for their name and fame, then how must the souls of Shakespeare and Webster have been stirred, after so long converse with things that stopped their ears, whether above or below the soil, at his exquisite appreciations of them; the souls of Titian and of Hogarth too; for, what has not been observed so generally as the excellence of his literary criticism, Charles Lamb is a fine critic of painting also. It was as loyal, self-forgetful work for others, for Shakespeare's self first, for instance, and then for Shakespeare's readers, that that too was done: he has the

true scholar's way of forgetting himself in his subject. For though "defrauded," as we saw, in his young years, "of the sweet food of academic institution," he is yet essentially a scholar, and all his work mainly retrospective, as I said; his own sorrows, affections, perceptions, being alone real to him of the present. "I cannot make these present times," he says once, "present to *me*."

9. Above all, he becomes not merely an expositor, permanently valuable, but for Englishmen almost the discoverer of the old English drama. "The book is such as I am glad there should be," he modestly says of the *Specimens of English Dramatic Poets who lived about the time of Shakespeare*; to which, however, he adds in a series of notes the very quintessence of criticism, the choicest savour and perfume of Elizabethan poetry being sorted, and stored here, with a sort of delicate intellectual epicureanism, which has had the effect of winning for these, then almost forgotten, poets, one generation after another of enthusiastic students. Could he but have known how fresh a source of culture he was evoking there for other generations, through all those years in which, a little wistfully, he would harp on the limitation of his time by business, and sigh for a better fortune in regard to literary opportunities!

10. To feel strongly the charm of an old poet or moralist, the literary charm of Burton, for instance, or Quarles, or The Duchess of Newcastle; and then to interpret that charm, to convey it to others—he seeming to himself but to hand on to others, in mere humble ministration, that of which for them he is really the creator—this is the way of his criticism; cast off in a stray letter often, or passing note, or lightest essay or conversation. It is in such a letter, for instance, that we come upon a singularly penetrative estimate of the genius and writings of Defoe.

11. Tracking, with an attention always alert, the whole process of their production to its starting-point in the deep places of the mind, he seems to realise the but half-conscious intuitions of Hogarth or Shakespeare, and develops the great ruling unities which have swayed their actual work; or "puts up," and takes, the one morsel of good stuff in an old, forgotten writer. Even in what he says casually there comes an aroma of old English; noticeable echoes, in chance turn and phrase, of the great masters of style, the old masters. Godwin, seeing in quotation a passage from *John Woodvil*, takes it for a choice fragment of an old dramatist, and goes to Lamb to assist him in finding the author. His power of delicate imitation in prose and verse reaches the length of a fine mimicry even, as in those last essays of Elia on Popular Fallacies, with their gentle reproduction or caricature of Sir Thomas Browne, showing, the more completely, his mastery, by disinterested study, of those elements of the man which were the real source of style in that great, solemn master of old English, who, ready to say what he has to say with fearless homeliness, yet continually

overawes one with touches of a strange utterance from worlds afar. For it is with the delicacies of fine literature especially, its gradations of expression, its fine judgment, its pure sense of words, of vocabulary—things, alas! dying out in the English literature of the present, together with the appreciation of them in our literature of the past—that his literary mission is chiefly concerned. And yet, delicate, refining, daintily epicurean, as he may seem, when he writes of giants, such as Hogarth or Shakespeare, though often but in a stray note, you catch the sense of veneration with which those great names in past literature and art brooded over his intelligence, his undiminished impressibility by the great effects in them. Reading, commenting on Shakespeare, he is like a man who walks alone under a grand stormy sky, and among unwonted tricks of light, when powerful spirits might seem to be abroad upon the air; and the grim humour of Hogarth, as he analyses it, rises into a kind of spectral grotesque; while he too knows the secret of fine, significant touches like theirs.

12. There are traits, customs, characteristics of houses and dress, surviving morsels of old life, such as Hogarth has transferred so vividly into *The Rake's Progress*, or *Marriage à la Mode*, concerning which we well understand how, common, uninteresting, or even worthless in themselves, they have come to please us at last as things picturesque, being set in relief against the modes of our different age. Customs, stiff to us, stiff dresses, stiff furniture—types of cast-off fashions, left by accident, and which no one ever meant to preserve—we contemplate with more than good-nature, as having in them the veritable accent of a time, not altogether to be replaced by its more solemn and self-conscious deposits; like those tricks of individuality which we find quite tolerable in persons, because they convey to us the secret of lifelike expression, and with regard to which we are all to some extent humourists. But it is part of the privilege of the genuine humourist to anticipate this pensive mood with regard to the ways and things of his own day; to look upon the tricks in manner of the life about him with that same refined, purged sort of vision, which will come naturally to those of a later generation, in observing whatever may have survived by chance of its mere external habit. Seeing things always by the light of an understanding more entire than is possible for ordinary minds, of the whole mechanism of humanity, and seeing also the manner, the outward mode or fashion, always in strict connexion with the spiritual condition which determined it, a humourist such as Charles Lamb anticipates the enchantment of distance; and the characteristics of places, ranks, habits of life, are transfigured for him, even now and in advance of time, by poetic light; justifying what some might condemn as mere sentimentality, in the effort to hand on unbroken the tradition of such fashion or accent. "The praise of beggars," "the cries of London," the traits of actors just grown "old," the spots

in "town" where the country, its fresh green and fresh water, still lingered on, one after another, amidst the bustle; the quaint, dimmed, just played-out farces, he had relished so much, coming partly through them to understand the earlier English theatre as a thing once really alive; those fountains and sun-dials of old gardens, of which he entertains such dainty discourse:—he feels the poetry of these things, as the poetry of things old indeed, but surviving as an actual part of the life of the present, and as something quite different from the poetry of things flatly gone from us and antique, which come back to us, if at all, as entire strangers, like Scott's old Scotch-border personages, their oaths and armour. Such gift of appreciation depends, as I said, on the habitual apprehension of men's life as a whole—its organic wholeness, as extending even to the least things in it—of its outward manner in connexion with its inward temper; and it involves a fine perception of the congruities, the musical accordance between humanity and its environment of custom, society, personal intercourse; as if all this, with its meetings, partings, ceremonies, gesture, tones of speech, were some delicate instrument on which an expert performer is playing.

13. These are some of the characteristics of Elia, one essentially an essayist, and of the true family of Montaigne, "never judging," as he says, "system-wise of things, but fastening on particulars;" saying all things as it were on chance occasion only, and by way of pastime, yet succeeding thus, "glimpse-wise," in catching and recording more frequently than others "the gayest, happiest attitude of things;" a casual writer for dreamy readers, yet always giving the reader so much more than he seemed to propose. There is something of the follower of George Fox about him, and the Quaker's belief in the inward light coming to one passive, to the mere wayfarer, who will be sure at all events to lose no light which falls by the way—glimpses, suggestions, delightful half-apprehensions, profound thoughts of old philosophers, hints of the innermost reason in things, the full knowledge of which is held in reserve; all the varied stuff, that is, of which genuine essays are made.

14. And with him, as with Montaigne, the desire of self-portraiture is, below all more superficial tendencies, the real motive in writing at all—a desire closely connected with that intimacy, that modern subjectivity, which may be called the *Montaignesque* element in literature. What he designs is to give you himself, to acquaint you with his likeness; but must do this, if at all, indirectly, being indeed always more or less reserved, for himself and his friends; friendship counting for so much in his life, that he is jealous of anything that might jar or disturb it, even to the length of a sort of insincerity, to which he assigns its quaint "praise"; this lover of stage plays significantly welcoming a little touch of the artificiality of play to sweeten the intercourse of actual life.

15. And, in effect, a very delicate and expressive portrait of him does put itself together for the duly meditative reader. In indirect touches of his own work, scraps of faded old letters, what others remembered of his talk, the man's likeness emerges; what he laughed and wept at, his sudden elevations, and longings after absent friends, his fine casuistries of affection and devices to jog sometimes, as he says, the lazy happiness of perfect love, his solemn moments of higher discourse with the young, as they came across him on occasion, and went along a little way with him, the sudden, surprised apprehension of beauties in old literature, revealing anew the deep soul of poetry in things, and withal the pure spirit of fun, having its way again; laughter, that most short-lived of all things (some of Shakespeare's even being grown hollow) wearing well with him. Much of all this comes out through his letters, which may be regarded as a department of his essays. He is an old-fashioned letter-writer, the essence of the old fashion of letter-writing lying, as with true essay-writing, in the dexterous availing oneself of accident and circumstance, in the prosecution of deeper lines of observation; although, just as with the record of his conversation, one loses something, in losing the actual tones of the stammerer, still graceful in his halting, as he halted also in composition, composing slowly and by fits, "like a Flemish painter," as he tells us, so "it is to be regretted," says the editor of his letters, "that in the printed letters the reader will lose the curious varieties of writing with which the originals abound, and which are scrupulously adapted to the subject."

16. Also, he was a true "collector," delighting in the personal finding of a thing, in the colour an old book or print gets for him by the little accidents which attest previous ownership. Wither's *Emblems*, "that old book and quaint," long-desired, when he finds it at last, he values none the less because a child had coloured the plates with his paints. A lover of household warmth everywhere, of that tempered atmosphere which our various habitations get by men's living within them, he "sticks to his favourite books as he did to his friends," and loved the "town," with a jealous eye for all its characteristics, "old houses" coming to have souls for him. The yearning for mere warmth against him in another, makes him content, all through life, with pure brotherliness, "the most kindly and natural species of love," as he says, in place of the *passion* of love. Brother and sister, sitting thus side by side, have, of course, their anticipations how one of them must sit at last in the faint sun alone, and set us speculating, as we read, as to precisely what amount of melancholy really accompanied for him the approach of old age, so steadily foreseen; make us note also, with pleasure, his successive wakings up to cheerful realities, out of a too curious musing over what is gone and what remains, of life. In his subtle capacity for enjoying the more refined points of earth, of human relationship,

he could throw the gleam of poetry or humour on what seemed common or threadbare; has a care for the sighs, and the weary, humdrum preoccupations of very weak people, down to their little pathetic "gentilities," even; while, in the purely human temper, he can write of death, almost like Shakespeare.

17. And that care, through all his enthusiasm of discovery, for what is accustomed, in literature, connected thus with his close clinging to home and the earth, was congruous also with that love for the accustomed in religion, which we may notice in him. He is one of the last votaries of that old-world sentiment, based on the feelings of hope and awe, which may be described as the religion of men of letters (as Sir Thomas Browne has his *Religion of the Physician*) religion as understood by the soberer men of letters in the last century, Addison, Gray, and Johnson; by Jane Austen and Thackeray, later. A high way of feeling developed largely by constant intercourse with the great things of literature, and extended in its turn to those matters greater still, this religion lives, in the main retrospectively, in a system of received sentiments and beliefs; received, like those great things of literature and art, in the first instance, on the authority of a long tradition, in the course of which they have linked themselves in a thousand complex ways to the conditions of human life, and no more questioned now than the feeling one keeps by one of the greatness—say! of Shakespeare. For Charles Lamb, such form of religion becomes the solemn background on which the nearer and more exciting objects of his immediate experience relieve themselves, borrowing from it an expression of calm; its necessary atmosphere being indeed a profound quiet, that quiet which has in it a kind of sacramental efficacy, working, we might say, on the principle of the *opus operatum*, almost without any co-operation of one's own, towards the assertion of the higher self. And, in truth, to men of Lamb's delicately attuned temperament mere physical stillness has its full value; such natures seeming to long for it sometimes, as for no merely negative thing, with a sort of mystical sensuality.

18. The writings of Charles Lamb are an excellent illustration of the value of reserve in literature. Below his quiet, his quaintness, his humour, and what may seem the slightness, the occasional or accidental character of his work, there lies, as I said at starting, as in his life, a genuinely tragic element. The gloom, reflected at its darkest in those hard shadows of *Rosamund Grey*, is always there, though not always realised either for himself or his readers, and restrained always in utterance. It gives to those lighter matters on the surface of life and literature among which he for the most part moved, a wonderful force of expression, as if at any moment these slight words and fancies might pierce very far into the deeper soul of things. In his writing, as in his life, that

quiet is not the low-flying of one from the first drowsy by choice, and needing the prick of some strong passion or worldly ambition, to stimulate him into all the energy of which he is capable; but rather the reaction of nature, after an escape from fate, dark and insane as in old Greek tragedy, following upon which the sense of mere relief becomes a kind of passion, as with one who, having narrowly escaped earthquake or shipwreck, finds a thing for grateful tears in just sitting quiet at home, under the wall, till the end of days.

19. He felt the genius of places; and I sometimes think he resembles the places he knew and liked best, and where his lot fell—London, sixty-five years ago, with Covent Garden and the old theatres, and the Temple gardens still unspoiled, Thames gliding down, and beyond to north and south the fields at Enfield or Hampton, to which, "with their living trees," the thoughts wander "from the hard wood of the desk"—fields fresher, and coming nearer to town then, but in one of which the present writer remembers, on a brooding early summer's day, to have heard the cuckoo for the first time. Here, the surface of things is certainly humdrum, the streets dingy, the green places, where the child goes a-maying, tame enough. But nowhere are things more apt to respond to the brighter weather, nowhere is there so much difference between rain and sunshine, nowhere do the clouds roll together more grandly; those quaint suburban pastorals gathering a certain quality of grandeur from the background of the great city, with its weighty atmosphere, and portent of storm in the rapid light on dome and bleached stone steeples.

1878.

SIR THOMAS BROWNE

English prose literature towards the end of the seventeenth century, in the hands of Dryden and Locke, was becoming, as that of France had become at an earlier date, a matter of design and skilled practice, highly conscious of itself as an art, and, above all, correct. Up to that time it had been, on the whole, singularly informal and unprofessional, and by no means the literature of the "man of letters," as we understand him. Certain great instances there had been of literary structure or architecture—*The Ecclesiastical Polity*, *The Leviathan*—but for the most part that earlier prose literature is eminently occasional, closely determined by the eager practical aims of contemporary politics and theology, or else due to a man's own native instinct to speak because he cannot help speaking. Hardly aware of the habit, he likes talking to himself; and when he writes (still in undress) he does but take the "friendly reader" into his confidence. The type of this literature, obviously, is not Locke or Gibbon, but, above all others, Sir Thomas Browne; as Jean Paul is a good instance of it in German literature, always in its developments so much later than the English; and as the best instance of it in French literature, in the century preceding Browne, is Montaigne, from whom indeed, in a great measure, all those tentative writers, or essayists, derive.

2. It was a result, perhaps, of the individualism and liberty of personal development, which, even for a Roman Catholic, were effects of the Reformation, that there was so much in Montaigne of the "subjective," as people say, of the singularities of personal character. Browne, too, bookish as he really is claims to give his readers a matter, "not picked from the leaves of any author, but bred amongst the weeds and tares" of his own brain. The faults of such literature are what we all recognise in it: unevenness, alike in thought and style; lack of design; and caprice—the lack of authority; after the full play of which, there is so much to refresh one in the reasonable transparency of Hooker, representing thus early the tradition of a classical clearness in English literature, anticipated by Latimer and More, and to be fulfilled afterwards in Butler and Hume. But then, in recompense for that looseness and whim, in Sir Thomas Browne for instance, we have in those "quaint" writers, as they themselves understood the term (*coint*, adorned, but adorned with all the curious ornaments of their own predilection, provincial or archaic, certainly unfamiliar, and selected without reference to the taste or usages of other people) the charm of an absolute sincerity, with all the ingenuous and racy effect of what is circumstantial and peculiar in their growth.

The whole creation is a mystery and particularly that of man. At the blast of His mouth were the rest of the creatures made, and at His bare word they started out of nothing. But in the frame of man He played the sensible operator, and seemed not so much to *create* as to *make* him. When He had separated the materials of other creatures, there consequently resulted a form and soul: but having raised the walls of man, He was driven to a second and harder creation—of a substance like Himself, an incorruptible and immortal soul.

3. There, we have the manner of Sir Thomas Browne, in exact expression of his mind!—minute and curious in its thinking, but with an effect, on the sudden, of a real sublimity or depth. His style is certainly an unequal one. It has the monumental aim which charmed, and perhaps influenced, Johnson—a dignity that can be attained only in such mental calm as follows long and learned pondering on the high subjects Browne loves to deal with. It has its garrulity, its various levels of painstaking, its mannerism, pleasant of its kind or tolerable, together with much, to us intolerable, but of which he was capable on a lazy summer afternoon down at Norwich. And all is so oddly mixed, showing, in its entire ignorance of self, how much he, and the sort of literature he represents, really stood in need of *technique*, of a formed taste in literature, of a literary architecture.

4. And yet perhaps we could hardly wish the result different, in him, any more than in the books of Burton and Fuller, or some other similar writers of that age—mental abodes, we might liken, after their own manner, to the little old private houses of some historic town grouped about its grand public structures, which, when they have survived at all, posterity is loth to part with. For, in their absolute sincerity, not only do these authors clearly exhibit themselves ("the unique peculiarity of the writer's mind," being, as Johnson says of Browne, "faithfully reflected in the form and matter of his work") but, even more than mere professionally instructed writers, they belong to, and reflect, the age they lived in. In essentials, of course, even Browne is by no means so unique among his contemporaries, and so singular, as he looks. And then, as the very condition of their work, there is an entire absence of personal restraint in dealing with the public, whose humours they come at last in a great measure to reproduce. To speak more properly, they have no sense of a "public" to deal with, at all—only a full confidence in the "friendly reader," as they love to call him. Hence their amazing pleasantry, their indulgence in their own conceits; but hence also those unpremeditated wildflowers of speech we should never have the good luck to find in any more formal kind of literature.

5. It is, in truth, to the literary purpose of the humourist, in the old-fashioned

sense of the term, that this method of writing naturally allies itself—of the humourist to whom all the world is but a spectacle in which nothing is really alien from himself, who has hardly a sense of the distinction between great and little among things that are at all, and whose half-pitying, half-amused sympathy is called out especially by the seemingly small interests and traits of character in the things or the people around him. Certainly, in an age stirred by great causes, like the age of Browne in England, of Montaigne in France, that is not a type to which one would wish to reduce all men of letters. Still, in an age apt also to become severe, or even cruel (its eager interest in those great causes turning sour on occasion) the character of the humourist may well find its proper influence, through that serene power, and the leisure it has for conceiving second thoughts, on the tendencies, conscious or unconscious, of the fierce wills around it. Something of such a humourist was Browne—not callous to men and their fortunes; certainly not without opinions of his own about them; and yet, undisturbed by the civil war, by the fall, and then the restoration, of the monarchy, through that long quiet life (ending at last on the day himself had predicted, as if at the moment he had willed) in which "all existence," as he says, "had been but food for contemplation."

6. Johnson, in beginning his *Life of Browne*, remarks that Browne "seems to have had the fortune, common among men of letters, of raising little curiosity after their private life." Whether or not, with the example of Johnson himself before us, we can think just that, it is certain that Browne's works are of a kind to directly stimulate curiosity about himself—about himself, as being manifestly so large a part of those works; and as a matter of fact we know a great deal about his life, uneventful as in truth it was. To himself, indeed, his life at Norwich, as he gives us to understand, seemed wonderful enough. "Of these wonders," says Johnson, "the view that can now be taken of his life offers no appearance." But "we carry with us," as Browne writes, "the wonders we seek without us," and we may note on the other hand, a circumstance which his daughter, Mrs. Lyttelton, tells us of his childhood: "His father used to open his breast when he was asleep, and kiss it in prayers over him, as 'tis said of Origen's father, that the Holy Ghost would take possession there." It was perhaps because the son inherited an aptitude for a like profound kindling of sentiment in the taking of his life, that, uneventful as it was, commonplace as it seemed to Johnson, to Browne himself it was so full of wonders, and so stimulates the curiosity of his more careful reader of to-day. "What influence," says Johnson again, "learning has had on its possessors may be doubtful." Well! the influence of his great learning, of his constant research on Browne, was its imaginative influence—that it completed his outfit as a poetic visionary, stirring all the strange "conceit" of his nature to its depths.

7. Browne himself dwells, in connexion with the first publication (extorted by circumstance) of the *Religio Medici*, on the natural "inactivity of his disposition"; and he does, as I have said, pass very quietly through an exciting time. Born in the year of the Gunpowder Plot, he was not, in truth, one of those clear and clarifying souls which, in an age alike of practical and mental confusion, can anticipate and lay down the bases of reconstruction, like Bacon or Hooker. His mind has much of the perplexity which was part of the atmosphere of the time. Not that he is without his own definite opinions on events. For him, Cromwell is a usurper, the death of Charles an abominable murder. In spite of what is but an affectation, perhaps, of the sceptical mood, he is a Churchman too; one of those who entered fully into the Anglican position, so full of sympathy with those ceremonies and observances which "misguided zeal terms superstition," that there were some Roman Catholics who thought that nothing but custom and education kept him from their communion. At the Restoration he rejoices to see the return of the comely Anglican order in old episcopal Norwich, with its ancient churches; the antiquity, in particular, of the English Church being, characteristically, one of the things he most valued in it, vindicating it, when occasion came, against the "unjust scandal" of those who made that Church a creation of Henry the Eighth. As to Romanists—he makes no scruple to "enter their churches in defect of ours." He cannot laugh at, but rather pities, "the fruitless journeys of pilgrims—for there is something in it of devotion." He could never "hear the *Ave Mary!* bell without an *oraison*." At a solemn procession he has "wept abundantly." How English, in truth, all this really is! It reminds one how some of the most popular of English writers, in many a half-conscious expression, have witnessed to a susceptibility in the English mind itself, in spite of the Reformation, to what is affecting in religious ceremony. Only, in religion as in politics, Browne had no turn for disputes; was suspicious of them, indeed; knowing, as he says with true acumen, that "a man may be in as just possession of truth as of a city, and yet be forced to surrender," even in controversies not necessarily maladroit—an image in which we may trace a little contemporary colouring.

8. The *Enquiries into Vulgar Errors* appeared in the year 1646; a year which found him very hard on "the vulgar." His suspicion, in the abstract, of what Bacon calls *Idola Fori*, the Idols of the Market-place, takes a special emphasis from the course of events about him:—"being erroneous in their single numbers, once huddled together, they will be error itself." And yet, congruously with a dreamy sweetness of character we may find expressed in his very features, he seems not greatly concerned at the temporary suppression of the institutions he values so much. He seems to possess some inward Platonic reality of them—church or monarchy—to hold by in idea, quite beyond the reach of

Roundhead or unworthy Cavalier. In the power of what is inward and inviolable in his religion, he can still take note: "In my solitary and retired imagination (*neque enim cum porticus aut me lectulus accepit, desum mihi*) I remember I am not alone, and therefore forget not to contemplate Him and His attributes who is ever with me."

9. His father, a merchant of London, with some claims to ancient descent, left him early in possession of ample means. Educated at Winchester and Oxford, he visited Ireland, France, and Italy; and in the year 1633, at the age of twenty-eight, became Doctor of Medicine at Leyden. Three years later he established himself as a physician at Norwich for the remainder of his life, having married a lady, described as beautiful and attractive, and affectionate also, as we may judge from her letters and postscripts to those of her husband, in an orthography of a homeliness amazing even for that age. Dorothy Browne bore him ten children, six of whom he survived.

10. Their house at Norwich, even then an old one it would seem, must have grown, through long years of acquisition, into an odd cabinet of antiquities — antiquities properly so called; his old Roman, or Romanised British urns, from Walsingham or Brampton, for instance, and those natural objects which he studied somewhat in the temper of a curiosity-hunter or antiquary. In one of the old churchyards of Norwich he makes the first discovery of *adipocere*, of which grim substance "a portion still remains with him." For his multifarious experiments he must have had his laboratory. The old window-stanchions had become magnetic, proving, as he thinks, that iron "acquires verticity" from long lying in one position. Once we find him re-tiling the place. It was then, perhaps, that he made the observation that bricks and tiles also acquire "magnetic alliciency"—one's whole house, one might fancy; as indeed, he holds the earth itself to be a vast lodestone.

11. The very faults of his literary work, its desultoriness, the time it costs his readers, that slow Latinity which Johnson imitated from him, those lengthy leisurely terminations which busy posterity will abbreviate, all breathe of the long quiet of the place. Yet he is by no means indolent. Besides wide book-learning, experimental research at home, and indefatigable observation in the open air, he prosecutes the ordinary duties of a physician; contrasting himself indeed with other students, "whose quiet and unmolested doors afford no such distractions." To most persons of mind sensitive as his, his chosen studies would have seemed full of melancholy, turning always, as they did, upon death and decay. It is well, perhaps, that life should be something of a "meditation upon death": but to many, certainly, Browne's would have seemed too like a lifelong following of one's own funeral. A museum is seldom a cheerful place—oftenest induces the feeling that nothing could ever have been young;

and to Browne the whole world is a museum; all the grace and beauty it has being of a somewhat mortified kind. Only, for him (poetic dream, or philosophic apprehension, it was this which never failed to evoke his wonderful genius for exquisitely impassioned speech) over all those ugly anatomical preparations, as though over miraculous saintly relics, there was the perpetual flicker of a surviving spiritual ardency, one day to reassert itself—stranger far than any fancied odylic gravelights!

12. When Browne settled at Norwich, being then about thirty-six years old, he had already completed the *Religio Medici*; a desultory collection of observations designed for himself only and a few friends, at all events with no purpose of immediate publication. It had been lying by him for seven years, circulating privately in his own extraordinarily perplexed manuscript, or in manuscript copies, when, in 1642, an incorrect printed version from one of those copies, "much corrupted by transcription at various hands," appeared anonymously. Browne, decided royalist as he was in spite of seeming indifference, connects this circumstance with the unscrupulous use of the press for political purposes, and especially against the king, at that time. Just here a romantic figure comes on the scene. Son of the unfortunate young Everard Digby who perished on the scaffold for some half-hearted participation in the Gunpowder Plot, Kenelm Digby, brought up in the reformed religion, had returned in manhood to the religion of his father. In his intellectual composition he had, in common with Browne, a scientific interest, oddly tinged with both poetry and scepticism: he had also a strong sympathy with religious reaction, and a more than sentimental love for a seemingly vanishing age of faith, which he, for one, would not think of as vanishing. A copy of that surreptitious edition of the *Religio Medici* found him a prisoner on suspicion of a too active royalism, and with much time on his hands. The Roman Catholic, although, secure in his definite orthodoxy, he finds himself indifferent on many points (on the reality of witchcraft, for instance) concerning which Browne's more timid, personally grounded faith might indulge no scepticism, forced himself, nevertheless, to detect a vein of rationalism in a book which on the whole much attracted him, and hastily put forth his "animadversions" upon it. Browne, with all his distaste for controversy, thus found himself committed to a dispute, and his reply came with the correct edition of the *Religio Medici* published at last with his name. There have been many efforts to formulate the "religion of the layman," which might be rightly understood, perhaps, as something more than what is called "natural," yet less than ecclesiastical, or "professional" religion. Though its habitual mode of conceiving experience is on a different plane, yet it would recognise the legitimacy of the traditional religious interpretation of that experience, generally and by implication; only, with a marked reserve as to religious particulars, both

of thought and language, out of a real reverence or awe, as proper only for a special place. Such is the lay religion, as we may find it in Addison, in Gray, in Thackeray; and there is something of a concession—a concession, on second thoughts—about it. Browne's *Religio Medici* is designed as the expression of a mind more difficult of belief than that of the mere "layman," as above described; it is meant for the religion of the man of science. Actually, it is something less to the point, in any balancing of the religious against the worldly view of things, than the religion of the layman, as just now defined. For Browne, in spite of his profession of boisterous doubt, has no real difficulties, and his religion, certainly, nothing of the character of a concession. He holds that there has never existed an atheist. Not that he is credulous; but that his religion is only the correlative of himself, his peculiar character and education, a religion of manifold association. For him, the wonders of religion, its supernatural events or agencies, are almost natural facts or processes. "Even in this material fabric, the spirits walk as freely exempt from the affection of time, place and motion, as beyond the extremest circumference." Had not Divine interference designed to raise the dead, nature herself is in act to do it—to lead out the "incinerated soul" from the retreats of her dark laboratory. Certainly Browne has not, like Pascal, made the "great resolution," by the apprehension that it is just in the contrast of the moral world to the world with which science deals that religion finds its proper basis. It is from the homelessness of the world which science analyses so victoriously, its dark unspirituality, wherein the soul he is conscious of seems such a stranger, that Pascal "turns again to his rest," in the conception of a world of wholly reasonable and moral agencies. For Browne, on the contrary, the light is full, design everywhere obvious, its conclusion easy to draw, all small and great things marked clearly with the signature of the "Word." The adhesion, the difficult adhesion, of men such as Pascal, is an immense contribution to religious controversy; the concession, again, of a man like Addison, of great significance there. But in the adhesion of Browne, in spite of his crusade against "vulgar errors," there is no real significance. The *Religio Medici* is a contribution, not to faith, but to piety; a refinement and correction, such as piety often stands in need of; a help, not so much to religious belief in a world of doubt, as to the maintenance of the religious mood amid the interests of a secular calling.

13. From about this time Browne's letters afford a pretty clear view of his life as it passed in the house at Norwich. Many of these letters represent him in correspondence with the singular men who shared his own half poetic, half scientific turn of mind, with that impressibility towards what one might call the thaumaturgic elements in nature which has often made men dupes, and which is certainly an element in the somewhat atrabiliar mental complexion of that

age in England. He corresponds seriously with William Lily, the astrologer; is acquainted with Dr. Dee, who had some connexion with Norwich, and has "often heard him affirm, sometimes with oaths, that he had seen transmutation of pewter dishes and flagons into silver (at least) which the goldsmiths at Prague bought of him." Browne is certainly an honest investigator; but it is still with a faint hope of something like that upon fitting occasion, and on the alert always for surprises in nature (as if nature had a rhetoric, at times, to deliver to us, like those sudden and surprising flowers of his own poetic style) that he listens to her everyday talk so attentively. Of strange animals, strange cures, and the like, his correspondence is full. The very errors he combats are, of course, the curiosities of error—those fascinating, irresistible, popular, errors, which various kinds of people have insisted on gliding into because they like them. Even his heresies were old ones—the very fossils of capricious opinion.

14. It is as an industrious local naturalist that Browne comes before us first, full of the fantastic minute life in the fens and "Broads" around Norwich, its various sea and marsh birds. He is something of a vivisectionist also, and we may not be surprised at it, perhaps, in an age which, for the propagation of truth, was ready to cut off men's ears. He finds one day "a *Scarabæus capricornus odoratus*," which he takes "to be mentioned by Monfetus, folio 150. He saith, '*Nucem moschatam et cinnamomum vere spirat*'—but to me it smelt like roses, santalum, and ambergris." "*Musca tuliparum moschata*," again, "is a small bee-like fly of an excellent fragrant odour, which I have often found at the bottom of the flowers of tulips." Is this within the experience of modern entomologists?

15. The *Garden of Cyrus*, though it ends indeed with a passage of wonderful felicity, certainly emphasises (to say the least) the defects of Browne's literary good qualities. His chimeric fancy carries him here into a kind of frivolousness, as if he felt almost too safe with his public, and were himself not quite serious, or dealing fairly with it; and in a writer such as Browne levity must of necessity be a little ponderous. Still, like one of those stiff gardens, half-way between the medieval garden and the true "English" garden of Temple or Walpole, actually to be seen in the background of some of the conventional portraits of that day, the fantasies of this indescribable exposition of the mysteries of the *quincunx* form part of the complete portrait of Browne himself; and it is in connexion with it that, once or twice, the quaintly delightful pen of Evelyn comes into the correspondence—in connexion with the "hortulane pleasure." "Norwich," he writes to Browne, "is a place, I understand, much addicted to the flowery part." Professing himself a believer in the operation "of the air and genius of gardens upon human spirits, towards virtue and sanctity," he is all for natural gardens as against "those which appear like gardens of paste-board and march-pane, and smell more of paint than of flowers and verdure." Browne is

in communication also with Ashmole and Dugdale, the famous antiquaries; to the latter of whom, who had written a work on the history of the embanking of fens, he communicates the discovery of certain coins, on a piece of ground "in the nature of an island in the fens."

16. Far more interesting certainly than those curious scientific letters is Browne's "domestic correspondence." Dobson, Charles the First's "English Tintoret," would seem to have painted a life-sized picture of Sir Thomas Browne and his family, after the manner of those big, urbane, family groups, then coming into fashion with the Dutch Masters. Of such a portrait nothing is now known. But in these old-fashioned, affectionate letters, transmitted often, in those troublous times, with so much difficulty, we have what is almost as graphic—a numerous group, in which, although so many of Browne's children died young, he was happy; with Dorothy Browne, occasionally adding her charming, ill-spelt postscripts to her husband's letters; the religious daughter who goes to daily prayers after the Restoration, which brought Browne the honour of knighthood; and, above all, two Toms, son and grandson of Sir Thomas, the latter being the son of Dr. Edward Browne, now become distinguished as a physician in London (he attended John, Earl of Rochester, in his last illness at Woodstock) and his childish existence as he lives away from his proper home in London, in the old house at Norwich, two hundred years ago, we see like a thing of to-day.

17. At first the two brothers, Edward and Thomas (the elder) are together in everything. Then Edward goes abroad for his studies, and Thomas, quite early, into the navy, where he certainly develops into a wonderfully gallant figure; passing away, however, from the correspondence, it is uncertain how, before he was of full age. From the first he is understood to be a lad of parts. "If you practise to write, you will have a good pen and style:" and a delightful, boyish journal of his remains, describing a tour the two brothers made in September 1662 among the Derbyshire hills. "I received your two last letters," he writes to his father from aboard the *Marie Rose*, "and give you many thanks for the discourse you sent me out of Vossius: *De motu marium et ventorum*. It seemed very hard to me at first; but I have now beaten it, and I wish I had the book." His father is pleased to think that he is "like to proceed not only a good navigator, but a good scholar": and he finds the much exacting, old classical prescription for the character of the brave man fulfilled in him. On 16th July 1666 the young man writes—still from the *Marie Rose*—

If it were possible to get an opportunity to send as often as I am desirous to write, you should hear more often from me, being now so near the grand action, from which I would by no means be absent. I extremely long for that thundering day: wherein I hope you shall hear we have behaved ourselves like men, and to the honour of our country. I thank you for your directions for my ears against the noise of the guns, but I have found that I could endure it; nor is it so intolerable as most conceive; especially when men are earnest, and intent upon their business, unto whom muskets sound but like pop-guns. It is impossible to express unto another how a smart sea-fight elevates the spirits of a man, and makes him despise all dangers. In and after all sea-fights, I have been very thirsty.

18. He died, as I said, early in life. We only hear of him later in connexion with a trait of character observed in Tom the grandson, whose winning ways, and tricks of bodily and mental growth, are duly recorded in these letters: the reader will, I hope, pardon the following extracts from them:—

Little Tom is lively. . . . Frank is fayne sometimes to play him asleep with a fiddle. When we send away our letters he scribbles a paper and will have it sent to his sister, and saith she doth not know how many fine things there are in Norwich. . . . He delights his grandfather when he comes home.

Tom gives you many thanks for his clothes (from London). He has appeared very fine this King's day with them.

Tom presents his duty. A gentleman at our election asked Tom who hee was for? and he answered, "For all four." The gentleman replied that he answered like a physician's son.

Tom would have his grandmother, his aunt Betty, and Frank, valentines: but hee conditioned with them that they should give him nothing of any kind that hee had ever had or seen before.

"Tom is just now gone to see two bears which are to be shown." "Tom, his duty. He is begging books and reading of them." "The players are at the Red Lion hard by; and Tom goes sometimes to see a play."

19. And then one day he stirs old memories—

The fairings were welcome to Tom. He finds about the house divers things that were your brother's (the late Edward's), and Betty sometimes tells him stories about him, so that he was importunate with her to write his life in a quarter of a sheet of paper, and read it unto him, and will have still some more added.

Just as I am writing (learnedly about a comet, 7th January 1680–81) Tom comes and tells me the blazing star is in the yard, and calls me to see it. It was but dim, and the sky not clear. . . . I am very sensible of this sharp weather.

20. He seems to have come to no good end, riding forth one stormy night. *Requiescat in pace!*

21. Of this long, leisurely existence the chief events were Browne's rare literary publications; some of his writings indeed having been left unprinted till after his death; while in the circumstances of the issue of every one of them there is something accidental, as if the world might have missed it altogether. Even the *Discourse of Vulgar Errors*, the longest and most elaborate of his works, is entirely discursive and occasional, coming to an end with no natural conclusion, but only because the writer chose to leave off just there; and few probably have been the readers of the book as a consecutive whole. At times indeed we seem to have in it observations only, or notes, preliminary to some more orderly composition. Dip into it: read, for instance, the chapter "Of the Ring-finger," or the chapters "Of the Long Life of the Deer," and on the "Pictures of Mermaids, Unicorns, and some Others," and the part will certainly seem more than the whole. Try to read it through, and you will soon feel cloyed;—miss very likely, its real worth to the fancy, the literary fancy (which finds its pleasure in inventive word and phrase) and become dull to the really vivid beauties of a book so lengthy, but with no real evolution. Though there are words, phrases, constructions innumerable, which remind one how much the work initiated in France by Madame de Rambouillet—work, done for England, we may think perhaps imperfectly, in the next century by Johnson and others—was really needed; yet the capacities of Browne's manner of writing, coming as it did so directly from the man, are felt even in his treatment of matters of science. As with Buffon, his full, ardent, sympathetic vocabulary, the poetry of his language, a poetry inherent in its elementary particles—the word, the epithet—helps to keep his eye, and the eye of the reader, on the object before it, and conduces directly to the purpose of the naturalist, the observer.

22. But, only one half observation, its other half consisting of very out-of-the-way book-lore, this work displays Browne still in the character of the antiquary, as that age understood him. He is a kind of Elias Ashmole, but dealing with natural objects; which are for him, in the first place, and apart from the remote religious hints and intimations they carry with them, curiosities. He seems to have no true sense of natural law, as Bacon understood it; nor even of that immanent reason in the natural world, which the Platonic tradition supposes. "Things are really true," he says, "as they correspond unto God's conception; and have so much verity as they hold of conformity unto that intellect, in whose idea they had their first determinations." But, actually, what he is busy in the record of, are matters more or less of the nature of caprices; as if things, after all, were significant of their higher verity only at random, and in a sort of surprises, like music in old instruments suddenly touched into

sound by a wandering finger, among the lumber of people's houses. Nature, "the art of God," as he says, varying a little a phrase used also by Hobbes, in a work printed later—Nature, he seems to protest, is only a little less magical, its processes only a little less in the way of alchemy, than you had supposed. We feel that, as with that disturbed age in England generally (and it is here that he, with it, is so interesting, curious, old-world, and unlike ourselves) his supposed experience might at any moment be broken in upon by a hundred forms of a natural magic, only not quite so marvellous as that older sort of magic, or alchemy, he is at so much pains to expose; and the large promises of which, its large words too, he still regretfully enjoys.

23. And yet the *Discourse of Vulgar Errors*, seeming, as it often does, to be a serious refutation of fairy tales—arguing, for instance, against the literal truth of the poetic statement that "The pigeon hath no gall," and such questions as "Whether men weigh heavier dead than alive?" being characteristic questions— is designed, with much ambition, under its pedantic Greek title *Pseudodoxia Epidemica*, as a criticism, a cathartic, an instrument for the clarifying of the intellect. He begins from "that first error in Paradise," wondering much at "man's deceivability in his perfection,"—"at such gross deceit." He enters in this connexion, with a kind of poetry of scholasticism which may interest the student of *Paradise Lost*, into what we may call the intellectual and moral by-play of the situation of the first man and woman in Paradise, with strange queries about it. Did Adam, for instance, already know of the fall of the Angels? Did he really believe in death, till Abel died? It is from Julius Scaliger that he takes his motto, to the effect that the true knowledge of things must be had from things themselves, not from books; and he seems as seriously concerned as Bacon to dissipate the crude impressions of a false "common sense," of false science, and a fictitious authority. Inverting, oddly, Plato's theory that all learning is but reminiscence, he reflects with a sigh how much of oblivion must needs be involved in the getting of any true knowledge. "Men that adore times past, consider not that those times were once present (that is, as our own are) and ourselves unto those to come, as they unto us at present." That, surely, coming from one both by temperament and habit so great an antiquary, has the touch of something like an influence in the atmosphere of the time. That there was any actual connexion between Browne's work and Bacon's is but a surmise. Yet we almost seem to hear Bacon when Browne discourses on the "use of doubts, and the advantages which might be derived from drawing up a calendar of doubts, falsehoods, and popular errors;" and, as from Bacon, one gets the impression that men really have been very much the prisoners of their own crude or pedantic terms, notions, associations; that they have been very indolent in testing very simple matters—with a wonderful kind of

"supinity," as he calls it. In Browne's chapter on the "Sources of Error," again, we may trace much resemblance to Bacon's striking doctrine of the *Idola*, the "shams" men fall down and worship. Taking source respectively, from the "common infirmity of human nature," from the "erroneous disposition of the people," from "confident adherence to authority," the errors which Browne chooses to deal with may be registered as identical with Bacon's *Idola Tribus, Fori, Theatri*; the idols of our common human nature; of the vulgar, when they get together; and of the learned, when they get together.

24. But of the fourth species of error noted by Bacon, the *Idola Specus*, the Idols of the Cave, that whole tribe of illusions, which are "bred amongst the weeds and tares of one's own brain," Browne tells us nothing by way of criticism; was himself, rather, a lively example of their operation. Throw those illusions, those "idols," into concrete or personal form, suppose them introduced among the other forces of an active intellect, and you have Sir Thomas Browne himself. The sceptical inquirer who rises from his cathartic, his purging of error, a believer in the supernatural character of pagan oracles, and a cruel judge of supposed witches, must still need as much as ever that elementary conception of the right method and the just limitations of knowledge, by power of which he should not just strain out a single error here or there, but make a final precipitate of fallacy.

25. And yet if the temperament had been deducted from Browne's work—that inherent and strongly marked way of deciding things, which has guided with so surprising effect the musings of the *Letter to a Friend*, and the *Urn-Burial*— we should probably have remembered him little. Pity! some may think, for himself at least, that he had not lived earlier, and still believed in the mandrake, for instance; its fondness for places of execution, and its human cries "on eradication, with hazard of life to them that pull it up." "In philosophy," he observes, meaning to contrast his free-thinking in that department with his orthodoxy in religion—in philosophy, "where truth seems double-faced, there is no man more paradoxical than myself:" which is true, we may think, in a further sense than he meant, and that it was the "paradoxical" that he actually preferred. Happy, at all events, he still remained—undisturbed and happy—in a hundred native prepossessions, some certainly valueless, some of them perhaps invaluable. And while one feels that no real logic of fallacies has been achieved by him, one feels still more how little the construction of that branch of logical inquiry really helps men's minds; fallacy, like truth itself, being a matter so dependent on innate gift of apprehension, so extra-logical and personal; the original perception counting for almost everything, the mere inference for so little! Yes! "A man may be in as just possession of truth as of a city, and yet be forced to surrender," even in controversies not necessarily maladroit.

26. The really stirring poetry of science is not in guesses, or facile divinations about it, but in its larger ascertained truths—the order of infinite space, the slow method and vast results of infinite time. For Browne, however, the sense of poetry which so overmasters his scientific procedure, depends chiefly on its vaguer possibilities; the empirical philosophy, even after Bacon, being still dominated by a temper, resultant from the general unsettlement of men's minds at the Reformation, which may be summed up in the famous question of Montaigne—*Que sçais-je?* The cold-blooded method of observation and experiment was creeping but slowly over the domain of science; and such unreclaimed portions of it as the phenomena of magnetism had an immense fascination for men like Browne and Digby. Here, in those parts of natural philosophy "but yet in discovery," "the America and untravelled parts of truth," lay for them the true prospect of science, like the new world itself to a geographical discoverer such as Raleigh. And welcome as one of the minute hints of that country far ahead of them, the strange bird, or floating fragment of unfamiliar vegetation, which met those early navigators, there was a certain fantastic experiment, in which, as was alleged, Paracelsus had been lucky. For Browne and others it became the crucial type of the kind of agency in nature which, as they conceived, it was the proper function of science to reveal in larger operation. "The subject of my last letter," says Dr. Henry Power, then a student, writing to Browne in 1648, the last year of Charles the First, "being so high and noble a piece of chemistry, invites me once more to request an experimental eviction of it from yourself; and I hope you will not chide my importunity in this petition, or be angry at my so frequent knockings at your door to obtain a grant of so great and admirable a mystery." What the enthusiastic young student expected from Browne, so high and noble a piece of chemistry, was the "re-individualling of an incinerated plant"—a violet, turning to freshness, and smelling sweet again, out of its ashes, under some genially fitted conditions of the chemic art.

27. *Palingenesis*, resurrection, effected by orderly prescription—the "re-individualling" of an "incinerated organism"—is a subject which affords us a natural transition to the little book of the *Hydriotaphia*, or *Treatise of Urn-Burial*—about fifty or sixty pages—which, together with a very singular letter not printed till after Browne's death, is perhaps, after all, the best justification of Browne's literary reputation, as it were his own curiously figured urn, and treasure-place of immortal memory.

28. In its first presentation to the public this letter was connected with Browne's *Christian Morals*; but its proper and sympathetic collocation would be rather with the *Urn-Burial*, of which it is a kind of prelude, or strikes the keynote. He is writing in a very complex situation—to a friend, upon

occasion of the death of a common friend. The deceased apparently had been little known to Browne himself till his recent visits, while the intimate friend to whom he is writing had been absent at the time; and the leading motive of Browne's letter is the deep impression he has received during those visits, of a sort of physical beauty in the coming of death, with which he still surprises and moves his reader. There had been, in this case, a tardiness and reluctancy in the circumstances of dissolution, which had permitted him, in the character of a physician, as it were to assist at the spiritualising of the bodily frame by natural process; a wonderful new type of a kind of mortified grace being evolved by the way. The spiritual body had anticipated the formal moment of death; the alert soul, in that tardy decay, changing its vesture gradually, and as if piece by piece. The infinite future had invaded this life perceptibly to the senses, like the ocean felt far inland up a tidal river. Nowhere, perhaps, is the attitude of questioning awe on the threshold of another life displayed with the expressiveness of this unique morsel of literature; though there is something of the same kind, in another than the literary medium, in the delicate monumental sculpture of the early Tuscan School, as also in many of the designs of William Blake, often, though unconsciously, much in sympathy with those unsophisticated Italian workmen. With him, as with them, and with the writer of the *Letter to a Friend upon the occasion of the death of his intimate Friend,*—so strangely! the visible function of death is but to refine, to detach from aught that is vulgar. And this elfin letter, really an impromptu epistle to a friend, affords the best possible light on the general temper of the man who could be moved by the accidental discovery of those old urns at Walsingham—funeral relics of "Romans, or Britons Romanised which had learned Roman customs"—to the composition of that wonderful book the *Hydriotaphia*. He had drawn up a short account of the circumstance at the moment; but it was after ten years' brooding that he put forth the finished treatise, dedicated to an eminent collector of ancient coins and other rarities, with congratulations that he "can daily command the view of so many imperial faces," and (by way of frontispiece) with one of the urns, "drawn with a coal taken out of it and found among the burnt bones." The discovery had resuscitated for him a whole world of latent observation, from life, from out-of-the-way reading, from the natural world, and fused into a composition, which with all its quaintness we may well pronounce classical, all the heterogeneous elements of that singular mind. The desire to "record these risen ashes and not to let them be buried twice among us," had set free, in his manner of conceiving things, something not wholly analysable, something that may be properly called genius, which shapes his use of common words to stronger and deeper senses, in a way unusual in prose writing. Let the reader, for instance, trace his peculiarly sensitive use of the epithets *thin* and *dark*, both here and in the *Letter to a Friend*.

29. Upon what a grand note he can begin and end chapter or paragraph! "When the funeral pyre was out, and the last valediction over:"—"And a large part of the earth is still in the urn unto us." Dealing with a very vague range of feelings, it is his skill to associate them to very definite objects. Like the Soul, in Blake's design, "exploring the recesses of the tomb," he carries a light, the light of the poetic faith which he cannot put off him, into those dark places, "the abode of worms and pismires," peering round with a boundless curiosity and no fear; noting the various casuistical considerations of men's last form of self-love; all those whims of humanity as a "student of perpetuity," the mortuary customs of all nations, which, from their very closeness to our human nature, arouse in most minds only a strong feeling of distaste. There is something congruous with the impassive piety of the man in his waiting on accident from without to take start for the work, which, of all his work, is most truly touched by the "divine spark." Delightsome as its eloquence is actually found to be, that eloquence is attained out of a certain difficulty and halting crabbedness of expression; the wretched punctuation of the piece being not the only cause of its impressing the reader with the notion that he is but dealing with a collection of notes for a more finished composition, and of a different kind; perhaps a purely erudite treatise on its subject, with detachment of all personal colour now adhering to it. Out of an atmosphere of all-pervading oddity and quaintness—the quaintness of mind which reflects that this disclosing of the urns of the ancients hath "left unto our view some parts which they never beheld themselves"—arises a work really ample and grand, nay! classical, as I said, by virtue of the effectiveness with which it fixes a type in literature; as, indeed, at its best, romantic literature (and Browne is genuinely romantic) in every period attains classical quality, giving true measure of the very limited value of those well-worn critical distinctions. And though the *Urn-Burial* certainly has much of the character of a poem, yet one is never allowed to forget that it was designed, candidly, as a scientific treatise on one department of ancient "culture" (as much so as Guichard's curious old French book on *Divers Manners of Burial*) and was the fruit of much labour, in the way especially of industrious selection from remote and difficult writers; there being then few or no handbooks, or anything like our modern shortcuts to varied knowledge. Quite unaffectedly, a curious learning saturates, with a kind of grey and aged colour most apt and congruous with the subject-matter, all the thoughts that arise in him. His great store of reading, so freely displayed, he uses almost as poetically as Milton; like him, profiting often by the mere sonorous effect of some heroic or ancient name, which he can adapt to that

same sort of learned sweetness of cadence with which so many of his single sentences are made to fall upon the ear.

30. Pope Gregory, that great religious poet, requested by certain eminent persons to send them some of those relics he sought for so devoutly in all the lurking-places of old Rome, took up, it is said, a portion of common earth, and delivered it to the messengers; and, on their expressing surprise at such a gift, pressed the earth together in his hand, whereupon the sacred blood of the Martyrs was beheld flowing out between his fingers. The veneration of relics became a part of Christian (as some may think it a part of natural) religion. All over Rome we may count how much devotion in fine art is owing to it; and, through all ugliness or superstition, its intention still speaks clearly to serious minds. The poor dead bones, ghastly and forbidding:—we know what Shakespeare would have felt about them.—"Beat not the bones of the buried: when he breathed, he was a man!" And it is with something of a similar feeling that Browne is full, on the common and general ground of humanity; an awe-stricken sympathy with those, whose bones "lie at the mercies of the living," strong enough to unite all his various chords of feeling into a single strain of impressive and genuine poetry. His real interest is in what may be called the curiosities of our common humanity. As another might be moved at the sight of Alexander's bones, or Saint Edmund's, or Saint Cecilia's, so he is full of a fine poetical excitement at such lowly relics as the earth hides almost everywhere beneath our feet. But it is hardly fair to take our leave amid these grievous images of so happy a writer as Sir Thomas Browne; so great a lover of the open air, under which much of his life was passed. His work, late one night, draws to a natural close:—"To keep our eyes open longer," he bethinks himself suddenly, "were but to act our Antipodes. The huntsmen are up in America!"

31. What a fund of open-air cheerfulness, there! in turning to sleep. Still, even when we are dealing with a writer in whom mere style counts for so much as with Browne, it is impossible to ignore his matter; and it is with religion he is really occupied from first to last, hardly less than Richard Hooker. And his religion, too, after all, was a religion of cheerfulness: he has no great consciousness of evil in things, and is no fighter. His religion, if one may say so, was all profit to him; among other ways, in securing an absolute staidness and placidity of temper, for the intellectual work which was the proper business of his life. His contributions to "evidence," in the *Religio Medici*, for instance, hardly tell, because he writes out of view of a really philosophical criticism. What does tell in him, in this direction, is the witness he brings to men's instinct of survival—the "intimations of immortality," as Wordsworth terms them, which were natural with him in surprising force. As was said of Jean Paul, his

special subject was the immortality of the soul; with an assurance as personal, as fresh and original, as it was, on the one hand, in those old half-civilised people who had deposited the urns; on the other hand, in the cynical French poet of the nineteenth century, who did not think, but knew, that *his* soul was imperishable. He lived in an age in which that philosophy made a great stride which ends with Hume; and his lesson, if we may be pardoned for taking away a "lesson" from so ethical a writer, is the force of men's temperaments in the management of opinion, their own or that of others;—that it is not merely different degrees of bare intellectual power which cause men to approach in different degrees to this or that intellectual programme. Could he have foreseen the mature result of that mechanical analysis which Bacon had applied to nature, and Hobbes to the mind of man, there is no reason to think that he would have surrendered his own chosen hypothesis concerning them. He represents, in an age, the intellectual powers of which tend strongly to agnosticism, that class of minds to which the supernatural view of things is still credible. The non-mechanical theory of nature has had its grave adherents since: to the non-mechanical theory of man—that he is in contact with a moral order on a different plane from the mechanical order—thousands, of the most various types and degrees of intellectual power, always adhere; a fact worth the consideration of all ingenuous thinkers, if (as is certainly the case with colour, music, number, for instance) there may be whole regions of fact, the recognition of which belongs to one and not to another, which people may possess in various degrees; for the knowledge of which, therefore, one person is dependent upon another; and in relation to which the appropriate means of cognition must lie among the elements of what we call individual temperament, so that what looks like a pre-judgment may be really a legitimate apprehension. "Men are what they are," and are not wholly at the mercy of formal conclusions from their formally limited premises. Browne passes his whole life in observation and inquiry: he is a genuine investigator, with every opportunity: the mind of the age all around him seems passively yielding to an almost foregone intellectual result, to a philosophy of disillusion. But he thinks all that a prejudice; and not from any want of intellectual power certainly, but from some inward consideration, some afterthought, from the antecedent gravitation of his own general character—or, will you say? from that unprecipitated infusion of fallacy in him—he fails to draw, unlike almost all the rest of the world, the conclusion ready to hand.

1886.

from SHAKESPEARE'S ENGLISH KINGS

[*On Richard the Second*]

[...] One gracious prerogative, certainly, Shakespeare's English kings possess: they are a very eloquent company, and Richard is the most sweet-tongued of them all. In no other play perhaps is there such a flush of those gay, fresh, variegated flowers of speech—colour and figure, not lightly attached to, but fused into, the very phrase itself—which Shakespeare cannot help dispensing to his characters, as in this "play of the Deposing of King Richard the Second," an exquisite poet if he is nothing else, from first to last, in light and gloom alike, able to see all things poetically, to give a poetic turn to his conduct of them, and refreshing with his golden language the tritest aspects of that ironic contrast between the pretensions of a king and the actual necessities of his destiny. What a garden of words! With him, blank verse, infinitely graceful, deliberate, musical in inflexion, becomes indeed a true "verse royal," that rhyming lapse, which to the Shakespearian ear, at least in youth, came as the last touch of refinement on it, being here doubly appropriate. His eloquence blends with that fatal beauty, of which he was so frankly aware, so amiable to his friends, to his wife, of the effects of which on the people his enemies were so much afraid, on which Shakespeare himself dwells so attentively as the "royal blood" comes and goes in the face with his rapid changes of temper. As happens with sensitive natures, it attunes him to a congruous suavity of manners, by which anger itself became flattering: it blends with his merely youthful hopefulness and high spirits, his sympathetic love for gay people, things, apparel—"his cote of gold and stone, valued at thirty thousand marks," the novel Italian fashions he preferred, as also with those real amiabilities that made people forget the darker touches of his character, but never tire of the pathetic rehearsal of his fall, the meekness of which would have seemed merely abject in a less graceful performer.

7. Yet it is only fair to say that in the painstaking "revival" of *King Richard the Second*, by the late Charles Kean, those who were very young thirty years ago were afforded much more than Shakespeare's play could ever have been before—the very person of the king based on the stately old portrait in Westminster Abbey, "the earliest extant contemporary likeness of any English sovereign," the grace, the winning pathos, the sympathetic voice of the player, the tasteful archæology confronting vulgar modern London with a scenic reproduction, for once really agreeable, of the London of Chaucer. In

the hands of Kean the play became like an exquisite performance on the violin.

8. The long agony of one so gaily painted by nature's self, from his "tragic abdication" till the hour in which he

> Sluiced out his innocent soul thro' streams of blood,

was for playwrights a subject ready to hand, and became early the theme of a popular drama, of which some have fancied surviving favourite fragments in the rhymed parts of Shakespeare's work.

> The king Richard of Yngland
> Was in his flowris then regnand:
> But his flowris efter sone
> Fadyt, and ware all undone:—

says the old chronicle. Strangely enough, Shakespeare supposes him an over-confident believer in that divine right of kings, of which people in Shakespeare's time were coming to hear so much; a general right, sealed to him (so Richard is made to think) as an ineradicable personal gift by the touch—stream rather, over head and breast and shoulders—of the "holy oil" of his consecration at Westminster; not, however, through some oversight, the genuine balm used at the coronation of his successor, given, according to legend, by the Blessed Virgin to Saint Thomas of Canterbury. Richard himself found that, it was said, among other forgotten treasures, at the crisis of his changing fortunes, and vainly sought reconsecration therewith—understood, wistfully, that it was reserved for his happier rival. And yet his coronation, by the pageantry, the amplitude, the learned care, of its order, so lengthy that the king, then only eleven years of age, and fasting, as a communicant at the ceremony, was carried away in a faint, fixed the type under which it has ever since continued. And nowhere is there so emphatic a reiteration as in *Richard the Second* of the sentiment which those singular rites were calculated to produce.

> Not all the water in the rough rude sea
> Can wash the balm from an anointed king,—

as supplementing another, almost supernatural, right.—"Edward's seven sons," of whom Richard's father was one,

> Were as seven phials of his sacred blood.

But this, too, in the hands of Shakespeare, becomes for him, like any other of those fantastic, ineffectual, easily discredited, personal graces, as capricious in its operation on men's wills as merely physical beauty, kindling himself to eloquence indeed, but only giving double pathos to insults which "barbarism itself" might have pitied—the dust in his face, as he returns, through the streets of London, a prisoner in the train of his victorious enemy.

> How soon my sorrow hath destroyed my face!

he cries, in that most poetic invention of the mirror scene, which does but reinforce again that physical charm which all confessed. The sense of "divine right" in kings is found to act not so much as a secret of power over others, as of infatuation to themselves. And of all those personal gifts the one which alone never altogether fails him is just that royal utterance, his appreciation of the poetry of his own hapless lot, an eloquent self-pity, infecting others in spite of themselves, till they too become irresistibly eloquent about him.

9. In the Roman Pontifical, of which the order of Coronation is really a part, there is no form for the inverse process, no rite of "degradation," such as that by which an offending priest or bishop may be deprived, if not of the essential quality of "orders," yet, one by one, of its outward dignities. It is as if Shakespeare had had in mind some such inverted rite, like those old ecclesiastical or military ones, by which human hardness, or human justice, adds the last touch of unkindness to the execution of its sentences, in the scene where Richard "deposes" himself, as in some long, agonising ceremony, reflectively drawn out, with an extraordinary refinement of intelligence and variety of piteous appeal, but also with a felicity of poetic invention, which puts these pages into a very select class, with the finest "vermeil and ivory" work of Chatterton or Keats.

> Fetch hither Richard that in common view
> He may surrender!—

And Richard more than concurs: he throws himself into the part, realises a type, falls gracefully as on the world's stage.—Why is he sent for?

> To do that office of thine own good will
> Which tired majesty did make thee offer.—
>
> Now mark me! how I will undo myself.

from SHAKESPEARE'S ENGLISH KINGS

10. "Hath Bolingbroke deposed thine intellect?" the Queen asks him, on his way to the Tower:—

> Hath Bolingbroke
> Deposed thine intellect? hath he been in thy heart?

And in truth, but for that adventitious poetic gold, it would be only "plume-plucked Richard."—

> I find myself a traitor with the rest,
> For I have given here my soul's consent
> To undeck the pompous body of a king.

He is duly reminded, indeed, how

> That which in mean men we entitle patience
> Is pale cold cowardice in noble breasts.

Yet at least within the poetic bounds of Shakespeare's play, through Shakespeare's bountiful gifts, his desire seems fulfilled.—

> O! that I were as great
> As is my grief.

And his grief becomes nothing less than a central expression of all that in the revolutions of Fortune's wheel goes *down* in the world.

11. No! Shakespeare's kings are not, nor are meant to be, great men: rather, little or quite ordinary humanity, thrust upon greatness, with those pathetic results, the natural self-pity of the weak heightened in them into irresistible appeal to others as the net result of their royal prerogative. One after another, they seem to lie composed in Shakespeare's embalming pages, with just that touch of nature about them, making the whole world akin, which has infused into their tombs at Westminster a rare poetic grace. It is that irony of kingship, the sense that it is in its happiness child's play, in its sorrows, after all, but children's grief, which gives its finer accent to all the changeful feeling of these wonderful speeches:—the great meekness of the graceful, wild creature, tamed at last.—

> Give Richard leave to live till Richard die!

his somewhat abject fear of death, turning to acquiescence at moments of extreme weariness:—

> My large kingdom for a little grave!
> A little little grave, an obscure grave!—

his religious appeal in the last reserve, with its bold reference to the judgment of Pilate, as he thinks once more of his "anointing."

12. And as happens with children he attains contentment finally in the merely passive recognition of superior strength, in the naturalness of the result of the great battle as a matter of course, and experiences something of the royal prerogative of poetry to obscure, or at least to attune and soften men's griefs. As in some sweet anthem of Handel, the sufferer, who put finger to the organ under the utmost pressure of mental conflict, extracts a kind of peace at last from the mere skill with which he sets his distress to music.—

> Beshrew thee, Cousin, that didst lead me forth
> Of that sweet way I was in to despair!

13. "With Cain go wander through the shades of night!"—cries the new king to the gaoler Exton, dissimulating his share in the murder he is thought to have suggested; and in truth there is something of the murdered Abel about Shakespeare's Richard. The fact seems to be that he died of "waste and a broken heart:" it was by way of proof that his end had been a natural one that, stifling a real fear of the face, the face of Richard, on men's minds, with the added pleading now of all dead faces, Henry exposed the corpse to general view; and Shakespeare, in bringing it on the stage, in the last scene of his play, does but follow out the motive with which he has emphasised Richard's physical beauty all through it—that "most beauteous inn," as the Queen says quaintly, meeting him on the way to death—residence, then soon to be deserted, of that wayward, frenzied, but withal so affectionate soul. Though the body did not go to Westminster immediately, his tomb,

> That small model of the barren earth
> Which serves as paste and cover to our bones,[1]

---

[1] Perhaps a *double entendre*:—of any ordinary grave, as comprising, in effect, the whole small earth now left to its occupant: or, of such a tomb as Richard's in particular, with its actual model, or effigy, of the clay of him. Both senses are so characteristic that it would be a pity to lose either.

from SHAKESPEARE'S ENGLISH KINGS

the effigy clasping the hand of his youthful consort, was already prepared there, with "rich gilding and ornaments," monument of poetic regret, for Queen Anne of Bohemia, not of course the "Queen" of Shakespeare, who however seems to have transferred to this second wife something of Richard's wildly proclaimed affection for the first. In this way, through the connecting link of that sacred spot, our thoughts once more associate Richard's two fallacious prerogatives, his personal beauty and his "anointing."

14. According to Johnson, *Richard the Second* is one of those plays which Shakespeare has "apparently revised;" and how doubly delightful Shakespeare is where he seems to have revised! "Would that he had blotted a thousand"—a thousand hasty phrases, we may venture once more to say with his earlier critic, now that the tiresome German superstition has passed away which challenged us to a dogmatic faith in the plenary verbal inspiration of every one of Shakespeare's clowns. Like some melodiously contending anthem of Handel's, I said, of Richard's meek "undoing" of himself in the mirror-scene; and, in fact, the play of *Richard the Second* does, like a musical composition, possess a certain concentration of all its parts, a simple continuity, an evenness in execution, which are rare in the great dramatist. With *Romeo and Juliet*, that perfect symphony (symphony of three independent poetic forms set in a grander one[1] which it is the merit of German criticism to have detected) it belongs to a small group of plays, where, by happy birth and consistent evolution, dramatic form approaches to something like the unity of a lyrical ballad, a lyric, a song, a single strain of music. Which sort of poetry we are to account the highest, is perhaps a barren question. Yet if, in art generally, unity of impression is a note of what is perfect, then lyric poetry, which in spite of complex structure often preserves the unity of a single passionate ejaculation, would rank higher than dramatic poetry, where, especially to the reader, as distinguished from the spectator assisting at a theatrical performance, there must always be a sense of the effort necessary to keep the various parts from flying asunder, a sense of imperfect continuity, such as the older criticism vainly sought to obviate by the rule of the dramatic "unities." It follows that a play attains artistic perfection just in proportion as it approaches that unity of lyrical effect, as if a song or ballad were still lying at the root of it, all the various expression of the conflict of character and circumstance falling at last into the compass of a single melody, or musical theme. As, historically, the earliest classic drama arose out of the chorus, from which this or that person, this or that episode, detached itself, so, into the unity of a choric song the perfect drama ever tends to return, its intellectual scope deepened, complicated, enlarged,

---

1 The Sonnet: the Aubade: the Epithalamium.

but still with an unmistakable singleness, or identity, in its impression on the mind. Just there, in that vivid single impression left on the mind when all is over, not in any mechanical limitation of time and place, is the secret of the "unities"—the true imaginative unity—of the drama.

1889.

DANTE GABRIEL ROSSETTI

It was characteristic of a poet who had ever something about him of mystic isolation, and will still appeal perhaps, though with a name it may seem now established in English literature, to a special and limited audience, that some of his poems had won a kind of exquisite fame before they were in the full sense published. *The Blessed Damozel*, although actually printed twice before the year 1870, was eagerly circulated in manuscript; and the volume which it now opens came at last to satisfy a long-standing curiosity as to the poet, whose pictures also had become an object of the same peculiar kind of interest. For those poems were the work of a painter, understood to belong to, and to be indeed the leader, of a new school then rising into note; and the reader of to-day may observe already, in *The Blessed Damozel*, written at the age of eighteen, a prefigurement of the chief characteristics of that school, as he will recognise in it also, in proportion as he really knows Rossetti, many of the characteristics which are most markedly personal and his own. Common to that school and to him, and in both alike of primary significance, was the quality of sincerity, already felt as one of the charms of that earliest poem—a perfect sincerity, taking effect in the deliberate use of the most direct and unconventional expression, for the conveyance of a poetic sense which recognised no conventional standard of what poetry was called upon to be. At a time when poetic originality in England might seem to have had its utmost play, here was certainly one new poet more, with a structure and music of verse, a vocabulary, an accent, unmistakably novel, yet felt to be no mere tricks of manner adopted with a view to forcing attention—an accent which might rather count as the very seal of reality on one man's own proper speech; as that speech itself was the wholly natural expression of certain wonderful things he really felt and saw. Here was one, who had a matter to present to his readers, to himself at least, in the first instance, so valuable, so real and definite, that his primary aim, as regards form or expression in his verse, would be but its exact equivalence to those *data* within. That he had this gift of transparency in language—the control of a style which did but obediently shift and shape itself to the mental motion, as a well-trained hand can follow on the tracing-paper the outline of an original drawing below it, was proved afterwards by a volume of typically perfect translations from the delightful but difficult "early Italian poets:" such transparency being indeed the secret of all genuine style, of all such style as can truly belong to one man and not to another. His own meaning was always personal and even recondite, in a certain sense learned and casuistical, sometimes complex or obscure; but the term was always, one could see, deliberately chosen from many competitors, as the just transcript of that peculiar phase of soul which he alone knew, precisely as he knew it.

2. One of the peculiarities of *The Blessed Damozel* was a definiteness of sensible imagery, which seemed almost grotesque to some, and was strange, above all, in a theme so profoundly visionary. The gold bar of heaven from which she leaned, her hair yellow like ripe corn, are but examples of a general treatment, as naively detailed as the pictures of those early painters contemporary with Dante, who has shown a similar care for minute and definite imagery in his verse; there, too, in the very midst of profoundly mystic vision. Such definition of outline is indeed one among many points in which Rossetti resembles the great Italian poet, of whom, led to him at first by family circumstances, he was ever a lover—a "servant and singer," faithful as Dante, "of Florence and of Beatrice"—with some close inward conformities of genius also, independent of any mere circumstances of education. It was said by a critic of the last century, not wisely though agreeably to the practice of his time, that poetry rejoices in abstractions. For Rossetti, as for Dante, without question on his part, the first condition of the poetic way of seeing and presenting things is particularisation. "Tell me now," he writes, for Villon's

> Dictes-moy où, n'en quel pays,
> Est Flora, la belle Romaine—

> Tell me now, in what hidden way is
> Lady Flora the lovely Roman:

—"way," in which one might actually chance to meet her; the unmistakably poetic effect of the couplet in English being dependent on the definiteness of that single word (though actually lighted on in the search after a difficult double rhyme) for which every one else would have written, like Villon himself, a more general one, just equivalent to place or region.

3. And this delight in concrete definition is allied with another of his conformities to Dante, the really imaginative vividness, namely, of his personifications—his hold upon them, or rather their hold upon him, with the force of a Frankenstein, when once they have taken life from him. Not Death only and Sleep, for instance, and the winged spirit of Love, but certain particular aspects of them, a whole "populace" of special hours and places, "the hour" even "which might have been, yet might not be," are living creatures, with hands and eyes and articulate voices.

> Stands it not by the door—
> Love's Hour—till she and I shall meet;
> With bodiless form and unapparent feet
> That cast no shadow yet before,
> Though round its head the dawn begins to pour
> The breath that makes day sweet?—
>
> Nay, why
> Name the dead hours? I mind them well:
> Their ghosts in many darkened doorways dwell
> With desolate eyes to know them by.

4. Poetry as a *mania*—one of Plato's two higher forms of "divine" mania—has, in all its species, a mere insanity incidental to it, the "defect of its quality," into which it may lapse in its moment of weakness; and the insanity which follows a vivid poetic anthropomorphism like that of Rossetti may be noted here and there in his work, in a forced and almost grotesque materialising of abstractions, as Dante also became at times a mere subject of the scholastic realism of the Middle Age.

5. In *Love's Nocturn* and *The Stream's Secret*, congruously perhaps with a certain feverishness of soul in the moods they present, there is at times a near approach (may it be said?) to such insanity of realism—

> Pity and love shall burn
> In her pressed cheek and cherishing hands;
> And from the living spirit of love that stands
> Between her lips to soothe and yearn,
> Each separate breath shall clasp me round in turn
> And loose my spirit's bands.

But even if we concede this; even if we allow, in the very plan of those two compositions, something of the literary conceit—what exquisite, what novel flowers of poetry, we must admit them to be, as they stand! In the one, what a delight in all the natural beauty of water, all its details for the eye of a painter; in the other, how subtle and fine the imaginative hold upon all the secret ways of sleep and dreams! In both of them, with much the same attitude and tone, Love—sick and doubtful Love—would fain inquire of what lies below the surface of sleep, and below the water; stream or dream being forced to speak by Love's powerful "control"; and the poet would have it foretell the fortune, issue, and event of his wasting passion. Such artifices, indeed, were not unknown in the old Provençal poetry of which Dante had learned something. Only, in Rossetti at least, they are redeemed by a serious purpose, by that sincerity of his, which allies itself readily to a serious beauty, a sort of grandeur of literary workmanship, to a great style. One seems to hear there a really new kind of poetic utterance, with effects which have nothing else like them; as there is nothing else, for instance, like the narrative of Jacob's Dream in *Genesis*, or Blake's design of the Singing of the Morning Stars, or Addison's Nineteenth Psalm.

6. With him indeed, as in some revival of the old mythopœic age, common things—dawn, noon, night—are full of human or personal expression, full of sentiment. The lovely little sceneries scattered up and down his poems, glimpses of a landscape, not indeed of broad open-air effects, but rather that of a painter concentrated upon the picturesque effect of one or two selected objects at a time—the "hollow brimmed with mist," or the "ruined weir," as he sees it from one of the windows, or reflected in one of the mirrors of his "house of life" (the vignettes for instance seen by Rose Mary in the magic beryl) attest, by their very freshness and simplicity, to a pictorial or descriptive power in dealing with the inanimate world, which is certainly also one half of the charm, in that other, more remote and mystic, use of it. For with Rossetti this sense of lifeless nature, after all, is translated to a higher service, in which it does but incorporate itself with some phase of strong emotion. Every one understands how this may happen at critical moments of life; what a weirdly expressive soul may have crept, even in full noonday, into "the white-flower'd elder-thicket," when Godiva saw it "gleam through the Gothic archways in the wall," at the end of her terrible ride. To Rossetti it is so always, because to him life is a crisis at every moment. A sustained impressibility towards the mysterious conditions of man's everyday life, towards the very mystery itself in it, gives a singular gravity to all his work: those matters never became trite to him. But throughout, it is the ideal intensity of love—of love based upon a perfect yet peculiar type of physical or material beauty—which is enthroned in the midst of those mysterious powers; Youth and Death, Destiny and Fortune, Fame, Poetic Fame, Memory, Oblivion, and the like. Rossetti is one of those who, in the words of Mérimée, *se passionnent pour la passion*, one of Love's lovers.

7. And yet, again as with Dante, to speak of his ideal type of beauty as material, is partly misleading. Spirit and matter, indeed, have been for the most part opposed, with a false contrast or antagonism by schoolmen, whose artificial creation those abstractions really are. In our actual concrete experience, the two trains of phenomena which the words *matter* and *spirit* do but roughly distinguish, play inextricably into each other. Practically, the church of the Middle Age by its æsthetic worship, its sacramentalism, its real faith in the resurrection of the flesh, had set itself against that Manichean opposition

of spirit and matter, and its results in men's way of taking life; and in this, Dante is the central representative of its spirit. To him, in the vehement and impassioned heat of his conceptions, the material and the spiritual are fused and blent: if the spiritual attains the definite visibility of a crystal, what is material loses its earthiness and impurity. And here again, by force of instinct, Rossetti is one with him. His chosen type of beauty is one,

> Whose speech Truth knows not from her thought,
> Nor Love her body from her soul.

Like Dante, he knows no region of spirit which shall not be sensuous also, or material. The shadowy world, which he realises so powerfully, has still the ways and houses, the land and water, the light and darkness, the fire and flowers, that had so much to do in the moulding of those bodily powers and aspects which counted for so large a part of the soul, here.

8. For Rossetti, then, the great affections of persons to each other, swayed and determined, in the case of his highly pictorial genius, mainly by that so-called material loveliness, formed the great undeniable reality in things, the solid resisting substance, in a world where all beside might be but shadow. The fortunes of those affections—of the great love so determined; its casuistries, its languor sometimes; above all, its sorrows; its fortunate or unfortunate collisions with those other great matters; how it looks, as the long day of life goes round, in the light and shadow of them: all this, conceived with an abundant imagination, and a deep, a philosophic, reflectiveness, is the matter of his verse, and especially of what he designed as his chief poetic work, "a work to be called *The House of Life*," towards which the majority of his sonnets and songs were contributions.

9. The dwelling-place in which one finds oneself by chance or destiny, yet can partly fashion for oneself; never properly one's own at all, if it be changed too lightly; in which every object has its associations—the dim mirrors, the portraits, the lamps, the books, the hair-tresses of the dead and visionary magic crystals in the secret drawers, the names and words scratched on the windows, windows open upon prospects the saddest or the sweetest; the house one must quit, yet taking perhaps, how much of its quietly active light and colour along with us!—grown now to be a kind of raiment to one's body, as the body, according to Swedenborg, is but the raiment of the soul—under that image, the whole of Rossetti's work might count as a *House of Life*, of which he is but the "Interpreter." And it is a "haunted" house. A sense of power in love, defying distance, and those barriers which are so much more than physical distance, of unutterable desire penetrating into the world of sleep, however "lead-bound," was one of those anticipative notes obscurely struck in *The Blessed Damozel*, and, in his later work, makes him speak sometimes almost

like a believer in mesmerism. Dream-land, as we said, with its "phantoms of the body," deftly coming and going on love's service, is to him, in no mere fancy or figure of speech, a real country, a veritable expansion of, or addition to, our waking life; and he did well perhaps to wait carefully upon sleep, for the lack of it became mortal disease with him. One may even recognise a sort of morbid and over-hasty making-ready for death itself, which increases on him; thoughts concerning it, its imageries, coming with a frequency and importunity, in excess, one might think, of even the very saddest, quite wholesome wisdom.

10. And indeed the publication of his second volume of *Ballads and Sonnets* preceded his death by scarcely a twelvemonth. That volume bears witness to the reverse of any failure of power, or falling-off from his early standard of literary perfection, in every one of his then accustomed forms of poetry—the song, the sonnet, and the ballad. The newly printed sonnets, now completing *The House of Life*, certainly advanced beyond those earlier ones, in clearness; his dramatic power in the ballad, was here at its height; while one monumental, gnomic piece, *Soothsay*, testifies, more clearly even than the *Nineveh* of his first volume, to the reflective force, the dry reason, always at work behind his imaginative creations, which at no time dispensed with a genuine intellectual structure. For in matters of pure reflection also, Rossetti maintained the painter's sensuous clearness of conception; and this has something to do with the capacity, largely illustrated by his ballads, of telling some red-hearted story of impassioned action with effect.

11. Have there, in very deed, been ages, in which the external conditions of poetry such as Rossetti's were of more spontaneous growth than in our own? The archaic side of Rossetti's work, his preferences in regard to earlier poetry, connect him with those who have certainly thought so, who fancied they could have breathed more largely in the age of Chaucer, or of Ronsard, in one of those ages, in the words of Stendhal—*ces siècles de passions où les âmes pouvaient se livrer franchement à la plus haute exaltation, quand les passions qui font la possibilité comme les sujets des beaux arts existaient.* We may think, perhaps, that such old time as that has never really existed except in the fancy of poets; but it was to find it, that Rossetti turned so often from modern life to the chronicle of the past. Old Scotch history, perhaps beyond any other, is strong in the matter of heroic and vehement hatreds and love, the tragic Mary herself being but the perfect blossom of them; and it is from that history that Rossetti has taken the subjects of the two longer ballads of his second volume: of the three admirable ballads in it, *The King's Tragedy* (in which Rossetti has dexterously interwoven some relics of James's own exquisite early verse) reaching the highest level of dramatic success, and marking perfection, perhaps, in this kind of poetry; which, in the earlier volume, gave us, among other pieces, *Troy Town*, *Sister Helen*, and *Eden Bower*.

12. Like those earlier pieces, the ballads of the second volume bring with them the question of the poetic value of the "refrain"—

> Eden bower's in flower:
> And O the bower and the hour!

—and the like. Two of those ballads—*Troy Town* and *Eden Bower*, are terrible in theme; and the refrain serves, perhaps, to relieve their bold aim at the sentiment of terror. In *Sister Helen* again, the refrain has a real, and sustained purpose (being here duly varied also) and performs the part of a chorus, as the story proceeds. Yet even in these cases, whatever its effect may be in actual recitation, it may fairly be questioned, whether, to the mere reader their actual effect is not that of a positive interruption and drawback, at least in pieces so lengthy; and Rossetti himself, it would seem, came to think so, for in the shortest of his later ballads, *The White Ship*—that old true history of the generosity with which a youth, worthless in life, flung himself upon death—he was contented with a single utterance of the refrain, "given out" like the keynote or tune of a chant.

13. In *The King's Tragedy*, Rossetti has worked upon motive, broadly human (to adopt the phrase of popular criticism) such as one and all may realise. Rossetti, indeed, with all his self-concentration upon his own peculiar aim, by no means ignored those general interests which are external to poetry as he conceived it; as he has shown here and there, in this poetic, as also in pictorial, work. It was but that, in a life to be shorter even than the average, he found enough to occupy him in the fulfilment of a task, plainly "given him to do." Perhaps, if one had to name a single composition of his to readers desiring to make acquaintance with him for the first time, one would select: *The King's Tragedy*—that poem so moving, so popularly dramatic, and lifelike. Notwithstanding this, his work, it must be conceded, certainly through no narrowness or egotism, but in the faithfulness of a true workman to a vocation so emphatic, was mainly of the esoteric order. But poetry, at all times, exercises two distinct functions: it may reveal, it may unveil to every eye, the ideal aspects of common things, after Gray's way (though Gray too, it is well to remember, seemed in his own day, seemed even to Johnson, obscure) or it may actually add to the number of motives poetic and uncommon in themselves, by the imaginative creation of things that are ideal from their very birth. Rossetti did something, something excellent, of the former kind; but his characteristic, his really revealing work, lay in the adding to poetry of fresh poetic material, of a new order of phenomena, in the creation of a new ideal.

1883.

POSTSCRIPT

αἴνει δὲ παλαιὸν μὲν οἶνον, ἄνθεα δ᾽ ὕμνων νεωτέρων

The words, *classical* and *romantic*, although, like many other critical expressions, sometimes abused by those who have understood them too vaguely or too absolutely, yet define two real tendencies in the history of art and literature. Used in an exaggerated sense, to express a greater opposition between those tendencies than really exists, they have at times tended to divide people of taste into opposite camps. But in that *House Beautiful*, which the creative minds of all generations—the artists and those who have treated life in the spirit of art—are always building together, for the refreshment of the human spirit, these oppositions cease; and the *Interpreter* of the *House Beautiful*, the true æsthetic critic, uses these divisions, only so far as they enable him to enter into the peculiarities of the objects with which he has to do. The term *classical*, fixed, as it is, to a well-defined literature, and a well-defined group in art, is clear, indeed; but then it has often been used in a hard, and merely scholastic sense, by the praisers of what is old and accustomed, at the expense of what is new, by critics who would never have discovered for themselves the charm of any work, whether new or old, who value what is old, in art or literature, for its accessories, and chiefly for the conventional authority that has gathered about it—people who would never really have been made glad by any Venus fresh-risen from the sea, and who praise the Venus of old Greece and Rome, only because they fancy her grown now into something staid and tame.

2. And as the term, *classical*, has been used in a too absolute, and therefore in a misleading sense, so the term, *romantic*, has been used much too vaguely, in various accidental senses. The sense in which Scott is called a romantic writer is chiefly this; that, in opposition to the literary tradition of the last century, he loved strange adventure, and sought it in the Middle Age. Much later, in a Yorkshire village, the spirit of romanticism bore a more really characteristic fruit in the work of a young girl, Emily Brontë, the romance of *Wuthering Heights*; the figures of Hareton Earnshaw, of Catherine Linton, and of Heathcliffe—tearing open Catherine's grave, removing one side of her coffin, that he may really lie beside her in death—figures so passionate, yet woven on a background of delicately beautiful, moorland scenery, being typical examples of that spirit. In Germany, again, that spirit is shown less in Tieck, its professional representative, than in Meinhold, the author of *Sidonia the Sorceress* and the *Amber-Witch*. In Germany and France, within the last hundred years, the term has been used to describe a particular school of writers; and,

consequently, when Heine criticises the *Romantic School* in Germany—that movement which culminated in Goethe's *Goetz von Berlichingen*; or when Théophile Gautier criticises the romantic movement in France, where, indeed, it bore its most characteristic fruits, and its play is hardly yet over where, by a certain audacity, or *bizarrerie* of motive, united with faultless literary execution, it still shows itself in imaginative literature, they use the word, with an exact sense of special artistic qualities, indeed; but use it, nevertheless, with a limited application to the manifestation of those qualities at a particular period. But the romantic spirit is, in reality, an ever-present, an enduring principle, in the artistic temperament; and the qualities of thought and style which that, and other similar uses of the word *romantic* really indicate, are indeed but symptoms of a very continuous and widely working influence.

3. Though the words *classical* and *romantic*, then, have acquired an almost technical meaning, in application to certain developments of German and French taste, yet this is but one variation of an old opposition, which may be traced from the very beginning of the formation of European art and literature. From the first formation of anything like a standard of taste in these things, the restless curiosity of their more eager lovers necessarily made itself felt, in the craving for new motives, new subjects of interest, new modifications of style. Hence, the opposition between the classicists and the romanticists—between the adherents, in the culture of beauty, of the principles of liberty, and authority, respectively—of strength, and order or what the Greeks called κοσμιότης.

4. Sainte-Beuve, in the third volume of the *Causeries du Lundi*, has discussed the question, *What is meant by a classic?* It was a question he was well fitted to answer, having himself lived through many phases of taste, and having been in earlier life an enthusiastic member of the romantic school: he was also a great master of that sort of "philosophy of literature," which delights in tracing traditions in it, and the way in which various phases of thought and sentiment maintain themselves, through successive modifications, from epoch to epoch. His aim, then, is to give the word *classic* a wider and, as he says, a more generous sense than it commonly bears, to make it expressly *grandiose et flottant*; and, in doing this, he develops, in a masterly manner, those qualities of measure, purity, temperance, of which it is the especial function of classical art and literature, whatever meaning, narrower or wider, we attach to the term, to take care.

5. The charm, therefore, of what is classical, in art or literature, is that of the well-known tale, to which we can, nevertheless, listen over and over again, because it is told so well. To the absolute beauty of its artistic form, is added the accidental, tranquil, charm of familiarity. There are times, indeed, at which these charms fail to work on our spirits at all, because they fail to excite us.

"*Romanticism*," says Stendhal, "is the art of presenting to people the literary works which, in the actual state of their habits and beliefs, are capable of giving them the greatest possible pleasure; *classicism*, on the contrary, of presenting them with that which gave the greatest possible pleasure to their grandfathers." But then, beneath all changes of habits and beliefs, our love of that mere abstract proportion—of music—which what is classical in literature possesses, still maintains itself in the best of us, and what pleased our grandparents may at least tranquillise us. The "classic" comes to us out of the cool and quiet of other times, as the measure of what a long experience has shown will at least never displease us. And in the classical literature of Greece and Rome, as in the classics of the last century, the essentially classical element is that quality of order in beauty, which they possess, indeed, in a pre-eminent degree, and which impresses some minds to the exclusion of everything else in them.

6. It is the addition of strangeness to beauty, that constitutes the romantic character in art; and the desire of beauty being a fixed element in every artistic organisation, it is the addition of curiosity to this desire of beauty, that constitutes the romantic temper. Curiosity and the desire of beauty, have each their place in art, as in all true criticism. When one's curiosity is deficient, when one is not eager enough for new impressions, and new pleasures, one is liable to value mere academical proprieties too highly, to be satisfied with worn-out or conventional types, with the insipid ornament of Racine, or the prettiness of that later Greek sculpture, which passed so long for true Hellenic work; to miss those places where the handiwork of nature, or of the artist, has been most cunning; to find the most stimulating products of art a mere irritation. And when one's curiosity is in excess, when it overbalances the desire of beauty, then one is liable to value in works of art what is inartistic in them; to be satisfied with what is exaggerated in art, with productions like some of those of the romantic school in Germany; not to distinguish, jealously enough, between what is admirably done, and what is done not quite so well, in the writings, for instance, of Jean Paul. And if I had to give instances of these defects, then I should say, that Pope, in common with the age of literature to which he belonged, had too little curiosity, so that there is always a certain insipidity in the effect of his work, exquisite as it is; and, coming down to our own time, that Balzac had an excess of curiosity—curiosity not duly tempered with the desire of beauty.

7. But, however falsely those two tendencies may be opposed by critics, or exaggerated by artists themselves, they are tendencies really at work at all times in art, moulding it, with the balance sometimes a little on one side, sometimes a little on the other, generating, respectively, as the balance inclines on this side or that, two principles, two traditions, in art, and in literature so far as it

partakes of the spirit of art. If there is a great overbalance of curiosity, then, we have the grotesque in art: if the union of strangeness and beauty, under very difficult and complex conditions, be a successful one, if the union be entire, then the resultant beauty is very exquisite, very attractive. With a passionate care for beauty, the romantic spirit refuses to have it, unless the condition of strangeness be first fulfilled. Its desire is for a beauty born of unlikely elements, by a profound alchemy, by a difficult initiation, by the charm which wrings it even out of terrible things; and a trace of distortion, of the grotesque, may perhaps linger, as an additional element of expression, about its ultimate grace. Its eager, excited spirit will have strength, the grotesque, first of all—the trees shrieking as you tear off the leaves; for Jean Valjean, the long years of convict life; for Redgauntlet, the quicksands of Solway Moss; then, incorporate with this strangeness, and intensified by restraint, as much sweetness, as much beauty, as is compatible with that. *Énergique, frais, et dispos*—these, according to Sainte-Beuve, are the characteristics of a genuine classic—*les ouvrages anciens ne sont pas classiques parce qu'ils sont vieux, mais parce qu'ils sont énergiques, frais, et dispos*. Energy, freshness, intelligent and masterly disposition:—these are characteristics of Victor Hugo when his alchemy is complete, in certain figures, like Marius and Cosette, in certain scenes, like that in the opening of *Les Travailleurs de la Mer*, where Déruchette writes the name of *Gilliatt* in the snow, on Christmas morning; but always there is a certain note of strangeness discernible there, as well.

8. The essential elements, then, of the romantic spirit are curiosity and the love of beauty; and it is only as an illustration of these qualities, that it seeks the Middle Age, because, in the over-charged atmosphere of the Middle Age, there are unworked sources of romantic effect, of a strange beauty, to be won, by strong imagination, out of things unlikely or remote.

9. Few, probably, now read Madame de Staël's *De l'Allemagne*, though it has its interest, the interest which never quite fades out of work really touched with the enthusiasm of the spiritual adventurer, the pioneer in culture. It was published in 1810, to introduce to French readers a new school of writers—the romantic school, from beyond the Rhine; and it was followed, twenty-three years later, by Heine's *Romantische Schule*, as at once a supplement and a correction. Both these books, then, connect romanticism with Germany, with the names especially of Goethe and Tieck; and, to many English readers, the idea of romanticism is still inseparably connected with Germany—that Germany which, in its quaint old towns, under the spire of Strasburg or the towers of Heidelberg, was always listening in rapt inaction to the melodious, fascinating voices of the Middle Age, and which, now that it has got Strasburg back again, has, I suppose, almost ceased to exist. But neither Germany, with

its Goethe and Tieck, nor England, with its Byron and Scott, is nearly so representative of the romantic temper as France, with Murger, and Gautier, and Victor Hugo. It is in French literature that its most characteristic expression is to be found; and that, as most closely derivative, historically, from such peculiar conditions, as ever reinforce it to the utmost.

10. For, although temperament has much to do with the generation of the romantic spirit, and although this spirit, with its curiosity, its thirst for a curious beauty, may be always traceable in excellent art (traceable even in Sophocles) yet still, in a limited sense, it may be said to be a product of special epochs. Outbreaks of this spirit, that is, come naturally with particular periods—times, when, in men's approaches towards art and poetry, curiosity may be noticed to take the lead, when men come to art and poetry, with a deep thirst for intellectual excitement, after a long *ennui*, or in reaction against the strain of outward, practical things: in the later Middle Age, for instance; so that medieval poetry, centering in Dante, is often opposed to Greek and Roman poetry, as romantic poetry to the classical. What the romanticism of Dante is, may be estimated, if we compare the lines in which Virgil describes the hazel-wood, from whose broken twigs flows the blood of Polydorus, not without the expression of a real shudder at the ghastly incident, with the whole canto of the *Inferno*, into which Dante has expanded them, beautifying and softening it, meanwhile, by a sentiment of profound pity. And it is especially in that period of intellectual disturbance, immediately preceding Dante, amid which the romance languages define themselves at last, that this temper is manifested. Here, in the literature of Provence, the very name of *romanticism* is stamped with its true signification: here we have indeed a romantic world, grotesque even, in the strength of its passions, almost insane in its curious expression of them, drawing all things into its sphere, making the birds, nay! lifeless things, its voices and messengers, yet so penetrated with the desire for beauty and sweetness, that it begets a wholly new species of poetry, in which the *Renaissance* may be said to begin. The last century was pre-eminently a classical age, an age in which, for art and literature, the element of a comely order was in the ascendant; which, passing away, left a hard battle to be fought between the classical and the romantic schools. Yet, it is in the heart of this century, of Goldsmith and Stothard, of Watteau and the *Siècle de Louis XIV.*—in one of its central, if not most characteristic figures, in Rousseau—that the modern or French romanticism really originates. But, what in the eighteenth century is but an exceptional phenomenon, breaking through its fair reserve and discretion only at rare intervals, is the habitual guise of the nineteenth, breaking through it perpetually, with a feverishness, an incomprehensible straining and excitement, which all experience to some degree, but yearning also, in the

genuine children of the romantic school, to be *énergique, frais, et dispos*—for those qualities of energy, freshness, comely order; and often, in Murger, in Gautier, in Victor Hugo, for instance, with singular felicity attaining them.

11. It is in the terrible tragedy of Rousseau, in fact, that French romanticism, with much else, begins: reading his *Confessions* we seem actually to assist at the birth of this new, strong spirit in the French mind. The wildness which has shocked so many, and the fascination which has influenced almost every one, in the squalid, yet eloquent figure, we see and hear so clearly in that book, wandering under the apple-blossoms and among the vines of Neuchâtel or Vevey actually give it the quality of a very successful romantic invention. His strangeness or distortion, his profound subjectivity, his passionateness—the *cor laceratum*—Rousseau makes all men in love with these. *Je ne suis fait comme aucun de ceux que j'ai sus. Mais si je ne vaux pas mieux, au moins je suis autre.*—"I am not made like any one else I have ever known: yet, if I am not better, at least I am different." These words, from the first page of the *Confessions*, anticipate all the Werthers, Renés, Obermanns, of the last hundred years. For Rousseau did but anticipate a trouble in the spirit of the whole world; and thirty years afterwards, what in him was a peculiarity, became part of the general consciousness. A storm was coming: Rousseau, with others, felt it in the air, and they helped to bring it down: they introduced a disturbing element into French literature, then so trim and formal, like our own literature of the age of Queen Anne.

12. In 1815 the storm had come and gone, but had left, in the spirit of "young France," the *ennui* of an immense disillusion. In the last chapter of Edgar Quinet's *Révolution Française*, a work itself full of irony, of disillusion, he distinguishes two books, Senancour's *Obermann* and Chateaubriand's *Génie du Christianisme*, as characteristic of the first decade of the present century. In those two books we detect already the disease and the cure—in *Obermann* the irony, refined into a plaintive philosophy of "indifference"—in Chateaubriand's *Génie du Christianisme*, the refuge from a tarnished actual present, a present of disillusion, into a world of strength and beauty in the Middle Age, as at an earlier period—in *René* and *Atala*—into the free play of them in savage life. It is to minds in this spiritual situation, weary of the present, but yearning for the spectacle of beauty and strength, that the works of French romanticism appeal. They set a positive value on the intense, the exceptional; and a certain distortion is sometimes noticeable in them, as in conceptions like Victor Hugo's *Quasimodo*, or *Gwynplaine*, something of a terrible grotesque, of the *macabre*, as the French themselves call it; though always combined with perfect literary execution, as in Gautier's *La Morte Amoureuse*, or the scene of the "maimed" burial-rites of the player, dead of

the frost, in his *Capitaine Fracasse*—true "flowers of the yew." It becomes grim humour in Victor Hugo's combat of Gilliatt with the devil-fish, or the incident, with all its ghastly comedy drawn out at length, of the great gun detached from its fastenings on shipboard, in *Quatre-Vingt-Treize* (perhaps the most terrible of all the accidents that can happen by sea) and in the entire episode, in that book, of the *Convention*. Not less surely does it reach a genuine pathos; for the habit of noting and distinguishing one's own most intimate passages of sentiment makes one sympathetic, begetting, as it must, the power of entering, by all sorts of finer ways, into the intimate recesses of other minds; so that pity is another quality of romanticism, both Victor Hugo and Gautier being great lovers of animals, and charming writers about them, and Murger being unrivalled in the pathos of his *Scènes de la Vie de Jeunesse*. Penetrating so finely into all situations which appeal to pity, above all, into the special or exceptional phases of such feeling, the romantic humour is not afraid of the quaintness or singularity of its circumstances or expression, pity, indeed, being of the essence of humour; so that Victor Hugo does but turn his romanticism into practice, in his hunger and thirst after practical *Justice!*—a justice which shall no longer wrong children, or animals, for instance, by ignoring in a stupid, mere breadth of view, minute facts about them. Yet the romanticists are antinomian, too, sometimes, because the love of energy and beauty, of distinction in passion, tended naturally to become a little *bizarre*, plunging into the Middle Age, into the secrets of old Italian story. *Are we in the Inferno?*—we are tempted to ask, wondering at something malign in so much beauty. For over all a care for the refreshment of the human spirit by fine art manifests itself, a predominant sense of literary charm, so that, in their search for the secret of exquisite expression, the romantic school went back to the forgotten world of early French poetry, and literature itself became the most delicate of the arts—like "goldsmith's work," says Sainte-Beuve, of Bertrand's *Gaspard de la Nuit*—and that peculiarly French gift, the gift of exquisite speech, *argute loqui*, attained in them a perfection which it had never seen before.

13. Stendhal, a writer whom I have already quoted, and of whom English readers might well know much more than they do, stands between the earlier and later growths of the romantic spirit. His novels are rich in romantic quality; and his other writings—partly criticism, partly personal reminiscences—are a very curious and interesting illustration of the needs out of which romanticism arose. In his book on *Racine and Shakespeare*, Stendhal argues that all good art was romantic in its day; and this is perhaps true in Stendhal's sense. That little treatise, full of "dry light" and fertile ideas, was published in the year 1823, and its object is to defend an entire independence and liberty in the choice and treatment of subject, both in art and literature, against those who upheld

the exclusive authority of precedent. In pleading the cause of romanticism, therefore, it is the novelty, both of form and of motive, in writings like the *Hernani* of Victor Hugo (which soon followed it, raising a storm of criticism) that he is chiefly concerned to justify. To be interesting and really stimulating, to keep us from yawning even, art and literature must follow the subtle movements of that nimbly-shifting *Time-Spirit*, or *Zeit-Geist*, understood by French not less than by German criticism, which is always modifying men's taste, as it modifies their manners and their pleasures. This, he contends, is what all great workmen had always understood. Dante, Shakespeare, Molière, had exercised an absolute independence in their choice of subject and treatment. To turn always with that ever-changing spirit, yet to retain the flavour of what was admirably done in past generations, in the classics, as we say—is the problem of true romanticism. "Dante," he observes, "was pre-eminently the romantic poet. He adored Virgil, yet he wrote the *Divine Comedy*, with the episode of Ugolino, which is as unlike the *Æneid* as can possibly be. And those who thus obey the fundamental principle of romanticism, one by one become classical, and are joined to that ever-increasing common league, formed by men of all countries, to approach nearer and nearer to perfection."

14. Romanticism, then, although it has its epochs, is in its essential characteristics rather a spirit which shows itself at all times, in various degrees, in individual workmen and their work, and the amount of which criticism has to estimate in them taken one by one, than the peculiarity of a time or a school. Depending on the varying proportion of curiosity and the desire of beauty, natural tendencies of the artistic spirit at all times, it must always be partly a matter of individual temperament. The eighteenth century in England has been regarded as almost exclusively a classical period; yet William Blake, a type of so much which breaks through what are conventionally thought the influences of that century, is still a noticeable phenomenon in it, and the reaction in favour of naturalism in poetry begins in that century, early. There are, thus, the born romanticists and the born classicists. There are the born classicists who start with *form*, to whose minds the comeliness of the old, immemorial, well-recognised types in art and literature, have revealed themselves impressively; who will entertain no matter which will not go easily and flexibly into them; whose work aspires only to be a variation upon, or study from, the older masters. "'Tis art's decline, my son!" they are always saying, to the progressive element in their own generation; to those who care for that which in fifty years' time every one will be caring for. On the other hand, there are the born romanticists, who start with an original, untried *matter*, still in fusion; who conceive this vividly, and hold by it as the essence of their work; who, by the very vividness and heat of their conception, purge away, sooner

or later, all that is not organically appropriate to it, till the whole effect adjusts itself in clear, orderly, proportionate form; which form, after a very little time, becomes classical in its turn.

15. The romantic or classical character of a picture, a poem, a literary work, depends, then, on the balance of certain qualities in it; and in this sense, a very real distinction may be drawn between good classical and good romantic work. But all critical terms are relative; and there is at least a valuable suggestion in that theory of Stendhal's, that all good art was romantic in its day. In the beauties of Homer and Pheidias, quiet as they now seem, there must have been, for those who confronted them for the first time, excitement and surprise, the sudden, unforeseen satisfaction of the desire of beauty. Yet the *Odyssey*, with its marvellous adventure, is more romantic than the *Iliad*, which nevertheless contains, among many other romantic episodes, that of the immortal horses of Achilles, who weep at the death of Patroclus. Æschylus is more romantic than Sophocles, whose *Philoctetes*, were it written now, might figure, for the strangeness of its motive and the perfectness of its execution, as typically romantic; while, of Euripides, it may be said, that his method in writing his plays is to sacrifice readily almost everything else, so that he may attain the fulness of a single romantic effect. These two tendencies, indeed, might be applied as a measure or standard, all through Greek and Roman art and poetry, with very illuminating results; and for an analyst of the romantic principle in art, no exercise would be more profitable, than to walk through the collection of classical antiquities at the Louvre, or the British Museum, or to examine some representative collection of Greek coins, and note how the element of curiosity, of the love of strangeness, insinuates itself into classical design, and record the effects of the romantic spirit there, the traces of struggle, of the grotesque even, though over-balanced here by sweetness; as in the sculpture of Chartres and Rheims, the real sweetness of mind in the sculptor is often overbalanced by the grotesque, by the rudeness of his strength.

16. Classicism, then, means for Stendhal, for that younger enthusiastic band of French writers whose unconscious method he formulated into principles, the reign of what is pedantic, conventional, and narrowly academical in art; for him, all good art is romantic. To Sainte-Beuve, who understands the term in a more liberal sense, it is the characteristic of certain epochs, of certain spirits in every epoch, not given to the exercise of original imagination, but rather to the working out of refinements of manner on some authorised matter; and who bring to their perfection, in this way, the elements of sanity, of order and beauty in manner. In general criticism, again, it means the spirit of Greece and Rome, of some phases in literature and art that may seem of equal authority with Greece and Rome, the age of Louis the Fourteenth, the age of Johnson;

though this is at best an uncritical use of the term, because in Greek and Roman work there are typical examples of the romantic spirit. But explain the terms as we may, in application to particular epochs, there are these two elements always recognisable; united in perfect art—in Sophocles, in Dante, in the highest work of Goethe, though not always absolutely balanced there; and these two elements may be not inappropriately termed the classical and romantic tendencies.

17. Material for the artist, motives of inspiration, are not yet exhausted: our curious, complex, aspiring age still abounds in subjects for æsthetic manipulation by the literary as well as by other forms of art. For the literary art, at all events, the problem just now is, to induce order upon the contorted, proportionless accumulation of our knowledge and experience, our science and history, our hopes and disillusion, and, in effecting this, to do consciously what has been done hitherto for the most part too unconsciously, to write our English language as the Latins wrote theirs, as the French write, as scholars should write. Appealing, as he may, to precedent in this matter, the scholar will still remember that if "the style is the man" it is also the age: that the nineteenth century too will be found to have had its style, justified by necessity—a style very different, alike from the baldness of an impossible "Queen Anne" revival, and an incorrect, incondite exuberance, after the mode of Elizabeth: that we can only return to either at the price of an impoverishment of form or matter, or both, although, an intellectually rich age such as ours being necessarily an eclectic one, we may well cultivate some of the excellences of literary types so different as those: that in literature as in other matters it is well to unite as many diverse elements as may be: that the individual writer or artist, certainly, is to be estimated by the number of graces he combines, and his power of interpenetrating them in a given work. To discriminate schools, of art, of literature, is, of course, part of the obvious business of literary criticism: but, in the work of literary production, it is easy to be overmuch occupied concerning them. For, in truth, the legitimate contention is, not of one age or school of literary art against another, but of all successive schools alike, against the stupidity which is dead to the substance, and the vulgarity which is dead to form.

from PLATO AND PLATONISM

EXTRACTS *from Chapters 1 to 5*

i. [*Three Kinds of Criticism*]

There are three different ways in which the criticism of philosophic, of all speculative opinion whatever, may be conducted. The doctrines of Plato's *Republic*, for instance, may be regarded as so much truth or falsehood, to be accepted or rejected as such by the student of to-day. That is the dogmatic method of criticism; judging every product of human thought, however alien or distant from one's self, by its congruity with the assumptions of Bacon or Spinoza, of Mill or Hegel, according to the mental preference of the particular critic. There is, secondly, the more generous, eclectic or syncretic method, which aims at a selection from contending schools of the various grains of truth dispersed among them. It is the method which has prevailed in periods of large reading but with little inceptive force of their own, like that of the Alexandrian Neo-Platonism in the third century, or the Neo-Platonism of Florence in the fifteenth. Its natural defect is in the tendency to misrepresent the true character of the doctrine it professes to explain, that it may harmonise thus the better with the other elements of a pre-conceived system.

6. Dogmatic and eclectic criticism alike have in our own century, under the influence of Hegel and his predominant theory of the ever-changing "Time-spirit" or *Zeit-geist*, given way to a third method of criticism, the historic method, which bids us replace the doctrine, or the system, we are busy with, or such an ancient monument of philosophic thought as *The Republic*, as far as possible in the group of conditions, intellectual, social, material, amid which it was actually produced, if we would really understand it. That ages have their genius as well as the individual; that in every age there is a peculiar *ensemble* of conditions which determines a common character in every product of that age, in business and art, in fashion and speculation, in religion and manners, in men's very faces; that nothing man has projected from himself is really intelligible except at its own date, and from its proper point of view in the never-resting "secular process"; the solidarity of philosophy, of the intellectual life, with common or general history; that what it behoves the student of philosophic systems to cultivate is the "historic sense": by force of these convictions many a normal, or at first sight abnormal, phase of speculation has found a reasonable meaning for us. As the strangely twisted pine-tree,

which would be a freak of nature on an English lawn, is seen, if we replace it, in thought, amid the contending forces of the Alpine torrent that actually shaped its growth, to have been the creature of necessity, of the logic of certain facts; so, beliefs the most fantastic, the "communism" of Plato, for instance, have their natural propriety when duly correlated with those facts, those conditions round about them, of which they are in truth a part.

7. In the intellectual as in the organic world the given product, its normal or abnormal characteristics, are determined, as people say, by the "environment." The business of the young scholar therefore, in reading Plato, is not to take his side in a controversy, to adopt or refute Plato's opinions, to modify, or make apology for, what may seem erratic or impossible in him; still less, to furnish himself with arguments on behalf of some theory or conviction of his own. His duty is rather to follow intelligently, but with strict indifference, the mental process there, as he might witness a game of skill; better still, as in reading *Hamlet* or *The Divine Comedy*, so in reading *The Republic*, to watch, for its dramatic interest, the spectacle of a powerful, of a sovereign intellect, translating itself, amid a complex group of conditions which can never in the nature of things occur again, at once pliant and resistant to them, into a great literary monument. To put Plato into his natural place, as a result from antecedent and contemporary movements of Greek speculation, of Greek life generally: such is the proper aim of the historic, that is to say, of the really critical study of him.

[From *Plato and the Doctrine of Motion*]

ii. [*"Perpetual Flux"*]

Heraclitus, a writer of philosophy in prose, yet of a philosophy which was half poetic figure, half generalised fact, in style crabbed and obscure, but stimulant, invasive, not to be forgotten—he too might be thought, as a writer of prose, one of the "fathers" of Plato. His influence, however, on Plato, though himself a Heraclitean in early life, was by way of antagonism or reaction; Plato's stand against any philosophy of motion becoming, as we say, something of a "fixed idea" with him. Heraclitus of Ephesus (what Ephesus must have been just then is denoted by the fact that it was one of the twelve cities of the Ionian League) died about forty years before Plato was born. Here then at Ephesus, the much frequented centre of the religious life of Ionia, itself so lately emancipated from its tyrants, Heraclitus, of ancient hereditary rank, an aristocrat by birth and temper, amid all the bustle of still undiscredited Greek democracy, had reflected, not to his peace of mind, on the mutable character of political as well as of physical existence; perhaps, early as it was, on the mutability of intellectual systems also, that modes of thought and practice had already been in and out of fashion. Empires certainly had lived and died around; and in Ephesus as elsewhere, the privileged class had gone to the wall. In this era of unrestrained youthfulness, of Greek youthfulness, one of the haughtiest of that class, as being also of nature's aristocracy, and a man of powerful intellectual gifts, Heraclitus, asserts the native liberty of thought at all events; becomes, we might truly say, sickly with "the pale cast" of his philosophical questioning. Amid the irreflective actors in that rapidly moving show, so entirely immersed in it superficial as it is that they have no feeling of themselves, he becomes self-conscious. He reflects; and his reflexion has the characteristic melancholy of youth when it is forced suddenly to bethink itself, and for a moment feels already old, feels the temperature of the world about it sensibly colder. Its very ingenuousness, its sincerity, will make the utterance of what comes to mind just then somewhat shrill or over-emphatic.

10. Yet Heraclitus, thus superbly turning aside from the vulgar to think, so early in the impetuous spring-tide of Greek history, does but reflect after all the aspect of what actually surrounds him, when he cries out—his philosophy was no matter of formal treatise or system, but of harsh, protesting cries—Πάντα χωρεῖ καὶ οὐδὲν μένει. All things give way: nothing remaineth. There had been enquirers before him of another sort, purely physical enquirers, whose bold, contradictory, seemingly impious guesses how and of what primary elements the world of visible things, the sun, the stars, the brutes, their own souls and bodies, had been composed, were themselves a part of the bold enterprise of that romantic age; a series of intellectual adventures, of a piece with its adventures in unknown lands or upon the sea. The resultant intellectual

chaos expressed the very spirit of gifted and sanguine but insubordinate youth (remember, that the word νεότης, *youth*, came to mean rashness, insolence!) questioning, deciding, rejecting, on mere rags and tatters of evidence, unbent to discipline, unmethodical, irresponsible. Those opinions too, coming and going, those conjectures as to what under-lay the sensible world, were themselves but fluid elements on the changing surface of existence.

11. Surface, we say; but was there really anything beneath it? That was what to the majority of his hearers, his readers, Heraclitus, with an eye perhaps on practice, seemed to deny. Perpetual motion, alike in things and in men's thoughts about them,—the sad, self-conscious, philosophy of Heraclitus, like one, knowing beyond his years, in this barely adolescent world which he is so eager to instruct, makes no pretence to be able to restrain that. Was not the very essence of thought itself also such perpetual motion? a baffling transition from the dead past, alive one moment since, to a present, itself deceased in turn ere we can say, It is here? A keen analyst of the facts of nature and mind, a master presumably of all the knowledge that then there was, a vigorous definer of thoughts, he does but refer the superficial movement of all persons and things around him to deeper and still more masterful currents of universal change, stealthily withdrawing the apparently solid earth itself from beneath one's feet. The principle of disintegration, the incoherency of fire or flood (for Heraclitus these are but very lively instances of movements, subtler yet more wasteful still) are inherent in the primary elements alike of matter and of the soul. Λέγει που Ἡράκλειτος, says Socrates in the *Cratylus*, ὅτι πάντα χωρεῖ καὶ οὐδὲν μένει. But the principle of lapse, of waste, was, in fact, in one's self. "No one has ever passed twice over the same stream." Nay, the passenger himself is without identity. Upon the same stream at the same moment we do, and do not, embark: for we are, and are not: εἰμέν τε καὶ οὐκ εἶμεν. And this rapid change, if it did not make all knowledge impossible, made it wholly relative, of a kind, that is to say, valueless in the judgment of Plato. Man, the individual, at this particular vanishing-point of time and place, becomes "the measure of all things." [...]

13. [...] In truth, what was sympathetic with the hour and the scene in the Heraclitean doctrine, was the boldly aggressive, the paradoxical and negative tendency there, in natural collusion, as it was, with the destructiveness of undisciplined youth; that sense of rapid dissolution, which, according to one's temperament and one's luck in things, might extinguish, or kindle all the more eagerly, an interest in the mere phenomena of existence, of one's so hasty passage through the world.

14. The theory of the perpetual flux was indeed an apprehension of which the full scope was only to be realised by a later age, in alliance with a larger

knowledge of the natural world, a closer observation of the phenomena of mind, than was possible, even for Heraclitus, at that early day. So, the seeds of almost all scientific ideas might seem to have been dimly enfolded in the mind of antiquity; but fecundated, admitted to their full working prerogative, one by one, in after ages, by good favour of the special intellectual conditions belonging to a particular generation, which, on a sudden, finds itself preoccupied by a formula, not so much new, as renovated by new application.

15. It is in this way that the most modern metaphysical, and the most modern empirical philosophies alike have illustrated emphatically, justified, expanded, the divination (so we may make bold to call it under the new light now thrown upon it) of the ancient theorist of Ephesus. The entire modern theory of "development," in all its various phases, proved or unprovable,—what is it but old Heracliteanism awake once more in a new world, and grown to full proportions?

16. Πάντα χωρεῖ, πάντα ῥεῖ.—It is the burden of Hegel on the one hand, to whom nature, and art, and polity, and philosophy, aye, and religion too, each in its long historic series, are but so many conscious movements in the secular process of the eternal mind; and on the other hand of Darwin and Darwinism, for which "type" itself properly *is* not but is only always *becoming*. The bold paradox of Heraclitus is, in effect, repeated on all sides, as the vital persuasion just now of a cautiously reasoned experience, and, in illustration of the very law of change which it asserts, may itself presently be superseded as a commonplace. Think of all that subtly disguised movement, *latens processus*, Bacon calls it (again as if by a kind of anticipation) which modern research has detected, measured, hopes to reduce to minuter or ally to still larger currents, in what had seemed most substantial to the naked eye, the inattentive mind. To the "observation and experiment" of the physical enquirer of to-day, the eye and the sun it lives by reveal themselves, after all, as Heraclitus had declared (scarcely serious, he seemed to those around him) as literally in constant extinction and renewal; the sun only going out more gradually than the human eye; the system meanwhile, of which it is the centre, in ceaseless movement nowhither. Our terrestrial planet is in constant increase by meteoric dust, moving to it through endless time out of infinite space. The Alps drift down the rivers into the plains, as still loftier mountains found their level there ages ago. The granite kernel of the earth, it is said, is ever changing in its very substance, its molecular constitution, by the passage through it of electric currents. And the Darwinian theory—that "species," the identifying forms of animal and vegetable life, immutable though they seem now, as of old in the Garden of Eden, are fashioned by slow development, while perhaps millions of years go by: well! every month is adding to its evidence. Nay, the

from PLATO AND PLATONISM

idea of development (that, too, a thing of growth, developed in the progress of reflexion) is at last invading one by one, as the secret of their explanation, all the products of mind, the very mind itself, the abstract reason; our certainty, for instance, that two and two make four. Gradually we have come to think, or to feel, that primary certitude. Political constitutions, again, as we now see so clearly, are "not made," cannot be made, but "grow." Races, laws, arts, have their origins and end, are themselves ripples only on the great river of organic life; and language is changing on our very lips.

17. In Plato's day, the Heraclitean flux, so deep down in nature itself—the flood, the fire—seemed to have laid hold on man, on the social and moral world, dissolving or disintegrating opinion, first principles, faith, establishing amorphism, so to call it, there also. All along indeed the genius, the good gifts of Greece to the world had had much to do with the mobility of its temperament. Only, when Plato came into potent contact with his countrymen (Pericles, Phidias, Socrates being now gone) in politics, in literature and art, in men's characters, the defect naturally incident to that fine quality had come to have unchecked sway. From the lifeless background of an unprogressive world—Egypt, Syria, frozen Scythia—a world in which the unconscious social aggregate had been everything, the conscious individual, his capacity and rights, almost nothing, the Greek had stepped forth, like the young prince in the fable, to set things going. To the philosophic eye however, about the time when the history of Thucydides leaves off, they might seem to need a regulator, ere the very wheels wore themselves out.

18. Mobility! We do not think that a necessarily undesirable condition of life, of mind, of the physical world about us. 'Tis the dead things, we may remind ourselves, that after all are most entirely at rest, and might reasonably hold that motion (vicious, fallacious, infectious motion, as Plato inclines to think) covers all that is best worth being. And as for philosophy—mobility, versatility, the habit of thought that can most adequately follow the subtle movement of things, that, surely, were the secret of wisdom, of the true knowledge of them. It means susceptibility, sympathetic intelligence, capacity, in short. It was the spirit of God that moved, moves still, in every form of real power, everywhere. Yet to Plato motion becomes the token of unreality in things, of falsity in our thoughts about them. It is just this principle of mobility, in itself so welcome to all of us, that, with all his contriving care for the future, he desires to withstand. Everywhere he displays himself as an advocate of the immutable. *The Republic* is a proposal to establish it indefectibly in a very precisely regulated, a very exclusive community, which shall be a refuge for elect souls from an ill-made world.

[From *Plato and the Doctrine of Motion*]

iii. [*The Eleatic School*]

In opposition then to the anthropomorphic religious poetry of Homer, Xenophanes elaborates the notion, or rather the abstract or purely verbal definition, of that which really is (τὸ ὄν) as inclusive of all time, and space, and mode; yet so that all which can be identified concretely with mode and space and time is but antithetic to it, as finite to infinite, seeming to being, contingent to necessary, the temporal, in a word, to the eternal. Once for all, in harshest dualism, the only true yet so barren existence is opposed to the world of phenomena—of colour and form and sound and imagination and love, of empirical knowledge. Objects, real objects, as we know, grow in reality towards us in proportion as we define their various qualities. And yet, from another point of view, definition, qualification, is a negative process: it is as if each added quality took from the object we are defining one or more potential qualities. The more definite things become as objects of sensible or other empirical apprehension, the more, it might be said from the logician's point of view, have we denied about them. It might seem that their increasing reality as objects of sense was in direct proportion to the increase of their distance from that perfect Being which is everywhere and at all times in every possible mode of being. A thing visibly white is found as one approaches it to be also smooth to the touch; and this added quality, says the formal logician, does but deprive it of all other possible modes of texture; *Omnis determinatio est negatio.* Vain puerilities! you may exclaim:—with justice. Yet such are the considerations which await the mind that suffers itself to dwell awhile on the abstract formula to which the "rational theology" of Xenophanes leads him. It involved the assertion of an absolute difference between the original and all that is or can be derived from it; that the former annuls, or is exclusive of, the latter, which has in truth no real or legitimate standing-ground as matter of knowledge; that, in opposite yet equally unanswerable senses, at both ends of experience there is—nothing! Of the most concrete object, as of the most abstract, it might be said, that it more properly is not than is.

9. From Xenophanes, as a critic of the polytheism of the Greek religious poets, that most abstract and arid of formulæ, *Pure Being*, closed in indifferently on every side upon itself, and suspended in the midst of nothing, like a hard transparent crystal ball, as he says; "The Absolute"; "The One"; passed to his fellow-citizen Parmenides, seeking, doubtless in the true spirit of philosophy, for the centre of the universe, of his own experience of it, for some common measure of the experience of all men. To enforce a reasonable unity and order, to impress some larger likeness of reason, as one knows it in one's self, upon the chaotic infinitude of the impressions that reach us from every

side, is what all philosophy as such proposes. Κόσμος; order; reasonable, delightful, order; is a word that became very dear, as we know, to the Greek soul, to what was perhaps most essentially Greek in it, to the Dorian element there. Apollo, the Dorian god, was but its visible consecration. It was what, under his blessing, art superinduced upon the rough stone, the yielding clay, the jarring metallic strings, the common speech of every day. Philosophy, in its turn, with enlarging purpose, would project a similar light of intelligence upon the at first sight somewhat unmeaning world we find actually around us:—project it; or rather discover it, as being really pre-existent there, if one were happy enough to get one's self into the right point of view. To certain fortunate minds the efficacious moment of insight would come, when, with delightful adaptation of means to ends, of the parts to the whole, the entire scene about one, bewildering, unsympathetic, unreasonable, on a superficial view, would put on, for them at least, κοσμιότης, that so welcome expression of fitness, which it is the business of the fine arts to convey into material things, of the art of discipline to enforce upon the lives of men. The primitive Ionian philosophers had found, or thought they found, such a principle (ἀρχή) in the force of some omnipresent physical element, air, water, fire; or in some common law, motion, attraction, repulsion; as Plato would find it in an eternally appointed hierarchy of genus and species; as the science of our day embraces it (perhaps after all only in fancy) in the expansion of a large body of observed facts into some all-comprehensive hypothesis, such as "evolution."

10. For Parmenides, at his early day, himself, as some remnants of his work in that direction bear witness, an acute and curious observer of the concrete and sensible phenomena of nature, that principle of reasonable unity seemed attainable only by a virtual negation, by the obliteration, of all such phenomena. When we have learned as exactly as we can all the curious processes at work in our own bodies or souls, in the stars, in or under the earth, their very definiteness, their limitation, will but make them the more antagonistic to that which alone really is, because it is always and everywhere itself, identical exclusively with itself. Phenomena!—by the force of such arguments as Zeno's, the instructed would make a clean sweep of them, for the establishment, in the resultant void, of the "One," with which it is impossible (παρὰ πάντα λεγόμενα) in spite of common language, and of what seems common sense, for the "Many"—the hills and cities of Greece, you and me, Parmenides himself, really to co-exist at all. "Parmenides," says one, "had stumbled upon the modern thesis that thought and being are the same."

11. Something like this—this impossibly abstract doctrine—is what Plato's "father in philosophy" had had to proclaim, in the midst of the busy, brilliant, already complicated life of the recently founded colonial town of Elea. It was

like the revelation to Israel in the midst of picturesque idolatries, "The Lord thy God is one Lord"; only that here it made no claim to touch the affections, or even to warm the imagination. Israel's Greek cousin was to undergo a harder, a more distant and repressive discipline in those matters, to which a peculiarly austere moral beauty, at once self-reliant and submissive, the æsthetic expression of which has a peculiar, an irresistible charm, would in due time correspond.

[From *Plato and the Doctrine of Rest*]

iv. [*The Mania for Nonentity*]

An infectious mania, it might seem,—that strange passion for nonentity, to which the Greek was so oddly liable, to which the human mind generally might be thought to have been constitutionally predisposed; for the doctrine of "The One" had come to the surface before in old Indian dreams of self-annihilation, which had been revived, in the second century after Christ, in the ecstasies (ecstasies of the pure spirit, leaving the body behind it) recommended by the Neo-Platonists; and again, in the Middle Age, as a finer shade of Christian experience, in the mystic doctrines of Eckhart and Tauler concerning that union with God which can only be attained by the literal negation of self, by a kind of moral suicide; of which something also may be found, under the cowl of the monk, in the clear, cold, inaccessible, impossible heights of the book of the *Imitation*. It presents itself once more, now altogether beyond Christian influence, in the hard and ambitious intellectualism of Spinoza; a doctrine of pure repellent substance—substance "in vacuo," to be lost in which, however, would be the proper consummation of the transitory individual life. Spinoza's own absolutely colourless existence was a practical comment upon it. Descartes; Malebranche, under the monk's cowl again; Leibnitz; Berkeley with his theory of the "Vision of all things in God"; do but present variations on the same theme through the seventeenth and eighteenth centuries. By one and all it is assumed, in the words of Plato, that to be colourless, formless, impalpable is the note of the superior grade of knowledge and existence, evanescing steadily, as one ascends towards that perfect (perhaps not quite attainable) condition of either, which in truth can only be attained by the suppression of all the rule and outline of one's own actual experience and thought.

[From *Plato and the Doctrine of Rest*]

v. [*Pythagoras*]

His devotion to the austere and abstract philosophy of Parmenides, its passivity or indifference, could not repress the opulent genius of Plato, or transform him into a cynic. Another ancient philosopher, Pythagoras, set the frozen waves in motion again, brought back to Plato's recognition all that multiplicity in men's experience to which Heraclitus had borne such emphatic witness; but as rhythm or melody now—in movement truly, but moving as disciplined sound and with the reasonable soul of music in it.

2. Pythagoras, or the founder of the Pythagorean philosophy, is the third of those earlier masters, who explain the intellectual conformation of Plato by way of antecedent. What he said, or was believed to have said, is almost everywhere in the very texture of Platonic philosophy, as *vera vox*, an authority with prescript claim on sympathetic or at least reverent consideration, to be developed generously in the natural growth of Plato's own thoughts.

3. Nothing remains of his writings: dark statements only, as occasion served, in later authors. Plato himself attributes those doctrines of his not to Pythagoras but to the Pythagoreans. But if no such name had come down to us we might have understood how, in the search for the philosophic unity of experience, a common measure of things, for a cosmical hypothesis, number and the truths of number would come to fill the place occupied by some omnipresent physical element, air, fire, water, in the philosophies of Ionia; by the abstract and exclusive idea of the unity of Being itself in the system of Parmenides. To realise unity in variety, to discover *cosmos*—an order that shall satisfy one's reasonable soul—below and within apparent chaos: is from first to last the continuous purpose of what we call philosophy. Well! Pythagoras seems to have found that unity of principle (ἀρχή) in the dominion of number everywhere, the proportion, the harmony, the music, into which number as such expands. Truths of number: the essential laws of measure in time and space:—Yes, these are indeed everywhere in our experience: must, as Kant can explain to us, be an element in anything we are able so much as to conceive at all. And music, covering all it does, for Pythagoras, for Plato and Platonism—music, which though it is of course much besides, is certainly a formal development of purely numerical laws: that too surely *is* something, independently of ourselves, in the real world without us, like a personal intelligible soul durably resident there for those who bring intelligence of it, of music, with them; to be known on the favourite Platonic principle of like by like (ὅμοιον ὁμοίῳ) though the incapable or uninstructed ear, in various degrees of dulness, may fail to apprehend it.

4. The *Golden Verses* of Pythagoras parted early into dust (that seems strange, if they were ever really written in a book) and antiquity itself knows little directly

about his doctrine. Yet Pythagoras is much more than a mere name, a term, for locating as well as may be a philosophical abstraction. Pythagoras, his person, his memory, attracted from the first a kind of fairy-tale of mystic science. The philosophy of number, of music and proportion, came, and has remained, in a cloud of legendary glory; the gradual accumulation of which Porphyry and Iamblichus, the fantastic masters of Neo-Platonism, or Neo-Pythagoreanism, have embodied in their so-called *Lives* of him, like some antique fable richly embossed with starry wonders. In this spirit there had been much writing about him: that he was a son of Apollo, nay, Apollo himself—the twilight, attempered, Hyperborean Apollo, like the sun in Lapland: that his person gleamed at times with a supernatural brightness: that he had exposed to those who loved him a golden thigh: how Abaris, the minister of that god, had come flying to him on a golden arrow: of his almost impossible journeys: how he was seen, had lectured indeed, in different places at the same time. As he walked on the banks of the Nessus the river had whispered his name: he had been, in the secondary sense, various persons in the course of ages; a courtesan once, for some ancient sin in him; and then a hero, Euphorbus, son of Panthus; could remember very distinctly so recent a matter as the Trojan war, and had recognised in a moment his own old armour, hanging on the wall, above one of his old dead bodies, in the temple of Athene at Argos; showing out all along only by hints and flashes the abysses of divine knowledge within him, sometimes by miracle. For if the philosopher really is all that Pythagoras or the Pythagoreans suppose; if the material world is so perfect a musical instrument, and he knows its theory so well, he might surely give practical and sensible proof of that on occasion, by himself improvising music upon it in direct miracle. And so there, in Porphyry and Iamblichus, the appropriate miracles are.

5. If the mistaken affection of the disciples of dreamy Neo-Platonic *Gnôsis* at Alexandria, in the third or fourth century of our era, has thus made it impossible to separate later legend from original evidence as to what he was, and said, and how he said it, yet that there was a brilliant, perhaps a showy, personality there, infusing the most abstract truths with what would tell on the fancy, seems more than probable, and, though he would appear really to have had from the first much of mystery or mysticism about him, the thaumaturge of Samos, "whom even the vulgar might follow as a conjuror," must have been very unlike the lonely "weeping" philosopher of Ephesus, or the almost disembodied philosopher of Elea. In the very person and doings of this earliest master of the doctrine of harmony, people saw that philosophy is

> Not harsh and crabbed, as dull fools suppose,
> But musical as is Apollo's lute.

And in turn he abounded in influence on the deeds, the persons, of others, as if he had really carried a magic lute in his hands to charm them.

[From *Plato and the Doctrine of Number*]

vi. [*The Centrifugal and the Centripetal*]

"The citizen of Athens," observed that great Athenian statesman of the preceding age, in whom, as a German philosopher might say, the mobile soul of Athens became conscious,—"The citizen of Athens seems to me to present himself in his single person to the greatest possible variety (πλεῖστα εἴδη) of thought and action, with the utmost degree of versatility." As we saw, the example of that mobility, that daring mobility, of character has seemed to many the special contribution of the Greek people to advancing humanity. It was not however of the Greek people in general that Pericles was speaking at the beginning of the Peloponnesian war, but of Athens in particular; of Athens, that perfect flower of Ionian genius, in direct contrast to, and now in bitter rivalry with, Sparta, the perfect flower of the Dorian genius. All through Greek history, as we also saw, in connexion with Plato's opposition to the philosophy of motion, there may be traced, in every sphere of the activity of the Greek mind, the influence of those two opposing tendencies:—the centrifugal and the centripetal tendencies, as we may perhaps not too fancifully call them.

4. There is the centrifugal, the irresponsible, the Ionian or Asiatic, tendency; flying from the centre, working with little forethought straight before it in the development of every thought and fancy; throwing itself forth in endless play of undirected imagination; delighting in colour and brightness, moral or physical; in beautiful material, in changeful form everywhere, in poetry, in music, in architecture and its subordinate crafts, in philosophy itself. In the social and political order it rejoices in the freest action of local and personal influences: its restless versatility drives it towards the assertion of the principles of individualism, of separatism—the separation of state from state, the maintenance of local religions, the development of the individual in that which is most peculiar and individual in him. Shut off land-wards from the primitive sources of those many elements it was to compose anew, shut off from all the rest of the world, to which it presented but one narrow entrance pierced through that rock of Tempe, so narrow that "in the opinion of the ancients it might be defended by a dozen men against all comers," it did recompose or fuse those many diverse elements into one absolutely original type. But what variety within! Its very claim was in its grace of *movement*, its freedom and easy happiness, its lively interests, the variety of its gifts to civilisation; but its weakness is self-evident, and was what had made the political unity of Greece impossible. The Greek spirit!—it might have become a hydra, to use Plato's own figure, a monster; the hand developing hideously into a hundred hands, or heads.

5. This inorganic, this centrifugal, tendency, Plato was desirous to cure by maintaining over against it the Dorian influence of a severe simplification

everywhere, in society, in culture, in the very physical nature of man. An enemy everywhere, though through acquired principle indeed rather than by instinct, to variegation, to what is cunning, or "myriad-minded" (as we say of Shakespere, as Plato thinks of Homer) he sets himself in mythology, in literature, in every kind of art, in the art of life, as if with conscious metaphysical opposition to the metaphysic of Heraclitus, to enforce the ideal of a sort of Parmenidean abstractness, and monotony or calm.

6. This, perhaps exaggerated, ideal of Plato is however only the exaggeration of that salutary, strictly European tendency, which, finding human mind, the human reason cool and sane, to be the most absolutely real and precious thing in the world, enforces everywhere the impress of its reasonable sanity; its candid reflexions upon things as they really are; its sense of logical proportion. It is that centripetal tendency, again, which links the individual units together, states to states, one period of organic growth to another, under the reign of a strictly composed, self-conscious order, in the universal light of the understanding.

[From *Plato and the Sophists*]

THE GENIUS OF PLATO

All true criticism of philosophic doctrine, as of every other product of human mind, must begin with an historic estimate of the conditions, antecedent and contemporary, which helped to make it precisely what it was. But a complete criticism does not end there. In the evolution of abstract doctrine as we find it written in the history of philosophy, if there is always, on one side, the fatal, irresistible, mechanic play of circumstance—the circumstances of a particular age, which may be analysed and explained; there is always also, as if acting from the opposite side, the comparatively inexplicable force of a personality, resistant to, while it is moulded by, them. It might even be said that the trial-task of criticism, in regard to literature and art no less than to philosophy, begins exactly where the estimate of general conditions, of the conditions common to all the products of this or that particular age—of the "environment"—leaves off, and we touch what is unique in the individual genius which contrived after all, by force of will, to have its own masterful way with that environment. If in reading Plato, for instance, the philosophic student has to re-construct for himself, as far as possible, the general character of an *age*, he must also, so far as he may, reproduce the portrait of a *person*. The Sophists, the Sophistical world, around him; his master, Socrates; the Pre-Socratic philosophies; the mechanic influence, that is to say, of past and present:—of course we can know nothing at all of the Platonic doctrine except so far as we see it in well-ascertained contact with all that; but there is also Plato himself in it.

2. —A personality, we may notice at the outset, of a certain complication. The great masters of philosophy have been for the most part its noticeably single-minded servants. As if in emulation of Aristotle's simplicity of character, his absorbing intellectualism—impressive certainly, heroic enough, in its way—they have served science, science *in vacuo*, as if nothing beside, faith, imagination, love, the bodily sense, could detach them from it for an hour. It is not merely that we know little of their lives (there was so little to tell!) but that we know nothing at all of their *temperaments*; of which, that one leading abstract or scientific force in them was in fact strictly exclusive. Little more than intellectual abstractions themselves, in them philosophy was wholly faithful to its colours, or its colourlessness; rendering not grey only, as Hegel said of it, but all colours alike, in grey.

3. With Plato it was otherwise. In him, the passion for truth did but bend, or take the bent of, certain ineradicable predispositions of his nature, in themselves

perhaps somewhat opposed to that. It is however in the blending of diverse elements in the mental constitution of Plato that the peculiar Platonic quality resides. Platonism is in one sense an emphatic witness to the unseen, the transcendental, the non-experienced, the beauty, for instance, which is not for the bodily eye. Yet the author of this philosophy of the unseen was,—Who can doubt it who has read but a page of him? this, in fact, is what has led and kept to his pages many who have little or no turn for the sort of questions Plato actually discusses:—The author of this philosophy of the unseen was one, for whom, as was said of a very different French writer, "the *visible* world really existed." Austere as he seems, and on well-considered principle really is, his temperance or austerity, æsthetically so winning, is attained only by the chastisement, the control, of a variously interested, a richly sensuous nature. Yes, the visible world, so pre-eminently worth eye-sight at Athens just then, really existed for him: exists still—there's the point!—is active still everywhere, when he seems to have turned away from it to invisible things.

4. To the somewhat sad-coloured school of Socrates, and its discipline towards apathy or contempt in such matters, he had brought capacities of bodily sense with the making in them of an *Odyssey*; or (shall we say?) of a poet after the order of Sappho or Catullus; as indeed also a practical intelligence, a popular management of his own powers, a skill in philosophic yet mundane Greek prose, which might have constituted him the most successful of Sophists. You cannot help seeing that his mind is a storehouse of all the liveliest imageries of men and things. Nothing, if it really arrests eye or ear at all, is too trivial to note. Passing through the crowd of human beings, he notes the sounds alike of their solemn hymns and of their pettiest handicraft. A conventional philosopher might speak of "dumb matter," for instance; but Plato has lingered too long in braziers' workshops to lapse into so stupid an epithet. And if the persistent hold of sensible things upon him thus reveals itself in trifles, it is manifest no less in the way in which he can tell a long story,—no one more effectively! and again, in his graphic presentment of whole scenes from actual life, like that with which *The Republic* opens. His Socrates, like other people, is curious to witness a new religious function: how they will do it. As in modern times, it would be a pleasant occasion also for meeting the acquaintance one likes best—Ξυνεσόμεθα πολλοῖς τῶν νέων αὐτόθι. "We shall meet a number of our youth there: we shall have a dialogue: there will be a torchlight procession in honour of the goddess, an equestrian procession: a novel feature!—What? Torches in their hands, passed on as they race? Aye, and an illumination, through the entire night. It will be worth seeing!"—that old midnight hour, as Carlyle says of another vivid scene, "shining yet on us, ruddy-bright through the centuries." Put alongside of that, and, for life-like charm, side by side

with Murillo's Beggar-boys (you catch them, if you look at his canvas on the sudden, actually moving their mouths, to laugh and speak and munch their crusts, all at once) the scene in the *Lysis* of the dice-players. There the boys are! in full dress, to take part in a religious ceremony. It is scarcely over; but they are already busy with the knuckle-bones, some just outside the door, others in a corner. Though Plato never tells one without due motive, yet he loves a story for its own sake, can make one of fact or fancy at a moment's notice, or re-tell other people's better: how those dear skinny grasshoppers of Attica, for instance, had once been human creatures, who, when the Muses first came on earth, were so absorbed by their music that they forgot even to eat and drink, till they died of it. And then the story of Gyges in *The Republic*, and the ring that can make its wearer invisible:—it goes as easily, as the ring itself round the finger.

5. Like all masters of literature, Plato has of course varied excellences; but perhaps none of them has won for him a larger number of friendly readers than this impress of visible reality. For him, truly (as he supposed the highest sort of knowledge must of necessity be) all knowledge was like knowing a *person*. The Dialogue itself, being, as it is, the special creation of his literary art, becomes in his hands, and by his masterly conduct of it, like a single living person; so comprehensive a sense does he bring to bear upon it of the slowly-developing physiognomy of the thing—its organic structure, its symmetry and expression—combining all the various, disparate subjects of *The Republic*, for example, into a manageable whole, so entirely that, looking back, one fancies this long dialogue of at least three hundred pages might have occupied, perhaps an afternoon.

6. And those who take part in it! If Plato did not create the "Socrates" of his Dialogues, he has created other characters hardly less life-like. The young Charmides, the incarnation of natural, as the aged Cephalus of acquired, temperance; his Sophoclean amenity as he sits there pontifically at the altar, in the court of his peaceful house; the large company, of varied character and of every age, which moves in those Dialogues, though still oftenest the young in all their youthful liveliness:—who that knows them at all can doubt Plato's hold on persons, that of persons on him? Sometimes, even when they are not formally introduced into his work, characters that had interested, impressed, or touched him, inform and colour it, as if with their personal influence, showing through what purports to be the wholly abstract analysis of some wholly abstract moral situation. Thus, the form of the dying Socrates himself is visible pathetically in the description of the suffering righteous man, actually put into his own mouth in the second book of *The Republic*; as the winning brilliancy of the lost spirit of Alcibiades infuses those pages of the sixth, which

discuss the nature of one by birth and endowments an aristocrat, amid the dangers to which it is exposed in the Athens of that day—the qualities which must make him, if not the saviour, the destroyer, of a society which cannot remain unaffected by his showy presence. *Corruptio optimi pessima!* Yet even here, when Plato is dealing with the inmost elements of personality, his eye is still on its object, on *character* as seen in *characteristics*, through those details, which make character a sensible fact, the changes of colour in the face as of tone in the voice, the gestures, the really physiognomic value, or the mere tricks, of gesture and glance and speech. What is visibly expressive in, or upon, persons; those flashes of temper which check yet give renewed interest to the course of a conversation; the delicate touches of intercourse, which convey to the very senses all the subtleties of the heart or of the intelligence:—it is always more than worth his while to make note of these.

7. We see, for instance, the sharp little pygmy bit of a soul that catches sight of any little thing so keenly, and makes a very proper lawyer. We see, as well as hear, the "rhapsodist," whose sensitive performance of his part is nothing less than an "interpretation" of it, artist and critic at once: the personal vanities of the various speakers in his Dialogues, as though Plato had observed, or overheard them, alone; and the inevitable prominence of youth wherever it is present at all, notwithstanding the real sweetness of manner and modesty of soul he records of it so affectionately. It is this he loves best to linger by; to feel himself in contact with a condition of life, which translates all it is, so immediately, into delightful colour, and movement, and sound. The eighth and ninth books of *The Republic* are a grave contribution, as you know, to abstract moral and political theory, a generalisation of weighty changes of character in men and states. But his observations on the concrete traits of individuals, young or old, which enliven us on the way; the difference in sameness of sons and fathers, for instance; the influence of servants on their masters; how the minute ambiguities of rank, as a family becomes impoverished, tell on manners, on temper; all the play of moral colour in the reflex of mere circumstance on what men really are:—the characterisation of all this has with Plato a touch of the peculiar fineness of Thackeray, one might say. Plato enjoys it for its own sake, and would have been an excellent writer of fiction.

8. There is plenty of humour in him also of course, and something of irony—salt, to keep the exceeding richness and sweetness of his discourse from cloying the palate. The affectations of sophists, or professors, their staginess or their inelegance, the harsh laugh, the swaggering ways, of Thrasymachus, whose determination to make the general company share in a private conversation, is significant of his whole character, he notes with a finely-pointed pencil, with something of the fineness of malice,—*malin*, as the French say. Once

Thrasymachus had been actually seen to blush. It is with a very different sort of fineness Plato notes the blushes of the young; of Hippocrates, for instance, in the *Protagoras*. The great Sophist was said to be in Athens, at the house of Callicles, and the diligent young scholar is up betimes, eager to hear him. He rouses Socrates before daylight. As they linger in the court, the lad speaks of his own intellectual aspirations; blushes at his confidence. It was just then that the morning sun blushed with his first beam, as if to reveal the lad's blushing face.—Καὶ ὃς εἶπεν ἐρυθριάσας, ἤδη γὰρ ὑπέφαινέ τι ἡμέρας ὥστε καταφανῆ αὐτὸν γενέσθαι. He who noted that so precisely had, surely, the delicacy of the artist, a fastidious eye for the subtleties of colour as soul made visibly expressive. "Poor creature as I am," says the Platonic Socrates, in the *Lysis*, concerning another youthful blush, "Poor creature as I am, I have one talent: I can recognise, at first sight, the lover and the beloved."

9. So it is with the audible world also. The exquisite monotony of the voice of the great sophist, for example, "once set in motion, goes ringing on like a brazen pot, which if you strike it continues to sound till some one lays his hand upon it." And if the delicacy of eye and ear, so also the keenness and constancy of his observation, are manifest in those elaborately wrought images for which the careful reader lies in wait: the mutiny of the sailors in the ship—ship of the state, or of one's own soul: the echoes and beams and shadows of that half-illuminated cavern, the human mind: the caged birds in the *Theætetus*, which are like the flighty, half-contained notions of an imperfectly educated understanding. *Real* notions are to be ingrained by persistent thoroughness of the "dialectic" method, as if by conscientious dyers. He makes us stay to watch such dyers busy with their purple stuff, as he had done; adding as it were ethic colour to what he sees with the eye, and painting while he goes, as if on the margin of his high philosophical discourse, himself scarcely aware; as the monkish scribe set bird or flower, with so much truth of earth, in the blank spaces of his heavenly meditation.

10. Now Plato is one for whom the visible world thus "really exists" because he is by nature and before all things, from first to last, unalterably a lover. In that, precisely, lies the secret of the susceptible and diligent eye, the so sensitive ear. The central interest of his own youth—of his profoundly impressible youth—as happens always with natures of real capacity, gives law and pattern to all that succeeds it. Τὰ ἐρωτικά, as he says, the experience, the discipline, of love, had been that for Plato; and, as love must of necessity deal above all with visible persons, this discipline involved an exquisite culture of the senses. It is "as lovers use," that he is ever on the watch for those dainty messages, those finer intimations, to eye and ear. If in the later development of his philosophy the highest sort of knowledge comes to seem like the knowledge of a person, the

relation of the reason to truth like the commerce of one person with another, the peculiarities of personal relationship thus moulding his conception of the properly invisible world of ideas, this is partly because, for a lover, the entire visible world, its hues and outline, its attractiveness, its power and bloom, must have associated themselves pre-eminently with the power and bloom of visible living persons. With these, as they made themselves known by word and glance and touch, through the medium of the senses, lay the forces, which, in that inexplicable tyranny of one person over another, shaped the soul.

11. Just there, then, is the secret of Plato's intimate concern with, his power over, the sensible world, the apprehensions of the sensuous faculty: he is a lover, a great lover, somewhat after the manner of Dante. For him, as for Dante, in the impassioned glow of his conceptions, the material and the spiritual are blent and fused together. While, in that fire and heat, what is spiritual attains the definite visibility of a crystal, what is material, on the other hand, will lose its earthiness and impurity. It is of the amorous temper, therefore, you must think in connexion with Plato's youth—of this, amid all the strength of the genius in which it is so large a constituent,—indulging, developing, refining, the sensuous capacities, the powers of eye and ear, of the fancy also which can re-fashion, of the speech which can best respond to and reproduce, their liveliest presentments. That is why when Plato speaks of visible things it is as if you saw them. He who in the *Symposium* describes so vividly the pathway, the ladder, of love, its joyful ascent towards a more perfect beauty than we have ever yet actually seen, by way of a parallel to the gradual elevation of mind towards perfect knowledge, knew all that, we may be sure—τὰ ἐρωτικά—all the ways of lovers, in the literal sense. He speaks of them retrospectively indeed, but knows well what he is talking about. Plato himself had not been always a mere Platonic lover; was rather, naturally, as he makes Socrates say of himself, ἥττων τῶν καλῶν—subject to the influence of fair persons. A certain penitential colour amid that glow of fancy and expression, hints that the final harmony of his nature had been but gradually beaten out, and invests the temperance, actually so conspicuous in his own nature, with the charms of a patiently elaborated effect of art.

12. For we must remind ourselves just here, that, quite naturally also, instinctively, and apart from the austere influences which claimed and kept his allegiance later, Plato, with a kind of unimpassioned passion, was a lover in particular of temperance; of temperance too, as it may be *seen*, as a visible thing—seen in Charmides, say! in that subdued and grey-eyed loveliness, "clad in sober grey"; or in those youthful athletes which, in ancient marble, reproduce him and the like of him with sound, firm outlines, such as temperance secures. Still, that some more luxurious sense of physical beauty had at one time

greatly disturbed him, divided him against himself, we may judge from his own words in a famous passage of the *Phædrus* concerning the management, the so difficult management, of those winged steeds of the body, which is the chariot of the soul.

13. Puzzled, in some degree, Plato seems to remain, not merely in regard to the higher love and the lower, Aphrodite Urania and Aphrodite Pandemus, as he distinguishes them in the *Symposium*; nor merely with the difficulty of arbitrating between some inward beauty, and that which is outward; with the odd mixture everywhere, save in its still unapprehended but eternal essence, of the beautiful with what is otherwise; but he is yet more harassed by the experience (it is in this shape that the world-old puzzle of the existence of evil comes to him) that even to the truest eyesight, to the best trained faculty of soul, the beautiful would never come to seem strictly concentric with the good. That seems to have taxed his understanding as gravely as it had tried his will, and he was glad when in the mere natural course of years he was become at all events less ardent a lover. 'Tis he is the authority for what Sophocles had said on the happy decay of the passions as age advanced: it was "like being set free from service to a band of madmen." His own distinguishing note is tranquil afterthought upon this conflict, with a kind of envy of the almost disembodied old age of Cephalus, who quotes that saying of Sophocles amid his placid sacrificial doings. Connect with this quiet scene, and contrast with the luxuriant power of the *Phædrus* and the *Symposium*, what, for a certain touch of later mysticism in it, we might call Plato's evening prayer, in the ninth book of *The Republic*.—

> When any one, being healthfully and temperately disposed towards himself, turns to sleep, having stirred the reasonable part of him with a feast of fair thoughts and high problems, being come to full consciousness, himself with himself; and has, on the other hand, committed the element of desire neither to appetite, nor to surfeiting, to the end that this may slumber well, and, by its pain or pleasure, cause no trouble to that part which is best in him, but may suffer it, alone by itself, in its pure essence, to behold and aspire towards some object, and apprehend what it knows not—some event, of the past, it may be, or something that now is, or will be hereafter; and in like manner has soothed hostile impulse, so that, falling to no angry thoughts against any, he goes not to rest with a troubled spirit, but with those two parts at peace within, and with that third part, wherein reason is engendered, on the move:—you know, I think, that in sleep of this sort he lays special hold on truth, and then least of all is there lawlessness in the visions of his dreams. *Republic*, 571.

14. For Plato, being then about twenty-eight years old, had listened to the "Apology" of Socrates; had heard from them all that others had heard or seen of his last hours; himself perhaps actually witnessed those last hours. "Justice itself"—the "absolute" Justice—had then become almost a visible object, and had greatly solemnised him. The rich young man, rich also in intellectual gifts, who might have become (we see this in the adroit management of his written work) the most brilliant and effective of Sophists; who might have developed dialogues into plays, tragedy, perhaps comedy, as he cared; whose sensuous or graphic capacity might have made him the poet of an *Odyssey*, a Sappho, or a Catullus, or, say! just such a poet as, just because he was so attractive, would have been disfranchised in the Perfect City; was become the creature of an immense seriousness, of a fully adult sense, unusual in Greek perhaps even more than in Roman writers, "of the weightiness of the matters concerning which he has to discourse, and of the frailty of man." He inherits, alien as they might be to certain powerful influences in his own temper, alike the sympathies and the antipathies of that strange, delightful teacher, who had given him (most precious of gifts!) an inexhaustible interest in himself. It is in this way he inherits a preference for those trying severities of thought which are characteristic of the Eleatic school; an antagonism to the successful Sophists of the day, in whom the old sceptical "philosophy of motion" seemed to be renewed as a theory of morals; and henceforth, in short, this master of visible things, this so ardent lover, will be a lover of the invisible, with—Yes! there it is constantly, in the Platonic dialogues, not to be explained away—with a certain asceticism, amid all the varied opulence, of sense, of speech and fancy, natural to Plato's genius.

15. The lover, who is become a lover of the invisible, but still a lover, and therefore, literally, a seer, of it, carrying an elaborate cultivation of the bodily senses, of eye and ear, their natural force and acquired fineness—gifts akin properly to τὰ ἐρωτικά, as he says, to the discipline of sensuous love—into the world of intellectual abstractions; seeing and hearing there too, associating for ever all the imagery of things seen with the conditions of what primarily exists only for the mind, filling that "hollow land" with delightful colour and form, as if now at last the mind were veritably dealing with living people there, living people who play upon us through the affinities, the repulsion and attraction, of *persons* towards one another, all the magnetism, as we call it, of actual human friendship or love:—There, is the *formula* of Plato's genius, the essential condition of the specially Platonic temper, of Platonism. And his style, because it really is Plato's style, conforms to, and in its turn promotes in others, that mental situation. He breaks as it were visible colour into the very texture of his work: his vocabulary, the very stuff he manipulates, has its delightful

æsthetic qualities; almost every word, one might say, its figurative value. And yet no one perhaps has with equal power literally sounded the unseen depths of thought, and, with what may be truly called "substantial" word and phrase, given locality there to the mere adumbrations, the dim hints and surmise, of the speculative mind. For him, all gifts of sense and intelligence converge in one supreme faculty of theoretic vision, θεωρία, the imaginative reason.

16. To trace that thread of physical colour, entwined throughout, and multiplied sometimes into large tapestried figures, is the business, the enjoyment, of the student of the Dialogues, as he reads them. For this or that special literary quality indeed we may go safely by preference to this or that particular Dialogue; to the *Gorgias*, for instance, for the readiest Attic wit, and a manly practical sense in the handling of philosophy; to the *Charmides*, for something like the effect of sculpture in modelling a person; to the *Timæus*, for certain brilliant chromatic effects. Yet who that reads the *Theætetus*, or the *Phædrus*, or the seventh book of *The Republic*, can doubt Plato's gift in precisely the opposite direction; that gift of sounding by words the depths of thought, a plastic power literally, moulding to term and phrase what might have seemed in its very nature too impalpable and abstruse to lend itself, in any case, to language? He gives names to the invisible acts, processes, creations, of abstract mind, as masterly, as efficiently, as Adam himself to the visible living creations of old. As Plato speaks of them, we might say, those abstractions too become visible living creatures. We read the speculative poetry of Wordsworth, or Tennyson; and we may observe that a great metaphysical force has come into language which is by no means purely technical or scholastic; what a help such language is to the understanding, to a real hold over the things, the thoughts, the mental processes, those words denote; a vocabulary to which thought freely commits itself, trained, stimulated, raised, thereby, towards a high level of abstract conception, surely to the increase of our general intellectual powers. That, of course, is largely due to Plato's successor, to Aristotle's life-long labour of analysis and definition, and to his successors the Schoolmen, with their systematic culture of a precise instrument for the registration, by the analytic intellect, of its own subtlest movements. But then, Aristotle, himself the first of the Schoolmen, had succeeded Plato, and did but formulate, as a terminology "of art," as technical language, what for Plato is still vernacular, original, personal, the product in him of an instinctive imaginative power—a sort of *visual* power, but causing others also to see what is matter of original intuition for him.

17. From first to last our faculty of thinking is limited by our command of speech. Now it is straight from Plato's lips, as if in natural conversation, that

the language came, in which the mind has ever since been discoursing with itself concerning itself, in that inward dialogue, which is the "active principle" of the dialectic method as an instrument for the attainment of truth. For, the essential, or dynamic, dialogue, is ever that dialogue of the mind with itself, which any converse with Socrates or Plato does but promote. The very words of Plato, then, challenge us straightway to larger and finer apprehension of the processes of our own minds; are themselves a discovery in the sphere of mind. It was he made us freemen of those solitary places, so trying yet so attractive: so remote and high, they seem, yet are naturally so close to us: he peopled them with intelligible forms. Nay more! By his peculiar gift of verbal articulation he divined the mere hollow spaces which a knowledge, then merely potential, and an experience still to come, would one day occupy. And so, those who cannot admit his actual speculative results, precisely *his* report on the invisible theoretic world, have been to the point sometimes, in their objection, that by sheer effectiveness of abstract language, he gave an illusive air of reality or substance to the mere nonentities of metaphysic hypothesis—of a mind trying to feed itself on its own emptiness.

18. Just there—in the situation of one, shaped, by combining nature and circumstance, into a seer who has a sort of sensuous love of the unseen—is the paradox of Plato's genius, and therefore, always, of Platonism, of the Platonic temper. His aptitude for things visible, with the gift of words, empowers him to express, as if for the eyes, what except to the eye of the mind is strictly invisible, what an acquired asceticism induces him to rank above, and sometimes, in terms of harshest dualism, oppose to, the sensible world. Plato is to be interpreted not merely by his antecedents, by the influence upon him of those who preceded him, but by his successors, by the temper, the intellectual alliances, of those who directly or indirectly have been sympathetic with him. Now it is noticeable that, at first sight somewhat incongruously, a certain number of Manicheans have always been of his company; people who held that matter was evil. Pointing significantly to an unmistakable vein of Manichean, or Puritan sentiment actually there in the Platonic Dialogues, these rude companions or successors of his, carry us back to his great predecessor, to Socrates, whose personal influence had so strongly enforced on Plato the severities, moral and intellectual, alike of Parmenides and of the Pythagoreans. The cold breath of a harshly abstract, a too incorporeal philosophy, had blown, like an east wind, on that last depressing day in the prison-cell of Socrates; and the venerable commonplaces then put forth, in which an overstrained pagan sensuality seems to be reacting, to be taking vengeance, on itself, turned now sick and suicidal, will lose none of their weight with Plato:—That "all who rightly touch philosophy, study nothing else than to *die*, and to be *dead*,"—that

"the soul reasons best, when, as much as possible, it comes to be alone with itself, bidding good-bye to the body, and, to the utmost of its power, rejecting communion with it, with the very touch of it, aiming at what *is*." It was, in short, as if for the soul to have come into a human body at all, had been the seed of disease in it, the beginning of its own proper death.

19. As for any adornments or provision for this body, the master had declared that a true philosopher as such would make as little of them as possible. To those young hearers, the words of Socrates may well have seemed to anticipate, not the visible world he had then delineated in glowing colour as if for the bodily eye, but only the chilling influence of the hemlock; and it was because Plato was only half convinced of the Manichean or Puritan element in his master's doctrine, or rather was in contact with it on one side only of his complex and genial nature, that Platonism became possible, as a temper for which, in strictness, the opposition of matter to spirit has no ultimate or real existence. Not to be "pure" from the body, but to identify it, in its utmost fairness, with the fair soul, by a gymnastic "fused in music," became, from first to last, the aim of education as he conceived it. That the body is but "a hindrance to the attainment of philosophy, if one takes it along with one as a companion in one's search" (a notion which Christianity, at least in its later though wholly legitimate developments, will correct) can hardly have been the last thought of Plato himself on quitting it. He opens his door indeed to those austere monitors. They correct the sensuous richness of his genius, but could not suppress it. The sensuous lover becomes a lover of the invisible, but still a lover, after his earlier pattern, carrying into the world of intellectual vision, of θεωρία, all the associations of the actual world of sight. Some of its invisible realities he can all but see with the bodily eye: the absolute Temperance, in the person of the youthful Charmides; the absolute Righteousness, in the person of the dying Socrates. Yes, truly! all true knowledge will be like the knowledge of a person, of living persons, and truth, for Plato, in spite of his Socratic asceticism, to the last, something to *look* at. The eyes which had noted physical things, so finely, vividly, continuously, would be still at work; and, Plato thus qualifying the Manichean or Puritan element in Socrates by his own capacity for the world of sense, Platonism has contributed largely, has been an immense encouragement towards, the redemption of matter, of the world of sense, by art, by all right education, by the creeds and worship of the Christian Church—towards the vindication of the dignity of the body.

20. It was doubtless because Plato was an excellent scholar that he did not begin to teach others till he was more than forty years old—one of the great scholars of the world, with Virgil and Milton: by which is implied that,

possessed of the inborn genius, of those natural powers, which sometimes bring with them a certain defiance of rule, of the intellectual habits of others, he acquires, by way of habit and rule, all that can be taught and learned; and what is thus derived from others by docility and discipline, what is *rangé*, comes to have in him, and in his work, an equivalent weight with what is unique, impulsive, underivable. Raphael—Raphael, as you see him in the Blenheim *Madonna*, is a supreme example of such scholarship in the sphere of art. Born of a romantically ancient family, understood to be the descendant of Solon himself, Plato had been in early youth a writer of verse. That he turned to a more vigorous, though pedestrian mode of writing, was perhaps an effect of his corrective intercourse with Socrates, through some of the most important years of his life,—from twenty to twenty-eight.

21. He belonged to what was just then the discontented class, and might well have taken refuge from active political life in political ideals, or in a kind of self-imposed exile. A traveller, adventurous for that age, he certainly became. After the *Lehr-jahre*, the *Wander-jahre!*—all round the Mediterranean coasts as far west as Sicily. Think of what all that must have meant just then, for eyes which could see. If those journeys had begun in angry flight from home, it was for purposes of self-improvement they were continued: the delightful fruit of them is evident in what he writes; and finding him in friendly intercourse with Dionysius the elder, with Dio, and Dionysius the younger, at the polished court of Syracuse, we may understand that they were a search also for "the philosophic king," perhaps for the opportune moment of realising "the ideal state." In that case, his quarrels with those capricious tyrants show that he was disappointed. For the future he sought no more to pass beyond the charmed theoretic circle, "speaking wisdom," as was said of Pythagoras, only "among the perfect." He returns finally to Athens; and there, in the quiet precincts of the *Acadêmus*, which has left a somewhat dubious name to places where people come to be taught or to teach, founds, not a state, nor even a brotherhood, but only the first college, with something of a common life, of communism on that small scale, with Aristotle for one of its scholars, with its chapel, its gardens, its library with the authentic text of his *Dialogues* upon the shelves: we may just discern the sort of place through the scantiest notices. His reign was after all to be in his writings. Plato himself does nothing in them to retard the effacement which mere time brings to persons and their abodes; and there had been that, moreover, in his own temper, which promotes self-effacement. Yet as he left it, the place remained for centuries, according to his will, to its original use. What he taught through the remaining forty years of his life, the method of that teaching, whether it was less or more esoteric than the teaching of the extant *Dialogues*, is but matter of surmise. Writers, who in their day

might still have said much we should have liked to hear, give us little but old, quasi-supernatural stories, told as if they had been new ones, about him. The year of his birth fell, according to some, in the very year of the death of Pericles (a significant date!) but is not precisely ascertainable: nor is the year of his death, nor its manner. *Scribens est mortuus*, says Cicero:—after the manner of a true scholar, "he died pen in hand."

from THE DOCTRINE OF PLATO, PART I.

The Theory of Ideas

[...] Of course we are not naturally formed to love, or be interested in, or attracted towards, the abstract as such; to notions, we might think, carefully deprived of all the incident, the colour and variety, which fits things—this or that—to the constitution and natural habit of our minds, fits them for attachment to what we really are. We cannot love or live upon *genus* and *species*, accident or substance, but for our minds, as for our bodies, need an orchard or a garden, with fruit and roses. Take a seed from the garden. What interest it has for us all lies in our sense of potential differentiation to come: the leaves, leaf upon leaf, the flowers, a thousand new seeds in turn. It is so with animal seed; and with humanity, individually, or as a whole, its expansion into a detailed, ever-changing, parti-coloured history of particular facts and persons. Abstraction, the introduction of general ideas, seems to close it up again; to reduce flower and fruit, odour and savour, back again into the dry and worthless seed. We might as well be colour-blind at once, and there is not a proper name left! We may contrast generally the mental world we actually live in, where classification, the reduction of all things to common types, has come so far, and where the particular, to a great extent, is known only as the member of a class, with that other world, on the other side of the generalising movement to which Plato and his master so largely contributed—a world we might describe as being under Homeric conditions, such as we picture to ourselves with regret, for which experience was intuition, and life a continuous surprise, and every object unique, where all knowledge was still of the concrete and the particular, face to face delightfully.

7. To that gaudy tangle of what gardens, after all, are meant to produce, in the decay of time, as we may think at first sight, the systematic, logical gardener put his meddlesome hand, and straightway all ran to seed; to *genus* and *species* and *differentia*, into formal classes, under general notions, and with—yes! with written labels fluttering on the stalks, instead of blossoms—a botanic or "physic" garden, as they used to say, instead of our flower-garden and orchard. And yet (it must be confessed on the other hand) what we actually see, see and hear, is more interesting than ever; the nineteenth century as compared with the first, with Plato's days or Homer's; the faces, the persons behind those masks which yet express so much, the flowers, or whatever it may happen to be they carry or touch. The concrete, and that even as a visible thing, has gained

immeasurably in richness and compass, in fineness, and interest towards us, by the process, of which those acts of generalisation, of reduction to class and generic type, have certainly been a part. And holding still to the concrete, the particular, to the visible or sensuous, if you will, last as first, thinking of that as essentially the one vital and lively thing, really worth our while in a short life, we may recognise sincerely what generalisation and abstraction have done or may do, are defensible as doing, just for that—for the particular gem or flower—what its proper service is to a mind in search, precisely, of a concrete and intuitive knowledge such as that.

8. Think, for a moment, of the difference, as regards mental attitude, between the naturalist who deals with things through ideas, and the layman (so to call him) in picking up a shell on the sea-shore; what it is that the subsumption of the individual into the species, its subsequent alliance to and co-ordination with other species, really does for the furnishing of the mind of the former. The layman, though we need not suppose him inattentive, or unapt to retain impressions, is in fact still but a child; and the shell, its colours and convolution, no more than a dainty, very easily destructible toy to him. Let him become a schoolboy about it, so to speak. The toy he puts aside; his mind is drilled perforce, to learn *about* it; and thereby is exercised, he may think, with everything except just the thing itself, as he cares for it; with other shells, with some general laws of life, and for a while it might seem that, turning away his eyes from the "vanity" of the particular, he has been made to sacrifice the concrete, the real and living product of nature, to a mere dry and abstract product of the mind. But when he comes out of school, and on the sea-shore again finds a fellow to his toy, perhaps a finer specimen of it, he may see what the service of that converse with the general has really been towards the concrete, towards what he sees—in regard to the particular thing he actually sees. By its juxtaposition and co-ordination with what is ever more and more not *it*, by the contrast of its very imperfection, at this point or that, with its own proper and perfect type, this concrete and particular thing has, in fact, been enriched by the whole colour and expression of the whole circumjacent world, concentrated upon, or as it were at focus in, it. By a kind of short-hand now, and as if in a single moment of vision, all that, which only a long experience, moving patiently from part to part, could exhaust, its manifold alliance with the entire world of nature, is legible upon it, as it lies there in one's hand.

9. So it is with the shell, the gem, with a glance of the eye; so it may be with the moral act, with a condition of the mind, or a feeling. You may draw, by use of this coinage (it is Hobbes's figure) this coinage of representative words and thoughts, at your pleasure, upon the accumulative capital of the

whole experience of humanity. Generalisation, whatever Platonists, or Plato himself at mistaken moments, may have to say about it, is a method, not of obliterating the concrete phenomenon, but of enriching it, with the joint perspective, the significance, the expressiveness, of all other things beside. What broad-cast light he enjoys!—that scholar, confronted with the sea-shell, for instance, or with some enigma of heredity in himself or another, with some condition of a particular soul, in circumstances which may never precisely so occur again; in the contemplation of that single phenomenon, or object, or situation. He not only sees, but understands (thereby only seeing the more) and will, therefore, also remember. The significance of the particular object he will retain, by use of his intellectual apparatus of notion and general law, as, to use Plato's own figure, fluid matter may be retained in vessels, not indeed of unbaked clay, but of alabaster or bronze. So much by way of apology for general ideas—abstruse, or intangible, or dry and seedy and wooden, as we may sometimes think them. [...]

[*The Idea of Beauty*]

20. [...] With the lover, who had graduated, was become a master, in the school of love, but had turned now to the love of intellectual and strictly invisible things, it was as if the faculty of physical vision, of the bodily eye, were still at work at the very centre of intellectual abstraction. Abstract ideas themselves became animated, living persons, almost corporeal, as if with hands and eyes. And it is, as a consequence, but partly also as a secondary reinforcing cause, of this mental condition, that the idea of Beauty becomes for Plato the central idea; the permanently typical instance of what an idea means; of its relation to particular things, and to the action of our thoughts upon them. It was to the lover dealing with physical beauty, a thing seen, yet unseen—seen by all, in some sense, and yet, truly, by one and not by another, as if through some capricious, personal self-discovery, by some law of affinity between the seer and what is seen, the knowing and the known—that the nature and function of an idea, as such, would come home most clearly. And then, while visible beauty is the clearest, the most certain thing, in the world (lovers will always tell you so) real with the reality of something hot or cold in one's hand, it also comes nearest of all things, so Plato assures us, to its eternal pattern or prototype. For some reason, the eternal idea of beauty had left visible copies of itself, shadows, antitypes, out of all proportion, in their truthfulness and adequacy, to any copy, left here with us, of Justice, for instance, or Equality, or the Perfect State. The typical instance of an abstract

idea, yet pre-occupying the mind with all the colour and circumstance of the relationship of person to person, the idea of Beauty, conveyed into the entire theory of ideas, the associations which belong properly to such relationships only. A certain measure of caprice, of capricious preference or repulsion, would thus be naturally incidental to the commerce of men's minds with what really is, with the world in which things really are, only so far as they are truly known. "Philosophers are *lovers* of truth and of that which *is*—impassioned lovers": *Τοῦ ὄντος τε καὶ ἀληθείας ἐραστάς, τοὺς φιλοσόφους.* They are the cornerstone, as readers of *The Republic* know, of the ideal state—those impassioned lovers, *ἐραστάς*, of that which really is, and in comparison wherewith, office, wealth, honour, the love of which has rent Athens, the world, to pieces, will be of no more than secondary importance.

THE DOCTRINE OF PLATO, PART II.

Dialectic

Three different forms of composition have, under the intellectual conditions of different ages, prevailed—three distinct literary methods, in the presentation of philosophic thought; the metrical form earliest, when philosophy was still a matter of intuition, imaginative, sanguine, often turbid or obscure, and became a *Poem*, Περὶ Φύσεως, "Concerning Nature"; according to the manner of Pythagoras, "his golden verses," of Parmenides or Empedokles, after whom Lucretius in his turn modelled the finest extant illustration of that manner of writing, of thinking.

2. It was succeeded by precisely the opposite manner, when native intuition had shrunk into dogmatic system, the dry bones of which rattle in one's ears, with Aristotle, or Aquinas, or Spinoza, as a formal treatise; the perfected philosophic temper being situate midway between those opposites, in the third essential form of the literature of philosophy, namely the essay; that characteristic literary type of our own time, a time so rich and various in special apprehensions of truth, so tentative and dubious in its sense of their *ensemble*, and issues. Strictly appropriate form of our modern philosophic literature, the essay came into use at what was really the invention of the relative, or "modern" spirit, in the Renaissance of the sixteenth century.[1]

3. The poem, the treatise, the essay: you see already that these three methods of writing are no mere literary accidents, dependent on the personal choice of this or that particular writer, but necessities of literary form, determined directly by matter, as corresponding to three essentially different ways in which the human mind relates itself to truth. If oracular verse, stimulant but enigmatic, is the proper vehicle of enthusiastic intuitions; if the treatise, with its ambitious array of premiss and conclusion, is the natural out-put of scholastic all-sufficiency; so, the form of the essay, as we have it towards the end of the sixteenth century, most significantly in Montaigne, representative essayist because the representative doubter, inventor of the name as, in essence, of the thing—of the essay, in its seemingly modest aim, its really large and adventurous possibilities—is indicative of Montaigne's peculiar function in

---

1. *Essay*—"A loose sally of the mind," says Johnson's Dictionary. Bailey's earlier Dictionary gives another suggestive use of the word "among miners"—*A little trench or hole, which they dig to search for ore.*

regard to his age, as in truth the commencement of our own. It provided him with precisely the literary form necessary to a mind for which truth itself is but a possibility, realisable not as general conclusion, but rather as the elusive effect of a particular personal experience; to a mind which, noting faithfully those random lights that meet it by the way, must needs content itself with suspension of judgment, at the end of the intellectual journey, to the very last asking: *Que scais-je?* Who knows?—in the very spirit of that old Socratic contention, that all true philosophy is but a refined sense of one's ignorance.

4. And as Aristotle is the inventor of the treatise, so the Platonic Dialogue, in its conception, its peculiar opportunities, is essentially an essay—an essay, now and then passing into the earlier form of philosophic poetry, the prose-poem of Heraclitus. There have been effective writers of dialogue since, Bruno, for instance, Berkeley, Landor, with whom, however, that literary form has had no strictly constitutional propriety to the kind of matter it conveyed, as lending itself (that is to say) structurally to a many-sided but hesitant consciousness of the truth. Thus, with Berkeley, its purpose is but to give a popular turn to certain very dogmatic opinions, about which there is no diffidence, there are no half-lights, in the writer's own mind. With Plato, on the other hand, with Plato least of all is the dialogue—that peculiar modification of the essay—anything less than essential, necessary, organic: the very form belongs to, is of the organism of, the matter which it embodies. For Plato's Dialogues, in fact, reflect, they refine upon while they fulfil, they idealise, the actual method, in which, by preference to anything like formal lecturing (the lecture being, so to speak, a treatise in embryo) Socrates conveyed his doctrine to others. We see him in those Dialogues of Plato, still loitering in the public places, the open houses, the suburban roads, of Athens, as if seeking truth from others; seeking it, doubtless, from himself, but along with, and by the help of, his supposed scholars, for whom, indeed, he can but bring their own native conceptions of truth to the birth; but always faithfully registering just so much light as is given, and, so to speak, never concluding.

5. The Platonic Dialogue is the literary transformation, in a word, of what was the intimately home-grown method of Socrates, not only of conveying truth to others, but of coming by it for himself. The essence of that method, of "dialectic" in all its forms, as its very name denotes, is dialogue, the habit of seeking truth by means of question and answer, primarily with one's self. Just there, lies the validity of the method—in a dialogue, an endless dialogue, with one's self; a dialogue concerning those first principles, or "universal definitions," or notions, those "ideas," which, according to Plato, are the proper objects of all real knowledge; concerning the adequacy of one's hold

upon them; the relationship to them of other notions; the plausible conjectures in our own or other minds, which come short of them; the elimination, by their mere presence in the mind, of positive ignorance or error. Justice, Beauty, Perfect Polity, and the like, in outlines of eternal and absolute certainty:—they were to be apprehended by "dialectic," literally, by a method (μέθοδος) a circuitous journey, presented by the Platonic dialogues in its most accomplished literary form.

6. For the certainty, the absolute and eternal character, of such ideas involved, with much labour and scruple, repeated acts of qualification and correction; many readjustments to experience; expansion, by larger lights from it; those exclusions and inclusions, *debitæ naturæ* (to repeat Bacon's phrase) demanded, that is to say, by the veritable nature of the facts which those ideas are designed to represent. "Representation" was, in fact, twofold, and comprehended many successive steps under each of its divisions. The thought was to be adjusted, first, to the phenomena, to the facts, daintily, to the end that the said thought might just cover those facts, and no more. To the thought, secondly, to the conception, thus articulated, it was necessary to adjust the term; the term, or "definition," by which it might be conveyed into the mind of another. The dialogue—the freedom, the variety and elasticity, of dialogue, informal, easy, natural, alone afforded the room necessary for that long and complex process. If one, if Socrates, seemed to become the teacher of another, it was but by thinking aloud for a few moments over his own lesson, or leaning upon that other as he went along that difficult way which each one must really prosecute for himself, however full such comradeship might be of happy occasions for the awakening of the latent knowledge, with which mind is by nature so richly stored. The Platonic Socrates, in fact, does not propose to teach anything: is but willing, "along with you," and if you concur, "to consider, to seek out, what the thing may be. Perchance using our eyes in common, rubbing away, we might cause Justice, for instance, to glint forth, as from fire-sticks."[1]

7. "And," again, "is not the road to Athens made for conversation?" Yes! It might seem that movement, after all, and any habit that promoted movement, promoted the power, the successes, the fortunate parturition, of the mind. A method such as this, a process (*processus*) a movement of thought, which is the very converse of mathematical or demonstrative reasoning, and incapable therefore of conventional or scholastic form, of "exactness," in fact; which proceeded to truth, not by the analysis and application of an axiom, but by a gradual suppression of error, of error in the form of partial or exaggerated truths

---

1. Σκέψασθαι καὶ συζητῆσαι ὅτι πότε ἔστιν· καί, τάχ᾽ ἄν, παρ᾽ ἄλληλα σκοποῦντες, καὶ τρίβοντες, ὥσπερ ἐκ πυρείων, ἐκλάμψαι ποιήσαιμεν τὴν δικαιοσύνην.

from THE DOCTRINE OF PLATO 247

on the subject-matter proposed, found its proper literary vehicle in a dialogue, the more flexible the better. It was like a journey indeed, that essay towards Justice, for example, or the true Polity; a journey, not along the simple road to Athens, but to a mountain's top. The proportions, the outline, the relation of the thing to its neighbours,—how do the inexperienced in such journeys mistake them, as they climb! What repeated misconceptions, embodying, one by one, some mere particularity of view, the perspective of this or that point of view, forthwith abandoned, some apprehension of mountain form and structure, just a little short, or, it may be, immeasurably short, of what Plato would call the "synoptic" view of the mountain as a whole. From this or that point, some insignificant peak presented itself as the mountain's veritable crest: inexperience would have sworn to the truth of a wholly illusive perspective, as the next turn in the journey assured one. It is only upon the final step, with free view at last on every side, uniting together and justifying all those various, successive, partial apprehensions of the difficult way—only on the summit, comes the intuitive comprehension of what the true form of the mountain really is; with a mental, or rather an imaginative hold upon which, for the future, we can find our way securely about it; observing perhaps that, next to that final intuition, the first view, the first impression, had been truest about it.

8. Such, in its full scope, is the journey or pilgrimage, the method (ὁδός, κίνησις, μέθοδος) of the Socratic, of the perfected Platonic dialectic, towards the truth, the true knowledge, of Bravery or Friendship, for instance; of Space or Motion, again, as suggested in the seventh book of *The Republic*; of the ideal City, of the immaculate Beauty. You are going about Justice, for example—that great complex elevation on the level surface of life, whose top, it may be, reaches to heaven. You fancy you have grasped its outline. Ἀλλὰ μεταθώμεθα. You are forced on, perhaps by your companion, a step further, and the view has already changed. "Persevere," Plato might say, "and a step may be made, upon which, again, the whole world around may change, the entire horizon and its relation to the point you stand on—a change from the half-light of conjecture to the full light of indefectible certitude." That, of course, can only happen by a *summary* act of intuition upon the entire perspective, wherein all those partial apprehensions, which one by one may have seemed inconsistent with each other, find their due place, or (to return to the Platonic Dialogue again, to the actual process of dialectic as there exposed) by that final impression of a subject, a theorem, in which the mind attains a hold, as if by a single imaginative act, through all the transitions of a long conversation, upon all the seemingly opposite contentions of all the various speakers at once. We see already why Platonic dialectic—the ladder, as Plato thinks, by which alone we can ascend into the entirely reasonable

world (νοητὸς τόπος) beginning with the boyish difficulties and crudities of Meno, for instance, is a process which may go on, at least with those gifted by nature and opportunity, as in the Perfect City,—may go on to the close of life, and, as Pythagorean theory suggests, perhaps does not end even then.

9. The process of dialectic, as represented in the Platonic Dialogues, may seem, therefore, inconsistent with itself, if you isolate this or that particular movement, in what is a very complex process, with many phases of development. It is certainly difficult, and that not merely on a first reading, to grasp the unity of the various statements Plato has made about it. Now it may seem to differ from ordinary reasoning by a certain plausibility only: it is logic, *plus* persuasion; helping, gently enticing, a child out of his natural errors; carefully explaining difficulties by the way, as one can best do, by question and answer with him; above all, never falling into the mistake of the *obscurum per obscurius*. At another time it may seem to aim at plausibility of another sort; at mutual complaisance, as Thrasymachus complains. It would be possible, of course, to present an insincere dialogue, in which certain of the disputants shall be mere men of straw. In the *Philebus* again, dialectic is only the name of the process (described there as exactly, almost as technically, as Aristotle, or some modern master of applied logic, might describe it) of the resolution of a genus into its species. Or it lapses into "eristic"—into an argument for its own sake; or sinks into logomachy, a mere dispute about words. Or yet again, an immense, a boundless promise is made for it, as in the seventh book of *The Republic*. It is a life, a systematised, but comprehensive and far-reaching, intellectual life, in which the reason, nay, the whole nature of man, realises all it was designed to be, by the beatific "vision of all time and all existence."

10. Now all these varying senses of the word "dialectic" fall within compass, if we remember that for Plato, as for every other really philosophic thinker, method must be *one*; that it must cover, or be understood to cover, the entire process, all the various processes, of the mind, in pursuit of properly representative ideas, of a reasoned reflex of experience; and that for Plato, this process is essentially a long discourse or reasoning of the mind with itself. It is that dynamic, or essential, dialogue of the mind with itself, which lends, or imputes, its active principle to the written or spoken dialogue, which, in return, lends its name to the method it figures—"dialectic." Well! in that long and complex dialogue of the mind with itself, many persons, so to speak, will necessarily take part; so many persons as there are possible contrasts or shades in the apprehension of some complex subject. The *advocatus diaboli* will be heard from time to time. The dog also, or, as the Greeks said, the wolf, will out with his story against the man; and one of the interlocutors will always be a child, turning round upon us innocently, candidly, with our own

admissions, or surprising us, perhaps at the last moment, by what seems his invincible ignorance, when we thought it rooted out of him. There will be a youth, inexperienced in the capacities of language, who will compel us to allow much time to the discussion of words and phrases, though not always unprofitably. And to the last, let us hope, refreshing with his enthusiasm, the weary or disheartened enquirer (who is always also of the company) the rightly sanguine youth, ingenuous and docile, to whom, surely, those friendly living ideas will be willing, longing, to come, after that Platonic law of affinity, so effectual in these matters—ὅμοῖον ὁμοίῳ.

11. With such a nature above all, bringing with it its felicities of temperament, with the sort of natures (as we may think) which intellectually can but thrive, a method like that, the dialectic method, will also have its felicities, its singular good fortunes. A voyage of discovery, prosecuted almost as if at random, the Socratic or Platonic "dialogue of enquiry," seems at times to be in charge of a kind of "Providence." Or again, it will be as when hunters or bird-catchers "beat the bush," as we say: Plato elaborates that figure in *The Republic*. Only, if they be knowing in the process, a fair percentage of birds will be found and taken. All the chances, or graces, of such a method, as actually followed in a whole life of free enquiry, *The Republic*, for a watchful reader, represents in little. And when, using still another figure, Socrates says: "I do not yet know, myself; but, we must just go where the argument carries us, as a vessel runs before the wind," he breathes the very soul of the "dialectic method":—ὅπη ἂν ὁ λόγος, ὥσπερ πνεῦμα, φέρῃ, ταύτῃ ἰτέον.

12. This dialectic method, this continuous discourse with one's self, being, for those who prosecute it with thoroughness, co-extensive with life itself—a part of the continuous company we keep with ourselves through life—will have its inequalities; its infelicities; above all, its final insecurity. "We argue rashly and adventurously," writes Plato, most truly, in the *Timæus*—aye, we, the Platonists, as such, sometimes—"by reason that, like ourselves, our discourses (our Platonic discourses, as such) have much participation in the temerity of chance." Of course, as in any other occasional conversation, with its dependence on the hour and the scene, the persons we are with, the humours of the moment, there will always be much of accident in this essentially informal, this un-methodical, method; and, therefore, opportunities for misuse, sometimes consciously. The candid reader notes instances of such, even in *The Republic*, not always on the part of Thrasymachus:—in this "new game of chess," played, as Plato puts it, not with counters, but with words, and not necessarily for the prize of truth, but, it may be, for the mere enjoyment of move and counter-move, of check-mating.

13. Since Zeno's paradoxes, in fact, the very air of Athens was become

sophisticated, infected with questionings, often vain enough; and the Platonic method had been, in its measure, determined by (the unfriendly might say, was in truth only a deposit from) that infected air. "Socrates," as he admits, "is easily refuted. Say rather, dear Agathon, that you cannot refute the truth." That is reassuring, certainly! For you might think sometimes, uneasily, of the Platonic Socrates, that, as he says of the Sophist, or of himself perhaps *en caricature*, in the *Euthydemus*, "Such is his skill in the war of words, that he can refute any proposition whatever, whether true or false"; that, in short, there is a dangerous facility abroad for proving all things whatever, equally well, of which Socrates, and his presumable allotment of truth, has but the general allotment.

14. The friendly, on the other hand, might rejoin even then, that, as Lessing suggests, the search for truth is a better thing for us than its possession. Plato, who supposes any knowledge worth the name to be "absolute and eternal"; whose constant contention it is, to separate *longo intervallo*, by the longest possible interval, science (ἐπιστήμη) as the possession of irresistible truth, from any and every sort of knowledge which falls short of that; would hardly have accepted the suggestion of Lessing. Yet, in spite of all that, in spite of the demand he makes for certainty and exactness and what is absolute, in all real knowledge, he does think, or inclines his reader to think, that truth, precisely because it resembles some high kind of relationship of persons to persons, depends a good deal on the receiver; and must be, in that degree, elusive, provisional, contingent, a matter of various approximation, and of an "economy," as is said; that it is partly a subjective attitude of mind:—that philosophic truth consists in the philosophic temper. "Socrates in Plato," remarks Montaigne acutely, "disputes, rather to the profit of the disputants, than of the dispute. He takes hold of the first subject, like one who has a more profitable end in view than to explain it; namely, to clear the understandings that he takes upon him to instruct and exercise."

15. Just there, in fact, is the justification of Plato's peculiar dialectical method, of its inexactness, its hesitancy, its scruples and reserve, as if he feared to obtrude knowledge on an unworthy receiver. The treatise, as the proper instrument of dogma—the Ethics of Aristotle, the Ethics of Spinoza—begins with a truth, or with a clear conviction of truth, in the axiom or definition, which it does but propose further to explain and apply.—The treatise, as the instrument of a dogmatic philosophy *begins* with an axiom or definition: the essay or dialogue, on the other hand, as the instrument of dialectic, does not necessarily so much as conclude in one; like that long dialogue with oneself, that dialectic process, which may be co-extensive with life. It does in truth little more than clear the ground, as we say, or the atmosphere, or the mental tablet,

that one may have a fair chance of knowing, or seeing, perhaps: it does but put one into a duly receptive attitude towards such possible truth, discovery, or revelation, as may one day occupy the ground, the tablet,—shed itself on the purified air; it does not provide a proposition, nor a system of propositions, but forms a temper.

16. What Plato presents to his readers is then, again, a paradox, or a reconciliation of opposed tendencies: on one side, the largest possible demand for infallible certainty in knowledge (it was he fixed that ideal of absolute truth, to which, vainly perhaps, the human mind, as such, aspires) yet, on the other side, the utmost possible inexactness, or contingency, in the method by which actually he proposes to attain it. It has been said that the humour of Socrates, of which the famous Socratic irony—the pretence to have a bad memory, to dislike or distrust long and formal discourse, to have taught nothing, to be but a mid-wife in relation to other people's thoughts—was an element, is more than a mere personal trait; that it was welcome as affording a means of escape from the full responsibilities of his teaching. It belonged, in truth, to the tentative character of dialectic, of question and answer as the method of discovery, of teaching and learning, to the position, in a word, of the philosophic *essayist*. That it was thus, might be illustrated abundantly from the Platonic dialogues. The irony, the Socratic humour, so serviceable to a diffident teacher, are, in fact, Plato's own. Κινδυνεύει, "it may chance to be," is, we may notice, a favourite catchword of his. The philosopher of Being, or, of the verb, "To be," is after all afraid of saying, "It is."

17. For, again, person dealing with person—with possible caprice, therefore, at least on one side—or intelligence with intelligence, is what Plato supposes in the reception of truth:—that, and not an exact mechanism, a precise machine, operating on, or with, an exactly ponderable matter. He has fears for truth, however carefully considered. To the very last falsehood will lurk, if not about truth itself, about this or that assent to it. The receiver may add the falsities of his own nature to the truth he receives. The proposition which embodies it very imperfectly, may not look to him, in those dark chambers of his individuality, of himself, into which none but he can ever get, to test the matter, what it looks to me, or to you. We may not even be thinking of, not looking at, the same thing, when we talk of Beauty, and the like; objects which, after all, to the Platonist are matters of θεωρία, of immediate intuition, of immediate vision, or, as Plato sometimes fancied, of an earlier personal experience; and which, as matter of such intuition, are incapable of analysis, and therefore, properly, incommunicable by words. Place, then, must be left to the last in any legitimate dialectic process for possible after-thoughts; for the introduction,

so to speak, of yet another interlocutor in the dialogue, which has, in fact, no necessary conclusion, and leaves off only because time is up, or when, as he says, one leaves off seeking through weariness (ἀποκάμνων). "What thought can think, another thought can mend." Another turn in the endless road may change the whole character of the perspective. You cannot, as the Sophist proposed to do (that was part of his foolishness) take and put truth into the soul. If you could, it might be established there, only as an "inward lie," as a mistake. "Must I take the argument, and literally insert it into your mind?" asks Thrasymachus. "Heaven forbid": answers Socrates. That is precisely what he fears most, for himself, and for others; and from first to last, demands, as the first condition of comradeship in that long journey in which he conceives teacher and learner to be but fellow-travellers, pilgrims side by side, sincerity, above all sincerity with one's self—that, and also freedom in reply. "Answer what you think, μεγαλοπρεπῶς—liberally." For it is impossible to make way otherwise, in a method which consists essentially in the development of knowledge by question and answer.

18. Misuse, again, is of course possible in a method which admits of no objective sanction or standard; the success of which depends on a loyalty to one's self, in the prosecution of it, of which no one else can be cognisant. And if we can misuse it with ourselves, how much more certainly can the expert abuse it with another. At every turn of the conversation, a door lies open to sophistry. Sophistry, logomachy, eristic: we may learn what these are, sometimes, from Plato's own practice. That justice is only useful as applied to things useless; that the just man is a kind of thief; and the like; is hardly so much as sophistry. And this too was possible in a method, which, with all its large outlook, has something of the irregularity, the accident, the heats and confusion, of life itself—a method of reasoning which can only in a certain measure be reasoned upon. How different the exactness which Aristotle supposes, and does his best to secure, in scientific procedure! For him, dialectic, Platonic dialectic, is, at best, a part of "eristic"—of the art, or trick, of merely popular and approximate debate, in matters where science is out of the question, and rhetoric has its office, not in providing for the intelligence, but in moulding the sentiments and the will. Conversely to that absoluteness and necessity which Plato himself supposes in all real knowledge, as "the spectacle of all time and all existence," it might seem that the only sort of truth attainable by his actual method, must be the truth of a particular time and place, for one and not for another. Διάλογος πειραστικός, "a Dialogue of search":—every one of Plato's Dialogues is in essence such like that whole, life-long, endless dialogue which dialectic, in its largest scope, does but formulate, and in which truly the last, the infallible word, after all, never gets spoken. Our pilgrimage

is meant indeed to end in nothing less than the *vision* of what we seek. But can we ever be quite sure that we are really come to that? By what sign or test?

19. Now oppose all this, all these peculiarities of the Platonic method, as we find it, to the exact and formal method of Aristotle, of Aquinas, of Spinoza, or Hegel; and then suppose one trained exclusively on Plato's dialogues. Is it the eternal certainty, after all, the immutable and absolute character of truth, as Plato conceived it, that he would be likely to apprehend? We have here another of those contrasts of tendency, constitutional in the genius of Plato, and which may add to our interest in him. Plato is to be explained, as we say, or interpreted, partly through his predecessors, and his contemporaries; but in part also by his followers, by the light his later mental kinsmen throw back on the conscious or unconscious drift of his teaching. Now there are in the history of philosophy two opposite Platonic traditions; two legitimate yet divergent streams of influence from him. Two very different yet equally representative scholars we may see in thought emerging from his school. The "theory of the Ideas," the high ideal, the uncompromising demand for absolute certainty, in any truth or knowledge worthy of the name; the immediate or intuitive character of the highest acts of knowledge; that all true theory is indeed "vision":—for the maintenance of that side of the Platonic position we must look onward to Aristotle, and the Schoolmen of all ages, to Spinoza, to Hegel; to those mystic aspirants to "vision" also, the so-called Neo-Platonists of all ages, from Proclus to Schelling. From the abstract, metaphysical systems of those, the ecstasy and illuminism of these, we may mount up to the actual words of Plato in the *Symposium*, the fifth book of *The Republic*, the *Phædrus*.

20. But it is in quite different company we must look for the tradition, the development, of Plato's actual method of learning and teaching. The Academy of Plato, the established seat of his philosophy, gave name to a school, of which Lucian, in Greek, and in Latin, Cicero, are the proper representatives,— Cicero, the perfect embodiment of what is still sometimes understood to be the "academic spirit," surveying all sides, arraying evidence, ascertaining, measuring, balancing, tendencies, but ending in suspension of judgment. If Platonism from age to age has meant, for some, ontology, a doctrine of "being," or the nearest attainable approach to or substitution for that; for others, Platonism has been in fact only another name for scepticism, in a recognisable philosophic tradition. Thus, in the Middle Age, it qualifies in the *Sic et Non* the confident scholasticism of Abelard. It is like the very trick and impress of the Platonic Socrates himself again, in those endless conversations of Montaigne—that typical sceptic of the age of the Renaissance—conversations with himself, with the living, with the dead through their writings, which his

Essays do but reflect. Typical Platonist or sceptic, he is therefore also the typical essayist. And the sceptical philosopher of Bordeaux does but commence the modern world, which, side by side with its metaphysical reassertions, from Descartes to Hegel, side by side also with a constant accumulation of the sort of certainty which is afforded by empirical science, has had assuredly, to check wholesomely the pretensions of one and of the other alike, its doubts.—"Their name is legion," says a modern writer. Reverent and irreverent, reasonable and unreasonable, manly and unmanly, morbid and healthy, guilty and honest, wilful, inevitable—they have been called, indifferently, in an age which thirsts for intellectual security, but cannot make up its mind. *Que scais-je?* it cries, in the words of Montaigne; but in the spirit also of the Platonic Socrates, with whom such dubitation had been nothing less than a religious duty or service.

21. Sanguine about any form of absolute knowledge, of eternal, or indefectible, or immutable truth, with our modern temperament as it is, we shall hardly become, even under the direction of Plato, and by the reading of the Platonic Dialogues. But if we are little likely to realise in his school, the promise of "ontological" science, of a "doctrine of Being," or any increase in our consciousness of metaphysical security, are likely, rather, to acquire there that other sort of Platonism, a habit, namely, of tentative thinking and suspended judgment, if we are not likely to enjoy the vision of his "eternal and immutable ideas," Plato may yet promote in us what we call "ideals"—the aspiration towards a more perfect Justice, a more perfect Beauty, physical and intellectual, a more perfect condition of human affairs, than any one has ever yet seen; that κόσμος, in which things *are* only as they are *thought* by a perfect mind, to which experience is constantly approximating us, but which it does not provide. There they stand, the two great landmarks of the intellectual or spiritual life as Plato conceived it: the ideal, the world of "ideas," "the great perhaps," for which it is his merit so effectively to have opened room in the mental scheme, to be known by us, if at all, through our affinities of nature with it, which, however, in our dealings with ourselves and others we may assume to be objective or real:—and then, over against our imperfect realisation of that ideal, in ourselves, in nature and history, amid the personal caprices (it might almost seem) of its discovery of itself to us, as the appropriate attitude on our part, the dialectical spirit, which to the last will have its diffidence and reserve, its scruples and second thoughts. Such condition of suspended judgment indeed, in its more genial development and under felicitous culture, is but the expectation, the receptivity, of the faithful scholar, determined not to foreclose what is still a question—the "philosophic temper," in short, for which a survival of query will be still the salt of truth, even in the most absolutely ascertained knowledge.

from LACEDÆMON

[...] Platonism is a highly conscious reassertion of one of the two constituent elements in the Hellenic genius, of the spirit of the highlands namely in which the early Dorian forefathers of the Lacedæmonians had secreted their peculiar disposition, in contrast with the mobile, the marine and fluid temper of the littoral Ionian people. *The Republic* of Plato is an embodiment of that Platonic reassertion or preference, of Platonism, as the principle of a society, ideal enough indeed, yet in various degrees practicable. It is not understood by Plato to be an erection *de novo*, and therefore only on paper. Its foundations might be laid in certain practicable changes to be enforced in the old schools, in a certain reformed music which must be taught there, and would float thence into the existing homes of Greece, under the shadow of its old temples, the sanction of its old religion, its old memories, the old names of things. Given the central idea, with its essentially renovating power, the well-worn elements of society as it is would rebuild themselves, and a new colour come gradually over all things as the proper expression of a certain new mind in them.

5. And in fact such embodiments of the specially Hellenic element in Hellenism, compacted in the natural course of political development, there had been, though in a less ideal form, in those many Dorian constitutions to which Aristotle refers. To Lacedæmon, in *The Republic* itself, admiring allusions abound, covert, yet bold enough, if we remember the existing rivalry between Athens and her neighbour; and it becomes therefore a help in the study of Plato's political ideal to approach as near as we may to that earlier actual embodiment of its principles, which is also very interesting in itself. The Platonic City of the Perfect would not have been cut clean away from the old roots of national life: would have had many links with the beautiful and venerable Greek cities of past and present. The ideal, poetic or romantic as it might seem, would but have begun where they had left off, where Lacedæmon, in particular, had left off. Let us then, by way of realising the better the physiognomy of Plato's theoretic building, suppose some contemporary student of *The Republic*, a pupil, say! in the Athenian Academy, determined to gaze on the actual face of what has so strong a family likeness to it. Stimulated by his master's unconcealed Laconism, his approval of contemporary Lacedæmon, he is at the pains to journey thither, and make personal inspection of a place, in Plato's general commendations of which he may suspect some humour or irony, but which has unmistakably lent many a detail to his ideal Republic, on paper, or in thought. [...]

11. From the first he notes "the antiquated appearance" of Lacedæmon, by no means a "growing" place, always rebuilding, remodelling itself, after the newest fashion, with shapeless suburbs stretching farther and farther on every side of it, grown too large perhaps, as Plato threatens, to be a body, a corporate unity, at all: not that, but still, and to the last, itself only a great village, a solemn, ancient, mountain village. Even here of course there had been movement, some sort of progress, if so it is to be called, linking limb to limb; but long ago. Originally a union, after the manner of early Rome, of perhaps three or four neighbouring villages which had never lost their physiognomy, like Rome it occupied a group of irregular heights, the outermost roots of Taygetus, on the bank of a river or mountain torrent, impetuous enough in winter, a series of wide shallows and deep pools in the blazing summer. It was every day however, all the year round, that Lacedæmonian youth plunged itself in the Eurotas. Hence, from this circumstance of the union there of originally disparate parts, the picturesque and expressive irregularity, had they had time to think it such, of the "city" properly so termed, the one open place or street, High Street, or *Corso*—Aphetais by name, lined, irregularly again, with various religious and other monuments. It radiated on all sides into a mazy coil, an ambush, of narrow crooked lanes, up and down, in which attack and defence would necessarily be a matter of hand-to-hand fighting. In the outskirts lay the citizens' houses, roomier far than those of Athens, with spacious, walled courts, almost in the country. Here, in contrast to the homes of Athens, the legitimate wife had a real dignity, the unmarried woman a singular freedom. There were no door-knockers: you shouted at the outer gate to be let in. Between the high walls lanes passed into country roads, sacred ways to ancient sacro-sanct localities, Therapnæ, Amyclæ, on this side or that, under the shade of mighty plane-trees.

12. Plato, as you may remember, gives a hint that, like all other visible things, the very trees—how they grow—exercise an æsthetic influence on character. The diligent legislator therefore would have his preferences, even in this matter of the trees under which the citizens of the Perfect City might sit down to rest. What trees? you wonder. The olive? the laurel, as if wrought in grandiose metal? the cypress? that came to a wonderful height in Dorian Crete: the oak? we think it very expressive of strenuous national character. Well! certainly the plane-tree for one, characteristic tree of Lacedæmon then and now; a very tranquil and tranquillising object, spreading its level or gravely curved masses on the air as regally as the tree of Lebanon itself. A vast grove of such was the distinguishing mark of Lacedæmon in any distant view of it; that, and, as at Athens, a colossal image, older than the days of Phidias—the *Demos* of Lacedæmon, it would seem, towering visibly above the people it

protected. Below those mighty trees, on an island in their national river, were the "playing-fields," where Lacedæmonian youth after sacrifice in the *Ephebeum* delighted others rather than itself (no "shirking" was allowed) with a sort of football, under rigorous self-imposed rules—tearing, biting—a sport, rougher even than our own, *et même très dangereux*, as our Attic neighbours, the French, say of the English game.

13. They were orderly enough perforce, the boys, the young men, within the city—seen, but not heard, except under regulations, when they made the best music in the world. Our visitor from Athens when he saw those youthful soldiers, or military students, as Xenophon in his pretty treatise on the polity of Lacedæmon describes, walking with downcast eyes, their hands meekly hidden in their cloaks, might have thought them young monks, had he known of such.

14. A little mountain town, however ambitious, however successful in its ambition, would hardly be expected to compete with Athens, or Corinth, itself a Dorian state, in art-production, yet had not only its characteristic preferences in this matter, in plastic and literary art, but had also many venerable and beautiful buildings to show. The Athenian visitor, who is standing now in the central space of Lacedæmon, notes here, as being a trait also of the "Perfect City" of academic theory, that precisely because these people find themselves very susceptible to the influences of form and colour and sound, to external æsthetic influence, but have withal a special purpose, a certain strongly conceived disciplinary or ethic ideal, that therefore a peculiar humour prevails among them, a self-denying humour, in regard to these things. Those ancient Pelopid princes, from whom the hereditary kings of historic Lacedæmon, come back from exile into their old home, claim to be descended, had had their palaces, with a certain Homeric, Asiatic splendour, of wrought metal and the like; considerable relics of which still remained, but as public or sacred property now. At the time when Plato's scholar stands before them, the houses of these later historic kings—two kings, as you remember, always reigning together, in some not quite clearly evolved differentiation of the temporal and spiritual functions—were plain enough; the royal doors, when beggar or courtier approached them, no daintier than Lycurgus had prescribed for all true Lacedæmonian citizens; rude, strange things to look at, fashioned only, like the ceilings within, with axe and saw, of old mountain oak or pine from those great Taygetan forests, whence came also the abundant iron, which this stern people of iron and steel had super-induced on that earlier dreamy age of silver and gold—steel, however, admirably tempered and wrought in its application to military use, and much sought after throughout Greece.

15. Layer upon layer, the relics of those earlier generations, a whole

succession of remarkable races, lay beneath the strenuous footsteps of the present occupants, as there was old poetic legend in the depths of their seemingly so practical or prosaic souls. Nor beneath their feet only: the relics of their worship, their sanctuaries, their tombs, their very houses, were part of the scenery of actual life. Our young Platonic visitor from Athens, climbing through those narrow winding lanes, and standing at length on the open platform of the Aphetais, finds himself surrounded by treasures, modest treasures of ancient architecture, dotted irregularly here and there about him, as if with conscious design upon picturesque effect, such irregularities sometimes carrying in them the secret of expression, an accent. Old Alcman for one had been alive to the poetic opportunities of the place; boasts that he belongs to Lacedæmon, "abounding in sacred tripods"; that it was here the Heliconian Muses had revealed themselves to him. If the private abodes even of royalty were rude it was only that the splendour of places dedicated to religion and the state might the more abound. Most splendid of them all, the *Stoa Pœkile*, a cloister or portico with painted walls, to which the spoils of the Persian war had been devoted, ranged its pillars of white marble on one side of the central space: on the other, connecting those high memories with the task of the living, lay the *Choros*, where, at the *Gymnopædia*, the Spartan youth danced in honour of Apollo.

16. Scattered up and down among the monuments of victory in battle were the *heroa*, tombs or chapels of the heroes who had purchased it with their blood—Pausanias, Leonidas, brought home from Thermopylæ forty years after his death. "A pillar too," says Pausanias, "is erected here, on which the paternal names are inscribed of those who at Thermopylæ sustained the attack of the Medes." Here in truth all deities put on a martial habit—Aphrodite, the Muses, Eros himself, Athene Chalcicecus, Athene of the Brazen House, an antique temple towering above the rest, built from the spoils of some victory long since forgotten. The name of the artist who made the image of the tutelary goddess was remembered in the annals of early Greek art, Gitiades, a native of Lacedæmon. He had composed a hymn also in her praise. Could we have seen the place he had restored rather than constructed, with its covering of mythological reliefs in brass or bronze, perhaps Homer's descriptions of a seemingly impossible sort of metallic architecture would have been less taxing to his reader's imagination. Those who in other places had lost their taste amid the facile splendours of a later day, might here go to school again.

17. Throughout Greece, in fact, it was the Doric style which came to prevail as the religious or hieratic manner, never to be surpassed for that purpose, as the Gothic style seems likely to do with us. Though it is not exclusively the invention of Dorian men, yet, says Müller, "the Dorian character created the

Doric architecture," and he notes in it, especially, the severity of the perfectly straight, smartly tapering line of its column; the bold projection of the capital; the alternation of long unornamented plain surfaces with narrower bands of decorated work; the profound shadows; the expression of security, of harmony, infused throughout; the magnificent pediment crowning the whole, like the cornice of mountain wall beyond, around, and above it. Standing there in the Aphetais, amid these venerable works of art, the visitor could not forget the natural architecture about him. As the Dorian genius had differentiated itself from the common Hellenic type in the heart of the mountains of Epirus, so here at last, in its final and most characteristic home, it was still surrounded by them:—ὀφρυᾷ τε καὶ κοιλαίνεται.

18. We know, some of us, what such mountain neighbourhood means. The wholesome vigour, the clearness and purity they maintain in matters such as air, light, water; how their presence multiplies the contrasts, the element of light and shadow, in things; the untouched perfection of the minuter ornament, flower or crystal, they permit one sparingly; their reproachful aloofness, though so close to us, keeping sensitive minds at least in a sort of moral alliance with their remoter solitudes. "The whole life of the Lacedæmonian community," says Müller, "had a secluded, impenetrable, and secret character." You couldn't really know it unless you were of it. [...]

23. A young Lacedæmonian, then, of the privileged class left his home, his tender nurses in those large, quiet old suburban houses early, for a public school, a schooling all the stricter as years went on, to be followed, even so, by a peculiar kind of barrack-life, the temper of which, a sort of military monasticism (it must be repeated) would beset him to the end. Though in the gymnasia of Lacedæmon no idle by-standers, no—well! Platonic loungers after truth or what not—were permitted, yet we are told, neither there nor in Sparta generally, neither there nor anywhere else, were the boys permitted to be alone. If a certain love of reserve, of seclusion, characterised the Spartan citizen as such, it was perhaps the cicatrice of that wrench from a soft home into the imperative, inevitable gaze of his fellows, broad, searching, minute, his regret for, his desire to regain, moral and mental even more than physical ease. And his education continued late; he could seldom think of marriage till the age of thirty. Ethically it aimed at the reality, æsthetically at the expression, of reserved power, and from the first set its subject on the thought of his personal dignity, of self-command, in the artistic way of a good musician, a good soldier. It is noted that "the general accent of the Doric dialect has itself the character not of question or entreaty, but of command or dictation." The place of deference, of obedience, was large in the education of Lacedæmonian

youth; and they never complained. It involved however for the most part, as with ourselves, the government of youth by itself; an implicit subordination of the younger to the older, in many degrees. Quite early in life, at school, they found that superiors and inferiors, ὅμοιοι and ὑπομείονες, there really were; and their education proceeded with systematic boldness on that fact. Εἴρην, μελλείρην, σιδεύνης, and the like—words, titles, which indicate an unflinching elaboration of the attitudes of youthful subordination and command with responsibility—remain as a part of what we might call their "public-school slang." They ate together "in their divisions" (ἀγέλαι) on much the same fare every day at a sort of messes; not reclined, like Ionians or Asiatics, but like heroes, the princely males, in Homer, sitting upright on their wooden benches; were "inspected" frequently, and by free use of *vivâ voce* examination "became adepts in presence of mind," in mental readiness and vigour, in the brief mode of speech Plato commends, which took and has kept its name from them; with no warm baths allowed; a daily plunge in their river required. Yes! The beauty of these most beautiful of all people was a male beauty, far remote from feminine tenderness; had the expression of a certain *ascêsis* in it; was like un-sweetened wine. In comparison with it, beauty of another type might seem to be wanting in edge or accent.

24. And they could be silent. Of the positive uses of the negation of speech, like genuine scholars of Pythagoras, the Lacedæmonians were well aware, gaining strength and intensity by repression. Long spaces of enforced silence had doubtless something to do with that expressive brevity of utterance, which could be also, when they cared, so inexpressive of what their intentions really were—something to do with the habit of mind to which such speaking would come naturally. In contrast with the ceaseless prattle of Athens, Lacedæmonian assemblies lasted as short a time as possible, all standing. A Lacedæmonian ambassador being asked in whose name he was come, replies: "In the name of the State, if I succeed; if I fail, in my own." What they lost in extension they gained in depth.

25. Had our traveller been tempted to ask a young Lacedæmonian to return his visit at Athens, permission would have been refused him. He belonged to a community bent above all things on keeping indelibly its own proper colour. Its more strictly mental education centered, in fact, upon a faithful training of the memory, again in the spirit of Pythagoras, in regard to what seemed best worth remembering. Hard and practical as Lacedæmonians might seem, they lived nevertheless very much by imagination; and to train the memory, to preoccupy their minds with the past, as in our own classic or historic culture of youth, was in reality to develope a vigorous imagination. In music (μουσική) as they conceived it, there would be no strictly selfish reading,

writing or listening; and if there was little a Lacedæmonian lad had to read or write at all, he had much to learn, like a true conservative, by heart: those unwritten laws of which the Council of Elders was the authorised depositary, and on which the whole public procedure of the state depended; the archaic forms of religious worship; the names of their kings, of victors in their games or in battle; the brief record of great events; the oracles they had received; the *rhetrai*, from Lycurgus downwards, composed in metrical Lacedæmonian Greek; their history and law, in short, actually set to music, by Terpander and others, as was said. What the Lacedæmonian learned by heart he was for the most part to sing, and we catch a glimpse, an echo, of their boys in school chanting; one of the things in old Greece one would have liked best to see and hear—youthful beauty and strength in perfect service—a manifestation of the true and genuine Hellenism, though it may make one think of the novices at school in some Gothic cloister, of our own old English schools, nay, of the young Lacedæmonian's cousins at Sion, singing there the law and its praises.

26. The Platonic student of the ways of the Lacedæmonians observes then, is interested in observing, that their education, which indeed makes no sharp distinction between mental and bodily exercise, results as it had begun in "music"—ends with body, mind, memory above all, at their finest, on great show-days, in the dance. Austere, self-denying Lacedæmon had in fact one of the largest theatres in Greece, in part scooped out boldly on the hill-side, built partly of enormous blocks of stone, the foundations of which may still be seen. We read what Plato says in *The Republic* of "imitations," of the imitative arts, imitation reaching of course its largest development on the stage, and are perhaps surprised at the importance he assigns, in every department of human culture, to a matter of that kind. But here as elsewhere to see was to understand. We should have understood Plato's drift in his long criticism and defence of imitative art, his careful system of rules concerning it, could we have seen the famous dramatic Lacedæmonian dancing. They danced a theme, a subject. A complex and elaborate art this must necessarily have been, but, as we may gather, as concise, direct, economically expressive, in all its varied sound and motion, as those swift, lightly girt, *impromptu* Lacedæmonian sayings. With no movement of voice or hand or foot, παραλειπόμενον, unconsidered, as Plato forbids, it was the perfect flower of their correction, of that minute patience and care which ends in a perfect expressiveness; not a note, a glance, a touch, but told obediently in the promotion of a firmly grasped mental conception, as in that perfect poetry or sculpture or painting, in which "the finger of the master is on every part of his work." We have nothing really like it, and to comprehend it must remember that, though it took place in part at least on the stage of a theatre—was in fact a ballet-dance, it had also the character

both of a liturgical service and of a military inspection; and yet, in spite of its severity of rule, was a natural expression of the delight of all who took part in it.

27. So perfect a spectacle the gods themselves might be thought pleased to witness; were in consequence presented with it as an important element in the religious worship of the Lacedæmonians, in whose life religion had even a larger part than with the other Greeks, conspicuously religious, δεισιδαίμονες, involved in religion or superstition, as the Greeks generally were. More closely even than their so scrupulous neighbours they associated the state, its acts and officers, with a religious sanction, religious usages, theories, traditions. While the responsibilities of secular government lay upon the Ephors, those mysteriously dual, at first sight useless, and yet so sanctimoniously observed kings, "of the house of Heracles," with something of the splendour of the old Achæan or Homeric kings, in life as also in death, the splendid funerals, the passionate archaic laments which then followed them, were in fact of spiritual or priestly rank, the living and active centre of a poetic religious system, binding them "in a beneficent connexion" to the past, and in the present with special closeness to the oracle of Delphi.

28. Of that catholic or general centre of Greek religion the Lacedæmonians were the hereditary and privileged guardians, as also the peculiar people of Apollo, the god of Delphi; but, observe! of Apollo in a peculiar development of his deity. In the dramatic business of Lacedæmon, centering in these almost liturgical dances, there was little comic acting. The fondness of the slaves for buffoonery and loud laughter, was to their master, who had no taste for the like, a reassuring note of his superiority. He therefore indulged them in it on occasion, and you might fancy that the religion of a people so strenuous, ever so full of their dignity, must have been a religion of gloom. It was otherwise. The Lacedæmonians, like those monastic persons of whom they so often remind one, as a matter of fact however surprising, were a very cheerful people; and the religion of which they had so much, deeply imbued everywhere with an optimism as of hopeful youth, encouraged that disposition, was above all a religion of sanity. The observant Platonic visitor might have taken note that something of that purgation of religious thought and sentiment, of its expression in literature, recommended in Plato's *Republic*, had been already quietly effected here, towards the establishment of a kind of cheerful daylight in men's tempers.

29. In furtherance then of such a religion of sanity, of that harmony of functions, which is the Aristotelian definition of health, Apollo, sanest of the national gods, became also the tribal or home god of Lacedæmon. That common Greek worship of Apollo they made especially their own, but (just

here is the noticeable point) with a marked preference for the human element in him, for the mental powers of his being over those elemental or physical forces of production, which he also mystically represents, and which resulted sometimes in an orgiastic, an unintellectual, or even an immoral service. He remains youthful and unmarried. In congruity with this, it is observed that, in a quasi-Roman worship, abstract qualities and relationships, ideals, become subsidiary objects of religious consideration around him, such as sleep, death, fear, fortune, laughter even. Nay, other gods also are, so to speak, Apollinised, adapted to the Apolline presence; Aphrodite armed, Enyalius in fetters, perhaps that he may never depart thence. Amateurs everywhere of the virile element in life, the Lacedæmonians, in truth, impart to all things an intellectual character. Adding a vigorous logic to seemingly animal instincts, for them courage itself becomes, as for the strictly philosophic mind at Athens, with Plato and Aristotle, an intellectual condition, a form of right knowledge.

30. Such assertion of the consciously human interest in a religion based originally on a preoccupation with the unconscious forces of nature, was exemplified in the great religious festival of Lacedæmon. As a spectator of the *Hyacinthia*, our Platonic student would have found himself one of a large body of strangers, gathered together from Lacedæmon and its dependent towns and villages, within the ancient precincts of Amyclæ, at the season between spring and summer when under the first fierce heat of the year the abundant hyacinths fade from the fields. Blue flowers, you remember, are the rarest, to many eyes the loveliest; and the Lacedæmonians with their guests were met together to celebrate the death of the hapless lad who had lent his name to them, Hyacinthus, son of Apollo, or son of an ancient mortal king who had reigned in this very place; in either case, greatly beloved of the god, who had slain him by sad accident as they played at quoits together delightfully, to his immense sorrow. That Boreas (the north-wind) had maliciously miscarried the discus, is a circumstance we hardly need to remind us that we have here, of course, only one of many transparent, unmistakable, parables or symbols of the great solar change, so sudden in the south, like the story of Proserpine, Adonis, and the like. But here, more completely perhaps than in any other of those stories, the primary elemental sense had obscured itself behind its really tragic analogue in human life, behind the figure of the dying youth. We know little of the details of the feast; incidentally, that Apollo was vested on the occasion in a purple robe, brought in ceremony from Lacedæmon, woven there, Pausanias tells us, in a certain house called from that circumstance *Chiton*. You may remember how sparing these Lacedæmonians were of such dyed raiment, of any but the natural and virgin colouring of the fleece; that purple or red,

however, was the colour of their royal funerals, as indeed Amyclæ itself was famous for purple stuffs—*Amyclææ vestes*. As the general order of the feast, we discern clearly a single day of somewhat shrill gaiety, between two days of significant mourning after the manner of All Souls' Day, directed from mimic grief for a mythic object, to a really sorrowful commemoration by the whole Lacedæmonian people—each separate family for its own deceased members.

31. It was so again with those other youthful demi-gods, the Dioscuri, themselves also, in old heroic time, resident in this venerable place: *Amyclæi fratres*, fraternal leaders of the Lacedæmonian people. Their statues at this date were numerous in Laconia, or the *docana*, primitive symbols of them, those two upright beams of wood, carried to battle before the two kings, until it happened that through their secret enmity a certain battle was lost, after which one king only proceeded to the field, and one part only of that token of fraternity, the other remaining at Sparta. Well! they were two stars, you know, at their original birth in men's minds, *Gemini*, virginal fresh stars of dawn, rising and setting alternately—those two half-earthly, half-celestial brothers, one of whom, Polydeuces, was immortal. The other, Castor, the younger, subject to old age and death, had fallen in battle, was found breathing his last. Polydeuces thereupon, at his own prayer, was permitted to die: with undying fraternal affection, had forgone one moiety of his privilege, and lay in the grave for a day in his brother's stead, but shone out again on the morrow; the brothers thus ever coming and going, interchangeably, but both alike gifted now with immortal youth.

32. In their origin, then, very obviously elemental deities, they were thus become almost wholly humanised, fraternised with the Lacedæmonian people, their closest friends of the whole celestial company, visitors, as fond legend told, at their very hearths, found warming themselves in the half-light at their rude fire-sides. Themselves thus visible on occasion, at all times in devout art, they were the starry patrons of all that youth was proud of, delighted in, horsemanship, games, battle; and always with that profound fraternal sentiment. Brothers, comrades, who could not live without each other, they were the most fitting patrons of a place in which friendship, comradeship, like theirs, came to so much. Lovers of youth they remained, those enstarred types of it, arrested thus at that moment of miraculous good fortune as a consecration of the clean, youthful friendship, "passing even the love of woman," which, by system, and under the sanction of their founder's name, elaborated into a kind of art, became an elementary part of education. A part of their duty and discipline, it was also their great solace and encouragement. The beloved and the lover, side by side through their long days of eager labour, and above all on the battlefield, became respectively, ἀΐτης, the hearer, and εἰσπνήλας,

the inspirer; the elder inspiring the younger with his own strength and noble taste in things.

33. What, it has been asked, what was there to occupy persons of the privileged class in Lacedæmon from morning to night, thus cut off as they were from politics and business, and many of the common interests of men's lives? Our Platonic visitor would have asked rather, Why this strenuous task-work, day after day; why this loyalty to a system, so costly to you individually, though it may be thought to have survived its original purpose; this laborious, endless, education, which does not propose to give you anything very useful or enjoyable in itself? An intelligent young Spartan might have replied: "To the end that I myself may be a perfect work of art, issuing thus into the eyes of all Greece." He might have observed—we may safely observe for him—that the institutions of his country, whose he was, had a beauty in themselves, as we may observe also of some at least of our own institutions, educational or religious: that they bring out, for instance, the lights and shadows of human character, and relieve the present by maintaining in it an ideal sense of the past. He might have added that he had his friendships to solace him; and to encourage him, the sense of honour.

34. Honour, friendship, loyalty to the ideal of the past, himself as a work of art! There was much of course in his answer. Yet still, after all, to understand, to be capable of, such motives, was itself but a result of that exacting discipline of character we are trying to account for; and the question still recurs, *To what purpose?* Why, with no prospect of Israel's reward, are you as scrupulous, minute, self-taxing, as he? A tincture of asceticism in the Lacedæmonian rule may remind us again of the monasticism of the Middle Ages. But then, monastic severity was for the purging of a troubled conscience, or for the hope of an immense prize, neither of which conditions is to be supposed here. In fact the surprise of Saint Paul, as a practical man, at the slightness of the reward for which a Greek spent himself, natural as it is about all pagan perfection, is especially applicable about these Lacedæmonians, who indeed had actually invented that so "corruptible" and essentially worthless parsley crown in place of the more tangible prizes of an earlier age. Strange people! Where, precisely, may be the spring of action in you, who are so severe to yourselves; you who, in the words of Plato's supposed objector that the rulers of the ideal state are not to be envied, have nothing you can really call your own, but are like hired servants in your own houses,—*qui manducatis panem doloris?*

35. Another day-dream, you may say, about those obscure ancient people,

it was ever so difficult really to know, who had hidden their actual life with so much success; but certainly a quite natural dream upon the paradoxical things we are told of them, on good authority. It is because they make us ask that question; puzzle us by a paradoxical idealism in life; are thus distinguished from their neighbours; that, like some of our old English places of education, though we might not care to live always at school there, it is good to visit them on occasion; as some philosophic Athenians, as we have now seen, loved to do, at least in thought.

PLATO'S ÆSTHETICS

When we remember Plato as the great lover, what the visible world was to him, what a large place the idea of Beauty, with its almost adequate realisation in that visible world, holds in his most abstract speculations as the clearest instance of the relation of the human mind to reality and truth, we might think that art also, the fine arts, would have been much for him; that the æsthetic element would be a significant one in his theory of morals and education. Τὰ τερπνὰ ἐν Ἑλλάδι (to use Pindar's phrase) all the delightful things in Hellas:—Plato least of all could have been unaffected by their presence around him. And so it is. Think what perfection of handicraft, what a subtle enjoyment therein, is involved in that specially Platonic rule, to mind one's business (τὸ τὰ αὑτοῦ πράττειν) that he who, like Fra Damiano of Bergamo, has a gift for ποικιλία, *intarsia* or *marqueterïe*, for example, should confine himself exclusively to that. Before him, you know, there had been no theorising about the beautiful, its place in life, and the like; and as a matter of fact he is the earliest critic of the fine arts. He anticipates the modern notion that art as such has no end but its own perfection,—"art for art's sake." Ἆρ' οὖν καὶ ἑκάστῃ τῶν τεχνῶν ἔστι τι συμφέρον ἄλλο ἢ ὅτι μάλιστα τελέαν εἶναι; We have seen again that not in theory only, by the large place he assigns to our experiences regarding visible beauty in the formation of his doctrine of ideas, but that in the practical sphere also, this great fact of experience, the reality of beauty, has its importance with him. The loveliness of virtue as a harmony, the winning aspect of those "images" of the absolute and unseen Temperance, Bravery, Justice, shed around us in the visible world for eyes that can see, the claim of the virtues as a visible representation by human persons and their acts of the eternal qualities of "the eternal," after all far out-weigh, as he thinks, the claim of their mere utility. And accordingly, in education, all will begin and end "in music," in the promotion of qualities to which no truer name can be given than symmetry, æsthetic fitness, tone. Philosophy itself indeed, as he conceives it, is but the sympathetic appreciation of a kind of music in the very nature of things.

2. There have been Platonists without Plato, and a kind of traditional Platonism in the world, independent of, yet true in spirit to, the Platonism of the Platonic Dialogues. Now such a piece of traditional Platonism we find in the hypothesis of some close connexion between what may be called the æsthetic qualities of the world about us and the formation of moral character, between æsthetics and ethics. Wherever people have been inclined to lay stress on the colouring, for instance, cheerful or otherwise, of the walls of

the room where children learn to read, as though that had something to do with the colouring of their minds; on the possible moral effect of the beautiful ancient buildings of some of our own schools and colleges; on the building of character, in any way, through the eye and ear; there the spirit of Plato has been understood to be, and rightly, even by those who have perhaps never read Plato's *Republic*, in which however we do find the connexion between moral character and matters of poetry and art strongly asserted. This is to be observed especially in the third and tenth books of *The Republic*. The main interest of those books lies in the fact, that in them we read what Plato actually said on a subject concerning which people have been so ready to put themselves under his authority.

3. It is said with immediate reference to metre and its various forms in verse, as an element in the general treatment of style or manner (λέξις) as opposed to the matter (λόγοι) in the imaginative literature, with which as in time past the education of the citizens of the Perfect City will begin. It is however at his own express suggestion that we may apply what he says, in the first instance, about metre and verse, to all forms of art whatever, to music (μουσική) generally, to all those matters over which the Muses of Greek mythology preside, to all productions in which the *form* counts equally with, or for more than, the *matter*. Assuming therefore that we have here, in outline and tendency at least, the mind of Plato in regard to the ethical influence of æsthetic qualities, let us try to distinguish clearly the central lines of that tendency, of Platonism in art, as it is really to be found in Plato.

4. "You have perceived have you not," observes the Platonic Socrates, "that acts of imitation, if they begin in early life, and continue, establish themselves in one's nature and habits, alike as to the body, the tones of one's voice, the ways of one's mind."

5. Yes, that might seem a matter of common observation; and what is strictly Platonic here and in what follows is but the emphasis of the statement. Let us set it however, for the sake of decisive effect, in immediate connexion with certain other points of Plato's æsthetic doctrine.

6. Imitation then, imitation through the eye and ear, is irresistible in its influence over human nature. And secondly, we, the founders, the people, of the Republic, of the city that shall be perfect, have for our peculiar purpose the simplification of human nature: a purpose somewhat costly, for it follows, thirdly, that the only kind of music, of art and poetry, we shall permit ourselves, our citizens, will be of a very austere character, under a sort of "self-denying ordinance." We shall be a fervently æsthetic community, if you will; but therewith also very fervent "renunciants," or ascetics.

7. In the first place, men's souls are, according to Plato's view, the creatures of what men see and hear. What would probably be found in a limited number only of sensitive people, a constant susceptibility to the aspects and other sensible qualities of things and persons, to the element of expression or form in them and their movements, to *phenomena* as such—this susceptibility Plato supposes in men generally. It is not so much the *matter* of a work of art, what is conveyed in and by colour and form and sound, that tells upon us educationally—the subject, for instance, developed by the words and scenery of a play—as the *form*, and its qualities, concision, simplicity, rhythm, or, contrariwise, abundance, variety, discord. Such "æsthetic" qualities, by what we might call in logical phrase, μετάβασις εἰς ἄλλο γένος, a derivation into another kind of matter, transform themselves, in the temper of the patient hearer or spectator, into terms of ethics, into the sphere of the desires and the will, of the *moral* taste, engendering, nursing there, strictly moral effects, such conditions of sentiment and the will as Plato requires in his City of the Perfect, or quite the opposite, but hardly in any case indifferent, conditions.

8. Imitation:—it enters into the very fastnesses of character; and we, our souls, ourselves, are for ever imitating what we see and hear, the forms, the sounds which haunt our memories, our imagination. We imitate not only if we play a part on the stage but when we sit as spectators, while our thoughts follow the acting of another, when we read Homer and put ourselves, lightly, fluently, into the place of those he describes: we imitate unconsciously the line and colour of the walls around us, the trees by the wayside, the animals we pet or make use of, the very dress we wear. Only, Ἵνα μὴ ἐκ τῆς μιμήσεως τοῦ εἶναι ἀπολαύσωσιν.—Let us beware how men attain the very truth of what they imitate.

9. That then is the first principle of Plato's æsthetics, his first consideration regarding the art of the City of the Perfect. Men, children, are susceptible beings, in great measure conditioned by the mere look of their "medium." Like those insects, we might fancy, of which naturalists tell us, taking colour from the plants they lodge on, they will come to match with much servility the aspects of the world about them.

10. But the people of the Perfect City would not be there at all except by way of a refuge, an experiment, or *tour de force*, in moral and social philosophy; and this circumstance determines the second constituent principle of Plato's æsthetic scheme. We, then, the founders, the citizens, of the Republic have a peculiar purpose. We are here to escape from, to resist, a certain vicious centrifugal tendency in life, in Greek and especially in Athenian life, which does but propagate a like vicious tendency in ourselves. We are to become—like little pieces in a machine! you may complain.—No, like performers rather,

individually, it may be, of more or less importance, but each with a necessary and inalienable part, in a perfect musical exercise which is well worth while, or in some sacred liturgy; or like soldiers in an invincible army, invincible because it moves as one man. We are to find, or be put into, and keep, every one his natural place; to cultivate those qualities which will secure mastery over ourselves, the subordination of the parts to the whole, musical proportion. To this end, as we saw, Plato, a remorseless idealist, is ready even to suppress the differences of male and female character, to merge, to lose the family in the social aggregate.

11. Imitation then, we may resume, imitation through the eye and ear, is irresistible in its influence on human nature. Secondly, the founders of the Republic are by its very purpose bound to the simplification of human nature: and our practical conclusion follows in logical order. We shall make, and sternly keep, a "self-denying" ordinance in this matter, in the matter of art, of poetry, of taste in all its varieties; a rule, of which Plato's own words, applied by him in the first instance to rhythm or metre, but like all he says on that subject fairly applicable to the whole range of musical or æsthetic effects, will be the brief summary: *Alternations will be few and far between*:—how differently from the methods of the poetry, the art, the choruses, we most of us love so much, not necessarily because our senses are inapt or untrained:—*Σμικραὶ αἱ μεταβολαί*. We shall allow no musical innovations, no Aristophanic cries, no imitations however clever of "the sounds of the flute or the lyre," no free imitation by the human voice of bestial or mechanical sounds, no such artists as are "like a mirror turning all about." There were vulgarities of nature, you see, in the youth of ideal Athens even. Time, of course, as such, is itself a kind of artist, trimming pleasantly for us what survives of the rude world of the past. Now Plato's method would promote or anticipate the work of time in that matter of vulgarities of taste. Yes, when you read his precautionary rules, you become fully aware that even in Athens there were young men who affected what was least fortunate in the habits, the pleasures, the sordid business of the class below them. But they would not be allowed quite their own way in the streets or elsewhere in a reformed world, to whose chosen imperial youth (*βασιλικὴ φυλή*) it would not be permitted even to think of any of those things—*οὐδενὶ προσέχειν τὸν νοῦν*. To them, what was illiberal, the illiberal crafts, would be (thanks to their well-trained power of intellectual abstraction!) as though it were not. And if art, like law, be, as Plato thinks, "a creation of mind, in accordance with right reason," we shall not wish our boys to sing like mere birds.

12. Yet what price would not the musical connoisseur pay to handle the instruments we may see in fancy passing out through the gates of the City of

the Perfect, banished, not because there is no one within its walls who knows the use of, or would receive pleasure from, them (a delicate susceptibility in these matters Plato, as was said, presupposes) but precisely because they are so seductive, must be conveyed therefore to some other essentially less favoured neighbourhood, like poison, say! moral poison, for one's enemies' water-springs. A whole class of painters, sculptors, skilled workmen of various kinds go into like banishment—they and their very tools; not, observe again carefully, because they are bad artists, but very good ones.—Ἀλλὰ μήν, ὦ Ἀδείμαντε, ἡδύς γε καὶ ὁ κεκραμένος. Art, as such, as Plato knows, has no purpose but itself, its own perfection. The proper art of the Perfect City is in fact the art of discipline. Music (μουσική) all the various forms of fine art, will be but the instruments of its one over-mastering social or political purpose, irresistibly conforming its so imitative subject units to type: they will be neither more nor less than so many variations, so to speak, of the trumpet-call.

13. Or suppose again that a poet finds his way to us, "able by his genius, as he chooses, or as his audience chooses, to become all things, or all persons, in turn, and able to transform us too into all things and persons in turn, as we listen or read, with a fluidity, a versatility of humour almost equal to his own, a poet myriad-minded, as we say, almost in Plato's precise words, as our finest touch of praise, of Shakespeare for instance, or of Homer, of whom he was thinking:—Well! we shall have been set on our guard. We have no room for him. Divine, delightful, being, "if he came to our city with his works, his poems, wishing to make an exhibition of them, we should certainly do him reverence as an object, sacred, wonderful, delightful, but we should not let him stay. We should tell him that there neither is, nor may be, any one like that among us, and so send him on his way to some other city, having anointed his head with myrrh and crowned him with a garland of wool, as something in himself half-divine, and for ourselves should make use of some more austere and less pleasing sort of poet, for his practical uses."—Τῷ αὐστηροτέρῳ καὶ ἀηδεστέρῳ ποιητῇ, ὠφελίας ἕνεκα. Not, as I said, that the Republic any more than Lacedæmon will be an artless place. Plato's æsthetic scheme is actually based on a high degree of sensibility to such influences in the people he is dealing with.—

Right speech, then, and rightness of harmony and form and rhythm minister to goodness of nature; not that good-nature which we so call with a soft name, being really silliness, but the frame of mind which in very truth is rightly and fairly ordered in regard to the moral habit.—Most certainly he said.—Must not these qualities, then, be everywhere pursued by the young men if they are to do each his own business?—Pursued, certainly.—Now painting, I suppose, is full of them (those qualities which are partly ethical, partly æsthetic) and all handicraft such as that; the weaver's art is full of them, and the inlayer's art and the building of houses, and the working of all the other apparatus of life; moreover the nature of our own bodies, and of all other living things. For in all these, rightness or wrongness of form is inherent. And wrongness of form, and the lack of rhythm, the lack of harmony, are fraternal to faultiness of mind and character, and the opposite qualities to the opposite condition—the temperate and good character:—fraternal, aye! and copies of them.—Yes, entirely so: he said.—

Must our poets, then, alone be under control, and compelled to work the image of the good into their poetic works, or not to work among us at all; or must the other craftsmen too be controlled, and restrained from working this faultiness and intemperance and illiberality and formlessness of character whether into the images of living creatures, or the houses they build, or any other product of their craft whatever; or must he who is unable so to do be forbidden to practise his art among us, to the end that our guardians may not, nurtured in images of vice as in a vicious pasture, cropping and culling much every day little by little from many sources, composing together some one great evil in their own souls, go undetected? Must we not rather seek for those craftsmen who have the power, by way of their own natural virtue, to track out the nature of the beautiful and seemly, to the end that, living as in some wholesome place, the young men may receive good from every side, whencesoever, from fair works of art, either upon sight or upon hearing anything may strike, as it were a breeze bearing health from kindly places, and from childhood straightway bring them unaware to likeness and friendship and harmony with fair reason?—Yes: he answered: in this way they would be by far best educated.—Well then, I said, Glaucon, on these grounds is not education in music of the greatest importance—because, more than anything else, rhythm and harmony make their way down into the inmost part of the soul, and take hold upon it with the utmost force, bringing with them rightness of form, and rendering its form right, if one be correctly trained; if not, the opposite? and again because he who has been trained in that department duly, would have the sharpest sense of oversights (τῶν παραλειπομένων) and of things not fairly turned out, whether by art or nature (μὴ καλῶς δημιουργηθέντων ἢ μὴ καλῶς φύντων) and disliking them, as he should, would commend things beautiful, and, by reason of his delight in these, receiving them into his soul, be nurtured of them, and become καλοκαγαθός, while he blamed the base, as he should, and hated it, while still young, before he was able to apprehend a reason, and when reason comes would welcome it, recognising it by its kinship to himself—most of all one thus taught?—Yes: he answered: it seems to me that for reasons such as these their education should be in music. *Republic*, 400.

14. Understand, then, the poetry and music, the arts and crafts, of the City of the Perfect—what is left of them there, and remember how the Greeks themselves were used to say that "the half is more than the whole." Liken its music, if you will, to Gregorian music, and call to mind the kind of architecture, military or monastic again, that must be built to such music, and then the kind of colouring that will fill its jealously allotted space upon the walls, the sort of carving that will venture to display itself on cornice or capital. The walls, the pillars, the streets—you see them in thought! nay, the very trees and animals, the attire of those who move along the streets, their looks and voices, their style—the hieratic Dorian architecture, to speak precisely, the Dorian manner everywhere, in possession of the whole of life. Compare it, for further vividness of effect, to Gothic building, to the Cistercian Gothic, if you will, when Saint Bernard had purged it of a still barbaric superfluity of ornament. It seems a long way from the Parthenon to Saint Ouen "of the aisles and arches," or *Notre-Dame de Bourges*; yet they illustrate almost equally the direction of the Platonic æsthetics. Those churches of the Middle Age have, as we all feel, their loveliness, yet of a stern sort, which fascinates while perhaps it repels us. We may try hard to like as well or better architecture of a more or less different kind, but coming back to them again find that the secret of final success is theirs. The rigid logic of their charm controls our taste, as logic proper binds the intelligence: we would have something of that quality, if we might, for ourselves, in what we do or make; feel, under its influence, very diffident of our own loose, or gaudy, or literally insignificant, decorations. "Stay then," says the Platonist, too sanguine perhaps,—"Abide," he says to youth, "in these places, and the like of them, and mechanically, irresistibly, the soul of them will impregnate yours. With whatever beside is in congruity with them in the order of hearing and sight, they will tell (despite, it may be, of unkindly nature at your first making) upon your very countenance, your walk and gestures, in the course and concatenation of your inmost thoughts."

15. And equation being duly made of what is merely personal and temporary in Plato's view of the arts, it may be salutary to return from time to time to the Platonic æsthetics, to find ourselves under the more exclusive influence of those qualities in the Hellenic genius he has thus emphasised. What he would promote, then, is the art, the literature, of which among other things it may be said that it solicits a certain effort from the reader or spectator, who is promised a great expressiveness on the part of the writer, the artist, if he for his part

will bring with him a great attentiveness. And how satisfying, how reassuring, how flattering to himself after all, such work really is—the work which deals with one as a scholar, formed, mature and manly. Bravery—ἀνδρεία or manliness—manliness and temperance, as we know, were the two characteristic virtues of that old pagan world; and in art certainly they seem to be involved in one another. Manliness in art, what can it be, as distinct from that which in opposition to it must be called the feminine quality there,—what but a full consciousness of what one does, of art itself in the work of art, tenacity of intuition and of consequent purpose, the spirit of construction as opposed to what is literally incoherent or ready to fall to pieces, and, in opposition to what is hysteric or works at random, the maintenance of a standard. Of such art ἦθος rather than πάθος will be the predominant mood. To use Plato's own expression there will be here no παραλειπόμενα, no "negligences," no feminine forgetfulness of one's self, nothing in the work of art unconformed to the leading intention of the artist, who will but increase his power by reserve. An artist of that kind will be apt, of course, to express more than he seems actually to say. He economises. He will not spoil good things by exaggeration. The rough, promiscuous wealth of nature he reduces to grace and order: reduces, it may be, lax verse to staid and temperate prose. With him, the rhythm, the music, the notes, will be felt to follow, or rather literally accompany as ministers, the sense,—ἀκολουθεῖν τὸν λόγον.

16. We may fairly prefer the broad daylight of Veronese to the contrasted light and shade of Rembrandt even; and a painter will tell you that the former is actually more difficult to attain. Temperance, the temperance of the youthful Charmides, super-induced on a nature originally rich and impassioned,—Plato's own native preference for that is only reinforced by the special needs of his time, and the very conditions of the ideal state. The diamond, we are told, if it be a fine one, may gain in value by what is cut away. It was after such fashion that the manly youth of Lacedæmon had been cut and carved. Lenten or monastic colours, brown and black, white and grey, give their utmost value for the eye (so much is obvious) to the scarlet flower, the lighted candle, the cloth of gold. And Platonic æsthetics, remember! as such, are ever in close connexion with Plato's ethics. It is life itself, action and character, he proposes to colour; to get something of that irrepressible conscience of art, that spirit of control, into the general course of life, above all into its energetic or impassioned acts.

17. Such Platonic quality you may trace of course not only in work of Doric, or, more largely, of Hellenic lineage, but at all times, as the very conscience of art, its saving salt, even in ages of decadence. You may analyse it, as a condition of literary style, in historic narrative, for instance; and then you have the stringent, short-hand art of Thucydides at his best, his masterly

feeling for master-facts, and the half as so much more than the whole. Pindar is in a certain sense his analogue in verse. Think of the amount of attention he must have looked for, in those who were, not to read, but to sing him, or to listen while he was sung, and to understand. With those fine, sharp-cut gems or chasings of his, so sparely set, how much he leaves for a well-drilled intelligence to supply in the way of connecting thought.

18. And you may look for the correlative of that in Greek clay, in Greek marble, as you walk through the British Museum. But observe it, above all, at work, checking yet reinforcing his naturally fluent and luxuriant genius, in Plato himself. His prose is a practical illustration of the value of that capacity for correction, of the effort, the intellectual astringency, which he demands of the poet also, the musician, of all true citizens of the ideal Republic, enhancing the sense of power in one's self, and its effect upon others, by a certain crafty reserve in its exercise, after the manner of a true expert. Χαλεπὰ τὰ καλά—he is faithful to the old Greek saying. Patience, "infinite patience," may or may not be, as was said, of the very essence of genius; but is certainly, quite as much as fire, of the mood of all true lovers. Ἴσως τὸ λεγόμενον ἀληθές, ὅτι χαλεπὰ τὰ καλά. Heraclitus had preferred the "dry soul," or the "dry light" in it, as Bacon after him the *siccum lumen*. And the dry beauty,—let Plato teach us, to love that also, duly.

ESSAYS POSTHUMOUSLY COLLECTED

1. "GREEK STUDIES"

A STUDY OF DIONYSUS
The Spiritual Form of Fire and Dew

Writers on mythology speak habitually of the *religion* of the Greeks. In thus speaking, they are really using a misleading expression, and should speak rather of *religions*; each race and class of Greeks—the Dorians, the people of the coast, the fishers—having had a religion of its own, conceived of the objects that came nearest to it and were most in its thoughts, and the resulting usages and ideas never having come to have a precisely harmonised system, after the analogy of some other religions. The religion of Dionysus is the religion of people who pass their lives among the vines. As the religion of Demeter carries us back to the cornfields and farmsteads of Greece, and places us, in fancy, among a primitive race, in the furrow and beside the granary; so the religion of Dionysus carries us back to its vineyards, and is a monument of the ways and thoughts of people whose days go by beside the winepress, and under the green and purple shadows, and whose material happiness depends on the crop of grapes. For them the thought of Dionysus and his circle, a little Olympus outside the greater, covered the whole of life, and was a complete religion, a sacred representation or interpretation of the whole human experience, modified by the special limitations, the special privileges of insight or suggestion, incident to their peculiar mode of existence.

2. Now, if the reader wishes to understand what the scope of the religion of Dionysus was to the Greeks who lived in it, all it represented to them by way of one clearly conceived yet complex symbol, let him reflect what the loss would be if all the effect and expression drawn from the imagery of the vine and the cup fell out of the whole body of existing poetry; how many fascinating trains of reflexion, what colour and substance would therewith have been deducted from it, filled as it is, apart from the more aweful associations of the Christian ritual, apart from Galahad's cup, with all the various symbolism of the fruit of the vine. That supposed loss is but an imperfect measure of all that the name of Dionysus recalled to the Greek mind, under a single imaginable form, an outward body of flesh presented to the senses, and comprehending, as its animating soul, a whole world of thoughts, surmises, greater and less experiences.

3. The student of the comparative science of religions finds in the religion

of Dionysus one of many modes of that primitive tree-worship which, growing out of some universal instinctive belief that trees and flowers are indeed habitations of living spirits, is found almost everywhere in the earlier stages of civilisation, enshrined in legend or custom, often graceful enough, as if the delicate beauty of the object of worship had effectually taken hold on the fancy of the worshipper. Shelley's *Sensitive Plant* shows in what mists of poetical reverie such feeling may still float about a mind full of modern lights, the feeling we too have of a life in the green world, always ready to assert its claim over our sympathetic fancies. Who has not at moments felt the scruple, which is with us always regarding animal life, following the signs of animation further still, till one almost hesitates to pluck out the little soul of flower or leaf?

4. And in so graceful a faith the Greeks had their share; what was crude and inane in it becoming, in the atmosphere of their energetic, imaginative intelligence, refined and humanised. The oak-grove of Dodona, the seat of their most venerable oracle, did but perpetuate the fancy that the sounds of the wind in the trees may be, for certain prepared and chosen ears, intelligible voices; they could believe in the transmigration of souls into mulberry and laurel, mint and hyacinth; and the dainty *Metamorphoses* of Ovid are but a fossilised form of one morsel here and there, from a whole world of transformation, with which their nimble fancy was perpetually playing. "Together with them," says the Homeric hymn to Aphrodite, of the Hamadryads, the nymphs which animate the forest trees, "with them, at the moment of their birth, grew up out of the soil, oak-tree or pine, fair, flourishing among the mountains. And when at last the appointed hour of their death has come, first of all, those fair trees are dried up; the bark perishes from around them, and the branches fall away; and therewith the soul of them deserts the light of the sun."

5. These then are the nurses of the vine, bracing it with interchange of sun and shade. They bathe, they dance, they sing songs of enchantment, so that those who seem oddly in love with nature, and strange among their fellows, are still said to be *nympholepti*; above all, they are weavers or spinsters, spinning or weaving with airiest fingers, and subtlest, many-coloured threads, the foliage of the trees, the petals of flowers, the skins of the fruit, the long thin stalks on which the poplar leaves are set so lightly that Homer compares to them, in their constant motion, the maids who sit spinning in the house of Alcinous. The nymphs of Naxos, where the grape-skin is darkest, weave for him a purple robe. Only, the ivy is never transformed, is visible as natural ivy to the last, pressing the dark outline of its leaves close upon the firm, white, quite human flesh of the god's forehead.

6. In its earliest form, then, the religion of Dionysus presents us with the most graceful phase of this graceful worship, occupying a place between the

ruder fancies of half-civilised people concerning life in flower or tree, and the dreamy after-fancies of the poet of the *Sensitive Plant*. He is the soul of the individual vine, first; the young vine at the house-door of the newly married, for instance, as the vine-grower stoops over it, coaxing and nursing it, like a pet animal or a little child; afterwards, the soul of the whole species, the spirit of fire and dew, alive and leaping in a thousand vines, as the higher intelligence, brooding more deeply over things, pursues, in thought, the generation of sweetness and strength in the veins of the tree, the transformation of water into wine, little by little; noting all the influences upon it of the heaven above and the earth beneath; and shadowing forth, in each pause of the process, an intervening person—what is to us but the secret chemistry of nature being to them the mediation of living spirits. So they passed on to think of Dionysus (naming him at last from the brightness of the sky and the moisture of the earth) not merely as the soul of the vine, but of all that life in flowing things of which the vine is the symbol, because its most emphatic example. At Delos he bears a son, from whom in turn spring the three mysterious sisters Œno, Spermo, and Elais, who, dwelling in the island, exercise respectively the gifts of turning all things at will into oil, and corn, and wine. In the *Bacchæ* of Euripides, he gives his followers, by miracle, honey and milk, and the water gushes for them from the smitten rock. He comes at last to have a scope equal to that of Demeter, a realm as wide and mysterious as hers; the whole productive power of the earth is in him, and the explanation of its annual change. As some embody their intuitions of that power in corn, so others in wine. He is the dispenser of the earth's hidden wealth, giver of riches through the vine, as Demeter through the grain. And as Demeter sends the airy, dainty-wheeled and dainty-winged spirit of Triptolemus to bear her gifts abroad on all winds, so Dionysus goes on his eastern journey, with its many intricate adventures, on which he carries his gifts to every people.

7. *A little Olympus outside the greater*, I said, of Dionysus and his companions; he is the centre of a cycle, the hierarchy of the creatures of water and sunlight in many degrees; and that fantastic system of tree-worship places round him, not the fondly whispering spirits of the more graceful inhabitants of woodland only, the nymphs of the poplar and the pine, but the whole satyr circle, intervening between the headship of the vine and the mere earth, the grosser, less human spirits, incorporate and made visible, of the more coarse and sluggish sorts of vegetable strength, the fig, the reed, the ineradicable weed-things which will attach themselves, climbing about the vine-poles, or seeking the sun between the hot stones. For as Dionysus, the *spiritual form* of the vine, is of the highest human type, so the fig-tree and the reed have animal souls, mistakeable in the thoughts of a later, imperfectly remembering age, for mere abstractions

of animal nature; Snubnose, and Sweetwine, and Silenus, the oldest of them all, so old that he has come to have the gift of prophecy.

8. Quite different from them in origin and intent, but confused with them in form, are those other companions of Dionysus, Pan and his children. Homespun dream of simple people, and like them in the uneventful tenour of his existence, he has almost no story; he is but a presence; the *spiritual form* of Arcadia, and the ways of human life there; the reflexion, in sacred image or ideal, of its flocks, and orchards, and wild honey; the dangers of its hunters; its weariness in noonday heat; its children, agile as the goats they tend, who run, in their picturesque rags, across the solitary wanderer's path, to startle him, in the unfamiliar upper places; its one adornment and solace being the dance to the homely shepherd's pipe, cut by Pan first from the sedges of the brook Molpeia.

9. Breathing of remote nature, the sense of which is so profound in the Homeric hymn to Pan, the pines, the foldings of the hills, the leaping streams, the strange echoings and dying of sound on the heights, "the bird, which among the petals of many-flowered spring, pouring out a dirge, sends forth her honey-voiced song," "the crocus and the hyacinth disorderly mixed in the deep grass"—things which the religion of Dionysus loves—Pan joins the company of the Satyrs. Amongst them, they give their names to insolence and mockery, and the finer sorts of malice, to unmeaning and ridiculous fear. But the best spirits have found in them also a certain human pathos, as in displaced beings, coming even nearer to most men, in their very roughness, than the noble and delicate person of the vine; dubious creatures, half-way between the animal and human kinds, speculating wistfully on their being, because not wholly understanding themselves and their place in nature; as the animals seem always to have this expression to some noticeable degree in the presence of man. In the later school of Attic sculpture they are treated with more and more of refinement, till in some happy moment Praxiteles conceived a model, often repeated, which concentrates this sentiment of true humour concerning them; a model of dainty natural ease in posture, but with the legs slightly crossed, as only lowly-bred gods are used to carry them, and with some puzzled trouble of youth, you might wish for a moment to smoothe away, puckering the forehead a little, between the pointed ears, on which the goodly hair of his animal strength grows low. Little by little, the signs of brute nature are subordinated, or disappear; and at last, Robetta, a humble Italian engraver of the fifteenth century, entering into the Greek fancy because it belongs to all ages, has expressed it in its most exquisite form, in a design of Ceres and her children, of whom their mother is no longer afraid, as in the Homeric hymn to Pan. The puck-noses have grown delicate, so that, with Plato's infatuated

lover, you may call them winsome, if you please; and no one would wish those hairy little shanks away, with which one of the small Pans walks at her side, grasping her skirt stoutly; while the other, the sick or weary one, rides in the arms of Ceres herself, who in graceful Italian dress, and decked airily with fruit and corn, steps across a country of cut sheaves, pressing it closely to her, with a child's peevish trouble in its face, and its small goat-legs and tiny hoofs folded over together, precisely after the manner of a little child.

10. There is one element in the conception of Dionysus, which his connexion with the satyrs, Marsyas being one of them, and with Pan, from whom the flute passed to all the shepherds of Theocritus, alike illustrates, his interest, namely, in one of the great species of music. One form of that wilder vegetation, of which the Satyr race is the soul made visible, is the reed, which the creature plucks and trims into musical pipes. And as Apollo inspires and rules over all the music of strings, so Dionysus inspires and rules over all the music of the reed, the water-plant, in which the ideas of water and of vegetable life are brought close together, natural property, therefore, of the spirit of life in the green sap. I said that the religion of Dionysus was, for those who lived in it, a complete religion, a complete sacred representation and interpretation of the whole of life; and as, in his relation to the vine, he fills for them the place of Demeter, is the life of the earth through the grape as she through the grain, so, in this other phase of his being, in his relation to the reed, he fills for them the place of Apollo; he is the inherent cause of music and poetry; he inspires; he explains the phenomena of enthusiasm, as distinguished by Plato in the *Phædrus*, the secrets of possession by a higher and more energetic spirit than one's own, the gift of self-revelation, of passing out of oneself through words, tones, gestures. A winged Dionysus, venerated at Amyclæ, was perhaps meant to represent him thus, as the god of enthusiasm, of the rising up on those spiritual wings, of which also we hear something in the *Phædrus* of Plato.

11. The artists of the Renaissance occupied themselves much with the person and the story of Dionysus; and Michelangelo, in a work still remaining in Florence, in which he essayed with success to produce a thing which should pass with the critics for a piece of ancient sculpture, has represented him in the fulness, as it seems, of this enthusiasm, an image of delighted, entire surrender to transporting dreams. And this is no subtle after-thought of a later age, but true to certain finer movements of old Greek sentiment, though it may seem to have waited for the hand of Michelangelo before it attained complete realisation. The head of Ion leans, as they recline at the banquet, on the shoulder of Charmides; he mutters in his sleep of things seen therein, but awakes as the flute-players enter, whom Charmides has hired for his birthday supper. The soul of Callias, who sits on the other side of Charmides, flashes

out; he counterfeits, with life-like gesture, the personal tricks of friend or foe; or the things he could never utter before, he finds words for now; the secrets of life are on his lips. It is in this loosening of the lips and heart, strictly, that Dionysus is the Deliverer, *Eleutherios*; and of such enthusiasm, or ecstasy, is, in a certain sense, an older patron than Apollo himself. Even at Delphi, the centre of Greek inspiration and of the religion of Apollo, his claim always maintained itself; and signs are not wanting that Apollo was but a later comer there. There, under his later reign, hard by the golden image of Apollo himself, near the sacred tripod on which the Pythia sat to prophesy, was to be seen a strange object—a sort of coffin or cinerary urn with the inscription, "Here lieth the body of Dionysus, the son of Semele." The pediment of the great temple was divided between them—Apollo with the nine Muses on that side, Dionysus, with perhaps three times three Graces, on this. A third of the whole year was held sacred to him; the four winter months were the months of Dionysus; and in the shrine of Apollo itself he was worshipped with almost equal devotion.

12. The religion of Dionysus takes us back, then, into that old Greek life of the vineyards, as we see it on many painted vases, with much there as we should find it now, as we see it in Bennozzo Gozzoli's mediæval fresco of the *Invention of Wine* in the Campo Santo at Pisa—the family of Noah presented among all the circumstances of a Tuscan vineyard, around the press from which the first wine is flowing, a painted idyll, with its vintage colours still opulent in decay, and not without its solemn touch of biblical symbolism. For differences, we detect in that primitive life, and under that Greek sky, a nimbler play of fancy, lightly and unsuspiciously investing all things with personal aspect and incident, and a certain mystical apprehension, now almost departed, of unseen powers beyond the material veil of things, corresponding to the exceptional vigour and variety of the Greek organisation. This peasant life lies, in unhistoric time, behind the definite forms with which poetry and a refined priesthood afterwards clothed the religion of Dionysus; and the mere scenery and circumstances of the vineyard have determined many things in its development. The noise of the vineyard still sounds in some of his epithets, perhaps in his best-known name—*Iacchus, Bacchus*. The masks suspended on base or cornice, so familiar an ornament in later Greek architecture, are the little faces hanging from the vines, and moving in the wind, to scare the birds. That garland of ivy, the æsthetic value of which is so great in the later imagery of Dionysus and his descendants, the leaves of which, floating from his hair, become so noble in the hands of Titian and Tintoret, was actually worn on the head for coolness; his earliest and most sacred images were wrought in the wood of the vine. The people of the vineyard had their feast, the *little* or *country Dionysia*, which still lived on, side by side with the greater ceremonies of a later time, celebrated

in December, the time of the storing of the new wine. It was then that the potters' fair came, *calpis* and *amphora*, together with lamps against the winter, laid out in order for the choice of buyers; for Keramus, the Greek Vase, is a son of Dionysus, of wine and of Athene, who teaches men all serviceable and decorative art. Then the goat was killed, and its blood poured out at the root of the vines; and Dionysus literally drank the blood of goats; and, being Greeks, with quick and mobile sympathies, δεισιδαίμονες, "superstitious," or rather "susceptible of religious impressions," some among them, remembering those departed since last year, add yet a little more, and a little wine and water for the dead also; brooding how the sense of these things might pass below the roots, to spirits hungry and thirsty, perhaps, in their shadowy homes. But the gaiety, that gaiety which Aristophanes in the *Acharnians* has depicted with so many vivid touches, as a thing of which civil war had deprived the villages of Attica, preponderates over the grave. The travelling country show comes round with its puppets; even the slaves have their holiday;[1] the mirth becomes excessive; they hide their faces under grotesque masks of bark, or stain them with wine-lees, or potters' crimson even, like the old rude idols painted red; and carry in midnight procession such rough symbols of the productive force of nature as the women and children had best not look upon; which will be frowned upon, and refine themselves, or disappear, in the feasts of cultivated Athens.

13. Of the whole story of Dionysus, it was the episode of his marriage with Ariadne about which ancient art concerned itself oftenest, and with most effect. Here, although the antiquarian may still detect circumstances which link the persons and incidents of the legend with the mystical life of the earth, as symbols of its annual change, yet the merely human interest of the story has prevailed over its earlier significance; the *spiritual form* of fire and dew has become a romantic lover. And as a story of romantic love, fullest perhaps of all the motives of classic legend of the pride of life, it survived with undiminished interest to a later world, two of the greatest masters of Italian painting having poured their whole power into it; Titian with greater space of ingathered shore and mountain, and solemn foliage, and fiery animal life; Tintoret with profounder luxury of delight in the nearness to each other, and imminent embrace, of glorious bodily presences; and both alike with consummate beauty of physical form. Hardly less humanised is the Theban legend of Dionysus, the legend of his birth from Semele, which, out of the entire body of tradition concerning him, was accepted as central by the Athenian imagination. For

---

1. There were some who suspected Dionysus of a secret democratic interest; though indeed he was *liberator* only of men's hearts, and ἐλευθερεύς only because he never forgot Eleutheræ, the little place which, in Attica, first received him.

the people of Attica, he comes from Bœotia, a country of northern marsh and mist, but from whose sombre, black marble towns came also the vine, the musical reed cut from its sedges, and the worship of the Graces, always so closely connected with the religion of Dionysus. "At Thebes alone," says Sophocles, "mortal women bear immortal gods." His mother is the daughter of Cadmus, himself marked out by many curious circumstances as the close kinsman of the earth, to which he all but returns at last, as the serpent, in his old age, attesting some closer sense lingering there of the affinity of man with the dust from whence he came. Semele, an old Greek word, as it seems, for the surface of the earth, the daughter of Cadmus, beloved by Zeus, desires to see her lover in the glory with which he is seen by the immortal Hera. He appears to her in lightning. But the mortal may not behold him and live. Semele gives premature birth to the child Dionysus; whom, to preserve it from the jealousy of Hera, Zeus hides in a part of his thigh, the child returning into the loins of its father, whence in due time it is born again. Yet in this fantastic story, hardly less than in the legend of Ariadne, the story of Dionysus has become a story of human persons, with human fortunes, and even more intimately human appeal to sympathy; so that Euripides, pre-eminent as a poet of pathos, finds in it a subject altogether to his mind. All the interest now turns on the development of its points of moral or sentimental significance; the love of the immortal for the mortal, the presumption of the daughter of man who desires to see the divine form as it is; on the fact that not without loss of sight, or life itself, can man look upon it. The travail of nature has been transformed into the pangs of the human mother; and the poet dwells much on the pathetic incident of death in childbirth, making Dionysus, as Callimachus calls him, a seven months' child, cast out among its enemies, motherless. And as a consequence of this human interest, the legend attaches itself, as in an actual history, to definite sacred objects and places, the venerable relic of the wooden image which fell into the chamber of Semele with the lightning-flash, and which the piety of a later age covered with plates of brass; the *Ivy-Fountain* near Thebes, the water of which was so wonderfully bright and sweet to drink, where the nymphs bathed the new-born child; the grave of Semele, in a sacred enclosure grown with ancient vines, where some volcanic heat or flame was perhaps actually traceable, near the lightning-struck ruins of her supposed abode.

14. Yet, though the mystical body of the earth is forgotten in the human anguish of the mother of Dionysus, the sense of his essence of fire and dew still lingers in his most sacred name, as the son of Semele, *Dithyrambus*. We speak of a certain wild music in words or rhythm as *dithyrambic*, like the dithyrambus, that is, the wild choral-singing of the worshippers of Dionysus. But Dithyrambus seems to have been, in the first instance, the name, not of

the hymn, but of the god to whom the hymn is sung; and, through a tangle of curious etymological speculations as to the precise derivation of this name, one thing seems clearly visible, that it commemorates, namely, the double birth of the vine-god; that he is born once and again; his birth, first of fire, and afterwards of dew; the two dangers that beset him; his victory over two enemies, the capricious, excessive heats and colds of spring.

15. He is πυριγενής, then, fire-born, the son of lightning; lightning being to light, as regards concentration, what wine is to the other strengths of the earth. And who that has rested a hand on the glittering silex of a vineyard slope in August, where the pale globes of sweetness are lying, does not feel this? It is out of the bitter salts of a smitten, volcanic soil that it comes up with the most curious virtues. The mother faints and is parched up by the heat which brings the child to the birth; and it pierces through, a wonder of freshness, drawing its everlasting green and typical coolness out of the midst of the ashes; its own stem becoming at last like a tangled mass of tortured metal. In thinking of Dionysus, then, as fire-born, the Greeks apprehend and embody the sentiment, the poetry, of all tender things which grow out of a hard soil, or in any sense blossom before the leaf, like the little mezereon-plant of English gardens, with its pale-purple, wine-scented flowers upon the leafless twigs in February, or like the almond-trees of Tuscany, or Aaron's rod that budded, or the staff in the hand of the Pope when Tannhäuser's repentance is accepted.

16. And his second birth is of the dew. The fire of which he was born would destroy him in his turn, as it withered up his mother; a second danger comes; from this the plant is protected by the influence of the cooling cloud, the lower part of his father the sky, in which it is wrapped and hidden, and of which it is born again, its second mother being, in some versions of the legend, Hyé—the Dew. The nursery, where Zeus places it to be brought up, is a cave in Mount Nysa, sought by a misdirected ingenuity in many lands, but really, like the place of the carrying away of Persephone, a place of fantasy, the oozy place of springs in the hollow of the hillside, nowhere and everywhere, where the vine was "invented." The nymphs of the trees overshadow it from above; the nymphs of the springs sustain it from below—the *Hyades*, those first leaping mænads, who, as the springs become rain-clouds, go up to heaven among the stars, and descend again, as dew or shower, upon it; so that the religion of Dionysus connects itself, not with tree-worship only, but also with ancient water-worship, the worship of the *spiritual forms* of springs and streams. To escape from his enemies Dionysus leaps into the sea, the original of all rain and springs, whence, in early summer, the women of Elis and Argos were wont to call him, with the singing of a hymn. And again, in thus commemorating Dionysus as born of the dew, the Greeks apprehend and embody the sentiment,

the poetry, of water. For not the heat only, but its solace—the *freshness* of the cup—this too was felt by those people of the vineyard, whom the prophet Melampus had taught to mix always their wine with water, and with whom the watering of the vines became a religious ceremony; the very dead, as they thought, drinking of and refreshed by the stream. And who that has ever felt the heat of a southern country does not know this poetry, the motive of the loveliest of all the works attributed to Giorgione, the *Fête Champêtre* in the Louvre; the intense sensations, the subtle and far-reaching symbolisms, which, in these places, cling about the touch and sound and sight of it? Think of the darkness of the well in the breathless court, with the delicate ring of ferns kept alive just within the opening; of the sound of the fresh water flowing through the wooden pipes into the houses of Venice, on summer mornings; of the cry *Acqua frésca!* at Padua or Verona, when the people run to buy what they prize, in its rare purity, more than wine, bringing pleasures so full of exquisite appeal to the imagination, that, in these streets, the very beggars, one thinks, might exhaust all the philosophy of the epicurean.

17. Out of all these fancies comes the vine-growers' god, the *spiritual form* of fire and dew. Beyond the famous representations of Dionysus in later art and poetry—the *Bacchanals* of Euripides, the statuary of the school of Praxiteles—a multitude of literary allusions and local customs carry us back to this world of vision unchecked by positive knowledge, in which the myth is begotten among a primitive people, as they wondered over the life of the thing their hands helped forward, till it became for them a kind of spirit, and their culture of it a kind of worship. Dionysus, as we see him in art and poetry, is the projected expression of the ways and dreams of this primitive people, brooded over and harmonised by the energetic Greek imagination; the religious imagination of the Greeks being, precisely, a unifying or identifying power, bringing together things naturally asunder, making, as it were, for the human body a soul of waters, for the human soul a body of flowers; welding into something like the identity of a human personality the whole range of man's experiences of a given object, or series of objects—all their outward qualities, and the visible facts regarding them—all the hidden ordinances by which those facts and qualities hold of unseen forces, and have their roots in purely visionary places.

18. Dionysus came later than the other gods to the centres of Greek life; and, as a consequence of this, he is presented to us in an earlier stage of development than they; that element of natural fact which is the original essence of all mythology being more unmistakeably impressed upon us here than in other myths. Not the least interesting point in the study of him is, that he illustrates very clearly, not only the earlier, but also a certain later influence of this element of natural fact, in the development of the gods of Greece. For the physical

sense, latent in it, is the clue, not merely to the original signification of the incidents of the divine story, but also to the source of the peculiar imaginative expression which its persons subsequently retain, in the forms of the higher Greek sculpture. And this leads me to some general thoughts on the relation of Greek sculpture to mythology, which may help to explain what the function of the imagination in Greek sculpture really was, in its handling of divine persons.

19. That Zeus is, in earliest, original, primitive intention, the open sky, across which the thunder sometimes sounds, and from which the rain descends—is a fact which not only explains the various stories related concerning him, but determines also the expression which he retained in the work of Pheidias, so far as it is possible to recall it, long after the growth of those later stories had obscured, for the minds of his worshippers, his primary signification. If men felt, as Arrian tells us, that it was a calamity to die without having seen the Zeus of Olympia; that was because they experienced the impress there of that which the eye and the whole being of man love to find above him; and the genius of Pheidias had availed to shed, upon the gold and ivory of the physical form, the blandness, the breadth, the smile of the open sky; the mild heat of it still coming and going, in the face of the father of all the children of sunshine and shower; as if one of the great white clouds had composed itself into it, and looked down upon them thus, out of the midsummer noonday: so that those things might be felt as warm, and fresh, and blue, by the young and the old, the weak and the strong, who came to sun themselves in the god's presence, as procession and hymn rolled on, in the fragrant and tranquil courts of the great Olympian temple; while all the time those people consciously apprehended in the carved image of Zeus none but the personal, and really human, characteristics.

20. Or think, again, of the Zeus of Dodona. The oracle of Dodona, with its dim grove of oaks, and sounding instruments of brass to husband the faintest whisper in the leaves, was but a great consecration of that sense of a mysterious will, of which people still feel, or seem to feel, the expression, in the motions of the wind, as it comes and goes, and which makes it, indeed, seem almost more than a mere symbol of the spirit within us. For Zeus was, indeed, the god of the winds also; Æolus, their so-called god, being only his mortal minister, as having come, by long study of them, through signs in the fire and the like, to have a certain communicable skill regarding them, in relation to practical uses. Now, suppose a Greek sculptor to have proposed to himself to present to his worshippers the image of this Zeus of Dodona, who is in the trees and on the currents of the air. Then, if he had been a really imaginative sculptor, working as Pheidias worked, the very soul of those moving, sonorous creatures would have passed through his hand, into the eyes and hair of the image; as they

can actually pass into the visible expression of those who have drunk deeply of them; as we may notice, sometimes, in our walks on mountain or shore.

21. Victory again—*Niké*—associated so often with Zeus—on the top of his staff, on the foot of his throne, on the palm of his extended hand—meant originally, mythologic science tells us, only the great victory of the sky, the triumph of morning over darkness. But that physical morning of her origin has its ministry to the later æsthetic sense also. For if *Niké*, when she appears in company with the mortal, and wholly fleshly hero, in whose chariot she stands to guide the horses, or whom she crowns with her garland of parsley or bay, or whose names she writes on a shield, is imaginatively conceived, it is because the old skyey influences are still not quite suppressed in her clear-set eyes, and the dew of the morning still clings to her wings and her floating hair.

22. The office of the imagination, then, in Greek sculpture, in its handling of divine persons, is thus to condense the impressions of natural things into human form; to retain that early mystical sense of water, or wind, or light, in the moulding of eye and brow; to arrest it, or rather, perhaps, to set it free, there, as human expression. The body of man, indeed, was for the Greeks, still the genuine work of Prometheus; its connexion with earth and air asserted in many a legend, not shaded down, as with us, through innumerable stages of descent, but direct and immediate; in precise contrast to our physical theory of our life, which never seems to fade, dream over it as we will, out of the light of common day. The oracles with their messages to human intelligence from birds and springs of water, or vapours of the earth, were a witness to that connexion. Their story went back, as they believed, with unbroken continuity, and in the very places where their later life was lived, to a past, stretching beyond, yet continuous with, actual memory, in which heaven and earth mingled; to those who were sons and daughters of stars, and streams, and dew; to an ancestry of grander men and women, actually clothed in, or incorporate with, the qualities and influences of those objects; and we can hardly over-estimate the influence on the Greek imagination of this mythical connexion with the natural world, at not so remote a date, and of the solemnising power exercised thereby over their thoughts. In this intensely poetical situation, the historical Greeks, the Athenians of the age of Pericles, found themselves; it was as if the actual roads on which men daily walk, went up and on, into a visible wonderland.

23. With such habitual impressions concerning the body, the physical nature of man, the Greek sculptor, in his later day, still free in imagination, through the lingering influence of those early dreams, may have more easily infused into human form the sense of sun, or lightning, or cloud, to which it was so closely akin, the spiritual flesh allying itself happily to mystical meanings, and readily expressing seemingly unspeakable qualities. But the human form is a limiting

influence also; and in proportion as art impressed human form, in sculpture or in the drama, on the vaguer conceptions of the Greek mind, there was danger of an escape from them of the free spirit of air, and light, and sky. Hence, all through the history of Greek art, there is a struggle, a *Streben*, as the Germans say, between the palpable and limited human form, and the floating essence it is to contain. On the one hand, was the teeming, still fluid world, of old beliefs, as we see it reflected in the somewhat formless *theogony* of Hesiod; a world, the Titanic vastness of which is congruous with a certain sublimity of speech, when he has to speak, for instance, of motion or space; as the Greek language itself has a primitive copiousness and energy of words, for wind, fire, water, cold, sound—attesting a deep susceptibility to the impressions of those things—yet with edges, most often, melting into each other. On the other hand, there was that limiting, controlling tendency, identified with the Dorian influence in the history of the Greek mind, the spirit of a severe and wholly self-conscious intelligence; bent on impressing everywhere, in the products of the imagination, the definite, perfectly conceivable human form, as the only worthy subject of art; less in sympathy with the mystical genealogies of Hesiod, than with the heroes of Homer, ending in the entirely humanised religion of Apollo, the clearly understood humanity of the old Greek warriors in the marbles of Ægina. The representation of man, as he is or might be, became the aim of sculpture, and the achievement of this the subject of its whole history; one early carver had opened the eyes, another the lips, a third had given motion to the feet; in various ways, in spite of the retention of archaic idols, the genuine human expression had come, with the truthfulness of life itself.

24. These two tendencies, then, met and struggled and were harmonised in the supreme imagination, of Pheidias, in sculpture—of Æschylus, in the drama. Hence, a series of wondrous personalities, of which the Greek imagination became the dwelling-place; beautiful, perfectly understood human outlines, embodying a strange, delightful, lingering sense of clouds and water and sun. Such a world, the world of really imaginative Greek sculpture, we still see, reflected in many a humble vase or battered coin, in Bacchante, and Centaur, and Amazon; evolved out of that "vasty deep"; with most command, in the consummate fragments of the Parthenon; not, indeed, so that he who runs may read, the gifts of Greek sculpture being always delicate, and asking much of the receiver; but yet visible, and a pledge to us, of creative power, as, to the worshipper, of the presence, which, without that material pledge, had but vaguely haunted the fields and groves.

25. This, then, was what the Greek imagination did for men's sense and experience of natural forces, in Athene, in Zeus, in Poseidon; for men's sense and experience of their own bodily qualities—swiftness, energy, power of

concentrating sight and hand and foot on a momentary physical act—in the close hair, the chastened muscle, the perfectly poised attention of the *quoit-player*; for men's sense, again, of ethical qualities—restless idealism, inward vision, power of presence through that vision in scenes behind the experience of ordinary men—in the idealised Alexander.

26. To illustrate this function of the imagination, as especially developed in Greek art, we may reflect on what happens with us in the use of certain names, as expressing summarily, this name for you and that for me—Helen, Gretchen, Mary—a hundred associations, trains of sound, forms, impressions, remembered in all sorts of degrees, which, through a very wide and full experience, they have the power of bringing with them; in which respect, such names are but revealing instances of the whole significance, power, and use of language in general. Well,—the mythical conception, projected at last, in drama or sculpture, is the *name*, the instrument of the identification, of the given matter,—of its unity in variety, its outline or definition in mystery; its *spiritual form*, to use again the expression I have borrowed from William Blake—form, with hands, and lips, and opened eyelids—spiritual, as conveying to us, in that, the soul of rain, or of a Greek river, or of swiftness, or purity.

27. To illustrate this, think what the effect would be, if you could associate, by some trick of memory, a certain group of natural objects, in all their varied perspective, their changes of colour and tone in varying light and shade, with the being and image of an actual person. You travelled through a country of clear rivers and wide meadows, or of high windy places, or of lowly grass and willows, or of the *Lady of the Lake*; and all the complex impressions of these objects wound themselves, as a second animated body, new and more subtle, around the person of some one left there, so that they no longer come to recollection apart from each other. Now try to conceive the image of an actual person, in whom, somehow, all those impressions of the vine and its fruit, as the highest type of the life of the green sap, had become incorporate;—all the scents and colours of its flower and fruit, and something of its curling foliage; the chances of its growth; the enthusiasm, the easy flow of more choice expression, as its juices mount within one; for the image is eloquent, too, in word, gesture, and glancing of the eyes, which seem to be informed by some soul of the vine within it: as Wordsworth says,

> Beauty born of murmuring sound
> Shall pass into her face—

so conceive an image into which the beauty, "born" of the vine, has passed; and you have the idea of Dionysus, as he appears, entirely fashioned at last

by central Greek poetry and art, and is consecrated in the Οἰνοφόρια and the
Ἀνθεστήρια, the great festivals of the *Winepress* and the *Flowers*.

28. The word *wine*, and with it the germ of the myth of Dionysus, is older than the separation of the Indo-Germanic race. Yet, with the people of Athens, Dionysus counted as the youngest of the gods; he was also the son of a mortal, dead in childbirth, and seems always to have exercised the charm of the latest born, in a sort of allowable fondness. Through the fine-spun speculations of modern ethnologists and grammarians, noting the changes in the letters of his name, and catching at the slightest historical records of his worship, we may trace his coming from Phrygia, the birthplace of the more mystical elements of Greek religion, over the mountains of Thrace. On the heights of Pangæus he leaves an oracle, with a perpetually burning fire, famous down to the time of Augustus, who reverently visited it. Southwards still, over the hills of Parnassus, which remained for the inspired women of Bœotia the centre of his presence, he comes to Thebes, and the family of Cadmus. From Bœotia he passes to Attica; to the villages first; at last to Athens; at an assignable date, under Peisistratus; out of the country, into the town.

29. To this stage of his town-life, that Dionysus of "enthusiasm" already belonged; it was to the Athenians of the town, to urbane young men, sitting together at the banquet, that those expressions of a sudden eloquence came, of the loosened utterance and finer speech, its colour and imagery. Dionysus, then, has entered Athens, to become urbane like them; to walk along the marble streets in frequent procession, in the persons of noble youths, like those who at the *Oschophoria* bore the branches of the vine from his temple, to the temple of *Athene of the Parasol*, or of beautiful slaves; to contribute through the arts to the adornment of life, yet perhaps also in part to weaken it, relaxing ancient austerity. Gradually, his rough country feasts will be outdone by the feasts of the town; and as comedy arose out of those, so these will give rise to tragedy. For his entrance upon this new stage of his career, his coming into the town, is from the first tinged with melancholy, as if in entering the town he had put off his country peace. The other Olympians are above sorrow. Dionysus, like a strenuous mortal hero, like Hercules or Perseus, has his alternations of joy and sorrow, of struggle and hard-won triumph. It is out of the sorrows of Dionysus, then,—of Dionysus in winter—that all Greek tragedy grows; out of the song of the sorrows of Dionysus, sung at his winter feast by the chorus of satyrs, singers clad in goat-skins, in memory of his rural life, one and another of whom, from time to time, steps out of the company to emphasise and develope this or that circumstance of the story; and so the song becomes dramatic. He will soon forget that early country life, or remember it but as the

dreamy background of his later existence. He will become, as always in later art and poetry, of dazzling whiteness; no longer dark with the air and sun, but like one ἐσκιατροφηκώς—brought up under the shade of Eastern porticoes or pavilions, or in the light that has only reached him softened through the texture of green leaves; honey-pale, like the delicate people of the city, like the flesh of women, as those old vase-painters conceive of it, who leave their hands and faces untouched with the pencil on the white clay. The ruddy god of the vineyard, stained with wine-lees, or coarser colour, will hardly recognise his double, in the white, graceful, mournful figure, weeping, chastened, lifting up his arms in yearning affection towards his late-found mother, as we see him on a famous Etruscan mirror. Only, in thinking of this early tragedy, of these town-feasts, and of the entrance of Dionysus into Athens, you must suppose, not the later Athens which is oftenest in our thoughts, the Athens of Pericles and Pheidias; but that little earlier Athens of Peisistratus, which the Persians destroyed, which some of us perhaps would rather have seen, in its early simplicity, than the greater one; when the old image of the god, carved probably out of the stock of an enormous vine, had just come from the village of Eleutheræ to his first temple in the *Lenæum*—the quarter of the winepresses, near the *Limnæ*—the marshy place, which in Athens represents the cave of Nysa; its little buildings on the hill-top, still with steep rocky ways, crowding round the ancient temple of Erechtheus and the grave of Cecrops, with the old miraculous olive-tree still growing there, and the old snake of Athene Polias still alive somewhere in the temple court.

30. The artists of the Italian Renaissance have treated Dionysus many times, and with great effect, but always in his joy, as an embodiment of that glory of nature to which the Renaissance was a return. But in an early engraving of Mocetto there is for once a Dionysus treated differently. The cold light of the background displays a barren hill, the bridge and towers of an Italian town, and quiet water. In the foreground, at the root of a vine, Dionysus is sitting, in a posture of statuesque weariness; the leaves of the vine are grandly drawn, and wreathing heavily round the head of the god, suggest the notion of his incorporation into it. The right hand, holding a great vessel languidly and indifferently, lets the stream of wine flow along the earth; while the left supports the forehead, shadowing heavily a face, comely, but full of an expression of painful brooding. One knows not how far one may really be from the mind of the old Italian engraver, in gathering from his design this impression of a melancholy and sorrowing Dionysus. But modern motives are clearer; and in a *Bacchus* by a young Hebrew painter, in the exhibition of the Royal Academy of 1868, there was a complete and very fascinating

realisation of such a motive; the god of the bitterness of wine, "of things too sweet"; the sea-water of the Lesbian grape become somewhat brackish in the cup. Touched by the sentiment of this subtler, melancholy Dionysus, we may ask whether anything similar in feeling is to be actually found in the range of Greek ideas;—had some antitype of this fascinating figure any place in Greek religion? Yes; in a certain darker side of the double god of nature, obscured behind the brighter episodes of Thebes and Naxos, but never quite forgotten, something corresponding to this deeper, more refined idea, really existed—the conception of Dionysus Zagreus; an image, which has left, indeed, but little effect in Greek art and poetry, which criticism has to put patiently together, out of late, scattered hints in various writers; but which is yet discernible, clearly enough to show that it really visited certain Greek minds here and there; and discernible, not as a late after-thought, but as a tradition really primitive, and harmonious with the original motive of the idea of Dionysus. In its potential, though unrealised scope, it is perhaps the subtlest dream in Greek religious poetry, and is, at least, part of the complete physiognomy of Dionysus, as it actually reveals itself to the modern student, after a complete survey.

31. The whole compass of the idea of Dionysus, a dual god of both summer and winter, became ultimately, as we saw, almost identical with that of Demeter. The Phrygians believed that the god slept in winter and awoke in summer, and celebrated his waking and sleeping; or that he was bound and imprisoned in winter, and unbound in spring. We saw how, in Elis and at Argos, the women called him out of the sea, with the singing of hymns, in early spring; and a beautiful ceremony in the temple at Delphi, which, as we know, he shares with Apollo, described by Plutarch, represents his mystical resurrection. Yearly, about the time of the shortest day, just as the light begins to increase, and while hope is still tremulously strung, the priestesses of Dionysus were wont to assemble with many lights at his shrine, and there, with songs and dances, awoke the new-born child after his wintry sleep, waving in a sacred cradle, like the great basket used for winnowing corn, a symbolical image, or perhaps a real infant. He is twofold then—a *Döppelganger*; like Persephone, he belongs to two worlds, and has much in common with her, and a full share of those dark possibilities which, even apart from the story of the rape, belong to her. He is a *Chthonian* god, and, like all the children of the earth, has an element of sadness; like Hades himself, he is hollow and devouring, an eater of man's flesh—*sarcophagus*—the grave which consumed unaware the ivory-white shoulder of Pelops.

32. And you have no sooner caught a glimpse of this image, than a certain perceptible shadow comes creeping over the whole story; for, in effect, we have seen glimpses of the sorrowing Dionysus, all along. Part of the interest of

the Theban legend of his birth is that he comes of the marriage of a god with a mortal woman; and from the first, like merely mortal heroes, he falls within the sphere of human chances. At first, indeed, the melancholy settles round the person of his mother, dead in childbirth, and ignorant of the glory of her son; in shame, according to Euripides; punished, as her own sisters allege, for impiety. The death of Semele is a sort of ideal or type of this peculiar claim on human pity, as the descent of Persephone into Hades, of all human pity over the early death of women. Accordingly, his triumph being now consummated, he descends into Hades, through the unfathomable Alcyonian lake, according to the most central version of the legend, to bring her up from thence; and that Hermes, the shadowy conductor of souls, is constantly associated with Dionysus, in the story of his early life, is not without significance in this connexion. As in Delphi the winter months were sacred to him, so in Athens his feasts all fall within the four months on this and the other side of the shortest day; as Persephone spends those four months—a third part of the year—in Hades. Son or brother of Persephone he actually becomes at last, in confused, half-developed tradition; and even has his place, with his dark sister, in the Eleusinian mysteries, as Iacchus; where, on the sixth day of the feast, in the great procession from Athens to Eleusis, we may still realise his image, moving up and down above the heads of the vast multitude, as he goes, beside "*the two*," to the temple of Demeter, amid the light of torches at noonday.

33. But it was among the mountains of Thrace that this gloomier element in the being of Dionysus had taken the strongest hold. As in the sunny villages of Attica the cheerful elements of his religion had been developed, so, in those wilder northern regions, people continued to brood over its darker side, and hence a current of gloomy legend descended into Greece. The subject of the *Bacchanals* of Euripides is the infatuated opposition of Pentheus, king of Thebes, to Dionysus and his religion; his cruelty to the god, whom he shuts up in prison, and who appears on the stage with his delicate limbs cruelly bound, but who is finally triumphant; Pentheus, the man of grief, being torn to pieces by his own mother, in the judicial madness sent upon her by the god. In this play, Euripides has only taken one of many versions of the same story, in all of which Dionysus is victorious, his enemy being torn to pieces by the sacred women, or by wild horses, or dogs, or the fangs of cold; or the mænad Ambrosia, whom he is supposed to pursue for purposes of lust, suddenly becomes a vine, and binds him down to the earth inextricably, in her serpentine coils.

34. In all these instances, then, Dionysus punishes his enemies by repaying them in kind. But a deeper vein of poetry pauses at the sorrow, and in the conflict does not too soon anticipate the final triumph. It is Dionysus himself who exhausts these sufferings. Hence, in many forms—reflexes of all the

various phases of his wintry existence—the image of Dionysus Zagreus, *the Hunter*—of Dionysus in winter—storming wildly on the dark Thracian hills, from which, like Ares and Boreas, he originally descends into Greece; the thought of the hunter concentrating into itself all men's forebodings over the departure of the year at its richest, and the death of all sweet things in the long-continued cold, when the sick and the old and little children, gazing out morning after morning on the dun sky, can hardly believe in the return any more of a bright day. Or he is connected with the fears, the dangers and hardships of the hunter himself, lost or slain sometimes, far from home, in the dense woods of the mountains, as he seeks his meat so ardently; becoming, in his chase, almost akin to the wild beasts—to the wolf, who comes before us in the name of Lycurgus, one of his bitterest enemies—and a phase, therefore, of his own personality, in the true intention of the myth. This transformation, this image of the beautiful soft creature become an enemy of human kind, putting off himself in his madness, wronged by his own fierce hunger and thirst, and haunting, with terrible sounds, the high Thracian farms, is the most tragic note of the whole picture, and links him on to one of the gloomiest creations of later romance, the werewolf, the belief in which still lingers in Greece, as in France, where it seems to become incorporate in the darkest of all romantic histories, that of Gilles de Retz.

35. And now we see why the tradition of human sacrifice lingered on in Greece, in connexion with Dionysus, as a thing of actual detail, and not remote, so that Dionysius of Halicarnassus counts it among the horrors of Greek religion. That the sacred women of Dionysus ate, in mystical ceremony, raw flesh, and drank blood, is a fact often mentioned, and commemorates, as it seems, the actual sacrifice of a fair boy deliberately torn to pieces, fading at last into a symbolical offering. At Delphi, the wolf was preserved for him, on the principle by which Venus loves the dove, and Hera peacocks; and there were places in which, after the sacrifice of a kid to him, a curious mimic pursuit of the priest who had offered it represented the still surviving horror of one who had thrown a child to the wolves. The three daughters of Minyas devote themselves to his worship; they cast lots, and one of them offers her own tender infant to be torn by the three, like a roe; then the other women pursue them, and they are turned into bats, or moths, or other creatures of the night. And fable is endorsed by history; Plutarch telling us how, before the battle of Salamis, with the assent of Themistocles, three Persian captive youths were offered to Dionysus *the Devourer*.

36. As, then, some embodied their fears of winter in Persephone, others embodied them in Dionysus, a devouring god, whose sinister side (as the best wine itself has its treacheries) is illustrated in the dark and shameful secret

society described by Livy, in which his worship ended at Rome, afterwards abolished by solemn act of the senate. He becomes a new Aidoneus, a hunter of men's souls; like him, to be appeased only by costly sacrifices.

37. And then, Dionysus recovering from his mid-winter madness, how intensely these people conceive the spring! It is that triumphant Dionysus, cured of his great malady, and sane in the clear light of the longer days, whom Euripides in the *Bacchanals* sets before us, as still, essentially, the Hunter, Zagreus; though he keeps the red streams and torn flesh away from the delicate body of the god, in his long vesture of white and gold, and fragrant with Eastern odours. Of this I hope to speak in another paper; let me conclude this by one phase more of religious custom.

38. If Dionysus, like Persephone, has his gloomy side, like her he has also a peculiar message for a certain number of refined minds, seeking, in the later days of Greek religion, such modifications of the old legend as may minister to ethical culture, to the perfecting of the moral nature. A type of second birth, from first to last, he opens, in his series of annual changes, for minds on the look-out for it, the hope of a possible analogy, between the resurrection of nature, and something else, as yet unrealised, reserved for human souls; and the beautiful, weeping creature, vexed by the wind, suffering, torn to pieces, and rejuvenescent again at last, like a tender shoot of living green out of the hardness and stony darkness of the earth, becomes an emblem or ideal of chastening and purification, and of final victory through suffering. It is the finer, mystical sentiment of the few, detached from the coarser and more material religion of the many, and accompanying it, through the course of its history, as its ethereal, less palpable, life-giving soul, and, as always happens, seeking the quiet, and not too anxious to make itself felt by others. With some unfixed, though real, place in the general scheme of Greek religion, this phase of the worship of Dionysus had its special development in the Orphic literature and mysteries. Obscure as are those followers of the mystical Orpheus, we yet certainly see them, moving, and playing their part, in the later ages of Greek religion. Old friends with new faces, though they had, as Plato witnesses, their less worthy aspect, in certain appeals to vulgar, superstitious fears, they seem to have been not without the charm of a real and inward religious beauty, with their neologies, their new readings of old legends, their sense of mystical second meanings, as they refined upon themes grown too familiar, and linked, in a sophisticated age, the new to the old. In this respect, we may perhaps liken them to the mendicant orders in the Middle Ages, with their florid, romantic theology, beyond the bounds of orthodox tradition, giving so much new matter to art and poetry. They are a picturesque addition, also, to the exterior of Greek life, with their white dresses, their dirges, their fastings and ecstasies,

their outward asceticism and material purifications. And the central object of their worship comes before us as a tortured, persecuted, slain god—the suffering Dionysus—of whose legend they have their own special and esoteric version. That version, embodied in a supposed Orphic poem, *The Occultation of Dionysus*, is represented only by the details that have passed from it into the almost endless *Dionysiaca* of Nonnus, a writer of the fourth century; and the imagery has to be put back into the shrine, bit by bit, and finally incomplete. Its central point is the picture of the rending to pieces of a divine child, of whom a tradition, scanty indeed, but harmonious in its variations, had long maintained itself. It was in memory of it, that those who were initiated into the Orphic mysteries tasted of the raw flesh of the sacrifice, and thereafter ate flesh no more; and it connected itself with that strange object in the Delphic shrine, the grave of Dionysus.

39. Son, first, of Zeus, and of Persephone whom Zeus woos, in the form of a serpent—the white, golden-haired child, the best-beloved of his father, and destined by him to be the ruler of the world, grows up in secret. But one day, Zeus, departing on a journey in his great fondness for the child, delivered to him his crown and staff, and so left him—shut in a strong tower. Then it came to pass that the jealous Here sent out the Titans against him. They approached the crowned child, and with many sorts of playthings enticed him away, to have him in their power, and then miserably slew him—hacking his body to pieces, as the wind tears the vine, with the axe *Pelekus*, which, like the swords of Roland and Arthur, has its proper name. The fragments of the body they boiled in a great cauldron, and made an impious banquet upon them, afterwards carrying the bones to Apollo, whose rival the young child should have been, thinking to do him service. But Apollo, in great pity for this his youngest brother, laid the bones in a grave, within his own holy place. Meanwhile, Here, full of her vengeance, brings to Zeus the heart of the child, which she had snatched, still beating, from the hands of the Titans. But Zeus delivered the heart to Semele; and the soul of the child remaining awhile in Hades, where Demeter made for it new flesh, was thereafter born of Semele—a second Zagreus—the younger, or Theban Dionysus.

THE BEGINNINGS OF GREEK SCULPTURE
I: The Heroic Age of Greek Art

The extant remains of Greek sculpture, though but a fragment of what the Greek sculptors produced, are, both in number and in excellence, in their fitness, therefore, to represent the whole of which they were a part, quite out of proportion to what has come down to us of Greek painting, and all those minor crafts which, in the Greek workshop, as at all periods when the arts have been really vigorous, were closely connected with the highest imaginative work. Greek painting is represented to us only by its distant reflexion on the walls of the buried houses of Pompeii, and the designs of subordinate though exquisite craftsmen on the vases. Of wrought metal, partly through the inherent usefulness of its material, tempting ignorant persons into whose hands it may fall to re-fashion it, we have comparatively little; while, in consequence of the perishableness of their material, nothing remains of the curious wood-work, the carved ivory, the embroidery and coloured stuffs, on which the Greeks set much store—of that whole system of refined artisanship, diffused, like a general atmosphere of beauty and richness, around the more exalted creations of Greek sculpture. What we possess, then, of that highest Greek sculpture is presented to us in a sort of threefold isolation; isolation, first of all, from the concomitant arts—the frieze of the Parthenon without the metal bridles on the horses, for which the holes in the marble remain; isolation, secondly, from the architectural group of which, with most careful estimate of distance and point of observation, that frieze, for instance, was designed to be a part; isolation, thirdly, from the clear Greek skies, the poetical Greek life, in our modern galleries. And if one here or there, in looking at these things, bethinks himself of the required substitution; if he endeavours mentally to throw them back into that proper atmosphere, through which alone they can exercise over us all the magic by which they charmed their original spectators, the effort is not always a successful one, within the grey walls of the Louvre or the British Museum.

2. And the circumstance that Greek sculpture is presented to us in such falsifying isolation from the work of the weaver, the carpenter, and the goldsmith, has encouraged a manner of regarding it too little sensuous. Approaching it with full information concerning what may be called the inner life of the Greeks, their modes of thought and sentiment amply recorded in the writings of the Greek poets and philosophers, but with no lively impressions of that mere craftsman's world of which so little has remained, students of antiquity have for the most part interpreted the creations of Greek sculpture, rather as

elements in a sequence of abstract ideas, as embodiments, in a sort of petrified language, of pure thoughts, and as interesting mainly in connexion with the development of Greek intellect, than as elements of a sequence in the material order, as results of a designed and skilful dealing of accomplished fingers with precious forms of matter for the delight of the eyes. Greek sculpture has come to be regarded as the product of a peculiarly limited art, dealing with a specially abstracted range of subjects; and the Greek sculptor as a workman almost exclusively intellectual, having only a sort of accidental connexion with the material in which his thought was expressed. He is fancied to have been disdainful of such matters as the mere tone, the fibre or texture, of his marble or cedar-wood, of that just perceptible yellowness, for instance, in the ivory-like surface of the Venus of Melos; as being occupied only with forms as abstract almost as the conceptions of philosophy, and translateable it might be supposed into any material—a habit of regarding him still further encouraged by the modern sculptor's usage of employing merely mechanical labour in the actual working of the stone.

3. The works of the highest Greek sculpture are indeed *intellectualised*, if we may say so, to the utmost degree; the human figures which they present to us seem actually to conceive thoughts; in them, that profoundly reasonable spirit of design which is traceable in Greek art, continuously and increasingly, upwards from its simplest products, the oil-vessel or the urn, reaches its perfection. Yet, though the most abstract and intellectualised of sensuous objects, they are still sensuous and material, addressing themselves, in the first instance, not to the purely reflective faculty, but to the eye; and a complete criticism must have approached them from both sides—from the side of the intelligence indeed, towards which they rank as great thoughts come down into the stone; but from the sensuous side also, towards which they rank as the most perfect results of that pure skill of hand, of which the Venus of Melos, we may say, is the highest example, and the little polished pitcher or lamp, also perfect in its way, perhaps the lowest.

4. To pass by the purely visible side of these things, then, is not only to miss a refining pleasure, but to mistake altogether the medium in which the most intellectual of the creations of Greek art, the Æginetan or the Elgin marbles, for instance, were actually produced; even these having, in their origin, depended for much of their charm on the mere material in which they were executed; and the whole black and grey world of extant antique sculpture needing to be translated back into ivory and gold, if we would feel the excitement which the Greek seems to have felt in the presence of these objects. To have this really Greek sense of Greek sculpture, it is necessary to connect it, indeed, with the inner life of the Greek world, its thought and sentiment, on the one hand; but

on the other hand to connect it, also, with the minor works of price, *intaglios*, coins, vases; with that whole system of material refinement and beauty in the outer Greek life, which these minor works represent to us; and it is with these, as far as possible, that we must seek to relieve the air of our galleries and museums of their too intellectual greyness. Greek sculpture could not have been precisely a *cold* thing; and, whatever a colour-blind school may say, pure thoughts have their coldness, a coldness which has sometimes repelled from Greek sculpture, with its unsuspected fund of passion and energy in material form, those who cared much, and with much insight, for a similar passion and energy in the coloured world of Italian painting.

5. Theoretically, then, we need that world of the minor arts as a complementary background for the higher and more austere Greek sculpture; and, as matter of fact, it is just with such a world—with a period of refined and exquisite *tectonics* (as the Greeks called all crafts strictly subordinate to architecture), that Greek art actually begins, in what is called the Heroic Age, that earliest, undefined period of Greek civilisation, the beginning of which cannot be dated, and which reaches down to the first Olympiad, about the year 776 B.C. Of this period we possess, indeed, no direct history, and but few actual monuments, great or small; but as to its whole character and outward local colouring, for its art, as for its politics and religion, Homer may be regarded as an authority. The Iliad and the Odyssey, the earliest pictures of that heroic life, represent it as already delighting itself in the application of precious material and skilful handiwork to personal and domestic adornment, to the refining and beautifying of the entire outward aspect of life; above all, in the lavish application of very graceful metal-work to such purposes. And this representation is borne out by what little we possess of its actual remains, and by all we can infer. Mixed, of course, with mere fable, as a description of the heroic age, the picture which Homer presents to us, deprived of its supernatural adjuncts, becomes continuously more and more realisable as the actual condition of early art, when we emerge gradually into historical time, and find ourselves at last among dateable works and real schools or masters.

6. The history of Greek art, then, begins, as some have fancied general history to begin, in a golden age, but in an age, so to speak, of real gold, the period of those first twisters and hammerers of the precious metals—men who had already discovered the flexibility of silver and the ductility of gold, the capacity of both for infinite delicacy of handling, and who enjoyed, with complete freshness, a sense of beauty and fitness in their work—a period of which that flower of gold on a silver stalk, picked up lately in one of the graves at Mycenæ, or the legendary golden honeycomb of Dædalus, might serve as the symbol. The heroic age of Greek art is the age of the hero as smith.

7. There are in Homer two famous descriptive passages in which this delight in curious metal-work is very prominent; the description in the Iliad of the shield of Achilles,[1] and the description of the house of Alcinous in the Odyssey.[2] The shield of Achilles is part of the suit of armour which Hephæstus makes for him at the request of Thetis; and it is wrought of variously coloured metals, woven into a great circular composition in relief, representing the world and the life in it. The various activities of man are recorded in this description in a series of idyllic incidents with such complete freshness, liveliness, and variety, that the reader from time to time may well forget himself, and fancy he is reading a mere description of the incidents of actual life. We peep into a little Greek town, and see in dainty miniature the bride coming from her chamber with torch-bearers and dancers, the people gazing from their doors, a quarrel between two persons in the market-place, the assembly of the elders to decide upon it. In another quartering is the spectacle of a city besieged, the walls defended by the old men, while the soldiers have stolen out and are lying in ambush. There is a fight on the river-bank; Ares and Athene, conspicuous in gold, and marked as divine persons by a scale larger than that of their followers, lead the host. The strange, mythical images of Kêr, Eris, and Kudoimos mingle in the crowd. A third space upon the shield depicts the incidents of peaceful labour—the ploughshare passing through the field, of enamelled black metal behind it, and golden before; the cup of mead held out to the ploughman when he reaches the end of the furrow; the reapers with their sheaves; the king standing in silent pleasure among them, intent upon his staff. There are the labourers in the vineyard in minutest detail; stakes of silver on which the vines hang; the dark trench about it, and one pathway through the midst; the whole complete and distinct, in variously coloured metal. All things and living creatures are in their places—the cattle coming to water to the sound of the herdsman's pipe, various music, the rushes by the water-side, a lion-hunt with dogs, the pastures among the hills, a dance, the fair dresses of the male and female dancers, the former adorned with swords, the latter with crowns. It is an image of ancient life, its pleasure and business. For the centre, as in some quaint chart of the heavens, are the earth and the sun, the moon and constellations; and to close in all, right round, like a frame to the picture, the great river Oceanus, forming the rim of the shield, in some metal of dark blue.

8. Still more fascinating, perhaps, because more completely realisable by the fancy as an actual thing—realisable as a delightful place to pass time in—is the description of the palace of Alcinous in the little island town of the Phæacians, to which we are introduced in all the liveliness and sparkle of the

---

1. *Il.* xviii. 468–608.   2. *Od.* vii. 37–132.

morning, as real as something seen last summer on the sea-coast; although, appropriately, Ulysses meets a goddess, like a young girl carrying a pitcher, on his way up from the sea. Below the steep walls of the town, two projecting jetties allow a narrow passage into a haven of stone for the ships, into which the passer-by may look down, as they lie moored below the roadway. In the midst is the king's house, all glittering, again, with curiously wrought metal; its brightness is "as the brightness of the sun or of the moon." The heart of Ulysses beats quickly when he sees it standing amid plantations ingeniously watered, its floor and walls of brass throughout, with continuous cornice of dark iron; the doors are of gold, the door-posts and lintels of silver, the handles, again, of gold—

> The walls were massy brass; the cornice high
> Blue metals crowned in colours of the sky;
> Rich plates of gold the folding-doors incase;
> The pillars silver on a brazen base;
> Silver the lintels deep-projecting o'er;
> And gold the ringlets that command the door.

Dogs of the same precious metals keep watch on either side, like the lions over the old gateway of Mycenæ, or the gigantic, human-headed bulls at the entrance of an Assyrian palace. Within doors the burning lights at supper-time are supported in the hands of golden images of boys, while the guests recline on a couch running all along the wall, covered with peculiarly sumptuous women's work.

9. From these two glittering descriptions manifestly something must be deducted; we are in wonder-land, and among supernatural or magical conditions. But the forging of the shield and the wonderful house of Alcinous are no merely incongruous episodes in Homer, but the consummation of what is always characteristic of him, a constant preoccupation, namely, with every form of lovely craftsmanship, resting on all things, as he says, like the shining of the sun. We seem to pass, in reading him, through the treasures of some royal collection; in him the presentation of almost every aspect of life is beautified by the work of cunning hands. The thrones, coffers, couches of curious carpentry, are studded with bossy ornaments of precious metal effectively disposed, or inlaid with stained ivory, or blue *cyanus*, or amber, or pale amber-like gold; the surfaces of the stone conduits, the sea-walls, the public washing-troughs, the ramparts on which the weary soldiers rest themselves when returned to Troy, are fair and smooth; all the fine qualities, in colour and texture, of woven stuff are carefully noted—the fineness, closeness, softness, pliancy, gloss, the

whiteness or nectar-like tints in which the weaver delights to work; to weave the sea-purple threads is the appropriate function of queens and noble women. All the Homeric shields are more or less ornamented with variously coloured metal, terrible sometimes, like Leonardo's, with some monster or grotesque. The numerous sorts of cups are bossed with golden studs, or have handles wrought with figures, of doves, for instance. The great brazen cauldrons bear an epithet which means *flowery*. The trappings of the horses, the various parts of the chariots, are formed of various metals. The women's ornaments and the instruments of their toilet are described—

πόρπας τε γναμπτάς θ᾿ἕλικας, κάλυκάς τε καὶ ὅρμους

—the golden vials for unguents. Use and beauty are still undivided; all that men's hands are set to make has still a fascination alike for workmen and spectators. For such dainty splendour Troy, indeed, is especially conspicuous. But then Homer's Trojans are essentially Greeks—Greeks of Asia; and Troy, though more advanced in all elements of civilisation, is no real contrast to the western shore of the Ægean. It is no *barbaric* world that we see, but the sort of world, we may think, that would have charmed also our comparatively jaded sensibilities, with just that quaint simplicity which we too enjoy in its productions; above all, in its wrought metal, which loses perhaps more than any other sort of work by becoming mechanical. The metal-work which Homer describes in such variety is all *hammer*-work, all the joinings being effected by pins or riveting. That is just the sort of metal-work which, in a certain *naïveté* and vigour, is still of all work the most expressive of actual contact with dexterous fingers; one seems to trace in it, on every particle of the partially resisting material, the touch and play of the shaping instruments, in highly trained hands, under the guidance of exquisitely disciplined senses—that *cachet*, or seal of nearness to the workman's hand, which is the special charm of all good metal-work, of early metal-work in particular.

10. Such descriptions, however, it may be said, are mere poetical ornament, of no value in helping us to define the character of an age. But what is peculiar in these Homeric descriptions, what distinguishes them from others at first sight similar, is a sort of internal evidence they present of a certain degree of reality, signs in them of an imagination stirred by surprise at the spectacle of real works of art. Such minute, delighted, loving description of details of ornament, such following out of the ways in which brass, gold, silver, or paler gold, go into the chariots and armour and women's dress, or cling to the walls—the enthusiasm of the *manner*—is the warrant of a certain amount of truth in all that. The Greek poet describes these things with the same

vividness and freshness, the same kind of fondness, with which other poets speak of flowers; speaking of them poetically, indeed, but with that higher sort of poetry which seems full of the lively impression of delightful things recently seen. Genuine poetry, it is true, is always naturally sympathetic with all beautiful sensible things and qualities. But with how many poets would not this constant intrusion of material ornament have produced a tawdry effect! The metal would all be tarnished and the edges blurred. And this is because it is not always that the products of even exquisite tectonics can excite or refine the æsthetic sense. Now it is probable that the objects of oriental art, the imitations of it at home, in which for Homer this actual world of art must have consisted, reached him in a quantity, and with a novelty, just sufficient to warm and stimulate without surfeiting the imagination; it is an exotic thing of which he sees just enough and not too much. The shield of Achilles, the house of Alcinous, are like dreams indeed, but this sort of dreaming winds continuously through the entire Iliad and Odyssey—a child's dream after a day of real, fresh impressions from things themselves, in which all those floating impressions re-set themselves. He is as pleased in touching and looking at those objects as his own heroes; their gleaming aspect brightens all he says, and has taken hold, one might think, of his language, his very vocabulary becoming *chryselephantine*. Homer's artistic descriptions, though enlarged by fancy, are not wholly imaginary, and the extant remains of monuments of the earliest historical age are like lingering relics of that dream in a tamer but real world.

11. The art of the heroic age, then, as represented in Homer, connects itself, on the one side, with those fabulous jewels so prominent in mythological story, and entwined sometimes so oddly in its representation of human fortunes—the necklace of Eriphyle, the necklace of Helen, which Menelaus, it was said, offered at Delphi to Athene Pronœa on the eve of his expedition against Troy—mythical objects, indeed, but which yet bear witness even thus early to the æsthetic susceptibility of the Greek temper. But, on the other hand, the art of the heroic age connects itself also with the actual early beginnings of artistic production. There are touches of reality, for instance, in Homer's incidental notices of its instruments and processes; especially as regards the working of metal. He goes already to the potter's wheel for familiar, life-like illustration. In describing artistic wood-work he distinguishes various stages of work; we see clearly the instruments for turning and boring, such as the old-fashioned drill-borer, whirled round with a string; he mentions the names of two artists, the one of an actual workman, the other of a craft turned into a proper name—stray relics, accidentally preserved, of a world, as we may believe, of such wide and varied activity. The forge of Hephæstus is a true forge; the magic tripods on which he is at work are really put together by

conceivable processes, known in early times. Compositions in relief similar to those which he describes were actually made out of thin metal plates cut into a convenient shape, and then beaten into the designed form by the hammer over a wooden model. These reliefs were then fastened to a differently coloured metal background or base, with nails or rivets, for there is no soldering of metals as yet. To this process the ancients gave the name of *empæstik*, such embossing being still, in our own time, a beautiful form of metal-work.

12. Even in the marvellous shield there are other and indirect notes of reality. In speaking of the shield of Achilles, I departed intentionally from the order in which the subjects of the relief are actually introduced in the Iliad, because, just then, I wished the reader to receive the full effect of the variety and elaborateness of the composition, as a representation or picture of the whole of ancient life embraced within the circumference of a shield. But in the order in which Homer actually describes those episodes he is following the method of a very practicable form of composition, and is throughout much closer than we might at first sight suppose to the ancient armourer's proceedings. The shield is formed of five superimposed plates of different metals, each plate of smaller diameter than the one immediately below it, their flat margins showing thus as four concentric stripes or rings of metal, around a sort of boss in the centre, five metals thick, and the outermost circle or ring being the thinnest. To this arrangement the order of Homer's description corresponds. The earth and the heavenly bodies are upon this boss in the centre, like a little distant heaven hung above the broad world, and from this Homer works out, round and round, to the river Oceanus, which forms the border of the whole; the subjects answering to, or supporting each other, in a sort of heraldic order—the city at peace set over against the city besieged—spring, summer, and autumn balancing each other—quite congruously with a certain heraldic turn common in contemporary Assyrian art, which delights in this sort of conventional spacing out of its various subjects, and especially with some extant metal chargers of Assyrian work, which, like some of the earliest Greek vases with their painted plants and flowers conventionally arranged, illustrate in their humble measure such heraldic grouping.

13. The description of the shield of Hercules, attributed to Hesiod, is probably an imitation of Homer, and, notwithstanding some fine mythological impersonations which it contains, an imitation less admirable than the original. Of painting there are in Homer no certain indications, and it is consistent with the later date of the imitator that we may perhaps discern in his composition a sign that what he had actually seen was a painted shield, in the pre-dominance in it, as compared with the Homeric description, of effects of colour over effects of form; Homer delighting in ingenious devices for *fastening* the metal, and

the supposed Hesiod rather in what seem like triumphs of heraldic *colouring*; though the latter also delights in effects of mingled metals, of mingled gold and silver especially—silver figures with dresses of gold, silver centaurs with pine-trees of gold for staves in their hands. Still, like the shield of Achilles, this too we must conceive as formed of concentric plates of metal; and here again that spacing is still more elaborately carried out, narrower intermediate rings being apparently introduced between the broader ones, with figures in rapid, horizontal, unbroken motion, carrying the eye right round the shield, in contrast with the repose of the downward or inward movement of the subjects which divide the larger spaces; here too with certain analogies in the rows of animals to the designs on the earliest vases.

14. In Hesiod then, as in Homer, there are undesigned notes of correspondence between the partly mythical ornaments imaginatively enlarged of the heroic age, and a world of actual handicrafts. In the shield of Hercules another marvellous detail is added in the image of Perseus, very daintily described as hovering in some wonderful way, as if really borne up by wings, above the surface. And that curious, haunting sense of magic in art, which comes out over and over again in Homer—in the golden maids, for instance, who assist Hephæstus in his work, and similar details which seem at first sight to destroy the credibility of the whole picture, and make of it a mere wonder-land—is itself also, rightly understood, a testimony to a real excellence in the art of Homer's time. It is sometimes said that works of art held to be miraculous are always of an inferior kind; but at least it was not among those who thought them inferior that the belief in their miraculous power began. If the golden images move like living creatures, and the armour of Achilles, so wonderfully made, lifts him like wings, this again is because the imagination of Homer is really under the stimulus of delightful artistic objects actually seen. Only those to whom such artistic objects manifest themselves through real and powerful impressions of their wonderful qualities, can invest them with properties magical or miraculous.

15. I said that the inherent usefulness of the material of metal-work makes the destruction of its acquired form almost certain, if it comes into the possession of people either barbarous or careless of the work of a past time. Greek art is for us, in all its stages, a fragment only; in each of them it is necessary, in a somewhat visionary manner, to fill up empty spaces, and more or less make substitution; and of the finer work of the heroic age, thus dimly discerned as an actual thing, we had at least till recently almost nothing. Two plates of bronze, a few rusty nails, and certain rows of holes in the inner surface of the walls of the "treasury" of Mycenæ, were the sole representatives of that favourite device of primitive Greek art, the lining of stone walls with

burnished metal, of which the house of Alcinous in the Odyssey is the ideal picture, and the temple of Pallas *of the Brazen House* at Sparta, adorned in the interior with a coating of reliefs in metal, a later, historical example. Of the heroic or so-called Cyclopean architecture, that "treasury," a building so imposing that Pausanias thought it worthy to rank with the Pyramids, is a sufficient illustration. Treasury, or tomb, or both (the selfish dead, perhaps, being supposed still to find enjoyment in the costly armour, goblets, and mirrors laid up there), this dome-shaped building, formed of concentric rings of stones gradually diminishing to a coping-stone at the top, may stand as the representative of some similar buildings in other parts of Greece, and of many others in a similar kind of architecture elsewhere, constructed of large many-sided blocks of stone, fitted carefully together without the aid of cement, and remaining in their places by reciprocal resistance. Characteristic of it is the general tendency to use vast blocks of stone for the jambs and lintels of doors, for instance, and in the construction of gable-shaped passages; two rows of such stones being made to rest against each other at an acute angle, within the thickness of the walls.

16. So vast and rude, fretted by the action of nearly three thousand years, the fragments of this architecture may often seem, at first sight, like works of nature. At Argos, Tiryns, Mycenæ, the skeleton of the old architecture is more complete. At Mycenæ the gateway of the *acropolis* is still standing with its two well-known sculptured lions—immemorial and almost unique monument of primitive Greek sculpture—supporting, herald-wise, a symbolical pillar on the vast, triangular, pedimental stone above. The heads are gone, having been fashioned possibly in metal by workmen from the East. On what may be called the *façade*, remains are still discernible of inlaid work in coloured stone, and within the gateway, on the smooth slabs of the pavement, the wheel-ruts are still visible. Connect them with those metal war-chariots in Homer, and you may see in fancy the whole grandiose character of the place, as it may really have been. Shut within the narrow enclosure of these shadowy citadels were the palaces of the kings, with all that intimacy which we may sometimes suppose to have been alien from the open-air Greek life, admitting, doubtless, below the cover of their rough walls, many of those refinements of princely life which the Middle Age found possible in such places, and of which the impression is so fascinating in Homer's description, for instance, of the house of Ulysses, or of Menelaus at Sparta. Rough and frowning without, these old *châteaux* of the Argive kings were delicate within with a decoration almost as dainty and fine as the network of weed and flower that now covers their ruins, and of the delicacy of which, as I said, that golden flower on its silver stalk, or the golden honeycomb of Dædalus, might be taken as representative. In these metal-like

structures of self-supporting polygons, locked so firmly and impenetrably together, with the whole mystery of the reasonableness of the arch implicitly within them, there is evidence of a complete artistic command over weight in stone, and an understanding of the "law of weight." But over weight only; the ornament still seems to be not strictly architectural, but, according to the notices of Homer, tectonic, borrowed from the sister arts, above all from the art of the metal-workers, to whom those spaces of the building are left which a later age fills with painting, or relief in stone. The skill of the Asiatic comes to adorn this rough native building; and it is a late, elaborate, somewhat voluptuous skill, we may understand, illustrated by the luxury of that Asiatic chamber of Paris, less like that of a warrior than of one going to the dance. Coupled with the vastness of the architectural works which actually remain, such descriptions as that in Homer of the chamber of Paris and the house of Alcinous furnish forth a picture of that early period—the tyrants' age, the age of the *acropoleis*, the period of great dynasties with claims to "divine right," and in many instances at least with all the culture of their time. The vast buildings make us sigh at the thought of wasted human labour, though there is a public usefulness too in some of these designs, such as the draining of the Copaic lake, to which the backs of the people are bent whether they will or not. For the princes there is much of that selfish personal luxury which is a constant trait of feudalism in all ages. For the people, scattered over the country, at their agricultural labour, or gathered in small hamlets, there is some enjoyment, perhaps, of the aspect of that splendour, of the bright warriors on the heights—a certain share of the nobler pride of the tyrants themselves in those tombs and dwellings. Some surmise, also, there seems to have been, of the "curse" of gold, with a dim, lurking suspicion of curious facilities for cruelty in the command over those skilful artificers in metal—some ingenious rack or bull "to pinch and peel"—the tradition of which, not unlike the modern Jacques Bonhomme's shudder at the old ruined French donjon or bastille, haunts, generations afterwards, the ruins of those "labyrinths" of stone, where the old tyrants had their pleasures. For it is a mistake to suppose that that wistful sense of eeriness in ruined buildings, to which most of us are susceptible, is an exclusively modern feeling. The name *Cyclopean*, attached to those desolate remains of buildings which were older than Greek history itself, attests their romantic influence over the fancy of the people who thus attributed them to a superhuman strength and skill. And the Cyclopes, like all the early mythical names of artists, have this note of reality, that they are names not of individuals but of classes, the guilds or companies of workmen in which a certain craft was imparted and transmitted. The Dactyli, the *Fingers*, are the first workers in iron; the savage Chalybes in Scythia the first smelters; actual names are given to the old, fabled Telchines—Chalkon, Argyron, Chryson—workers in brass, silver, and gold, respectively. The tradition of their activity haunts the several regions where those metals were found. They make the trident of Poseidon; but then Poseidon's trident is a real fisherman's instrument, the tunny-fork. They are credited, notwithstanding, with an evil sorcery, unfriendly to men, as poor humanity remembered the makers of chains, locks, Procrustean beds; and, as becomes this dark recondite mine and metal work, the traditions about them are gloomy and grotesque, confusing mortal workmen with demon guilds.

17. To this view of the heroic age of Greek art as being, so to speak, an age of real gold, an age delighting itself in precious material and exquisite handiwork in all tectonic crafts, the recent extraordinary discoveries at Troy and Mycenæ are, on any plausible theory of their date and origin, a witness. The æsthetic critic needs always to be on his guard against the confusion of mere curiosity or antiquity with beauty in art. Among the objects discovered at Troy—mere curiosities, some of them, however interesting and instructive—the so-called royal cup of Priam, in solid gold, two-handled and double-lipped, (the smaller lip designed for the host and his libation, the larger for the guest,) has, in the very simplicity of its design, the grace of the economy with which it exactly fulfils its purpose, a positive beauty, an absolute value for the æsthetic sense, while strange and new enough, if it really settles at last a much-debated expression of Homer; while the "diadem," with its twisted chains and flowers of pale gold, shows that those profuse golden fringes, waving so comely as he moved, which Hephæstus wrought for the helmet of Achilles, were really within the compass of early Greek art.

18. And the story of the excavations at Mycenæ reads more like some well-devised chapter of fiction than a record of sober facts. Here, those sanguine, half-childish dreams of buried treasure discovered in dead men's graves, which seem to have a charm for every one, are more than fulfilled in the spectacle of those antique kings, lying in the splendour of their crowns and breastplates of embossed plate of gold; their swords, studded with golden imagery, at their sides, as in some feudal monument; their very faces covered up most strangely in golden masks. The very floor of one tomb, we read, was thick with gold-dust—the heavy gilding fallen from some perished kingly vestment; in another was a downfall of golden leaves and flowers; and, amid this profusion of thin fine fragments, were rings, bracelets, smaller crowns as if for children, dainty butterflies for ornaments of dresses, and that golden flower on a silver stalk—all of pure, soft gold, unhardened by alloy, the delicate films of which one must touch but lightly, yet twisted and beaten, by hand and hammer, into wavy, spiral relief, the cuttle-fish with its long undulating arms appearing frequently.

19. It is the very image of the old luxurious life of the princes of the heroic age, as Homer describes it, with the arts in service to its kingly pride. Among the other costly objects was one representing the head of a cow, grandly designed in gold with horns of silver, like the horns of the moon, supposed to be symbolical of Here, the great object of worship at Argos. One of the interests of the study of mythology is that it reflects the ways of life and thought of the people who conceived it; and this religion of Here, the special religion of Argos, is congruous with what has been here said as to the place of art in the civilisation of the Argives; it is a reflexion of that splendid and wanton old feudal life. For Here is, in her original essence and meaning, equivalent to Demeter—the one living spirit of the earth, divined behind the veil of all its manifold visible energies. But in the development of a common mythological motive the various peoples are subject to the general limitations of their life and thought; they can but work outward what is within them; and the religious conceptions and usages, ultimately derivable from one and the same rudimentary instinct, are sometimes most diverse. Out of the visible, physical energies of the earth and its system of annual change, the old Pelasgian mind developed the person of Demeter, mystical and profoundly aweful, yet profoundly pathetic, also, in her appeal to human sympathies. Out of the same original elements, the civilisation of Argos, on the other hand, developes the religion of Queen Here, a mere Demeter, at best, of gaudy flower-beds, whose toilet Homer describes with all its delicate fineries; though, characteristically, he may still allow us to detect, perhaps, some traces of the mystical person of the earth, in the all-pervading scent of the ambrosial unguent with which she anoints herself, in the abundant tresses of her hair, and in the curious variegation of her ornaments. She has become, though with some reminiscence of the mystical earth, a very limited human person, wicked, angry, jealous—the lady of Zeus in her castle-sanctuary at Mycenæ, in wanton dalliance with the king, coaxing him for cruel purposes in sweet sleep, adding artificial charms to her beauty.

20. Such are some of the characteristics with which Greek art is discernible in that earliest age. Of themselves, they almost answer the question which next arises—Whence did art come to Greece? or was it a thing of absolutely native growth there? So some have decidedly maintained. Others, who lived in an age possessing little or no knowledge of Greek monuments anterior to the full development of art under Pheidias, and who, in regard to the Greek sculpture of the age of Pheidias, were like people criticising Michelangelo, without knowledge of the earlier Tuscan school—of the works of Donatello and Mino da Fiesole—easily satisfied themselves with theories of its importation ready-made from other countries. Critics in the last century, especially, noticing some characteristics which early Greek work has in common, indeed, with Egyptian

art, but which are common also to all such early work everywhere, supposed, as a matter of course, that it came, as the Greek religion also, from Egypt—that old, immemorial half-known birthplace of all wonderful things. There are, it is true, authorities for this derivation among the Greeks themselves, dazzled as they were by the marvels of the ancient civilisation of Egypt, a civilisation so different from their own, on the first opening of Egypt to Greek visitors. But, in fact, that opening did not take place till the reign of Psammetichus, about the middle of the seventh century B.C., a relatively late date. Psammetichus introduced and settled Greek mercenaries in Egypt, and, for a time, the Greeks came very close to Egyptian life. They can hardly fail to have been stimulated by that display of every kind of artistic workmanship gleaming over the whole of life; they may in turn have freshened it with new motives. And we may remark, that but for the peculiar usage of Egypt concerning the tombs of the dead, but for their habit of investing the last abodes of the dead with all the appurtenances of active life, out of that whole world of art, so various and elaborate, nothing but the great, monumental works in stone would have remained to ourselves. We should have experienced in regard to it, what we actually experience too much in our knowledge of Greek art—the lack of a fitting background, in the smaller tectonic work, for its great works in architecture, and the bolder sort of sculpture.

21. But, one by one, at last, as in the medieval parallel, monuments illustrative of the earlier growth of Greek art before the time of Pheidias have come to light, and to a just appreciation. They show that the development of Greek art had already proceeded some way before the opening of Egypt to the Greeks, and point, if to a foreign source at all, to oriental rather than Egyptian influences; and the theory which derived Greek art, with many other Greek things, from Egypt, now hardly finds supporters. In Greece all things are at once old and new. As, in physical organisms, the actual particles of matter have existed long before in other combinations; and what is really new in a new organism is the new cohering force—the *mode* of life,—so, in the products of Greek civilisation, the actual elements are traceable elsewhere by antiquarians who care to trace them; the elements, for instance, of its peculiar national architecture. Yet all is also emphatically *autochthonous*, as the Greeks said, new-born at home, by right of a new, informing, combining spirit playing over those mere elements, and touching them, above all, with a wonderful sense of the nature and destiny of man—the dignity of his soul and of his body—so that in all things the Greeks are as discoverers. Still, the original and primary motive seems, in matters of art, to have come from without; and the view to which actual discovery and all true analogies more and more point is that of a connexion of the origin of Greek art, ultimately with Assyria, proximately with Phœnicia, partly through

Asia Minor, and chiefly through Cyprus—an original connexion again and again re-asserted, like a surviving trick of inheritance, as in later times it came in contact with the civilisation of Caria and Lycia, old affinities being here linked anew; and with a certain Asiatic tradition, of which one representative is the Ionic style of architecture, traceable all through Greek art—an Asiatic curiousness, or ποικιλία, strongest in that heroic age of which I have been speaking, and distinguishing some schools and masters in Greece more than others; and always in appreciable distinction from the more clearly defined and self-asserted Hellenic influence. Homer himself witnesses to the intercourse, through early, adventurous commerce, as in the bright and animated picture with which the history of Herodotus begins, between the Greeks and Eastern countries. We may, perhaps, forget sometimes, thinking over the greatness of its place in the history of civilisation, how small a country Greece really was; how short the distances onwards, from island to island, to the coast of Asia, so that we can hardly make a sharp separation between Asia and Greece, nor deny, besides great and palpable acts of importation, all sorts of impalpable Asiatic influences, by way alike of attraction and repulsion, upon Greek manners and taste. Homer, as we saw, was right in making Troy essentially a Greek city, with inhabitants superior in all culture to their kinsmen on the Western shore, and perhaps proportionally weaker on the practical or moral side, and with an element of languid Ionian voluptuousness in them, typified by the cedar and gold of the chamber of Paris—an element which the austere, more strictly European influence of the Dorian Apollo will one day correct in all genuine Greeks. The Ægean, with its islands, is, then, a bond of union, not a barrier; and we must think of Greece, as has been rightly said, as its whole continuous shore.

22. The characteristics of Greek art, indeed, in the heroic age, so far as we can discern them, are those also of Phœnician art, its delight in metal among the rest, of metal especially as an element in architecture, the covering of everything with plates of metal. It was from Phœnicia that the costly material in which early Greek art delighted actually came—ivory, amber, much of the precious metals. These the adventurous Phœnician traders brought in return for the mussel which contained the famous purple, in quest of which they penetrated far into all the Greek havens. Recent discoveries present the island of Cyprus, the great source of copper and copper-work in ancient times, as the special mediator between the art of Phœnicia and Greece; and in some archaic figures of Aphrodite with her dove, brought from Cyprus and now in the British Museum—objects you might think, at first sight, taken from the niches of a French Gothic cathedral—are some of the beginnings, at least, of Greek sculpture manifestly under the influence of Phœnician masters. And,

again, mythology is the reflex of characteristic facts. It is through Cyprus that the religion of Aphrodite comes from Phœnicia to Greece. Here, in Cyprus, she is connected with some other kindred elements of mythological tradition, above all with the beautiful old story of Pygmalion, in which the thoughts of art and love are connected so closely together. First of all, on the prows of the Phœnician ships, the tutelary image of Aphrodite *Euplœa*, the protectress of sailors, comes to Cyprus—to Cythera; it is in this simplest sense that she is, primarily, *Anadyomene*. And her connexion with the arts is always an intimate one. In Cyprus her worship is connected with an architecture, not colossal, but full of dainty splendour—the art of the shrine-maker, the maker of reliquaries; the art of the toilet, the toilet of Aphrodite; the Homeric hymn to Aphrodite is full of all that; delight in which we have seen to be characteristic of the true Homer.

23. And now we see why Hephæstus, that crook-backed and uncomely god, is the husband of Aphrodite. Hephæstus is the god of fire, indeed; as fire he is flung from heaven by Zeus; and in the marvellous contest between Achilles and the river Xanthus in the twenty-first book of the Iliad, he intervenes in favour of the hero, as mere fire against water. But he soon ceases to be thus generally representative of the functions of fire, and becomes almost exclusively representative of one only of its aspects, its function, namely, in regard to early art; he becomes the patron of smiths, bent with his labour at the forge, as people had seen such real workers; he is the most perfectly developed of all the Dædali, Mulcibers, or Cabeiri. That the god of fire becomes the god of all art, architecture included, so that he makes the houses of the gods, and is also the husband of Aphrodite, marks a threefold group of facts; the prominence, first, of a peculiar kind of art in early Greece, that beautiful metal-work, with which he is bound and bent; secondly, the connexion of this, through Aphrodite, with an almost wanton personal splendour; the connexion, thirdly, of all this with Cyprus and Phœnicia, whence, literally, Aphrodite comes. Hephæstus is the "spiritual form" of the Asiatic element in Greek art.

24. This, then, is the situation which the first period of Greek art comprehends; a people whose civilisation is still young, delighting, as the young do, in ornament, in the sensuous beauty of ivory and gold, in all the lovely productions of skilled fingers. They receive all this, together with the worship of Aphrodite, by way of Cyprus, from Phœnicia, from the older, decrepit Eastern civilisation, itself long since surfeited with that splendour; and they receive it in frugal quantity, so frugal that their thoughts always go back to the East, where there is the fulness of it, as to a wonder-land of art. Received thus in frugal quantity, through many generations, that world of Asiatic tectonics stimulates the sensuous capacity in them, accustoms the hand to produce and

the eye to appreciate the more delicately enjoyable qualities of material things. But nowhere in all this various and exquisite world of design is there as yet any adequate sense of man himself, nowhere is there an insight into or power over human form as the expression of human soul. Yet those arts of design in which that younger people delights have in them already, as *designed* work, that spirit of reasonable order, that expressive congruity in the adaptation of means to ends, of which the fully developed admirableness of human form is but the consummation—a consummation already anticipated in the grand and animated figures of epic poetry, their power of thought, their laughter and tears. Under the hands of that younger people, as they imitate and pass largely and freely beyond those older craftsmen, the fire of the reasonable soul will kindle, little by little, up to the Theseus of the Parthenon and the Venus of Melos.

25. The ideal aim of Greek sculpture, as of all other art, is to deal, indeed, with the deepest elements of man's nature and destiny, to command and express these, but to deal with them in a manner, and with a kind of expression, as clear and graceful and simple, if it may be, as that of the Japanese flower-painter. And what the student of Greek sculpture has to cultivate generally in himself is the capacity for appreciating the expression of thought in outward form, the constant habit of associating sense with soul, of tracing what we call expression to its sources. But, concurrently with this, he must also cultivate, all along, a not less equally constant appreciation of intelligent *workmanship* in work, and of *design* in things designed, of the rational control of matter everywhere. From many sources he may feed this sense of intelligence and design in the productions of the minor crafts, above all in the various and exquisite art of Japan. Carrying a delicacy like that of nature itself into every form of imitation, reproduction, and combination—leaf and flower, fish and bird, reed and water—and failing only when it touches the sacred human form, that art of Japan is not so unlike the earliest stages of Greek art as might at first sight be supposed. We have here, and in no mere fragments, the spectacle of a universal application to the instruments of daily life of fitness and beauty, in a temper still unsophisticated, as also unelevated, by the divination of the spirit of man. And at least the student must always remember that Greek art was throughout a much richer and warmer thing, at once with more shadows, and more of a dim magnificence in its surroundings, than the illustrations of a classical dictionary might induce him to think. Some of the ancient temples of Greece were as rich in æsthetic curiosities as a famous modern museum. That Asiatic ποικιλία, that spirit of minute and curious loveliness, follows the bolder imaginative efforts of Greek art all through its history, and one can hardly be too careful in keeping up the sense of this daintiness of execution through the entire course of its development. It is not only that the minute

object of art, the tiny vase-painting, *intaglio*, coin, or cameo, often reduces into the palm of the hand lines grander than those of many a life-sized or colossal figure; but there is also a sense in which it may be said that the Venus of Melos, for instance, is but a supremely well-executed object of *vertu*, in the most limited sense of the term. Those solemn images of the temple of Theseus are a perfect embodiment of the human ideal, of the reasonable soul and of a spiritual world; they are also the best *made* things of their kind, as an urn or a cup is well made.

26. A perfect, many-sided development of tectonic crafts, a state such as the art of some nations has ended in, becomes for the Greeks a mere opportunity, a mere starting-ground for their imaginative presentment of man, moral and inspired. A world of material splendour, moulded clay, beaten gold, polished stone;—the informing, reasonable soul entering into that, reclaiming the metal and stone and clay, till they are as full of living breath as the real warm body itself; the presence of those two elements is continuous throughout the fortunes of Greek art after the heroic age, and the constant right estimate of their action and reaction, from period to period, its true philosophy.

from FURTHER CHAPTERS ON GREEK SCULPTURE

i. [*The First True School of Greek Sculpture*]

And, at last, about the year 576 B.C., we come to the first true school of sculptors, the first clear example, as we seem to discern, of a communicable style, reflecting and interpreting some real individuality (the double personality, in this case, of two brothers) in the masters who evolved it, conveyed to disciples who came to acquire it from distant places, and taking root through them at various centres, where the names of the masters became attached, of course, to many fair works really by the hands of the pupils. Dipœnus and Scyllis, these first true *masters*, were born in Crete; but their work is connected mainly with Sicyon, at that time the chief seat of Greek art. "In consequence of some injury done them," it is said, "while employed there upon certain sacred images, they departed to another place, leaving their work unfinished; and, not long afterwards, a grievous famine fell upon Sicyon. Thereupon, the people of Sicyon, inquiring of the Pythian Apollo how they might be relieved, it was answered them, 'if Dipœnus and Scyllis should finish those images of the gods'; which thing the Sicyonians obtained from them, humbly, at a great price." That story too, as we shall see, illustrates the spirit of the age. For their sculpture they used the white marble of Paros, being workers in marble especially, though they worked also in ebony and in ivory, and made use of gilding. "Figures of cedar-wood, partly incrusted with gold"—κέδρου ζῴδια χρυσῷ διηνθισμένα—Pausanias says exquisitely, describing a certain work of their pupil, Dontas of Lacedæmon. It is to that that we have definitely come at last, in the school of Dipœnus and Scyllis.

10. Dry and brief as these details may seem, they are the witness to an active, eager, animated period of inventions and beginnings, in which the Greek workman triumphs over the first rough mechanical difficulties which beset him in the endeavour to record what his soul conceived of the form of priest or athlete then alive upon the earth, or of the ever-living gods, then already more seldom seen upon it. Our own fancy must fill up the story of the unrecorded patience of the workshop, into which we seem to peep through these scanty notices—the fatigue, the disappointments, the steps repeated, ending at last in that moment of success, which is all Pausanias records, somewhat uncertainly.

11. And as this period begins with the chest of Cypselus, so it ends with a work in some respects similar, also seen and described by Pausanias—the

throne, as he calls it, of the *Amyclæan Apollo*. It was the work of a well-known artist, Bathycles of Magnesia, who, probably about the year 550 B.C., with a company of workmen, came to the little ancient town of Amyclæ, near Sparta, a place full of traditions of the heroic age. He had been invited thither to perform a peculiar task—the construction of a throne; not like the throne of the Olympian Zeus, and others numerous in after times, for a seated figure, but for the image of the local Apollo; no other than a rude and very ancient pillar of bronze, thirty cubits high, to which, Hermes-wise, head, arms, and feet were attached. The thing stood upright, as on a base, upon a kind of tomb or reliquary, in which, according to tradition, lay the remains of the young prince Hyacinth, son of the founder of that place, beloved by Apollo for his beauty, and accidentally struck dead by him in play, with a quoit. From the drops of the lad's blood had sprung up the purple flower of his name, which bears on its petals the letters of the ejaculation of woe; and in his memory the famous games of Amyclæ were celebrated, beginning about the time of the longest day, when the flowers are stricken by the sun and begin to fade—a festival marked, amid all its splendour, with some real melancholy, and serious thought of the dead. In the midst of the "throne" of Bathycles, this sacred receptacle, with the strange, half-humanised pillar above it, was to stand, probably in the open air, within a consecrated enclosure. Like the chest of Cypselus, the throne was decorated with reliefs of subjects taken from epic poetry, and it had supporting figures. Unfortunately, what Pausanias tells us of this monument hardly enables one to present it to the imagination with any completeness or certainty; its dimensions he himself was unable exactly to ascertain, and he does not tell us its material. There are reasons, however, for supposing that it was of metal; and amid these ambiguities, the decorations of its base, the grave or altar-tomb of Hyacinth, shine out clearly, and are also, for the most part, clear in their significance.

12. "There are wrought upon the altar figures, on the one side of Biris, on the other of Amphitrite and Poseidon. Near Zeus and Hermes, in speech with each other, stand Dionysus and Semele, and, beside her, Ino. Demeter, Kore, and Pluto are also wrought upon it, the Fates and the Seasons above them, and with them Aphrodite, Athene, and Artemis. They are conducting Hyacinthus to heaven, with Polybœa, the sister of Hyacinthus, who died, as is told, while yet a virgin.... Hercules also is figured on the tomb; he too carried to heaven by Athene and the other gods. The daughters of Thestius also are upon the altar, and the Seasons again, and the Muses."

13. It was as if many lines of solemn thought had been meant to unite, about the resting-place of this local Adonis, in imageries full of some dim promise of immortal life.

14. But it was not so much in care for old idols as in the making of new ones that Greek art was at this time engaged. This whole first period of Greek art might, indeed, be called *the period of graven images*, and all its workmen sons of Dædalus; for Dædalus is the mythical, or all but mythical, representative of all those arts which are combined in the making of lovelier idols than had heretofore been seen. The old Greek word which is at the root of the name Dædalus, the name of a craft rather than a proper name, probably means to work curiously—all curiously beautiful wood-work is Dædal work; the main point about the curiously beautiful chamber in which Nausicaa sleeps, in the Odyssey, being that, like some exquisite Swiss *châlet*, it is wrought in wood. But it came about that those workers in wood, whom Dædalus represents, the early craftsmen of Crete especially, were chiefly concerned with the making of religious images, like the carvers of Berchtesgaden and Oberammergau, the sort of daintily finished images of the objects of public or private devotion which such workmen would turn out. Wherever there was a wooden idol in any way fairer than others, finished, perhaps, sometimes, with colour and gilding, and appropriate real dress, there the hand of Dædalus had been. That such images were quite detached from pillar or wall, that they stood free, and were statues in the proper sense, showed that Greek art was already liberated from its earlier Eastern associations; such free-standing being apparently unknown in Assyrian art. And then, the effect of this Dædal skill in them was, that they came nearer to the proper form of humanity. It is the wonderful life-likeness of these early images which tradition celebrates in many anecdotes, showing a very early instinctive turn for, and delight in naturalism, in the Greek temper. As Cimabue, in his day, was able to charm men, almost as with illusion, by the simple device of half-closing the eyelids of his personages, and giving them, instead of round eyes, eyes that seemed to be in some degree sentient, and to feel the light; so the marvellous progress in those Dædal wooden images was, that the eyes were open, so that they seemed to look,—the feet separated, so that they seemed to walk. Greek art is thus, almost from the first, essentially distinguished from the art of Egypt, by an energetic striving after truth in organic form. In representing the human figure, Egyptian art had held by mathematical or mechanical proportions exclusively. The Greek apprehends of it, as the main truth, that it is a living organism, with freedom of movement, and hence the infinite possibilities of motion, and of expression by motion, with which the imagination credits the higher sort of Greek sculpture; while the figures of Egyptian art, graceful as they often are, seem absolutely incapable of any motion or gesture, other than the one actually designed. The work of the Greek sculptor, together with its more real anatomy, becomes full also of human soul.

15. That old, primitive, mystical, first period of Greek religion, with its profound, though half-conscious, intuitions of spiritual powers in the natural world, attaching itself not to the worship of visible human forms, but to relics, to natural or half-natural objects—the roughly hewn tree, the unwrought stone, the pillar, the holy cone of Aphrodite in her dimly-lighted cell at Paphos—had passed away. The second stage in the development of Greek religion had come; a period in which poet and artist were busily engaged in the work of incorporating all that might be retained of the vague divinations of that earlier visionary time, in definite and intelligible human image and human story. The vague belief, the mysterious custom and tradition, develope themselves into an elaborately ordered ritual—into personal gods, imaged in ivory and gold, sitting on beautiful thrones. Always, wherever a shrine or temple, great or small, is mentioned, there, we may conclude, was a visible idol, there was conceived to be the actual dwelling-place of a god. And this understanding became not less but more definite, as the temple became larger and more splendid, full of ceremony and servants, like the abode of an earthly king, and as the sacred presence itself assumed, little by little, the last beauties and refinements of the visible human form and expression.

16. In what we have seen of this first period of Greek art, in all its curious essays and inventions, we may observe this demand for beautiful idols increasing in Greece—for sacred images, at first still rude, and in some degree the holier for their rudeness, but which yet constitute the beginnings of the religious style, consummate in the work of Pheidias, uniting the veritable image of man in the full possession of his reasonable soul, with the true religious mysticity, the signature there of something from afar. One by one these new gods of bronze, or marble, or flesh-like ivory, take their thrones, at this or that famous shrine, like the images of this period which Pausanias saw in the temple of Here at Olympia—the throned *Seasons*, with Themis as the mother of the *Seasons* (divine rectitude being still blended, in men's fancies, with the unchanging physical order of things) and *Fortune*, and *Victory* "having wings," and Kore and Demeter and Dionysus, already visibly there, around the image of Here herself, seated on a throne; and all chryselephantine, all in gold and ivory. Novel as these things are, they still undergo consecration at their first erecting. The figure of Athene, in her brazen temple at Sparta, the work of Gitiades, who makes also the image and the hymn, in triple service to the goddess; and again, that curious story of Dipœnus and Scyllis, brought back with so much awe to remove the public curse by completing their sacred task upon the images, show how simply religious the age still was—that this widespread artistic activity was a religious enthusiasm also; those early sculptors have still, for their contemporaries, a divine mission, with some kind of hieratic or sacred quality in their gift, distinctly felt.

17. The development of the artist, in the proper sense, out of the mere craftsman, effected in the first division of this period, is now complete; and, in close connexion with that busy graving of religious images, which occupies its second division, we come to something like real personalities, to men with individual characteristics—such men as Ageladas of Argos, Callon and Onatas of Ægina, and Canachus of Sicyon. Mere fragment as our information concerning these early masters is at the best, it is at least unmistakeably information about men with personal differences of temper and talent, of their motives, of what we call *style*. We have come to a sort of art which is no longer broadly characteristic of a general period, one whose products we might have looked at without its occurring to us to ask concerning the artist, his antecedents, and his school. We have to do now with types of art, fully impressed with the subjectivity, the intimacies of the artist.

[From *The Beginnings of Greek Sculpture, Part II.—The Age of Graven Images*]

ii. (a) [*The "Discobolus" of Myron*]

"Ample is the glory stored up for Olympian winners." And what Pindar's contemporaries asked of him for the due appreciation, the consciousness, of it, by way of song, that the next generation sought, by way of sculptural memorial in marble, and above all, as it seems, in bronze. The keen demand for athletic statuary, the honour attached to the artist employed to make his statue at Olympia, or at home, bear witness again to the pride with which a Greek town, the pathos, it might be, with which a family, looked back to the victory of one of its members. In the courts of Olympia a whole population in marble and bronze gathered quickly,—a world of portraits, out of which, as the purged and perfected essence, the ideal soul, of them, emerged the *Diadumenus*, for instance, the *Discobolus*, the so-called *Jason* of the Louvre. Olympia was in truth, as Pindar says again, a *mother* of gold-crowned contests, the mother of a large offspring. All over Greece the enthusiasm for gymnastic, for the life of the *gymnasia*, prevailed. It was a gymnastic which, under the happy conditions of that time, was already surely what Plato pleads for, already one half music, μουσική, a matter, partly, of character and of the soul, of the fair proportion between soul and body, of the soul with itself. Who can doubt it who sees and considers the still irresistible grace, the contagious pleasantness, of the *Discobolus*, the *Diadumenus*, and a few other precious survivals from the athletic age which immediately preceded the manhood of Pheidias, between the Persian and the Peloponnesian wars?

10. Now, this predominance of youth, of the youthful form, in art, of bodily gymnastic promoting natural advantages to the utmost, of the physical

perfection developed thereby, is a sign that essential mastery has been achieved by the artist—the power, that is to say, of a full and free realisation. For such youth, in its very essence, is a matter properly within the limits of the visible, the empirical, world; and in the presentment of it there will be no place for symbolic hint, none of that reliance on the helpful imagination of the spectator, the legitimate scope of which is a large one, when art is dealing with religious objects, with what in the fulness of its own nature is not really expressible at all. In any passable representation of the Greek *discobolus*, as in any passable representation of an English cricketer, there can be no successful evasion of the natural difficulties of the thing to be done—the difficulties of competing with nature itself, or its maker, in that marvellous combination of motion and rest, of inward mechanism with the so smoothly finished surface and outline—finished *ad unguem*—which enfold it.

11. Of the gradual development of such mastery of natural detail, a veritable counterfeit of nature, the veritable *rhythmus* of the runner, for example—twinkling heel and ivory shoulder—we have hints and traces in the historians of art. One had attained the very turn and texture of the crisp locks, another the very feel of the tense nerve and full-flushed vein, while with another you saw the bosom of Ladas expand, the lips part, as if for a last breath ere he reached the goal. It was like a child finding little by little the use of its limbs, the testimony of its senses, at a definite moment. With all its poetic impulse, it is an age clearly of faithful observation, of what we call realism, alike in its iconic and heroic work; alike in portraiture, that is to say, and in the presentment of divine or abstract types. Its workmen are close students now of the living form as such; aim with success at an ever larger and more various expression of its details; or replace a conventional statement of them by a real and lively one. That it was thus is attested indirectly by the fact that they busied themselves, seemingly by way of a *tour de force*, and with no essential interest in such subject, alien as it was from the pride of health which is characteristic of the gymnastic life, with the expression of physical pain, in Philoctetes, for instance. The adroit, the swift, the strong, in full and free exercise of their gifts, to the delight of others and of themselves, though their sculptural record has for the most part perished, are specified in ancient literary notices as the sculptor's favourite subjects, repeated, remodelled, over and over again, for the adornment of the actual scene of athletic success, or the market-place at home of the distant Northern or Sicilian town whence the prizeman had come.—A countless series of popular illustrations to Pindar's Odes! And if art was still to minister to the religious sense, it could only be by clothing celestial spirits also as nearly as possible in the bodily semblance of the various athletic combatants, whose patrons respectively they were supposed to be.

12. The age to which we are come in the story of Greek art presents to us indeed only a chapter of scattered fragments, of names that are little more, with but surmise of their original significance, and mere reasonings as to the sort of art that may have occupied what are really empty spaces. Two names, however, connect themselves gloriously with certain extant works of art; copies, it is true, at various removes, yet copies of what is still found delightful through them, and by copyists who for the most part were themselves masters. Through the variations of the copyist, the restorer, the mere imitator, these works are reducible to two famous original types—the *Discobolus* or quoit-player, of Myron, the *beau idéal* (we may use that term for once justly) of athletic motion; and the *Diadumenus* of Polycleitus, as, binding the fillet or crown of victory upon his head, he presents the *beau idéal* of athletic repose, and almost begins to think.

13. Myron was a native of Eleutheræ, and a pupil of Ageladas of Argos. There is nothing more to tell by way of positive detail of this so famous artist, save that the main scene of his activity was Athens, now become the centre of the artistic as of all other modes of life in Greece. *Multiplicasse veritatem videtur*, says Pliny. He was in fact an earnest realist or naturalist, and rose to central perfection in the portraiture, the idealised portraiture, of athletic youth, from a mastery first of all in the delineation of inferior objects, of little lifeless or living things. Think, however, for a moment, how winning such objects are still, as presented on Greek coins;—the ear of corn, for instance, on those of Metapontum; the microscopic cockle-shell, the dolphins, on the coins of Syracuse. Myron, then, passes from pleasant truth of that kind to the delineation of the worthier sorts of animal life,—the ox, the dog—to nothing short of illusion in the treatment of them, as ancient connoisseurs would have you understand. It is said that there are thirty-six extant epigrams on his brazen cow. That animal has her gentle place in Greek art, from the Siren tomb, suckling her young there, as the type of eternal rejuvenescence, onwards to the procession of the Elgin frieze, where, still breathing deliciously of the distant pastures, she is led to the altar. We feel sorry for her, as we look, so lifelike is the carved marble. The sculptor who worked there, whoever he may have been, had profited doubtless by the study of Myron's famous work. For what purpose he made it, does not appear;—as an architectural ornament; or a votive offering; perhaps only because he liked making it. In hyperbolic epigram, at any rate, the animal breathes, explaining sufficiently the point of Pliny's phrase regarding Myron—*Corporum curiosus*. And when he came to his main business with the quoit-player, the wrestler, the runner, he did not for a moment forget that they too were animals, young animals, delighting in natural motion, in free course through the yielding air, over uninterrupted

space, according to Aristotle's definition of pleasure: "the unhindered exercise of one's natural force." *Corporum tenus curiosus:*—he was a "curious workman" as far as the living body is concerned. Pliny goes on to qualify that phrase by saying that he did not express the sensations of the mind—*animi sensus*. But just there, in fact, precisely in such limitation, we find what authenticates Myron's peculiar value in the evolution of Greek art. It is of the essence of the athletic prizeman, involved in the very ideal of the quoit-player, the cricketer, not to give expression to mind, in any antagonism to, or invasion of, the body; to mind as anything more than a function of the body, whose healthful balance of functions it may so easily perturb;—to disavow that insidious enemy of the fairness of the bodily soul as such.

14. Yet if the art of Myron was but little occupied with the reasonable soul (*animus*), with those mental situations the expression of which, though it may have a pathos and a beauty of its own, is for the most part adverse to the proper expression of youth, to the beauty of youth, by causing it to be no longer youthful, he was certainly a master of the animal or physical soul there (*anima*); how it is, how it displays itself, as illustrated, for instance, in the *Discobolus*. Of voluntary animal motion the very soul is undoubtedly there. We have but translations into marble of the original in bronze. In that, it was as if a blast of cool wind had congealed the metal, or the living youth, fixed him imperishably in that moment of rest which lies between two opposed motions, the *backward* swing of the right arm, the movement *forwards* on which the left foot is in the very act of starting. The matter of the thing, the stately bronze or marble, thus rests indeed; but the artistic form of it, in truth, scarcely more, even to the eye, than the rolling ball or disk, may be said to rest, at every moment of its course,—just metaphysically, you know.

15. This mystery of combined motion and rest, of rest in motion, had involved, of course, on the part of the sculptor who had mastered its secret, long and intricate consideration. Archaic as it is, primitive still in some respects, full of the primitive youth it celebrates, it is, in fact, a learned work, and suggested to a great analyst of literary style, singular as it may seem, the "elaborate" or "contorted" manner in literature of the later Latin writers, which, however, he finds "laudable" for its purpose. Yet with all its learned involution, thus so oddly characterised by Quintilian, so entirely is this quality subordinated to the proper purpose of the *Discobolus* as a work of art, a thing to be looked at rather than to think about, that it makes one exclaim still, with the poet of athletes, "The natural is ever best!"— τὸ δὲ φυᾷ ἄπαν κράτιστον. Perhaps that triumphant, unimpeachable naturalness is after all the reason why, on seeing it for the first time, it suggests no new view of the beauty of human form, or point of view for the regarding of it; is acceptable rather as embodying (say, in one perfect

flower) all one has ever fancied or seen, in old Greece or on Thames' side, of the unspoiled body of youth, thus delighting itself and others, at that perfect, because unconscious, point of good-fortune, as it moves or rests just there for a moment, between the animal and spiritual worlds. "Grant them," you pray in Pindar's own words, "grant them with feet so light to pass through life!"

ii. (b) [*The "Diadumenus" of Polycleitus*]

Myron, by patience of genius, had mastered the secret of the expression of movement, had plucked out the very heart of its mystery. Polycleitus, on the other hand, is above all the master of rest, of the expression of rest after toil, in the victorious and crowned athlete, *Diadumenus*. In many slightly varying forms, marble versions of the original in bronze of Delos, the *Diadumenus*, indifferently, mechanically, is binding round his head a ribbon or fillet. In the Vaison copy at the British Museum it was of silver. That simple fillet is, in fact, a *diadem*, a crown, and he assumes it as a victor; but, as I said, mechanically, and, prize in hand, might be asking himself whether after all it had been worth while. For the active beauty of the *Agonistes* of which Myron's art is full, we have here, then, the passive beauty of the victor. But the later incident, the realisation of rest, is actually in affinity with a certain earliness, so to call it, in the temper and work of Polycleitus. He is already something of a reactionary; or pauses, rather, to enjoy, to convey enjoyably to others, the full savour of a particular moment in the development of his craft, the moment of the perfecting of restful form, before the mere consciousness of technical mastery in delineation urges forward the art of sculpture to a bewildering infinitude of motion. In opposition to the ease, the freedom, of others, his aim is, by a voluntary restraint in the exercise of such technical mastery, to achieve nothing less than the impeccable, within certain narrow limits. He still hesitates, is self-exacting, seems even to have checked a growing readiness of hand in the artists about him. He was renowned as a graver, found much to do with the chisel, introducing many a fine after-thought, when the rough-casting of his work was over. He studied human form under such conditions as would bring out its natural features, its static laws, in their entirety, their harmony; and in an *academic* work, so to speak, no longer to be clearly identified in what may be derivations from it, he claimed to have fixed the *canon*, the common measure, of perfect man. Yet with Polycleitus certainly the measure of man was not yet "the measure of an angel," but still only that of mortal youth; of youth, however, in that scrupulous and uncontaminate purity of form which recommended itself even to the Greeks as befitting messengers from the gods, if such messengers should come.

23. And yet a large part of Myron's contemporary fame depended on his religious work—on his statue of Here, for instance, in ivory and gold—that too, doubtless, expressive, as appropriately to its subject as to himself, of a passive beauty. We see it still, perhaps, in the coins of Argos. And has not the crowned victor, too, in that mechanic action, in his demure attitude, something which reminds us of the religious significance of the Greek athletic service? It was a sort of worship, you know—that department of public life; such worship as Greece, still in its superficial youth, found itself best capable of. At least those solemn contests began and ended with prayer and sacrifice. Their most honoured prizes were a kind of religiously symbolical objects. The athletic life certainly breathes of abstinence, of rule and the keeping under of one's self. And here in the *Diadumenus* we have one of its priests, a priest of the religion whose central motive was what has been called "the worship of the body,"—its modest priest.

ii. (c) [*The "Discobolus at Rest"*]

He is neither the victor at rest, as with Polycleitus, nor the combatant already in motion, as with Myron; but, as if stepping backward from Myron's precise point of interest, and with the heavy *discus* still in the left hand, he is preparing for his venture, taking stand carefully on the right foot. Eye and mind concentre, loyally, entirely, upon the business in hand. The very finger is reckoning while he watches, intent upon the cast of another, as the metal glides to the goal. Take him, to lead you forth quite out of the narrow limits of the Greek world. You have pure humanity there, with a glowing, yet restrained joy and delight in itself, but without vanity; and it *is* pure. There is nothing certainly supersensual in that fair, round head, any more than in the long, agile limbs; but also no impediment, natural or acquired. To have achieved just that, was the Greek's truest claim for furtherance in the main line of human development. He had been faithful, we cannot help saying, as we pass from that youthful company, in what comparatively is perhaps little—in the culture, the administration, of the visible world; and he merited, so we might go on to say—he merited Revelation, something which should solace his heart in the inevitable fading of that. We are reminded of those strange prophetic words of the Wisdom, the *Logos*, by whom God made the world, in one of the *sapiential*, half-Platonic books of the Hebrew Scriptures:—"I was by him, as one brought up with him; rejoicing in the habitable parts of the earth. My delights were with the sons of men."

[From *The Age of Athletic Prizemen: A Chapter in Greek Art*]

2. "MISCELLANEOUS STUDIES"

PROSPER MÉRIMÉE[1]

For one born in eighteen hundred and three much was recently become incredible that had at least warmed the imagination even of the sceptical eighteenth century. Napoleon, sealing the tomb of the Revolution, had foreclosed many a problem, extinguished many a hope, in the sphere of practice. And the mental parallel was drawn by Heine. In the mental world too a great outlook had lately been cut off. After Kant's criticism of the mind, its pretensions to pass beyond the limits of individual experience seemed as dead as those of old French royalty. And Kant did but furnish its innermost theoretic force to a more general criticism, which had withdrawn from every department of action, underlying principles once thought eternal. A time of disillusion followed. The typical personality of the day was Obermann, the very genius of *ennui*, a Frenchman disabused even of patriotism, who has hardly strength enough to die. More energetic souls, however, would recover themselves, and find some way of making the best of a changed world. Art: the passions, above all, the ecstasy and sorrow of love: a purely empirical knowledge of nature and man: these still remained, at least for pastime, in a world of which it was no longer proposed to calculate the remoter issues:—art, passion, science, however, in a somewhat novel attitude towards the practical interests of life. The *désillusionné*, who had found in Kant's negations the last word concerning an unseen world, and is living, on the morrow of the Revolution, under a monarchy made out of hand, might seem cut off from certain ancient natural hopes, and will demand, from what is to interest him at all, something in the way of artificial stimulus. He has lost that sense of large proportion in things, that all-embracing prospect of life as a whole (from end to end of time and space, it had seemed), the utmost expanse of which was afforded from a cathedral tower of the Middle Age: by the church of the thirteenth century, that is to say, with its consequent aptitude for the co-ordination of human effort. Deprived of that exhilarating yet pacific outlook, imprisoned now in the narrow cell of its own subjective experience, the action of a powerful nature will be intense, but exclusive and peculiar. It will come to art, or science, to the experience of life itself, not as

---

1. A lecture delivered at the Taylor Institution, Oxford, and at the London Institution. Published in the *Fortnightly Review*, Dec. 1890, and now reprinted by the kind permission of the proprietors. *[Editorial note in* Miscellaneous Studies.*]*

to portions of human nature's daily food, but as to something that must be, by the circumstances of the case, exceptional; almost as men turn in despair to gambling or narcotics, and in a little while the narcotic, the game of chance or skill, is valued for its own sake. The vocation of the artist, of the student of life or books, will be realised with something—say! of fanaticism, as an end in itself, unrelated, unassociated. The science he turns to will be a science of crudest fact; the passion extravagant, a passionate love of passion, varied through all the exotic phases of French fiction as inaugurated by Balzac; the art exaggerated, in matter or form, or both, as in Hugo or Baudelaire. The development of these conditions is the mental story of the nineteenth century, especially as exemplified in France.

2. In no century would Prosper Mérimée have been a theologian or metaphysician. But that sense of negation, of theoretic insecurity, was in the air, and conspiring with what was of like tendency in himself made of him a central type of disillusion. In him the passive *ennui* of Obermann became a satiric, aggressive, almost angry conviction of the littleness of the world around; it was as if man's fatal limitations constituted a kind of stupidity in him, what the French call *bêtise*. Gossiping friends, indeed, linked what was constitutional in him and in the age with an incident of his earliest years. Corrected for some childish fault, in passionate distress, he overhears a half-pitying laugh at his expense, and has determined, in a moment, never again to give credit—to be for ever on his guard, especially against his own instinctive movements. Quite unreserved, certainly, he never was again. Almost everywhere he could detect the hollow ring of fundamental nothingness under the apparent surface of things. Irony surely, habitual irony, would be the proper complement thereto, on his part. In his infallible self-possession, you might even fancy him a mere man of the world, with a special aptitude for matters of fact. Though indifferent in politics, he rises to social, to political eminence; but all the while he is feeding all his scholarly curiosity, his imagination, the very eye, with the, to him ever delightful, relieving, reassuring spectacle, of those straightforward forces in human nature, which are also matters of fact. There is the formula of Mérimée! the enthusiastic amateur of rude, crude, naked force in men and women wherever it could be found; himself carrying ever, as a mask, the conventional attire of the modern world—carrying it with an infinite, contemptuous grace, as if that, too, were an all-sufficient end in itself. With a natural gift for words, for expression, it will be his literary function to draw back the veil of time from the true greatness of old Roman character; the veil of modern habit from the primitive energy of the creatures of his fancy, as the *Lettres à une Inconnue* discovered to general gaze, after his death, a certain depth of passionate force which had surprised him in himself. And how forcible will be their outlines in

an otherwise insignificant world! Fundamental belief gone, in almost all of us, at least some relics of it remain—queries, echoes, reactions, after-thoughts; and they help to make an atmosphere, a mental atmosphere, hazy perhaps, yet with many secrets of soothing light and shade, associating more definite objects to each other by a perspective pleasant to the inward eye against a hopefully receding background of remoter and ever remoter possibilities. Not so with Mérimée! For him the fundamental criticism has nothing more than it can do; and there are no half-lights. The last traces of hypothesis, of supposition, are evaporated. Sylla, the false Demetrius, Carmen, Colomba, that impassioned self within himself, have no atmosphere. Painfully distinct in outline, inevitable to sight, unrelieved, there they stand, like solitary mountain forms on some hard, perfectly transparent day. What Mérimée gets around his singularly sculpturesque creations is neither more nor less than empty space.

3. So disparate are his writings that at first sight you might fancy them only the random efforts of a man of pleasure or affairs, who, turning to this or that for the relief of a vacant hour, discovers to his surprise a workable literary gift, of whose scope, however, he is not precisely aware. His sixteen volumes nevertheless range themselves in three compact groups. There are his letters—those *Lettres à une Inconnue*, and his letters to the librarian Panizzi, revealing him in somewhat close contact with political intrigue. But in this age of novelists, it is as a writer of novels, and of fiction in the form of highly descriptive drama, that he will count for most:—*Colomba*, for instance, by its intellectual depth of motive, its firmly conceived structure, by the faultlessness of its execution, vindicating the function of the novel as no tawdry light literature, but in very deed a fine art. The *Chronique du Règne de Charles IX.*, an unusually successful specimen of historical romance, links his imaginative work to the third group of Mérimée's writings, his historical essays. One resource of the disabused soul of our century, as we saw, would be the empirical study of facts, the empirical science of nature and man, surviving all dead metaphysical philosophies. Mérimée, perhaps, may have had in him the making of a master of such science, disinterested, patient, exact: scalpel in hand, we may fancy, he would have penetrated far. But quite certainly he had something of genius for the exact study of history, for the pursuit of exact truth, with a keenness of scent as if that alone existed, in some special area of historic fact, to be determined by his own peculiar mental preferences. Power here too again,—the crude power of men and women which mocks, while it makes its use of, average human nature: it was the magic function of history to put one in living contact with that. To weigh the purely physiognomic import of the memoir, of the pamphlet saved by chance, the letter, the anecdote, the very gossip by which one came face to face with energetic personalities: there

lay the true business of the historic student, not in that pretended theoretic interpretation of events by their mechanic causes, with which he dupes others if not invariably himself. In the great hero of the *Social War*, in Sylla, studied, indeed, through his environment, but only so far as that was in dynamic contact with himself, you saw, without any manner of doubt, on one side, the solitary height of human genius; on the other, though on the seemingly so heroic stage of antique Roman story, the wholly inexpressive level of the humanity of every day, the spectacle of man's eternal *bêtise*. Fascinated, like a veritable son of the old pagan Renaissance, by the grandeur, the concentration, the satiric hardness of ancient Roman character, it is to Russia nevertheless that he most readily turns—youthful Russia, whose native force, still unbelittled by our western civilisation, seemed to have in it the promise of a more dignified civilisation to come. It was as if old Rome itself were here again; as, occasionally, a new quarry is laid open of what was thought long since exhausted, ancient marble, *cipollino* or *verde antique*. Mérimée, indeed, was not the first to discern the fitness for imaginative service of the career of "the false Demetrius," pretended son of Ivan the Terrible; but he alone seeks its utmost force in a calm, matter-of-fact, carefully ascertained presentment of the naked events. Yes! In the last years of the Valois, when its fierce passions seemed to be bursting France to pieces, you might have seen, far away beyond the rude Polish dominion of which one of those Valois princes had become king, a display more effective still of exceptional courage and cunning, of horror in circumstance, of *bêtise*, of course, of *bêtise* and a slavish capacity of being duped, in average mankind: all that under a mask of solemn Muscovite court-ceremonial. And Mérimée's style, simple and unconcerned, but with the eye ever on its object, lends itself perfectly to such purpose—to an almost phlegmatic discovery of the facts, in all their crude natural colouring, as if he but held up to view, as a piece of evidence, some harshly dyed oriental carpet from the sumptuous floor of the Kremlin, on which blood had fallen.

4. A lover of ancient Rome, its great character and incident, Mérimée valued, as if it had been personal property of his, every extant relic of it in the art that had been most expressive of its genius—architecture. In that grandiose art of building, the most national, the most tenaciously rooted of all the arts in the stable conditions of life, there were historic documents hardly less clearly legible than the manuscript chronicle. By the mouth of those stately Romanesque churches, scattered in so many strongly characterised varieties over the soil of France, above all in the hot, half-pagan south, the people of empire still protested, as he understood, against what must seem a smaller race. The Gothic enthusiasm indeed was already born, and he shared it—felt intelligently the fascination of the Pointed Style, but only as a further

transformation of old Roman structure; the round arch is for him still the great architectural form, *la forme noble*, because it was to be seen in the monuments of antiquity. Romanesque, Gothic, the manner of the Renaissance, of Lewis the Fourteenth:—they were all, as in a written record, in the old abbey church of Saint-Savin, of which Mérimée was instructed to draw up a report. Again, it was as if to his concentrated attention through many months that deserted sanctuary of Benedict were the only thing on earth. Its beauties, its peculiarities, its odd military features, its faded mural paintings, are no merely picturesque matter for the pencil he could use so well, but the lively record of a human society. With what appetite! with all the animation of George Sand's *Mauprat*, he tells the story of romantic violence having its way there, defiant of law, so late as the year 1611; of the family of robber nobles perched, as abbots *in commendam*, in those sacred places. That grey, pensive old church in the little valley of Poitou, was for a time like *Santa Maria del Fiore* to Michelangelo, the mistress of his affections—of a practical affection; for the result of his elaborate report was the Government grant which saved the place from ruin. In architecture, certainly, he had what for that day was nothing less than intuition—an intuitive sense, above all, of its logic, of the *necessity* which draws into one all minor changes, as elements in a reasonable development. And his care for it, his curiosity about it, were symptomatic of his own genius. Structure, proportion, design, a sort of architectural coherency: that was the aim of his method in the art of literature, in that form of it, especially, which he will live by, in fiction.

5. As historian and archæologist, as a man of erudition turned artist, he is well seen in the *Chronique du Règne de Charles IX.*, by which we pass naturally from Mérimée's critical or scientific work to the products of his imagination. What economy in the use of a large antiquarian knowledge! what an instinct amid a hundred details, for the detail that carries physiognomy in it, that really tells! And again what outline, what absolute clarity of outline! For the historian of that puzzling age which centres in the "Eve of Saint Bartholomew," outward events themselves seem obscured by the vagueness of motive of the actors in them. But Mérimée, disposing of them as an artist, not in love with half-lights, compels events and actors alike to the clearness he desired; takes his side without hesitation; and makes his hero a Huguenot of pure blood, allowing its charm, in that charming youth, even to Huguenot piety. And as for the incidents—however freely it may be undermined by historic doubt, all reaches a perfectly firm surface, at least for the eye of the reader. The *Chronicle of Charles the Ninth* is like a series of masterly drawings in illustration of a period—the period in which two other masters of French fiction have found their opportunity, mainly by the development of its actual historic

characters. Those characters—Catherine de Medicis and the rest—Mérimée, with significant irony and self-assertion, sets aside, preferring to think of them as essentially commonplace. For him the interest lies in the creatures of his own will, who carry in them, however, so lightly! a learning equal to Balzac's, greater than that of Dumas. He knows with like completeness the mere fashions of the time—how courtier and soldier dressed themselves, and the large movements of the desperate game which fate or chance was playing with those pretty pieces. Comparing that favourite century of the French Renaissance with our own, he notes a decadence of the more energetic passions in the interest of general tranquillity, and perhaps (only perhaps!) of general happiness. "Assassination," he observes, as if with regret, "is no longer a part of our manners." In fact, the duel, and the whole morality of the duel, which does but enforce a certain regularity on assassination, what has been well called *le sentiment du fer*, the sentiment of deadly steel, had then the disposition of refined existence. It was, indeed, very different, and *is*, in Mérimée's romance. In his gallant hero, Bernard de Mergy, all the promptings of the lad's virile goodness are in natural collusion with that *sentiment du fer*. Amid his ingenuous blushes, his prayers, and plentiful tears between-while, it is a part of his very sex. With his delightful, fresh-blown air, he is for ever tossing the sheath from the sword, but always as if into bright natural sunshine. A winsome, yet withal serious and even piteous figure, he conveys his pleasantness, in spite of its gloomy theme, into Mérimée's one quite cheerful book.

6. Cheerful, because, after all, the gloomy passions it presents are but the accidents of a particular age, and not like the mental conditions in which Mérimée was most apt to look for the spectacle of human power, allied to madness or disease in the individual. For him, at least, it was the office of fiction to carry one into a different if not a better world than that actually around us; and if the *Chronicle of Charles the Ninth* provided an escape from the tame circumstances of contemporary life into an impassioned past, *Colomba* is a measure of the resources for mental alteration which may be found even in the modern age. There was a corner of the French Empire, in the manners of which assassination still had a large part.

7. "The beauty of Corsica," says Mérimée, "is grave and sad. The aspect of the capital does but augment the impression caused by the solitude that surrounds it. There is no movement in the streets. You hear there none of the laughter, the singing, the loud talking, common in the towns of Italy. Sometimes, under the shadow of a tree on the promenade, a dozen armed peasants will be playing cards, or looking on at the game. The Corsican is naturally silent. Those who walk the pavement are all strangers: the islanders stand at their doors: every one seems to be on the watch, like a falcon on its nest. All around

the gulf there is but an expanse of tanglework; beyond it, bleached mountains. Not a habitation! Only, here and there, on the heights about the town, certain white constructions detach themselves from the background of green. They are funeral chapels or family tombs."

8. Crude in colour, sombre, taciturn, Corsica, as Mérimée here describes it, is like the national passion of the Corsican—that morbid personal pride, usurping the place even of grief for the dead, which centuries of traditional violence had concentrated into an all-absorbing passion for bloodshed, for bloody revenges, in collusion with the natural wildness, and the wild social condition of the island still unaffected even by the finer ethics of the duel. The supremacy of that passion is well indicated by the cry, put into the mouth of a young man in the presence of the corpse of his father deceased in the course of nature—a young man meant to be commonplace. "Ah! Would thou hadst died *malamorte*—by violence! We might have avenged thee!" In Colomba, Mérimée's best known creation, it is united to a singularly wholesome type of personal beauty, a natural grace of manner which is irresistible, a cunning intellect patiently diverting every circumstance to its design; and presents itself as a kind of genius, allied to fatal disease of mind. The interest of Mérimée's book is that it allows us to watch the action of this malignant power on Colomba's brother, Orso della Rebbia, as it discovers, rouses, concentrates to the leaping-point, in the somewhat weakly diffused nature of the youth, the dormant elements of a dark humour akin to her own. Two years after his father's murder, presumably at the instigation of his ancestral enemies, the young lieutenant is returning home in the company of two humorously conventional English people, himself now half Parisianised, with an immense natural cheerfulness, and willing to believe an account of the crime which relieves those hated Barricini of all complicity in its guilt. But from the first, Colomba, with "voice soft and musical," is at his side, gathering every accident and echo and circumstance, the very lightest circumstance, into the chain of necessity which draws him to the action every one at home expects of him as the head of his race. He is not unaware. Her very silence on the matter speaks so plainly. "You are forming me!" he admits. "Well! 'Hot shot, or cold steel!'—you see I have not forgotten my Corsican." More and more, as he goes on his way with her, he finds himself accessible to the damning thoughts he has so long combated. In horror, he tries to disperse them by the memory of his comrades in the regiment, the drawing-rooms of Paris, the English lady who has promised to be his bride, and will shortly visit him in the humble *manoir* of his ancestors. From his first step among them the villagers of Pietranera, divided already into two rival camps, are watching him in suspense—Pietranera, perched among those deep forests where the stifled sense of violent death is everywhere. Colomba places in his hands the

little chest which contains the father's shirt covered with great spots of blood. "Behold the lead that struck him!" and she laid on the shirt two rusted bullets. "Orso! you will avenge him!" She embraces him with a kind of madness, kisses wildly the bullets and the shirt, leaves him with the terrible relics already exerting their mystic power upon him. It is as if in the nineteenth century a girl, amid Christian habits, had gone back to that primitive old pagan version of the story of the Grail, which identifies it not with the Most Precious Blood, but only with the blood of a murdered relation crying for vengeance. Awake at last in his old chamber at Pietranera, the house of the Barricini at the other end of the square, with its rival tower and rudely carved escutcheons, stares him in the face. His ancestral enemy is there, an aged man now, but with two well-grown sons, like two stupid dumb animals, whose innocent blood will soon be on his so oddly lighted conscience. At times, his better hope seemed to lie in picking a quarrel and killing at least in fair fight, one of these two stupid dumb animals; with rude ill-suppressed laughter one day, as they overhear Colomba's violent utterances at a funeral feast, for she is a renowned *improvisatrice*. "Your father is an old man," he finds himself saying, "I could crush with my hands. 'Tis for you I am destined, for you and your brother!" And if it is by course of nature that the old man dies not long after the murder of these sons (self-provoked after all), dies a fugitive at Pisa, as it happens, by an odd accident, in the presence of Colomba, no violent death by Orso's own hand could have been more to her mind. In that last hard page of Mérimée's story, mere dramatic propriety itself for a moment seems to plead for the forgiveness, which from Joseph and his brethren to the present day, as we know, has been as winning in story as in actual life. Such dramatic propriety, however, was by no means in Mérimée's way. "What I must have is the hand that fired the shot," she had sung, "the eye that guided it; aye! and the *mind* moreover—the mind, which had conceived the deed!" And now, it is in idiotic terror, a fugitive from Orso's vengeance, that the last of the Barricini is dying.

9. Exaggerated art! you think. But it was precisely such exaggerated art, intense, unrelieved, an art of fierce colours, that is needed by those who are seeking in art, as I said of Mérimée, a kind of artificial stimulus. And if his style is still impeccably correct, cold-blooded, impersonal, as impersonal as that of Scott himself, it does but conduce the better to his one exclusive aim. It is like the polish of the stiletto Colomba carried always under her mantle, or the beauty of the fire-arms, that beauty coming of nice adaptation to purpose, which she understood so well—a task characteristic also of Mérimée himself, a sort of fanatic joy in the perfect pistol-shot, at its height in the singular story he has translated from the Russian of Pouchkine. Those raw colours he preferred; Spanish, Oriental, African, perhaps, irritant certainly to cisalpine

eyes, he undoubtedly attained the colouring you associate with sun-stroke, only possible under a sun in which dead things rot quickly.

10. Pity and terror, we know, go to the making of the essential tragic sense. In Mérimée, certainly, we have all its terror, but without the pity. Saint-Clair, the consent of his mistress barely attained at last, rushes madly on self-destruction, that he may die with the taste of his great love fresh on his lips. All the grotesque accidents of violent death he records with visual exactness, and no pains to relieve them; the ironic indifference, for instance, with which, on the scaffold or the battle-field, a man will seem to grin foolishly at the ugly rents through which his life has passed. Seldom or never has the mere pen of a writer taken us so close to the cannon's mouth as in the *Taking of the Redoubt*, while *Matteo Falcone*—twenty-five short pages—is perhaps the cruellest story in the world.

11. Colomba, that strange, fanatic being, who has a code of action, of self-respect, a conscience, all to herself, who with all her virginal charm only does not make you hate her, is, in truth, the type of a sort of humanity Mérimée found it pleasant to dream of—a humanity as alien as the animals, with whose moral affinities to man his imaginative work is often directly concerned. Were they so alien, after all? Were there not survivals of the old wild creatures in the gentlest, the politest of us? Stories that told of sudden freaks of gentle, polite natures, straight back, *not* into Paradise, were always welcome to men's fancies; and that could only be because they found a psychologic truth in them. With much success, with a credibility insured by his literary tact, Mérimée tried his own hand at such stories: unfrocked the bear in the amorous young Lithuanian noble, the wolf in the revolting peasant of the Middle Age. There were survivals surely in himself, in that stealthy presentment of his favourite themes, in his own art. You seem to find your hand on a serpent, in reading him.

12. In such survivals, indeed, you see the operation of his favourite motive, the sense of wild power, under a sort of mask, or assumed habit, realised as the very genius of nature itself; and that interest, with some superstitions closely allied to it, the belief in the vampire, for instance, is evidenced especially in certain pretended Illyrian compositions—prose translations, the reader was to understand, of more or less ancient popular ballads; *La Guzla*, he called the volume, *The Lyre*, as we might say; only that the instrument of the Illyrian minstrel had but one string. Artistic deception, a trick of which there is something in the historic romance as such, in a book like his own *Chronicle of Charles the Ninth*, was always welcome to Mérimée; it was part of the machinery of his rooted habit of intellectual reserve. A master of irony also, in *Madame Lucrezia* he seems to wish to expose his own method cynically; to explain his art—how he takes you in—as a clever, confident conjuror might do. So properly were the readers of *La Guzla* taken in that he followed up

his success in that line by the *Theatre of Clara Gazul*, purporting to be from a rare Spanish original, the work of a nun, who, under tame, conventual reading, had felt the touch of mundane, of physical passions; had become a dramatic poet, and herself a powerful actress. It may dawn on you in reading her that Mérimée was a kind of Webster, but with the superficial mildness of our nineteenth century. At the bottom of the true drama there is ever, logically at least, the ballad: the ballad dealing in a kind of short-hand (or, say! in grand, simple, universal outlines) with those passions, crimes, mistakes, which have a kind of fatality in them, a kind of necessity to come to the surface of the human *mind*, if not to the surface of our *experience*, as in the case of some frankly supernatural incidents which Mérimée re-handled. Whether human love or hatred has had most to do in shaping the universal fancy that the dead come back, I cannot say. Certainly that old ballad literature has instances in plenty, in which the voice, the hand, the brief visit from the grave, is a natural response to the cry of the human creature. That ghosts should return, as they do so often in Mérimée's fiction, is but a sort of natural justice. Only, in Mérimée's prose ballads, in those admirable, short, ballad-like stories, where every word tells, of which he was a master, almost the inventor, they are a kind of half-material ghosts—a vampire tribe—and never come to do people good; congruously with the mental constitution of the writer, which, alike in fact and fiction, could hardly have horror enough—theme after theme. Mérimée himself emphasises this almost constant motive of his fiction when he adds to one of his volumes of short stories some letters on a matter of fact—a Spanish bull-fight, in which those old Romans, he regretted, might seem, decadently, to have survived. It is as if you saw it. In truth, Mérimée was the unconscious parent of much we may think of dubious significance in later French literature. It is as if there were nothing to tell of in this world but various forms of hatred, and a love that is like lunacy; and the only other world, a world of maliciously active, hideous, dead bodies.

13. Mérimée, a literary artist, was not a man who used two words where one would do better, and he shines especially in those brief compositions which, like a minute intaglio, reveal at a glance his wonderful faculty of design and proportion in the treatment of his work, in which there is not a touch but counts. That is an art of which there are few examples in English; our somewhat diffuse, or slipshod, literary language hardly lending itself to the concentration of thought and expression, which are of the essence of such writing. It is otherwise in French, and if you wish to know what art of that kind can come to, read Mérimée's little romances; best of all, perhaps, *La Vénus d'Ille* and *Arsène Guillot*. The former is a modern version of the beautiful old story of the Ring given to Venus, given to her, in this case, by a somewhat

sordid creature of the nineteenth century, whom she looks on with more than disdain. The strange outline of the Canigou, one of the most imposing outlying heights of the Pyrenees, down the mysterious slopes of which the traveller has made his way towards nightfall into the great plain of Toulouse, forms an impressive background, congruous with the many relics of irrepressible old paganism there, but in entire contrast to the *bourgeois* comfort of the place where his journey is to end, the abode of an aged antiquary, loud and bright just now with the celebration of a vulgar worldly marriage. In the midst of this well-being, prosaic in spite of the neighbourhood, in spite of the pretty old wedding customs, morsels of that local colour in which Mérimée delights, the old pagan powers are supposed to reveal themselves once more (malignantly, of course), in the person of a magnificent bronze statue of Venus recently unearthed in the antiquary's garden. On her finger, by ill-luck, the coarse young bridegroom on the morning of his marriage places for a moment the bridal ring only too effectually (the bronze hand closes, like a wilful living one, upon it), and dies, you are to understand, in her angry metallic embraces on his marriage night. From the first, indeed, she had seemed bent on crushing out men's degenerate bodies and souls, though the supernatural horror of the tale is adroitly made credible by a certain vagueness in the events, which covers a quite natural account of the bridegroom's mysterious death.

14. The intellectual charm of literary work so thoroughly designed as Mérimée's depends in part on the sense as you read, hastily perhaps, perhaps in need of patience, that you are dealing with a composition, the full secret of which is only to be attained in the last paragraph, that with the last word in mind you will retrace your steps, more than once (it may be) noting then the minuter structure, also the natural or wrought flowers by the way. Nowhere is such method better illustrated than by another of Mérimée's quintessential pieces, *Arséne Guillot*, and here for once with a conclusion ethically acceptable also. Mérimée loved surprises in human nature, but it is not often that he surprises us by tenderness or generosity of character, as another master of French fiction, M. Octave Feuillet, is apt to do; and the simple pathos of *Arséne Guillot* gives it a unique place in Mérimée's writings. It may be said, indeed, that only an essentially pitiful nature could have told the exquisitely cruel story of Matteo Falcone precisely as Mérimée has told it; and those who knew him testify abundantly to his own capacity for generous friendship. He was no more wanting than others in those natural sympathies (sending tears to the eyes at the sight of suffering age or childhood) which happily are no extraordinary component in men's natures. It was, perhaps, no fitting return for a friendship of over thirty years to publish posthumously those *Lettres à une Inconnue*, which reveal that reserved, sensitive, self-centred nature, a

little pusillanimously in the power, at the disposition of another. For just there lies the interest, the psychological interest, of those letters. An amateur of power, of the spectacle of power and force, followed minutely but without sensibility on his part, with a kind of cynic pride rather for the mainspring of his method, both of thought and expression, you find him here taken by surprise at last, and somewhat humbled, by an unsuspected force of affection in himself. His correspondent, unknown but for these letters except just by name, figures in them as, in truth, a being only too much like himself, seen from one side; reflects his taciturnity, his touchiness, his incredulity except for self-torment. Agitated, dissatisfied, he is wrestling in her with himself, his own difficult qualities. He demands from her a freedom, a frankness, he would have been the last to grant. It is by first thoughts, of course, that what is forcible and effective in human nature, the force, therefore, of carnal love, discovers itself; and for her first thoughts Mérimée is always pleading, but always complaining that he gets only her second thoughts; the thoughts, that is, of a reserved, self-limiting nature, well under the yoke of convention, like his own. Strange conjunction! At the beginning of the correspondence he seems to have been seeking only a fine intellectual companionship; the lady, perhaps, looking for something warmer. Towards such companionship that likeness to himself in her might have been helpful, but was not enough of a complement to his own nature to be anything but an obstruction in love; and it is to that, little by little, that his humour turns. He—the *Megalopsychus*, as Aristotle defines him—acquires all the lover's humble habits: himself displays all the tricks of love, its casuistries, its exigency, its superstitions, aye! even its vulgarities; involves with the significance of his own genius the mere hazards and inconsequence of a perhaps average nature; but too late in the day—the years. After the attractions and repulsions of half a lifetime, they are but friends, and might forget to be that, but for his death, clearly presaged in his last weak, touching letter, just two hours before. There, too, had been the blind and naked force of nature and circumstance, surprising him in the uncontrollable movements of his own so carefully guarded heart.

15. The intimacy, the effusion, the so freely exposed personality of those letters does but emphasise the fact that *impersonality* was, in literary art, Mérimée's central aim. Personality *versus* impersonality in art:—how much or how little of one's self one may put into one's work: whether anything at all of it: whether one *can* put there anything else:—is clearly a far-reaching and complex question. Serviceable as the basis of a precautionary maxim towards the conduct of our work, self-effacement, or impersonality, in literary or artistic creation, is, perhaps, after all, as little possible as a strict realism. "It has always been my rule to put nothing of myself into my works," says another

great master of French prose, Gustave Flaubert; but, luckily as we may think, he often failed in thus effacing himself, as he too was aware. "It has always been my rule to put nothing of myself into my works" (to be *disinterested* in his literary creations, so to speak), "yet I have put much of myself into them": and where he failed Mérimée succeeded. There they stand—Carmen, Colomba, the "False" Demetrius—as detached from him as from each other, with no more filial likeness to their maker than if they were the work of another person. And to his method of conception, Mérimée's much-praised literary style, his method of expression, is strictly conformable—impersonal in its beauty, the perfection of nobody's style—thus vindicating anew by its very impersonality that much worn, but not untrue saying, that the style is the man:—a man, impassible, unfamiliar, impeccable, veiling a deep sense of what is forcible, nay, terrible, in things, under the sort of personal pride that makes a man a nice observer of all that is most conventional. Essentially unlike other people, he is always fastidiously in the fashion—an expert in all the little, half-contemptuous elegances of which it is capable. Mérimée's superb self-effacement, his impersonality, is itself but an effective personal trait, and, transferred to art, becomes a markedly peculiar quality of literary beauty. For, in truth, this creature of disillusion who had no care for half-lights, and, like his creations, had no atmosphere about him, gifted as he was with pure *mind*, with the quality which secures flawless literary structure, had, on the other hand, nothing of what we call *soul* in literature:—hence, also, that singular harshness in his ideal, as if, in theological language, he were incapable of grace. He has none of those subjectivities, colourings, peculiarities of mental refraction, which necessitate *varieties* of style—could we spare such?—and render the perfections of it no merely negative qualities. There are masters of French prose whose art has begun where the art of Mérimée leaves off.

RAPHAEL[1]

By his immense productiveness, by the even perfection of what he produced, its fitness to its own day, its hold on posterity, in the suavity of his life, some would add in the "opportunity" of his early death, Raphael may seem a signal instance of the luckiness, of the good fortune, of genius. Yet, if we follow the actual growth of his powers, within their proper framework, the age of the Renaissance—an age of which we may say, summarily, that it enjoyed itself, and found perhaps its chief enjoyment in the attitude of the scholar, in the enthusiastic acquisition of knowledge for its own sake:—if we thus view Raphael and his works in their environment we shall find even his seemingly mechanical good fortune hardly distinguishable from his own patient disposal of the means at hand. Facile master as he may seem, as indeed he is, he is also one of the world's typical scholars, with Plato, and Cicero, and Virgil, and Milton. The *formula* of his genius, if we must have one, is *this*: genius by accumulation; the transformation of meek scholarship into genius—triumphant power of genius.

2. Urbino, where this prince of the Renaissance was born in 1483, year also of the birth of Luther, leader of the other great movement of that age, the Reformation—Urbino, under its dukes of the house of Montefeltro, had wherewithal just then to make a boy of native artistic faculty from the first a willing learner. The gloomy old fortress of the feudal masters of the town had been replaced, in those later years of the *Quattro-cento*, by a consummate monument of *Quattro-cento* taste, a museum of ancient and modern art, the owners of which lived there, gallantly at home, amid the choicer flowers of living humanity. The ducal palace was, in fact, become nothing less than a school of ambitious youth in all the accomplishments alike of war and peace. Raphael's connexion with it seems to have become intimate, and from the first its influence must have overflowed so small a place. In the case of the lucky Raphael, for once, the actual conditions of early life had been suitable, propitious, accordant to what one's imagination would have required for the childhood of the man. He was born amid the art he was, not to transform, but to perfect, by a thousand reverential retouchings. In no palace, however, but in a modest abode, still shown, containing the workshop of his father, Giovanni Santi. But here, too, though in frugal form, art, the arts, were present. A store

---

1. A lecture delivered to the University Extension Students, Oxford, 2 August, 1892. Published in the *Fortnightly Review*, Oct. 1892, and now reprinted by the kind permission of the proprietors. *[Editorial note in* Miscellaneous Studies.*]*

of artistic objects was, or had recently been, made there, and now especially, for fitting patrons, religious pictures in the old Umbrian manner. In quiet nooks of the Apennines Giovanni's works remain; and there is one of them, worth study, in spite of what critics say of its crudity, in the National Gallery. Concede its immaturity, at least, though an immaturity visibly susceptible of a delicate grace, it wins you nevertheless to return again and again, and ponder, by a sincere expression of sorrow, profound, yet resigned, be the cause what it may, among all the many causes of sorrow inherent in the ideal of maternity, human or divine. But if you keep in mind when looking at it the facts of Raphael's childhood, you will recognise in his father's picture, not the anticipated sorrow of the "Mater Dolorosa" over the dead son, but the grief of a simple household over the mother herself taken early from it. That may have been the first picture the eyes of the world's great painter of Madonnas rested on; and if he stood diligently before it to copy, and so copying, quite unconsciously, and with no disloyalty to his original, refined, improved, substituted,—substituted himself, in fact, his finer self—he had already struck the persistent note of his career. As with his age, it is his vocation, ardent worker as he is, to enjoy himself—to enjoy himself amiably, and to find his chief enjoyment in the attitude of a scholar. And one by one, one after another, his masters, the very greatest of them, go to school to him.

3. It was so especially with the artist of whom Raphael first became certainly a learner—Perugino. Giovanni Santi had died in Raphael's childhood, too early to have been in any direct sense his teacher. The lad, however, from one and another, had learned much, when, with his share of the patrimony in hand, enough to keep him, but not to tempt him from scholarly ways, he came to Perugia, hoping still further to improve himself. He was in his eighteenth year, and how he looked just then you may see in a drawing of his own in the University Galleries, of somewhat stronger mould than less genuine likenesses may lead you to expect. There is something of a fighter in the way in which the nose springs from the brow between the wide-set, meditative eyes. A strenuous lad! capable of plodding, if you dare apply that word to labour so impassioned as his—to any labour whatever done at Perugia, centre of the dreamiest Apennine scenery. Its various elements (one hardly knows whether one is thinking of Italian nature or of Raphael's art in recounting them), the richly-planted lowlands, the sensitive mountain lines in flight one beyond the other into clear distance, the cool yet glowing atmosphere, the romantic morsels of architecture, which lend to the entire scene I know not what expression of reposeful antiquity, arrange themselves here as for set purpose of pictorial effect, and have gone with little change into his painted backgrounds. In the midst of it, on titanic old Roman and Etruscan foundations, the later Gothic town had

piled itself along the lines of a gigantic land of rock, stretched out from the last slope of the Apennines into the plain. Between its fingers steep dark lanes wind down into the olive gardens; on the finger-tips military and monastic builders had perched their towns. A place as fantastic in its attractiveness as the human life which then surged up and down in it in contrast to the peaceful scene around. The Baglioni who ruled there had brought certain tendencies of that age to a typical completeness of expression, veiling crime—crime, it might seem, for its own sake, a whole octave of fantastic crime—not merely under brilliant fashions and comely persons, but under fashions and persons, an outward presentment of life and of themselves, which had a kind of immaculate grace and discretion about them, as if Raphael himself had already brought his unerring gift of selection to bear upon it all for motives of art. With life in those streets of Perugia, as with nature, with the work of his masters, with the mere exercises of his fellow-students, his hand rearranges, refines, renews, as if by simple contact; but it is met here half-way in its renewing office by some special aptitude for such grace in the subject itself. Seemingly innocent, full of natural gaiety, eternally youthful, those seven and more deadly sins, embodied and attired in just the jaunty dress then worn, enter now and afterwards as spectators, or assistants, into many a sacred foreground and background among the friends and kinsmen of the Holy Family, among the very angels, gazing, conversing, standing firmly and unashamed. During his apprenticeship at Perugia Raphael visited and left his work in more modest places round about, along those seductive mountain or lowland roads, and copied for one of them Perugino's "Marriage of the Virgin" significantly, did it by many degrees better, with a very novel effect of motion everywhere, and with that grace which natural motion evokes, introducing for a temple in the background a lovely bit of his friend Bramante's sort of architecture, the true Renaissance or perfected *Quattro-cento* architecture. He goes on building a whole lordly new city of the like as he paints to the end of his life. The subject, we may note, as we leave Perugia in Raphael's company, had been suggested by the famous mystic treasure of its cathedral church, the marriage ring of the Blessed Virgin herself.

4. Raphael's copy had been made for the little old Apennine town of Città di Castello; and another place he visits at this time is still more effective in the development of his genius. About his twentieth year he comes to Siena—that other rocky Titan's hand, just lifted out of the surface of the plain. It is the most grandiose place he has yet seen; it has not forgotten that it was once the rival of Florence; and here the patient scholar passes under an influence of somewhat larger scope than Perugino's. Perugino's pictures are for the most part religious contemplations, painted and made visible, to accompany the action of divine service—a visible pattern to priests, attendants, worshippers,

of what the course of their invisible thoughts should be at those holy functions. Learning in the workshop of Perugino to produce the like—such works as the Ansidei Madonna—to produce them very much better than his master, Raphael was already become a freeman of the most strictly religious school of Italian art, the so devout Umbrian soul finding there its purest expression, still untroubled by the naturalism, the intellectualism, the antique paganism, then astir in the artistic soul everywhere else in Italy. The lovely work of Perugino, very lovely at its best, of the early Raphael also, is in fact "conservative," and at various points slightly behind its day, though not unpleasantly. In Perugino's allegoric frescoes of the *Cambio*, the Hall of the Money-changers, for instance, under the mystic rule of the Planets in person, pagan personages take their place indeed side by side with the figures of the New Testament, but are no Romans or Greeks, neither are the Jews Jews, nor is any one of them, warrior, sage, king, precisely of Perugino's own time and place, but still contemplations only, after the manner of the personages in his church-work; or, say, dreams—monastic dreams—thin, do-nothing creatures, conjured from sky and cloud. Perugino clearly never broke through the meditative circle of the Middle Age.

5. Now Raphael, on the other hand, in his final period at Rome, exhibits a wonderful narrative power in painting; and the secret of that power—the power of developing a story in a picture, or series of pictures—may be traced back from him to Pinturicchio, as that painter worked on those vast, well-lighted walls of the cathedral library at Siena, at the great series of frescoes illustrative of the life of Pope Pius the Second. It had been a brilliant personal history, in contact now and again with certain remarkable public events—a career religious yet mundane, you scarcely know which, so natural is the blending of lights, of interest in it. How unlike the Peruginesque conception of life in its almost perverse other-worldliness, which Raphael now leaves behind him, but, like a true scholar, will not forget. Pinturicchio then had invited his remarkable young friend hither, "to assist him by his counsels," who, however, pupil-wise, after his habit also learns much as he thus assists. He stands depicted there in person in the scene of the canonisation of Saint Catherine; and though his actual share in the work is not to be defined, connoisseurs have felt his intellectual presence, not at one place only, in touches at once finer and more forcible than were usual in the steady-going, somewhat Teutonic, Pinturicchio, Raphael's elder by thirty years. The meek scholar you see again, with his tentative sketches and suggestions, had more than learned his lesson; through all its changes that flexible intelligence loses nothing; does but add continually to its store. Henceforward Raphael will be able to tell a story in a picture, better, with a truer economy, with surer judgment, more naturally and easily than any one else.

6. And here at Siena, of all Italian towns perhaps most deeply impressed

with medieval character—an impress it still retains—grotesque, parti-coloured—parti-coloured, so to speak, in its genius—Satanic, yet devout of humour, as depicted in its old chronicles, and beautiful withal, dignified; it is here that Raphael becomes for the first time aware of that old pagan world, which had already come to be so much for the art-schools of Italy. There were points, as we saw, at which the school of Perugia was behind its day. Amid those intensely Gothic surroundings in the cathedral library where Pinturicchio worked, stood, as it remained till recently, unashamed there, a marble group of the three Graces—an average Roman work in effect—the sort of thing we are used to. That, perhaps, is the only reason why for our part, except with an effort, we find it conventional or even tame. For the youthful Raphael, on the other hand, at that moment, antiquity, as with "the dew of herbs," seemed therein "to awake and sing" out of the dust, in all its sincerity, its cheerfulness and natural charm. He has turned it into a picture; has helped to make his original only too familiar, perhaps, placing the three sisters against his own favourite, so unclassic, Umbrian background indeed, but with no trace of the Peruginesque ascetic, Gothic meagreness in themselves; emphasising rather, with a hearty acceptance, the nude, the flesh; making the limbs, in fact, a little heavy. It was but one gleam he had caught just there in medieval Siena of that large pagan world he was, not so long afterwards, more completely than others to make his own. And when somewhat later he painted the exquisite, still Peruginesque, Apollo and Marsyas, semi-medieval habits again asserted themselves with delightfully blent effects. It might almost pass for a parable—that little picture in the Louvre—of the contention between classic art and the romantic, superseded in the person of Marsyas, a homely, quaintly poetical young monk, surely! Only, Apollo himself also is clearly of the same brotherhood; has a touch, in truth, of Heine's fancied Apollo "in exile," who, Christianity now triumphing, has served as a hired shepherd, or hidden himself under the cowl in a cloister; and Raphael, as if at work on choir-book or missal, still applies symbolical gilding for natural sunlight. It is as if he wished to proclaim amid newer lights—this scholar who never forgot a lesson—his loyal pupilage to Perugino, and retained still something of medieval stiffness, of the monastic thoughts also, that were born and lingered in places like Borgo San Sepolcro or Città di Castello. *Chef-d'œuvre!* you might exclaim, of the peculiar, tremulous, half-convinced, monkish treatment of that after all damnable pagan world. And our own generation certainly, with kindred tastes, loving or wishing to love pagan art as sincerely as did the people of the Renaissance, and medieval art as well, would accept, of course, of work conceived in that so seductively mixed manner, ten per cent of even Raphael's later, purely classical presentments.

7. That picture was suggested by a fine old intaglio in the Medicean collection at Florence, was painted, therefore, after Raphael's coming thither, and therefore also a survival with him of a style limited, immature, literally provincial; for in the phase on which he had now entered he is under the influence of style in its most fully determined sense, of what might be called the thorough-bass of the pictorial art, of a fully realised intellectual system in regard to its processes, well tested by experiment, upon a survey of all the conditions and various applications of it—of style as understood by Da Vinci, then at work in Florence. Raphael's sojourn there extends from his twenty-first to his twenty-fifth year. He came with flattering recommendations from the Court of Urbino; was admitted as an equal by the masters of his craft, being already in demand for work, then and ever since duly prized; was, in fact, already famous, though he alone is unaware—is in his own opinion still but a learner, and as a learner yields himself meekly, systematically to influence; would learn from Francia, whom he visits at Bologna; from the earlier naturalistic works of Masolino and Masaccio; from the solemn prophetic work of the venerable dominican, Bartolommeo, disciple of Savonarola. And he has already habitually this strange effect, not only on the whole body of his juniors, but on those whose manner had been long since formed; they lose something of themselves by contact with him, as if they went to school again.

8. Bartolommeo, Da Vinci, were masters certainly of what we call "the ideal" in art. Yet for Raphael, so loyal hitherto to the traditions of Umbrian art, to its heavy weight of hieratic tradition, dealing still somewhat conventionally with a limited, non-natural matter—for Raphael to come from Siena, Perugia, Urbino, to sharp-witted, practical, masterful Florence was in immediate effect a transition from reverie to realities—to a world of facts. Those masters of the ideal were for him, in the first instance, masters also of realism, as we say. Henceforth, to the end, he will be the analyst, the faithful reporter, in his work, of what he *sees*. He will realise the function of style as exemplified in the practice of Da Vinci, face to face with the world of nature and man as they are; selecting from, asserting one's self in a transcript of its veritable *data*; like drawing to like there, in obedience to the master's preference for the embodiment of the creative form within him. Portrait-art had been nowhere in the school of Perugino, but it was the triumph of the school of Florence. And here a faithful analyst of what he sees, yet lifting it withal, unconsciously, inevitably, recomposing, glorifying, Raphael too becomes, of course, a painter of portraits. We may foresee them already in masterly series, from Maddalena Doni, a kind of younger, more virginal sister of La Gioconda, to cardinals and popes—to that most sensitive of all portraits, the "Violin-player," if it be really his. But then, on the other hand, the influence of such portraiture will be

felt also in his inventive work, in a certain reality there, a certain convincing loyalty to experience and observation. In his most elevated religious work he will still keep, for security at least, close to nature, and the truth of nature. His modelling of the visible surface is lovely because he understands, can see the hidden causes of momentary action in the face, the hands—how men and animals are really made and kept alive. Set side by side, then, with that portrait of Maddalena Doni, as forming together a measure of what he has learned at Florence, the "Madonna del Gran Duca," which still remains there. Call it on revision, and without hesitation, the loveliest of his Madonnas, perhaps of all Madonnas; and let it stand as representative of as many as fifty or sixty types of that subject, onwards to the Sixtine Madonna, in all the triumphancy of his later days at Rome. Observe the veritable atmosphere about it, the grand composition of the drapery, the magic relief, the sweetness and dignity of the human hands and faces, the noble tenderness of Mary's gesture, the unity of the thing with itself, the faultless exclusion of all that does not belong to its main purpose; it is like a single, simple axiomatic thought. Note withal the novelty of its effect on the mind, and you will see that this master of style (that's a consummate example of what is meant by *style*) has been still a willing scholar in the hands of Da Vinci. But then, with what ease also, and simplicity, and a sort of natural success not his!

9. It was in his twenty-fifth year that Raphael came to the city of the popes, Michelangelo being already in high favour there. For the remaining years of his life he paces the same streets with that grim artist, who was so great a contrast with himself, and for the first time his attitude towards a gift different from his own is not that of a scholar, but that of a rival. If he did not become the scholar of Michelangelo, it would be difficult, on the other hand, to trace anywhere in Michelangelo's work the counter influence usual with those who had influenced him. It was as if he desired to add to the strength of Michelangelo that sweetness which at first sight seems to be wanting there. *Ex forti dulcedo:* and in the study of Michelangelo certainly it is enjoyable to detect, if we may, sweet savours amid the wonderful strength, the strangeness and potency of what he pours forth for us: with Raphael, conversely, something of a relief to find in the suavity of that so softly moving, tuneful existence, an assertion of strength. There was the promise of it, as you remember, in his very look as he saw himself at eighteen; and you know that the lesson, the prophecy of those holy women and children he has made his own, is that "the meek shall possess." So, when we see him at Rome at last, in that atmosphere of greatness, of the strong, he too is found putting forth strength, adding that element in due proportion to the mere sweetness and charm of his genius; yet a sort of strength, after all, still congruous with the line of development that

genius has hitherto taken, the special strength of the scholar and his proper reward, a purely cerebral strength—the strength, the power of an immense understanding.

10. Now the life of Raphael at Rome seems as we read of it hasty and perplexed, full of undertakings, of vast works not always to be completed, of almost impossible demands on his industry, in a world of breathless competition, amid a great company of spectators, for great rewards. You seem to lose him, feel he may have lost himself, in the multiplicity of his engagements; might fancy that, wealthy, variously decorated, a courtier, cardinal *in petto*, he was "serving tables." But, you know, he was forcing into this brief space of years (he died at thirty-seven) more than the natural business of the larger part of a long life; and one way of getting some kind of clearness into it, is to distinguish the various divergent outlooks or applications, and group the results of that immense intelligence, that still untroubled, flawlessly operating, completely informed understanding, that purely cerebral power, acting through his executive, inventive or creative gifts, through the eye and the hand with its command of visible colour and form. In that way you may follow him along many various roads till brain and eye and hand suddenly fail in the very midst of his work—along many various roads, but you can follow him along each of them distinctly.

11. At the end of one of them is the *Galatea*, and in quite a different form of industry, the *datum* for the beginnings of a great literary work of pure erudition. Coming to the capital of Christendom, he comes also for the first time under the full influence of the antique world, pagan art, pagan life, and is henceforth an enthusiastic archæologist. On his first coming to Rome a papal bull had authorised him to inspect all ancient marbles, inscriptions, and the like, with a view to their adaptation in new buildings then proposed. A consequent close acquaintance with antiquity, with the very touch of it, blossomed literally in his brain, and, under his facile hand, in artistic creations, of which the *Galatea* is indeed the consummation. But the frescoes of the Farnese palace, with a hundred minor designs, find their place along that line of his artistic activity; they do not exhaust his knowledge of antiquity, his interest in and control of it. The mere fragments of it that still cling to his memory would have composed, had he lived longer, a monumental illustrated survey of the monuments of ancient Rome.

12. To revive something of the proportionable spirit at least of antique building in the architecture of the present, came naturally to Raphael as the son of his age; and at the end of another of those roads of diverse activity stands Saint Peter's, though unfinished. What a proof again of that immense intelligence, by which, as I said, the element of strength supplemented the element of mere sweetness and charm in his work, that at the age of thirty,

known hitherto only as a painter, at the dying request of the venerable Bramante himself, he should have been chosen to succeed him as the director of that vast enterprise! And if little in the great church, as we see it, is directly due to him, yet we must not forget that his work in the Vatican also was partly that of an architect. In the Loggie, or open galleries of the Vatican, the last and most delicate effects of *Quattro-cento* taste come from his hand, in that peculiar arabesque decoration which goes by his name.

13. Saint Peter's, as you know, had an indirect connexion with the Teutonic reformation. When Leo X. pushed so far the sale of indulgences to the overthrow of Luther's Catholicism, it was done after all for the not entirely selfish purpose of providing funds to build the metropolitan church of Christendom with the assistance of Raphael; and yet, upon another of those diverse outways of his so versatile intelligence, at the close of which we behold his unfinished picture of the Transfiguration, what has been called Raphael's Bible finds its place—that series of biblical scenes in the Loggie of the Vatican. And here, while he has shown that he could do something of Michelangelo's work a little more soothingly than he, this graceful Roman Catholic rivals also what is perhaps best in the work of the rude German reformer—of Luther, who came to Rome about this very time, to find nothing admirable there. Place along with them the Cartoons, and observe that in this phase of his artistic labour, as Luther printed his vernacular German version of the Scriptures, so Raphael is popularising them for an even larger world; he brings the simple, to their great delight, face to face with the Bible as it is, in all its variety of incident, after they had so long had to content themselves with but fragments of it, as presented in the symbolism and in the brief lections of the Liturgy:—*Biblia Pauperum*, in a hundred forms of reproduction, though designed for popes and princes.

14. But then, for the wise, at the end of yet another of those divergent ways, glows his painted philosophy in the *Parnassus* and the *School of Athens*, with their numerous accessories. In the execution of those works, of course, his antiquarian knowledge stood him in good stead; and here, above all, is the pledge of his immense understanding, at work on its own natural ground on a purely intellectual deposit, the apprehension, the transmission to others of complex and difficult ideas. We have here, in fact, the sort of intelligence to be found in Lessing, in Herder, in Hegel, in those who, by the instrumentality of an organised philosophic system, have comprehended in one view or vision what poetry has been, or what Greek philosophy, as great complex dynamic facts in the world. But then, with the artist of the sixteenth century, this synoptic intellectual power worked in perfect identity with the pictorial imagination and a magic hand. By him large theoretic conceptions are addressed, so to speak, to the intelligence of the eye. There had been efforts at such abstract or theoretic

painting before, or say rather, leagues behind him. Modern efforts, again, we know, and not in Germany alone, to do the like for that larger survey of such matters which belongs to the philosophy of our own century; but for one or many reasons they have seemed only to prove the incapacity of philosophy to be expressed in terms of art. They have seemed, in short, so far, not fit to be seen literally—those ideas of culture, religion, and the like. Yet Plato, as you know, supposed a kind of visible loveliness about ideas. Well! in Raphael, painted ideas, painted and visible philosophy, are for once as beautiful as Plato thought they must be, if one truly apprehended them. For note, above all, that with all his wealth of antiquarian knowledge in detail, and with a perfect technique, it is after all the beauty, the grace of poetry, of pagan philosophy, of religious faith that he thus records.

15. Of religious faith also. The *Disputa*, in which, under the form of a council representative of all ages, he embodies the idea of theology, *divinarum rerum notitia*, as constantly resident in the Catholic Church, ranks with the "Parnassus" and the "School of Athens," if it does not rather close another of his long lines of intellectual travail—a series of compositions, partly symbolic, partly historical, in which the "Deliverance of St. Peter from Prison," the "Expulsion of the Huns," and the "Coronation of Charlemagne," find their places; and by which, painting in the great official chambers of the Vatican, Raphael asserts, interprets the power and charm of the Catholic ideal as realised in history. A scholar, a student of the visible world, of the natural man, yet even more ardently of the books, the art, the life of the old pagan world, the age of the Renaissance, through all its varied activity, had, in spite of the weakened hold of Catholicism on the critical intellect, been still under its influence, the glow of it, as a religious ideal, and in the presence of Raphael you cannot think it a mere after-glow. Independently, that is, of less or more evidence for it, the whole creed of the Middle Age, as a scheme of the world as it should be, as we should be glad to find it, was still welcome to the heart, the imagination. Now, in Raphael, all the various conditions of that age discover themselves as characteristics of a vivid personal genius, which may be said therefore to be conterminous with the genius of the Renaissance itself. For him, then, in the breadth of his immense cosmopolitan intelligence, for Raphael, who had done in part the work of Luther also, the Catholic Church—through all its phases, as reflected in its visible local centre, the papacy—is alive still as of old, one and continuous, and still true to itself. Ah! what is local and visible, as you know, counts for so much with the artistic temper!

16. Old friends, or old foes with but new faces, events repeating themselves, as his large, clear, synoptic vision can detect, the invading King of France, Louis XII., appears as Attila: Leo X. as Leo I.: and he thinks of, he sees, at

one and the same moment, the coronation of Charlemagne and the interview of Pope Leo with Francis I., as a dutiful son of the Church: of the deliverance of Leo X. from prison, and the deliverance of St. Peter.

17. I have abstained from anything like description of Raphael's pictures in speaking of him and his work, have aimed rather at preparing you to look at his work for yourselves, by a sketch of his life, and therein especially, as most appropriate to this place, of Raphael as a scholar. And now if, in closing, I commend one of his pictures in particular to your imagination or memory, your purpose to see it, or see it again, it will not be the Transfiguration nor the Sixtine Madonna, nor even the "Madonna del Gran Duca," but the picture we have in London—the Ansidei, or Blenheim, Madonna. I find there, at first sight, with something of the pleasure one has in a proposition of Euclid, a sense of the power of the understanding, in the economy with which he has reduced his material to the simplest terms, has disentangled and detached its various elements. He is painting in Florence, but for Perugia, and sends it a specimen of its own old art—Mary and the babe enthroned, with St. Nicolas and the Baptist in attendance on either side. The kind of thing people there had already seen so many times, but done better, in a sense not to be measured by degrees, with a wholly original freedom and life and grace, though he perhaps is unaware, done better as a whole, because better in every minute particular, than ever before. The scrupulous scholar, aged twenty-three, is now indeed a master; but still goes carefully. Note, therefore, how much mere exclusion counts for in the positive effect of his work. There is a saying that the true artist is known best by what he omits. Yes, because the whole question of good taste is involved precisely in such jealous omission. Note this, for instance, in the familiar Apennine background, with its blue hills and brown towns, faultless, for once—for once only—and observe, in the Umbrian pictures around, how often such background is marred by grotesque, natural, or architectural detail, by incongruous or childish incident. In this cool, pearl-grey, quiet place, where colour tells for double—the jewelled cope, the painted book in the hand of Mary, the chaplet of red coral—one is reminded that among all classical writers Raphael's preference was for the faultless Virgil. How orderly, how divinely clean and sweet the flesh, the vesture, the floor, the earth and sky! Ah, say rather the hand, the method of the painter! There is an unmistakeable pledge of strength, of movement and animation in the cast of the Baptist's countenance, but reserved, repressed. Strange, Raphael has given him a staff of transparent crystal. Keep then to that picture as the embodied formula of Raphael's genius. Amid all he has here already achieved, full, we may think, of the quiet assurance of what is to come, his attitude is still that of the scholar; he seems still to be saying, before all things, from first to last, "I am utterly purposed that I will not offend."

from PASCAL[1]

[...] Observe, he is not a sceptic converted, a returned infidel, but is seen there [in the *Pensées*] as if at the very centre of a perpetually maintained tragic crisis holding the faith steadfastly, but amid the well-poised points of essential doubt all around him and it. It is no mere calm supersession of a state of doubt by a state of faith; the doubts never die, they are only just kept down in a perpetual *agonia*. Everywhere in the "Letters" he had seemed so great a master—a master of himself—never at a loss, taking the conflict so lightly, with so light a heart: in the great Atlantean travail of the "Thoughts" his feet sometimes "are almost gone." In his soul's agony, theological abstractions seem to become personal powers. It was as if just below the surface of the green undulations, the stately woods, of his own strange country of Auvergne, the volcanic fires had suddenly discovered themselves anew. In truth into his typical diagnosis, as it may seem, of the tragedy of the human soul, there have passed not merely the personal feelings, the temperament of an individual, but his malady also, a physical malady. Great genius, we know, has the power of elevating, transmuting, serving itself by the accidental conditions about it, however unpromising—poverty, and the like. It was certainly so with Pascal's long-continued physical sufferings. That *aigreur*, which is part of the native colour of Pascal's genius, is reinforced in the "Pensées" by insupportable languor, alternating with supportable pain, as he died little by little through the eight years of their composition. They are essentially the utterance of a soul *malade*—a soul of great genius, whose malady became a new quality of that genius, perfecting it thus, by its very defect, as a type on the intellectual stage, and thereby guiding, reassuring sympathetically, manning by a sense of good company that large class of persons who are *malade* in the same way. "*La maladie est l'état naturel des Chrétiens*," says Pascal himself. And we concede that every one of us more or less is ailing thus, as another has told us that life itself is a disease of the spirit.

17. From Port-Royal also came, about the year 1670, a painful book, the "Life of Pascal," a portrait painted slowly from the life or living death, but with an almost exclusive preference for traits expressive of disease. The *post-mortem* examination of Pascal's brain revealed, we are now told, the secret, not merely of that long prostration, those sudden passing torments, but of something

---

1. Published in the *Contemporary Review*, Feb. 1895, and now reprinted by the kind permission of the of the proprietors. *[Editorial note in* Miscellaneous Studies.*]*

analogous to them in Pascal's genius and work. Well! the light cast indirectly on the literary work of Pascal by Mme. Périer's "Life" is of a similar kind. It is a veritable chapter in morbid pathology, though it may have truly a beauty for experts, the beauty which belongs to all refined cases even of cerebral disturbance. That he should have sought relief from his singular wretchedness, in that sombre company, is like the second stroke of tragedy upon him. At moments Pascal becomes almost a sectarian, and seems to pass out of the genial broad heaven of the Catholic Church. He had lent himself in those last years to a kind of pieties which do not make a winning picture, which always have about them, even when they show themselves in men physically strong, something of the small compass of the sick-chamber. His medieval or oriental self-tortures, all the painful efforts at absolute detachment, a perverse asceticism taking all there still was to spare from the denuded and suffering body, might well, you may think, have died with him, but are here recorded, chiefly by way of showing the world, the Jesuits, that the Jansenists, too, had a saint quite after their mind.

18. But though, at first sight, you may find a pettiness in those minute pieties, they have their signification as a testimony to the wholeness of Pascal's assent, the entirety of his submission, his immense sincerity, the heroic grandeur of his achieved faith. The seventeenth century presents survivals of the gloomy mental habits of the Middle Age, but for the most part of a somewhat theatrical kind, imitations of Francis and Dominic or of their earlier imitators. In Pascal they are original, and have all their seriousness. *Que je n'en sois jamais séparé—pas séparé éternellement*, he repeats, or makes that strange sort of MS. amulet, of which his sister tells us, repeat for him. *Cast me not away from Thy presence; and take not Thy Holy Spirit from me.* It is *table rase* he is trying to make of himself, that He might reign there absolutely alone, who, however, as he was bound to think, had made and blest all those things he declined to accept. Deeper and deeper, then, he retreated into the renunciate life. He could not, had he wished, deprive himself of that his greatest gift—literally a gift he might have thought it not to be buried but accounted for—the gift of *le beau dire*, of writing beautifully. "*Il avoit renoncé depuis longtemps aux sciences purement humains.*" To him who had known them so well, and as if by intuition, those abstract and perdurable forms of service might well have seemed a part of "the Lord's doing, marvellous in our eyes," as his favourite Psalm cxix., the psalm *des petites heures*, the cxviii. of the Vulgate, says.[2] These, too, he counts now as but a variety of *le néant* and vanity of things. He no longer records, therefore, the mathematical

---

2. The words here cited are, however, from Psalm cxviii., the cxvii. of the Vulgate, and not from Pascal's favourite Psalm. (C.L.S.) *[Shadwell's editorial note in* Miscellaneous Studies.*]*

aperçus that may visit him; and in his scruples, his suspicions of visible beauty, he interests us as precisely an inversion of what is called the æsthetic life.

19. Yet his faith, as in the days of the Middle Age, had been supported, rewarded, by what he believed to be visible miracle among the strange lights and shades of that retired place. Pascal's niece, the daughter of Madame Périer, a girl ten years of age, suffered from a disease of the eyes pronounced to be incurable. The disease was a peculiarly distressing one, the sort of affliction which, falling on a young child, may lead one to question the presence of divine justice in the world, makes one long that miracles were possible. Well! Pascal, for one, believed that on occasion that profound aspiration had been followed up by the power desired. A thorn from the crown of Jesus, as was believed, had been lately brought to the Port-Royal du Faubourg S. Jacques in Paris, and was one day applied devoutly to the eye of the suffering child. What followed was an immediate and complete cure, fully attested by experts. *Ah! Thou hast given him his heart's desire: and hast not denied him the request of his lips.* Pascal, and the young girl herself, faithfully to the end of a long life, believed the circumstances to have been miraculous. Otherwise, we do not see that Pascal was ever permitted to enjoy (so to speak) the religion for which he had exchanged so much; that the sense of acceptance, of assurance, had come to him; that for him the Spouse had ever penetrated the veil of the ordinary routine of the means of grace; nothing that corresponded as a matter of clear personal intercourse of the very senses to the greatness of his surrender—who had emptied himself of all other things. Besides, there was some not wholly-explained delay in his reception, in those his last days, of the Sacrament. It was brought to him just in time—"*Voici celui que vous avez tant désiré*"—the ministrant says to the dying man. Pascal was then aged thirty-nine—an age you may remember fancifully noted as fatal to genius.

20. Pascal's "Thoughts," then, we shall not rightly measure but as the outcome, the utterance, of a soul diseased, a soul permanently ill at ease. We find in their constant tension something of insomnia, of that sleeplessness which can never be a quite healthful condition of mind in a human body. Sometimes they are cries, cries of obscure pain rather than thoughts—those great fine sayings which seem to betray by their depth of sound the vast unseen hollow places of nature, of humanity, just beneath one's feet or at one's side. Reading them, so modern still are those thoughts, so rich and various in suggestion, that one seems to witness the mental seed-sowing of the next two centuries, and perhaps more, as to those matters with which he concerns himself. Intuitions of a religious genius, they may well be taken also as the final considerations of the natural man, as a religious inquirer on doubt and faith, and their place in things. [...]

NOTRE-DAME D'AMIENS[1]

The greatest and purest of Gothic churches, Notre-Dame d'Amiens, illustrates, by its fine qualities, a characteristic secular movement of the beginning of the thirteenth century. Philosophic writers of French history have explained how, in that and in the two preceding centuries, a great number of the more important towns in eastern and northern France rose against the feudal establishment, and developed severally the local and municipal life of the commune. To guarantee their independence therein they obtained charters from their formal superiors. The Charter of Amiens served as the model for many other communes. Notre-Dame d'Amiens is the church of a commune. In that century of Saint Francis, of Saint Louis, they were still religious. But over against monastic interests, as identified with a central authority—king, emperor, or pope—they pushed forward the local, and, so to call it, secular authority of their bishops, the flower of the "secular clergy" in all its mundane astuteness, ready enough to make their way as the natural Protectors of such townships. The people of Amiens, for instance, under a powerful episcopal patron, invested their civic pride in a vast cathedral, outrivalling neighbours, as being in effect their parochial church, and promoted there the new, revolutionary, Gothic manner, at the expense of the derivative and traditional, Roman or Romanesque, style, the imperial style, of the great monastic churches. Nay, those grand and beautiful *people's* churches of the thirteenth century, churches pre-eminently of "Our Lady," concurred also with certain novel humanistic movements of religion itself at that period, above all with the expansion of what is reassuring and popular in the worship of Mary, as a tender and accessible, though almost irresistible, intercessor with her severe and awful Son.

2. Hence the splendour, the space, the novelty, of the great French cathedrals in the first Pointed style, monuments for the most part of the artistic genius of laymen, significant pre-eminently of that Queen of Gothic churches at Amiens. In most cases those early Pointed churches are entangled, here or there, by the constructions of the old round-arched style, the heavy, Norman or other, Romanesque chapel or aisle, side by side, though in strong contrast with, the soaring new Gothic of nave or transept. But of that older manner of the round arch, the *plein-cintre*, Amiens has nowhere, or almost nowhere, a trace. The

---

1. Published in the *Nineteenth Century*, March 1894, and now reprinted by the kind permission of the proprietors. *[Editorial note in* Miscellaneous Studies.*]*

Pointed style, fully pronounced, but in all the purity of its first period, found here its completest expression. And while those venerable, Romanesque, profoundly characteristic, monastic churches, the gregarious product of long centuries, are for the most part anonymous, as if to illustrate from the first a certain personal tendency which came in with the Gothic manner, we know the name of the architect under whom, in the year A.D. 1220, the building of the church of Amiens began—a layman, Robert de Luzarches.

3. Light and space—floods of light, space for a vast congregation, for all the people of Amiens, for their movements, with something like the height and width of heaven itself enclosed above them to breathe in;—you see at a glance that this is what the ingenuity of the Pointed method of building has here secured. For breadth, for the easy flow of a processional torrent, there is nothing like the "ambulatory," the aisle of the choir and transepts. And the entire area is on one level. There are here no flights of steps upward, as at Canterbury, no descending to dark crypts, as in so many Italian churches—a few low, broad steps to gain the choir, two or three to the high altar. To a large extent the old pavement remains, though almost worn-out by the footsteps of centuries. Priceless, though not composed of precious material, it gains its effect by ingenuity and variety in the patterning, zig-zags, chequers, mazes, prevailing respectively, in white and grey, in great square, alternate spaces—the original floor of a medieval church for once untouched. The massive square bases of the pillars of a Romanesque church, harshly angular, obstruct, sometimes cruelly, the standing, the movements, of a multitude of persons. To carry such a multitude conveniently round them is the matter-of-fact motive of the gradual chiselling away, the softening of the angles, the graceful compassing, of the Gothic base, till in our own Perpendicular period it all but disappears. You may study that tendency appropriately in the one church of Amiens; for such in effect Notre-Dame has always been. That circumstance is illustrated by the great font, the oldest thing here, an oblong trough, perhaps an ancient saintly coffin, with four quaint prophetic figures at the angles, carved from a single block of stone. To it, as to the baptistery of an Italian town, not so long since all the babes of Amiens used to come for christening.

4. Strange as it may seem, in this "queen" of Gothic churches, *l'église ogivale par excellence*, there is nothing of mystery in the vision, which yet surprises, over and over again, the eye of the visitor who enters at the western doorway. From the flagstone at one's foot to the distant keystone of the *chevet*, noblest of its species—reminding you of how many largely graceful things, sails of a ship in the wind, and the like!—at one view the whole is visible, intelligible;—the integrity of the first design; how later additions affixed themselves thereto; how the rich ornament gathered upon it; the increasing richness of the choir;

its glazed triforium; the realms of light which expand in the chapels beyond; the astonishing boldness of the vault, the astonishing lightness of what keeps it above one; the unity, yet the variety of perspective. There is no mystery here, and indeed no repose. Like the age which projected it, like the impulsive communal movement which was here its motive, the Pointed style at Amiens is full of excitement. Go, for repose, to classic work, with the simple vertical law of pressure downwards, or to its Lombard, Rhenish, or Norman derivatives. Here, rather, you are conscious restlessly of that sustained equilibrium of oblique pressure on all sides, which is the essence of the hazardous Gothic construction, a construction of which the "flying buttress" is the most significant feature. Across the clear glass of the great windows of the triforium you see it, feel it, at its Atlas-work audaciously. "A pleasant thing it is to behold the sun" those first Gothic builders would seem to have said to themselves; and at Amiens, for instance, the walls have disappeared; the entire building is composed of its windows. Those who built it might have had for their one and only purpose to enclose as large a space as possible with the given material.

5. No; the peculiar Gothic buttress, with its double, triple, fourfold flights, while it makes such marvels possible, securing light and space and graceful effect, relieving the pillars within of their massiveness, is not a restful architectural feature. Consolidation of matter naturally on the move, security for settlement in a very complex system of construction—that is avowedly a part of the Gothic situation, the Gothic problem. With the genius which contended, though not always quite successfully, with this difficult problem, came also novel æsthetic effect, a whole volume of delightful æsthetic effects. For the mere *melody* of Greek architecture, for the sense as it were of music in the opposition of successive sounds, you got *harmony*, the richer music generated by opposition of sounds in one and the same moment; and were gainers. And then, in contrast with the classic manner, and the Romanesque survivals from it, the vast complexity of the Gothic style seemed, as if consciously, to correspond to the richness, the expressiveness, the thousandfold influence of the Catholic religion, in the thirteenth century still in natural movement in every direction. The later Gothic of the fifteenth and sixteenth centuries tended to conceal, as it now took for granted, the structural use of the buttress, for example; seemed to turn it into a mere occasion for ornament, not always pleasantly:—while the ornament was out of place, the structure failed. Such falsity is far enough away from what at Amiens is really of the thirteenth century. In this pre-eminently "secular" church, the execution, in all the defiance of its method, is direct, frank, clearly apparent, with the result not only of reassuring the intelligence, but of keeping one's curiosity also continually on the alert, as we linger in these restless aisles.

6. The integrity of the edifice, together with its volume of light, has indeed been diminished by the addition of a range of chapels, beyond the proper limits of the aisles, north and south. Not a part of the original design, these chapels were formed for private uses in the fourteenth century, by the device of walling in and vaulting the open spaces between the great buttresses of the nave. Under the broad but subdued sunshine which falls through range upon range of windows, reflected from white wall and roof and gallery, soothing to the eye, while it allows you to see the delicate carved work in all its refinement of touch, it is only as an after-thought, an artificial after-thought, that you regret the lost stained glass, or the vanished mural colour, if such to any large extent there ever were. The best stained glass is often that stained by weather, by centuries of weather, and we may well be grateful for the amazing cheerfulness of the interior of Amiens, as we actually find it. Windows of the richest remain, indeed, in the apsidal chapels; and the rose-windows of the transepts are known, from the prevailing tones of their stained glass, as Fire and Water, the western rose symbolising in like manner Earth and Air, as respectively green and blue. But there is no reason to suppose that the interior was ever so darkened as to prevent one's seeing, really and clearly, the dainty ornament, which from the first abounded here; the floriated architectural detail; the broad band of flowers and foliage, thick and deep and purely sculptured, above the arches of nave and choir and transepts, and wreathing itself continuously round the embedded piers which support the roof; with the woodwork, the illuminated metal, the magnificent tombs, the jewellers' work in the chapels. One precious, early thirteenth-century window of *grisaille* remains, exquisite in itself, interesting as evidence of the sort of decoration which originally filled the larger number of the windows. *Grisaille*, with its lace-work of transparent grey, set here and there with a ruby, a sapphire, a gemmed medallion, interrupts the clear light on things hardly more than the plain glass, of which indeed such windows are mainly composed. The finely designed frames of iron for the support of the glass, in the windows from which even this decoration is gone, still remain, to the delight of those who are knowing in the matter.

7. Very ancient light, this seems, at any rate, as if it had been lying imprisoned thus for long centuries; were in fact the light over which the great vault originally closed, now become almost substance of thought, one might fancy,—a mental object or medium. We are reminded that after all we must of necessity look on the great churches of the Middle Age with other eyes than those who built or first worshipped in them; that there is something verily worth having, and a just equivalent for something else lost, in the mere effect of time, and that the salt of all æsthetic study is in the question,—What, precisely what, is this

to *me*? You and I, perhaps, should not care much for the mural colouring of a medieval church, could we see it as it was; might think it crude, and in the way. What little remains of it at Amiens has parted, indeed, in the course of ages, with its shrillness and its coarse grain. And in this matter certainly, in view of Gothic polychrome, our difference from the people of the thirteenth century is radical. We have, as it was very unlikely they should have, a curiosity, a very pleasurable curiosity, in the mere working of the stone they built with, and in the minute facts of their construction, which their colouring, and the layer of plaster it involved, disguised or hid. We may think that in architecture stone is the most beautiful of all things. Modern hands have replaced the colour on some of the tombs here—the effigies, the tabernacles above—skilfully as may be, and have but deprived them of their dignity. Medieval colouring, in fact, must have improved steadily, as it decayed, almost till there came to be no question of colour at all. In architecture, close as it is to men's lives and their history, the visible result of time is a large factor in the realised æsthetic value, and what a true architect will in due measure always trust to. A false restoration only frustrates the proper ripening of his work.

8. If we may credit our modern eyes, then, those old, very secular builders aimed at, they achieved, an immense cheerfulness in their great church, with a purpose which still pursued them into their minuter decoration. The conventional vegetation of the Romanesque, its blendings of human or animal with vegetable form, in cornice or capital, have given way here, in the first Pointed style, to a pleasanter, because more natural, mode of fancy; to veritable forms of vegetable life, flower or leaf, from meadow and woodside, though still indeed with a certain survival of the grotesque in a confusion of the leaf with the flower, which the subsequent Decorated period will wholly purge away in its perfect garden-borders. It was not with monastic artists and artisans that the sheds and workshops around Amiens Cathedral were filled, as it rose from its foundations through fifty years; and those lay schools of art, with their communistic sentiment, to which in the thirteenth century the great episcopal builders must needs resort, would in the natural course of things tend towards naturalism. The subordinate arts also were no longer at the monastic stage, borrowing inspiration exclusively from the experiences of the cloister, but belonged to guilds of laymen—smiths, painters, sculptors. The great confederation of the "city," the commune, subdivided itself into confederations of citizens. In the natural objects of the first Pointed style there is the freshness as of nature itself, seen and felt for the first time; as if, in contrast, those older cloistral workmen had but fed their imagination in an embarrassed, imprisoned, and really decadent manner, or mere reminiscence of, or prescriptions about, things visible.

9. Congruous again with the popularity of the builders of Amiens, of their motives, is the wealth, the freedom and abundance, of popular, almost secular, teaching, here afforded, in the carving especially, within and without; an open Bible, in place of later legend, as at monastic Vézelay,—the Bible treated as a book about men and women, and other persons equally real, but blent with lessons, with the liveliest observations, on the lives of men as they were then and now, what they do, and how they do it, or did it then, and on the doings of nature which so greatly influence what man does; together with certain impressive metaphysical and moral ideas, a sort of popular scholastic philosophy, or as if it were the virtues and vices Aristotle defines, or the characters of Theophrastus, translated into stone. Above all, it is to be observed that as a result of this spirit, this "free" spirit, in it, art has at last become personal. The artist, as such, appears at Amiens, as elsewhere, in the thirteenth century; and, by making his personal way of conception and execution prevail there, renders his own work vivid and organic, and apt to catch the interest of other people. He is no longer a Byzantine, but a Greek—an unconscious Greek. Proof of this is in the famous *Beau-Dieu* of Amiens, as they call that benign, almost classically proportioned figure, on the central pillar of the great west doorway; though in fact neither that, nor anything else on the west front of Amiens, is quite the best work here. For that we must look rather to the sculpture of the portal of the south transept, called, from a certain image there, *Portail de la Vierge dorée*, gilded at the expense of some unknown devout person at the beginning of the last century. A presentation of the mystic, the delicately miraculous, story of Saint Honoré, eighth Bishop of Amiens, and his companions, with its voices, its intuitions, and celestial intimations, it has evoked a correspondent method of work at once *naïve* and nicely expressive. The *rose*, or *roue*, above it, carries on the outer rim seventeen personages, ascending and descending—another piece of popular philosophy—the wheel of fortune, or of human life.

10. And they were great brass-founders, surely, who at that early day modelled and cast the tombs of the Bishops Evrard and Geoffrey, vast plates of massive black bronze in half-relief, like abstract thoughts of those grand old prelatic persons. The tomb of Evrard, who laid the foundations (*qui fundamenta hujus basilicæ locavit*), is not quite as it was. Formerly it was sunk in the pavement, while the tomb of Bishop Geoffrey opposite (it was he closed in the mighty vault of the nave: *hanc basilicam culmen usque perduxit*), itself vaulted-over the space of the grave beneath. The supreme excellence of those original workmen, the journeymen of Robert de Luzarches and his successor, would seem indeed to have inspired others, who have been at their best here, down to the days of Louis the Fourteenth. It prompted, we may think, a high level of execution,

through many revolutions of taste in such matters; in the marvellous furniture of the choir, for instance, like a whole wood, say a thicket of old hawthorn, with its curved topmost branches spared, slowly transformed by the labour of a whole family of artists, during fourteen years, into the stalls, in number one hundred and ten, with nearly four thousand figures. Yet they are but on a level with the Flamboyant carved and coloured enclosures of the choir, with the histories of John the Baptist, whose face-bones are here preserved, and of Saint Firmin—popular saint, who protects the houses of Amiens from fire. Even the screens of forged iron around the sanctuary, work of the seventeenth century, appear actually to soar, in their way, in concert with the airy Gothic structure; to let the daylight pass as it will; to have come, they too, from smiths, odd as it may seem at just that time, with some touch of inspiration in them. In the beginning of the fifteenth century they had reared against a certain bald space of wall, between the great portal and the western "rose," an organ, a lofty, many-chambered, veritable house of church-music, rich in azure and gold, finished above at a later day, not incongruously, in the quaint, pretty manner of Henri-Deux. And those who are interested in the curiosities of ritual, of the old provincial Gallican "uses," will be surprised to find one where they might least have expected it. The reserved Eucharist still *hangs* suspended in a pyx, formed like a dove, in the midst of that lamentable "glory" of the eighteenth century in the central bay of the sanctuary, all the poor, gaudy, gilt rays converging towards it. There are days in the year in which the great church is still literally filled with reverent worshippers, and if you come late to service you push the doors in vain against the closely serried shoulders of the good people of Amiens, one and all in black for church-holiday attire. Then, one and all, they intone the *Tantum ergo* (did it ever sound so in the Middle Ages?) as the Eucharist, after a long procession, rises once more into its resting-place.

11. If the Greeks, as at least one of them says, really believed there could be no true beauty without bigness, that thought certainly is most specious in regard to architecture; and the thirteenth-century church of Amiens is one of the three or four largest buildings in the world, out of all proportion to any Greek building, both in that and in the multitude of its external sculpture. The chapels of the nave are embellished without by a double range of single figures, or groups, commemorative of the persons, the mysteries, to which they are respectively dedicated—the gigantic form of Christopher, the Mystery of the Annunciation.

12. The builders of the church seem to have projected no very noticeable towers; though it is conventional to regret their absence, especially with visitors from England, where indeed cathedral and other towers are apt to

be good, and really make their mark. Robert de Luzarches and his successors aimed rather at the domical outline, with its central point at the centre of the church, in the spire or *flèche*. The existing spire is a wonderful mass of carpentry of the beginning of the sixteenth century, at which time the lead that carefully wraps every part of it was heavily gilt. The great western towers are lost in the west front, the grandest, perhaps the earliest, example of its species—three profound, sculptured portals; a double gallery above, the upper gallery carrying colossal images of twenty-two kings of the House of Judah, ancestors of Our Lady; then the great rose; above it the ringers' gallery, half masking the gable of the nave, and uniting at their topmost storeys the twin, but not exactly equal or similar, towers, oddly oblong in plan, as if never intended to carry pyramids or spires. They overlook an immense distance in those flat, peat-digging, black and green regions, with rather cheerless rivers, and are the centre of an architectural region wider still—of a group to which Soissons, far beyond the woods of Compiègne, belongs, with St. Quentin, and, towards the west, a too ambitious rival, Beauvais, which has stood however—what we now see of it—for six centuries.

13. It is a spare, rather sad world at most times that Notre-Dame d'Amiens thus broods over; a country with little else to be proud of; the sort of world, in fact, which makes the range of conceptions embodied in these cliffs of quarried and carved stone all the more welcome as a hopeful complement to the meagreness of most people's present existence, and its apparent ending in a sparely built coffin under the flinty soil, and grey, driving sea-winds. In Notre-Dame, therefore, and her sisters, there is not only a common method of construction, a single definable type, different from that of other French latitudes, but a correspondent common sentiment also; something which speaks, amid an immense achievement just here of what is beautiful and great, of the necessity of an immense effort in the natural course of things, of what you may see quaintly designed in one of those hieroglyphic carvings—*radix de terra sitienti:* "a root out of a dry ground."

THE CHILD IN THE HOUSE[1]

As Florian Deleal walked, one hot afternoon, he overtook by the wayside a poor aged man, and, as he seemed weary with the road, helped him on with the burden which he carried, a certain distance. And as the man told his story, it chanced that he named the place, a little place in the neighbourhood of a great city, where Florian had passed his earliest years, but which he had never since seen, and, the story told, went forward on his journey comforted. And that night, like a reward for his pity, a dream of that place came to Florian, a dream which did for him the office of the finer sort of memory, bringing its object to mind with a great clearness, yet, as sometimes happens in dreams, raised a little above itself, and above ordinary retrospect. The true aspect of the place, especially of the house there in which he had lived as a child, the fashion of its doors, its hearths, its windows, the very scent upon the air of it, was with him in sleep for a season; only, with tints more musically blent on wall and floor, and some finer light and shadow running in and out along its curves and angles, and with all its little carvings daintier. He awoke with a sigh at the thought of almost thirty years which lay between him and that place, yet with a flutter of pleasure still within him at the fair light, as if it were a smile, upon it. And it happened that this accident of his dream was just the thing needed for the beginning of a certain design he then had in view, the noting, namely, of some things in the story of his spirit—in that process of brain-building by which we are, each one of us, what we are. With the image of the place so clear and favourable upon him, he fell to thinking of himself therein, and how his thoughts had grown up to him. In that half-spiritualised house he could watch the better, over again, the gradual expansion of the soul which had come to be there—of which indeed, through the law which makes the material objects about them so large an element in children's lives, it had actually become a part; inward and outward being woven through and through each other into one inextricable texture—half, tint and trace and accident of homely colour and form, from the wood and the bricks; half, mere soul-stuff, floated thither from who knows how far. In the house and garden of his dream he saw a child moving, and could divide the main streams at least of the winds that had played on him, and study so the first stage in that mental journey.

2. The *old house*, as when Florian talked of it afterwards he always called it, (as all children do, who can recollect a change of home, soon enough but

---

[1]. Published in *Macmillan's Magazine*, Aug. 1878. *[Editorial note in Miscellaneous Studies.]*

not too soon to mark a period in their lives) really was an old house; and an element of French descent in its inmates—descent from Watteau, the old court-painter, one of whose gallant pieces still hung in one of the rooms—might explain, together with some other things, a noticeable trimness and comely whiteness about everything there—the curtains, the couches, the paint on the walls with which the light and shadow played so delicately; might explain also the tolerance of the great poplar in the garden, a tree most often despised by English people, but which French people love, having observed a certain fresh way its leaves have of dealing with the wind, making it sound, in never so slight a stirring of the air, like running water.

3. The old-fashioned, low wainscoting went round the rooms, and up the staircase with carved balusters and shadowy angles, landing half-way up at a broad window, with a swallow's nest below the sill, and the blossom of an old pear-tree showing across it in late April, against the blue, below which the perfumed juice of the find of fallen fruit in autumn was so fresh. At the next turning came the closet which held on its deep shelves the best china. Little angel faces and reedy flutings stood out round the fireplace of the children's room. And on the top of the house, above the large attic, where the white mice ran in the twilight—an infinite, unexplored wonderland of childish treasures, glass beads, empty scent-bottles still sweet, thrum of coloured silks, among its lumber—a flat space of roof, railed round, gave a view of the neighbouring steeples; for the house, as I said, stood near a great city, which sent up heavenwards, over the twisting weather-vanes, not seldom, its beds of rolling cloud and smoke, touched with storm or sunshine. But the child of whom I am writing did not hate the fog because of the crimson lights which fell from it sometimes upon the chimneys, and the whites which gleamed through its openings, on summer mornings, on turret or pavement. For it is false to suppose that a child's sense of beauty is dependent on any choiceness or special fineness, in the objects which present themselves to it, though this indeed comes to be the rule with most of us in later life; earlier, in some degree, we see inwardly; and the child finds for itself, and with unstinted delight, a difference for the sense, in those whites and reds through the smoke on very homely buildings, and in the gold of the dandelions at the road-side, just beyond the houses, where not a handful of earth is virgin and untouched, in the lack of better ministries to its desire of beauty.

4. This house then stood not far beyond the gloom and rumours of the town, among high garden-wall, bright all summer-time with Golden-rod, and brown-and-golden Wall-flower—*Flos Parietis*, as the children's Latin-reading father taught them to call it, while he was with them. Tracing back the threads of his complex spiritual habit, as he was used in after years to do, Florian found

that he owed to the place many tones of sentiment afterwards customary with him, certain inward lights under which things most naturally presented themselves to him. The coming and going of travellers to the town along the way, the shadow of the streets, the sudden breath of the neighbouring gardens, the singular brightness of bright weather there, its singular darknesses which linked themselves in his mind to certain engraved illustrations in the old big Bible at home, the coolness of the dark, cavernous shops round the great church, with its giddy winding stair up to the pigeons and the bells—a citadel of peace in the heart of the trouble—all this acted on his childish fancy, so that ever afterwards the like aspects and incidents never failed to throw him into a well-recognised imaginative mood, seeming actually to have become a part of the texture of his mind. Also, Florian could trace home to this point a pervading preference in himself for a kind of comeliness and dignity, an *urbanity* literally, in modes of life, which he connected with the pale people of towns, and which made him susceptible to a kind of exquisite satisfaction in the trimness and well-considered grace of certain things and persons he afterwards met with, here and there, in his way through the world.

5. So the child of whom I am writing lived on there quietly; things without thus ministering to him, as he sat daily at the window with the birdcage hanging below it, and his mother taught him to read, wondering at the ease with which he learned, and at the quickness of his memory. The perfume of the little flowers of the lime-tree fell through the air upon them like rain; while time seemed to move ever more slowly to the murmur of the bees in it, till it almost stood still on June afternoons. How insignificant, at the moment, seem the influences of the sensible things which are tossed and fall and lie about us, so, or so, in the environment of early childhood. How indelibly, as we afterwards discover, they affect us; with what capricious attractions and associations they figure themselves on the white paper, the smooth wax, of our ingenuous souls, as "with lead in the rock for ever," giving form and feature, and as it were assigned house-room in our memory, to early experiences of feeling and thought, which abide with us ever afterwards, thus, and not otherwise. The realities and passions, the rumours of the greater world without, steal in upon us, each by its own special little passage-way, through the wall of custom about us; and never afterwards quite detach themselves from this or that accident, or trick, in the mode of their first entrance to us. Our susceptibilities, the discovery of our powers, manifold experiences—our various experiences of the coming and going of bodily pain, for instance—belong to this or the other well-remembered place in the material habitation—that little white room with the window across which the heavy blossoms could beat so peevishly in the wind, with just that particular catch or throb, such a sense of teasing in

it, on gusty mornings; and the early habitation thus gradually becomes a sort of material shrine or sanctuary of sentiment; a system of visible symbolism interweaves itself through all our thoughts and passions; and irresistibly, little shapes, voices, accidents—the angle at which the sun in the morning fell on the pillow—become parts of the great chain wherewith we are bound.

6. Thus far, for Florian, what all this had determined was a peculiarly strong sense of home—so forcible a motive with all of us—prompting to us our customary love of the earth, and the larger part of our fear of death, that revulsion we have from it, as from something strange, untried, unfriendly; though life-long imprisonment, they tell you, and final banishment from home is a thing bitterer still; the looking forward to but a short space, a mere childish *goûter* and dessert of it, before the end, being so great a resource of effort to pilgrims and wayfarers, and the soldier in distant quarters, and lending, in lack of that, some power of solace to the thought of sleep in the home churchyard, at least—dead cheek by dead cheek, and with the rain soaking in upon one from above.

7. So powerful is this instinct, and yet accidents like those I have been speaking of so mechanically determine it; its essence being indeed the early familiar, as constituting our ideal, or typical conception, of rest and security. Out of so many possible conditions, just this for you and that for me, brings ever the unmistakeable realisation of the delightful *chez soi*; this for the Englishman, for me and you, with the closely-drawn white curtain and the shaded lamp; that, quite other, for the wandering Arab, who folds his tent every morning, and makes his sleeping-place among haunted ruins, or in old tombs.

8. With Florian then the sense of home became singularly intense, his good fortune being that the special character of his home was in itself so essentially home-like. As after many wanderings I have come to fancy that some parts of Surrey and Kent are, for Englishmen, the true landscape, true home-counties, by right, partly, of a certain earthy warmth in the yellow of the sand below their gorse-bushes, and of a certain grey-blue mist after rain, in the hollows of the hills there, welcome to fatigued eyes, and never seen farther south; so I think that the sort of house I have described, with precisely those proportions of red-brick and green, and with a just perceptible monotony in the subdued order of it, for its distinguishing note, is for Englishmen at least typically home-like. And so for Florian that general human instinct was reinforced by this special home-likeness in the place his wandering soul had happened to light on, as, in the second degree, its body and earthly tabernacle; the sense of harmony between his soul and its physical environment became, for a time at least, like perfectly played music, and the life led there singularly tranquil and filled with a curious sense of self-possession. The love of security, of an habitually

undisputed standing-ground or sleeping-place, came to count for much in the generation and correcting of his thoughts, and afterwards as a salutary principle of restraint in all his wanderings of spirit. The wistful yearning towards home, in absence from it, as the shadows of evening deepened, and he followed in thought what was doing there from hour to hour, interpreted to him much of a yearning and regret he experienced afterwards, towards he knew not what, out of strange ways of feeling and thought in which, from time to time, his spirit found itself alone; and in the tears shed in such absences there seemed always to be some soul-subduing foretaste of what his last tears might be.

9. And the sense of security could hardly have been deeper, the quiet of the child's soul being one with the quiet of its home, a place "inclosed" and "sealed." But upon this assured place, upon the child's assured soul which resembled it, there came floating in from the larger world without, as at windows left ajar unknowingly, or over the high garden walls, two streams of impressions, the sentiments of beauty and pain—recognitions of the visible, tangible, audible loveliness of things, as a very real and somewhat tyrannous element in them—and of the sorrow of the world, of grown people and children and animals, as a thing not to be put by in them. From this point he could trace two predominant processes of mental change in him—the growth of an almost diseased sensibility to the spectacle of suffering, and, parallel with this, the rapid growth of a certain capacity of fascination by bright colour and choice form—the sweet curvings, for instance, of the lips of those who seemed to him comely persons, modulated in such delicate unison to the things they said or sang,—marking early the activity in him of a more than customary sensuousness, "the lust of the eye," as the Preacher says, which might lead him, one day, how far! Could he have foreseen the weariness of the way! In music sometimes the two sorts of impressions came together, and he would weep, to the surprise of older people. Tears of joy too the child knew, also to older people's surprise; real tears, once, of relief from long-strung, childish expectation, when he found returned at evening, with new roses in her cheeks, the little sister who had been to a place where there was a wood, and brought back for him a treasure of fallen acorns, and black crow's feathers, and his peace at finding her again near him mingled all night with some intimate sense of the distant forest, the rumour of its breezes, with the glossy blackbirds aslant and the branches lifted in them, and of the perfect nicety of the little cups that fell. So those two elementary apprehensions of the tenderness and of the colour in things grew apace in him, and were seen by him afterwards to send their roots back into the beginnings of life.

10. Let me note first some of the occasions of his recognition of the element of pain in things—incidents, now and again, which seemed suddenly to

awake in him the whole force of that sentiment which Goethe has called the *Weltschmerz*, and in which the concentrated sorrow of the world seemed suddenly to lie heavy upon him. A book lay in an old book-case, of which he cared to remember one picture—a woman sitting, with hands bound behind her, the dress, the cap, the hair, folded with a simplicity which touched him strangely, as if not by her own hands, but with some ambiguous care at the hands of others—Queen Marie Antoinette, on her way to execution—we all remember David's drawing, meant merely to make her ridiculous. The face that had been so high had learned to be mute and resistless; but out of its very resistlessness, seemed now to call on men to have pity, and forbear; and he took note of that, as he closed the book, as a thing to look at again, if he should at any time find himself tempted to be cruel. Again, he would never quite forget the appeal in the small sister's face, in the garden under the lilacs, terrified at a spider lighted on her sleeve. He could trace back to the look then noted a certain mercy he conceived always for people in fear, even of little things, which seemed to make him, though but for a moment, capable of almost any sacrifice of himself. Impressible, susceptible persons, indeed, who had had their sorrows, lived about him; and this sensibility was due in part to the tacit influence of their presence, enforcing upon him habitually the fact that there are those who pass their days, as a matter of course, in a sort of "going quietly." Most poignantly of all he could recall, in unfading minutest circumstance, the cry on the stair, sounding bitterly through the house, and struck into his soul for ever, of an aged woman, his father's sister, come now to announce his death in distant India; how it seemed to make the aged woman like a child again; and, he knew not why, but this fancy was full of pity to him. There were the little sorrows of the dumb animals too—of the white angora, with a dark tail like an ermine's, and a face like a flower, who fell into a lingering sickness, and became quite delicately human in its valetudinarianism, and came to have a hundred different expressions of voice—how it grew worse and worse, till it began to feel the light too much for it, and at last, after one wild morning of pain, the little soul flickered away from the body, quite worn to death already, and now but feebly retaining it.

11. So he wanted another pet; and as there were starlings about the place, which could be taught to speak, one of them was caught, and he meant to treat it kindly; but in the night its young ones could be heard crying after it, and the responsive cry of the mother-bird towards them; and at last, with the first light, though not till after some debate with himself, he went down and opened the cage, and saw a sharp bound of the prisoner up to her nestlings; and therewith came the sense of remorse,—that he too was become an accomplice in moving, to the limit of his small power, the springs and handles of that

great machine in things, constructed so ingeniously to play pain-fugues on the delicate nerve-work of living creatures.

12. I have remarked how, in the process of our brain-building, as the house of thought in which we live gets itself together, like some airy bird's-nest of floating thistle-down and chance straws, compact at last, little accidents have their consequence; and thus it happened that, as he walked one evening, a garden gate, usually closed, stood open; and lo! within, a great red hawthorn in full flower, embossing heavily the bleached and twisted trunk and branches, so aged that there were but few green leaves thereon—a plumage of tender, crimson fire out of the heart of the dry wood. The perfume of the tree had now and again reached him, in the currents of the wind, over the wall, and he had wondered what might be behind it, and was now allowed to fill his arms with the flowers—flowers enough for all the old blue-china pots along the chimney-piece, making *fête* in the children's room. Was it some periodic moment in the expansion of soul within him, or mere trick of heat in the heavily-laden summer air? But the beauty of the thing struck home to him feverishly; and in dreams all night he loitered along a magic roadway of crimson flowers, which seemed to open ruddily in thick, fresh masses about his feet, and fill softly all the little hollows in the banks on either side. Always afterwards, summer by summer, as the flowers came on, the blossom of the red hawthorn still seemed to him absolutely the reddest of all things; and the goodly crimson, still alive in the works of old Venetian masters or old Flemish tapestries, called out always from afar the recollection of the flame in those perishing little petals, as it pulsed gradually out of them, kept long in the drawers of an old cabinet. Also then, for the first time, he seemed to experience a passionateness in his relation to fair outward objects, an inexplicable excitement in their presence, which disturbed him, and from which he half longed to be free. A touch of regret or desire mingled all night with the remembered presence of the red flowers, and their perfume in the darkness about him; and the longing for some undivined, entire possession of them was the beginning of a revelation to him, growing ever clearer, with the coming of the gracious summer guise of fields and trees and persons in each succeeding year, of a certain, at times seemingly exclusive, predominance in his interests, of beautiful physical things, a kind of tyranny of the senses over him.

13. In later years he came upon philosophies which occupied him much in the estimate of the proportion of the sensuous and the ideal elements in human knowledge, the relative parts they bear in it; and, in his intellectual scheme, was led to assign very little to the abstract thought, and much to its sensible vehicle or occasion. Such metaphysical speculation did but reinforce what was instinctive in his way of receiving the world, and for him, everywhere, that

sensible vehicle or occasion became, perhaps only too surely, the necessary concomitant of any perception of things, real enough to be of any weight or reckoning, in his house of thought. There were times when he could think of the necessity he was under of associating all thoughts to touch and sight, as a sympathetic link between himself and actual, feeling, living objects; a protest in favour of real men and women against mere grey, unreal abstractions; and he remembered gratefully how the Christian religion, hardly less than the religion of the ancient Greeks, translating so much of its spiritual verity into things that may be seen, condescends in part to sanction this infirmity, if so it be, of our human existence, wherein the world of sense is so much with us, and welcomed this thought as a kind of keeper and sentinel over his soul therein. But certainly, he came more and more to be unable to care for, or think of soul but as in an actual body, or of any world but that wherein are water and trees, and where men and women look, so or so, and press actual hands. It was the trick even his pity learned, fastening those who suffered in anywise to his affections by a kind of sensible attachments. He would think of Julian, fallen into incurable sickness, as spoiled in the sweet blossom of his skin like pale amber, and his honey-like hair; of Cecil, early dead, as cut off from the lilies, from golden summer days, from women's voices; and then what comforted him a little was the thought of the turning of the child's flesh to violets in the turf above him. And thinking of the very poor, it was not the things which most men care most for that he yearned to give them; but fairer roses, perhaps, and power to taste quite as they will, at their ease and not task-burdened, a certain desirable, clear light in the new morning, through which sometimes he had noticed them, quite unconscious of it, on their way to their early toil.

14. So he yielded himself to these things, to be played upon by them like a musical instrument, and began to note with deepening watchfulness, but always with some puzzled, unutterable longing in his enjoyment, the phases of the seasons and of the growing or waning day, down even to the shadowy changes wrought on bare wall or ceiling—the light cast up from the snow, bringing out their darkest angles; the brown light in the cloud, which meant rain; that almost too austere clearness, in the protracted light of the lengthening day, before warm weather began, as if it lingered but to make a severer workday, with the school-books opened earlier and later; that beam of June sunshine, at last, as he lay awake before the time, a way of gold-dust across the darkness; all the humming, the freshness, the perfume of the garden seemed to lie upon it—and coming in one afternoon in September, along the red gravel walk, to look for a basket of yellow crab-apples left in the cool, old parlour, he remembered it the more, and how the colours struck upon him, because a wasp on one bitten apple stung him, and he felt the passion of sudden, severe pain. For this too

brought its curious reflexions; and, in relief from it, he would wonder over it—how it had then been with him—puzzled at the depth of the charm or spell over him, which lay, for a little while at least, in the mere absence of pain; once, especially, when an older boy taught him to make flowers of sealing-wax, and he had burnt his hand badly at the lighted taper, and been unable to sleep. He remembered that also afterwards, as a sort of typical thing—a white vision of heat about him, clinging closely, through the languid scent of the ointments put upon the place to make it well.

15. Also, as he felt this pressure upon him of the sensible world, then, as often afterwards, there would come another sort of curious questioning how the last impressions of eye and ear might happen to him, how they would find him—the scent of the last flower, the soft yellowness of the last morning, the last recognition of some object of affection, hand or voice; it could not be but that the latest look of the eyes, before their final closing, would be strangely vivid; one would go with the hot tears, the cry, the touch of the wistful bystander, impressed how deeply on one! or would it be, perhaps, a mere frail retiring of all things, great or little, away from one, into a level distance?

16. For with this desire of physical beauty mingled itself early the fear of death—the fear of death intensified by the desire of beauty. Hitherto he had never gazed upon dead faces, as sometimes, afterwards, at the *Morgue* in Paris, or in that fair cemetery at Munich, where all the dead must go and lie in state before burial, behind glass windows, among the flowers and incense and holy candles—the aged clergy with their sacred ornaments, the young men in their dancing-shoes and spotless white linen—after which visits, those waxen, resistless faces would always live with him for many days, making the broadest sunshine sickly. The child had heard indeed of the death of his father, and how, in the Indian station, a fever had taken him, so that though not in action he had yet died as a soldier; and hearing of the "resurrection of the just," he could think of him as still abroad in the world, somehow, for his protection—a grand, though perhaps rather terrible figure, in beautiful soldier's things, like the figure in the picture of Joshua's Vision in the Bible—and of that, round which the mourners moved so softly, and afterwards with such solemn singing, as but a worn-out garment left at a deserted lodging. So it was, until on a summer day he walked with his mother through a fair churchyard. In a bright dress he rambled among the graves, in the gay weather, and so came, in one corner, upon an open grave for a child—a dark space on the brilliant grass—the black mould lying heaped up round it, weighing down the little jewelled branches of the dwarf rose-bushes in flower. And therewith came, full-grown, never wholly to leave him, with the certainty that even children do sometimes die, the physical horror of death, with its wholly selfish recoil

from the association of lower forms of life, and the suffocating weight above. No benign, grave figure in beautiful soldier's things any longer abroad in the world for his protection! only a few poor, piteous bones; and above them, possibly, a certain sort of figure he hoped not to see. For sitting one day in the garden below an open window, he heard people talking, and could not but listen, how, in a sleepless hour, a sick woman had seen one of the dead sitting beside her, come to call her hence; and from the broken talk evolved with much clearness the notion that not all those dead people had really departed to the churchyard, nor were quite so motionless as they looked, but led a secret, half-fugitive life in their old homes, quite free by night, though sometimes visible in the day, dodging from room to room, with no great goodwill towards those who shared the place with them. All night the figure sat beside him in the reveries of his broken sleep, and was not quite gone in the morning—an odd, irreconcileable new member of the household, making the sweet familiar chambers unfriendly and suspect by its uncertain presence. He could have hated the dead he had pitied so, for being thus. Afterwards he came to think of those poor, home-returning ghosts, which all men have fancied to themselves—the *revenants*—pathetically, as crying, or beating with vain hands at the doors, as the wind came, their cries distinguishable in it as a wilder inner note. But, always making death more unfamiliar still, that old experience would ever, from time to time, return to him; even in the living he sometimes caught its likeness; at any time or place, in a moment, the faint atmosphere of the chamber of death would be breathed around him, and the image with the bound chin, the quaint smile, the straight, stiff feet, shed itself across the air upon the bright carpet, amid the gayest company, or happiest communing with himself.

17. To most children the sombre questionings to which impressions like these attach themselves, if they come at all, are actually suggested by religious books, which therefore they often regard with much secret distaste, and dismiss, as far as possible, from their habitual thoughts as a too depressing element in life. To Florian such impressions, these misgivings as to the ultimate tendency of the years, of the relationship between life and death, had been suggested spontaneously in the natural course of his mental growth by a strong innate sense for the soberer tones in things, further strengthened by actual circumstances; and religious sentiment, that system of biblical ideas in which he had been brought up, presented itself to him as a thing that might soften and dignify, and light up as with a "lively hope," a melancholy already deeply settled in him. So he yielded himself easily to religious impressions, and with a kind of mystical appetite for sacred things; the more as they came to him through a saintly person who loved him tenderly, and believed that this early

pre-occupation with them already marked the child out for a saint. He began to love, for their own sakes, church lights, holy days, all that belonged to the comely order of the sanctuary, the secrets of its white linen, and holy vessels, and fonts of pure water; and its hieratic purity and simplicity became the type of something he desired always to have about him in actual life. He pored over the pictures in religious books, and knew by heart the exact mode in which the wrestling angel grasped Jacob, how Jacob looked in his mysterious sleep, how the bells and pomegranates were attached to the hem of Aaron's vestment, sounding sweetly as he glided over the turf of the holy place. His way of conceiving religion came then to be in effect what it ever afterwards remained—a sacred history indeed, but still more a sacred ideal, a transcendent version or representation, under intenser and more expressive light and shade, of human life and its familiar or exceptional incidents, birth, death, marriage, youth, age, tears, joy, rest, sleep, waking—a mirror, towards which men might turn away their eyes from vanity and dullness, and see themselves therein as angels, with their daily meat and drink, even, become a kind of sacred transaction—a complementary strain or burden, applied to our every-day existence, whereby the stray snatches of music in it re-set themselves, and fall into the scheme of some higher and more consistent harmony. A place adumbrated itself in his thoughts, wherein those sacred personalities, which are at once the reflex and the pattern of our nobler phases of life, housed themselves; and this region in his intellectual scheme all subsequent experience did but tend still further to realise and define. Some ideal, hieratic persons he would always need to occupy it and keep a warmth there. And he could hardly understand those who felt no such need at all, finding themselves quite happy without such heavenly companionship, and sacred double of their life, beside them.

18. Thus a constant substitution of the typical for the actual took place in his thoughts. Angels might be met by the way, under English elm or beech-tree; mere messengers seemed like angels, bound on celestial errands; a deep mysticity brooded over real meetings and partings; marriages were made in heaven; and deaths also, with hands of angels thereupon, to bear soul and body quietly asunder, each to its appointed rest. All the acts and accidents of daily life borrowed a sacred colour and significance; the very colours of things became themselves weighty with meanings like the sacred stuffs of Moses' tabernacle, full of penitence or peace. Sentiment, congruous in the first instance only with those divine transactions, the deep, effusive unction of the House of Bethany, was assumed as the due attitude for the reception of our every-day existence; and for a time he walked through the world in a sustained, not unpleasurable awe, generated by the habitual recognition, beside every circumstance and event of life, of its celestial correspondent.

19. Sensibility—the desire of physical beauty—a strange biblical awe, which made any reference to the unseen act on him like solemn music—these qualities the child took away with him, when, at about the age of twelve years, he left the old house, and was taken to live in another place. He had never left home before, and, anticipating much from this change, had long dreamed over it, jealously counting the days till the time fixed for departure should come; had been a little careless about others even, in his strong desire for it—when Lewis fell sick, for instance, and they must wait still two days longer. At last the morning came, very fine; and all things—the very pavement with its dust, at the roadside—seemed to have a white, pearl-like lustre in them. They were to travel by a favourite road on which he had often walked a certain distance, and on one of those two prisoner days, when Lewis was sick, had walked farther than ever before, in his great desire to reach the new place. They had started and gone a little way when a pet bird was found to have been left behind, and must even now—so it presented itself to him—have already all the appealing fierceness and wild self-pity at heart of one left by others to perish of hunger in a closed house; and he returned to fetch it, himself in hardly less stormy distress. But as he passed in search of it from room to room, lying so pale, with a look of meekness in their denudation, and at last through that little, stripped white room, the aspect of the place touched him like the face of one dead; and a clinging back towards it came over him, so intense that he knew it would last long, and spoiling all his pleasure in the realisation of a thing so eagerly anticipated. And so, with the bird found, but himself in an agony of home-sickness, thus capriciously sprung up within him, he was driven quickly away, far into the rural distance, so fondly speculated on, of that favourite country-road.

Explanatory Notes

The aim of these notes is to be 'explanatory' in a broad sense, and to aid understanding by providing cross-references. Wherever the text itself gives us to understand that it is referring to something, but does not provide a sufficiently clear or accurate idea of what that something is (or where to look for it), I have tried to identify Pater's sources and discover the objects of his allusions. For present purposes I have deemed this to be part of the business of 'explanation', since it resolves mysteries which Pater, consciously or not, has himself introduced. In cases in which scholarship is able to point to sources, but where Pater's own prose does not, by itself, alert the reader to any borrowing or allusion, I have generally abstained from comment, since this would likely double the total volume of the notes. For more detailed critical commentary on Pater's sources and influences the reader is referred to the following, to each of which I am indebted, and which I cite and acknowledge in my own notes using a short title:

'**Hill**': Pater, *The Renaissance: Studies in Art and Poetry (the 1893 Text)*, ed. Donald L. Hill (Berkeley: University of California Press, 1980).
'**Clark**': Pater, *The Renaissance*, ed. Kenneth Clark (London: Collins, 1961).
'**Inman (1981)**': Billie Andrew Inman, *Walter Pater's Reading: A Bibliography of His Library Borrowings and Literary References, 1858–1873* (New York: Garland, 1981).
'**Inman (1990)**': Billie Andrew Inman, *Walter Pater and His Reading, 1874–1877: With a Bibliography of His Library Borrowings, 1878–1894* (New York: Garland, 1990).
'**Østermark-Johansen**': Pater, *Imaginary Portraits*, ed. Lene Østermark-Johansen (London: MHRA, 2014).

The titles of Pater's own volumes are abbreviated as follows:

Ren.	The Renaissance	**GS**	Greek Studies
Marius	Marius the Epicurean	**MS**	Miscellaneous Studies
IP	Imaginary Portraits	**Gaston**	Gaston de Latour
App.	Appreciations	**EG**	Essays from the Guardian
PP	Plato and Platonism		

Cross-references to passages included in the present anthology are given by essay title and paragraph number (¶), while adversions to works by Pater which are unrepresented here are, where a precise reference is needed, given by page number in the Library Edition. Pater is 'WP' throughout. Other abbreviations are adopted locally and should be sufficiently clear.

In referring to most works that are neither by nor about Pater, I have thought it more useful to give 'chapter and verse' citations than page-references to particular editions. Titles which exist in a sole edition, or a sole English edition, or of which one edition is much the most common or easily accessible, are treated as exceptional and so cited with page references. The English Bible is quoted from the Authorized Version, except for some of the Psalms which, as indicated, Pater has quoted from the *Book of Common Prayer*. Vasari in English is quoted from the translation by A.B. Hinds (1900). In occasional quotations from Pater's fragment entitled 'The Æsthetic Life' (Houghton Library, Harvard, *MS Eng 1150*, item 7) I have supplied some of the punctuation and omitted some of the alternative words left by Pater between lines.

Quotations from Pater retain the 'æ' and 'œ' ligatures, since they have been judged worth preserving in the text itself; but otherwise I have kept to the modern habit and printed 'ae' and 'oe' in separated type. Only here in the notes is the juxtaposition of the two conventions likely to be noticed, but I hope without too much discomfort.

Passing mentions of authors and artists, well-known books or works of art, have not been glossed unless an interpretative comment on their relevance or associations appeared likely to be helpful, or a sense of chronology seemed desirable. Some things have been glossed more than once, where I suppose it reasonable for the reader to have forgotten the previous instances, or, especially, where an unfamiliarity with the Greek alphabet might make repeated words or phrases less easily recognised than they would otherwise be. Where Pater himself has translated (or closely paraphrased) a quotation from a language other than English, but which he gives in the original also, I have provided a more literal rendering only in cases where it helped to clarify a point or illuminate a leaning in Pater's version. But where there might be doubt—for those who do not read the particular language in question—whether or not Pater has fully translated the quotation, I have given explicit confirmation and, where necessary, located the relevant English words.

THE RENAISSANCE
§Preface

¶2. **"To see the object as in itself it really is"**: Matthew Arnold, in *On Translating Homer* (1862) and 'The Function of Criticism at the Present Time' (1864); cf. Introduction, p. 17.

¶3. *La Gioconda*: i.e. the 'Mona Lisa', the subject of WP's famous 'purple panel' in 'Leonardo Da Vinci', ¶29-30. **hills of Carrara**: source of Carrara marble. WP must have in mind Michelangelo's devotion to the stone of these quarries. In 'The Poetry of Michelangelo' (*Ren.*), he writes: 'He loved the very quarries of Carrara [...]; and on the crown of the head of the David there still remains a morsel of uncut stone, as if by one touch to maintain its connexion with the place from which it was hewn' (Lib. Edn., pp. 76-77). **Pico of Mirandola**: cf. herein WP's essay on this C15th philosopher. **a recent critic of Sainte-Beuve**: i.e. a critical essay by Saint-Beuve. Hill proposes 'critique' as a 'conjectural emendation', but 'critic'—as a *piece of criticism*—is a not uncommon English equivalent of 'critique' in this period. Charles Augustin Sainte-Beuve (1804-69) was an important French literary critic. The source is an 1867 review-essay (collected in the *Nouveaux Lundis*) on Du Bellay, to whom WP devotes an essay. *De se borner* (etc.): 'To limit oneself to a close knowledge of beautiful things, and a self-cultivation as meticulous amateurs, as accomplished humanists'.

¶4. **"The ages are all equal [etc.]"**: from Blake's marginalia to the third of Joshua Reynolds' *Discourses*, quoted in Gilchrist's *Life of William Blake* (1863), vol. 1, p. 263.

¶5. *Resolution and Independence*: also known as 'The Leech-Gatherer'. *Ode on the*

Recollections of Childhood: 'Ode: Intimations of Immortality'. Two of Wordsworth's most famous poems.

¶6. **I have explained […] what I understand by the word**: 'For us the Renaissance is the name of a many-sided but yet united movement, in which the love of the things of the intellect and the imagination for their own sake, the desire for a more liberal and comely way of conceiving life, make themselves felt, urging those who experience this desire to search out first one and then another means of intellectual or imaginative enjoyment, and directing them not only to the discovery of old and forgotten sources of this enjoyment, but to the divination of fresh sources thereof—new experiences, new subjects of poetry, new forms of art.' 'Two Early French Stories', *Ren.*, Lib. Edn, p. 2. **those who originally used it to denote that revival of classical antiquity in the fifteenth century**: perhaps principally Jacob Burckhardt (1818–97), in *The Civilization of the Renaissance in Italy* (1860); but also other mid-C19th historians: Michelet especially, given WP's emphasis on the French Renaissance and its medieval antecedents. He may also have in mind those who used the term in a more limited sense before the C19th. **two little compositions in early French**: the subjects of the first essay in *Ren.*, 'Two Early French Stories': (i) the tale of the intimate friendship of Amis and Amile (*Li Amitiez de Ami et Amile*), and (ii) the love-story of *Aucassin and Nicolette*. Both are C13th narratives which WP had read in *Nouvelles françoises en prose du XIIIe siècle*, ed. Louis Moland and Charles d'Héricault (1856). **Joachim du Bellay**: see herein WP's essay on this C16th French poet. *ascêsis*: 'self-discipline', 'training'; cf. 'Style', ¶10, and esp. 'Lacedæmon', ¶23.

¶8. **Pericles**: *de facto* ruler of Athens in its Golden Age, c. 461–29 B.C. **Lorenzo de' Medici**, 'the Magnificent' (1449–92): Lord of Florence, poet, and patron of the arts.

¶9. Johann Joachim **Winckelmann** (1717–68): important German antiquary and philhellene historian of art. Cf. extract from WP's long essay 'Winckelmann'.

§*Pico Della Mirandola*

First published in the *Fortnightly Review*, October 1871. Giovanni Pico della Mirandola (1463–94) was one of the pre-eminent philosophers associated with the Florentine Neo-Platonism of the late C15th.

¶1. **The restored Greek literature**: a revival in the study and knowledge of ancient Greek literature was one of the most important aspects of the classical humanist culture of the C15th 'Renaissance'.

¶2. Heinrich **Heine** (1797–1856): major German Romantic poet and man of letters; *Gods in Exile*: an essay, published in 1853, in which Heine imagines the Greek gods living *incognito* in the Christian age, and discusses this notion as found in medieval culture and folk traditions. Cf. 'Leonardo Da Vinci', ¶24; 'Winckelmann', ¶42; *PP*, ch. 1–5 extracts, extr. (v), ¶4; and 'Raphael', ¶6. See also the stories 'Denys L'Auxerrois' (*IP*) and 'Apollo in Picardy' (*MS*). **"Let me briefly remind the reader [etc.]"**: WP translates, with some omissions.

¶3. *éclaircissement*: the 'Enlightenment'.

¶4. **the historic sense**: cf. 'Style', ¶9, and *PP*, ch. 1–5 extracts, extr. (i), ¶6. In the unpublished essay-fragment 'The Æsthetic Life', WP writes: 'That historic sense, which is one of the signal intellectual privileges of our age, justifying men's successive changes of mood, or habit, as of logical necessity in a great dramatic evolution, has co-ordinated the revolutions of taste, also, in that reasonable series, connected schools of art with the longer cycles of human development, and, by thus interpreting the variations of the beautiful, greatly extended our appreciation of it.' **Plato and Homer must be made to speak agreeably to Moses**: the 'Neo-Platonic' philosophy of Pico, and of his contemporaries and followers, was a syncretic philosophy based upon the collation of philosophical and religious sources from various traditions, interpreted so as to make them mutually illuminative and bring them into harmony. The synthesis of classical pagan traditions with Christianity was thus one of its basic functions. *in recessu divinius aliquid*: 'something more divine [latent] in the depths', as compared with what appears on the surface; from Pico's preface to his *Heptaplus*, a commentary on *Genesis*.

¶5. **"madhouse-cell"**: allusion to the shared heading ('Madhouse Cells') of two of Robert Browning's best-known dramatic monologues, 'Porphyria's Lover' and 'Johannes Agricola in Meditation'. **life, written by his nephew Francis**: this biography by Giovanni Francesco Pico della Mirandola (1470–1533) prefaces Pico's posthumous *Opera Omnia* (1498). **translated [...] by Sir Thomas More**: WP quotes henceforward from More's English version, written 1504, published 1510.

¶6. **Marsilio Ficino** (1433–99): besides Pico, the most important philosopher of the Florentine Neo-Platonic movement. The account of Pico's arrival is told by Ficino in his dedicatory '*proemium*' to Lorenzo de' Medici, prefacing his translations of the *Enneads* of Plotinus (1492). **translation of Plato into Latin**: the first Latin versions of the works of Plato, and therefore a major milestone in early modern philosophy. Published as *Divini Platonis Opera Omnia*, 1484. Ernest **Renan** (1823–92): important French historian, philologist and philosopher, whose works on early Christianity (e.g. his *Life of Jesus*, 1863), were well known, and major sources for some of WP's later work, including *Marius*. Hill locates the source for the remarks to which WP alludes: *Averroès et l'averroïsme* (1852), in Renan, *Oeuvres complètes*, vol. 3, p. 293. **many a needy Greek scholar**: the westward migration of Byzantine scholars after the fall of Constantinople has traditionally been seen as a major cause of the revival of Greek literature in Italy and western Europe. The scholars brought both knowledge and manuscripts. **"of feature and shape seemly and beauteous [etc.]"**: from More. WP changes 'not too picked' to 'abundant'.

¶7. **from a Greek word which signifies *to shut***: i.e. μύω (*muô*), 'I close', 'I shut'. **wonderful walk with Tobit**: as in the Book of Tobit (Apocrypha). WP may have in mind Verrocchio's painting of 'Tobias and the Angel', bought by the National Gallery, London, in 1867; or (as Hill supposes) Botticini's 'Tobias and the Angel', which WP could have seen in the Uffizi. **in dedicating this translation to Lorenzo de' Medici**: see ¶6n. above.

¶8. **nine hundred bold paradoxes**: Pico's 900 Theses were published in 1486 (*Conclusiones Philosophicae, Cabalasticae et Theologicae*) and accompanied by a challenge from the author to any scholar who wished to come to Rome and debate them. Papal intervention prevented such a disputation and obliged Pico to retract some of the theses.

¶9. **The oration**: Pico's 'Oration on the Dignity of Man' ('*Oratio de Hominis Dignitate*'), which accompanied the 900 Theses, has proven to be his most famous and enduring work. *nodus et vinculum mundi*: translated by WP in next clause; Hill locates the phrase in Pico's *Heptaplus* V:7. **"interpreter of nature"**: from the exordium to Pico's *Oration*. For Bacon's use, see *Novum Organum* I: '*Aphorismi de Interpretatione Naturae et Regno Hominis*', no. 1. Cf. WP's quotation of the latter as subtitle to 'Leonardo Da Vinci'. ***Tritum est in scholis*** (etc.): from the second preface to Pico's *Heptaplus*; WP's own translation.

¶10. creative ***Logos***: God as demiurge or 'the Word' (see Hill for discussion) in one of the frescoes at the ***Campo Santo*** ('Sacred Field'), the medieval walled cemetery at Pisa, of which the soil, or part of it, was said to have been transported there from the hill of Golgotha (cf. ¶15 below), and whose frescoes had inspired the formation of the Pre-Raphaelite Brotherhood. **mote in the beam**: cannot fail to bring to mind Matthew 7:3: 'And why beholdest thou the mote that is in thy brother's eye, but considerest not the beam that is in thine own eye?' Yet the 'beam' here is apparently a beam or shaft of light, not a beam of wood. ***Le silence éternel*** [...] ***m'effraie***: Pascal, *Pensées*, Laf. fr. 201, Sel. fr. 233: 'The eternal silence of these infinite spaces frightens me'.

¶11. **"wandering over the crooked hills of delicious pleasure"**: from More, substituting 'wandering over' for 'followed'. Girolamo **Savonarola's famous "bonfire of vanities"**: a mass burning of 'vain' books, images, etc., which took place in 1497 at the instigation of this charismatic friar. **love-songs in the vulgar tongue**: the *Life* tells us that Pico had destroyed the texts of his own Italian vernacular love-poems. His Latin poems survive. **Platonic commentary**: Pico's famous '*Commento*', his early Platonic treatise on love, is in part a commentary on a canzone by his friend, the poet Girolamo **Beniveni** (1453–1542). **Camilla Rucellai** (1465–1520): a follower of Savonarola, and the wife of a prosperous Florentine gentleman, she withdrew from married to conventual life and was noted for a putative gift of prophecy. The story told by WP had been related by George Eliot in *Romola* (1862–63), ch. 29. **those thoughts on the religious life**: the *Duodecim Regulae* and *Duodecim arma*, which **More** translates into verse as the 'Twelve Rules' and 'Twelve Weapons of Spiritual Battle'. The other **English translator** is More's friend, the Roman Catholic priest Richard Whitford (or Whytford), in *The Following of Christ*, his translation of the Latin ***Imitation of Christ*** attributed to Thomas à Kempis. But in fact the 'Rules' of Pico were added to this book only in the Rouen edition of 1585, long after Whitford's death, so the decision to include it cannot have been his own. **"It is not hard to know God [etc.]"**: '*On connaît Dieu facilement, pourvu qu'on ne se contraigne pas à le définir*'; from the *Pensées* of French essayist Joseph **Joubert** (1754–1824). As Hill notes, the saying had been quoted in Arnold's essay 'Joubert' (1864). **Angelo Politian** (Poliziano; 1454-94): important humanist scholar and poet at Florence under Lorenzo de' Medici.

¶12. **Charles the Eighth entered Florence**: Pico died on 17 November 1494. The entry of Charles VIII of France into Florence, his armies being *en route* to Naples, is an important event in the First Italian War.

¶13. ***Heptaplus***: see ¶4n. above.

¶15. **When the ship-load of sacred earth** (etc.): see ¶10n. above. **Maremma**: region of the west coast of Italy, including parts of Tuscany and the Lazio. **"Mighty Mother"**: '*Magna Mater*' is usually the epithet of Cybele, who comes into Greco-Roman mythology from Phrygia, and is associated with orgiastic worship involving emasculated priests; but she was sometimes identified with other deities (including the Greek Demeter), to whom the status of mother-goddess was transferrable.

¶16. *cæsiis et vigilibus oculis*: given in More's English in ¶6: 'his eyes grey, and quick of look'. *decenti rubore interspersa*: likewise: 'intermingled with comely reds'. **a true humanist**: most simply, a 'humanist' was a scholar during the Renaissance who was learned in classical texts and culture, and 'humanism' an intellectual movement and system of educational reform which promoted the 'revival of antiquity' and endorsed the study and imitation of ancient literature. But because of this movement's investment in the acquisition of 'humane' arts, the *studia humanitatis* (study of *humanitas*), it is also necessarily involved with a system of values to the cultivation of which the academic humanities are supposed to contribute. Thus WP's claim that Pico is a 'true' humanist is a way of insisting that *more* than the simplest sense of the word should be regarded as appropriate to him; and the explanation that follows is a characteristically Paterian celebration of imaginative historical sympathy and curiosity. Cf. 'Preface', ¶3; 'Winckelmann', ¶29; 'Coleridge', ¶4'; 'Notre Dame d'Amiens', ¶1; and see Introduction, pp. 35-36. For further discussion see Richmond Crinkley, *Walter Pater: Humanist* (1970).

§ Sandro Botticelli

First published in the *Fortnightly Review*, August 1870.

¶1. **In Leonardo's treatise on painting**: i.e. in his posthumously published *Trattato della Pittura*, Bk II (§57: '*Precetti del pittore*'). **quietly becoming important**: Botticelli had been considered a very minor artist, little discussed, at the start of the C19th, but was destined to become one of the great names in Renaissance painting by the mid C20th. Though he had been mentioned and even celebrated by a range of earlier English authors, WP's essay is an important part of the English revival of interest in B during the 1870s. Herbert Horne's major book *Botticelli* (1908) was dedicated to WP.

¶2. **the gossip which Vasari accumulated**: i.e. in his *Lives of the Most Excellent Painters, Sculptors and Architects* (from 1550), a work to which WP often turns. The modern 'criticism' which dispels Vasari's myths certainly includes Crowe and Cavalcaselle's *New History of Painting in Italy*—in this case, vol. 2 (1864). **legend of Lippo and Lucrezia**: Vasari tells us that Lippo Lippi abducted Lucrezia Buti from a Florentine convent, and that she was the mother of Lippi's son, the painter Filippino Lippi, a story doubted by Crowe and Cavalcaselle (who propose that Filippino was adopted) but still current today and widely accepted as true. **rehabilitated the character of Andrea del Castagno**: said to have been the murderer of Domenico Veneziano, another important painter. **Savonarola**: see 'Pico Della Mirandola', ¶11n. **1515, according to the received date**: thus in Vasari, but modern scholarship has fixed the true date of B's death as 1510. **comment on the *Divine Comedy***: Vasari mentions this, though the commentary, if it ever existed, is not extant. B also provided designs for the 1481 edition of Dante's *Commedia*, with a commentary by Latin poet and humanist Cristoforo Landino. He subsequently worked on a fuller series of illustrations, in ink on vellum, ninety-two of which survive, and most of which were reposing out of sight and largely out of mind in the collection of the Duke of Hamilton in WP's day, so that he is unlikely to have known about them and cannot have seen them.

¶3. **edition of 1481**: see above. **the copy in the Bodleian Library** (Oxford): present shelfmark Auct. 2Q 1.11. The engraving to which WP refers is the one at the start of canto III, though this is the same image as that for canto II. **the scene of those who "go down quick into hell"**: from WP's description of the image, this refers to *Inferno* XIX:1–30, the punishment of Simon Magus and the Simoniacs. Yet the quotation, 'go down quick into hell', from Psalm 55:15 ('quick' in the sense 'alive'), does not seem appropriate to that canto, and would more correctly refer to *Inf.* XXXIII, the punishment of treachery to guests. The latter episode was illustrated by B only in the later series of drawings, and not in the 1481 volume. **scene of the Centaurs**: engraving for *Inf.* XII.

¶4. **Giotto, the tried companion of Dante**: Dante and Giotto were contemporaries, and the latter is mentioned at *Purg.* XI:94–96. Legend has it that Dante visited Giotto as he worked on the frescoes of the Scrovegni Chapel in Padua, a story Vasari records. In a fresco in the Bargello Chapel, Florence, traditionally attributed to Giotto, one of the figures is said to be a portrait of Dante. WP likely has this in mind. An 1852 painting by D.G. Rossetti shows Dante sitting for the supposed portrait. **Masaccio and Ghirlandajo** are both important C15th Florentine painters. **a mood [...] which it clothes [...] with visible circumstance**: cf. 'Style', ¶21.

¶5. **One picture of his**: National Gallery, London, inv. 1126 (acquired in 1882, and therefore after WP's essay); but the attribution to B, endorsed by Vasari, has long been given up, and it is now attributed to Francesco Botticini. In 1870 it belonged to the Duke of Hamilton. **Matteo Palmieri** (1406–75): important Florentine statesman and writer, who commissioned the 'Assumption' for the chapel that was to contain his tomb. The poem to which WP refers—in fact *La Città di Vita* (*City of Life*), not *Divina* (Hill explains the source of the error)—was found, upon a posthumous inspection by Church censors, to contain heretical suggestions, and the chapel was subsequently closed. The painting, remaining in place, was also for some time inaccessible; Vasari says that the condemnation applied to it also. ***Glorias***: cf. *OED*, 'glory': 'a representation of the heavens opening and revealing celestial beings'. **portrait of Dante**: see ¶5n. above.

¶6. **what Dante scorns**: see *Inf.* III:34–42: 'This miserable mode / Maintain the melancholy souls of those / Who lived withouten infamy or praise. // Commingled are they with that caitiff choir / Of Angels, who have not rebellious been, / Nor faithful were to God, but were for self. // The heavens expelled them, not to be less fair; / Nor them the nethermore abyss receives, / For glory none the damned would have from them' (trans. Longfellow). **that middle world in which men take no side in great conflicts** (etc.): see also 'Two Early French Stories' (*Ren.*): 'the student of the Renaissance has this advantage over the student of the emancipation of the human mind in the Reformation, or the French Revolution, that in tracing the footsteps of humanity to higher levels, he is not beset at every turn by the inflexibilities and antagonisms of some well-recognised controversy, with rigidly defined opposites, exhausting the intelligence and limiting one's sympathies. [...] Here there are no fixed parties, no exclusions: all breathes of that unity of culture in which "whatsoever things are comely" are reconciled, for the elevation and adorning of our spirits.' (Lib. Edn, pp. 26–27). **great refusals**: see *Inf.* III:59–60: 'I looked, and I beheld the shade of him / Who made through cowardice the great refusal' (trans. Longfellow). This refers to Celestine V, Pope in 1294 for five months terminating with his abdication. The painter Fra **Angelico** (died 1455) is known especially for bright and ethereal images. **Orcagna's *Inferno***: in the Strozzi Chapel, Santa Maria Novella, Florence, painted around the middle of the C14th. The fresco depicts Hell according to Dante's *Commedia*, and is now more commonly attributed to Orcagna's brother, Nardo di Cione, though Vasari claims that they worked together.

¶7. **Sistine Madonna**: by Raphael; now at the Dresden Gallery. **"Desire of all nations"**: Haggai 4:7: 'And I will shake all nations, and the desire of all nations shall come: and I will fill this house with glory, saith the LORD of hosts'. **Once, indeed, he guides her hand** (etc.): in the so-called 'Madonna of the Magnificat', now in the Uffizi. *Ave*: the salutation of the Archangel Gabriel to the Virgin Mary, and consequently also the '*Ave Maria*' prayer (the 'Hail Mary'). *Magnificat*: refers to Mary's words to St Elizabeth (Luke 1:46ff.: 'My soul doth magnify the Lord', etc.), which form the basis of an important Marian hymn. *Gaude Maria [virgo]*: 'Rejoice, O Virgin Mary', a Marian reponsorial song or chant. **those others**: WP is not referring to other figures in the 'Madonna of the Magnificat', nor, I believe, to other paintings by B (for his Annunciations do not depict children), but is imaginatively transforming the curly-haired angels in this and other similar compositions 'back' into the earthlier creatures they suggest by their appearance. The 'look of wistful inquiry' is there on the angels' faces in the picture, but WP wants to see them as ordinary children, as though in Sunday-best, and not as true angels. **intolerable**: in a strict Latinate sense, 'too much to bear'; refers to the 'honour' of being made the mother of God. *enfants du choeur*: 'choir-boys'.

¶8. **picture in the *Uffizii***: the 'Birth of Venus'. **Men go forth to their labours until the evening**: Psalm 104:23: 'Man goeth forth unto his work and to his labour until the evening' (*AV*). **"showing his teeth"**: idiomatic way of referring to the foam on the surface of the water.

¶9. **Simonetta** Vespucci (1453–76) was famed as the pre-eminent beauty of her day. **Giuliano de' Medici** (1453–78) ruled Florence alongside Lorenzo the Magnificent, his brother. The 'Return of Judith to Bethulia' in the Uffizi is the painting to which WP refers. *Justice*: one of the series of 'Theological and Cardinal Virtues' painted for the Mercatanzia in Florence by Piero del Pollaiuolo (c. 1443–96) and B. The latter painted only one of the seven, representing 'Fortitude', and Hill supposes that WP has this painting in mind. But 'Fortitude' does not hold a sword, and Pollaiuolo's 'Justice' fits WP's description perfectly; so it is likely that he has simply misattributed that painting, or attributes all of the seven, to B. All are now in the Uffizi. *Veritas*: 'Truth', as depicted in the *Calumnia*, i.e. 'The Calumny of Apelles', in the Uffizi. We know that the nude figure, who much resembles the goddess of 'The Birth of Venus', is meant to represent 'Truth', because she is so described by Lucian (*On Calumny*) in a description of the lost ancient painting by Apelles upon which this composition by B is based.

§ *Leonardo Da Vinci*

First published in the *Fortnightly Review*, November 1869. The Latin epigraph means 'Man, Minister and Interpreter of Nature', and is taken from Francis Bacon, *Novum Organum* I:

'*Aphorismi de Interpretatione Naturae et Regno Hominis*', no. 1. Cf. 'Pico Della Mirandola', ¶9n.

¶1. **Vasari's life of Leonardo [...] variations from the first edition**: in the 1550 text of the *Vite*, Leonardo's religious scepticism is emphasised much more strongly than in the revised text of 1568. E.g. in 1550 he has an 'heretical' outlook, 'esteeming it better, perhaps, to be a philosopher than a Christian'. **fixed the outward type of Christ**: i.e. in the *Last Supper*, Milan. ***Battle of the Standard***: also called 'The Battle of Anghiari', this mural in the Palazzo Vecchio, Florence, is now believed by some art historians to remain intact beneath the present frescoes by Vasari. Jules **Michelet** (1798–1874): major French historian, who speaks of LdV in grandiloquent terms in his *Histoire de France*, vol. 9, Intro., §11.

¶2. **Carlo Amoretti** (1741–1816): in the *Memorie storiche su la vita, gli studi e le opere di Leonardo da Vinci* (1804).

¶3. ***Château de Clou*** (Clos Lucé): estate near Amboise where LdV lived in the last few years of his life, in the service of François I of France.

¶4. **Andrea del Verrocchio**: c. 1435–88. **pyxes**: ceremonial boxes used in Christian churches to hold the consecrated host. Pietro **Perugino**: c. 1446/52–1523. **ambries**: the *OED*, under 'aumbry', gives, *inter alia*, these meanings: 'A container for storing books'; 'A place for storing things [...]'; 'A cupboard, locker, or recess in the wall of a church or church building, to hold books, communion vessels, vestments, etc.'

¶5. **Leonardo was allowed to finish an angel in the left-hand corner**: according to Vasari, and with some support from modern scholars. The picture is now in the Uffizi.

¶6. ***Santa Maria Novella***: major church in Florence. **tombs of the Medici**: in the Medici Chapels, San Lorenzo, Florence. Vasari's 'Life of Verrocchio' provides these details.

¶7. ***Modesty and Vanity***: now attributed to Bernardino Luini, but putatively based on a design by LdV; Rothschild collection (Prégny, inv. 91). ***Virgin of the Balances***: Louvre, inv. 785; at present there is no official attribution, but it is no longer thought to be by LdV. [*Virgin and Child with*] ***Saint Anne***: Louvre, inv. 776. **lost picture of *Paradise***: as Vasari tells us.

¶8. **"the true mistress of higher intelligences"**: loosely quoted, at third hand, from one of LdV's manuscripts. Hill explores possible sources.

¶9. **perforation of mountains** (etc.): Vasari is the source for these 'impossibilities'. **raising [...] the church of *San Giovanni*** (Florence): i.e. lifting it and placing steps beneath it, without its collapse. **the motion of great waters**: among LdV's drawings are a number of striking studies of the movement of water.

¶10. **he would follow such about the streets of Florence**: see Vasari. **he caricatures Dante even**: in the Royal Collections (inv. 912493) is a drawing in red chalk of grotesque heads 'after Leonardo', including a caricature of Dante. It has been in the Royal Collections since the end of the C17[th]. Other copies exist.

¶11. ***Medusa* of the *Uffizii*** (inv. 1479): now attributed to an anonymous Flemish painter, c. 1600; but Luigi Lanzi (1732–1810) identified it with the Medusa painting described by Vasari, and throughout the C19[th] it was considered a work by LdV. **Vasari's story of an earlier Medusa**: i.e. on a round piece of wood (a 'shield'): 'To a room, to which he alone had access, Lionardo took lizards, newts, maggots, snakes, butterflies, locusts, bats, and other animals of the kind, out of which he composed a horrible and terrible monster, of poisonous breath, issuing from a dark and broken rock [...]. Ser Piero went to his rooms one morning to fetch it. When he knocked at the door Lionardo opened it and told him to wait a little, and, returning to the room, put the round panel in the light on his easel, and having arranged the window to make the light dim, he called his father in. Ser Piero, taken unaware, started back', etc.

¶12. **Raffaelle du Fresne**: see his *Trattato della Pittura di Leonardo da Vinci* (1651). **Paracelsus** and **Cardan** (Girolamo Cardano): both famous C16th physicians and polymaths with esoteric interests.

¶13. **Ludovico Sforza** (1451–1508): Duke of Milan from 1494. **Francesco** Sforza (1401–66): Duke from 1450, and father of Ludovico.

¶14. **mellow, unbroken surfaces of Giotto and Arnolfo** (di Cambio): i.e. the Duomo of Florence, very different in style from the more novel and more 'Northern' Duomo of Milan.

¶16. **that *subtilitas naturæ* which Bacon notices**: *Novum Organum* I, §10: 'The subtilty of nature is far beyond that of sense or of the understanding: so that the specious meditations, speculations, and theories of mankind are but a kind of insanity, only there is no one to stand by and observe it.' **Fra Luca Paccioli** (died 1520): LdV, his friend, provided illustrations to his *De divina proportione* (1509). **Marc Antonio della Torre** (1481–1512): LdV furnished him with some anatomical drawings, mentioned by Vasari and extant in the Royal Collections. **He explained [...] above the polar**: Hill shows that these details are taken from Henry Hallam's *Introduction to the Literature of Europe* (4th edn, 1854, vol. 1, pp. 219–20n.). Hill also thinks WP's sentence 'incomplete and unintelligible', which does not seem to me to be the case: the omission of 'and' before 'knew' is an admissable stylistic effect, in keeping with WP's familiar idiom; and if (as Hallam points out) LdV was wrong about the 'equatorial waters', so that 'knew' is not strictly appropriate, it is characteristic of WP to see the supposed fact from LdV's point of view, and thus subjectivize knowledge—perhaps with some irony—rather than change 'knew' to something implying '*thought* he knew'.

¶17. **Clement** (Charles Clément): in *Michel-Ange, Léonard de Vince, Raphael* (1861), p. 196. Alexis-François **Rio**: in *De L'Art chrétien* (1861–67), vol. 3, p. 92 (see Hill). **a stray leaf from his portfolio** (etc.): Accademia, Venice; Popham, *Drawings*, no. 256. **Madonna of the Balances**: see ¶7 (and n.) above. **Madonna of the Lake** (*Madonna del Lago*): now at the Bob Jones University Museum and Gallery, and attributed to Marco d'Oggiono, though the composition may possibly be based on a design by LdV, with whom he studied. **Madonna of the Rocks**: Louvre, inv. 777. **La Gioconda**: the 'Mona Lisa' of the Louvre. **Saint Anne**: see ¶7 (and n.) above.

¶18. **Lucretia Crivelli**: 1452–1508; **Cecilia Galerani**: 1473–1536; **Ludovico** Sforza: see ¶13 (and n.); **Duchess Beatrice** d'Este: 1475–97, wife of Ludovico. **La Belle Feronière**: Louvre, inv. 778; sitter uncertain, attribution questionable. **in the Ambrosian library** (Biblioteca and Pinacoteca Ambrosiana, Milan): inv. 99 1971 000099, now called 'The Musician', attribution dubious. **portrait of Beatrice d'Este**: Ambrosiana, inv. 100 1971 000100, now tentatively attributed to Giovanni Ambrogio De Predis; sitter uncertain.

¶20. *müde sich gedacht*: translated by WP; from Goethe, '*Antike und Modern*' ('Ancient and Modern'), in *Über Kunst und Altertum*, vol. 2 (1818). [WP's fn.]: *Quanto più, un' arte porta* (etc): 'the more an art requires fatigue of the body, so much the more contemptible it is'. Goethe's novel *Elective Affinities* was published in 1809; his drama *Faust*, Pt 1, in 1808, and Pt 2 in 1832.

¶21. **the heads of a woman and a little child; a young man; a slave**: these drawings remain unidentified, although Clark is clear that none of them is by LdV. **a small Madonna and Child**: Hill gives references to illustrations of this Leonardesque drawing.

¶22. **a little drawing in red chalk**: Louvre, inv. 2252 (recto), now attributed to Giovanni Agostino da Lodi. In the second edition of *Ren*. (1877) this image was used as a frontispiece vignette. **Another drawing**: unidentified. *bulla*: globular amulet worn as a pendant by Roman boys before their reaching the age of sixteen years.

¶23. **Andrea Salaino**: Clark: 'there was no such painter as Andrea Salaino. The name seems to be a confusion between Andrea Solario and Giacomo Salai. The latter was the boy with curly hair who joined Leonardo in 1490.' *belli capelli ricci e inanellati*: 'lovely rich and curly hair' (Vasari). **Francesco Melzi**: LdV's pupil, who died c. 1570, and to whom his works and collections were bequeathed. *Canonica al Vaprio*: Vaprio d'Adda, near Milan.

¶24. **a hand, rough enough by contrast** (etc.): but see ¶7n. above. Bernardino **Luini** (died 1532): painter associated with LdV's workshop; attributed to him are several Leonardesque paintings of Salome (the 'Daughter of Herodias') with the head of John the Baptist, including examples in Florence, Boston, Vienna and Madrid. *Saint John the Baptist*: Louvre, inv. 775; the two copies mentioned are both by imitators of LdV. *Bacchus*: Louvre, inv. 780, attributed to the workshop of LdV; this painting began as a John the Baptist and was transformed into a Bacchus in the C17th. **Théophile Gautier**: see '*Léonard de Vinci*', in Gautier, Houssaye and Saint Victor, *Les Dieux et semidieux de la peinture* (*The Gods and Demigods of Painting*, 1864); but he is speaking of the St John, not the Bacchus. Perhaps, if he has not simply misremembered, WP has reconstructed Gautier's chain of thought, and the proximity and similarity of the Bacchus is supposed to explain the mental occurence to Gautier of **Heine's notion of decayed gods**, for which cf. 'Pico Della Mirandola', ¶2 (and n. for cross-refs).

¶25. **Goethe's pensive sketch**: '*Giuseppe Bossi: über Leonardo da Vincis Abendmahl zu Mailand*' ('On LdV's *Last Supper* at Milan'), in *Über Kunst und Altertum*, vol. 1 (1817). **Duchess Beatrice** and **Ludovico**: see ¶13 (and n.) above. **drawing [...] at the *Brera***: inv. 280. **Mino da Fiesole**: Florentine sculptor of the mid C15th.

¶26. **Raphael**: but Perugino is now the presumed author of the frescoes **in the refectory** (*cenacolo*) **of Saint Onofrio**. For Raphael and Perugino, cf. 'Raphael'. **[N.b.]** In the fourth edition (1893), on which the Lib. Edn (and the present text) is based, WP excised two much-discussed sentences at the end of this paragraph: 'It is the image of what the history it symbolises has been more and more ever since, paler and paler as it recedes from us. Criticism came with its appeal from mystical unrealities to originals, and restored no life-like reality but these transparent shadows, spirits which have not flesh and bones.' (Quoted from 1873.)

¶27. **in 1498 the French entered Milan**: the invasion, by the new King Louis XII, in fact occurred in 1499. **Bartolomeo Colleoni on horseback**: still in its place. The notion here represented regarding Verrocchio's death is not in Vasari. **one of the rooms of the great tower still shown** (etc.): WP probably visited this room in the Château de

Loches, which is *still* shown, the wall-paintings having been partially restored. *Infelix Sum*: 'Unhappy am I'.

¶28. **straight from the cabinet of Francis the First**: as Hill observes, the paintings WP probably has foremost in mind did not come 'straight from' Fontainebleau. **the *Saint Anne* [...] cartoon, now in London**: Clark points out that the Burlington House cartoon is *not* the same one which 'drew a crowd in 1500' (as WP would have read in Vasari). This must have been another version of the composition. **"triumph" of Cimabue** (c. 1240–1302): his painting of the Virgin for Santa Maria Novella, Florence, caused such marvel that it was carried in a solemn procession from the painter's house to its place in the church (Vasari). **an undraped Monna Lisa** (etc.): Clément (*op. cit.*) in 1861 mentions this, but Rio (*op. cit.*) had written about it in 1855; cf. ¶17n. above. **Ginevra di Benci**: National Gallery of Art, Washington, D.C., inv. 1967.6.1.a; still officially attributed to LdV with a firm identification of the presumed sitter. **Lisa** (1479–1542), wife of the Florentine merchant **Francesco del Giocondo**, is traditionally identified as the model for—

¶29. —*La Gioconda* (the 'Mona Lisa'): Louvre inv. 779. ***Melancholia* of Dürer**: i.e. '*Melencolia* 1', an engraving of 1514, perhaps the artist's most famous single image. **folio of drawings, once in the possession of Vasari** (etc.): 'There are some of his drawings in our book executed with the greatest patience and judgment, among them being some female heads so beautiful and with such charming hair that Leonardo da Vinci was always imitating them' (Vasari, 'Life of Verrocchio'). **the legend that by artificial means [...] that subtle expression was protracted on the face**: Vasari: 'while Leonardo was drawing her portrait he engaged people to play and sing, and jesters to keep her merry, and remove that melancholy which painting usually gives to portraits.'

¶30. **"the ends of the world are come"**: 1 Corinthians 10:11: 'Now all these things happened unto them for ensamples: and they are written for our admonition, upon whom the ends of the world are come.' **Leda, Saint Anne**: these were the subjects of other paintings by LdV, in which the figures named may be said to betray a likeness to the 'Mona Lisa' and to indicate the cultivation of a Leonardesque 'type' of feminine beauty. WP's suggestive prose, however, would seem to mean much more than merely this prosaic fact. Hill summarizes the range of comparable notions and possible sources that critics have proposed. Swinburne's 'Notes on Designs of the Old Masters at Florence', *Fortnightly Review*, 4 (July 1868), is probably the most direct source. The originals of LdV's two paintings of 'Leda and the Swan' are lost, but copies and studies are extant.

¶31. **Cæsar Borgia** (1475/6–1507): powerful *condottiere*; at first a cardinal, and then, resigning that office, Duke of Valentinois. Son of Pope Alexander VI, and brother of Lucrezia Borgia. LdV was retained as his military engineer and architect. **strange tower of Siena, elastic like a bent bow**: elastic in the sense 'impulsive', 'propulsive', implying energetic or spontaneous momentum; the 'bow' simile suggests tension, not that the tower is actually curved—although Ruskin's 'graceful as a bow just bent', describing the Rialto Bridge (*Stones of Venice*, vol. 2 [1853], ch. 1, §1), perhaps echoes here. Yeats's 'beauty like a tightened bow' ('No Second Troy') evokes a comparable tension. Presumably the Torre del Mangia in the Piazza del Campo is meant: LdV, visiting in 1502, notes the movements of the bells in this tower.

¶32. *Battle of the Standard*: see ¶1n. above. **Michelangelo chose for his cartoon** (etc.): the 'Battle of Cascina', known only through copies, was intended for the same hall in the Palazzo Vecchio, Florence, in which LdV was to paint the 'Battle of Anghiari'. **the background of his *Holy Family* in the *Uffizii***: an arrangement of male nudes dominates the background of this famous painting (the 'Doni Tondo') by Michelangelo. **fragment of Rubens**: Louvre, inv. 20271. **a drawing of his at Florence**: unidentified. None of the drawings at the Uffizi currently associated with LdV seems to answer to the description.

¶33. **"fly before the storm"**: one of LdV's manuscripts is headed by the motto 'flee from storms', a fact to which great emphasis is given by Clément (*op. cit.*, cf. ¶17n. above).

¶34. *A Monsieur Lyonard* (etc.): 'To M. Leonardo, the King's painter for Amboise'.

§ *The School of Giorgione*

First published in the *Fortnightly Review*, October 1877, this essay did not appear in the first or second editions of *Ren.*, but was added in 1888.

¶ 1. **"imaginative reason"**: the term is used by Matthew Arnold near the end of the essay 'Pagan and Mediæval Religious Sentiment' (1864), which had been collected into his *Essays in Criticism* (First Series, 1865). Cf. WP's use of the phrase elsewhere in this essay (¶9–10), and in 'The Genius of Plato', ¶15. It is also used in WP's essay 'On Wordsworth' (April 1874, *Fortnightly Review*), though omitted from the longer Wordsworth essay in *App*. Cf. also 'imaginative intellect' ('Winckelmann', ¶31, 33) and 'imaginative intelligence' ('Study of Dionysus', ¶4).

¶2. Gotthold Ephraim **Lessing**'s essay *Laocoon* (1766), subtitled 'On the Limits of Painting and Poetry', was an important work of critical theory. **Titian's *Lace-girl***: the attribution was not generally accepted even at WP's time of writing, as Hill demonstrates, and the painting, privately owned, is now attributed to Sofonisba Anguissola (died 1625). **Rubens's *Descent from the Cross***: WP is probably thinking of the 'Descent' painted for Antwerp Cathedral, c. 1612–14. **Titian [...] in the *Ariadne***: i.e. the 'Bacchus and Ariadne', National Gallery, London. **Presentation of the Virgin**: Accademia, Venice; the 'quaint figure' is the Virgin Mary as a small child.

¶3. *Anders-streben*: a 'striving toward the other', or 'otherward-straining'. I do not find that any critic has been able to locate the term in German writing earlier than WP's essay, so its provenance remains (or becomes increasingly) dubious. In his explanation of the term, however, WP is translating from the French of Baudelaire. Compare: '**the arts are able, not indeed to supply the place of each other, but reciprocally to lend each other new forces**', with Baudelaire: '*les arts aspirent, sinon à se suppléer l'un l'autre, du moins à se prêter réciproquement des forces nouvelles*' ('*L'Oeuvre et la vie d'Eugène Delacroix*', 1863, collected into *L'Art romantique*, 1868). The debt was noted by Germain d'Hangest (*Walter Pater: L'Homme et l'oeuvre*, 1961).

¶4. *Arena* **chapel**: at Padua, containing an important fresco cycle by Giotto. **Giotto's tower at Florence**: i.e. the campanile of the Duomo. **strangely twisted staircases** (etc.): the double-spiral staircases at the *châteaux* of Chambord and Blois are particularly famous. Cf. 'Joachim Du Bellay', esp. ¶1.

¶5. *All art constantly aspires towards the condition of music*: besides the 'gemlike flame', this must be the most famous sentence in WP. Hill is eager to stress the fact that it is not, as has sometimes been claimed, taken directly from Hegel. Cf. WP's passing return to the theme in 'Style', ¶30.

¶6. **M. Alphonse Legros** (1837-1911): French painter, sculptor and engraver, who lived and worked in England from the early 1860s. The etching to which WP refers is probably, as Hill proposes, '*Le Coup de Vent*' (cat. 110, Malassis and Thibaudeau, 1877).

¶7. **that song of Mariana's page in *Measure for Measure***: 'Take o take those lips away', which begins Act IV, sc. 1, and which WP, in his essay on '*Measure for Measure*' (*App.*), calls 'one of the loveliest songs of Shakespeare' (Lib. Edn., p. 176).

¶8. **the fashion of a time, which elevates the trivialities of speech, and manner, and dress** (etc.): cf. WP's unpublished essay-fragment 'The Æsthetic Life': 'in truth the fashion is always charming. The dexterity, the tact, of those whose interest lies there, does contrive to bring grace out of it, making minute permissible points of difference tell, […] transforming mere utilities into unlooked-for, subtle grace.'

¶11. **much has been taken by recent criticism** (etc.): WP is thinking primarily of the work of Crowe and Cavalcaselle (discussed below). The process has continued, and now the number of attributions to G which may be regarded as reasonably certain is extremely small.

¶12. **no Giotto, no Angelico, no Botticelli**: presumably Giotto is associated by WP with **naturalism**, Angelico with **religious mysticism**, and Botticelli (given what is said of him in 'Sandro Botticelli') with **philosophical theories**. Vittore **Carpaccio**: Venetian painter (c. 1465-1525/6) who had studied under Gentile **Bellini** (c. 1429-1507). The latter was the brother of Giovanni **Bellini** (c. 1430-1516) and the son of Jacopo **Bellini** (c. 1400-70?), both of these also important painters. **the marking of its precious stone**: WP is thinking again of the 'crust of marble and gold on the walls of the *Duomo* of Murano, or of Saint Mark's', as described above. **Of all art such as this, […] Giorgione is the initiator**: taken literally, this would have been a contentious statement in WP's time, and will find no consent today. But the 'Giorgionesque' element in northern Italian painting certainly represents a flourishing of what will later turn into 'genre' painting and the 'conversation piece', and which has few close precedents before the end of the C15[th].

¶13. **Born so near to Titian**: G's dates are c. 1478-1510 (the birth date conjectural, based on his estimated age at death). Titian's are c. 1488/90-1576. **companion pupils of the aged Giovanni Bellini**: in the case of G, this putative fact of biography is stated by Carlo Ridolfi (1594-1658) in his *Vite degli Illustri Pittori Veneti e dello Stato* (1648). **the relationship of Sordello to Dante, in Browning's poem**: in *Sordello* (1840), the poet-speaker addresses Dante: 'for he is thine! / Sordello, thy forerunner, Florentine! / A herald-star I know thou didst absorb / Relentless into the consummate orb / That scared it from its right to roll along / A sempiternal path with dance and song / Fulfilling its allotted period / Serenest of the progeny of God / Who yet resigns it not! His darling stoops / With no quenched lights, desponds with no blank troops / Of disenfranchised brilliances, for, blent / Utterly with thee, its shy element / Like thine upburneth prosperous and clear' (I:347-59). **Sordello's one fragment of lovely verse**: I do not see any evidence that WP 'misread' Browning, as Inman suggests (1990, pp. 393-94); but it is hardly clear whether he is still thinking of Browning's Sordello or of the historical Sordello. He may be conflating them. There are many poems by Sordello extant, and the most celebrated of these is no 'fragment', but a substantial complete *sirventès*. In Browning, however, the few lines we are given from Sordello's song on 'Elys' at II:152-55 ('Her head that's sharp and perfect like a pear, / So close and smooth are laid the few fine locks / Coloured like honey oozed from topmost rocks / Sun-blanched the livelong summer') are, by the end of the poem, all that is said to remain—not of his work generally, but merely of that one song: 'all that's left / Of the Goito lay' (VI:869-70). It seems most probable that WP has these lines in mind.

¶14. **old Venetian humanity**: for the associations of 'humanity' here, cf. Introduction, pp. 35-36, and see 'Pico Della Mirandola', ¶16n., etc. **only one is certainly from Giorgione's hand**: WP, since he is grudgingly following Crowe and Cavalcaselle here, is almost certainly thinking of the 'Concert' of the Palazzo Pitti, inv. 185, now more usually given to Titian. *fondaco dei Tedeschi*: important Renaissance palazzo in Venice, near the *Rialto* bridge; it served the Germanic merchants as storehouse, official premises and residence. Only fragments remain of G's frescoes there. **the "new Vasari"**: i.e. Crowe and Cavalcaselle; here, particularly their *History of Painting in North Italy* (1871).

¶15. **The *Concert* [...] is undoubtedly Giorgione's**: so say Crowe and Cavalcaselle. It is now commonly attributed to Titian.

¶16. The following attributions are all made by Crowe and Cavalcaselle (vol. 2, ch. 1). To **Pellegrino da San Daniele** (1467-1547) **the *Holy Family* in the Louvre** (inv. 70), now officially attributed to Sebastiano del Piombo (1485-1547). **the *Fête Champêtre*** (or 'Concert' of the Louvre, inv. 71) to **an imitator of Sebastiano del Piombo**, though it is now widely and officially attributed to Titian, and still regularly claimed for G. **the *Tempest*** (Accademia, Venice) to **Paris Bordone** (1500-71) or **"some advanced craftsman of the sixteenth century"** (in fact 'an advanced sixteenth-century craftsman', and the phrasing is ambiguous: if it was ever touched by G, it has at any rate been transformed so completely 'as to appear—in part at least—by Paris Bordone'); it is, however, still widely credited to G. **the *Knight embracing a Lady*** (Dresden Gall., inv. 221) to **"a Brescian hand"** (in fact it is described as a 'dry, hard specimen of Brescian art'), though Clark in 1961 states that the accepted attribution is to Girolamo Romanino (1480s-1560s), and now it is exhibited under the title '*Ein Liebespaar*', and attributed to Altobello Melone (1490/1-1547). ***Jacob meeting Rachel*** (Dresden Gall., inv. 192) to **a pupil** ['disciple'] **of Palma** [Il Vecchio] (c. 1480-1528), though it is now generally attributed to Palma himself. **the *Ordeal [of Moses]*** (Uffizi, inv. 945) and **the *Finding of Moses*** (by which Hill understands Pitti, inv. 161, although WP may conceivably have been thinking of Brera, inv. 144) to **Bellini**; but in fact Crowe and Cavalcaselle attribute the 'Ordeal' to G (still common), and the Pitti 'Finding of Moses' to Bonifazio Veronese (1487-1553), Berenson concurring with the latter claim. (The Brera picture is also said to be by Bonifazio.)

¶17. The biographical details are taken from Crowe and Cavalcaselle, relying largely on Vasari and Ridolfi (see ¶13n. above). **Catherine of Cornara** (or Cornaro, 1454-1510), last Queen of Cyprus, lived at Asolo, and Vasari says that he has seen a portrait of her by G (not extant). **Tuzio Costanzo** commissiond G's 'Castelfranco Altarpiece' for the family chapel, after the death of his son, Matteo. *condottiere*: a mercenary captain whose military services were contracted to political powers. **Castelfranco**: Giorgione's birthplace; **the altar-piece** here is one of the few paintings whose attribution to G remains reasonably secure: it is a Madonna and Child with **the warrior-saint, Liberale** (or St Nicasius) and St Francis of Assisi, painted c. 1500. **original little study in oil**: i.e. NG269 at the **National Gallery**, London, now attributed to a C17th imitator of G; WP, like Crowe and Cavalcaselle, takes it to be an original study for the Altarpiece. **"they rejoiced greatly,"** says Vasari (etc.): in the *Lives*. **Ridolfi**: see ¶13n. above.

¶20. **the kiss, caught with death itself**: see end of ¶17 above. **some momentary conjunction of mirrors** (etc.): Vasari: 'Giorgione is said to have once engaged in an argument with some scupltors [...]. They maintained that sculpture was superior to painting, because it presented so many various aspects, whereas painting only showed one side of a figure. [...] He painted a nude figure turning its back; at its feet was a limpid fount of water, the reflection from which showed the front. On one side was a burnished corselet which had been taken off, and gave a side view, because the shining metal reflected everything. On the other side was a looking-glass, showing the other side of the figure [...]. This work was greatly admired and praised for its ingenuity and beauty.' *il fuoco Giorgionesco*: 'the Giorgionesque fire'. The phrase is not in Vasari, and critics have supposed it to be WP's own, the attribution a ruse. In fact Anton Maria Zanetti the Younger (1706–78), in his work *Della pittura veneziana e delle opere pubbliche de' veneziani maestri* (1771), uses the phrase when speaking of the colouring of Titian's 'St Mark Enthroned' in Santa Maria della Salute, Venice (Bk II, p. 105 of the 1771 edn). I do not know if this is the origin of the phrase. It seems to have been commonly adopted by Italian critics in the early C19th.

¶21. **in an ingenious passage of the** *Republic*: Plato, *Rep.*, 531a–b: 'The teachers of harmony [says Socrates] compare the sounds and consonances which are heard only, and their labour, like that of the astronomers, is in vain. Yes, by heaven! he [Glaucon] said; and 'tis as good as a play to hear them talking about their condensed notes, as they call them; they put their ears close alongside of the strings like persons catching a sound from their neighbour's wall—one set of them declaring that they distinguish an intermediate note and have found the least interval which should be the unit of measurement; the others insisting that the two sounds have passed into the same—either party setting their ears before their understanding.' (Trans. Jowett.)

¶22. Matteo **Bandello** (c. 1480–1562) is known for his *Novelle* ('novels' or stories, of the same kind as in Boccaccio's *Decameron*). Crowe and Cavalcaselle, in the same chapter on G (vol. 3, ch. 1), propose that the subject of a painting formerly supposed to be by G (now known as 'The Lovers', Royal Collections, inv. 403928, and tentatively attributed to Titian), 'might have been derived from the novels of Bandello'. **play is in many instances that to which people really apply their own best powers** (etc.): cf. *Gaston*, end of ch. 4: 'Always on the lookout for the sincerities of human nature (sincerity counting for life-giving *form*, whatever the *matter* might be) as he delighted in watching children, Montaigne loved also to watch grown people when they were most like children; at their games, therefore, and in the mechanical and customary parts of their existence, as discovering the real soul in them.' (Lib. Edn., p. 90.)

¶23. **literally empyrean**: the original Greek word implies 'in the fire'. See *OED* for 'empyrean' as noun: 'The highest or most exalted part or sphere of heaven; (in ancient cosmology) the sphere of the pure element of fire'.

¶24. **one peak of rich blue**: WP is thinking of the 'Jacob and Rachel' of the Dresden Gall., now attributed to Palma (see ¶16n. above).

¶25. *vraie vérité*: the 'true truth', 'the essential truth', a favourite phrase of WP's; cf. 'Style', ¶26, and see Introduction, p. 27.

§ Joachim Du Bellay

Published for the first time in *Ren.* (1873). Du Bellay (c. 1522–60) was a French poet and critic, writing important works in both Latin and the vernacular. He was one of the leading lights of the poetic group or movement known as the 'Pléiade'.

¶1. ***Château de Gaillon***: this and the others named are all famous *châteaux* built or rebuilt in the C16th, Gaillon being the residence of the Archbishops of Rouen in Eure, northern France. **Isräel Silvestre** (the Younger): C17th draughtsman and engraver. **donjon**: castle tower or keep. ***Maître Roux***: French epithet of the Italian mannerist painter Rosso Fiorentino (1494–1540), resident in France in the final decade of his life, where he worked at and around the royal *château* of Fontainebleau. He was thus closely involved with the so-called **school of Fontainebleau**. **glass-painters of Chartres or Le Mans**: i.e. of their cathedrals. On Chartres Cathedral, cf. *Gaston*, ch. 2. **Saint Martin's summer**: a brief return to warm weather at the start of November. Pierre de **Ronsard** (1524–85): pre-eminent French vernacular poet of his age, and an important figure in the 'Pléiade'. For a fuller consideration of Ronsard, see *Gaston*, ch. 3. **the house of Jacques Cœur**, a wealthy merchant, is a palatial building of the mid C15th in Bourges. **the *Maison de Justice* at Rouen** dates from the beginning of the C16th.

¶2. ***une netteté remarquable d'exécution***: translated by WP, but more closely: 'a remarkable nicety [or neatness] of execution'. I cannot identify a source. **François Clouet** (died 1572) and his father Jean (died 1541) were both painters known especially for portraiture. Hans **Hemling** (Memling): Flemish painter of German origin, died 1494. **the Van Eycks** were a family of Flemish painters, the most important of whom was Jan Van Eyck (died 1441). François **Villon** (1431–after 1463): great French late-medieval poet, author of the *Testament* (1461). ***Hours of Anne of Brittany***: a celebrated Book of Hours belonging to this French Queen (1476–1514); magnificently illustrated by the miniaturist Jean Bourdichon in the first decade of the C16th. ***chansons de geste***: medieval French narrative poems of historical and romantic exploits. **granite church at Folgoat**: i.e. the church of Notre-Dame at Le Folgoët, Brittany. **in the song of Roland**: ll. 2249–51, in the Old French epic telling of Roland and the wars of Charlemagne. Hill shows that WP's attention had been drawn to these lines (on Turpin's 'white and fair hands') by Andrew Lang.

¶3. **castigation**: in a Latinate sense, 'chastisement', etymologically implying 'chastening'.

¶4. **Pindaric ode**: a lyric verse form of mixed line-length and repeating tripartite structure of ***strophe***, matching ***antistrophe***, and *epode* (in a different form), on the model of the classical Greek poet Pindar, though Ronsard does not follow the structures exactly.

His Pindarics, published in the *First Book of Odes* (1550), are each consistent in line-length and make their stanzaic variations in the *epode* by altering the rhyme-scheme. The example WP gives from Belleau is not a Pindaric, but illustrates instead the characteristic of 'changefulness and variety of metre'. *Avril, la grace, et le ris* (etc.): from '*Avril*', taken from the '*Première Jour*' of *La Bergerie* by Remy Belleau (1528-77). Since WP will later refer to the translations by Andrew Lang, the stanzas may be given in Lang's English version: 'April, with thy gracious wiles, / Like the smiles, / Smiles of Venus; and thy breath / Like her breath, the gods' delight, / (From their height / They take the happy air beneath;) // It is thou that, of thy grace, / From their place / In the far-off isles dost bring / Swallows over earth and sea, / Glad to be / Messengers of thee and spring.' Lang, *Poetical Works* (Longmans, 1923), vol. 2, p. 142. [Jean-] **Antoine de Baif** (1532-89), **Pontus de Tyard** (c. 1521-1605), **Étienne Jodelle** (1532-73), and **Jean Daurat** [or Dorat] (1508-88), are all French poets and intellectuals who, with Ronsard, JdB and Belleau, were associated with the 'Pléiade'.

¶5. *La Deffense et Illustration de la langue Françoyse*: *The Defence and Illustration of the French Language* (1549), JdB's major prose work, and one of the most important early works of poetic theory to concern itself specifically with the French vernacular. 'Illustration' in the sense 'enrichment'. **"It is a remarkable fact," says M. Sainte-Beuve** (etc.): in an essay on 'Joachim Du Bellay', first published in the *Revue des deux mondes*, 24 (Oct. 1840). On Sainte-Beuve, cf. 'Preface', ¶3 (and n.), and *App.*, 'Postscript', ¶4 (and n.).

¶6. *cette élégance et copie* (etc): 'that elegance and fecundity which are in the Greek and Roman [tongues]': *Defense* I.9 (trans. Gladys M. Turquet [London, 1939]). **"Those who speak thus," says Du Bellay** (etc.): *Def.* I.10. **"Languages," he says again** (etc.): *Def.* I.1, with omissions before 'Therefore'.

¶7. *nous favorisons toujours les étrangers* (WP translates): *Def.* I.9. **"I do not believe that one can learn [etc.]"**: *Def.* I.5. **"To prove this [etc.]"**: *ibid.*

¶8. *cette dernière main que nous désirons*: 'that final touch [which painters give to their pictures], which we desire' (trans. Turquet), *Def.* I.5. *péris et mises en reliquaires de livres*: '[As if, like the Greek and Latin, it had] perished and been put into the reliquary of books' (trans. Turquet), *Def.* I.11. *pauvre plante et vergette*: 'poor plant and little shoot' (trans. Turquet), *Def.* I.3. *le discours fatal des choses mondaines*: *Def.* II.4; Turquet has 'the immutable order of earthly things', '*discours*' being taken as basically synonymous with *cours*, i.e. 'course, order': a more accurate translation than WP's. *parfait en toute élégance et vénusté de paroles* (WP translates): *Def.* I.9, but applied there to Greek.

¶9. **Du Bellay was born in [...] 1525**: c. 1522 is the date now generally given. *ce petit Liré*: JdB was born near the village of Liré, between Nantes and Angers, and celebrates it as 'my little Liré' ('*mon petit Lyré*') in the sonnet '*Heureux qui, comme Ulysse, a fait un beau voyage*' (*Regrets*, son. 31). **"The time of my youth," says Du Bellay** (etc.): from JdB's Latin elegiac epistle to Jean de Morel ('*Elegia: Ad Ianum Morellum*'), appended to his posthumous Latin collection, *Xenia* (1569), ll. 113-14. Many of the details following are also taken from this elegy, but Hill proposes persuasively that WP's immediate source is a French paraphrase thereof, in the biographical sketch included by Charles Marty-Laveaux in his 1866 edition of JdB's French works. **too late to make him [...] a trifler in Greek** and Latin verse: in fact JdB was an excellent and well-recognised Latin poet also.

¶10. her early days in the court of Catherine (etc.): Mary Stuart, married first to François II, had spent her youth at the French court. Her mother-in-law, Catherine de Médicis, belonged to the Medici dynasty of Tuscan dukes. François de **Malherbe** (1555–1628): important French poet and critic. *ce fleur particulier*, **which Ronsard himself tells us every garden has**: in the 1587 '*Préface*' to his epic *Franciade* (1578), defending his choice of French vernacular, Ronsard writes: 'I counsel you to use all dialects indifferently [...]. Among them, the courtly idiom will always be the most beautiful, owing to the king's majesty; but without the aid of the others, it cannot be perfect; for every garden has its own particular flower'.

¶11. *la petite pucelle Angevine*: 'the little maiden of Anjou'. The phrase, excepting the definite article, comprises the first line of the first '*chanson*' in Ronsard's *Second Book of Amours*. **the letter *è* Grecque** (etc.): these are considerations (i.e. the use of the letter Y, and vocalic *vs.* consonantal uses of I) which occupy Ronsard in the '*Avertissement au Lecteur*' in his *Odes* of 1550, in which he explains his orthographical practice. **ephemeral existence**: Hill points out that WP here closely paraphrases Marty-Laveaux (see ¶9n. above), vol. 1, p. iv.

¶12. **unscanned verse of Villon**: not truly without metrical method, but Villon's prosody has not always been well understood. In any case Villon's versification is less theoretically fastidious and self-consciously regulated than that of Ronsard and JdB. *la poésie chantée*: 'sung verse', poetry set to music (e.g. medieval troubadour verse).

¶13. Claude **Goudimel** (died 1572): French composer known especially for settings of poetry (*chansons*). **"Lord of terrible aspect"**: Love as portrayed by Dante in the *Vita Nuova* (the precise phrase appears in D.G. Rossetti's 1861 translation), as opposed to **Love the boy, or the babe**, i.e. the child Cupid or Eros. *ondelette*: wavelet; *fontelette*: little fountain; *doucelette*: sweet-little-[one]; *Cassandrette*: diminutive of the name of Ronsard's beloved in the 1552 *Amours de Cassandre*, which he confers, in her honour, upon a kind of flower: see *First Book of Amours*, son. 116. Diminutives are used with great frequency in the verse of the Pléiade poets, an aspect of their '*style mignard*' which shows Neo-Catullan influence. *le beau sejour du commun jour* (WP translates): quoted from Ronsard's ode '*De L'Élection de son sepulchre*', *Fourth Book of Odes*, no. 4.

¶14. *une fadeur exquise*: translated by WP, but *fadeur* usually means 'blandness' or 'insipidity'; source, if any, unknown.

¶15. *ce pays du Vendomois*: 'the country of the Vendôme'. *La Beauce*: a region between the Loire and the Seine, with Chartres as its major city. The character of this country is portrayed in the early chapters of *Gaston*.

¶16. *Sonnetz a la louange d'Olive*: 'Sonnets in Praise of Olive', a Petrarchistic sequence published in 1549. *D'amour, de grace, et de haulte valeur* (etc.): *Olive*, son. 2: 'With grace, and love, and high valour, the divine fires were girdled, and the heavens were invested in a precious mantle of burning, many-coloured rays; all was filled with beauty, with happiness—the becalmed sea, and the gracious winds—when she was born here, in these humble places; she who has accrued to herself all the honour in the world. She took her complexion from the whitening lily, her hair from gold, her two lips from the roses, and from the sun she took her resplendent eyes. Heaven, in its generosity, put into her spirit, sealed up there, its own seeds, and from the Gods her name wins immortality.'

¶17. **M. Sainte-Beuve thought he found** (etc.): i.e. in his review-essay 'Joachim Du Bellay', on the publication of vol. 1 of Marty-Laveaux's edition (see ¶9n. above). The essay appeared in the *Journal des savants* in Aug. 1867, and was later collected into the *Nouveaux lundis*. As Hill notes, Sainte-Beuve does not use the term *poésie intime* in relation to JdB, but Marty-Laveaux himself in his biographical note (vol. 1, p. x) had made reference to the phrase. ***Antiquités de Rome*** ('Antiquities of Rome') and ***Regrets***: two sonnet-collections by JdB, both published in 1558 on his return to France from Rome.

¶18. **among the ruins of ancient Rome**: as described in the *Antiquités de Rome*. ***la grandeur du rien*** (WP translates): *Antiq.*, son. 13. ***le grand tout***: translated by WP, but otherwise, 'the great All'; *Antiq.*, son. 9 and 22. ***La douceur Angevine***: translated by WP, but otherwise, 'the Angevin mildness'; from *Regrets*, son. 31, which furnishes also the image of the smoking chimney. Cf. ¶9n.

¶19. **the eighteen lines of one famous ode**: i.e. Ronsard's *First Book of Odes* (1555), no. 17, the '*Ode à Cassandre*', or '*A sa maistresse*' ('To his Mistress'), beginning '*Mignonne, allons voir si la rose*'. **Du Bellay has almost been the poet of one poem**: the poem is from a Latin epigram by **Andrea Navagero** (Andreas Naugerius, 1483–1529), an important Italian scholar and Latin poet. The epigram titled '*Vota ad Auras*' ('Prayer to the Winds'), from his *Lusus* (1530), is only six lines, whereas JdB's imitation expands to eighteen (each elegiac couplet in the Latin becoming a six-line stanza in the French). ***D'UN VANNEUR DE BLE AUX VENTS***: 'A Wheat-Winnower, to the Winds'; *Divers Jeux rustiques* (1558), no. 3. Lang's English version ('Hymn to the Winds') reads: 'To you, troop so fleet, / That with winged wandering feet, / Through the wide world pass, / And with soft murmuring / Toss the green shades of spring / In woods and grass, / Lily and violet / I give, and blossoms wet, / Roses and dew; / This branch of blushing roses, / Whose fresh bud uncloses; / Wind-flowers, too. // Ah, winnow with sweet breath, / Winnow the holt and heath / Round this retreat; / Where all the golden morn / We fan the gold o' the corn, / In the sun's heat.' Lang, *op. cit.*, p. 138; cf. ¶4n. above.

§ *Winckelmann*

An early publication, revised for *Ren.* (1873), but first appearing in the *Westminster Review*, January 1867. Johann Joachim Winckelmann (1717–68) was an important German historian of art, antiquarian and philhellene. The Latin subtitle or epigraph, added in the third edition (1888), means 'I too was in Arcadia' or 'I too have been in Arcadia', and is a version of the title of a famous painting by Poussin, '*Et in Arcadia Ego*' ('Even in Arcadia am I' or 'I too am in Arcadia'), which displays the phrase as an inscription on a tomb. The speaker is usually taken to be Death, and Arcadia is significant as the idyllic country of classical and neo-classical pastoral poetry.

¶19. **one of the frescoes of the Vatican**: Raphael's '*Disputa*', in the *Camera della Segnatura*. **Another fresco**: Raphael's 'Parnassus'. **sources of Castalia**: in classical mythology, the sacred fount of the Muses on Mount Parnassus. **this other "city of God"**:

see Psalm 46:4: 'There is a river, the streams whereof shall make glad the city of God, the holy place of the tabernacles of the most High' (*AV*). **Scyles […] in the beautiful story of Herodotus**: Scyles is a Scythian king enamoured of Greek customs, who is said to have spent certain intervals living secretly as a Greek, in Greek attire (Herodotus IV.78).

¶ 20. **"the artist is the child of his time"**: Schiller, *Letters on the Aesthetic Education of Man*, letter 9.

¶21. **Athena Polias**: Athena 'of the city', in her guise as benign protectress of city states, Athens especially. **"the classical polytheism [etc.]"**: J.H. Newman, *Essay on the Development of Christian Doctrine* (1845), ch. 4, §1.

¶ 22. **"rise up with wings as eagles"**: see Isaiah 40:31: 'But they that wait upon the LORD shall renew their strength; they shall mount up with wings as eagles; they shall run, and not be weary; and they shall walk, and not faint'.

¶23. ἡ πτεροῦ δύναμις (translated by WP): from Plato, *Phaedrus*, 246d. **those which Pausanias found** (etc.): see Pausanias, Bk VIII: Arcadia. (Hill refers to II.4.5, but that passage is concerned with Corinth, not Arcadia.) **Athenæus tells the story** (etc.): *Deipnosophistae* XIV.2. **in whom they live and move and have their being**: see Acts 17:28, in which Paul addresses the pagans of Athens: 'For in him we live, and move, and have our being; as certain also of your own poets have said, For we are also his offspring'. **addolorata**: the Virgin Mary, in Roman Catholic tradition, as 'Lady of Sorrows'. On the 'worship of sorrow', cf. 'Study of Dionysus', ¶29ff., and see also 'The Myth of Demeter and Persephone' (two parts, *GS*). **the vertiginous prophetess at the very centre of Greek religion**: the Delphic oracle. **The Dorian worship of Apollo** (etc.): cf. 'Lacedæmon', ¶17, etc.; *PP* ch. 1–5 extracts, extr. (iii), ¶9, and extr. (vi), *passim*; 'Study of Dionysus', ¶23; and 'Beginnings of Greek Sculpture, I', ¶21. **Chthonian divinities**: underworld gods.

¶24. On Fra **Angelico** (1387–1455), cf. 'Sandro Botticelli', ¶6n. *tanquam lana alba et tanquam nix*: Revelation 1:14 in the Vulgate (*AV*: '[His head and his hairs were white] like wool, as white as snow').

¶25. **Venus of Melos**: statue in the Louvre. **"lordship of the soul"**: quoted, apparently, from the fourth choral song (l. 1200) of *Atalanta in Calydon* (1865), Swinburne's pseudo-Hellenic verse tragedy, which had been published a couple of years before WP's essay. But in Swinburne the main sense seems to be lordship *over* the soul (i.e. self-discipline), whereas here the main sense is *the soul's quality of lordliness*.

¶26. Those **"Mothers"** (etc.): refers to the protagonist's visit to the 'realm of the Mothers' in Goethe's *Faust*, Pt 2, 1.7. **"nimbly and sweetly recommending itself"**: *Macbeth* 1.6:1–3: 'the air / Nimbly and sweetly recommends itself / Unto our gentle senses'.

¶ 27. **"By no people," says Winckelmann** (etc.): paraphrased from a paragraph near the start of Pt 1, ch. 4, §1 of JJW's *History of the Art of Antiquity*. Some of the sentences are not found in the first edition (1764), but come from later revised texts. Herodotus V.47 furnishes the story of Philip of Croton, and Pausanias VIII.24.4, IX.10.4 and IX.22.1 provide the details of the second sentence. **Charito-blepharos**: 'graceful-eyebrowed'. *palæstra*: gymnasium.

¶28. Ὄμνυμι πάντας θεοὺς (etc., translated by WP): Xenophon, *Symposium* IV.11.

¶29. **Hegel's beautiful comparison**: refers to a certain statue of Memnon supposed to have emitted a sound when struck by the rays of the sun at dawn. Hegel uses this image in *Phenomenology of Mind* VII.A.(c), and in *Aesthetics*, Pt 2, *abschnitt* 1, ch. 1.C.3(a).

¶32. **Heiterkeit** and **Allgemeinheit**: terms used by Hegel in the *Aesthetics*.

¶33. **Robert Browning**: see also WP's review-essay 'Browning' (*EG*). 'Dîs Aliter Visum, or *Le Byron de nos Jours*' ('The Gods Thought Otherwise, or The Byron of our Times'): poem from Browning's *Dramatis Personae* (1864), spoken by a woman to an old friend, a poet. Ten years ago, and before her now unhappy marriage, they missed their chance of love. The monologue is a mixture of regret, nostalgia and upbraiding.

¶36. **The *Laocoon***: well-known statue group in the Vatican galleries, showing the Trojan priest and his two sons set upon by sea-serpents, as depicted in *Aeneid* II.

¶37. **Winckelmann compares it to a quiet sea** (etc.): *History of the Art of Antiquity*, Pt I, ch. 4, §3: 'The forms of beautiful youth resemble the unity of the surface of the sea, which at some distance appears smooth and still, like a mirror, although constantly in movement with its heaving swell' (trans. G. Henry Lodge, London, 1850, pp. 47-48 [ch. 2, ¶28]). **"beautiful multitude"**: Keats, *Endymion* III:817. **Panathenaic frieze**: the frieze of the Parthenon, much of which is in the British Museum. **the *adorante* of the museum of Berlin**: a Hellenistic bronze statue of a praying boy, still in the Staatliche Museum, Berlin. WP mentions it again in 'The Age of Athletic Prizemen', where it is called 'Winckelmann's antique favourite' (*GS*, Lib. Edn, pp. 295, 297).

¶38. **"This sense," says Hegel** (etc.): translated or paraphrased quite closely from the *Aesthetics*, Pt 3, *abschnitt* 2, ch. 1.3. Phryne, seen bathing thus at a festival, was said to have become the model for a legendary painting by Apelles showing Aphrodite rising from the sea.

¶39. **like a relic of classical antiquity** (etc.): closely echoes a sentence in WP's earlier essay 'Diaphaneité', at that time still unpublished, which attempts to delineate a kind of ideal character or temperament: 'Such a character is like a relic from the classical age, laid open by accident to our alien modern atmosphere' (*MS*, Lib. Edn, p. 251). **The beauty of the Greek statues [...] significance of its own**: these sentences are almost exactly reproduced from 'Diaphaneité': 'The beauty of the Greek statues was a sexless beauty; the statues of the gods had the least traces of sex. Here there is a moral sexlessness, a kind of impotence, an ineffectual wholeness of nature, yet with a divine beauty and significance of its own' (p. 253).

¶40. **"the tyranny of the senses"**: the phrase is in relatively common usage in the C19[th], the idea broadly Platonic. On art as an 'escape' therefrom, Hill finds precedents in both Schiller (particularly *Aesthetic Education*, letter 24) and Hegel. Cf. 'The Child in the House', ¶9, 12. **Plato's false astronomer**: *Republic*, 529-30, in which Socrates says: 'that knowledge only which is of being and of the unseen can make the soul look upwards, and whether a man gapes at the heavens or blinks on the ground, seeking to learn some particular sense, I would deny that he can learn, for nothing of that sort is matter of science; his soul is looking downwards, not upwards [...]. The spangled heavens should be used as a pattern and with a view to that higher knowledge; their beauty is like the beauty of figures or pictures excellently wrought by the hand of Daedalus, or some other great artist, which we may chance to behold; any geometrician who saw them would appreciate the exquisiteness of their workmanship, but he would never dream of thinking that in them he could find the true equal or the true double, or the truth of any other proportion. [...] And will not a true astronomer have the same feeling when he looks at the movements of the stars? Will he not think that heaven and the things in heaven are framed by the Creator of them in the most perfect manner? But he will never imagine that the proportions of night and day, or of both to the month, or of the month to the year, or of the stars to these and to one another, and any other things that are material and visible can also be eternal and subject to no deviation—that would be absurd; and it is equally absurd to take so much pains in investigating their exact truth.' (Trans. Jowett.) *I did but taste a little honey* (etc.): 1 Samuel 14:43: 'Then Saul said to Jonathan, Tell me what thou hast done. And Jonathan told him, and said, I did but taste a little honey with the end of the rod that was in mine hand, and, lo, I must die'.

¶41. **Theocritus**: Hellenistic Greek poet of the C3rd B.C., whose 'Idylls' are the earliest major classical models of pastoral verse.

¶42. **Gilliatt, in Victor Hugo's *Travailleurs de la Mer*** (*Toilers of the Sea*, 1866): Gilliatt is the hero of the novel, a lonely young man of Guernsey, mistusted by the community, who falls in love with the niece of a ship-owner. When the ship is wrecked, she promises to marry the man who recovers the engine from the wreckage—which Gilliat does, after a dramatic fight with an octopus, only to find that his beloved has fallen in love with another. He renounces his claim and drowns himself. **the bleeding mouth of Fantine**: in Hugo's *Les Misérables* (1862), Fantine sells her own front teeth in order to pay the medical expenses of her daughter, who is in the care of unscrupulous extortioners, and whose illness is fictitious. **mournful mysteries of Adonis, of Hyacinthus, of Demeter**: on Adonis and Hyacinthus, cf. 'Lacedæmon', ¶30, and Greek Sculpture (Further Extracts), extr. (i), ¶11–13; on Demeter, see 'The Myth of Demeter and Persephone' (two parts, *GS*). Cf. also ¶23n. above on the 'worship of sorrow'. **Hyperion gives way to Apollo, Oceanus to Poseidon**: refers to the overthrow of the Titans by the Olympian gods in Greek mythology. ***Master of the Passion***: in Hill's opinion, probably the late-C15th 'Master of the Berlin Passion', a German or Netherlandish engraver. **"ready to melt out their essence fine into the winds"**: another reference to Keats' *Endymion*: 'For 'twas the morn: Apollo's upward fire / Made every eastern cloud a silvery pyre / Of brightness so unsullied, that therein / A melancholy spirit well might win / Oblivion, and melt out his essence fine / Into the winds' (1:95–100); cf. ¶37n. **in which[,] like Helen of Troy [...] spectres of the middle age**: the Lib. Edn omits the comma after 'which', presumably by a simple typesetting oversight, but I have restored it in accordance with the 1893 text (WP's last revisions) and earlier editions. The mention of Helen in this context perhaps refers to her magical or ghostly reappearance in Goethe's *Faust* (and in Marlowe's *Doctor Faustus*), and/or to the myth of 'Helen in Egypt'—the notion, espoused by Euripides and Stesichorus, that Helen had remained in Egypt during the time of the Trojan War, while a spectral pseudo-Helen was at the centre of the great events. On the classical pagan gods as spooky presences in the middle ages, cf. 'Pico Della Mirandola', ¶2 (and n.); also *PP*, ch. 1–5 extracts, extr. (v), ¶4. And see 'Denys L'Auxerrois' (*IP*) and 'Apollo in Picardy' (*MS*).

¶43. **the form of the *basilica***: the basic shape of the basilican church (the usual plan of Christian churches) is inspired by the basilicas of the Roman world, which were non-religious buildings used for official, legal and ceremonial business. **"worship of sorrow"**: see ¶23n. above. **"smiled through its tears"**: in Hegel this describes the 'espression of lament' in Romantic art (*Aesthetics*, Pt 1, ch. 3.A.1(c).β). Raphael's **Saint Agatha at Bologna**: in fact the painting is now attributed to Guercino. Goethe's *Iphigenie* [*auf Tauris*] (1779-86) is a dramatic work based on the *Iphigenia in Tauris* of Euripides.

§ Conclusion

WP's most famous 'essay', this appeared in the first edition of *Ren*. (1873), was excised from the second (1877) after having occasioned much controversy, and was restored, with a number of revisions, in the third (1888). See Introduction for a discussion of its fortunes. Its earliest appearance, however, was in a rather different context, for it formed the final part of a review-essay called 'Poems by William Morris' in the *Westminster Review*, October 1868. The rest of the essay on Morris was revised for the first edition of *App.*, where it goes under the title 'Æsthetic Poetry'; but this too was omitted from later editions. **Greek epigraph**: 'Heraclitus says that all things are in flight and nothing stands still'; from Plato's *Cratylus*, 402a. Cf. *PP*, ch. 1-5 extracts, extr. (ii), ¶10-11, 16, *et passim*.

¶1. **the tendency of modern thought**: cf. 'Coleridge', ¶2, 35; *PP*, ch. 1-5 extracts, extr. (ii), ¶15-16; and 'Doctrine of Plato: Pt II: Dialectic', ¶2, 20-21. The thoughts explored here are informed both by modern experimental science and by philosophy ancient and modern. One of the classical points of reference for such thinking, and for the expressions and figurations used by WP, is—as the epigraph advertises—the philosophy of Heraclitus: cf. *PP*, ch. 1-5 extracts, extr. (ii). WP's later and fuller thoughts on Heraclitus and 'perpetual flux' are explored in *Marius*, beginning in Pt II (ch. 8) and then adjusted from Pt III onward (see especially ch. 16, 'Second Thoughts').

¶2. **constantly re-forming itself on the stream**: this figure draws upon the aqueous imagery associated with Heraclitean 'flux'. See again, e.g., Plato, *Cratylus*, 402a: 'Heraclitus [...] compares present reality to the flow of a river, saying that one can never step into the same stream twice'.

¶3. *Philosophiren ist dephlegmatisiren* [,] *vivificiren*: 'To philosophize is to dephlegmatize [i.e. rouse], to vivify'; but WP offers his own paraphrase. From the philosophical fragments of the German Romantic writer Novalis (Baron Friedrich von Hardenberg, 1772-1801). I have replaced the comma between *dephlegmatisiren* and *vivificiren*, which is missing from the Lib. Edn but present in the fourth edition (upon which it was based) and all previous versions. Doubtless it is a mere typesetting error.

¶4. **"Philosophy is the microscope of thought"**: Victor Hugo, *Les Misérables* (1862) v: Jean Valjean, Bk II, ch. 2: '*La philosophie, c'est le miscroscope de la pensée*'. In the first edition of *Ren*. the quotation had been printed in French. **in the clear, fresh writings of Voltaire**: as several critics have noted, Rousseau's *Confessions* VI does not speak about Voltaire in particular.

¶5. *les hommes sont tous condamnés* (etc.; WP translates above the French): from Victor Hugo's novella *Le Dernier Jour d'un condamné* (*The Last Day of a Condemned Man*, 1829/32), ch. 3. **then our place knows us no more**: allusion to Psalm 103:15-16: 'As for man, his days are as grass: as a flower of the field, so he flourisheth. For the wind passeth over it, and it is gone; and the place thereof shall know it no more' (*AV*). **"the children of this world"**: a reference to the Parable of the Unjust Steward in Luke 16:1–13. The steward, whose dishonesty has been discovered, is dismissed by his master, but ingratiates himself with the master's debtors by doctoring their bills in order to reduce their debts. 'And the lord commended the unjust steward, because he had done wisely: for the children of this world are in their generation wiser than the children of light.' WP thus makes clear, without full explicitness, that his remarks at this point concern 'the children of *this* world' as opposed implicitly to 'the children of light', thereby suggesting that the ethic described is specifically that of the religious sceptic. A remembrance of the parable, taking account of the master's ironic commendation of the unjust steward's 'wisdom', may also add a tint of irony to WP's expression, 'the wisest'. **the love of art for its own sake**: thus in the fourth edition (1893), which includes WP's final revisions; but in the first and third editions and in 'Poems by William Morris' the phrase had been 'the love of art for art's sake'. This is one of the more significant of the minor revisions made by WP to his most controversial piece of writing, since it appears to show his avoidance of what had become a too-familiar aestheticist credo or slogan.

APPRECIATIONS

§*Style*

First published in the *Fortnightly Review*, December 1888. Much of the essay is concerned with Flaubert, about whom Pater had written one review-essay already ('The Life and Letters of Flaubert', *Pall Mall Gazette*, August 1888) and would publish another in the following year ('*Correspondance de Gustave Flaubert*', *Athenaeum*, August 1889).

¶1. **"good round-hand"**: metaphor taken from handwriting. **of *Lycidas* for instance**: possibly WP has in mind Ruskin's elucidation of Milton's poem in 'Of King's Treasuries' (*Sesame and Lilies*, 1865). Cf. ¶11n. below.

¶2. **"the literature of power and the literature of knowledge"**: a famous distinction elaborated in De Quincey's *Letters to a Young Man whose Education has been Neglected* (1823), and in 'The Poetry of Pope' (1848).

¶7. ***Exclusiones debitæ naturæ***: 'exclusions owed to nature'; Francis Bacon, *Novum Organum* I, §105: 'But the induction which is to be available for the discovery and demonstration of sciences and arts, must analyse nature by proper rejections and exclusions [*naturam separare debet, per rejectiones et exclusiones debitas*]; and then, after a sufficient number of negatives, come to a conclusion on the affirmative instances'. (Trans. James Spedding, 1855.) Cf. 'Doctrine of Plato, Pt II: Dialectic', ¶6 (and n.).

¶8. *le cuistre*: implies smugness and priggishness as well as pedantry.

¶9. **Wordsworth**, and **the consecrated poetic associations of a century** (etc.): alludes not only to the qualities of Wordsworth's verse, but to his polemical 'Preface' to *Lyrical Ballads* (1798). ***ascertain, communicate, discover***: we 'misuse' these words by failing to remain aware of their most literal meanings: i.e., respectively, to make an approach towards certainty in a matter, or to bring someone else towards such assurance; to make something common or communal (from Latin *communis*); to reveal something by removing what covers or conceals it (i.e. to disclose or divulge, implying the pre-existence of the thing). **"*its*," which ought to have been in Shakespeare**: i.e., it would be absurd for a modern writer to undertake never to use the word 'its' on the grounds that Shakespeare instead uses 'his' and 'hers' to refer to inanimate objects. In fact Shakespeare sometimes does use 'its'.

"second intention": in logic, 'first intentions' are one's 'primary conceptions of things, formed by the first or direct application of the mind to the things themselves', whereas 'secondary conceptions [are] formed by the application of thought to first intentions in their relations to each other' (*OED*). Distance from a word's origins, transference between languages, and historical changes in usage all contribute to a sensitive writer's (or reader's) apprehension of precise distinctions, associations, the linguistic standing of one word in relation to another, etc.—and hence the implications of particular verbal choices.

¶ 10. **"To go preach to the first passer-by"**: Montaigne, *Essays* III.8; the wording is very close to the translation by Charles Cotton. *ascêsis*: 'self-discipline' (from Greek); cf. *Ren.*, 'Preface', ¶6 (and n.), and 'Lacedæmon', ¶23.

¶11. *Lycidas*: poem by John Milton, 1637; see ¶1 (and n.) above. [*The History of Henry*] *Esmond*: 1852 novel by W.M. Thackeray. John Henry **Newman's** *Idea of a University*: book-length essay, 1852. **"The artist," says Schiller** (etc.): Schiller, *Votivtafeln* (*Votive Tablets*), no. 43 ('*Der Meister*'): '*Jeden anderen Meister erkennt man an dem was er ausspricht, / Was er weise verschweigt zeigt mir den Meister des Styls*' ('Every other kind of master can be known by what he says; but it is what he wisely *conceals* that shows me the master of style'). Cf. discussion of artistic omission and selectivity in 'A Prince of Court Painters' (*IP*). In the unpublished essay-fragment 'The Æsthetic Life', WP writes: 'Well! does not all right conduct of artistic matters always involve selection? Does not the aim of all art lie in the establishment of an ideal depending partly on negative qualifications, culture in its most general sense being in large measure negative or renunciant, a fine habit of ignoring or forgetting?'

¶13. **Currently**: i.e. as one goes along; in the flow of reading.

¶15. Henry Longueville **Mansel** (1820-71): philosopher and theologian; the book to which WP refers is his *Prolegomena Logica: An Inquiry into the Psychological Character of Logical Processes* (1851/60). **critical tracing out**: cf. 'Dante Gabriel Rossetti', ¶1. **Yet of poetic literature too**: cf. comments on prose and verse virtues in 'English Literature' (*EG*).

¶ 16. **"The altar-fire has touched those lips!"** Isaiah 6:6-7: 'Then flew one of the seraphims unto me, having a live coal in his hand, which he had taken with the tongs from off the altar: And he laid it upon my mouth, and said, Lo, this hath touched thy lips; and thine iniquity is taken away, and thy sin purged'. Emanuel **Swedenborg** (1688-1722): Swedish natural philosopher and mystic; cf. 'Coleridge', ¶29, and 'Dante Gabriel Rossetti', ¶9. **Tracts for the Times**: theological publications by members of the Oxford (or 'Tractarian') Movement in the Church of England, 1833-41, including important writings by such as Keble, Newman and Pusey.

¶17. **a curious series of letters**: i.e. Flaubert's correspondence with Louise Colet, which began in 1846, soon after their first meeting and the beginning of their almost immediate erotic entanglement. A poet and writer for journals, married, a noted beauty, and well known in artistic circles, Colet became the anonymous **Madame X**. of early editions of the correspondence. Most of the letters quoted by WP are addressed to her (henceforth 'LC'). **[Inset quotation(s)]**: para. 1, from letter to LC, 13 Sept. 1846; para. 2, to Alfred le Poittevin, 13 May and 1 May 1845; para. 3, to LC, 17 Sept. 1846 (sentences 1–2) and to le Poittevin, [?] Sept. 1845, with omissions; para. 4, to LC, 18 Sept. 1846, omitting from GF's list the 'end' of the nightingale, which is 'to sing'.

¶**18.** **[Inset quotation]**: the 'commentator' is Guy de Maupassant, in an '*Étude sur Flaubert*' (*Revue Bleue*, Jan. 1884; repr. as preface to F's *Oeuvres*, 1885).

¶**20.** "**soul and body reunited**": 'The Reunion of the Soul & the Body', one of Blake's illustrations for Robert Blair's poem *The Grave* (cf. 'Sir Thomas Browne', ¶29). **[Inset quotation]**: from letter to LC, 18 Sept. 1846.

¶**22.** **those labourers in the parable**: see Matthew 20:1–16. **[Inset quotation(s)]**: from letter to LC, 11 Aug. 1846 (sentences 1–2); the rest to Maxime Du Camp, 7 Apr. 1846.

¶**23.** **[Inset quotation(s)]**: from various letters: to LC, [?] Oct. 1847 (sentences 1–2); to LC, early 1847 (sent. 3); to LC, 14–15 Aug. 1846 (sent. 4–5); the rest to Ernest Chevalier, 26 Dec. 1838. **What Buffon said**: the saying is attributed to the Comte de **Buffon** (1707–88) by Hérault de Séchelles in his *Visite à Buffon* (1785).

¶**24.** **[Inset quotation]**: from letter to LC, end of Sept. 1847.

¶**26.** *vraie vérité*: cf. 'School of Giorgione', ¶25 (and n.). "**entire, smooth, and round**": Horace, *Satires* II.7:86: '*totus teres atque rotundus*'.

¶**27.** "**The style is the man**": Buffon (see ¶23n. above) in his *Discours sur le Style* (*Discourse on Style*, 1753): '*Le style c'est l'homme même*'.

¶**28.** **[Inset quotation]**: Maupassant, *op. cit.* (see ¶18n. above).

¶**30.** **music [...] as the typically perfect art**: cf. 'School of Giorgione', ¶5ff.

¶**31.** **the soul of humanity** (etc.): cf. Introduction, pp. 35–36; 'Pico Della Mirandola', ¶16n.; 'Charles Lamb', ¶17; and *Marius*, ch. 15.

§ *Wordsworth*

An earlier review-essay on Wordsworth was published in the *Fortnightly Review*, April 1874. This piece from *App.* is a much longer essay reproducing, in altered form, some of the earlier material. Two further review-essays on recent editions of Wordsworth, one in the *Athenaeum* (26 January 1889) and the other in the *Guardian* (27 February 1889), also re-use material from the 1874 essay.

¶**1.** *Fancy* and *Imagination*: in English criticism, this distinction is associated primarily with Coleridge, who elaborates upon it in his *Biographia Literaria* (ch. 4–13) and elsewhere. It is discussed by WW in the 'Preface' to his *Poems* of 1815, in which collection he classified his earlier poems under the heads 'Poems of the Fancy' and 'Poems of the Imagination', *inter alia*.

¶**2.** **excesses of 1795**: refers to the events of the French Revolution, which had initially filled WW with hopeful enthusiasm. 1795 saw the establishment of the *Directoire*, but the 'Reign of Terror' had already run its course over the previous two years. **that old fancy which made the poet's art an enthusiasm**: i.e. the theory of poetic inspiration as a divine mania or *furor*, an idea connected particularly with Plato (in the *Ion* and *Phaedrus*) and Neo-Platonism.

¶3. *disciplina arcani*: 'discipline of the secret'; term used in early Christianity with reference to the deliberately secretive guardianship of religious mysteries.

¶5. **Senancour** and **Théophile Gautier** (etc.): cf. 'Postscript', ¶11, and 'Prosper Mérimée', ¶1. **[Inset quotations]**: respectively, from WW's *Prelude* X:277–78 ('The' for 'And'), XII:319–20, and IV:329–30; and from 'The Pet-Lamb: A Pastoral', l. 28 ('thine' for 'thy').

¶6. **"efficacious spirit"**: *Prelude* XII:219. **"particular spots" of time**: *ibid.*, l. 208, where WW famously introduces the idea of 'spots of time', though without using the word 'particular'.

¶8. **"full of souls"**: Leibniz uses such a phrase on several occasions. Versions of panpsychism and animism seem to have appealed to WP. Cf. *Marius*, ch. 20: 'Were not all visible objects—the whole material world indeed, [...] "full of souls"?'

¶9. **"a sort of thought in sense"**: from Shelley's 1839 poem 'Peter Bell the Third' (a satirical response to WW's 'Peter Bell'), l. 312.

¶10. **leech-gatherer**: see WW's 'Resolution and Independence' (or 'The Leech-Gatherer'). **woman "stepping westward"**: see 'Stepping Westward'. **aged thorn** and **lichened rock**: see 'The Thorn', with its comparison to a lichened rock at ll. 10–15. **the poet of Surrey, say!**: no doubt the implication is that the county of Surrey is less stirring to the imagination than the Lake District.

¶11. **"Grave livers," stately speech** (etc.): references to 'Resolution and Independence', and the leech-gatherer's 'stately speech; / Such as grave Livers do in Scotland use, / Religious men, who give to God and man their dues' (ll. 96–98).

¶12. **"related in a selection of language really used by men"**: from WW's 'Preface' to *Lyrical Ballads* (1798).

¶13. **Michael by the sheepfold, Ruth by the wayside**: refers to the narrative poems 'Michael' and 'Ruth'. Wilhelm **Meinhold** (1797–1851): German writer; cf. 'Postscript', ¶2 (and n.). **the girl who rung her father's knell**: see 'The Westmoreland Girl' (Pt 2). **the unborn infant feeling about its mother's heart**: see 'The Thorn', st. 13: 'And grey-haired Wilfred of the Glen / Held that the unborn infant wrought / About its mother's heart, and brought / Her senses back again'. **"who, in his heart, was half a shepherd on the stormy seas"**: 'The Brothers', ll. 42–43 (paraphrased). **the wild woman teaching her child to pray for her betrayer**: see 'The Mad Mother'. **making of the shepherd's staff** and **laying the first stone of the sheepfold**: both incidents in 'Michael'.

¶14. **"the little rock-like pile"**: *Prelude* VII:327.

¶15. **the old heresy of Origen** (Christian theologian flourishing in the early C3[rd]): i.e. of the pre-existency of the human soul. **"the first diviner influence of this world"**: *Prelude* XII:182.

¶17. *anima mundi*: 'soul of the world'. **others had become indifferent to the distinctions of good and evil**: refers primarily to the Albigensian Heresy (Catharism); see 'Two Early French Stories' in *Ren.* ('Aucassin and Nicolette' in the first edition). **like the sign of the *macrocosm* to Faust in his cell**: Goethe, *Faust*, Pt I, sc. 1 ('Night').

¶18. **those two lofty books of *The Prelude***: Bks XII–XIII.

¶20. **a clause from one of Shakespeare's sonnets**: apparently not the words 'weep to have' (quoting son. 64) at *Prelude* V:25, because in the 1850 version of the poem, the only text known to WP, the phrase is given in quotation marks and hence cannot be 'unconscious'. The singing bird in the ruined nave at *Prelude* 11:121–30 may be an echo of son. 73, but does not reproduce a particular 'clause'. WP may have in mind the words 'If this be error', later in the same book (l. 419): a direct 'quotation' (even if 'unconscious') from son. 116. But possibly several other plausible passages might be adduced.

¶22. **Grandet**: miserly father in Balzac's novel *Eugénie Grandet* (1833). **Javert**: detective in Hugo's *Les Misérables* (1862). **Saint Catherine of Siena** (1347–80): remembered especially for her visionary 'mystical marriage' with Christ, described in her letters. ***House Beautiful***: refers to Bunyan's *The Pilgrim's Progress*; cf. 'Dante Gabriel Rossetti', ¶8, and 'Postscript', ¶1.

¶23. **that old Greek moralist**: Aristotle, whose ethical thinking is based on a notion of 'proper function' and concerned with the practical achievement of such function. **a cup of water to a poor man**: perhaps remembering Matthew 10:42. **"antique Rachel," sitting in the company of Beatrice**: see Dante, *Inferno* 11:102 ('*l'antica Rachele*').

¶24. **whatever may become of the fruit, make sure of the flowers and the leaves**: cf. *Ren.*, 'Conclusion'. **the battle** (etc.): i.e. in the cause of Utilitarianism: see WP's footnote.

¶25. the morality of ***being*** as distinct from ***doing*** is further elaborated in *Marius*. **"on the great and universal passions of men [etc.]"**: from WW's 'Preface' to *Lyrical Ballads* ('on' added by WP). **"the operations of the elements [etc.]"**: *ibid.* ('on' for 'with' throughout). **"of man suffering, amid awful forms and powers"**: the true line is 'Man suffering among awful Powers and Forms' (*Prelude* VIII:16).

§ *Coleridge*

An early essay on Coleridge, furnishing considerable material for this later piece, was WP's first publication, 'Coleridge's Writings', which appeared anonymously in the *Westminster Review* for January 1866. This was concerned primarily with Coleridge's philosophical thought. As WP's footnote indicates, another substantial part of the final essay, dealing with Coleridge (here 'STC') as a poet, originates in a prefatory memoir contributed to T.H. Ward's anthology of *English Poets*, vol. 3, in 1880.

¶1. **an unbroken continuity of life**: seems to fuse together Darwinism, the Hegelian conception of history, and the idea of 'humanism' or 'humanity' often expressed in WP (e.g. in *Marius*, ch. 15; but cf. 'Style', ¶31, and 'Charles Lamb', ¶17; and see Introduction, pp. 35–36).

¶2. **οὐσία ἀχρώματος, ἀσχημάτιστος, ἀναφής**: 'colourless, formless, untouchable essence'; paraphrase from Plato, *Phaedrus*, 247c.

¶3. **"apprehend the absolute"**: possibly WP quotes the phrase from Emerson's 1836 essay 'Nature' (§6: 'Idealism'). But similar phrases are common in Hegel and other German philosophical writers of idealist tendencies.

¶4. **"weep", "shriek"** (etc.): the original version of the essay had no quotation marks in this sentence—a circumstance which might be supposed to suggest that reference to precise sources was not intended. **Crœsus thought it a paradox** (etc.): see Herodotus I.29–33. **"children in the market-place"**: see Matthew 11:16–19 and Luke 7:31–35. The children ('calling unto their fellows, And saying, We have piped unto you, and ye have not danced; we have mourned unto you, and ye have not lamented') represent 'the men of this generation', who fail to accept Christ and the Baptist. The implications of this allusion are ambiguous.

¶5. **"I was driven from life in motion [etc.]"**: quoted from one one STC's autobiographical notes, as reproduced in ch. 1 of James Gillman's *Life of Coleridge* (1838). **as Madame de Staël observed**: they had met in London in 1813, and this became a much-repeated literary anecdote. **"I am much better [etc.]"**: letter to Joseph Cottle, 14 Apr. 1798.

¶6. **"rich graciousness and courtesy"**: source unlocated. **"His voice rose [etc.]"**: from Hazlitt's *My First Acquaintance with Poets* (1823), describing his first encounter with STC in 1798, and quoting a line from Milton's *Comus* (l. 556). **"He talks like an angel [etc.]"**: attributed to Lord Egmont; quoted in De Quincey's *Recollections of the Lakes and the Lake Poets* (1862), in the ch. on STC (earlier published as a series of articles). WP paraphrases.

¶7. *Aids to Reflection*: prose work, 1825. *The Friend*: soon-aborted regular periodical published through 1809–10 by STC, who was responsible for most of the content. *Biographia Literaria*: one of STC's most important works of criticism, 1817.

¶8. **"he wanted better bread [etc.]"**: De Quincey, *op. cit.* (cf. ¶6n. above); the phrase is proverbial, but associated particularly with John Lyly, who uses in in the dedicatory epistle to *Euphues: The Anatomy of Wit* (1578), and also in *Mother Bombie* (1594), I.3. **"hungered for eternity"**: from Charles Lamb's 'The Death of Coleridge' (1834; 'had a hunger'). **"Beautiful Soul"**: i.e. the supposed author of the 'confessions' which make up Bk VI of Goethe's *Wilhelm Meister's Apprenticeship*. **"singing in the sails"**: perhaps referring to STC's 'Rime of the Ancient Mariner', ll. 368–83, though not a direct quotation.

¶9. **[Long quotation]**: from STC's notebooks (entry: 14 Apr. 1805). Several sentences omitted after 'inner nature'.

¶11. Friedrich Wilhelm Joseph **Schelling** (1775–1854): German idealist philosopher.

¶13. **Schelling's "Philosophy of Nature"**: i.e. his *'Naturphilosophie'*, as elaborated in his *Ideas Concerning a Philosophy of Nature* (1797) and other works. *Es giebt kein Plagiat in der Philosophie*: from Heine's *Die romantische Schule* (*The Romantic School*, 1835), Bk III. Giordano **Bruno** (1548–1600): Italian philosopher and monk, executed for heresy; see *Gaston*, ch. 7: 'The Lower Pantheism' (earlier published as an independent essay, 'Giordano Bruno', 1889). **"Whatever is, is according to reason [etc.]"**: 'What is rational is real; / And what is real is rational': Hegel, preface to *Philosophy of Right* (trans. S.W. Dyde, London, 1896). **Plotinus**: Neo-Platonic philosopher of the C3rd A.D. Georges **Cuvier** (1769–1832): French natural scientist known particularly for his pioneering work in the nascent field of paleontology. **"shadow of approaching humanity"**: STC, *Aids to Reflection* (4th edn, corr., 1839), 'Moral and Religious Aphorisms', comment to no. 36.

¶14. **"In the Shakespearian drama [etc.]"**: from the seventh of STC's 1818 lectures on literature.

¶15. [Inset quotation]: *ibid.*, earlier in the lecture.

¶16. [Inset quotation]: from STC's notes for a lecture delivered in 1812. See Coleridge, *Lectures on Literature 1808–1819*, ed. R.A. Foakes (1987), vol. 1, p. 495. It had been given in the *Literary Remains*, ed. H.N. Coleridge (1836–39), vol. 2., pp. 67–68, which established the text WP must have read. There are omissions, and WP repunctuates.

¶28. Percy's *Relics [of Ancient English Poetry]*: influential anthology of British ballads (1765). James **Macpherson's** *Ossian*: a body of supposed ancient Gaelic poems published (in feigned English 'translation') in 1760–65; the poems enjoyed great popularity in Britain and abroad. Sir Walter **Scott** compiled a well-known anthology of Scotch ballads, *The Minstrelsy of the Scottish Border* (1802–03), and was one of the chief writers who initiated the fashion in English Romantic and Victorian poetry for imitations of old ballads. **Young-eyed poesy** (etc.): from STC's 'Monody on the Death of Chatterton'. Thomas Chatterton, a poet and literary forger known for his hoax-medieval writings, died in 1770 at the age of seventeen, and was celebrated by the Romantic poets of the succeeding generations.

¶29. Samuel **Purchas**'s *Pilgrims*: evolving and expanding work published from 1613, concerned chiefly with the accounts of travellers and explorers. This is the book STC claims to have been reading before the nap in which he received the inspiration for his poetic fragment 'Kubla Khan'. Richard **Hakluyt**: editor-compiler of the voluminous classic, *The Principal Navigations, Voyages, Traffiques and Discoveries of the English Nation* (1589–1600), which was one of Purchas's main inspirations. **Thomas Burnet** (died 1715): English theologian and natural philosopher, whose *Sacred Theory of the Earth* (1681–90) was well known to STC's circle; his *Archaeologiae Philosophicae* (1692) is the source of the Latin epigraph to STC's 'Rime of the Ancient Mariner' (1817 text), from which WP quotes: "***Facile credo, plures* [etc.]**": 'I readily believe there to be more invisible than visible natures in the universe.' **the stealing of Dionysus**: one of the Homeric Hymns (VII) to Dionysus relates a story of the god's abduction from the sea-shore by a band of pirates, who think him a prince. In Andrew Lang's translation: 'But anon strange matters appeared to them: first there flowed through all the swift black ship a sweet and fragrant wine [...]. And straightway a vine stretched hither and thither along the sail, hanging with many a cluster, and dark ivy twined round the mast blossoming with flowers, and gracious fruit and garlands grew on all the thole-pins [...] [T]he God changed into the shape of a lion at the bow; and loudly he roared, and in midship he made a shaggy bear [...]. [T]he men all at once leaped overboard into the strong sea, shunning dread doom, and there were changed into dolphins.' **"Morning Stars singing together"**: one of Blake's illustrations to *The Book of Job*. **"Only once!"**: related in Gilchrist's *Life of William Blake* (1863), vol. 1, p. 128. **His "spirits"**: Blake claimed to experience regular visions in which he conversed with spirits and angels. **Swedenborg**: cf. 'Style', ¶16 (and n.), and 'Dante Gabriel Rossetti', ¶9. **The blot upon the brain** (etc.): from Tennyson's *Maud* (1855), Pt II, §4. *spectra*: 'appearances'.

¶33. [Inset quotation]: in the line 'They stood aloof[,] the scars remaining,' I have, after some hesitation, re-supplied the first comma, which WP's text lacks in all editions.

¶35. **delicate and tender justice**: cf. Introduction, pp. 33–34.

¶36. **the *ennuyé***: character type oppressed by *ennui*, and pre-eminently represented in literature by Chateaubriand's **René**, Byron's **Childe Harold** and Goethe's **Werther**. *τρυφῆς, ἁβρότητος, χλιδῆς* (etc.): 'father of delicacy, luxury, fineness, graces, longing and desire'; Plato, *Symposium*, 197d, in which the subject is Love (*Eros*). *Πατήρ* ('father' or 'author') transliterates to '*Patêr*', and one wonders if WP was humorously conscious of this fact.

§ *Charles Lamb*

First published in the *Fortnightly Review*, October 1878, with the significant surtitle 'The Character of the Humourist'. See WP's further characterisation of Lamb's prose and thought in the 1886 review-essay 'English Literature' (*EG*). It is important to bear in mind how much more popular and highly esteemed Charles Lamb (1775–1834) was in the C19th than he is at present. 'Elia' is his literary *alter ego*, the supposed speaker of the *Essays of Elia* (here '*EE*').

¶1. **distinction between the *Fancy* and the *Imagination***: refers back to the start of the essay on 'Wordsworth'.

¶2. **Coleridge and other kindred critics**: see, e.g., Hazlitt's essay 'On Wit and Humour'.

¶3. **The author of the *English Humourists of the Eighteenth Century***: Thackeray.

¶4. **"sweet food of academic institution"**: from 'Oxford in the Vacation' (*EE*). **infirmity of speech**: a stutter.

¶5. **his earliest biographer**: Sir Thomas Noon Talfourd (1795–1854) in the *Letters and Life* (1837). **"feverish, romantic tie of love"**, and **"charities of home"**: from a letter to Coleridge, 10 Dec. 1797. **voluntarily yielding to restraint**: after the murder of Elizabeth Lamb in September 1796, Mary was committed to a private 'mad house', but released into CL's guardianship in the following year. On a number of subsequent occasions (the first being in 1800), Mary returned temporarily to institutional care. ***Rosamund Grey [Gray]***: tragic story by CL, first published in 1798, and his best-known work of prose fiction.

¶7. ***Weltschmerz***: 'world-pain', a term first used by the German Romantic author Jean Paul (1763–1825); cf. 'The Child in the House', ¶10. **stolen sleep at Arundel Castle**: see 'The Praise of Chimney-Sweepers' (*EE*). ***Pity's Gift***: CL's brother John Lamb published a pamphlet against cruelty to animals in 1810. CL himself often extends his pity and sympathy to animals, but which particular work or passage WP has in mind is unobvious. It is possible that he takes the 'Dissertation upon Roast Pig' in this spirit, though its wrongfooting ironies make it hardly a clear-cut 'Pity's Gift' (this designaton referring probably to a 1798 volume of that name by Samuel Jackson Pratt, subtitled: '*A collection of interesting tales, to excite the compassion of youth for the animal creation*'). Otherwise WP may be thinking of the poem 'Thoughtless Cruelty', included in *Poetry for Children* (1809). Yet this poem and several others conveying comparable sentiments have since been confidently attributed to Mary Lamb.

¶8. **exquisite appreciations**: CL's criticism was held in high esteem in WP's day, and has since been largely neglected. He contributed significantly to the revival of interest in early modern English drama which culminated later in the C19th. **"I cannot make these present times present to *me*"**: letter to Thomas Manning, 1 Mar. 1800.

¶9. **"The book is such as I am glad there should be"**: letter to Manning, 26 Feb. 1808;

Specimens appeared in the same year. **the limitation of his time by business**: CL worked as a clerk for the East India Company in the City of London. He (and 'Elia') frequently referred to the drudgery of office work, in contrast with literary pursuits.

¶10. Robert **Burton** (1577–1640): author of *The Anatomy of Melancholy* (first published in 1621). Francis **Quarles** (1592–1644): popular poet and author of one of the most famous English emblem-books, the *Emblems* (first 1634). Margaret Cavendish, **Duchess of Newcastle** (1623–73): wide-ranging writer, natural philosopher and eccentric personality; author of the philosophical prose fantasy *The Blazing-World* (1666). All these are writers to whom CL alludes with interest, affection or enthusiasm in his writings, especially his letters. **penetrative estimate of [...] Defoe**: i.e. in a letter to Walter Wilson, 16 Dec. 1822.

¶11. [William] **Godwin, seeing in quotation a passage from *John Woodvil*** (etc.): story recounted by Hazlitt in 'Elia, and Geoffrey Crayon' (*Spirit of the Age*). **caricature of Sir Thomas Browne**: Elia's 'Popular Fallacies' are in part inspired by Browne's *Pseudodoxia Epidemica* or *Discourse on Vulgar Errors* (see 'Sir Thomas Browne').

¶12. *The Rake's Progress*, or *Marriage à la Mode*: two famous sequences of pictures by Hogarth, both published in book form. **"The praise of beggars"**, and **"the cries of London"**: referring to 'A Complaint of the Decay of Beggars in the Metropolis', elided perhaps in WP's phrase with 'The Praise of Chimney-Sweepers' (both *EE*). In the latter, Elia notes the street-cries of the sweeps, while in the former he expresses a more general love of 'the Cries of London' (as also in 'The Superannuated Man'). **the traits of actors just grown "old"**: see 'On Some of the Old Actors' (*EE*), and other essays on theatre. **the spots in "town"**: the beginning of 'The Old Benchers of the Middle Temple' (*EE*) may be uppermost in WP's mind. **as a thing once really alive**: cf. 'Pico Della Mirandola', ¶5, 16. **fountains and sun-dials**: another reference to 'The Old Benchers of the Middle Temple'.

¶13. **"never judging system-wise [etc.]"**: from a letter to Southey, 15 Mar. 1799. **"glimpse-wise"**: if this is a quotation, I do not know the source. **"the gayest, happiest attitude of things"**: from Mark Akenside's poem, *The Pleasures of the Imagination* (1744), I:30. **George Fox** (1624–91): dissenting preacher and founder of The Religious Society of Friends. **held in reserve**: see ¶18n. below.

¶14. *Montaignesque* element in literature: cf. 'Doctrine of Plato, Part II: Dialectic', ¶3, 20, etc.; also 'Sir Thomas Browne', ¶1–2; and *Gaston*, ch. 4–5. **a sort of insincerity, to which he assigns its quaint "praise"**: probably 'irony', celebrated in 'New Year's Eve' (*EE*). CL, writing as a 'Friend' of Elia, remarks that the latter 'too much affected that dangerous figure—irony' ('Preface', *Last Essays of Elia*). WP associates 'irony' with 'reserve'.

¶15. **"like a Flemish painter"**: 'I am as slow as a Fleming painter when I compose anything'; letter to Southey, 29 Oct. 1798. **the editor of his letters**: Thomas Noon Talfourd (1837, often reprinted). The quotation is from the Preface.

¶16. **Wither's *Emblems*, "that old book and quaint"**: quotation from CL's *Rosamund Gray*, ch. 1; repeated in a letter to Southey, 18 Oct. 1798. George Wither (1588–1667) was an English poet. **"sticks to his favourite books [etc.]"**: comment by Talfourd in the *Letters*, apropos of CL's correspondence with Southey in 1798. **"old houses"** (etc.): WP probably has in mind 'The South-Sea House' (*EE*), second paragraph. **"the most kindly** and natural species of love": from a letter to Coleridge, 14 Nov. 1796.

¶17. *Religion of the Physician*: i.e. as portrayed by Browne's *Religio Medici*: see 'Sir Thomas Browne'. **A high way of feeling [...] on the authority of a long tradition** (etc.): cf. the passage on Fronto in *Marius*, ch. 15 ('And he proceeded to expound the idea of Humanity', etc.), and the protagonist's reflections thereon in ch. 16 ('But, without him there is a venerable system of sentiment and idea', etc.). See also 'Style', ¶31. *opus operatum*: 'the work wrought', usually in the sense of a spiritual effect of the operation of grace, brought about by religious sacrament or rite; cf. CL's ironic use of the phrase in the final paragraph of 'The Superannuated Man' (*EE*).

¶18. **the value of reserve in literature**: see ¶13–14 above, and Introduction, pp. 23–24. Cf. also 'Winckelmann', ¶35–36; 'Doctrine of Plato, Pt II: Dialectic', ¶15, 21; 'Lacedæmon', ¶23; 'Plato's Æsthetics', ¶15, 18; 'Prosper Mérimée', ¶2, 12, 14; and 'Raphael', ¶17.

¶19. **"with their living trees"** (etc.): see CL's letter to Thomas Manning, 28 May 1819: 'This dead, everlasting dead desk—how it weighs the spirit of a gentleman down! This dead wood of the desk instead of your living trees!'

§ *Sir Thomas Browne*

First published in *Macmillan's Magazine*, May 1886. Sir Thomas Browne (1605–82) was an English physician and polymath resident in Norwich, and is known as the author of several oft-reprinted works of non-fiction in which he developed an idiosyncratic, elaborately Latinate prose style.

¶1. *Ecclesiastical Polity* (1594–97): theological work by Richard Hooker. *Leviathan* (1651): philosophical work by Thomas Hobbes. On **Montaigne** and **all those tentative writers, or essayists**, cf. 'Doctrine of Plato, Part II: Dialectic', ¶3, 20, etc.

¶2. **"not picked from the leaves of any author [etc.]"**: TB, *Religio Medici* I.35; cf. Matthew 13:24–30. Hugh **Latimer**: c. 1487–1555; Thomas **More**: 1478–1535; Joseph **Butler**: 1692–1753; David **Hume**: 1711–76. [Inset quotation]: from *Rel. Med.* I.35.

¶4. **the books of Burton and Fuller**: Robert Burton, *Anatomy of Melancholy* (1621); Thomas Fuller, *Worthies of England* (1662), etc. **"the unique peculiarity of the writer's mind [etc.]"**: supposedly from Johnson's *Life of Browne* (1756), but like Inman (1990) I am unable to find it there or elsewhere.

¶5. **the humourist to whom [...] nothing is really alien from himself**: cf. WP's comments on Montaigne in *Gaston*, ch. 4–5. Montaigne had written on his study ceiling the motto: 'NIHIL HUMANI ALIENI MIHI PUTO': 'I consider nothing human alien to me'. **half-pitying, half-amused sympathy [...] small interests and traits** (etc.): cf. 'Charles Lamb', ¶7, 12–14. **"all existence had been but food for contemplation"**: this seems not, as far as I can see, to have been taken from TB, but rather loosely paraphrased from the initial footnote in the 'Supplementary Memoir' included in vol. 1 of Simon Wilkin's edition of TB (first published 1836), a copy of which WP borrowed in 1883. A mix-up in WP's note-taking would be sufficient explanation. The footnote itself is quoted from an article on Browne in the *Athenaeum*, 93 (1829), and its phrase—'food of serious contemplation'—exactly echoes Christopher Harvey's prefatory poem to Izaak Walton's

Compleat Angler (1653).

¶6. *Life of Browne*: see ¶4n. above. The first is a genuine quotation, with 'their' for 'his', and adding the first comma; the second quotation is accurate; and the final three words of the third are WP's addition, arguably constituting a very loose paraphrase. **the example of Johnson himself**: he being notably the subject of a large and famous biography, Boswell's *Life* (1791). **"we carry with us the wonders we seek without us"**: *Rel. Med.* 1.15. **"His father used to open his breast [etc.]"**: this was communicated in writing to White Kennet, Bishop of Peterborough, in 1712, who made a note of it in his own copy of TB's works. Printed in Wilkin's 'Supplementary Memoir'.

¶7. On the **first publication** of the *Religio Medici* (a pirate edition of 1642), see ¶12 below. The book ('The Religion of a Physician'), published by the author in 1643, is one of TB's most famous works. **year of the Gunpowder Plot**: 1605. **"misguided zeal terms superstition"**: *Rel. Med.* 1.3. **"unjust scandal"**: *ibid.*, 1.5. **"enter their churches in defect of ours"**: *ibid.*, 1.3. **"the fruitless journeys of pilgrims [etc.]"**: *ibid.*, 1.3. **"hear the *Ave Mary!* bell without an *oraison*"**: confuses two similar moments, *Rel. Med.* 1.3 and 1.7. **"wept abundantly"**: *ibid.*, 1.3. **"a man may be in as just possession of truth [etc.]"**: *ibid.*, 1.6; **contemporary colouring**, because the image recalls the sieges of royalist strongholds during the English Civil Wars.

¶8. *Enquiries into Vulgar Errors* (*Pseudodoxia Epidemica*): TB's longest work, first published in 1646 and subsequently revised several times. *Idola Fori*: see ¶23-24n. below. **"being erroneous in their single numbers [etc.]"**: *Vulgar Errors* 1.3. **"In my solitary and retired imagination [etc.]"**: the Latin means: 'for neither when the colonnades, nor when the couch, receives me, do I lose possession of myself' (Horace, *Satires* 1.3:133-34).

¶10. his old **Roman, or Romanised British urns**: see ¶28 (and n.) below. *Adipocere*: 'In an Hydropicall body ten years buried in a Church-yard, we met with a fat concretion, where the nitre of the Earth, and the salt and lixivious liquor of the body, had coagulated large lumps of fat, into the consistence of the hardest castle-soap; whereof part remaineth with us' (TB, *Urn-Burial* III). The name 'adipocere' was applied to this waxy substance much later. **"magnetic alliciency"** (power of attraction), and **the earth [...] a vast lodestone**: see *Vulgar Errors* II.2.

¶11. **"whose quiet and unmolested doors [etc.]"**: *Vulgar Errors*, 'To the Reader'. **odylic gravelights**: refers to the vitalist theories of WP's own century, and the 'odylic force' of which Karl Reichenbach had written, beginning in the 1840s. Some people of particular sensitivity could, he said, detect currents of odylic force emanating from recent graves.

¶12. **"much corrupted by transcription at various hands"**: TB's actual words are: 'being communicated unto one, it became common unto many, and was by transcription successively corrupted untill it arrived in a most depraved copy at the presse' (*Rel. Med.*, 'To the Reader'). **Kenelm Digby**: wide-ranging writer and thinker (1603-65), whose *Animadversions* on *Rel. Med.*, which he claimed to have written in less than twenty-four hours, had been published in 1643, based upon the unauthorised version of the text. **"Even in this material fabric [etc.]"**: *Rel. Med.* 1.35. **Had not Divine interference designed** (etc.): *ibid.*, 1.46. **"incinerated soul"**: apparently not a quotation, but a re-application of the adjectival participle, taken from a letter to be spoken of in ¶26, to a different noun, in order to suggest an analogy. On **Pascal**, cf. WP's essay 'Pascal'.

¶13. **William Lily** [Lilly]: writer and astrologer (1602-81). **Dr. Dee** (1527-c. 1609): eminent Elizabethan astrologer and natural philosopher, with an interest in magic and alchemy, and famous for his putative communications with spirits and angels. **"often heard him affirm [etc.]"**: TB writing to Elias Ashmole, March 1674 (letter no. 192 in TB ed. Keynes). WP slightly adapts the wording, and the ironic parenthesis is his.

¶14. *Scarabæus capricornus odoratus*: the musk-beetle, capricorn beetle, cerambyx or 'goat-chafer', which diffuses a musky odour. '*Nucem moschatam et cinnamomum vere spirat*': 'truly it smells of nutmeg and cinnamon'. *Musca tuliparum moschata*: a 'musky tulip-fly', it would seem.

¶15. *Garden of Cyrus*: a work by TB published with *Urn-Burial* in 1658; contains his most esoteric thinking, centred on the significance of the 'quincunx' pattern of five points, its uses and mystical significance. Richard **Temple**, Viscount Cobham (1675-1749): his gardens at Stow were celebrated by Pope (see 'Epistle to Burlington'). Horace **Walpole** (1717-97), author, antiquarian and an early Gothic revivalist, had impressive gardens at Strawberry Hill, and wrote a discourse *On Modern Gardening* (1780). *quincunx*: see above. **"hortulane pleasure"**: i.e. the pleasure of gardens; Evelyn writing to TB, 28 Jan. 1659/60 (Keynes no. 181). **"Norwich is a place [etc.]"**: *ibid.*, with slight adjustments to wording. Elias **Ashmole** (1617-92): polymath, writer and collector. Sir William **Dugdale** (1605-86): antiquary and writer. **"in the nature of an island in the fens"**: actually Dugdale to TB, not *vice versa* as stated: probably WP, having returned the book, has misunderstood his own notes. It seems Dugdale had previously told TB about the discovery of 'certain coins', supposedly in Ashmole's possession, and in the letter from which WP quotes (that of 9 Nov. 1658, i.e. Keynes no. 196, with WP altering 'fenne' to 'fens') he confesses he had been mistaken.

¶16. William **Dobson** (c. 1611-46): celebrated English painter of portraits. The painting in question is at Chatsworth, and the identification of the sitters is in question. **Edward Browne**: 1644-1708. **attended John [Wilmot], Earl of Rochester, in his last illness**: recorded in *Munk's Roll* of Fellows of the Royal College of Physicians, vol. 1 (1861). Rochester (1647-80) was the celebrated poet and notorious libertine, whose alleged deathbed conversion was legendary.

¶17. **"If you practise to write [etc.]"**: TB to his sons Edward and Thomas, at Cambridge, July 1663 (Keynes no. 14). **"I received your two last letters [etc.]"**: Thomas Browne the younger to his father, 16 July 1666 (read by WP in Wilkin but not included in Keynes). The book by Isaac **Vossius** is *On the Motions of Sea and Wind* (1663). **"like to proceed not only a good navigator, but a good scholar"**: TB to Thomas the younger, May/June 1667 (Keynes no. 18). The original reads 'noble navigator', and 'not only' is supplied in square brackets by Wilkin. **[Inset quotation]**: date given in text; WP abstracts from a longer passage.

¶18. **[Inset quotations]**: all from letters to Edward Browne; Keynes nos 48 (8 Apr. 1677, PS.); 162 (29 May 1682, Dorothy Browne's PS., with WP's parenthesis); 70 (10 May 1679); 60 (14 Feb. 1678/9); 145 (26 Dec. 1681); 130 (28 Feb. 1680/1); and 120 (29 Nov. 1680).

¶19. **[Inset quotations]**, with WP's parentheses: Keynes nos 113 (15 Sept. 1680) and

125 (7 Jan. 1680/1).

¶21. **Madame de Rambouillet** (1588–1665): pre-eminent literary *salonnière* in Paris during the second quarter of the C17th. Here she is associated with developing standards of clarity in French writing, and so mentioned alongside Dr Johnson, pre-eminent critic and lexicographer of the English C18th. Comte de **Buffon** (1707–88): French polymath and author of the 36-volume *Histoire Naturelle*; cf. 'Style', ¶23, 27n.

¶22. **Elias Ashmole**: see ¶15n. above. **"Things are really true [etc.]"**: *Vulgar Errors* I.1. **"the art of God"**: *Rel. Med.* I.16. **phrase used also by Hobbes**: i.e. in the opening of the *Leviathan*: 'Nature, the art whereby God hath made and governs the world', etc.

¶23. *Pseudodoxia Epidemica*: the title means 'false opinions widespread among the people' (i.e. '*epidemic*'). **"that first error in Paradise"** (etc.): *Vulgar Errors* I.1. **Julius [Caesar] Scaliger** (1484–1558): important Italian humanist scholar, poet and literary theorist. **motto**: i.e. the epigraph to *Vulgar Errors*, appearing on the title page: '*Ex Libris colligere quae prodiderunt Authore longe est periculosissimum; rerum ipsarum cognitio vera e rebus ipsis est*' ('To gather out of books what authors have put forth is most dangerous; true knowledge of things themselves comes from the things themselves'). **"Men that adore times past [etc.]"**: *Vulgar Errors* I.6. **"use of doubts [etc.]"**: taken from Wilkin's 'Editor's Preface' to *Vulgar Errors*, rather than from TB himself: another possible note-taking error. **"supinity"**: implies both 'proneness' (literally and figuratively) and mere laziness of intellect. See *Vulgar Errors* I.4. **Bacon's *Idola Tribus*, *Fori*, *Theatri*** and (in ¶24) ***specus***: see *Novum Organum* I, §38ff.

¶24. **"bred amongst the weeds [etc.]"**: see ¶2 above. **final precipitate of fallacy**: 'precipitate' (noun) in the chemical sense.

¶25. **"on eradication, [etc.]"**: 'eradication' in the strict etymological sense ('rooted out'); *Vulgar Errors* II.6. **"In philosophy [etc.]"**: *Rel. Med.* I.6.

¶26. *Que sçais-je?*: 'What do I know?' Cf. 'Doctrine of Plato, Pt II: Dialectic', ¶3, 20 (and notes). **"but yet in discovery"**: *Vulgar Errors* II.2. **"the America and untravelled parts of truth,"**: *ibid.*, 'To the Reader'. **"The subject of my last letter," says Dr. Henry Power** (etc.): letter to TB, 10 Feb. 1647/8 (Keynes no. 174).

¶27. *Palingenesis*: 'rebirth', 'resurrection'; here refers specifically to the classic alchemical experiment to which Power has alluded. **"incinerated organism"**: WP's paraphrase, the more generalised noun ('organism' for 'plant') allowing for the transition of his own critical attention to *Urn-Burial*. *Hydriotaphia, or Treatise of Urn-Burial* (1658) is another of TBs most famous works, stimulated by the discovery of some ancient burial urns in Norfolk. **very singular letter**: TB's posthumously published *Letter to a Friend, upon Occasion of the Death of his Intimate Friend.*

¶28. *Christian Morals*: published posthumously in 1716. **"Romans, or Britons Romanised which had learned Roman customs"**: see *Urn-Burial* II. **dedicated to an eminent collector**: TB's friend Thomas Le Gros.

¶29. **Blake's design**: one of his illustrations to Blair's *The Grave* (cf. 'Style', ¶20 and n.). **well-worn critical distinctions**: cf. 'Postscript'. **Guichard's [...] *Divers Manners of Burial***: Claude Guichard, *Funérailles et diverses manieres d'ensevelir des Romains, Grecs, et autres nations* (1581).

¶30. **Pope Gregory**: i.e. Gregory the Great. **"Beat not the bones of the buried [etc.]"**: from *Love's Labour's Lost* V.2:658–59. **To keep our eyes open longer [etc.]"**: from the famous conclusion to TB's *Garden of Cyrus*.
¶31. **as Wordsworth terms them**: i.e. in the famous 'Ode: Intimations of Immortality from Recollections of Early Childhood'. **Jean Paul** (Johann Paul Friedrich Richter, 1763–1825): German Romantic author; cf. ¶1. **cynical French poet of the nineteenth century**: possibly Alfred de Musset (1810–57) in his *'Lettre à Lamartine'*; more probably Baudelaire in *'Bénédiction'*, ll. 61–64. **the force of men's temperaments in the management of opinion**: cf. esp. *Marius*, ch. 20, as quoted in Introduction, pp. 26–27.

§ *Shakespeare's English Kings*

This essay first appeared in *Scribner's Magazine* on 5 April 1889. The present extract omits WP's introduction and his relatively brief remarks on some of the other history plays, but continues to the end of the essay. *Richard II* is the play with which he is chiefly occupied here. References to this work ('*R2*') in the notes below relate to Charles R. Forker's Arden edition (third series), which is based largely on the first quarto (1597).

¶6. **a true "verse royal"**: alluding to the medieval and early modern use of terms such as '*chant royal*' in French, and 'ballade royal' or 'rhythm royal' in English—which were *not* uniformly applied to what has since been known as 'rhyme royal'. It had sometimes been said that the appellation 'royal', applied to this last form, derived from King James I of Scotland's choice of that stanza for 'The Kingis Quair' (cf. 'Dante Gabriel Rossetti', ¶11); but WP quite probably knew this supposition to be false. The **'rhyming lapse'** in *R2*, and common in early Shakespeare, is the rhyming couplet that provides a flourish amid a context of blank verse, especially at the end of a speech or scene. The suggestion seems to be that Richard's blank verse, with its occasional rhymes, is more truly 'royal' than what we call 'rhyme royal'. **as the "royal blood" comes and goes in the face**: cf. *R2* II.1:117–19: 'Darest with thy frozen admonition / Make pale our cheek, chasing the royal blood / With fury from his native residence?' **"his cote of gold and stone [etc.]"**: from Holinshed's *Chronicles* (a major source for *R2*) for the year 1399.

¶7. **Charles Kean** (1811–68), son of another celebrated actor, Edmund Kean, staged the first successful modern revival of *R2* in 1857, with a long run and a reprise in the same year. He cut the text dramatically and printed it, with commentary, for purchase in the theatre. **"the earliest extant contemporary likeness [etc.]"**: source unknown, but not from Kean's annotated script. The latter does, however, point out that 'The costume of the king in [Act I, sc. 1] is taken from the curious and authentic portrait of Richard' which remains at Westminster Abbey.

¶8. **"tragic abdication"**: i.e. in IV.1. **Sluiced out his innocent soul thro' streams of blood**: I.1:103 (not in fact applied to Richard). **The king Richard of Ynglande** (etc.): from Andrew of Wyntoun's *Orygynale Cronykil of Scotland* (before 1425), IX.18. **that divine right of kings, of which people in Shakespeare's time were coming to hear so much**: i.e. under the influence of political theorists such as Jean Bodin (1530–96) and, in England, though after the date of composition of *R2*, especially during the reign of James I, a firm and outspoken believer in this principle. **Richard himself found that, it was said** (etc.): the story is told in the *Annales Ricardi Secundi* of the contemporaneous chronicler Thomas of Walsingham. **Not all the water in the rough rude sea** (etc.): III.2:54–55. **"Edward's seven sons"** and subsequent inset quotation: I.2:11–12. **"barbarism itself"**: V.2:36. **How soon my sorrow hath destroyed my face!**: IV.1:291.

¶9. **Chatterton**: see 'Coleridge', ¶28n. **Fetch hither Richard** (etc.): IV.1:156–57. **To do that office of thine own good will** (etc.): IV.1:178–79. **Now mark me! how I will undo myself**: IV.1:203.

¶10. **Hath Bolingbroke / Deposed thine intellect?**: V.1:27–28. **"plume-plucked Richard"**: IV.1:109. **I find myself a traitor with the rest** (etc.): IV.1:248–50. **That which in mean men we entitle patience** (etc.): I.2:33–34, though Richard is not present when these words are spoken by the Duchess of Gloucester. **O! that I were as great / As is my grief**: III.3:136–37.

¶11. **No! Shakespeare's kings are not, nor are meant to be, great men**: this must have influenced the famous lines in T.S. Eliot's 'The Love Song of J. Alfred Prufrock': 'No! I am not Prince Hamlet, nor was meant to be', etc. **Give Richard leave to live till Richard die!**: III.3:174. **My large kingdom for a little grave!** (etc.): III.3:153–54. **bold reference to the judgment of Pilate**: IV.1:239–42.

¶12. **Beshrew thee, Cousin** (etc.): III.2:204–05.

¶13. **"With Cain go wander through the shades of night!"**: V.6:43. **"waste and a broken heart"**: precise source unknown; but the idea that Richard 'wilfullie [...] starved himselfe' is mentioned in Holinshed under the year 1400, who claims to take the notion from Thomas Walsingham (see ¶8n. above). **"most beauteous inn"**: V.1:13. **That small model of the barren earth** (etc.): III.2:153–54. **Queen Anne of Bohemia, not of course the "Queen" of Shakespeare**: the latter is Isabella of Valois, whom Richard had married in 1396, two years after the death of Anne of Bohemia.

¶14. **According to [Samuel] Johnson**: i.e. in his 1765 edition of the play. **"Would that he had blotted a thousand"**: i.e. a thousand lines, in revision; this famous remark on Shakespeare by Ben Jonson is taken from his *Timber, or Discoveries* (1641). **the mirror-scene**: i.e. IV.1. **German criticism**: Charles R. Forker, in the *R2* volume of the series *Shakespeare: The Critical Tradition* (1998), gives a reference to G.G. Gervinus, *Shakespeare Commentaries* (1877), pp. 205–08. **Which sort of poetry we are to account the highest**: cf. 'School of Giorgione', ¶5–10.

§*Dante Gabriel Rossetti*

This essay was written in 1883, the year following that in which Rossetti had died, and included as an introduction to a selection from his poems in T.H. Ward's anthology of *English Poets*, vol. 4, in its revised and expanded second edition.

¶1. One of DGR's most famous poems, **'The Blessed Damozel'** was written in 1847. It appeared in *The Germ*, 2 (1850) and *The Oxford and Cambridge Magazine*, 11 (1856), and so was well known before its inclusion in DGR's *Poems* (1870). **new school then rising into note**: Pre-Raphaelitism, whether in its first or later phases. Regarding the '**tracing-paper**' metaphor for stylistic '**control**', cf. 'Style', ¶15; the general points made about 'transparency' and 'sincerity' here are illustrative of the general tenets considered there. **"early Italian poets"**: DGR's book of verse translations, *The Early Italian Poets*, was published in 1861.

¶2. **The gold bar of heaven** (etc): images from the opening stanzas of 'The Blessed Damozel'. **"servant and singer"**, and **"of Florence and of Beatrice"**: from DGR's poem 'Dante at Verona'. **family circumstances**: DGR's father was a scholar of Dante. **critic of the last century**: probably Addison in *The Spectator*, 339 (29 March 1712): 'poetry delights in clothing abstracted ideas in allegories and sensible images'. **Dictes-moy où** (etc.): from a famous *ballade* in **Villon**'s *Testament*; DGR's translation, 'A Ballad of Dead Ladies', was widely celebrated.

¶3. **a whole "populace" of special hours**: see *House of Life* (1881 version), son. XVI. **"the hour [...] which might have been, yet might not be"**: *ibid.*, son. LV. **[Inset quotations]**: two separate extracts from 'The Stream's Secret'.

¶5. **[Inset quotation]**: also from 'The Stream's Secret'. **Jacob's Dream**: see Genesis 28:10-22. **Addison's Nineteenth Psalm**: i.e. the 'Ode' beginning 'The Spacious Firmament on high'.

¶6. **"hollow brimmed with mist"**, **"ruined weir"**, **magic beryl**: all taken from DGR's narrative poem 'Rose Mary'. **"the white-flower'd elder-thicket"** (etc.): from Tennyson's 'Godiva' (1842). *se passionnent pour la passion*: translated by WP, but more directly: '[those who] have a passion for passion', or 'are in love with love'.

¶7. **Manichean opposition of spirit and matter** (etc.): cf. 'The Genius of Plato', ¶18-19 (and n.). **[Inset quotation]**: from DGR's lyric 'Love-Lily'.

¶8. **"a work to be called The House of Life"**: this description is quoted from the 1870 text of DGR's sonnet sequence, which continued to grow until its final 1881 version was printed, and might have continued to do so if the poet had lived to oversee further editions.

¶9. **according to Swedenborg**: e.g. in the *De Commercio Animae & Corporis* (*On the Relation of Soul and* Body, 1769), §IX-X. On Swedenborg, cf. 'Style', ¶16 and 'Coleridge', ¶29 (and notes). *House of Life*, **of which he is but the "Interpreter"**: playful allusion to Bunyan's *Pilgrim's Progress*; cf. 'Wordsworth', ¶22, and 'Postscript', ¶1. **"lead-bound"**: this may at first seem to be applied to 'sleep', but in fact probably refers to 'desire', making it a delicate allusion to one of the odes of Anacreon (usually numbered 44), in which the poet dreams he is pursued by a Cupid with lead-bound feet. **"phantoms of the body"**: see DGR's 'Love's Nocturn', ll. 65-66: 'Master, from thy shadowkind / Call my body's phantom now'.

¶10. **his second volume of** *Ballads and Sonnets* (etc.): published in October 1881. DGR died on 9 April 1882.

¶11. *ces siècles de passions où les âmes* (etc.): 'those ages of passions, where souls could surrender freely to the higher exaltation; when there existed those passions that make for the possibility, as well as the subjects, of the fine arts'. A close paraphrase from two sentences in Stendhal's *Histoire de la peinture en Italie* (*History of Painting in Italy*, 1817), from the Introduction and ch. 2 respectively. **the two longer ballads of his second volume**: this ought to mean 'Rose Mary' and 'The King's Tragedy', for no other interpretation suggests itself, and WP himself calls the third ballad in that volume, i.e. 'The White Ship', the 'shortest' of them. But 'Rose Mary' is ostensibly a story of DGR's own invention, and, if so, cannot be said to have been taken from 'Old Scotch history'. **relics of James's own exquisite early verse**: i.e. 'The Kingis Quair', a poem in C15th Scots attributed to James I of Scotland.

¶12. **[Inset quotation]**: from 'Eden Bower'. *The White Ship*—**that old true history** (etc.): the ballad is based on the wreck of the 'White Ship' off the coast of Normandy in 1120, which killed Prince William, the only heir of King Henry I of England. **a single utterance of the refrain, "given out"** (etc.): i.e. the refrains are included in the initial stanza, and then omitted throughout, returning only in the final stanza.

¶13. **Gray too [...] seemed even to Johnson, obscure**: the implication appears to be that it would now occur to nobody to think the lucid Augustan verse of Thomas Gray 'obscure'. Johnson considers Gray's poetry marred by logical and rhetorical confusions, as discovered in passages of which he 'would glady find the meaning' (*Lives of the Poets*).

§*Postscript*

First published under the title 'Romanticism' in *Macmillan's Magazine*, November 1876. **Greek epigraph**: 'Praise the wine that is old; but of song, praise the newer flowers'. Pindar, *Olympian Odes* 9:48–49.

¶1. **Interpreter** of the *House Beautiful*: reference to Bunyan's *Pilgrim's Progress*. Cf. 'Wordsworth', ¶22, and 'Dante Gabriel Rossetti', ¶8.

¶2. Wilhelm **Meinhold** (1797–1851): German writer whose romances, *Sidonia the Sorceress* (translated by Jane, Lady Wilde, in 1849) and the *Amber-Witch* (translated by Lucie, Lady Duff-Gordon, in 1843) were popular in England, and particular favourites of D.G. Rossetti and his circle. **Heine**'s long essay on the *Romantic School* was published in 1833. **Goethe**'s *Goetz von Berlichingen* is a play of 1773 based on the life of an historical poet-knight of the Renaissance.

¶3. κοσμιότης (*kosmiotês*): 'propriety', 'orderliness', 'decorum'. Cf. *PP*, ch. 1–5 extracts, extr. (iii), below.

¶4. Charles Augustin **Sainte-Beuve** (1804–69): French critic; *Causeries du Lundi*: his regular weekly column (the 'Monday chit-chats') in *Le Constitutionnel*, later published in book form. The essay WP quotes here and below was published on 21 Oct. 1850. *grandiose et flottant*: literally, 'grandiose and floating'; i.e. a broader and more capacious ('**generous**') meaning than the term had usually been given.

¶5. "*Romanticism*," says Stendhal (etc.): in his study *Racine et Shakespeare* (1823/25), cited explicitly by WP below.

¶7. **trees shrieking as you tear off the leaves**: see Dante, *Inferno* XIII (the Wood of the Suicides). **Jean Valjean**: a central character in Victor Hugo's *Les Misérables* (1862). **Redgauntlet**: protagonist in the historical novel of that name by Walter Scott (1824). *les ouvrages anciens [...] énergiques, frais, et dispos*: 'the ancient works are not classical merely because they are old, but because they are energetic, fresh, and well-formed' (see ¶4n. for source). **Marius** and **Cosette**: characters in *Les Misérables*.

¶9. **Madame de Staël** (1766–1817): French intellectual and woman of letters; *De l'Allemagne* (1810/13): her book-length study of the literary and philosophical culture of Germany, which did much to popularise German Romanticism in France, and to which Heine's *Romantische Schule* (*The Romantic School*; see ¶2n. above) was a response. Goethe is much better known to English readers than the poet, novelist and man of letters Johann Ludwig **Tieck** (1773–1853), one of the most important of the early German Romantics. **now that it [Germany] has got Strasburg back again**: i.e. following the Frankfurt Treaty of 1871; for it had previously been, as it is now, a part of France. Henri **Murger** (1822–61): French writer of prose and verse, best remembered for his prose work *Scènes de la vie de bohème* (*Scenes of the Bohemian Life*), upon which Puccini's *La Bohème* was based.

¶10. **the lines in which Virgil describes the hazel-wood**: *Aeneid* III:22–68. **the whole canto of the *Inferno***: canto XIII. Thomas **Stothard**, R.A. (1755–1834): British painter and illustrator.

¶11. *cor laceratum*: 'the lacerated heart'.

¶12. **Werthers, Renés, Obermanns**: all famous fictional personages characterised by some combination of melancholy, lassitude, alienation and *ennui* (see Goethe, *The Sorrows of Young Werther*, 1774/87; Chateaubriand, *René*, 1802; Senancour, *Obermann*, 1804/33); cf. Essay on 'Style', ¶5, and 'Prosper Mérimée', ¶1. **"young France"**: in the 1820s and 1830s a group of young Romantic writers and artists, including Gautier and Gérard de Nerval, came to be known as the *Jeunes-France* (after the periodical *La Jeune France*). **Chateaubriand's *Génie du Christianisme*** (*The Genius of Christianity*, meaning primarily Roman Catholicism): a book written in exile during the Revolution, and published in 1802. ***René*** and ***Atala***: both novels by Chateaubriand (1802 and 1801 respectively). **Quasimodo**: the hunchback in Hugo's *Notre-Dame de Paris* (*The Hunchback of Notre-Dame*, 1831). **Gwynplaine**: protagonist in Hugo's *L'Homme qui rit* (*The Man who Laughs*, or *The Laughing Man*, 1869), whose face is mutilated into a permanent grin. **true "flowers of the yew"**: resembles a direct quotation, possibly from verse, but I have not found a source. Taking account of the adjective 'true', could it be that the speech marks do not imply *verbatim* quotation, and that WP is coyly alluding to Tennyson's *In Memoriam*, 2 ('Old Yew, which graspest at the stones'), which, as critics had pointed out, would appear to imply erroneously that the yew tree bore no flowers? The allusion would therefore suggest: Yes, indeed they do have flowers, and these (figuratively, or in the sense that really matters) are they. The yew is of course associated with graveyards. Hugo's **Quatre-Vingt-Treize** (*Ninety-Three*, 1874) depicts the counter-revolutionary uprisings of 1793; the **Convention** is a judicial body or 'tribunal' assembled to conduct the trial of a captured royalist counter-revolutionary. *Scènes de la Vie de Jeunesse*: *Scenes of the Life of Youth* (1851). **Are we in the *Inferno*?**: not directly quoting Dante, but possibly a quotation from elsewhere. **like "goldsmith's work"**: Aloysius **Bertrand's** collection of prose poems *Gaspard de la Nuit* was published posthumously in 1842 with an introduction by Sainte-Beuve. *argute loqui*: 'of cunning speech', a phrase applied to the Gallic Celts by Cato in the *Origines*, fr. 34.

¶13. **"dry light"**: figure for a certain kind of wisdom or reason: the phrase is taken from Heraclitus *via* Bacon (cf. 'Plato's Æsthetics', ¶18 and n.). ***Hernani***: an historical play by Hugo, set in golden-age Spain, and first produced in 1830 to much opposition from conservative or 'classicist' critics. On the Hegelian concept of *Time-Spirit*, or *Zeit-Geist*: cf. *PP*, ch. 1-5 extracts, extr. (i), ¶6. **"Dante," he [Stendhal] observes** (etc.): in *Racine et Shakespeare* (see ¶5n. above).

¶15. **Pheidias**: classical Greek sculptor; cf. 'Beginnings of Greek Sculpture, I', ¶20n; also 'Lacedæmon', ¶12, 'Study of Dionysus', ¶19, etc. **the immortal horses of Achilles**: Xanthus and Balius; see *Iliad* XVII:426-40. **the sculpture of Chartres and Rheims**: i.e. of their Gothic cathedrals. For an appreciative description of 'Notre-Dame de Chartres', see *Gaston*, ch. 2.

¶17. **"the style is the man"**: cf. 'Style', ¶27-29 and notes. **incondite**: unformed or poorly constructed.

PLATO AND PLATONISM

Unless otherwise noted, all chapters from *PP* were published there for the first time in 1893.

§ Extracts from Chapters 1 to 5

i. **Three Kinds of Criticism** ['Plato and the Doctrine of Motion' (ch. 1), ¶5-7. This chapter had been previously published under the title 'A Chapter on Plato' in *Macmillan's Magazine*, May 1892.]

¶5. **Neo-Platonism of Florence**: an important movement in the late C15th; see 'Pico Della Mirandola'.

¶6. **Zeit-geist**: in a Hegelian sense; cf. *App.*, 'Postscript', ¶13. **"secular process"**: the temporal process of history (literally 'of the ages'). This is distinct from older, providential conceptions of history, and specifically associated by WP with Hegel's philosophy of history (see below, extr. [ii], ¶16n.). **"communism" of Plato**: as outlined in the *Republic*.

ii. **"Perpetual Flux"** ['Plato and the Doctrine of Motion' (ch. 1), ¶9-11, 13-18. For publication history, see note to extr. (i) above.]

¶9. **lately emancipated from its tyrants**: Heraclitus was a grown man by the time the Ionian Revolt began, and the liberation of Ionia, including Ephesus, from Persian rule was not accomplished until the very last years (probably) of his life. But the Persians had ruled somewhat distantly compared with the Lydians under Croesus, who had held Ephesus from 560 B.C. until defeated by the Persians in 547. So WP may be referring to the tyranny of Croesus, from which the city-state had been 'emancipated' by the conquering Persians some decade or so before the birth of Heraclitus. **sickly with "the pale cast"**: a reference to the III.1 soliloquy in *Hamlet*.

¶10. **Πάντα χωρεῖ καὶ οὐδὲν μένει**: translated by WP, but otherwise, 'all things are in motion and nothing stands still'; attributed to Heraclitus. See Plato, *Cratylus*, 402a, which WP more directly quotes below:—

¶11. **Λέγει πού Ἡράκλειτος** (etc.): 'Heraclitus says, I think, that all things are in motion and nothing stands still'. See above. This quotation had earlier been used by WP as the epigraph to *Ren.*, 'Conclusion'. **"No one has ever passed twice over the same stream"**:

another saying attributed to Heraclitus, although variously attested in three rather different fragments (B12, B49a, B91). εἶμέν τε καὶ οὐκ εἶμεν (translated by WP): part of fr. B49a.

¶13. "[Man is] the measure of all things": saying attributed to Protagoras; see Plato's *Theaetetus*, 152a.

¶14. apprehension [...] realised by a later age (etc.): cf. *Ren.*, 'Conclusion', ¶1–2, and 'Coleridge', ¶2.

¶16. πάντα χωρεῖ, πάντα ῥεῖ: 'All things are in motion, all things flow'; sayings attributed to Heraclitus (cf. ¶10–11). secular process of the eternal mind: cf. extr. (i), ¶7 (and n.). *latens processus*: 'latent process', which it is the business of the natural philosopher to find out; see Bacon's *Novum Organum* II, *passim*, but esp. §1–2, 5–7. constant increase by meteoric dust: the later C19th saw considerable research into the terrestrial accumulation of cosmic or meteoric dust, a substance that became central to J. Norman Lockyer's far-reaching 'Meteoric Hypothesis'. This was the title of a book he published in 1890; see especially his ch. 10 on terrestrial deposits. Political constitutions [...] cannot be made, but "grow": although others had written to the same effect, WP appears to be quoting or paraphrasing either or both of the following well-known works: James Mackintosh, *Discourse on the Law of Nature and Nations* (1799); Joseph de Maistre, *Essai sur le Principe Générateur des Constitutions Politiques* (*Essay on the Generative Principle of Political Constitutions*, 1809).

¶17. when the history of Thucydides leaves off: i.e. 411 B.C.

iii. The Eleatic School ['Plato and the Doctrine of Rest' (ch. 2), ¶8–11.]

¶8. τὸ ὄν: 'being', 'that which exists'. *Omnis determinatio est negatio*: 'all determination is negation', a formulation adopted by Hegel from Spinoza.

¶9. Κόσμος: i.e. *kosmos*. the Dorian element: cf. 'Lacedæmon', ¶17, etc.; *PP*, ch. 1–5 extracts, extr. (vi), *passim*; 'Study of Dionysus', ¶23; and 'Beginnings of Greek Sculpture, I', ¶21. Κοσμιότης (*kosmiotês*): 'propriety', 'orderliness', 'decorum'; from *kosmos*. ἀρχή (*archê*): 'principle', 'beginning', 'rule'.

¶10. παρὰ πάντα λεγόμενα: translated by WP after the parenthesis; otherwise 'against all arguments'. Plato, *Parmenides*, 127e. "Parmenides," says one (etc.): Benjamin Jowett, in the Introduction to his translation of Plato's *Phaedo*.

¶11. "The Lord thy God is one Lord": Deuteronomy 6:4; WP has 'thy' for 'our'.

iv. The Mania for Nonentity ['Plato and the Doctrine of Rest' (ch. 2), ¶15.]

Eckhart and Tauler: Eckhart von Hochheim ('Meister Eckhart', died c. 1328) and Joannes Tauler (died 1361) were German theological writers and preachers of a mystical bent. book of the *Imitation*: Thomas à Kempis (died 1471), *De Imitatione Christi* (*Imitation of Christ*).

v. Pythagoras ['Plato and the Doctrine of Number' (ch. 3), ¶1–5.]

¶2. intellectual conformation: the first and all subsequent editions read 'confirmation', which I believe to be a typesetters' error and have therefore emended. For WP's use of the word 'conformation' in this sense elsewhere in *PP*, see Lib. Edn, p. 60: 'the actual conformation of Plato's thoughts'; and cf. p. 23: 'the material conformation of Greece'.

vera vox: 'the true voice'.

¶3. **as Kant can explain to us**: i.e. the necessity of space and time, being *a priori* forms of 'intuition', as preconditions of human experience. These are central notions in the *Critique of Pure Reason* and Kant's philosophy generally. ὅμοιον ὁμοίῳ: 'like to like'. See Plato, *Lysis*, 214b; *Symposium*, 195b; and *Gorgias*, 510b. Cf. also Aristotle, *Eudemian Ethics*, 1235a.

¶4. ***Golden Verses* of Pythagoras**: WP appears to be referring to the authentic writings of Pythagoras, and *not* to the brief text known spuriously by this name since antiquity. **Porphyry and Iamblichus**: both important Neo-Platonic philosophers flourishing at the end of the C3rd and beginning of the C4th A.D.; the latter was the student of the former, who had himself studied with Plotinus. Both wrote lives of Pythagoras which survive. Yet much of what WP cites from the legendary traditions of Pythagoras had been reported much earlier by Aristotle (fr. 191), to whom they refer.

¶5. **Neo-Platonic *Gnôsis* at Alexandria**: this would seem to refer back to Iamblichus and Porphyry, and is therefore somewhat misleading, since both of them, and Plotinian Neo-Platonism generally, had been rather hostile to what may be properly called Alexandrian Gnosticism. **"whom even the vulgar might follow as a conjuror"**: source unlocated, but the syntax gives the impression of being translated from Greek or Latin. **"weeping" philosopher of Ephesus**: Heraclitus; see extr. (ii) above. **almost disembodied philosopher of Elea**: Parmenides; see extr. (iii) above. **Not harsh and crabbed** (etc.): from Milton's *Comus* (ll. 476–78); the preceding line being: 'How charming is divine Philosophy'.

vi. The Centrifugal and the Centripetal ['Plato and the Sophists' (ch. 5), ¶3–6.] For the antithesis of Ionian and Dorian, see extr. (iii), ¶8 (and n.) above, and cross-refs given.

¶3. The **great Athenian statesman** is Pericles, whose 'Funeral Oration' is recorded in Thucydides (the passage quoted is from II.41.1).

¶4. **"in the opinion of the ancients [etc.]"**: *ten* men is the usual number given: may WP be forgiven for adopting the appropriate term, rhetorically speaking, in the Imperial system? See Livy XLIV.6. The closest wording to WP's seeming quotation which I can locate is from Connop Thirlwall's often-reprinted *History of Greece* (1835), vol. 1, p. 5. **Plato's own figure**: at *Republic*, 426e, in a discussion of poor governance: ineffective lawmakers do not realise that they are 'cutting off a Hydra's head'.

§ *The Genius of Plato*

First published in the *Contemporary Review*, February 1892.

¶1. **The Sophists**: a class of professional intellectuals offering their teaching in rhetoric and various areas of philosophical enquiry to paying citizens.

¶2. **not grey only, as Hegel said of it** (etc.): in a famous passage at the end of the Preface to his *Philosophy of Right*, Hegel had said: 'Philosophy, as the thought of the world, does not appear until reality has completed its formative process, and made itself ready'. Thus 'only in the maturity of reality does the ideal appear as counterpart to the real'. 'When Philosophy paints its grey in grey, one form of life has grown old, and by means of grey it cannot be rejuvenated, but only known. The owl of Minerva takes its flight only when the shades of night are gathering'. (Trans. S.W. Dyde, 1896).

¶3. **"the *visible* world really existed"**: Théophile Gautier said this of himself, as recorded in the Goncourt *Journal* for 1 May 1857: '*Je suis un homme pour qui le monde visible existe*'.

¶4. **Sappho or Catullus**: it is significant that both are rather sensual poets. **braziers' workshops**: metalworkers are among the craftspeople mentioned by Socrates on many occasions (metalworkers particularly in *Rep.* IV), but if WP has a source making Plato one who 'has lingered' among the brassworkers, I have not found it. The remark also calls to mind the story of Pythagoras and the harmonious blacksmith, which purports to explain the discovery of the laws of harmony: the philosopher, walking past a blacksmith's forge, hears the harmonious hammerings caused, according to the legend, by the ratio of the sizes of the hammers. Perhaps the implication is that Plato, if he follows in the footsteps of Pythagoras, and if he closely observes nature and the arts and crafts (as WP says that he does), would know that matter is not 'dumb'. *Ξυνεσόμεθα πολλοῖς τῶν νέων αὐτόθι*: *Rep.*, 328a. The Greek quoted corresponds with the first part of WP's ensuing translation, up to the first colon. WP freely re-orders the sequence of the original. **as Carlyle says**: *Past and Present* (1843), Pt II, describing a festival at Bury St Edmunds in the C12th. **the scene in the *Lysis* of the dice-players**: 206e–207b. **grasshoppers of Attica**: see *Phaedrus*, 259b–d. **the story of Gyges**: see *Rep.*, 359d–360c: Gyges seduces the queen, kills the king and usurps the throne by use of a magical ring which makes him invisible, and which he has found on the finger of a superhuman corpse inside a hollow brazen horse, down a subterranean cavern.

¶6. **If Plato did not create the "Socrates" of his Dialogues**: note that Socrates, a real historical personage, is differently represented in the writings of Plato's contemporary, Xenophon. See WP's discussion in 'Plato and Socrates' (*PP*, ch. 4). **the description of the suffering righteous man**: *Rep.*, 361b–d. The speaker in fact is Glaucon, but the whole dialogue is notionally related by Socrates. *Corruptio optimi pessima*: 'the corruption of the best is the worst'.

¶7. **makes a very proper lawyer**: see *Theaetetus*, 172c–176a, the famous comparison of the Philosopher and the Lawyer. **the "rhapsodist"**: Ion, in the dialogue named after him. In spite of what WP says, Socrates in the *Ion* appears to conclude that the rhapsode has no 'art' or 'knowledge', but only 'inspiration'; though they both readily agree that **"interpretation"** is what he does.

¶8. **Thrasymachus**: an historical sophist who participates in the dialogue of Plato's *Republic*, where he is bluff, impetuous in argument, and given to overstatement. His 'blush' is mentioned at 350d. *Καὶ ὃς εἶπεν ἐρυθριάσας* (etc.): *Protagoras*, 312a. In Jowett's English: 'He answered, with a blush upon his face (for the day was just beginning to dawn, so that I could see him)'. **"Poor creature as I am, I have one talent [etc.]"**: *Lysis*, 204b–c.

¶9. **"once set in motion, goes ringing on [etc.]"**: *Protagoras*, 329a. **the caged birds in the *Theætetus***: 197c–200c. **dyers busy with their purple stuff**: see *Rep.*, 429d–430b.

¶10. *Τὰ ἐρωτικά* (*ta erôtika*): matters of love, 'erotics'.

¶11. *ἥττων τῶν καλῶν* (WP translates): from *Meno*, 76c.

¶12. "clad in sober grey": apparently a quotation from the opening line of Joseph Warton's 'Ode to Evening': 'Hail, meek-ey'd maiden, clad in sober grey'. **famous passage of the *Phædrus*:** 246a–254e.

¶13. **Aphrodite Urania** (the 'heavenly' form of the goddess) **and Aphrodite Pandemus** (*pan-demos*: 'of all the people'): these epithets mark a distinction between the goddess as a patron of spiritual love on the one hand, and common or sensual love on the other; see *Symposium*, 181a–182a. **"like being set free from service to a band of madmen":** *Rep.*, 329b–d, where Cephalus recalls having personally heard Sophocles say so. **[Inset quotation]:** *Rep.*, 571d–572b.

¶14. **the "Apology" of Socrates:** the oration given by Socrates in his own defence at his trial in 399 B.C. for 'corruption of the young' and religious impiety, at which he was sentenced to death. The speech and the events of the trial are recorded in the *Apology* of Plato. **just such a poet [...] disfranchised in the Perfect City:** see *Rep.* x, and WP's discussion in 'Plato's Æsthetics', ¶11–14. **"of the weightiness of the matters [etc.]":** cf. *Phaedo*, 107a–b; Simmias speaks. **Eleatic school:** cf. extr. (iii) above. **"philosophy of motion":** cf. extr. (ii) above.

¶15. **theoretic vision,** θεωρία (*theôria*): contemplation, speculation, 'theory' as opposed to practice; but also, more fundamentally, a *viewing* or *spectatorship*. Ruskin in *Modern Painters* had made much of the relationship between the simple perception and appreciation of objects in their visible character (*aesthesis*), and the apprehension of the spiritual and moral significance or truths they may convey (*theoria*). On the **imaginative reason**, an important term in WP, cf. 'School of Giorgione', ¶1 (and n.), 9, 10.

¶16. **the Schoolmen:** i.e. the scholastics, referring usually to the academics of universities in medieval and sometimes early modern Europe.

¶17. **the dialectic method:** essentially, a system of learning, teaching and conducting philosophical enquiry by means of question and answer, or disputation; but for WP's sense of the term, cf. 'Doctrine of Plato, Pt. II: Dialectic'.

¶18. **Manicheans:** followers of a dualistic religion originating in the Sasanian Empire but spreading both east and west during late antiquity, and much persecuted; but also, by extension, any person favouring a markedly dualistic conception of cosmology, in which the material world is evil or contemptible: cf. 'Dante Gabriel Rossetti', ¶7. **that last depressing day in the prison-cell of Socrates:** see ¶14n. above. **"all who rightly touch philosophy [etc.]":** *Phaedo*, 64a. **"the soul reasons best [etc.]":** *Phaedo*, 65c.

¶19. **"a hindrance to the attainment of philosophy [etc.]":** freeish paraphrase from *Phaedo*, 66a, perhaps also glancing back to 65a. **austere monitors:** 'monitor' in the literal Latinate sense, a *thing which gives warning*, an 'admonisher'. θεωρία: see ¶15n. above.

¶20. **one of the great scholars of the world** (etc.): cf. 'Raphael', ¶1. **rangé:** 'orderly', 'regular'. **Blenheim *Madonna*:** cf. 'Raphael', ¶4, 17.

¶21. **the discontented class:** the point here is not entirely clear. Two of Plato's relatives, an uncle (Charmides) and a cousin once removed (Critias), along with other wealthy Athenians, had been prominent statesmen during the short-lived rule of the anti-democratic 'Thirty Tyrants' (404–03 B.C.) in Plato's early manhood. WP may be thinking of the period before the Thirty took power, or he may have in mind the aftermath of the régime, and the re-establishment of the democracy, naturally occasioning a fall from grace for those associated with the oligarchy: Critias and Charmides were killed. **self-imposed exile**: perhaps refers to Plato's removal to Megara after the execution of Socrates. *Lehr-jahre*: years of apprenticeship. *Wander-jahre*: journeyman's years. **Dionysius the elder, Dio, and Dionysius the younger**: successive Tyrants of Syracuse; Plato was tutor to Dio (or Dion), and later engaged by him to tutor his son, Dionysius the younger. **"the philosophic king"**: as described in *Rep.* VI. **"the ideal state"**: as elaborated in *Rep.* generally. **"speaking wisdom [...] among the perfect"**: 1 Corinthians 2:6: 'Howbeit we speak wisdom among them that are perfect'. WP alludes to the supposed secretiveness of the school of Pythagoras. **the *Acadêmus***, i.e. the 'Academy' of Plato, named after the legendary hero Academus (*Akadêmos*) who was said to have previously owned the plot of land, just outside the walls of Athens. **a somewhat dubious name** (for institutions of education): presumably because Academus was supposed to have been the first abductor of Helen, while she was still unmarried; but also perhaps because it implies seclusion, as when we speak of 'the groves of academe'. *Scribens est mortuus*: 'he died while writing'; from Cicero, *De Senectute* 13.

§ *The Doctrine of Plato, Part I. — The Theory of Ideas*

The first passage given here (¶6–9) is a defence of generalised or abstract 'ideas' as contributing to one's sense of particularities — a reconciliation of the aesthetic with the idealist outlook. The second part (¶20), on the idea of beauty in Plato, begins with the notion that Plato had turned his youthful amorous disposition into a 'love' of philosophy and ideas. For this notion, cf. 'The Genius of Plato', ¶10–14.

¶7. *differentia*: 'difference'; in scholastic logic, 'a characteristic by which a given species is distinguished from all other species of the same genus' (*OED*).

¶9. Hobbes's figure: *Leviathan*, Pt I, ch. 4: 'For words are wise mens counters, they do but reckon by them: but they are the mony of fooles, that value them by the authority of an Aristotle, a Cicero, or a Thomas, or any other Doctor whatsoever, if but a man.' Hobbes does not give precedent for the latter part of WP's sentence. **Plato's own figure**: an allusion to *Gorgias*, 493a–b, in which the simile relies on some complex wordplay: (i) a pun on πιθανός (*pithanos*, 'persuadable', 'fickle') and πίθος (*pithos*, 'wine-jar'); and (ii) a pun on ἀμύητος (*amuêtos*, 'uninitiated', 'profane'), which by a trick of dubious etymologizing is made to mean also 'unclosed'. Hence Plato says that the mind or soul, because it is so easily swayed, is called a 'jar'; and the mind or soul of the ignorant ('uninitiated') is more specifically a *leaky* jar, i.e. 'unclosed' — perhaps suggesting to WP the unsealed, because unbaked, clay to which he refers. No mention is made in the *Gorgias* passage of alabaster or bronze, and I can find no other precedent in Plato for these particulars.

¶20. "Philosophers are *lovers* of truth [etc.]": *Rep.*, 501d. WP's qualifying afterthought, '*impassioned* lovers', seems to be added in order to bring out the sexual sense of the word ἐραστής (*erastês*, 'lover').

§ The Doctrine of Plato, Part II.—Dialectic

For another treatment of similar themes, but focussed rather on Montaigne than on Plato, see *Gaston*, ch. 5 ('Suspended Judgement').

¶1. The philosophers mentioned are all known or thought to have written in verse. On **Pythagoras** and his 'golden verses', cf. *PP*, ch. 1–5 extracts, extr. (v), above. **Lucretius**, a much later writer than the others, wrote the long Latin poem *De Rerum Natura* (*On Nature*), which WP sees as the culmination of the Greek tradition of verse-philosophy.
¶3. *Que scais-je?*: WP translates, but more literally the phrase means 'What do I know?' It was a motto of Montaigne's.
¶6. *debitæ naturæ*: 'debts to nature'. See Francis Bacon, *Sermones Fideles*, §2, 12, and *De Sapientia Veterum*, §12. The phrase is applied here in a wider sense than that of the common usage, in which the 'debt to nature' (always singluar) is merely a euphemism for mortality. For the fuller sense, cf. 'Style', ¶7 (and n.). **"along with you [...] to consider, to seek out, [etc.]"**: WP gives the original Greek in his footnote, but it is a composite quotation from *Meno*, 80d, and *Rep.*, 435a.
¶7. **"And [...] is not the road to Athens [etc.]"**: *Symp.*, 173b. *processus*: cf. *PP*, ch. 1–5 extracts, extr. (ii), above, ¶16 (and n.).
¶8. ὁδός (*hodos*): 'road', 'way'. κίνησις (*kinêsis*): 'motion', 'movement'. μέθοδος (*methodos*): 'method', 'system'. Ἀλλὰ μεταθώμεθα: 'but let us go further along', or 'pursue the matter', or perhaps 'shift our ground'; *Rep.*, 334e. **"Persevere [...] indefectible certitude"**: WP, or the printer, omits to close the direct speech; I have therefore added the terminal quotation mark after 'certitude'. νοητὸς τόπος: literally 'mental place'; the noetic or intelligible realm, as opposed to the visible world (see *Rep.*, 508c and 517b). **difficulties and crudities of Meno**: i.e. in the dialogue named after this youthful interlocutor of Socrates.
¶9. **a certain plausibility**: i.e. a persuasive agreeableness helping and encouraging hearers to grasp the intention; while, below, '**plausibility of another sort**' implies the danger of a specious appearance of credibility—agreeableness taken too far toward coercive platitude. Etymologically, 'plausible' means 'seeking ap*plause*, approval'. *obscurum per obscurius*: '[to cast light on] something obscure by means of something still more obscure'. **eristic**: 'the art of disputation' (*OED*), or verbal wrangling. **logomachy**: disputation *about* the meanings of words themselves. **"vision of all time and all existence"**: *Rep.*, 486a.
¶10. *advocatus diaboli*: 'the devil's advocate'. The **dog** or **wolf** implies cynicism. ὅμοιον ὁμοίῳ: 'like to like'; cf. *PP*, ch. 1–5 extracts, extr. (v), above, ¶3 (and n.).
¶11. Plato elaborates that figure in *The Republic*: 432b–d. ὅπῃ ἂν ὁ λόγος (etc.): *Rep.*, 394d; WP translates ('I do not [...] before the wind').
¶12. **"We argue rashly and adventurously [etc.]"**: a very loose and expansive paraphrase from *Timaeus*, 34c. **"new game of chess"** (etc.): *Rep.*, 487c.
¶13. Zeno's paradoxes: cf. *PP*, ch. 1–5 extracts, extr. (iii), above. **"Socrates," as he admits** (etc.): *Symp.*, 201c. **"Such is his skill [etc.]"**: *Euthydemus*, 272a–b.
¶14. **as Lessing suggests**: Gotthold Ephraim Lessing, in his *Anti-Goeze* (1778). *longo intervallo*: 'by a long distance'; cf. *Aeneid* V:320. ἐπιστήμη (*epistêmê*): 'understanding', 'knowledge', 'science'. **"Socrates in Plato,"** remarks Montaigne (etc.): *Essays* III.8.

¶17. **exactly ponderable**: i.e. weighable, measurable, with precision or certainty by the mind. *θεωρία* (*theôria*): cf. 'The Genius of Plato', ¶15 (and n.). *ἀποκάμνων*: 'growing tired', or 'flagging'. **"Must I take the argument [etc.]"**: *Rep.*, 345b. **"Answer what you think, *μεγαλοπρεπῶς*—liberally"**: seemingly a variation on a theme in *Meno*, 70b, perhaps combined with *Gorgias*, 521a.

¶18. **That justice is only useful as applied to things useless**: see *Rep.*, 333d. **that the just man is a kind of thief**: see *Rep.*, 334a. **"the spectacle of all time and all existence"**: *Rep.*, 486a; cf. 'Doctrine of Plato, Pt II: Dialectic', ¶9.

¶19. **Proclus** (412–85): Neo-Platonic philosopher. Friedrich Wilhelm Joseph von **Schelling** (1775–1854): German idealist philosopher.

¶20. **Lucian**: Grecophone writer of the C2nd A.D. working in diverse genres, including dialogues and several kinds of non-fiction, frequently humorous; cf. *Marius*, ch. 24, in which he appears as a character. On **Cicero**, a more obvious choice in this context, cf. 'Style', ¶1, 6, 27; 'The Genius of Plato', ¶21; and 'Raphael', ¶1. **the *Sic et Non*** (*Yes and No*): a work by Peter **Abelard** (1079–1142) concerned with the application of logical processes to ostensibly contradictory statements on theology. On Abelard, the eminent scholastic theologian and philosopher, legendary in later ages for his ill-fated affair with Heloïse d'Argenteuil, see WP's 'Two Early French Stories' in *Ren.* ('Aucassin and Nicolette' in the first edition). **"Their name is legion,"** says a **modern writer**: source unlocated.

¶21. *κόσμος* (*kosmos*): 'order', 'world-order', etc.; cf. *PP*, ch. 1–5 extracts, extr. (iii), ¶9.

§Lacedæmon

This is a study of the state of Sparta (Lacedaemon), as seen from the point of view of an imaginary Athenian visitor who is supposed to be a student of Plato's. The chapter first appeared as a separate essay in the *Contemporary Review*, June 1892. WP is much influenced by Karl Otfried Müller's *History and Antiquities of the Doric Race*, first published in German in 1824, and in an English translation by Henry Tufnell and George Cornewall Lewis in 1830 (London: Murray, 2 vols). References below are to the text of this English edition.

¶4. **Dorian** and **Ionian**: more than a geographical distinction. The Dorians and Ionians were two of the major ethnic groups in ancient Greece, with many differences of culture as WP describes. They represent opposite sides of the Peloponnesian War (431–04 B.C.) fought during Plato's childhood and youth. Cf. *PP*, ch. 1–5 extracts, extr. (iii), and cross-refs given there. *de novo*: 'from new', 'from scratch'.

¶5. **Dorian constitutions to which Aristotle refers**: see *Politics* II.9, IV.9, etc.

¶11. **as Plato threatens**: *Rep.*, 423b–c. **Lacedæmonian youth plunged itself in the Eurotas**: see ¶23 below. **High Street, or *Corso***: the latter being a kind of Italian equivalent for the former (British English), i.e. a central street. **Therapnæ, Amyclæ**: two towns near Sparta, the former reputed the birthplace of Castor and Pollux, the latter the site of a famous temple of Apollo and the festival of the *Hyacinthia*.

¶12. **Plato, as you may remember**: perhaps WP is combining the sense of *Rep.*, 401b–c with that of *Phaedrus*, 229a–230d. **Phidias** (or Pheidias): Greek sculptor; see 'Beginnings of Greek Sculpture, I', ¶20n. *Demos*: 'populace'; this colossal statue representing the

Spartan 'People' is mentioned by Pausanias at III.11.10. *Ephebeum*: an exercise hall for youths (*ephêboi*). *et même très dangereux*: 'and even very dangerous'.

¶13. **as Xenophon [...] describes** (etc.): see *Constitution of the Lacedaemonians* III.4.

¶14. **Those ancient Pelopid princes**: Menelaus (grandson of Pelops) and his successors had been, in legend, kings of Mycenaean Sparta. The historical Doric kings of Plato's time in fact claimed Achaean (i.e. non-Dorian) descent from the mythical Hercules, who in legend had been granted territories in Sparta, and whose descendants had been ousted by the Pelopids. In that sense they had, as WP says, '**come back from exile into their old home**', but *not* as the descendents of the Pelopid line. It is unclear where WP may have encountered this idea. See Müller's *Doric Race* I.3, and cf. Plato's *Laws*, 682e. **two kings [...] always reigning together**: the *Archagetai*, both hereditary, and representing two lines (the Agiad and Eurypontid dynasties) descended originally from the twin brothers Eurystenes and Procles. **Lycurgus**: legendary lawgiver and framer of the Spartan constitution, notionally in the C9th B.C. On his prescriptions for domestic architecture, see Müller, *Doric Race* IV.1.

¶15. **Alcman**: lyric poet of the C7th B.C. who lived and worked in Sparta, though probably of Lydian origin. **"abounding in sacred tripods"** (etc.): see Greek Anthology VII.709. The epigram is in fact not attributed to Alcman himself, but is a later composition by Alexander of Aetolia in which Alcman is the supposed speaker. *Stoa Pœkile*: 'painted porch'. *Choros*: a place for dancing; this was the site of the *Gymnopædia*, an annual festival during which the youths (*ephêboi*) performed a kind of military dance.

¶16. **"A pillar too,"** says Pausanias (etc.): III.14. **Athene Chalciœcus** (i.e. **of the Brazen House**) **and Gitiades**: cf. 'Beginnings of Greek Sculpture, I', ¶16, and Greek Sculpture (Further Extracts), extr. (i), ¶16. **Homer's descriptions of [...] metallic architecture**: cf. 'Beginnings of Greek Sculpture, I', ¶8, 15, 17.

¶17. **Müller**: see headnote above. **"the Dorian character [etc.]"**: *Doric Race* IV.1, §4. ὀφρῦᾳ τε καὶ κοιλαίνεται: 'beetling and hollowed-out', a saying mentioned by Strabo (*Geog.* VIII.6.23), but applied to Corinth. WP borrows it for Sparta.

¶18. **"The whole life of the Lacedæmonian community [etc.]"**: I have not been able to locate an exact source in *Doric Race*, although the basic notion is several times expressed. Possibly another work is quoted.

¶23. **"the general accent of the Doric dialect [etc.]"**: *Doric Race* IV.9, §33. **as with ourselves [...] subordination of the younger to the older**: the comparison is with English schools—especially public schools—with their official and unofficial hierarchies. For the Spartan system, see *Doric Race* IV.5, §2. ὅμοιοι and ὑπομείονες: respectively, the 'equals' or higher-ranking citizens, and the 'inferiors' or lesser-ranking citizens, who had fewer political rights. Εἴρην, μελλείρην, σιδεύνης: terms defining successive stages in the growth of a Spartan youth: respectively, (i) one who has completed his twentieth year; (ii) one in the phase immediately preceding that condition; (iii) the youth in a still earlier stage, aged around fifteen to seventeen. ἀγέλαι: the 'groups' into which the Spartan youths were divided for their training. *vivâ voce*: oral examination by question and answer (a term well known to WP's Oxford University audiences); see *Doric Race* IV.8, §2. **"became adepts in presence of mind"**: not quoting Müller, it seems, but perhaps paraphrasing

Plutarch, *Lycurgus* 18.2. **the brief mode of speech Plato commends**: *Protagoras*, 342a–343c. **which took and has kept its name from them**: i.e. 'laconic'. *ascêsis*: 'training', 'practice', 'self-discipline'; cf. 'Preface' (*Ren.*), ¶6, and 'Style', ¶10.

¶24. **A Lacedæmonian ambassador** (etc.): cf. *Doric Race* IV.9, §5.

¶25. μουσική (*mousikê*): 'music' in a wide sense, i.e. the arts over which the Muses presided; cf. 'Plato's Æsthetics', ¶3, and Greek Sculpture (Further Extracts), extr. (ii.a); and see *Doric Race* IV.6. *rhetrai*: 'sayings', the traditional maxims of Spartan law. **Terpander**: lyrist of the C7[th] B.C. **cousins at Sion** (etc.): a reference to Judaic liturgy of roughly the same period as that of the Spartan customs described.

¶26. **the foundations of which may still be seen**: even yet. **what Plato says in** *The Republic* **of "imitations"** (etc.): especially in Bk X. **Lacedæmonian sayings**: i.e. laconicisms. παραλειπόμενον: translated by WP; cf. 'Plato's Æesthetics', ¶15.

¶27. δεισιδαίμονες: cf. 'Study of Dionysus', ¶12. **the Ephors**: the council of five senior magistrates at Sparta.

¶28. **purgation [...] recommended in Plato's** *Republic*: see 399e and 567c.

¶29. **Enyalius**: the 'Warlike'; sometimes an epithet of the war-god Ares, sometimes rather the son of Ares.

¶30. **the** *Hyacinthia*: a festival of the mythical youth Hyacinthus, celebrated at Amyclae. **Hyacinthus** and **Apollo**: cf. Greek Sculpture (Further Extracts), extr. (i), ¶11; and see 'Apollo in Picardy' (*MS*), which reimagines the accidental death of Hyacinthus in the setting of a medieval monastery. **symbols of the great solar change**: i.e. the myth represents the coming of summer, the fatal discus being the sun that withers the flowers. **Proserpine, Adonis, and the like**: on Adonis cf. 'Winckelmann', ¶42, and Greek Sculpture (Further Extracts), extr. (i), ¶11–13; and see WP's meditations on Persephone-Proserpine in the 'The Myth of Demeter and Persephone' (two parts, *GS*). *Chiton*: this being the name of a kind of robe or tunic; see Pausanias III.16.2. *Amyclææ vestes*: 'cloths of Amyclae', purple-dyed.

¶31. *Amyclæi fratres*: 'the brothers of Amyclae', i.e. Castor and Pollux (Polydeuces), together called the 'Dioscuri'. **the** *docana*: see Plutarch, *De Fraterno Amore* I. **a certain battle was lost** (etc.): see Herodotus V.75.

¶32. **"passing even the love of woman"**: 2 Samuel 1:26. ἀΐτης and εἰσπνήλας: terms used at Sparta for the two parties in a pederastic relationship. The affection and guidance of the older man, as the lover ('inspirer'), is figured as an inspiration or literally *in-breathing*, while the boy (beloved) is the 'listener' or 'hearer'. See discussion in *Doric Race* IV.4, §6–8, in which Müller argues that the relationship was, though 'not entirely mental', nevertheless free from the 'pollution' or 'vice' of actual sexual contact.

¶34. **the surprise of Saint Paul**: see, e.g., 1 Corinthians 9:24–27: 'Know ye not that they which run in a race run all, but one receiveth the prize? So run, that ye may obtain. And every man that striveth for the mastery is temperate in all things. Now they do it to obtain a corruptible crown; but we an incorruptible'. This leads naturally into WP's reference to the parsley crown, below. On asceticism and self-restraint, see also 1 Timothy 4, and Colossians 2:16–23. **parsley crown**: an honorific prize for athletes. *qui manducatis panem doloris?*: 'you who eat the bread of sorrows?' Psalm 127 ('*Nisi Dominus*'), v. 2.

§Plato's Æsthetics

¶1. *Τὰ τερπνὰ ἐν Ἑλλάδι* (translated by WP): Pindar, *Pythian Odes* 10.19. *τὸ τὰ αὑτοῦ πράττειν* (translated by WP): see Plato, *Rep.*, 433a(ff.), and *Charmides*, 162a(ff.). **ποικιλία**: decorative craftwork in various colours; sometimes embroidery, but here apparently used in the sense of *intarsia* or *marqueterie*, i.e. wood inlay or decoration by the application of contrasting wood veneers. **Fra Damiano of Bergamo** (died 1549): celebrated Italian master of *intarsia*. *Ἆρ᾽ οὖν καὶ ἑκάστῃ τῶν τεχνῶν* (etc.): in Jowett's translation: 'And the interest of any art is the perfection of it—this and nothing else?' *Rep.*, 341d. (*N.b.* the semicolon ending the quotation is a Greek question mark.)

¶3. It may help to transliterate **λέξις** (*lexis*), **λόγοι** (*logoi*), and **μουσική** (*mousikē*). On music as embracing **all productions in which the *form* counts equally with, or for more than, the *matter***, cf. 'School of Giorgione', ¶5–10.

¶4. "You have perceived have you not [etc.]": Plato, *Rep.*, 395d.

¶7. *μετάβασις εἰς ἄλλο γένος* (translated by WP): see Aristotle, *Analytica Posteriora*, 75a38, and *De Caelo*, 268b. **in the temper of the patient hearer or spectator**: all previous editions read: 'in the temper of the patient the hearer or spectator'. This seems incorrect. It is just conceivable that what was meant was 'the patient, the hearer or spectator'; but I think the present emendation more probably representative of WP's intention.

¶8. *Ἵνα μὴ ἐκ τῆς μιμήσεως* (etc., translated by WP): i.e. lest by imitating one should become what one imitates. *Rep.*, 395c–d.

¶10. **a certain vicious centrifugal tendency** (etc.): cf. *PP*, ch. 1–5 extracts, extr. (vi). **to suppress the differences of male and female character** (etc.): see *Rep.* v.

¶11. *Σμικραὶ αἱ μεταβολαί*: translated by WP above; but otherwise, 'the changes [or transitions] are slight'. *Rep.*, 397b. The list of forbidden 'imitations' refers to Bks III and x. **βασιλικὴ φυλή**: 'ruling class'. *οὐδενὶ προσέχειν τὸν νοῦν*: *Rep.*, 396a. **illiberal**: i.e. originally, 'unfitting for a free citizen'; hence also 'base', 'vulgar', 'mean'. **"a creation of mind, in accordance with right reason"**: Plato, *Laws*, 890d. This claim, made by the speaker Cleinias, applies to both law and art.

¶12. *Ἀλλὰ μήν, ὦ Ἀδείμαντε* (etc.): 'And yet, Adeimantus, the mixed kind [of art] is also pleasing'. Socrates in Plato, *Rep.*, 397d.

¶13. In the first sentence, all previous editions print open speech-marks at '**able**', which are never closed, direct quotation then beginning anew in the next sentence with '**if he came to our city**'. I have inserted the closing speech-marks after '**genius**', since the phrase thus contained is a direct rendering of Plato ['*δυνάμενον ὑπὸ σοφίας*'], while the succeeding clauses represent WP's own amplifying and explanatory paraphrases. The whole mixture of quotations and elaboration comes from *Rep.*, 398a. **myriad-minded**: epithet applied to Shakespeare by Coleridge. *Τῷ αὐστηροτέρῳ καὶ ἀηδεστέρῳ ποιητῇ, ὠφελίας ἕνεκα*: translated by WP as 'some more austere [...]'; *Rep.*, 398b. **[Inset quotation]**: *Rep.*, 400e–402a, with some licence taken. **καλοκἀγαθός** (or *καλὸς κἀγαθός*): 'both beautiful and good', 'of the perfect character'.

¶14. **"the half is more than the whole"**: see Hesiod, *Works and Days*, l. 40. **Cistercian Gothic [...] when Saint Bernard had purged it**: Bernard of Clairvaux (died 1153) was the figurehead for a movement towards less abundant ornamentation in Cistercian architecture.

¶15. **as a scholar, formed, mature and manly**: the use of the term 'manly' here, which need not strictly be coterminous with 'male', relies on two considerations: (i) the classical association between 'virtue' and masculinity, the word *virtus* (literally 'man-ness') being the lexical basis of Latin thinking on the matter (the Greek *andreia*, discussed by WP in the next sentence, having something of the same generalised moral significance); and (ii) the condition of modern education in WP's own day, which, as he says in 'Style', ¶7, 'still to so large an extent limits real scholarship to men'. ἀνδρεία: 'manliness'. ἦθος (*ethos*): 'custom', 'manners', 'character', 'temperament', 'bearing'. πάθος (*pathos*): 'feeling', 'emotional experience', 'passion', 'sensation'. παραλειπόμενα: 'negligences'; cf. Lacedæmon, ¶26. ἀκολουθεῖν τὸν λόγον: [music and rhythm must] 'follow the words' (i.e. the 'sense' of the words); *Rep.*, 398d.

¶17. **in those who were, not to read, but to sing him**: Pindar's odes in celebration of athletic victories were ostensibly written to be sung chorally.

¶18. Χαλεπὰ τὰ καλά: 'fine things are difficult', a saying occasionally quoted in Plato; see *Rep.*, 435c, 497d. Ἴσως τὸ λεγόμενον ἀληθές (etc.): 'it may be that the saying is true, that fine things are difficult'; 435c. **"dry soul"**, **"dry light"**: alternative readings from a saying attributed to Heraclitus (Diels fr. 118), in which the adjective 'dry' seems to have been positioned ambiguously with respect to the nouns 'light' and 'soul'. *siccum lumen*: 'dry light'; see Francis Bacon, *Advancement of Learning* (1605), third paragraph following the dedication: Bacon quotes Heraclitus. And cf. 'Style', ¶13.

GREEK STUDIES

§A Study of Dionysus: The Spiritual Form of Fire and Dew

First published in the *Fortnightly Review*, December 1876, this followed WP's two-part study of 'The Myth of Demeter and Persephone', published in the same periodical in January and February of the same year. His essay on 'The Bacchanals of Euripides', also included in *GS*, was probably written around this time too, but was not published until May 1889, in *Macmillan's Magazine*; it is an important complement to the 'Study', and completes the picture of WP's Dionysus.

¶3. **Shelley's *Sensitive Plant***: a long poem of c. 1820 in which a 'sensitive plant' is nurtured by a mother-like 'Lady' who tends the garden in which it grows.

¶4. **Dodona**: an important oracle in Epirus, where prophecies were drawn from an interpretation of the rustling of the leaves. **"Together with them [etc.]"**: Homeric hymn (v) to Aphrodite, ll. 264-66, 69-72.

¶5. *nympholepti*: 'taken by the nymphs', nympholepsy being otherwise considered a form of frenzied possession by the gods or spirits of the woods, akin to 'panic' fear (i.e. possession by Pan). **the maids who sit spinning in the house of Alcinous**: see *Odyssey* VII:103-07. **The nymphs of Naxos**: nurses of the infant Dionysus in some versions of the myth of his life (e.g. in Diodorus Siculus, *Bibl. Hist.* v.52). The **purple robe** is a traditional attribute of D. Concerning its origin, WP may have had in mind some such retelling as in Apollonius Rhodius, *Argonautica* IV:424-34.

¶6. **naming him [...] from the brightness of the sky and the moisture of the earth**: this is somewhat obscure. It would appear to imply that the name 'Dionysus' is etymologically compounded of words signifying *brightness of sky* and *mositure of earth*. For the first part (*dio-*, connected with Zeus) there is foundation, assuming as WP does that Zeus is fundamentally the god of sky. The second part of the name is usually connected with Mount Nysa, where the infant D is raised by the Hyades (rain-bearing water nymphs); so Nysa may be associated with rainwater for WP. Another consideration is that one of the epithets of Dionysus, as a deity of fertilizing moisture, is Hyes (*Huês*), etymologically related to rain and water. **Œno** (wine), **Spermo** (corn or wheat), and **Elais** (olive): the magical powers to which WP alludes were conferred by D (with Demeter's aid, in some versions) upon these, his three granddaughters. **honey and milk** (etc.): see Euripides, *Bacchae*, ll. 699-713.

¶7. **Snubnose, and Sweetwine, and Silenus**: Silenus ('snub-nosed') is the name of a paticular satyr, the avuncular leader of lesser satyrs, and the tutor or companion of D. 'Snub-nose' and 'Sweet-wine' are English translations of Greek names applied to individual satyrs in the inscriptions of vase-paintings, etc., given as examples in Karl Otfried Müller's *Ancient Art and its Remains* (trans. John Leitch, 2nd edn, London, 1852), pp. 497-99.

¶8. **the brook Molpeia** (or Melpeia): the place in Arcadia where Pan 'discovered the music of the pan-pipes': see Pausanias IV.38.11.

¶9. **"the bird, which among the petals [etc.]"**, **"the crocus and the hyacinth [etc.]"**: from the Homeric hymn (XIX) to Pan, ll. 17-18, 25-26. **they give their names to insolence and mockery** (etc.): i.e. 'satire', in its range of ancient and modern senses. **unmeaning and ridiculous fear**: i.e. 'panic'; cf. '*nympholepti*' in ¶5n. above. **Praxiteles**: Pausanias (I.20.1) and Pliny (*Nat. Hist.* XXXIV.69) speak of a famous statue of a satyr by this sculptor of the C4th B.C., and WP attributes to him the original of a class of later replicas (known as the 'Resting' or 'Leaning Satyr' type) of which there is a fine example in the Capitoline Museum, Rome (inv. 739). The attribution is now a popular one. There is a copy of Cristofano **Robetta**'s engraving of **Ceres and her children** (c. 1500-20) in the British Museum (inv. 1845,0825.792). **no longer afraid**: see Homeric hymn (XIX) to Pan, ll. 35-39.

¶10. **enthusiasm, as distinguished by Plato in the *Phædrus***: see especially 244a and ff. **A winged Dionysus, venerated at Amyclæ**: see Pausanias III.19.6.

¶11. Michelangelo's *Bacchus* is now in the Bargello, Florence. **The head of Ion leans** (etc.): this passage, which looks like a retelling of some specific Greek source, appears rather to be a free *fantasia* based upon several characters and situations found in various works by Plato. The scene recalls the preface to the *Charmides* as well as the end of the *Symposium*. Charmides and Callias appear together in the *Protagoras*, and also in Xenophon's *Symposium*. The birthday party is an odd detail without obvious precedent, but the *Symposia* of both Plato and Xenophon are set at celebratory parties of other sorts. *Eleutherios*: 'the Deliverer', 'the Liberator'. **the Pythia**: oracular priestess of Apollo. **"Here lieth the body of Dionysus [etc.]"**: as attested by Philochorus, *Fragments* 328.

¶12. *Iacchus, Bacchus*: these epithets are supposed to signify the loud cries of his worshippers. *calpis* and *amphora*: two forms of jug or pitcher. **Keramus** (or Ceramus): literally 'pottery', or the potter's clay, but personified as a legendary heroic figure worshipped by Athenian potters. That D and Ariadne were his parents is a circumstance mentioned by Pausanias (1.3.1). δεισιδαίμονες: cf. 'Lacedæmon', ¶27. **Aristophanes in the *Acharnians***: this comedy, written and set in Athens around 424 B.C., during the war with the Peloponnesians and Boeotians, depicts the rural *Dionysia* at ll. 202ff.

¶13. **marriage with Ariadne**: D finds Ariadne abandoned by Theseus on the island of Naxos, and they are married. **two of the greatest masters of Italian painting**: Titian, in the famous *Bacchus and Ariadne* in the National Gallery, London; Tintoretto, in a composition generally known by the same name, in the Palazzo Ducale, Venice. **"At Thebes alone"**: Sophocles, fr. 773. **Cadmus**: brother of Europa and father of Semele, he was the founder and ruler of Thebes. Having killed a sacred dragon, he sowed the teeth, on Athene's orders, and so produced the *spartoi*. He himself was later transformed into a snake. **Euripides**: the reference is to the *Bacchae*. See WP's 'The Bachannals of Euripides' (*GS*). **as Callimachus calls him**: Callimachus says this of Apollo in his 'Hymn to Delos', and the same thing is said of D elsewhere (e.g. by Lucian in the *Dialogue* of Poseidon and Hermes), but never, as far as I can see, by Callimachus. **venerable relic of the wooden image**: see Pausanias IX.12.4. ***Ivy-Fountain***: see Plutarch, *Lysander* XXVIII.4. **the grave of Semele**: see Pausanias IX.12.3–4, 16.7.

¶15. πυριγενής: 'fire-born'. **Aaron's rod that budded**: see Numbers 17:8. **the staff in the hand of the Pope** (etc.): the staff puts out new shoots, as a sign from God that Tannhäuser's sin of cohabitation with the pagan Venus in her subterranean abode is not unforgivable. The sign comes too late to prevent him from returning to Venus in despair of absolution. Among the various C19[th] reimaginings of the tale are the opera by Wagner, poems by Swinburne and Morris, and paintings by Burne-Jones and others.

¶16. **Hyades**: rain nymphs. **mænads**: female followers or worhsippers of D, known for frenzied behaviour and revelry. **Melampus**: legendary prophet, associated with the importation of the worship of D. Regarding his advice to wine-drinkers, see Athenaeus, *Deipnosophistae* 11.23. **Giorgione, *Fête Champêtre***: often now attributed to Titian; cf. 'School of Giorgione', ¶16, 23. ***Acqua frésca!***: 'Fresh water!'

¶19. **Pheidias**: the great Greek sculptor; cf. 'Beginnings of Greek Sculpture, I', ¶20n. **Arrian tells us**: *Discourses of Epictetus* 1.6.

¶20. **The oracle of Dodona**: see ¶4n. above.

¶22. **work of Prometheus**: in Greek mythology, Prometheus was sometimes supposed to have created mankind out of earth and water. **age of Pericles**: c. 461–29 B.C.

¶23. ***Streben***: cf. 'School of Giorgione', ¶3–4. **the Dorian influence**: cf. 'Lacedæmon', ¶17, etc.; *PP*, ch. 1–5 extracts, extr. (iii), ¶9, and extr. (vi), *passim*; and 'Beginnings of Greek Sculpture, I', ¶21. **humanised religion of Apollo**: cf. 'Lacedæmon', ¶28–29. **marbles of Ægina**: see WP's 'The Marbles of Ægina' (*GS*).

¶24. **"vasty deep"**: Shakespeare, *Henry IV, Pt 1*, III.1:50.

¶25. **the *quoit-player***: i.e. the statue of the 'discobolus', attributed to Myron. Cf. Greek Sculpture (Further Extracts), extr. (ii.a).

¶26. **Helen, Gretchen, Mary**: obvious associations for these names would include characteristics ascribed, respectively, to Helen of Troy; the tragic heroine of Goethe's *Faust*; and the Virgin Mary. **borrowed from William Blake**: as in Blake's paintings of the 'Spiritual Forms' of Pitt, Nelson and Napoleon.

¶27. **Lady of the Lake**: a long poem by Walter Scott (1810). **Beauty born of murmuring sound** (etc.): from Wordsworth, 'Lucy' (iv), ll. 29–30. *Οἰνοφόρια* **and the** *Ἀνθεστήρια*: *Oinophoria* and *Anthestêria*, both Dionysian festivals.

¶28. **separation of the Indo-Germanic race**: i.e. the period in which the Western and Indian branches of the Indo-European language family, presumed to have a common central-Asian origin, were bifurcated. **youngest of the gods**: see Herodotus II.145. **under Peisistratus**: i.e. c. 561–27 B.C.

¶29. **Oschophoria**: an Athenian festival of D. **Athene of the Parasol**: at the Athenian festival of the *Scira* or *Scirophoria*, the image of Athene Sciras was carried beneath a white canopy or parasol (*skiron*). *ἐσκιατροφηκώς*: 'brought up in the shade', 'kept indoors'. **texture of green leaves**: 'texture' in the literal sense, a weaving-together. **famous Etruscan mirror**: in the Berlin Staatliche Museum. **the Lenæum**: a temple or precincts sacred to D in Athens. **the Limnæ**: another sanctuary of D in the marshes to the south of the Areopagus. **snake of Athene Polias**: the sacred snake of the goddess was said to reside in the part of the Erechtheum given over to her.

¶30. There is an example of Girolamo **Mocetto**'s engraving of D (c. 1490–1530) in the British Museum (inv. 1859,0806.303). **young Hebrew painter**: Simeon Solomon (1840–1905), British Jewish artist associated with the Rossetti circle; he was influenced by Pre-Raphaelitism and French Symbolism, and became a significant figure in the British Aesthetic Movement. His homosexuality was well known, and in 1873 he had been gaoled for indecent acts in a public convenience. For much of his later life he resided in a workhouse in London, where he was visited by admirers and collectors including many central literary characters of the 1880s and 1890s, and continued to produce drawings and paintings in a distinctive Symbolist style. **"of things too sweet"**: phrase taken from Swinburne's provocative poem of ambiguous gender and eroticism, 'Fragoletta' (1866), l. 66. Swinburne and Solomon had been close friends before 1873. **Dionysus Zagreus**: a form of D probably originating in Crete, the myths of whom closely resemble those of the Egyptian Osiris. He is torn to pieces by the Titans and buried, but the heart is given by Athene to Zeus, who swallows it and brings forth a new D (Iacchus). His worship was associated with barbarous rituals, such as the rending of victims and the eating of raw flesh.

¶31. **described by Plutarch**: *De E apud Delphos* 9. **Chthonian god**: a god of the underworld. **eater of man's flesh**: D is sometimes given the epithet *ὠμηστής*, 'eater of raw flesh'. **sarcophagus**: this word commonly used for coffins of stone means literally 'flesh-eater'. **the ivory-white shoulder of Pelops**: it is usually the grieving Demeter who is said to have eaten, absent-mindedly, the shoulder of Pelops—thereafter replaced, when he was restored to life, by one carved from ivory. Unless WP has come upon some variant of the myth, it is likely that this image is merely meant to add detail and emphasis to his collation of cannibalistic motifs in Greek mythology, indicating a thematic strain to which the story of D-Zagreus (mangled, consumed and restored) and the rites of his cult belong.

¶32. **Alcyonian lake**: fabled bottomless lake in the region of Lerna. See Pausanias

II.37.5-6. **Eleusinian mysteries**: the *Eleusinia*, a festival and mystery cult of Demeter and Persephone, with secretive and enigmatic rituals. **"*the two*"**: i.e. Demeter and Persephone.

¶34. **the name of Lycurgus**: the name comes from '*lukos*' ('wolf'). Lycurgus, king of the Edones in Thrace, banned the worship of D, and is thus presented in legend as the enemy of the god. **Gilles de Retz** (de Rais; died 1440): Marshal of France during the English Wars, and a comrade of Joan of Arc; also among the richest men in France at that time. He was tried and eventually put to death for a remarkable catalogue of crimes, which, besides black magic, included the abduction, sexual abuse, murder and mutilation of hundreds of children. In subsequent French folklore he became associated both with the werewolf and with the sinister fairytale character of 'Bluebeard'.

¶35. **Dionysius of Halicarnassus**: see *Antiq. Rom.* I.38.1-4. **curious mimic pursuit of the priest**: at the festival of the *Agrionia*, the knife-wielding priest of D reportedly staged a chase of the women descended from the family of the Minyades; see Plutarch, *Quest. Grae.* XXXVIII. That passage is also a source for WP's version of the tale of the **three daughters of Minyas**, Leucippe, Arsinoë and Alcathoë. The ill-fated child, son of Leucippe, was named Hippasus. The detail of **bats**, **moths**, etc., is drawn from the accounts of Antoninus Liberalis (*Met. Syn.* X) and/or Aelian (*Varia Hist.* III.42).

¶36. **Aidoneus**: i.e. Hades.

¶37. **Of this I hope to speak in another paper**: i.e. 'The Bacchanals of Euripides'; see headnote above.

¶38. **as Plato witnesses**: see *Rep.*, 364e. **Occultation of Dionysus**, *Dionysiaca* of Nonnus: as Inman (1990) demonstrates in detail (pp. 272-73, 275-79), the story as WP gives it in the following paragraph (¶39) is not substantially based on Nonnus, as the reader might naturally suppose, but is rather a collage from various sources, including modern scholarly works such as Ludwig Preller's *Griechische Mythologie* (*Greek Mythology*, 1854, 2nd edn 1860-61) and Friedrich Gottlieb Welcker's *Griechische Götterlehre* (*The Greek Lore of the Gods*, 1857-63), both of which WP had borrowed from the Taylorian Library in Oxford. Even though WP says the content of the lost Orphic poem is 'represented *only*' by Nonnus, he has clearly looked elsewhere to find scraps of the 'imagery' which he wants to put 'back into the shrine, bit by bit'. He appears to intend a speculative reconstruction, from various sources, of the putative contents of the lost Orphic poem and the tradition embodied in it, rather than a synopsis of the version found in Nonnus alone.

¶39. **See above for sources. Here**: i.e. Hera.

§ *The Beginnings of Greek Sculpture, I:*
The Heroic Age of Greek Art

The first of two studies entitled 'The Beginnings of Greek Sculpture' for the *Fortnightly Review*, this essay appeared in the February 1880 number. It represents the start of a series of four completed essays on Greek scuplture, all collected posthumously in *GS*; but the series was meant to have been expanded further still, as Shadwell's 'Preface' to *GS* tells us.

¶2. **the modern sculptor's usage** (etc.): the term 'modern' here should be understood to encompass the Renaissance and all subsequent periods, during which artists have commonly relied on workshop assistants to work the stone of sculptures.

¶6. **that flower of gold on a silver stalk**: the famous excavations at **Mycenæ** in 1876 were led by Heinrich Schliemann, who had previously excavated the presumed site of Troy. The flower is mentioned briefly in his book *Mycenae* (1878), ch. 7 (p. 204 in the English edition of the same year), but is not illustrated or much described. **golden honeycomb of Dædalus**: Diodorus Siculus records that Daedalus had crafted for the temple of Aphrodite at Mt Eryx a golden honeycomb indistinguishable from a real honeycomb (IV.78).

¶7. **Kêr** is a goddess of death or doom, **Eris** a goddess of discord; in Hesiod both are daughters of Night. **Kudoimos** is the spirit of the confusion and tumult of battle; see *Iliad* XVIII:535.

¶8. **"as the brightness of the sun or of the moon"**: *Odyssey* VII:84–85; but also at IV:45–46, where it describes the palace of Menelaus. **The walls were massy brass** (etc.): from Pope's verse translation; *Od.* VII:112–17 in Pope, 86–90 in the Greek. **lions over the old gateway of Mycenæ**: excavated and described by Schliemann (1878); see ¶6n above.

¶9. *cyanus* (κύανος): a dark blue enamel used especially on armour. **Leonardo's [shield]**: refers to a lost work, described by Vasari; cf. 'Leonardo Da Vinci', ¶11 (and n.). **an epithet which means *flowery***: at *Od.* III:440, the λέβης (cauldron or basin) is ἀνθεμόεις (flowery, i.e. decorated with flowery designs). πόρπας τε γναμπτάς θ᾽ἕλικας (etc.): 'brooches and twisting bracelets and rosette ear-rings [*or* cups] and necklaces'; *Il.* XVIII:401. **Use and beauty are still undivided**: if this brings to mind William Morris's famous injunction, 'Have nothing in your houses that you do not know to be useful, or believe to be beautiful', it is noteworthy that Morris's lecture was first given in the same month (February 1880) in which WP's essay was published.

¶10. *chryselephantine*: i.e. made from ivory and gold.

¶11. **necklace of Eriphyle**: made by Hephaestus and given as a wedding gift by Cadmus to Harmonia; later given by Polyneices to Eriphyle as he asks her to persuade her husband, Amphiaraus, to participate in the raid of the 'Seven against Thebes'. **necklace of Helen**: this story is recorded by Demetrius of Phalerum in the *scholia* to *Od.* III.267. **potter's wheel**: see *Il.* XVIII:599–601. **old-fashioned drill-borer**: see *Od.* IX:381–86 for the simile that describes the piercing of the eye of the Cylops. **the names of two artists**: Phereclus (son of Harmonides), a woodworker and ship-carpenter of the Trojan fleet, is mentioned at *Il.* V:59–68. The other name, '**of a craft turned into a proper name**', probably refers to Daedalus (*Il.* XVIII:592). On Daedalus, see Greek Sculpture (Further Extracts), extr. (i), ¶14 (and n.). *empæstik*: beaten metalwork, otherwise known as *repoussé*.

¶13. **shield of Hercules**: refers to an early Greek epic, once attributed to Hesiod.

¶14. **hovering in some wonderful way**: see *Shield of Heracles*, ll. 216–220. **the golden maids [...] who assist Hephæstus**: see *Il.* XVIII:417–21. **armour of Achilles [...] lifts him like wings**: see *Il.* XIX:384–86.

¶15. **the "treasury" of Mycenæ**: the so-called 'Treasury of Atreus', also known as the 'Tomb of Agamemnon', a well-preserved Bronze Age *tholos* tomb at Mycenae. **temple of Pallas *of the Brazen House***: cf. 'Lacedæmon', ¶16, and Greek Sculpture (Further Extracts), extr. (i), ¶16. **worthy to rank with the Pyramids**: it appears that WP has confused the so-called 'Treasury of Minyas' at Orchomenos—the building Pausanias mentions as being no less wonderful than the pyramids (IX.36.5)—with the 'Treasury of Atreus' at Mycenae. They are similar structures, '*tholos*' or beehive tombs.

¶16. **that Asiatic chamber of Paris**: see *Il.* III:390-94 (here in Lang's translation): 'Come hither; Alexandros [i.e. Paris] summoneth thee to go homeward. There is he in his chamber and inlaid bed, radiant in beauty and vesture; nor wouldst thou deem him to be come from fighting his foe, but rather to be faring to the dance, or from the dance to be just resting and set down.' *acropoleis*: plural of *acropolis*, a citadel built at a high elevation, often a focal point of ancient Greek cities. **the draining of the Copaic lake**: Lake Kopais in Boeotia was drained in Mycenaean times for agricultural purposes. **"to pinch and peel"**: from Keats, 'Isabella, or, The Pot of Basil', ll. 119-20: 'Half-ignorant, they turn'd an easy wheel, / That set sharp racks at work, to pinch and peel'. **Jacques Bonhomme**: popular name for Guillaume Cale, leader of the Jacquerie (peasants' revolt) of 1358 in northern France, who was captured, tortured and killed; cf. 'Prosper Mérimée', ¶11. **Dactyli**: 'Fingers', legendary beings devoted to metalwork, sometimes confused with the Telchines and Cabeiri (cf. ¶23 below). **Chalybes**: a people dwelling on the Anatolian coast of the Black Sea, known to the Greeks as early and proficient workers of iron. **Telchines**: a race of mysterious and sinister mythical creatures, sometimes regarded as craftsmen, inventors and artists, and associated especially with metallurgy. **Procrustean beds**: in Greek mythology, the smith Procrustes invited visitors and travellers to sleep in a particular iron bed, and each victim was stretched or mutilated in order to make them fit it perfectly.

¶17. **recent extraordinary discoveries at Troy and Mycenæ**: Heinrich Schliemann had led these excavations in the 1870s. **royal cup of Priam**: see Schliemann's *Troy and its Remains* (1875), p. 326 (in the English edition); illustrated in pl. XVI, nos 239 and 240. It is an elongated shallow vessel in the shape of a boat, standing like a gravy boat on a foot-base, and lipped at either end. **a much-debated expression of Homer**: i.e. the phrase δέπας ἀμφικύπελλον (see *Il.* I:584, VI:220), previously interpreted as a cup with two bowls, perhaps at either end (vertically). Schliemann thinks that the common double-handled cups, as well as the double-lipped cups (which are also two-handled), are all to be considered examples of the type of vessel meant by Homer. See *Troy and its Remains*, pp. 14-15, 313-14, 326, etc. **"diadem"**: *ibid.*, pp. 335-36, pl. XIX.

¶18. **the story of the excavations at Mycenæ**: as recounted in Schliemann's *Mycenae* (1878). **golden masks**: perhaps the most famous objects from the excavations. The finest of them soon became known as the 'Mask of Agamemnon'.

¶19. **head of a cow [...] in gold with horns of silver**: this '*rhyton*' is in fact of silver, with horns of gold; see Schliemann's *Mycenae*, pp. 215-18, and ill. nos 327, 328. **equivalent to Demeter**: cf. 'Study of Dionysus', ¶1 and 6, and 'The Myth of Demeter and Persephone' (two parts, *GS*). **Pelasgian**: refers to the indigenous peoples of Greece before the ascendency of the Greeks. **whose toilet Homer describes**: see *Il.* XIV:169-86.

¶20. **Pheidias** (or Phidias): this great classical Greek sculptor, flourishing in the mid C5[th] B.C., is an important point of reference for WP in the rest of the essays on Greek sculpture.

¶21. ποικιλία: 'embroidery', or any parti-coloured decoration; by extension, also 'intricacy', 'ornamentation', 'subtlety of working' or 'versatility' generally. **clearly defined and self-asserted Hellenic influence** (etc.): i.e. the Doric influence; cf. 'Lacedæmon',

¶17, etc., and *PP*, ch. 1-5 extracts, extr. (iii), ¶9, and extr. (vi), *passim*. For the **Dorian Apollo**, see also 'Lacedæmon', ¶28-29.

¶22. **Aphrodite with her dove**: I have been unable to determine exactly which figures (necessarily acquired before 1880) WP was thinking of. Many of the small Cypriot figures in the BM collection are holding birds, but they are not now generally thought to represent Aphrodite. *Anadyomene*: epithet of Venus-Aphrodite as depicted rising from the sea. **the true Homer**: as distinct from the pseudo-Homer of the Homeric Hymns.

¶23. **Achilles and the river Xanthus**: see *Il*. XXI:328ff. **Dædali**: see the following extract (no. i), ¶13 (and notes). **Mulcibers**: Mulciber is another name for Vulcan, the Roman equivalent of Hephaestus, and may represent an originally separate Italian deity associated with blacksmithery. **Cabeiri**: a group or race of very ancient deities, sometimes represented as crab-like creatures, and often associated with metalwork, for which they used their crabs' claws. **"spiritual form"**: cf. 'Study of Dionysus', esp. ¶7-8, 13, 16-17, 26.

¶25. *ποικιλία*: see ¶21n. above.

§ *EXTRACTS FROM* **Further Chapters on Greek Sculpture**

i. The First True School of Greek Sculpture [from the second of the two studies jointly entitled 'The Beginnings of Greek Sculpture', i.e. 'The Age of Graven Images', first published in the *Fortnightly Review*, March 1880; this extr. reproduces ¶9-17.] WP tells us that he is dealing here with 'the first historical period of Greek art, a period coming down to about the year 560 B.C., and the government of Pisistratus at Athens' (*GS*, pp. 228-29).

¶9. **"In consequence of some injury done them [etc.]"**: Pliny, *Nat. Hist.* XXXVI.4. **"Figures of cedar-wood [etc.]"**: Pausanias VI.19.12.

¶11. **chest of Cypselus**: an ancient chest carved with reliefs; not extant but described in some detail by Pausanias, who had seen it in the temple of Here at Olympia (V.17.5 to 19.10). WP had spoken of it at the beginning of the essay (*GS*, pp. 225-28). **Amyclæan Apollo**: see Pausanias III.18.9 to 19.2. **Hyacinth** and **Apollo**: cf. Lacedæmon', ¶30, and WP's story 'Apollo in Picardy' (*MS*). **ejaculation of woe**: the petals of the flower known to the Greeks as the hyacinth (possibly the larkspur) bear markings which resemble the letters 'AI', thus putatively signifying the boy's dying cry. **games of Amyclæ**: cf. 'Lacedæmon', ¶30.

¶12. **"There are wrought upon the altar [etc.]"**: Pausanias III.19.3-5.

¶13. **this local Adonis**: like Adonis he was a mortal youth, beloved of a deity, killed by ill-chance, and subject to cultic worship. Cf. 'Winckelmann', ¶42, and 'Lacedæmon', ¶30.

¶14. *the period of graven images*: a comment on the religious nature of the works with which the sculptors seem chiefly to have been employed, 'graven images' being a relatively frequent phrase in the English Old Testament to refer to crafted idols generally. **the root of the name Dædalus**: see Pausanias IX.3.2. **Dædal work**: i.e. crafted objects that are *δαίδαλος* (*daidalos*), 'curiously or intricately worked'. 'Dedale' is the archaic English form of this word, as in Spenser. **chamber in which Nausicaa sleeps**: see *Od*. VII:15-19, where the adjective employed is *πολυδαίδαλος* (*poly+daidalos*). **carvers of Berchtesgaden and Oberammergau**: these regions of Bavaria have a long tradition of wood-carving. **Cimabue**: Italian painter (died c. 1302) traditionally regarded as the initiator of the transition from

Byzantine style to the increasing naturalism of Giotto and his followers.

¶15. **holy cone of Aphrodite**: at Paphos Aphrodite was worshipped in the form of a white conical stone. **human image and human story** (etc.): cf. 'Lacedæmon', ¶29–32, and 'Study of Dionysus', *passim*, esp. ¶4, 13, 32, etc. See also 'The Myth of Demeter and Persephone' (two parts, *GS*).

¶16. **Pheidias**: cf. 'Beginnings of Greek Sculpture, I', ¶20n. **the images […] which Pausanias saw in the temple of Here at Olympia**: see ¶10–11n. above. Athene's **brazen temple at Sparta**: cf. 'Lacedæmon', ¶16, and 'Beginnings of Greek Sculpture, I', ¶15.

ii. (a) The "*Discobolus*" of *Myron* ['The Age of Athletic Prizemen', first published in the *Contemporary Review*, February 1894, ¶9–15.] The 'discus-thrower' is well known and the attribution to Myron is solid, though the original is lost and the work is known only through Roman copies.

¶9. **"Ample is the glory [etc.]"**: Pindar, *Olympian Odes* 11:7–8. The *Diadumenus* is the subject of the next extr., while the *Jason* is a type otherwise known as the *Sandal-Binder* or *Hermes Fastening his Sandal*. **a mother of gold-crowned contests**: see Pindar, *Olympian Odes* 8:1. μουσική (*mousikê*): 'music' in the widest, classical sense, embracing all the arts over which the Muses presided (cf. 'Plato's Æsthetics', ¶3). **between the Persian and the Peloponnesian wars**: i.e. 449–431 B.C.

¶10. *ad unguem*: 'to the very fingernails', i.e. utterly, to perfection.

¶11. *rhythmus*: rhythm. **Ladas**: a winning runner at Olympia, and the subject of a statue by Myron which is now entirely lost. From ancient descriptions it would seem to have represented the athlete in an active pose. **Philoctetes**: the wounded mythical hero, well known to later ages from the tragedy of Sophocles, was the subject of a statue by Pythagoras of Samos which was celebrated in antiquity but is no longer extant.

¶12. *beau idéal*: something representing the highest standard of attainment. WP is using the term '**for once justly**' because Myron's statues of young athletes are both '*beau*' (beautiful, handsome) and 'ideal' types of human perfection.

¶13. *Multiplicasse veritatem videtur*: 'he seems to have expanded the reach of [artistic] truthfulness', or 'mutliplied the possibilities of realism'; Pliny, *Nat. Hist.* XXXIV.58 (or 24 in some texts). **thirty-six extant epigrams on his brazen cow**: some of these are collected in Bk IX of the Greek Anthology. **Siren tomb**: i.e. the 'Harpy Tomb' (C5th B.C.), acquired by the British Museum in 1848. *Corporum curiosus*: Pliny (XXXIV.58 again) adds: '*corporum tenus curiosus animi sensus non expressisse*': Myron was 'careful as far the the body was concerned, [but] not to express the feelings of the mind'. **"the unhindered exercise of one's natural force"**: see Aristotle, *Nicomachean Ethics* VII.12. 'Natural state' is a more usual translation than 'natural force'.

¶14. *animus* in Latin is the rational soul, mind or intellect; the *anima* is the physical life, the vital principal, the soul more generally.

¶15. **a great analyst of literary style** (etc.): Quintilian, *Institutio Oratoria* II.13: 'What is so distorted and elaborate as the *Discobolus* of Myron? […] The most laudable thing about it is that very novelty and difficulty.' τὸ δὲ φυᾷ ἅπαν κράτιστον (translated by WP): Pindar, *Olympian Odes* 9:100. **"Grant them […] with feet so light to pass through life!"**:

Pindar, *Olympian Odes* 13:114-15.

ii. (b) The "Diadumenus" of Polycleitus ['The Age of Athletic Prizemen', first published in the *Contemporary Review*, February 1894, ¶22-23.] This statue-type depicting the 'diadem-crowned' athlete is also well known, and the attribution of the lost original, again known only through Roman copies, is generally accepted.

¶22. **the Vaison copy**, discovered in excavations at Vaison in the south of France, was acquired by the **British Museum** in 1870. According to A.H. Smith's *Catalogue of Sculpture in the Department of Greek and Roman Antiquities, British Museum*, vol. 1 (1892), 'The band was made of bronze, and holes remain for its attachment' (cat. 500). Some earlier information seen by WP may have suggested silver instead of bronze. **the *Agonistes***: a contestant; a person involved in an *agôn* (struggle). **claimed to have fixed the *canon***: Polycleitus is said to have written a treatise on the ideal proportions of the human form, his 'Canon' ('rule' or 'measure'). His statue known as the *Doryphoros*, closely related to the *Diadumenos*, seems also to have been known in antiquity as the 'Canon', for it was thought to illustrate his principles. **"the measure of an angel"**: Revelation 21:17: 'And he measured the wall thereof, an hundred and forty and four cubits, according to the measure of a man, that is, of the angel.' **as befitting messengers from the gods**: a play on words, referring back to the 'angel' of the first half of the sentence: the English word 'angel' comes, *via* Latin, from the Greek word for a 'messenger'.

ii. (c) The "Discobolus at Rest" ['The Age of Athletic Prizemen', ¶26 = the final paragraph; for publication history see note to extr. (ii.b.) above.] The statue under discussion is more generally known as the *Discopohoros* or *Discophorus*: the discus-bearer, as distinct from discus-thrower. It has been attributed sometimes to Polycleitus, sometimes to his follower, Naucydes of Argos. WP supposes it to be the work of Alcamenes. The Vatican version (Museo Pio Clementino, inv. 2349) is one of several Roman copies of the lost original.

sapiential: relating to wisdom, and specifically the 'Books of Wisdom' in the Old Testament, from one of which WP now quotes. **"I was by him [etc.]"**: Proverbs 8:30-31: 'Then I was by him, as one brought up with him: and I was daily his delight, rejoicing always before him; Rejoicing in the habitable part of his earth; and my delights were with the sons of men.'

MISCELLANEOUS STUDIES

§ *Prosper Mérimée*

The major French author Prosper Mérimée (1803-70) is best remembered today as the author of *Carmen* (1845)—later adapted by Ludovic Halévy for the opera by Bizet—and for a few other works of shorter fiction which are discussed or mentioned by WP. The first sentence of the initial footnote is WP's own, as printed in the essay's first publication in the *Fortnightly Review*, December 1890, and reproduced in *MS*.

¶1. **sealing the tomb of the Revolution**: the First Republic came to an end in 1804,

Napoleon Bonaparte becoming Emperor and thereby disappointing many republican and revolutionary hopes in Europe. With Napoleon's fall and exile, the Empire itself collapsed in 1814-15, and the Bourbon monarchy was restituted until the Revolution of 1830. **the mental parallel**: WP may be thinking particularly of **Heine**'s 'fragment' on *Religion and Philosophy in Germany* (1834/35). **Kant's criticism of the mind**: i.e. principally in such works as the three *Critques*, published between 1781-90. Kant distinguishes between the 'thing-in-itself' or '*noumenon*', to which the mind has no immediate access, and its 'phenomenal' appearance to the perceiving human subject. **Obermann**: melancholic protagonist of the widely influential French novel of the same name (1804) by Senancour; cf. 'Style', ¶5, and *App.*, 'Postscript', ¶11. *désillusionné*: 'one who is disillusioned'.

¶2. *bêtise*: it is important, especially later in the essay, that this French word—signifying, as WP says, 'a kind of stupidity'—is associated with the brutish, *bête* meaning 'beast'. **an incident of his earliest years**: the story is recorded in the Goncourt *Journal*, 13 January 1864. **political eminence**: besides various earlier duties in the civil service and his position as Inspector General of Historic Monuments, PM served as a senator during the reign of Napoleon III, in the early years of the Second Empire. *Lettres à une Inconnue*: *Letters to an Unknown Woman*. This correspondence with Jenny Daquin was published posthumously in 1874. **nothing more than it can do**: *sic* in all available versions. Those who are unable to find sufficient sense in this might consider reading 'that' for 'than'; but I have resisted the temptation to make the emendation. Unfortunately there is no extant manuscript to solve the problem. The **'half-lights'** should be taken to correspond with 'atmosphere' in the preceding sentence, with its 'light and shade', and **'fundamental criticism'** is that which deals with questions of 'fundamental belief'. For PM it is a matter of All or Nothing, although for the majority of 'us', as WP says, there may be an ambiguous middle-ground. Accepting the given reading (with 'than'), the meaning might be construed: Now that fundamental criticism can no longer function as it once could—that is, can no longer 'do' its job as before—one should no longer hope to benefit from its concomitant psychological atmospherics to the same extent; and if not to the full extent, then not at all. Fundamental belief gone, its criticism disabled, the 'atmosphere' must go too. **Sylla** (or Sulla): Roman politician and general during the Social War (*bellum sociale*) of 91-88 B.C. He is a prominent character in PM's historical essay *La Guerre Sociale* (*Études sur l'Histoire Romaine*, 1844). **the false Demetrius**: another historical figure, a pretended heir to Ivan the Terrible; subject of PM's study *Les faux Démetrius* (1852). **Carmen** and **Colomba** are the heroines of PM's two novellas named after them (1845, 1840), while **'that impassioned self within himself'** refers again to the *Lettres à une Inconnue*.

¶3. Sir Anthony **Panizzi**: Librarian at the British Museum, politically well-connected in Britain, and a friend to the prominent Italian Republican Giuseppe Mazzini. Panizzi's correspondence with PM is frequently political in nature. *Chronique du Règne de Charles IX*.: *Chronicle of the Reign of Charles IX* (1560-74), an historical novel portraying the beginnings of the French Wars of Religion, including the St Bartholomew's Day Massacre of 1572. See WP's discussion in ¶5 below. I have re-inserted a comma after '**matter-of-fact**', missing in *MS* but present in the original *Fortnightly Review* article. **last years of the Valois**: the Valois dynasty had held the French throne since the C14th, although Charles IX was to be the penultimate Valois monarch. Henri III was the last, and is the '**one of those Valois princes**' who had been King of Poland (1573–75) before his accession to the French throne.

¶4. *la forme noble*: literally 'the noble form'; WP explains. **Saint-Savin**: a Romanesque abbey in the *département* of Vienne. PM's study of it in the mid 1830s was made in his official capacity as Inspector General of Historic Monuments. **George Sand's *Mauprat***: an 1837 novel set in pre-Revolutionary France, telling a tale of lawless clans. Sand was friendly with PM. The latter's *Notice sur les peintures de l'église de Saint-Savin* (*Note on the Paintings of the Church of Saint-Savin*, 1845) tells in lurid detail how, in **1611**, a minor nobleman named Henri de Neuchèze arrived with a bandit militia and, driving out the monks, took possession of the abbey in order to set up residence there, doing much damage to the structure of the buildings. *in commendam*: 'in trust'; refers to the status of provisional or honorary occupants of ecclesiastical benefices. ***Santa Maria del Fiore***: the Cathedral of Florence.

¶5. **"Eve of Saint Bartholomew"**: infamous massacre of Huguenots (Prostestants) by French Catholics in 1572, centred in Paris (see ¶3n. above). WP has treated this historical episode in *Gaston*. **Catherine de Medicis**, mother of Charles IX, was popularly blamed for the massacre. The **two other masters of French fiction**, named by WP a few lines below, are **Balzac** in the four-part novel *Sur Catherine de Médicis* (1830–42, rev. 1846), and **Dumas**, especially in *La Reine Margot* (*Queen Margot*, 1845) and *Le Page du Duc de Savoie* (*The Page of the Duke of Savoy*, 1855). **"Assassination […] is no longer a part of our manners"**: '*L'assassinat n'est plus dans nos moeurs*'; from PM's Preface to the *Chronique du Règne de Charles IX*.

¶7. This is a collage of sentences from ch. 3 of *Colomba*. Other quotations in the paragraph following are also from this story.

¶8. See above. *improvisatrice*: 'improvisor' (feminine), an impromptu speaker or reciter.

¶9. **But it was […] that is needed**: *sic* also in the 1890 text. The **story** translated by PM from **Pouchkine** (Pushkin) is presumably *Le Coup de pistolet* (*The Shot*), though he had also translated other stories from the same author.

¶10. **Pity and terror**: central concepts in Aristotle's famous theoretical discussion of tragedy in the *Poetics*. **Saint-Clair**: the protagonist in PM's story *Le Vase étrusque* (*The Etruscan Vase*, 1830).

¶11. **unfrocked the bear** (etc.): in *Lokis* (1869); **the wolf** (etc.): in *La Jacquerie* (*The Peasants' Revolt*, 1828).

¶12. **Illyrian**: of the coastal regions to the east of the Adriatic, i.e. the western Balkans, including historical Dalmatia, Croatia, Istria. ***La Guzla***: as WP implies, the volume (1827) is named after a string instrument, in English called the 'gusle'. **a kind of Webster**: reference to the English Jacobean dramatist John Webster, whose reputation was on the rise at the end of the C19[th], especially following J.A. Symonds' edition for the Mermaid Series (1888). **some letters**: the *Lettres d'Espagne* (*Letters from Spain*) included in PM's volume of stories *Mosaïque* (*Mosaic*, 1833) and subsequently reprinted elsewhere.

¶13. **the Ring given to Venus**: a traditional medieval or late-antique legend, well known to the German Romantics, which provides the outline of PM's plot.

¶14. The first sentence of this paragraph recalls the process of composition described in 'Style', ¶15. **M. Octave Feuillet**: French author (1821-90), about whose novel *La Morte* (*Death*) WP had written an appreciative review-essay in 1886, included in the second and subsequent editions of *App*. *Megalopsychus*: one exhibiting the quality of 'greatness of soul' (magnanimity); see Aristotle, *Nicomachean Ethics* IV.

¶15. **Personality *versus* impersonality in art**: cf. 'Style', ¶29. This question would become central to Anglophone poetic theory in the age of Modernism; see T.S. Eliot's essay 'Tradition and the Individual Talent' (1919) for his advocacy of 'impersonality'. **"It has always been my rule [etc]"**: '*Je me suis toujours défendu de* rien mettre de moi *dans mes oeuvres, et pourtant j'en ai mis beaucoup*'; Flaubert, letter to Louise Colet, 15 August 1846. **the style is the man**: cf. 'Style', ¶27-29 (esp. ¶27n.). **mind** and **soul** as literary-critical terms refer back to 'Style': see ¶14ff.

§ *Raphael*

As WP's footnote explains, this essay was first given as one of Oxford University's 'Extension Lectures', a programme delivered in various locations to non-members of the University. First published in the *Fortnightly Review*, October 1892.

¶1. **the world's typical scholars**: cf. 'The Genius of Plato', ¶20.

¶2. The **ducal palace** at **Urbino** had been built (incorporating some earlier structures) under Federico da Montefeltro, beginning in the mid C15[th], and was the home of one of the most sophisticated humanist courts in Italy. The painting by **Giovanni Santi** in the National Gallery, London, is the 'Virgin and Child' now catalogued as NG751. **"Mater Dolorosa"**: 'the Sorrowing Mother'; i.e. the Virgin Mary in grieving for the crucified Christ. **the grief of a simple household** (etc.): R's mother died when he was eight years old. WP appears to suppose (without committing to a definite statement) that the picture was painted after that date (1491), though Giovanni Santi lived only until 1494. The National Gallery currently estimates the date of the composition at 'perhaps about 1488'.

¶3. **a drawing [...] in the University Galleries**: now in the Ashmolean Museum, Oxford, inv. WA1846.158; i.e. Joannides, *Drawings of R.*, cat. 9. **The Baglioni**: a dynasty of *condottieri* (mercenaries) holding the lordship of Perugia in R's time. WP's view of them may owe something to his reading of Burckhardt's *Civilization of the Renaissance in Italy* (1860). **"Marriage of the Virgin"**: in the Musée des Beaux-Arts, Caen, the attribution not universal but widely accepted. R's copy—though the chronological relation between the two pictures has sometimes been questioned—is now at the Brera, Milan.

¶4. **Ansidei Madonna** (Blenheim Madonna): in the National Gallery, London. [*Collegio del*] **Cambio**: the Exchange, or 'college' of the Exchange Guild, occupying the Palazzo dei Priori at Perugia. The *Sala delle Udienze* contains Perugino's frescoes.

¶5. **Pinturicchio**'s frescoes at the Duomo in Pisa are still well preserved. **"to assist him by his counsels"**: source, if any, unidentified. **He stands depicted there** (etc.): the identification of R's likeness is still popularly made at the Piccolomini Library today.

¶6. **parti-coloured**: the Duomo at Siena is indeed strikingly multi-coloured, with dark green bands in the stonework to interior and exterior, and famous mosaic floors inlaid with marbles of many kinds. **a marble group of the three Graces**: evidently removed in WP's day, it has since been replaced and at present may still be seen there. **"the dew of herbs"**, **"to awake and sing"**: Isaiah 26:19: 'Awake and sing, ye that dwell in dust: for thy dew is as the dew of herbs, and the earth shall cast out the dead'. **He has turned it into a picture**: 'The Three Graces', now at the Musée Condé, Chantilly. The old story that the painting was inspired by the statue is not universally accepted as fact. **Apollo and Marsyas**: the painting was bought by the Louvre in 1883, as attributed to R, and displayed as such; but critics of the time and afterwards, including Berenson, commonly attributed it to Perugino, or sometimes Pinturicchio. The Louvre now catalogues it as a Perugino (inv. RF370). **Heine's fancied Apollo "in exile"**: cf. 'Pico Della Mirandola', ¶2 (and n. for cross-refs). **Chef-d'œuvre**: an artist's greatest work. **ten per cent** (etc.): i.e., we would willingly have ten works in this 'mixed' style in place of a hundred of R's 'purely classical' pictures.

¶8. **Maddalena Doni**: this portrait is now in the Palazzo Pitti, Florence. In composition it is apparently modelled upon **La Gioconda** (the 'Mona Lisa'); cf. 'Leonardo Da Vinci', ¶29–30. **"Violin-player"**: now usually attributed to Sebastiano del Piombo, it is (or was) in the collection of the late Guy de Rothschild in Paris. **"Madonna del Gran Duca"**: a Madonna and Child now in the Palazzo Pitti. **Sixtine Madonna**: Madonna and Child with St Barbara and Sixtus II, now in the Dresden Gallery.

¶9. *Ex forti dulcedo*: 'From the strong, sweetness'. See Judges 14:14: 'and out of the strong came forth sweetness'. **"the meek shall possess"**: Matthew 5:5 and Psalm 37:11, in some translations (*AV*: 'shall inherit').

¶10. **cardinal *in petto***: a cardinal-elect, but not yet announced ('*in petto*' meaning 'in secret', literally 'in the chest'). According to Vasari, Pope Leo had intimated to R that he might be made a cardinal on his completing the suite of frescoes then in hand.

¶11. *Galatea*: the *Triumph of Galatea*, a set of frescoes by R at the Villa Farnesina, Rome. **literary work of pure erudition**: this is the '**monumental illustrated survey of the monuments of ancient Rome**' mentioned at the end of the paragraph. The project is described in R's famous letter to Leo X, written in 1519/20 with the aid of Baldassare Castiglione, and possibly intended as a preface to the proposed work. **frescoes of the Farnese palace**: including the *Galatea* series and the *Psyche* ceiling in the *Loggie di Psiche*.

¶12. R was architect at **St Peter's** Basilica between the death of **Bramante** (1514) and his own death (1520). *Quattro-cento*: i.e. 'C15th'. **arabesque decoration which goes by his name**: R's influential arabesques in the Vatican *Loggie* had been inspired, according to Vasari, by the wall decorations of the newly excavated *Domus Aurea* of Nero.

¶13. the '**Transfiguration**' is in the Vatican Galleries. **Cartoons**: R's designs for the tapestries of the Sistine Chapel, widely disseminated in the form of engravings. *Biblia Pauperum*: 'Bible of the Poor', a term often used to describe a kind of picture-Bible which arranges scriptural stories from the Old and New Testaments according to typological correspondences.

¶14. **Plato, as you know**: cf. 'The Genius of Plato', *passim*, and 'Doctrine of Plato, Pt I: The Theory of Ideas', ¶20.

¶15. *Disputa*: 'Disputation (on the Sacrament)', located in the *Stanza della Segnatura*, along with the *Parnassus* and *School of Athens*. *divinarum rerum notitia*: 'knowledge of divine matters', a motto included in R's depiction of Theology on the ceiling of the

Stanza della Segnatura. Cf. *Institutes* of Justinian, I.1: 'Jurisprudence is the knowledge of matters human and divine' ('*Iurisprudentia est divinarum atque humanarum rerum notitia*').

¶16. **Old friends** (etc.): the French King Louis XII's military ambitions in Italy had been thwarted in part thanks to the intervention of Pope Julius II, the patron of R. The defeated Huns in R's frescoes, therefore, might easily be taken as an allusion to the French. The 'Meeting of Leo I (the Great) and Attila', or 'Repulse of Attila', in which Leo I is painted to resemble Leo X (the new pope under whom R was working), is in the *Stanza di Eliodoro* at the Vatican Palace. So is the 'Deliverance' or 'Liberation of St Peter', to which WP also refers; the correlation with recent history is explained by the fact that Leo X, as cardinal, had briefly been taken prisoner by the French at the Battle of Ravenna (1512). In the *Stanza dell' Incendio* appears the 'Coronation of Charlemagne', which again appears to shadow a contemporary event: the treaty of 1515 in which the new King of France, François I, had (like Charlemagne) taken on the role of 'Defender' of the Church.

¶17. **appropriate to this place**: i.e., the University of Oxford, where the lecture was first given. The **Ansidei, or Blenheim, Madonna** (see ¶4n. above) is part of an altarpiece commissioned by Niccolò Ansidei of Perugia to adorn his family chapel at the church of S. Fiorenzo. **the true artist is known best by what he omits**: cf. 'Style', ¶11 (and n.). **"I am utterly purposed that I will not offend"**: Psalm 17:3 (in the Prayer Book version by Coverdale).

§*Pascal*

The essay from which this extract is taken was left unfinished by WP at his death in 1894. A.C. Benson comments: 'it is his last work; the work on which he was engaged in the last hours of his life; the essay, indeed, never received the last touches of that careful hand, and though substantially complete, it breaks off in the middle of a sentence' (*Walter Pater*, ch. 6). Posthumous publication in the *Contemporary Review*, December 1894, was arranged by WP's literary executors.

¶16. Here WP is turning his attention to Pascal's *Pensées*, considered at first in comparison with the *Lettres Provinciales* (**"Letters"**). *agonia*: 'agony', a state of struggle or contention. **his feet sometimes "are almost gone"**: Psalms 73:2: 'But as for me, my feet were almost gone; my steps had well nigh slipped' (*AV*). **a physical malady**: BP's ill health has been variously attributed to consumption, cancer of the stomach or intestines (or a carcinomatous meningitis resulting therefrom), and damage to the brain. *aigreur*: 'bitterness'. *malade*: 'ill', 'sick'. *La maladie est l'état naturel des Chrétiens*: 'Sickness is the natural state of Christians': quoted from the biography of BP by his sister, which prefaced early editions of his works; cf. ¶17 below. **life itself is a disease of the spirit**: an aphorism of Novalis, quoted in Carlyle's essay 'Novalis' (1829).

¶17. **Port-Royal**: an important Catholic convent in Paris, which was the focus of the Jansenist movement. **"Life of Pascal"**: *La Vie de M. Blaise Pascal*, by his sister, Gilberte Périer. **post-mortem examination**: this 'revealed disorders of the stomach and adjacent organs, together with a serious lesion of the brain' (Donald Adamson, *Blaise Pascal* [London and New York, 1995], ch. 1, n. 64 [p. 235]). **that sombre company**: BP made frequent visits to the Jansenist convent of Port-Royal, of which his sister was a member. **almost a sectarian**: i.e., as an apologist for Jansenism amid heated controversies within the Catholic Church. **self-tortures**: in later life, for instance, he wore a belt of metal spikes beneath his clothing, which he used both as a means of self-mortification and as a stimulant during periods of torpidity brought on by ill health.

¶18. **Francis and Dominic**: significant as saintly founders of important monastic orders. *Que je n'en sois jamais séparé* (etc.): 'Let me never be separated [from Him]—not separated eternally'; WP has here put together two lines from BP's 'Memorial', a manuscript prayer which he carried inside the lining of his coat (i.e. the '**MS. amulet**'), and which was recovered after his death. *Cast me not away from Thy presence* (etc.): Psalms 51:11 (*AV* or Prayer Book version). ***table rase***: '*tabula rasa*', or 'blank slate', a concept used in theories of the mind since the time of Aristotle. **renunciate**: based on an unclear manuscript, both printed texts have 'renuncient', a very unclassical misspelling not attested elsewhere in WP (who correctly uses 'renunciant'). Prof. Higgins, who has re-transcribed the original manuscript, points out to me that in fact what WP wrote here was 'renunciate'. In this case, avoiding a distracting solecism which was never authorial, I have returned to the manuscript reading. **Not to be buried but accounted for**: a reference to the 'parable of the talents', Matthew 25:14–30, Luke 19:12–27. ***le beau dire***: 'speaking beautifully', 'elegant expression'. ***Il avoit renoncé depuis longtemps aux sciences purement humains***: 'He had for a long time given himself over to purely human sciences' (i.e. 'humane arts', as opposed to his mathematical studies); from Charles Bossut's introduction to BP's works (1779, repr. frequently). **"the Lord's doing, marvellous in our eyes"**: as Shadwell's footnote indicates, WP has muddled the numbering; the right reference is Psalms 118:23. ***des petits heures***: 'of the wee hours'. ***le néant***: 'non-existence', 'non-being'; absolute nullity, negation or absence.

¶19. **Port-Royal du Faubourg S. Jacques**: Jansenist convent in Paris founded in 1626, an offshoot of the pre-existing convents of Port-Royal des Champs and Port-Royal de Paris. ***Ah! Thou hast given him his heart's desire*** (etc.): Psalm 21:2 (in the Prayer Book version by Coverdale). **Spouse**: i.e. Christ. "***Voici celui que vous avez tant désiré***": 'Here is the thing you have so much desired!' Quoted from Mme Périer's *Vie* (see ¶17n. above).

¶20. **vast unseen hollow places [...] just beneath one's feet or at one's side**: this image is significantly echoed at the close of WP's incomplete essay, as it stands: 'About the time when he was bidding adieu to the world, Pascal had an accident. As he drove round a corner on the Seine to cross the bridge at Neuilly, the horses were precipitated down the bank into the water. Pascal escaped, but with a nervous shock, a certain hallucination, from which he never recovered. As he walked or sat he was apt to perceive a yawning depth beside him; would set stick or chair there to reassure himself. We are now told, indeed, that that circumstance has been greatly exaggerated. But how true to Pascal's temper, as revealed in his work, that alarmed precipitous character in it! Intellectually the abyss was evermore at his side.' **natural man**: in itself this term might bring to mind theories of the 'state of nature' in Enlightenment thought (e.g. Rousseau), but such a meaning is evidently inappropriate. A more germane precedent is 1 Corinthians 2:14, in which St Paul distinguishes between 'natural' and 'spiritual' man: 'But the natural man receiveth not the things of the Spirit of God: for they are foolishness unto him: neither can he know them, because they are spiritually discerned.' If this is what he had in mind, then WP is emphasising a contradiction in BP's character between the 'religious genius' (parallel to Paul's 'spiritual man') and the 'natural man'. BP, then, approaches 'doubt and faith' from two directions; or, perhaps, from one or the other, depending on the reader's point of view. T.S. Eliot may have been half-remembering this when he made a similar point in 'The Pensées of Pascal', calling BP 'a man of the world among ascetics, and an ascetic among men of the world.' But cf. also WP's use of the phrase 'natural man' in 'Raphael', ¶15.

§ Notre-Dame d'Amiens

This piece was first published in the last year of WP's life (1894), as one of two completed pieces on 'Some Great Churches in France' for the March and June issues of The Nineteenth Century. The second of these was 'Vézelay', also collected in MS. Ruskin had written enthusiastically about the great Gothic Cathedral of Amiens a decade earlier in The Bible of Amiens (1884).

¶1. **Philosophic writers of French history**: WP may be thinking of Augustin Thierry, whose discussion of such matters in the Lettres sur l'Histoire de France (Letters on the History of France), especially in the expanded edition of 1827, were widely influential; but the same theme was dealt with by many later historians, including Jules Michelet and François Guizot. **"secular clergy"**: ordained clergy who do not belong to a monastic or other religious institution.

¶2. **the first Pointed style**: the early 'Gothic' style of architecture, which, starting in the mid C12th, made use of pointed arches in place of the earlier rounded arches of Romanesque style. **plein-cintre**: 'full-curve', i.e. the rounded arch.

¶3. **Perpendicular period**: in English architecture, the final period of the Gothic style, beginning around the middle of the C14th and lasting into the Tudor period. The style was distinguished by pronounced verticality.

¶4. **l'église ogivale par excellence**: 'the ogival church par excellence', 'ogival' meaning that kind of architecture characterised by the use of the curved-and-pointed arch, i.e. the 'Gothic' style. WP is quoting from the major French architectural historian and theorist Viollet-le-Duc, who bestows this praise upon Amiens in his Dictionnaire Raisonné de l'Architecture Française du XIe au XVIe Siècle (1854–68), vol. 2, p. 330. **chevet**: the areas of the church beyond the sanctuary; the apse. **triforium**: a blind-arched space on the interior wall of a church building, usually in a horizontal series, as of windows, although without glazing or opening. **"A pleasant thing it is to behold the sun"**: Ecclesiastes 11:7: 'Truly the light is sweet, and a pleasant thing it is for the eyes to behold the sun'.

¶5. **direct, frank, clearly apparent**: WP shows his debts to Ruskin's architectural values; see the latter's Seven Lamps of Architecture (1849), ch. 2: 'The Lamp of Truth'.

¶6. **floriated**: flowery, or decorated with flowers. **grisaille**: the grey monochrome painting or underpainting in stained glass designs.

¶7. **What, precisely what, is this to me?**: cf. Ren., 'Preface', ¶2. **false restoration**: note that William Morris, who had founded the Society for the Protection of Ancient

Buildings in 1877, was campaigning about this time against unnecessary, misleading and destructive restoration of historical buildings.

¶8. **Decorated period**: technical term referring usually to a phase of English Gothic architecture dominant from the mid C13th to mid C14th, but here applied to French Gothic.

¶9. **Vézelay**: this Romanesque Abbey, attached to a Benedictine monastery, was the subject of another essay by WP (see headnote above). **other persons equally real**: the three persons of the Holy Trinity. **Theophrastus**: Greek philosopher and head of the Peripatetic School after Aristotle; attributed to him is a work on *Characters*, composed of thirty studies of the various types of human character. **art has at last become personal**: cf. Greek Sculpture (Further Extracts), extr. (i). **Beau-Dieu**: 'the handsome God', a statue much admired by Ruskin (*Bible of Amiens*, ch. 4, §36). **Portail de la Vierge dorée**: 'Portal of the gilt Virgin'. **story of Saint Honoré**: i.e. of St Honoratus, a late-C6th Bishop of Amiens. Ruskin tells the story thus, referring to the narrative of the carvings of which WP speaks: 'So here is St. Honoré, who doesn't want to be a bishop, sitting sulkily in the corner; he hugs his book with both hands, and won't get up to take his crosier; and here are all the city aldermen of Amiens come to *poke* him up; and all the monks in the town in a great puzzle what they shall do for a bishop if St. Honoré won't be […]. At last St. Honoré consents to be bishop, and here he sits in a throne, and has his book now grandly on his desk instead of his knees, and he directs one of his village curates how to find relics in a wood […]. After this, St. Honoré performs grand mass, and the miracle occurs of the appearance of a hand blessing the wafer, which occurrence afterwards was painted for the arms of the abbey. Then St. Honoré dies; and here is his tomb with his statue on the top; and miracles are being performed at it—a deaf man having his ear touched, and a blind man groping his way up to the tomb with his dog.' Ruskin, *The Two Paths*, Lecture IV (1857): 'Influence of Imagination in Architecture'. **rose, or roue**: circular ('rose') windows are known also as '*roue*' ('wheel') windows in French.

¶10. ***qui fundamenta hujus basilicæ locavit***: 'who lay the foundations of this basilica'. ***hanc basilicam culmen usque perduxit***: 'he brought this basilica [i.e. oversaw its construction] as far as the roof'. Ruskin comments that this 'may or may not mean that the vaulting was closed' (*Bible of Amiens*, ch. 4, §24 fn.). **Flamboyant**: technical term for a style of late Gothic architecture dominant in France from the mid C14th into the C16th; WP is here speaking of the polychrome relief sculptures of the ambulatory, dating to the late C15th and the C16th. **manner of Henri-Deux**: the style associated with the reign (1546–59) of Henri II of France. **Gallican "uses"**: the ritual practices of the French or 'Gallican' Church as it had existed before the Revolution (the term 'Gallican' being comparable with 'Anglican'). **reserved Eucharist**: it is traditional for some part of the consecrated sacrament to be 'reserved' in a safe place in the church, for use under exceptional circumstances. The **pyx** is the receptacle in which the eucharistic host is kept, though it is not usually suspended in plain view. **"glory"**: see 'Sandro Botticelli', ¶5n. ***Tantum ergo***: a Latin hymn, or part thereof, sung during the veneration of the Eucharistic sacrament: '*Tantum ergo Sacramentum / Veneremur cernui*' ('Therefore, bowing, let us venerate so great a sacrament'), etc.

¶11. **Specious**: WP's meaning is that this supposed notion of the Greeks seems most persuasive in the case of architecture, but is still to be resisted.

¶12. **domical**: in the form of a dome. *flèche*: a spire (literally 'arrow') constructed of wood. The Basilica of **Saint-Quentin** and **Soissons** Cathedral are both major Gothic buildings. **Beauvais** Cathedral, under construction at the same time as Amiens, was its '**ambitious rival**' in the sheer height of the choir vaulting, some 20ft taller than the nave at Amiens. The vaulting collapsed in 1284 and had to be rebuilt to a more cautious plan.

¶13. *radix de terra sitienti*: these words, in Christian thought taken to refer prophetically to the coming of Christ, come from Isaiah 53:2 in the Vulgate: '*Et ascendet sicut virgultum coram eo; et sicut radix de terra sitienti*' ('For he shall grow up before him as a tender plant, and as a root out of a dry ground', *AV*).

§ *The Child in the House*

This early foray into essayistic fiction was published in *Macmillan's Magazine*, August 1878, with the surtitle 'Imaginary Portraits 1', but it was not included in *IP* in 1887.

¶2. Jean-Antoine **Watteau** (1684–1721): French painter of the Rococo period. See 'A Prince of Court Painters' (*IP*), which is focussed on Watteau and his relationship to the family of a younger painter, Jean-Baptiste Pater (1695–1736), from whom WP liked to fancy he was descended.

¶4. *Flos Parietis*: 'flower of the wall'. The Latin term in fact referred, in the early modern period, to a kind of saltpetre (aphronitre), whereas the botanical name of the wallflower genus is *Erysimum*. **urbanity** literally: 'urbane' is derived from the Latin *urbanus* ('urban'), and ultimately *urbs* ('city').

¶5. "**with lead in the rock for ever**": see Job 19:23–24: 'Oh that my words were now written! oh that they were printed in a book! That they were graven with an iron pen and lead in the rock for ever!'

¶6. *goûter*: *OED*: 'A light afternoon repast; five-o'clock tea'; from the French, 'to taste'. **the thought of sleep in the home churchyard**: cf. *Gaston*, ch. 2, on the 'amiable little child who had a kind of genius for tranquillity, and on his first coming hither had led Gaston to what he held to be the choicest, pleasantest places, as being impregnable by noise. In his small stock of knowledge, he knew, like all around him, that he was going to die, and took kindly to the thought of a small grave in the little green close, as to a natural sleeping-place, in which he would be at home beforehand.' (Lib. Edn, pp. 42–43.)

¶7. *chez soi*: 'home', 'at home'; the feeling of home.

¶8. **home-counties**: in ordinary use this refers to the counties surrounding London.

¶9. **tyrannous element**: cf. ¶12 below, and 'Winckelmann', ¶40 (and n.). "**the lust of the eye**": 1 John 2:16: 'For all that is in the world, the lust of the flesh, and the lust of the eyes, and the pride of life, is not of the Father, but is of the world.'

¶10. *Weltschmerz*: 'world-sorrow'; cf. 'Charles Lamb', ¶7. Jacques-Louis **David's drawing** of the condemned **Marie Antoinette** is a famous image, the original of which is in the Louvre. **the white angora**: a long-haired Angora cat, which in WP's day was hardly distinguishable from a Persian cat. **face like a flower**: a pansy, perhaps?

¶12. **making** *fête*: i.e. decorating as though for (i) an elaborate party, or (ii) a church festival, with lavish floral displays. **tyranny of the senses**: cf. ¶9 (and n.) above.

¶16. **"resurrection of the just"**: see Luke 14:14: 'And thou shalt be blessed; for they cannot recompense thee: for thou shalt be recompensed at the resurrection of the just.' **Joshua's Vision**: Joshua 5:13–15: 'behold, there stood a man over against him with his sword drawn in his hand: and Joshua went unto him, and said unto him, Art thou for us, or for our adversaries? And he said, Nay; but as captain of the host of the LORD am I now come. And Joshua fell on his face to the earth, and did worship', etc. *revenants*: ghosts or vampires. **crying, or beating with vain hands** (etc.): as Østermark-Johansen notes, this seems to be remembering the ghost of Cathy at the casement in *Wuthering Heights*.

¶17. **"lively hope"**: see 1 Peter 1:3: 'Blessed be the God and Father of our Lord Jesus Christ, which according to his abundant mercy hath begotten us again unto a lively hope by the resurrection of Jesus Christ from the dead'. **the wrestling angel** and **Jacob**: see Genesis 32:22–30. **his mysterious sleep**: refers to the dream of 'Jacob's ladder', Genesis 28:10–22. **bells and pomegranates** on **Aaron's vestment**: see Exodus 28:33(–34): 'And beneath upon the hem of it thou shalt make pomegranates of blue, and of purple, and of scarlet, round about the hem thereof; and bells of gold between them round about'.

¶18. **mere messengers seemed like angels**: the word 'angel' literally means a 'messenger' (from the Greek ἄγγελος). **effusive unction**: see Matthew 26:6–7(ff.): 'Now when Jesus was in Bethany, in the house of Simon the leper, There came unto him a woman having an alabaster box of very precious ointment, and poured it on his head, as he sat at meat.'